The Economics of Sports

The Addison-Wesley Series in Economics

The Economics of Sports

SECOND EDITION

Michael Leeds

TEMPLE UNIVERSITY

Peter von Allmen

MORAVIAN COLLEGE

PEARSON

Addison
Wesley

Boston San Francisco New York
London Toronto Sydney Tokyo Singapore Madrid
Mexico City Munich Paris Cape Town Hong Kong Montreal

Editor-in-Chief: Denise Clinton
Acquisitions Editor: Adrienne D'Ambrosio
Director of Development: Sylvia Mallory
Managing Editor: James Rigney
Senior Production Supervisor: Katherine Watson
Project Coordination and Electronic Page Makeup: Electronic Publishing Services Inc., NYC
Manufacturing Buyer: Hugh Crawford
Design Manager and Cover Designer: Regina Hagen Kolenda
Cover Photo: ©Masterfile

We gratefully acknowledge the following for permission to use copyrighted material: p. 5, ©AllSport/Craig Jones. All Rights Reserved; p. 45, ©Archive Photos; p. 86, Eric Jamison/AP Wide World Photos; p. 110 © Gerard David/Contact Press images/PictureQuest; p. 142, ©Larry C. Morris/New York Times Co./Archive Photos; p. 154, AP Wide World Photos; p. 173, AP/Wide World Photos; p. 214, ©Bruce Hoertel/The Gamma Liaison Network; p. 249, Corbis; p. 287, Archive Photos/PictureQuest; p. 293, ©Donald Miralle/AllSport; p. 323, ©Bettmann/CORBIS; p. 340, ©Bettman/CORBIS; p. 348, © Pittsburgh Courier Archives/Archive Photos; p. 372, ©Robert Laberce/AllSport; p. 417, Courtesy of AAFLA.

Library of Congress Cataloging-in-Publication Data
    Leeds, Michael A. (Michael A.)
      The economics of sports / Michael Leeds, Peter von Allmen.--2nd ed.
        p. cm.--(The Addison-Wesley series in economics.)
      Includes index.
      ISBN 0-321-23774-9
      1. Sports--Economic aspects.   I. Von Allmen, Peter.   II. Title.   III. Series
    GV716 .L44 2005
    338.4'3796--dc22   2004046602

ISBN 0-321-23774-9

2 3 4 5 6 7 8 9 10—PHH—08 07 06 05

For our parents
Carolyn and Erwin von Allmen
Stella Leeds and in memory of Paul Leeds

Brief Contents

Detailed Contents

Preface

When we began the process of writing the first edition of *The Economics of Sports*, we had little idea what we were in for. Not only were we new to the process of text authorship, but we also could not have anticipated just how helpful and supportive our students and colleagues would be in the project. As the writing process drew to a close and the book was published, the support did not wane. Instead, we found that our colleagues continued to send us helpful suggestions, shared classroom pleasures and challenges that might help to improve the second edition, and suggested new and different coverage. Students also continued to share their suggestions. For all of this support and help, we are most grateful. We can only hope that our own enthusiasm, as well as the enthusiasm others have shared with us, is reflected in this second edition.

Since the publication of the first edition, so much has changed, yet some things remain the same. Sports still grab and hold the attention of our students in a way that many other industries cannot. Students who show no interest in multiplier effects or the functioning of labor markets anxiously follow their city's plans to build a new stadium and the latest free agent signing by their home team.[1] Many instructors have noticed this tendency in their students and sought to motivate their students by using sports to illustrate economic principles. Over time, isolated examples have evolved into full-fledged courses on the economics of sports.

Before the first edition was published, economics of sports classes were handicapped by the lack of an appropriate text. While many outstanding books on the economics of sports existed, none was designed with the instruction of economic concepts as its central focus. In the second edition, we retained the features from the first edition that made learning about sports economics easier, while at the same time updating the examples, adding significant events such as the baseball settlement of 2002, and adding a new chapter to significantly expand our coverage of competitive balance. In addition, every chapter contains more end-of-chapter problems and discussion questions.

Our goal in writing this edition was to keep the text comprehensive yet accessible. The text is designed to serve as the foundation for undergraduate courses in

---

[1] In one memorable labor class, one of us tried to illustrate the preference shown in some "old boy networks" to graduates of Ivy League universities by asking what an employer might think if an applicant showed up in an orange and black tie. An eager student immediately replied, "He'd see the applicant is a Flyers fan!"

sports economics. The nature of the subject matter makes this a unique challenge. Unlike area courses like industrial organization or labor economics, which are self-contained fields in the broader area of economics, sports economics cuts across a wide array of economic disciplines. To deal with this problem, we have split the text into five sections, three of which are devoted to illustrating prominent areas of economics: industrial organization, public finance, and labor economics. We hope that this division provides students with an overview of much of economics and inspires them to pursue each field in its own right. Because we focus largely on professional sports in the first three sections of the book, we include a closing section devoted to amateur sports. This final section provides insights into theories related to the not-for-profit sector of the economy like the theory of bureaucracy. Each of the five parts of this text presents significant economic theory and recent evidence and research for that area of economics.

To make the text accessible, we have written it assuming that students have had one semester of microeconomics principles. Balancing exposition against an economist's desire for theoretical rigor presented a challenge that almost equaled that of providing a comprehensive text. In order to help the students understand the economics and to make the treatment more entertaining, we have included a generous component of sports history to place the events and economic theory in perspective.

INTENDED AUDIENCE

Economics of sports classes are taught at a variety of levels, ranging from undergraduate courses with principles of economics as the only prerequisites, to the graduate level. This text is designed to offer a high level of flexibility to the instructor. All the material in the main body of the text should be accessible to students with a single semester of microeconomics principles. In order to enrich courses taught at a higher level, we have included appendices containing intermediate level material at the end of several chapters. In order to ensure that all students begin the course with a common background we provide a substantial review of principles-level material in Chapter 2. This material can either be covered explicitly with lecture support, or left to the students to read on their own, as needed. For instructors interested in presenting the results of econometric research, Chapter 2 contains an appendix on the fundamentals of regression. In advanced undergraduate and graduate level courses, the text can serve as a foundation for common understanding of basic concepts.

ORGANIZATION OF THE TEXT AND COVERAGE OPTIONS

The text is divided into five parts. The first two chapters provide an introduction to the topic of sports economics, a review of principles-level tools, and an illustration of how economic principles apply to the sports industry. Chapters 3, 4, and 5 focus on the industrial organization of the sports industry. Here, we discuss the competitive landscape, the implications of monopoly power, and the notion of profit maximization. Chapter 4 focuses specifically on issues of antitrust and regulation and how they have impacted the formation, success, and, sometimes, the failure of leagues. Chapter 5 is new to this edition and describes why leagues are concerned about competitive balance, how competitive balance is measured, and how leagues might attempt to alter the balance of competition in a league. Chapter 6 and Chapter 7 focus on public finance. In this portion of the text, students learn the economics behind the stadium boom that has affected so many U.S. cities—why teams seem to have so much power over municipalities, and why municipalities fight so hard to keep the teams they have as well as court new ones. Chapters 8 through 10 focus on labor issues related to sports. Chapter 8 introduces human capital theory. It also discusses monopsony and tournament theory. Chapter 9 covers the economics of unions in the context of the sports industry, and Chapter 10 discusses discrimination. Finally, Chapter 11 focuses on the economics of amateur sports, especially major collegiate sports. Because major college sports are really an industry itself, this chapter serves as a capstone to the text, incorporating the theories and concepts from many of the previous chapters.

ACKNOWLEDGEMENTS

In a project such as this, the list of people who contributed to its completion extends far beyond those whose names appear on the cover. We owe personal and professional debts of sincere gratitude to a great many people. First, we thank our editorial team at Pearson Addison Wesley, including Adrienne D'Ambrosio, Sylvia Mallory, Denise Clinton, Regina Hagen, Katy Watson, and Dottie Dennis. Lisa Kinne and her team at EPS also added greatly to the quality of the manuscript. We are also grateful for the advice, encouragement, and suggestions from the community of sports economists, without whose input and support we could not have completed this project. We would like to thank all of those who read and reviewed the second edition of the manuscript, including Andrew Allen, Jeff Ankrom, David Berri, Roger Blair, Ross Booth, Barry Chiswick, Norman Cloutier, Edward Coulson, Michael Davis, Ranjit Dighe, John Fizel, Glenn Gerstner, John Goddard, Randy Grant, Peter Groothuis, Larry Hadley, Jill Harris, John Harter, Brad Humphreys, Todd Jewell, Philip Lane, Jo Beth Mertens, Patrick Rishe, Cory Sinclair, and Stefan Szymanski. Their suggestions for improvements were excellent, and we tried our best to incorporate them wherever possible. Our student assistants, Vera Korshunova, Erin McCormick, and Nina Safavi helped ease the burden of finding much of the data presented here. Michelle Matuczinski provided expert secretarial support. Finally, we would like to thank our families: Eva, Daniel, Melanie, Heather, Daniel, Thomas, and Eric, all of whom provided unwavering support.

Michael Leeds

Peter von Allmen

Introduction and Review of Economic Concepts

Introduction

All I remember about my wedding day in 1967 is that the Cubs dropped a double-header.

— GEORGE WILL[1]

If you are like most students—or even like most Americans—you spend a lot more time thinking about sports than about economics. Nevertheless, even if you are not conscious of it, economics affects your every day in a wide variety of ways. From the loss of a major employer in your community to the price you pay for orange juice after an ice storm in Florida, economics has an impact on your life. The challenge that faces students of economics is to learn just how all-encompassing the effects are and to develop the tools to understand them. That is where sports comes in. Sports are a pervasive factor in how people feel about their communities and themselves.

Sports teams give colleges, towns, even religious groups a sense of identity. In the fall semester at large universities, many significant events in students' lives revolve around the football field. From pregame rallies to stadiums filled with 80,000 screaming fans to postgame euphoria, a big win for the home team makes the whole campus come alive. Conversely, a city or even an entire country can suffer when the home team does poorly. After Scotland lost in a recent World Cup soccer final, a Scottish fan wrote to a local paper that he was so ashamed of being a Scotsman that he was moving to England and changing his name to Smith. Religious rivalries are sometimes played out on the pitch or gridiron, as seen in Scotland by the bitter rivalry between largely Protestant fans of the Glasgow Rangers and largely Catholic fans of Glasgow Celtic. The success of Notre Dame and the loyalty of its "subway" alumni have been an important touchstone for the Catholic community in the United States, and American Jews felt great pride in the fact that Hall of Famers Hank Greenberg and Sandy Koufax sat out important games rather than played on Yom Kippur.

---

[1]George F. Will, *Bunts* (New York: Scribner, 1998), p. 22.

3

As a result, topics that you might dismiss as boring in a typical economics class become the subject of impassioned arguments when applied to sports. For example, one of the most talked about topics today in the sports world is the construction of new arenas. To understand the debate over whether your community should build (or should have built) a new stadium for the local franchise requires economic tools and analysis. Likewise, before participating in the debate about whether the salaries paid to professional athletes are too high, you must first understand the fundamental economic concept of **market power**—a person's or group's ability to set prices.

Without the benefit of economics, many commonplace events in the world of sports seem inexplicable. For example, why did National Hockey League (NHL) star Keith Primeau sit out almost half of the 1999–2000 season rather than play and earn several million dollars? Such behavior is not limited to players. The owners of the Houston National Football League (NFL) franchise paid over $700 million just for permission to join the league in 2002. The reasons behind the actions of both Primeau and the NFL lie in the market power that comes from having special or unique characteristics. Keith Primeau is one of a limited number of superstars in hockey whose presence can change a team from an also-ran to a contender. Such players have the bargaining power that comes from being one of the very few highly productive sellers of labor. The Houston franchise is willing to pay the existing teams in the NFL an exorbitant entry fee because joining the NFL immediately gives it access to enormous streams of revenue from gate receipts and television broadcast rights. The NFL can charge such fees because it offers a unique product to the public.

Even before the sports pages became clogged with financial data, the sports industry emerged as a never-ending source of current events topics driven, at least in part, by economics. Among the four major sports in the United States (baseball, football, hockey, and basketball), there are 121 major league teams, hundreds of minor league teams, and thousands of people participating in individual sports and sports-related activities. *Street & Smith's SportsBusiness Journal* recently estimated that the sports industry in this country generates $195 billion in annual revenues, roughly the same as General Motors.[2] From an economic standpoint, something new and interesting in sports happens every day. After all, it is the only industry to which an entire section of every major daily newspaper is devoted.

A quick perusal of your newspaper's sports section reveals feature articles that are just as likely to focus on player salaries, new stadium deals, and league expansion as they are on the result of last night's game. Moreover, while the result of last night's game rarely appears on the newspaper's front page, news of player strikes or new taxes designed to fund a new arena almost certainly will. This level of attention is not new. In 1972, Marvin Miller, the executive director of

---

[2]See http://www.gm.com/company/investor_information/gm_financials/index.html. Bill King, "Passion That Can't Be Counted Puts Billions of Dollars in Play," *Street & Smith's SportsBusiness Journal: By the Numbers*, v. 9, no. 36 (2003), pp. 148–149.

Happy Duke fans enjoy a win over North Carolina.

the union representing major league baseball players, expressed shock at how much attention the first major strike in professional sports received:

> I would learn that the media coverage of five hundred players in major league baseball far exceeded the ink spent on even a lengthy steel strike of five hundred thousand workers that affected the entire economy.[3]

THREE MAJOR AREAS OF ECONOMICS EXPLORED

In your principles of economics course, you studied the building blocks of economics, such as supply and demand analysis, and their relevance to the world around you. Catering to a wide variety of backgrounds and tastes, introductory

---

[3]Marvin Miller, *A Whole Different Ballgame* (New York: Carol Publishing Group, 1991), p. 43.

courses typically take a general approach to economics. Microeconomics texts offer many applications and examples drawn from a broad sampling of industries. In this book, we take the opposite approach. We start from a narrow set of examples and use them to teach economic theory.

The sports industry as we define it includes the four major professional sports—baseball, hockey, football, and basketball—and individual sports such as golf and tennis and intercollegiate and Olympic events. The variety of the sports industry will allow you to study several areas of economics in a single course that covers one industry, rather than the other way around. While doing so, you will also learn about some of the defining moments in American sports.

In addition to reviewing basic economic principles, this text addresses three areas of economic theory—industrial organization, public finance, and labor economics. **Industrial organization** is the study of firms and markets as they relate to employees, consumers, government, and perhaps most importantly, each other. For example, the teams in the National Basketball Association (NBA) may compete fiercely on the court, but off the court they cooperate far more than firms in other industries. To some extent, this cooperation is understandable, even necessary. Imagine the chaos that would result if teams did not follow a common schedule! At other times, however, by acting as a single entity rather than as competing firms, teams may exert too much market power. Because the league has no competitors, fans who want to watch the highest level of basketball must patronize the NBA, which gives it power over its consumers. Finally, the NBA wields great power over local governments that vie for the right to host teams. Theories of industrial organization help us to understand the costs and possible benefits of having leagues with so much economic power.

Public finance is the study of how governments provide goods and services and of the ways that governments pay for them. For example, as local municipalities compete for the right to host a team in a given league, they may decide to underwrite some of the team's expenses, such as part of the cost of an arena. To make these payments, the municipality will likely need to raise taxes or cut funding to other programs. Exactly who should pay how much has become a very controversial issue for local and state officials. Economists and policymakers use public finance theory to analyze the costs and benefits of public subsidies for stadium construction.

Labor economics is the study of how labor markets determine the level of employment and salaries. For example, one of the functions of a minor league system is to provide training for young, inexperienced players. Minor league teams provide training in the hope that the players will become more productive and eventually play at the major league level. Labor economics helps stakeholders determine whether the team, the player, or both should pay for this training. Labor economics also shows how one can use statistics to measure productivity and therefore to determine the value of a player to the team. Finally, data on salaries and performance can be used to see whether players on the whole are exploited or whether specific groups of players are the victims of discrimination.

The goal of applied economics is to inform **policy.** For example, in Part II of this text, we discuss Major League Baseball's (MLB) antitrust exemption and whether the exemption allows team owners to take unfair advantage of players, city governments, and fans. In Part III, we discuss the wisdom of public subsidies for stadiums when many team owners could easily finance the construction themselves. In Part IV, we discuss the economics of discrimination and policies such as Title IX, which has led to dramatically increased funding for women's intercollegiate sports but has recently come under attack for its alleged impact on men's sports.

In the interest of full disclosure, we readily admit that one of our goals as economics professors is to increase your interest in economics through the use of sports. We hope that when you see how the economic principles in this text apply to sports, you will start to become passionate about (OK, at least like) economics for its own sake and become motivated to seek out other areas in which to apply it.

One of the most important reasons to study economics is to develop the tools necessary to become an informed citizen. The economic theories introduced in this text are all readily transferable to other industries. For example, the tools we introduce to help you understand the debate over stadium financing can easily be applied to the public funding of a new zoo in your community. The same questions may be asked in each case. If the project does not receive funding, will it be built anyway? Who will benefit if the project is funded? What is the cost? If public funding is provided, how can we as citizens decide who should be taxed and how much?

THE ROLE OF MODELS

Economists as well as scholars in all the social sciences rely heavily on simplifications of the real world, known as **models.** Models allow economists to isolate particular economic forces or actions. They can use a good model to make predictions and provide explanations about the world quickly and inexpensively.

Economists use models because, unlike in the physical sciences, many experiments in the social sciences are physically or legally impossible while others are prohibitively expensive. For example, to determine the effect of an increase in the number of firms in an industry, economists cannot actually increase the number of firms. Instead, economists rely on models of industry structure to make reliable predictions at almost no cost at all.

An important criterion in evaluating a model is its parsimony, or simplicity. Because the real world is simply too complex to model precisely, models make simplifying assumptions. A set of assumptions for a model of, say, perfectly competitive markets includes the size of firms relative to the size of the market, the amount of information available to firms and consumers, and the ability of individual firms and consumers to take certain courses of action (e.g., the ability to enter an industry). We introduce and make heavy use of models throughout the text. As you read, be aware of the simplifications and assumptions inherent in the models. They are often the key to what makes the models so effective, but they may also prevent the models from providing meaningful explanations under slightly different circumstances.

A good model is based on reasonable assumptions.[4] For example, it is reasonable to assume that a college football player who is thinking of forgoing his senior year knows approximately what his salary would be in his first year in the NFL; this is a **weak assumption,** meaning that it is likely to be true much of the time. Assuming that he knows what his salary will be after 10 years in the league is a **strong assumption**: it is probably not true, and so it is very risky to assume.

Most of the models that we use are well known in the industrial organization, public finance, and labor literatures. One of the most important things to remember about models is that they must be appropriate to the task. Just as the standard monopoly model is not appropriate for the study of competitive industries, a model of wage determination that requires a measure of productivity (such as batting average) is not appropriate to study sports in which worker productivity is not easily measured (such as tennis). We do not assume that you have had more than a one-semester course in principles of microeconomics, so we fully describe each model each time we employ it.

POSITIVE VERSUS NORMATIVE ECONOMICS

One of the defining elements of sports is that they appeal to people at an emotional level. Fans love *their* teams even though they have no ownership stake in them. Because of the passion that surrounds sports, it is especially important to separate fact from emotion. **Positive economics** is the study of economic phenomena from an objective viewpoint; it requires no emotional or subjective judgments. It is often described as the study of "what is." For example, if a team increased its ticket prices by 5 percent and saw its ticket sales decrease by 10 percent as a result, the team receives less total revenue as a result of the price increase. Such a conclusion requires no subjective input on the part of the economist; it just is.

Conversely, **normative economics** is sometimes referred to as the study of "what ought to be." For example, saying that corporations should pay higher prices for luxury boxes so that general admission tickets can be more affordable is a statement of opinion not fact. Normative statements involve the values—the *norms*—of the speaker. Most of the discussion in this text focuses on developing the tools of positive economics, though we sometimes use these tools to address normative issues, especially in Part III, where we discuss stadium funding.

---

[4]Alternatively, one may favor models that make good predictions, no matter how unrealistic the assumptions. For a rigorous treatment of this view, see Milton Friedman, *Essays on Positive Economics* (Chicago: University of Chicago Press, 1953).

BIOGRAPHIES

One of the best ways to learn about a larger institution, such as a team or league, is to learn about the people who have had a formative role in defining that institution. To this end, each chapter contains a biography designed to introduce you to a highly influential person in the economics of sports. In many cases, it was the experience or actions of just a few famous (or infamous) characters that changed the course of the industry. You may not know the names Bill Veeck, Branch Rickey, or Pete Rozelle, but these people were all at the center of watershed events in sports history. The text describes the events in which they participated in detail from an economic standpoint. The biographies will help you to appreciate the men and women behind the action.

SPORTS HISTORY AND BALANCE OF COVERAGE

The title of this book indicates that it will cover the economics of sports rather than the economics of the NFL or any other single sport. This is intentional. Because we view this as an economics text that uses sports as a running example rather than as a book about sports that discusses economics, we draw on a wide variety of team and individual sports at both the professional and amateur levels. Thus, you should prepare yourself for lots of baseball. Whereas your authors are split with respect to their preferences in sports—one is a die-hard baseball fan while the other is an equally rabid ice hockey fan—the existing literature is decidedly not. The literature on the economics of sports reveals a pronounced slant toward baseball.

The reasons for the emphasis on baseball are twofold. First, baseball has the longest and best-documented history of any of the four major sports in the United States. Organized baseball has been played in the United States for over 150 years. In addition, baseball has long been heralded as the "great American pastime." Americans have historically felt a unique sense of ownership of the game. Thus, its history has been documented in extraordinary detail. By comparison, basketball and football, while perhaps more popular today than baseball, did not have well-organized leagues until much later. The NFL did not stabilize as a league until well into the 1940s, and the NBA was not even formed until the late 1940s. The NHL has a long history, but hockey has never been as popular in the United States as in Canada. We make every attempt to even out the coverage of team sports across all major sports and to include a wide variety of examples from other sports, such as professional golf, tennis, and auto racing. We also include major international sports, such as soccer.

Second, some economic phenomena occur only in baseball (such as the antitrust exemption) or have their origins in baseball. While other sports have frequently imitated baseball, such as in their adoption of the reserve clause, baseball has generally served as a model for other sports. That makes it inevitable that we use it frequently to illustrate theories in action.

THE ORGANIZATION OF THE TEXT

The text is divided into four parts. Part I includes this chapter and Chapter 2, which provides an extensive review of basic economic theory. In Chapter 2, we cover the basics of supply and demand, including a discussion of antiscalping laws that seek to protect the very people who try to circumvent them. It also reviews the basics of profit maximization, including important cost concepts such as fixed, variable, opportunity, and sunk costs.

Part II contains Chapters 3, 4, and 5 and focuses on the industrial organization of sports. In Chapter 3, we review the competitive and monopoly market structures and discuss the implications for profit maximization in each case. In Chapter 4, we extend the discussion of monopoly, including an extensive discussion of the challenges that concentrated markets create for consumers. Chapter 5 describes the desirability of competitive balance, how it can be measured, how it has changed over time, and how leagues have dealt with unbalanced competition.

Part III includes two chapters on public finance. In Chapter 6, we analyze how firms might get local municipalities to pay for new arenas and describe how fiscal and neighborhood constraints have helped to determine the shape of facilities over the years. In Chapter 7, we extend this analysis by asking why local governments would make such an investment and, if such an investment is to be made, how to best fund it.

Part IV covers the labor economics of professional sports. In Chapter 8, we provide an introduction to basic labor market theories such as human capital, and we use them to explain the determination of wages. In Chapter 9, we look at the rich history of union activity in professional sports. From the recent lockouts in the NHL and NBA to the strikes in the NFL and MLB, the relations between organized labor and the leagues provide a fascinating snapshot of the union–management negotiating process. In this context, we discuss the importance of information, available substitutes, and profitability as they relate to outcomes of union–management standoffs.

In Chapter 10, we discuss the history and implications of discrimination in professional sports. From the informal yet strictly enforced "color lines" that marked the NFL and MLB until 1946 and 1947, respectively, to the possibility that hockey teams may view French Canadian defensemen as less productive than English Canadians, sports provide many examples of discriminatory behavior. In this chapter, we introduce a theoretical model that economists often use to analyze the effects of economic discrimination by employers, employees, and consumers. We then discuss the implications of discrimination using this model of wages, profits, and winning percentages.

Finally, in Chapter 11 we broaden our study of sports to include amateur athletics at the Olympic and major college levels. We discuss the history of amateurism and the consequences that misperceptions about this history have had for the National Collegiate Athletic Association (NCAA). This chapter also examines the effects of admissions and eligibility standards designed to prevent the use of nonstudent athletes. As part of this discussion, we include a section on the uneven racial impact of these rules.

ADDITIONAL SUPPORT AND SOURCES

As you progress through the course, we encourage you to make full use of the Internet as a powerful and easy-to-use source of further reading. First and foremost, the publisher of this text, Addison Wesley, maintains a website specifically designed to support the book. Log on to **www.aw-bc.com/leeds_vonallmen** and you will find a set of interesting links to other quality sites as well as information we provide directly to assist you. The site is updated regularly so that it contains links to sites and stories that are sure to be of interest.

In addition, virtually every major (and almost every minor) league team and individual sports league or association has its own web site. These sites are continually updated with new information about news (including economic events) from around the league. Finally, many sports magazines maintain websites that have current and archived information that can be very useful for term papers, projects, and general information. One caution: beware of low-quality information that is rampant on noncommercial, individual user websites. The information they convey is often based on opinion rather than on fact and is of little or no value.

Let the games begin!

CHAPTER 2

Review of the Economist's Arsenal

To be a sports fan these days is to be taking a course in economics.

— ALLEN BARRA[1]

INTRODUCTION

The sports business is full of apparent anomalies. For example:

- In 1919 the Boston Red Sox took the best left-hander in baseball out of the pitching rotation.
- Collectors pay much more for Mickey Mantle baseball cards than for Hank Aaron baseball cards, even though Aaron had better career statistics.
- Sports fans regularly seek ways around antiscalping laws designed to protect them.
- Most teams typically fail to sell out but do not lower their ticket prices.
- Teams justify hefty increases in ticket prices by pointing to expensive new free agents, yet they do not raise prices when they re-sign those same players.

Such behavior strikes the casual observer as unprofitable, self-defeating, even irrational. To the economist, however, such behavior is perfectly normal. In fact, all of the above anomalies can be easily resolved by appealing to basic economic theory. This chapter will reacquaint you with some of the most basic economic principles: supply and demand, simple market models, and simple cost concepts. Although we introduce more advanced tools in appendixes and later chapters, you should be familiar with the core ideas presented here from your principles of microeconomics class. Throughout this chapter, we reintroduce and summarize each concept before using it to resolve a real-world paradox.

---

[1]Allen Barra, "In Anti-trust We Trust," *Salon Magazine,* May 19, 2000, at http://www.salon.com/news/feature/2000/05/19/antitrust/index.html.

2.1   OPPORTUNITY COST AND COMPARATIVE ADVANTAGE

In 1915 a young left-hander for the Boston Red Sox emerged as one of the dominant pitchers in the game, helping the Red Sox to World Series championships in 1916 and 1918. In the 1918 World Series, he won two games and set a record for consecutive scoreless innings that stood until 1961. From 1915 through 1918, he won 78 games and lost only 40, and he allowed slightly over 2 runs per game. In 1919, however, he pitched in only 17 games and won only 16 more games in the rest of his career, yet no Boston fans complained. The reason was that the young pitcher was none other than George Herman "Babe" Ruth, who went on to redefine baseball as a power-hitting right fielder for the Red Sox and later for the New York Yankees.

Babe Ruth confronted the Red Sox with a classic economic problem. If Babe Ruth remained a pitcher, his attention would be divided and he would never reach his potential as a hitter. If the team put him in the outfield, they would lose his services as a pitcher. Either choice would deprive the Red Sox of a valuable service. Economists call the loss the Red Sox would incur by either choice an **opportunity cost.**

Like the Red Sox, we face opportunity costs in our everyday lives. Our limited time, income, and resources constantly force us to choose between possible actions. The value of the action we forgo is the opportunity cost of the action we choose. In this case, Boston gladly endured the loss of the best left-handed pitcher in the league in order to get the greatest hitter in the history of baseball.[2]

Both Babe Ruth and the Red Sox benefited from Ruth's forgoing an activity in which he excelled so he could specialize in an activity at which he was even better. Such decisions play a vital role in a variety of economic settings. We frequently buy goods and services from others when we could do the job more efficiently ourselves: professors employ research assistants; working parents hire day care providers; students buy latte from a coffee bar. In each case, we pay someone else to provide the good or service because doing it ourselves would keep us from an activity that we value even more highly. Employing someone to provide the less-valued good or service allows us to focus on more valuable activities and make ourselves better off.

Nowhere is this principle more frequently applied—or more misunderstood—than in the area of international trade. The United States may want to import televisions from Japan even if it is more efficient at making TVs. It does so because concentrating on making wheat or pharmaceuticals and sending them to Japan in exchange for TVs creates more total value than manufacturing the TVs in the United States. To see why, think back to Babe Ruth and the Red Sox. As the best pitcher and the best hitter on the Red Sox, Babe Ruth had an **absolute advantage** in both activities. His absolute advantage as a hitter, however, was much greater than his absolute advantage as a pitcher. Comparatively

---

[2]For more information, see Edward Scahill, "Did Babe Ruth Have a Comparative Advantage as a Pitcher?" *Journal of Economic Education*, v. 21, no. 4 (Fall 1990), pp. 402–410.

speaking, Babe Ruth was relatively better at hitting than at pitching. In other words, despite having an absolute advantage at both activities, Babe Ruth had a **comparative advantage** as a hitter. This means that the Red Sox would win far more games from having Babe Ruth play every day as a right fielder than they would lose by not having him pitch every fourth day. Similarly, a team that has four outstanding outfielders but lacks a decent shortstop can make itself better off by trading one of its outfielders for a shortstop, even if the outfielder is a better player. Since a team can use only three outfielders at a time, the fourth outfielder will have a limited role with the team and thus have a limited impact on the team's record. The shortstop, however, may add a great deal to the team if he is superior to any of the shortstops the team already has.

At the national level, if the United States had a comparative advantage in the production of pharmaceuticals, it would be better off specializing in pharmaceuticals instead of TVs even if it had an absolute advantage over Japan in both products. The opportunity cost of sacrificing pharmaceuticals in order to make TVs ourselves is higher than the cost of sending pharmaceuticals to Japan in exchange for TVs. Like Babe Ruth, we would be better off specializing in what we are relatively best at and leaving the rest to others.

2.2   A REINTRODUCTION TO SUPPLY AND DEMAND

The supply and demand model is among the simplest weapons in an economist's arsenal, yet it has remarkable power to explain the world around us. Supply and demand show us how producers and consumers respond to market incentives. Together, they determine what those incentives will be, how much of the good or service is produced, and what value society places on it. In a different course, we might use these tools to explain the financial meltdown of Asian economies or the impact of minimum wage laws on employment. In this section, we introduce the concepts of supply and demand and use them to show why Mickey Mantle cards cost so much more than Hank Aaron cards. In Section 2.3, we explore what can happen when governments interfere with the market allocation mechanism. As an example, we discuss why Michigan football fans have found creative ways to circumvent antiscalping laws designed to protect them. In Section 2.4, we review basic models of perfectly competitive and monopoly markets, and we apply them to ticket-pricing strategy.

Demand, Supply, and Equilibrium

A consumer's **demand** for baseball cards (or for any good or service) is the relationship between the price of those cards and the number of cards that he or she is willing and able to buy. It is a sequence of answers to the question, "If baseball cards cost this much, how many of them would you buy?" Figure 2.1 shows that this relationship is invariably negative: as the price of cards falls, the number of cards that the consumer buys rises. The **demand curve** representing this relationship is thus downward-sloping. Economists call the

FIGURE 2.1

The Demand for Baseball
Cards

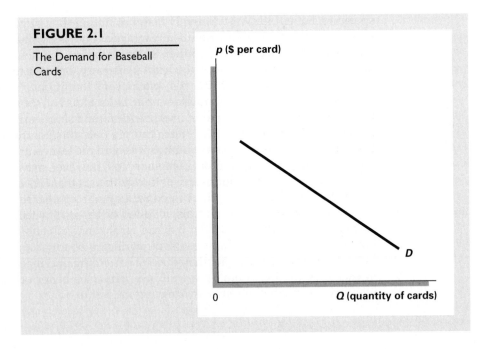

negative relationship between price and quantity the **law of demand.** A change in the price of a good causes a **change in quantity demanded,** moving quantity up along the demand curve when prices rise and down the curve when prices fall.

The relationship between price and quantity is negative for two reasons. First, as the price of baseball cards falls, consumers buy more baseball cards and less of other goods (such as football cards, comic books, or snack food). Just the opposite happens when the price of baseball cards rise. Economists call the switch to goods that have become relatively cheaper the **substitution effect,** because consumers *substitute* baseball cards for items that they would have bought had baseball cards not fallen in price.

Moreover, when a good becomes less expensive, consumers can afford more of that good (and others as well), because their purchasing power rises even if their income remains fixed. For example, if the price of baseball cards falls, consumers can afford more baseball cards as well as more hockey cards. Since the lower prices make consumers' money go further, economists call this impact the **purchasing power** (or **income**) **effect.**

The **supply** of baseball cards relates price to the number of cards that producers are willing and able to provide. As the price of baseball cards increases, each card producer has an incentive to produce more cards. At the same time, other producers have an incentive to stop what they are doing and start producing cards. Some economists call the positive relationship between price and quantity the **law of supply.**

Unlike consumers, who view the price of an item as the sacrifice they must make, producers view the price as a reward. As a result, higher prices encourage producers to make more, and the **supply curve** is upward-sloping, as seen in Figure 2.2. Again, if the price of cards changes, the quantity moves along the supply curve, a movement that economists call a **change in quantity supplied.** Taken alone, demand tells nothing about the amount consumers actually buy or the price they pay. Similarly, supply alone does not tell the amount producers sell or the price they receive. The two relationships are simply the quantity that consumers are willing and able to buy or that producers are willing and able to produce at various prices.

To find out what happens in the marketplace, one must look at supply and demand together. Figure 2.3 shows that the two curves cross at the point labeled e. Economists call e the **equilibrium point** because at that point, the actions of consumers and producers are in balance. Consumers can buy all the cards they are willing and able to buy at the equilibrium price (p_e). Similarly, producers can provide all the cards they are willing and able to sell at p_e. As a result, neither consumers nor producers have any desire to alter their actions, the price stays at p_e, and the quantity at Q_e.

At a price higher than p_e (such as p_h) **disequilibrium** occurs, because producers are willing and able to sell Q_s while consumers are willing and able to buy only Q_d. Unable to sell all the cards they want, producers face a **surplus** or **excess supply.** Frustrated producers lower their prices in order to attract more customers. The lower price encourages consumers to buy more cards and discourages producers from selling them. As Q_d rises and Q_s falls, the excess supply falls until it equals zero, and equilibrium is restored at p_e.

FIGURE 2.2

The Supply of Baseball Cards

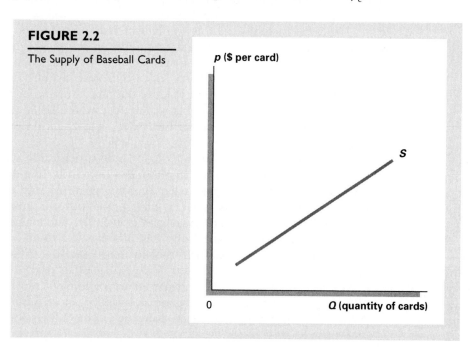

p ($ per card)

S

0   *Q* (quantity of cards)

FIGURE 2.3

Equilibrium in the Baseball
Card Market

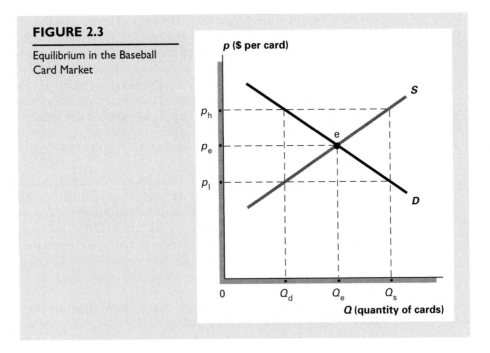

At a price below the equilibrium (p_l), buyers are willing and able to purchase more cards than sellers are willing and able to sell. The **shortage** or
excess demand for cards at p_l drives the price upward until the shortage disappears at p_e.

We cannot actually see the supply and demand curves of the products we
consume. We do, however, observe equilibrium prices. For example, baseball
trading card prices are published regularly in price guides. In 1955, the
Bowman Company produced a set of cards known as the "TV set," with pictures of players appearing on the face of the card bordered by what appears to
be a television set. Included in that set are the cards of Mickey Mantle, perhaps
the greatest switch-hitting power hitter ever, and Hank Aaron, baseball's all-
time leader in home runs.

According to Beckett's *Baseball Card Monthly* price guide, which tracks card
values, the April 2003 prices of Mantle and Aaron cards from the 1955 Bowman
set were $800 and $225, respectively.[3] Such a large difference in price is difficult
to justify, given that Hank Aaron is the all-time leader in home runs and had
more hits (H), runs scored (R), runs batted in (RBIs), and a higher batting average (Avg) than Mantle (see Table 2.1). We can use the simple supply and
demand model as an analytical tool to investigate the difference in prices.

---

[3]*Beckett's Baseball Card Monthly,* July 1999, p. 21.

Table 2.1

Career Statistics of Hank Aaron and Mickey Mantle

	AB	*H*	*R*	*HR*	*RBI*	*Avg*	*Card Price*
Hank Aaron	12,364	3,771	2,174	755	2,297	.305	$225
Mickey Mantle	8,102	2,415	1,677	536	1,509	.298	$800

Source: Beckett's Baseball Monthly, April, 2003.

Because the forces of supply and demand determine prices, the explanation must lie in differences in supply, in demand, or in both.

Supply and Demand Curves and the Price of Baseball Cards

The supply and demand relationships are not permanently fixed. The demand or supply relationship between price and quantity can change for many different reasons. This section reviews why the supply or demand curve might shift and the effects that shifts have on the equilibrium price and quantity.

Factors that Affect the Location of the Demand Curve   Economists call a shift of the demand curve a change in demand. A **change in demand** stems from a change in any of five sets of underlying factors: consumer income, the prices of substitutes or complements, consumer tastes, the number of consumers in the market, and the expectations that consumers hold. A change in the price of the item causes only a change in the quantity demanded, moving quantity along a given demand curve.

Consumers typically buy more of a good if their incomes increase, but frequent exceptions exist. If a hockey fan living in Providence, R.I., gets a raise, he may buy more hockey cards of the Providence Bruins, the local minor league team. Alternatively, he may choose to buy fewer cards of the Providence Bruins and more cards of players on the NHL's Boston Bruins. If he buys more cards of the Providence Bruins as his income rises, then the cards are **normal goods** (because that is what normally happens). If he buys fewer, then they are **inferior goods.** The term *inferior* has a very limited meaning here. Inferior goods need not be undesirable or poorly made. They are simply goods that one buys less of as one's income rises.

When the price of a substitute good increases, the demand curve shifts to the right. If a card collector views Mickey Mantle cards and Yogi Berra cards as reasonable substitutes, an increase in the price of Yogi Berra cards causes the demand curve for Mickey Mantle cards to shift to the right.

The opposite effect occurs when the price of a complement increases. For example, older cards need protection from bending and other mishaps that reduce the value of the card. The best way to prevent such mishaps is to keep the cards in protective sleeves. If the price of the sleeves rises, the demand for cards falls. This occurs because collectors tend to use the two products together and think of them as a single commodity. When the price of sleeves rises, the price of a card with a sleeve also rises, reducing demand for the **composite commodity.**

Tastes and the number of consumers in the market also affect demand. The aging of the baby boomers has led them to look back nostalgically upon the baseball players from an earlier era, increasing their tastes for old baseball cards and shifting the demand curve of a typical baby boomer to the right. While the nostalgia felt by baby boomers is not unusual, the number of people yearning for a bygone era is larger than ever, shifting the demand curve farther to the right.

Finally, expectations of future prices can affect demand. A collector who believes that the prices of cards will rise in the near future is willing to buy more cards at any given price than a collector who believes that prices will remain stable. The expectation of a price increase shifts the collector's demand curve to the right. Similarly, if the collector believes that prices will fall, his demand curve shifts to the left.

Factors that Affect the Location of the Supply Curve

As was the case for demand, the position of the supply curve also depends on several underlying factors. A **change in supply** results from a change in input prices, technology, taxes, expectations held by producers, and natural events that destroy or promote products or resources. Again, a change in price causes a change in the quantity supplied, moving quantity along a given supply curve.

In the case of baseball cards, if, on the one hand, the price of paper products rises, the cost of producing each baseball card rises as well. At any given price, the net return to making and selling cards is lower than before, and the incentive to provide cards falls. Card manufacturers produce fewer cards at any given price, and the supply curve shifts to the left from S_0 to S_1 in Figure 2.4. On the other hand, a technological breakthrough that reduces the cost of making cards increases the profitability of making cards and encourages producers to make and sell more cards. The increase in technology shifts the supply curve rightward to S_2.

A sales tax on cards introduces a wedge between the price the consumer pays and the price the producer receives. The difference between what the consumer pays and what the producer receives means that the market has two supply curves, as seen in Figure 2.5. The curve S_0 shows the supply curve from the firm's perspective. Its supply relationship is not changed by the tax: if it receives the price p_0, it is willing and able to provide Q_0. However, the consumer now must pay $p_0 + t$ in order to get the producer to provide Q_0. Figure 2.5 shows that the vertical difference between the two supply curves equals the amount of the tax. For example, a $0.10 per card tax on producers results in a new supply curve that lies $0.10 above the original.

Finally, if producers expect prices to rise in the future, they have an incentive to wait until prices rise before selling their product. At any price, producers are willing to provide less today, thinking that they will be able to sell for more tomorrow, and the supply curve again shifts to the left.

FIGURE 2.4

Changes in the Supply
of Baseball Cards

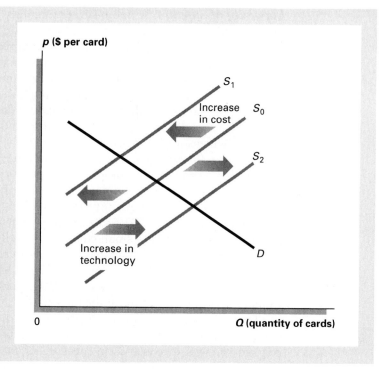

FIGURE 2.5

A Change in Supply Due
to a Tax

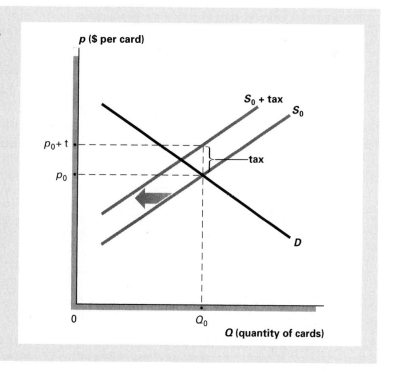

Elasticity of Supply   Economists are often less interested in how much producers produce than in how sensitive their production decisions are to changes in price. At first, one might be tempted to express this sensitivity in terms of slope. If the card producer had a steep supply curve such as S_0 in Figure 2.6, then it appears that the firm does not respond very much to an increase in price. As price rises from p_0 to p_1, the firm's output grows from Q_0 cards to only Q_1. If, however, the firm's supply curve is relatively flat (S_1), the producer responds to the price increase by expanding output from Q'_0 to Q'_1. Slope, however, is a misleading measure of sensitivity.

Suppose, for example, that the price of a pack of baseball cards rises from $0.10 to $0.11 and that the company that produces them responds by printing 200 more packs of cards. The slope of the supply curve is the change in price divided by the change in quantity, or $0.01/(200 packs).

The problem is that 200 packs can represent a big change in the number of packs produced or a very small change, depending on the producer's starting point: how many packs it had been printing to begin with. Increasing production by 200 packs means much more to the producer if it expands from 1,000 packs to 1,200 than if it expands from 10,000 packs to 10,200. As a result, slope cannot tell us how meaningful the increase of 200 packs really is.

Economists account for the producer's starting point by using percentage changes in price and output rather than absolute changes.[4] They use these percentage changes to construct a measure of the sensitivity of production to changes in price known as the **elasticity of supply** (which we denote as ε_s). The elasticity of supply is the percentage change in quantity that results from a given percentage change in price:

$$\varepsilon_s = \frac{\%\Delta Q^s}{\%\Delta p}$$

In the above example, the $0.01 increase in the price of a pack of cards corresponds to a percentage change of $0.01/$0.10 = 0.10, or 10 percent. If the company originally produced 1,000 packs of cards, then the percentage change in quantity is $(1{,}200 - 1{,}000)/1{,}000 = 0.2$, or 20 percent, and the elasticity of supply is $\varepsilon_s = 0.2/0.1 = 2.0$. When the price of a pack of cards rises by 10 percent, producers increase their output by 20 percent. The percentage increase in output is twice the percentage rise in price.

If the company originally produced 10,000 packs of cards, the percentage increase in output is $(10{,}200 - 10{,}000)/10{,}000 = 0.02$, or 2 percent, and the elasticity of supply becomes $\varepsilon_s = 0.02/0.10 = 0.20$. In this case, a 10 percent increase in the price of a pack of cards brings only a 2 percent increase in production, and the firm is much less responsive to changes in price.

Although the supply curve's location and elasticity are important for many of the issues we deal with later in the book, they cannot resolve our question

---

[4]We define the percentage change of the variable X (% ΔX) as $\Delta X/X = (X_1 - X_0)/X_0$.

FIGURE 2.6

Relatively Elastic Versus
Inelastic Supply

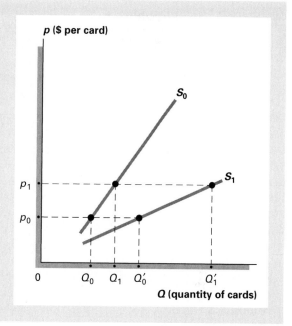

about the relative prices of Mantle and Aaron cards. Because the Bowman Company produced the cards for the same series in the same year, we know that it printed the same number of each card. If we assume that the same number of cards have survived in perfect (mint) condition, the supply of each card is equal and fixed. Thus, the quantity supplied is completely unresponsive to changes in price, and the supply curve is a vertical line. Because price changes do not affect the quantity supplied, the supply curve in Figure 2.7 is **perfectly inelastic.**

Elasticity of Demand As with supply, we are often interested in the sensitivity of demand to changes in price rather than absolute levels of price and quantity. The **elasticity of demand** (ε_d) is the percentage change in quantity demanded for a given percentage change in price. The only difference between the elasticity of demand and the elasticity of supply is that the elasticity of demand measures movement along the demand curve rather than the supply curve:

$$\varepsilon_d = \frac{\%\Delta Q^d}{\%\Delta p}$$

For example, if the price of a card increases from $0.10 to $0.11 and the quantity demanded falls from 1,000 to 750 cards, the elasticity of demand is

$$\frac{(1000 - 750)\Big/1000}{(0.10 - 0.11)\Big/0.10} = -2.5.$$

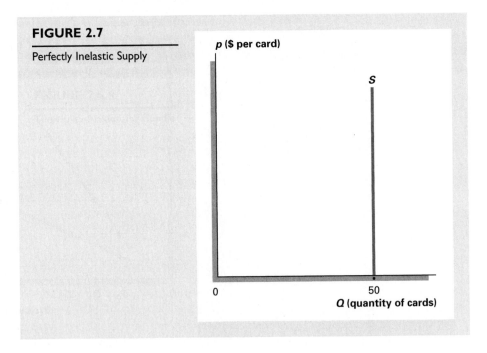

FIGURE 2.7

Perfectly Inelastic Supply

Elasticities of demand fall between zero (perfectly inelastic) and minus infinity (infinitely elastic).[5] When the elasticity lies between 0 and −1, we say that demand is **inelastic,** because the percentage change in quantity is less than the percentage change in price. When the elasticity is less than −1, we say that demand is **elastic.**

Resolving the Card Price Paradox   We can now use the simple supply and demand model to show that the difference in value between Mickey Mantle and Hank Aaron stems from economic forces rather than accident or error. We previously noted that there is no reason to believe that the supply curves of Mantle and Aaron cards differ from each other. Because a fixed number of cards of each player were produced, we assume that supply is perfectly inelastic. As a result, differences in price must be the result of differences in demand. What factors might contribute to such a large difference in demand?

Mickey Mantle spent his entire career in New York, while Aaron spent his career in Milwaukee and Atlanta, which are much smaller cities. Even if Aaron and Mantle are equally popular with their hometown fans, the difference in population causes the demand curve for Mickey Mantle cards to lie far to the right of the demand curve for Hank Aaron cards. To see why, assume that a typical fan prefers players and memorabilia for his hometown team and that each Braves fan has the same individual demand for Hank Aaron cards that

[5]Some microeconomics textbooks eliminate the negative sign by taking the absolute value of the elasticity formula. We use the negative number because it reinforces the notion that price and quantity move in opposite directions along the demand curve.

each Yankee fan has for Mickey Mantle cards. To make life even easier, assume that there are only two Braves fans—Ray and Roy—and that only 50 mint condition cards for each player exist.[6] Each has a demand curve for Hank Aaron cards, given by D_{Ray} and D_{Roy} in Figure 2.8, which tell us how many Hank Aaron cards Ray or Roy is willing and able to buy. We are not, however, interested in how many cards an individual Braves fan buys at each price. We want to know how many cards all Braves fans *combined* buy at each price. In this example, all we have to do is find how many cards Ray buys at each price and add that amount to the number that Roy buys at the same price. Thus, if Ray buys 22 cards at $225 while Roy buys 28, the market demand at $225 is 50 cards.

Suppose Ray and Roy have identical twins in New York who are just as rabid about Mickey Mantle as Ray and Roy are about Hank Aaron. Because New York is a larger city, the twins in New York have several friends who also root for the Yankees. Adding all of the individual demand curves for Mickey Mantle cards pushes the market demand curve for his cards to the right, increasing their price relative to Hank Aaron cards.

In addition to having more people, the New York metropolitan area has fans who are, on average, wealthier than Braves fans in either Milwaukee or Atlanta. If baseball cards are normal goods, the higher level of income causes the demand curve for Mickey Mantle cards to shift out still farther relative to the demand for Hank Aaron cards.

FIGURE 2.8

The Relationship Between Individual Demand and Market Demand for Baseball Cards

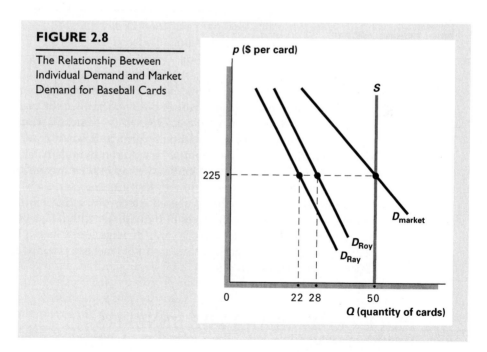

---

[6]In practice, the process of determining market demand is the same whether there are two Braves fans or 2 million. Assuming there are only two fans just simplifies the illustration.

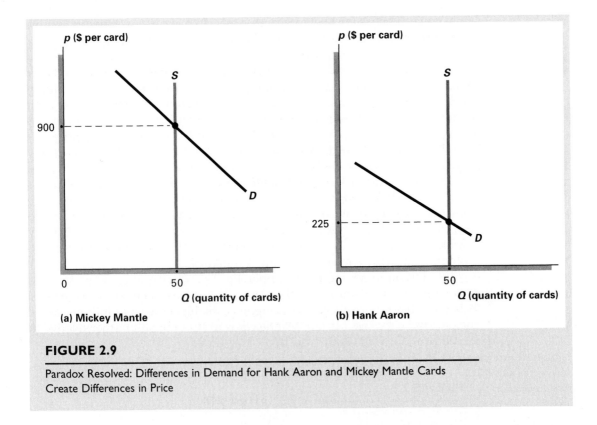

FIGURE 2.9

Paradox Resolved: Differences in Demand for Hank Aaron and Mickey Mantle Cards
Create Differences in Price

Finally, one must account for the unfortunate possibility that the tastes of baseball fans for baseball cards reflect the prejudices of the population at large. As we shall see in Chapter 10, most economists regard discrimination as a taste or distaste for members of a particular group. If some card collectors prefer Mickey Mantle, who was white, to Hank Aaron, who is black, simply because of their races, the demand for Mantle cards would be greater than the demand for Aaron cards.

Figure 2.9 shows that the combined effects of the differences in market size, income, and tastes and preferences of individuals with a taste for discrimination result in greater demand for Mantle cards than for Aaron cards. The differences in demand coupled with the identical, perfectly inelastic supply curves create the difference in equilibrium price.

2.3   PRICE CEILINGS AND THE BENEFITS OF SCALPING

A few days before football games against traditional rivals such as Michigan State or Ohio State, a strange ritual often occurred in front of the University of Michigan's Student Union. Students walked about with tickets to that

Saturday's game in one hand and a pencil in the other. When someone offered to buy the ticket, the student would agree to do so—but only if the potential buyer also bought a pencil.

The key to understanding such an odd sales arrangement lies in the state of Michigan's antiscalping laws. According to the law, no one can sell tickets for more than the value printed on the ticket (its *face value*). The face value of the ticket, however, was well below what a free market would dictate. In economic terms, the law placed a **price ceiling** on tickets, keeping their price far below equilibrium. If the face value of a ticket is $15, and no sales are permitted above this price, the price ceiling (p^c) is $15. Such a ceiling is shown in Figure 2.10.

A price ceiling creates two problems for buyers and sellers. First, the price ceiling ($p^c = \$15$ in Figure 2.10) creates excess demand for tickets, since the quantity of tickets demanded (Q^d) is much greater than the quantity of tickets supplied (Q^s). To make matters worse, there is no guarantee that the people who place the greatest value on tickets will be able to get them. By limiting price to p^c, we know only that all buyers are willing and able to pay at least p^c to see the University of Michigan football team. If price does not serve as an allocation mechanism, someone who is just willing to pay the face value for a ticket may get one while someone who values it far more highly may not.

If those with tickets could sell freely to those without, a mutually beneficial trade could be arranged. Suppose, for example, that Daniel is a rabid Michigan fan who is willing to pay $100 for a ticket to see Michigan play Michigan State.

FIGURE 2.10

The Effect of a Price Ceiling

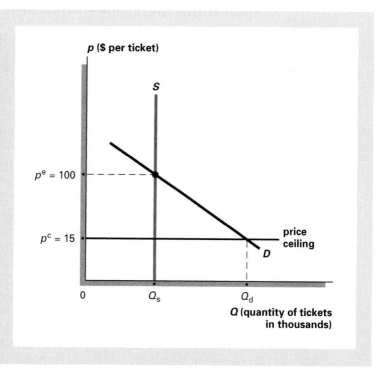

Melanie—the lucky recipient of a ticket—thinks a ticket is worth only $15. If Daniel pays Melanie $70 for the ticket, he would pay $30 less than the ticket is worth to him while Melanie would receive $55 more than the ticket is worth to her. Daniel and Melanie would both benefit from such an exchange, yet the law prohibits it. That is why Melanie can be found on State Street in Ann Arbor, offering her ticket for the face value of $15, but only to those who are willing to pay $55 for her pencil. That is why Daniel is there as well, happy to pay a premium price for a pencil![7]

2.4   MARKET STRUCTURES: FROM PERFECT COMPETITION TO MONOPOLY

So far, we have implicitly made the unrealistic assumption that all goods are bought and sold in **competitive markets.** While this assumption may work for some goods, such as potatoes, it is not always accurate. As we will see in Chapters 3 and 4, it is usually inaccurate for professional and elite amateur sports markets. In this section, we review both competitive and monopolistic market structures. We then use these simple models to see why the Philadelphia Phillies do not lower their ticket prices even though they regularly fail to sell out. We also use them to explain why the Texas Rangers raised ticket prices when they signed Alex Rodriguez to a quarter-billion dollar contract.

A Note on the Definition of Output

Before analyzing any market, economists must determine how to measure output. In some markets, such as the pizza market, defining output (Q) is easy. It is the number of pizzas produced per period. In the sports industry, defining and measuring output is more complicated. If we think of output as that which the firm sells in order to obtain revenue, we could measure output as attendance or television appearances. If we focus on production, it may be more useful to measure output by the game, because the team must combine inputs to produce games throughout the course of the season. Finally, if a team's popularity, and hence its revenue, depend on its performance, the appropriate output is wins or winning percentage rather than simply games played. Our problem resembles the one facing those who study higher education. From the standpoint of revenue, a college or university may define output as the number of students enrolled. From the standpoint of input utilization, it may define output as the amount that its students learn, perhaps measured by their future incomes. Unfortunately, there is no simple resolution to this issue. To force a universal definition of output would cloud the issue as often as it would clarify it. In this text, we address this thorny issue by defining output according to the aspect of the market we wish to focus on.

---

[7]A note of caution: it is doubtful that this practice is legal in most areas—and thus it is not one that we would advocate or condone.

Perfect Competition

Competitive markets have many producers and consumers, all buying and selling a homogeneous product. Buyers and sellers are small compared with the overall size of the market, so no single firm or consumer can alter the market price unilaterally. We further assume that buyers and sellers have good information about prices. Thus, if a firm in a competitive market tries to raise the price it charges, consumers will simply purchase an equivalent product elsewhere at the market price.

Although the *market* demand curve for a good sold in a competitive market is still downward-sloping, each *individual* competitive firm faces an L-shaped demand curve. The horizontal part of the curve shows the market price that is determined by market supply and demand. If a firm raises its price above that charged by its rivals in a perfectly competitive market, its sales fall to zero. The vertical part of the demand curve coincides with the vertical (price) axis and shows that the firm will not sell any output if it charges a price above the prevailing market price.

Figure 2.11 shows how a competitive market works for potatoes. Market demand and market supply dictate an equilibrium price of $4/bag in Figure 2.11a. Each farmer thus faces a demand curve that is horizontal at p = $4 in Figure 2.11b. If a farmer attempts to charge more than $4, his sales fall to zero.

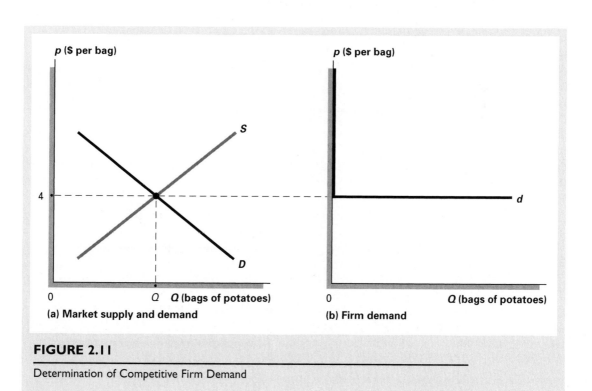

(a) Market supply and demand

(b) Firm demand

FIGURE 2.11

Determination of Competitive Firm Demand

Since each producer is so small relative to the size of the entire market, a farmer can sell all the bags he wants at the market price without causing the market price to fall. Economists call firms in this position **price-takers.**

Because the farmer can sell each additional bag of potatoes for $4, the extra revenue he receives from selling an additional bag—his **marginal revenue** (*MR*)—equals the price he charges for that last bag ($MR = p$). The farmer weighs the additional revenue received against the additional costs endured to produce an additional bag of potatoes, his **marginal cost** (*MC*). The farmer maximizes profits by producing and selling additional bags of potatoes until the extra revenue earned from selling the last bag (*MR*) equals the cost of producing that last bag (*MC*), as seen in Figure 2.12.

We can envision marginal revenue and marginal cost by imagining that the farmer keeps all of his money in a safe. When an additional bag of potatoes is produced and sold, the farmer must take some money out of the safe to pay the expenses associated with selling one more bag. The revenue from the sale goes back into the safe. If marginal revenue exceeds marginal cost, the total amount of money in the safe rises when the farmer sells another bag because he puts more money in the safe than he takes out. If selling an additional bag increases the total amount of money in the safe, the farmer wants to sell more potatoes. If marginal cost exceeds marginal revenue, selling more potatoes causes the farmer to take more money out of the safe than he puts in, and the farmer wants to cut back on the amount of potatoes grown and sold. When the farmer puts just as much money into the safe as he takes out of it, $MR = MC$, and there is no incentive to increase or reduce production.

FIGURE 2.12

Marginal Revenue and Marginal Cost

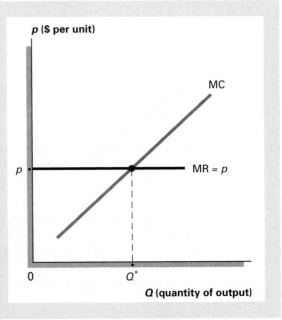

Finally, economists assume that competitive firms can freely enter and exit the market. Thus, if potato farmers are making large profits, more farmers will plant potatoes. The increase in the number of farmers growing potatoes shifts the market supply curve to the right. The rightward shift of the supply curve causes prices to fall, reducing individual firm profits. This result is probably the single most important outcome of the competitive market. When firms in a competitive industry are profitable, other firms enter, causing price and profits to fall.

Free entry by producers benefits consumers in two important ways. It ensures that firms in the industry cannot restrict output in order to drive up prices and earn excessive profits. More importantly, competitive markets are **economically efficient.** An economically efficient outcome maximizes society's gains from exchange. In this context, profits attract new farmers and stimulate production by existing farmers so that society's desire for potatoes is satisfied. We discuss the concept of economic efficiency extensively in Chapter 4.

Monopoly and Other Imperfectly Competitive Market Structures

In reality, most goods have some characteristics that distinguish them from other commodities. Consumers may have no clear preferences over the type of potatoes they buy, but they may prefer buying tickets to see the Colorado Rockies play baseball to buying tickets to see the Denver Broncos play football. If we measure output as the number of fans in attendance, and if sports fans in Denver feel that there are no perfect substitutes for a Rockies game, the Rockies have **market power** that enables them to raise prices without losing all of their customers. As a result, the demand curve for Rockies games is downward-sloping rather than L-shaped. If the Rockies had no competitors at all and consumers had the choice of seeing a Rockies game or seeing nothing, we would call the Rockies a **monopoly.** To keep things simple for now, we shall focus on this extreme form of market power, in which a single firm is the only producer. In such a case, the demand curve faced by the individual firm is the market demand curve, because the firm does not share the market with any other firms.

Most sports franchises exercise some degree of market power. This power stems from several sources. Baseball fans' preference for watching baseball games rather than other sporting events gives the Rockies a degree of market power. The Rockies' market power increases if baseball fans in Denver prefer watching a Rockies home game to watching a St. Louis Cardinals home game. Even if fans in Denver feel that attending a Cardinals home game is just as good as attending a Rockies home game, the two games are not readily substitutable for each other because it is much more difficult and expensive for a Rockies fan to get to a Cardinals game in St. Louis. Finally, potential competitors (i.e., teams competing for an audience against other forms of entertainment) often face substantial **barriers to entry**—such as access to playing facilities or a television contract—that prevent them from providing a reasonable alternative.

Like a competitive firm, a monopoly maximizes profit when its marginal revenue equals its marginal cost. *Unlike* a competitive firm, a monopolist does not passively accept the price and quantity that are dictated by the intersection of supply and demand. The monopolist can set price and output at the level that maximizes its profits.

As a monopoly, the Rockies face the downward-sloping market demand curve and must lower their ticket prices if they want to sell more tickets next year. Since the Rockies cannot easily identify all the fans who bought tickets at a higher price this year, they will have to reduce the price of all the tickets they sell next year.[8] The extra revenue they receive from selling an additional ticket changes for two reasons. First, the team gains additional revenue from selling the extra tickets, although at a lower price than in the previous year. Second, the team loses revenue because it must lower the price of all tickets in order to sell more tickets. For example, suppose the Rockies sold 2 million tickets last year at $10 each and want to sell 3 million this year. If they attract the additional fans by charging $8 for all 3 million tickets, they gain $8 million in revenue from selling 1 million extra tickets at $8 apiece and lose $2 on each of the 2 million tickets they could have sold for $10 each. As a result, the additional revenue from increasing sales by 1 million tickets is only $4 million (new revenue = $8 × 3 million = $24 million; original revenue = $10 × 2 million = $20 million), not $8 million as the price alone suggests. As a result, the monopolist's marginal revenue curve lies below the demand curve, as seen in Figure 2.13.

FIGURE 2.13

Demand and Marginal Revenue from Ticket Sales

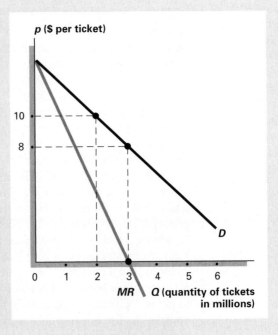

[8]For now we ignore the complication raised by season tickets and by price discrimination.

As long as the Rockies are not selling out, the marginal cost of accommodating an extra spectator is close to zero. It costs the team relatively little to sell one more ticket and to admit and clean up after one more fan. As a result, economic analyses of ticket sales typically assume that the marginal cost of an extra spectator equals zero. When ticket sales reach the capacity of the stadium, the marginal cost effectively becomes infinite since the team cannot sell any more seats at any price. Figure 2.14 illustrates this with a marginal cost curve that is effectively zero until the team reaches its capacity of approximately 50,000. At this point the marginal cost curve becomes vertical.

Figure 2.14 shows that monopoly power allows the monopoly to charge a much higher price than would a competitive industry. A perfectly competitive industry operates where the market demand curve cuts the MC curve, producing Q^c and charging a very low price (in this simple example, $p^c = \$3$). The monopolist produces $Q^m < Q^c$ because the MR curve cuts the horizontal axis at a much lower level of output. When the demand curve is a straight line, the

FIGURE 2.14

Rockies Attendance and Prices

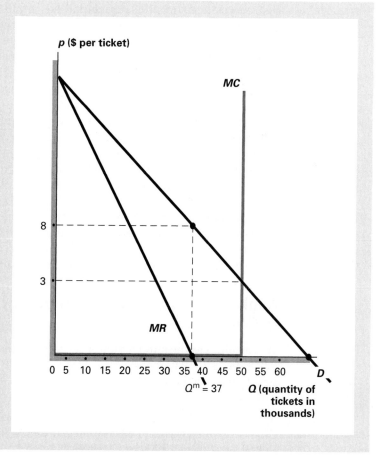

marginal revenue curve cuts the horizontal (quantity) axis exactly half as far out as the demand curve cuts the axis.

To find the highest price the producer can charge and still sell Q^m (37,000 tickets per game in this example), we look at the demand curve. In addition to telling us how much people are willing and able to buy at a given set of prices, the demand curve tells us the maximum amount consumers are willing and able to pay for a given amount. The demand curve in Figure 2.14 tells us that the Rockies can sell 37,000 tickets if they charge no more than $8 per ticket.

We can now use this simple model of monopoly behavior to determine whether the Philadelphia Phillies or Philadelphia Flyers is irrational in their ticket policy. On the surface, it appears that *someone* is doing *something* wrong. After all, the Flyers regularly sell out while, even in their glory years, the Phillies could only half-fill Veterans Stadium on average. It seems that either the Flyers charge too little or the Phillies charge too much.

In fact, both teams may be following optimal strategies. Having at least a degree of market power in the market for sports entertainment, both the Phillies and the Flyers face downward-sloping demand and marginal revenue curves. We continue to assume that marginal costs are zero, so their marginal cost curves lie along the horizontal axis at all attendance levels below full capacity. However, the teams reach full capacity at very different points. Until their recent move, the Phillies played in Veterans Stadium, which had a capacity of almost 65,000 per game, while the Flyers play in the Wachovia Center, which can hold only 19,500 per game.[9] Because the Wachovia Center is so much smaller, the marginal cost curve for Flyers games becomes vertical much earlier than the marginal cost curve for the Phillies, as seen in Figure 2.15.

The different MC curves mean that the Phillies and the Flyers will follow different pricing policies even if they have identical demand curves. Because the MC curve for the Phillies is horizontal over such a large range of attendance, the marginal revenue curve probably crosses the marginal cost curve along the horizontal axis, as seen in Figure 2.15b. This means that the Phillies were maximizing their profits from attendance even though they played in a stadium that was more than half-empty. By contrast, the Flyers' marginal revenue curve is far more likely to cross the marginal cost curve after the marginal cost curve has become vertical. The Flyers maximize their profits from attendance by charging a relatively high price and selling out the Wachovia Center.

Applying the Models: Evaluating an Increase in Costs

We can also use the simple monopoly model to explain the puzzling response of ticket prices to player costs. Professional franchises typically blame increases in ticket prices on the spiraling salaries of their players. "Don't blame us," they say,

---

[9]For facilities capacities, see *Inside the Ownership of Professional Sports Teams*, ed. by Mathew Freeman (Chicago: Team Marketing Report, 2000). We shall discuss why the Phillies play in a stadium that is "too big" for them in Chapter 6.

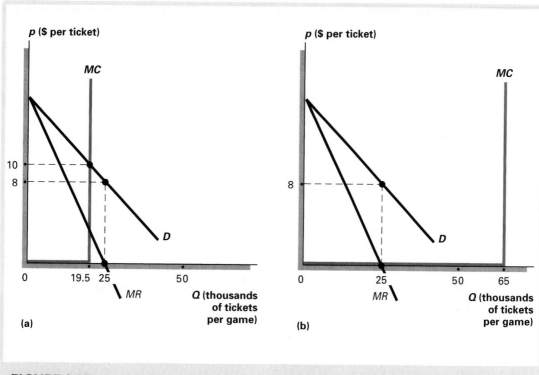

FIGURE 2.15

(a) Flyers Attendance and Prices; (b) Phillies Attendance and Prices

"as our costs go up, we have to raise prices to keep pace." This explanation has been accepted without question by most fans and columnists. Unfortunately, the claim flies in the face of basic economic theory.

We have shown that teams determine how many tickets to sell—and how much to charge for their tickets—by equating the marginal revenue and marginal cost of selling an additional ticket. We have also shown that the marginal cost of providing an extra seat is generally very low until the team approaches the seating capacity of its venue. Perhaps surprisingly, the model completely ignores the cost of guaranteed player contracts. That is because such contracts are **fixed costs** that do not vary with output (recall we are measuring output as attendance). Because player contracts do not affect marginal costs, they have no bearing on ticket prices.

To see why Alex Rodriguez's salary represents a fixed cost to the New York Yankees, just ask yourself how much the Yankees must pay him if the team draws only 1 million fans and how much they must pay him if the team draws over 3 million fans. A player's salary—like any fixed cost—does not change as output rises. The $252 million over 10 years that the Yankees are

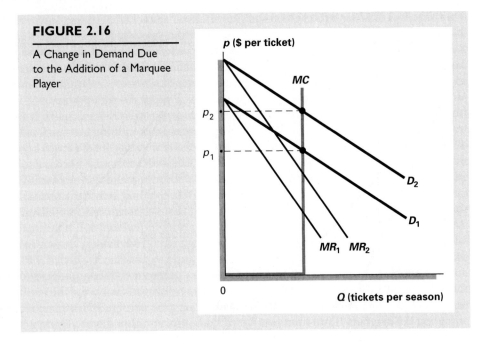

FIGURE 2.16

A Change in Demand Due to the Addition of a Marquee Player

paying Alex Rodriguez has the same impact that a $252 million legal judgment against the team might have. All else equal (or, as economists say, *ceteris paribus*), the price and quantity of tickets that maximized profits before the payment still do so after the payment. The only difference is that profits are lower than before. Why, then, do teams raise ticket prices after signing free agents?

The key can be found on the demand side of the ledger, not the supply side. Teams raise ticket prices when they sign a *new* free agent if they feel that the new player makes fans willing to pay higher prices than before. Teams charge higher ticket prices because the demand curve (and hence the marginal revenue curve) shifts outward, as seen in Figure 2.16. The higher demand and marginal revenue curves lead to a higher equilibrium price and (subject to capacity) quantity than before. In short, teams charge higher prices when they sign free agents because they *can* do so not because they *must*.

2.5 THE DEVELOPMENT OF PROFESSIONAL SPORTS

Before closing this chapter, we briefly look back at the development of organized and professional sports. It is no coincidence that professional soccer and professional baseball developed almost simultaneously in England and in the United States. While all "ball sports" have antecedents dating back to antiquity, baseball and soccer were the first sports to become widely popular, professional national pastimes.[10] Both sports developed and flourished when and where they did as the result of broad-based economic phenomena. Historians of sport determined early on that there was a link between the prosperity that came in the wake of the Industrial Revolution in the mid-19th century and the development of sport.[11] Specifically, in order for a society to adopt a pastime, it first must have time to pass.[12]

Soccer and baseball started as leisure activities of the relatively wealthy. They became professional sports only after the Industrial Revolution had sufficiently raised the living standards of the public at large so that a steady fan base could financially support a professional organization.

The modern version of soccer developed in the elite "public schools" of England (e.g., Eton, Charterhouse, Westminster, Harrow, and Rugby). Starting from a vaguely defined primitive sport, soccer evolved at each of the public schools in much the same way that different species of animals develop from a common ancestor when they live on separate islands. Each school developed its own version of soccer based on the unique characteristics of the terrain on which it was played. At most schools, rough or muddy grounds made violent contact impractical. Schools that had large, open fields, such as the Rugby School, developed much rougher versions of the sport. Soccer's popularity soon spread to Cambridge University and Oxford University and was played in clubs formed by public school and university graduates. It is no coincidence that one of the most popular of the early clubs called itself "The Old Etonians."

In the United States, baseball also first appeared among the more prosperous elements of society. An early form of baseball was an adaptation of English games played by the Puritan upper-middle class in New England by the late 18th century. The first organized game did not appear until 1842, with the formation of the New York Knickerbocker Club.

Though they lacked the social imprimatur of the British public school, baseball clubs also strove to establish or maintain the social positions of their members. Games between baseball clubs in the pre–Civil War era were less a competition than an exercise in "manly upright fellowship, harmony, and decorum. For them, excellence in performance meant exhibiting character as well as skill. . . . "[13]

In the second half of the 19th century, the benefits of the Industrial Revolution began to spread to all segments of society in England and in the United States. The higher standard of living of working-class families led to a

---

[10]The ancient sports were typically associated with religious festivals, whereas movements such as the *Turnverein* in the early 19th-century German states were more expressions of nationalism than entertainment.

[11]For a good historical overview, see William Baker, *Sports in the Western World* (Totowa, N.J.: Rowman & Littlefield, 1982); and Robert Burk, *Never Just a Game: Players, Owners, and American Baseball to 1920* (Chapel Hill: University of North Carolina Press, 1994).

[12]More advanced students can refer to Appendix 2A to see the material presented in a more sophisticated manner that introduces and uses indifference curves and budget constraints to present the same material.

[13]Burk, *Never Just a Game* (1994), p. 6.

broader pursuit of leisure activities. Rising real wage rates gave people the option of devoting at least some time to leisure. As a result, soccer spread northward from the public schools around London into the industrial heartland of England and Scotland, and baseball spread south and west from New York. In addition, playing baseball became a way for members of immigrant communities to assert their "Americanness." Thus, by the turn of the century, in England, soccer clubs of working-class people had largely displaced "Old Etonians," while in America, first-generation Americans of German and Irish descent had largely displaced "Yankee" baseball players.

The most significant result of the popularity of soccer and baseball among the working class was the growing professionalization of the games. Working-class athletes lacked the independent means of earlier participants, so they could not afford to play regularly without being compensated for the opportunity cost of their time. The upper-class sportsmen on both sides of the Atlantic saw their roles change from amateur participants to financial backers of professional teams. While they remained firmly in charge of the management and financing of the clubs, the old guard roundly condemned the "moral declension" that accompanied both the increasing professionalism of sports and the participation of working-class athletes. Their concern did not keep them from recognizing that they could profit from marketing a superior, professional product to a public that now had the money and leisure time to attend sporting events regularly. We will return to the discussion of the spread of sports activities to the working class in Chapter 11 in the context of the history of amateurism.

2.6   CHOICES UNDER UNCERTAINTY

Implicit in all of our analysis to this point is the assumption that everyone knows the consequences of his or her actions with certainty. Life, however, is far less certain and far more interesting than that. When consumers make choices, they allocate their income to maximize their levels of well-being, or **utility.** In a world of perfect knowledge and information, maximizing one's utility is a straightforward exercise. Because real-world consumers do not have perfect knowledge or information as they make choices, they must instead maximize **expected utility.** Throughout this book, we will encounter situations in which uncertainty enters into the decision-making process. From the fans who do not know whether their favorite team will win to the owners who do not know how well a free agent or draft pick will perform, those involved encounter uncertainty at every turn in the world of sports.

Consider, for example, the case of Thomas, a rabid Chicago Bears fan. He wants to purchase tickets to the Bears final home game of the season. Because it is the last home game, he must purchase the ticket several months in advance to be assured of a seat. When Thomas buys his ticket, it is unclear whether the Bears will still have a chance to make the playoffs when game day arrives. He will enjoy the game much more if it has implications for the team's status in the playoffs. In economic terms, Thomas derives substantially more utility from a meaningful Bears game than from one with no playoff implications (especially if the Bears have already been eliminated). As a result, a ticket to a game that the Bears need to win is worth more than a ticket to a game where it does not matter if they lose. We must now adjust our definition of the commodity from simply "a seat" to "a seat for a specific type of game." A meaningful game is a qualitatively different commodity from a meaningless game. Unfortunately, Thomas must purchase his ticket before he knows the implications of the game, an extremely common dilemma facing sports fans.

When a person makes consumption decisions under uncertainty, he must calculate his anticipated level of utility, which is his expected utility from consuming the good. Expected utility $[E(U)]$ is the weighted sum of utilities derived from all possible outcomes, where the weights equal the probabilities of the outcomes. For example, Thomas's expected utility of attending the Bears game is his utility from seeing a meaningful game (U_M) times the probability that he will see a meaningful game (Pr_M), plus his utility from seeing a meaningless game (U_N) times the probability of a meaningless game (Pr_N):

$$E(U) = Pr_M(U_M) + Pr_N(U_N)$$

If the Bears have an equal chance of playing a game with playoff implications and playing a game without playoff implications on Sunday, then the probability of each event is 0.5. If Thomas receives 30 units of happiness from seeing a meaningless game and 100 units of happiness from seeing a game with playoff implications, then his expected utility from attending the game is 65:

$$E(U) = 0.5(100) + 0.5(30) = 65$$

Such reasoning may seem abstract, but it has important implications for ticket sales. As the quality of the team improves, the odds of seeing games with playoff implications (Pr_M) rise, and the expected utility of fans like Thomas rises. As a result, better teams should draw more fans.

Table 2.2 shows the relationship between performance in 2001 and attendance in 2002 for both the National Football League and Major League Baseball. The figures show that attendance at baseball games follows performance much more closely than it does for football.[14] The apparent fickleness of baseball fans probably stems from the fact that football has a much shorter season. As a result, far fewer fans have the opportunity to attend games. For example, the San Diego Padres and San Diego Chargers both play in Qualcomm Stadium, but the Padres can accommodate approximately 4.9 million fans over the course of a season, whereas the Chargers can seat only about 456,000. This means that the Chargers will find it easier to fill Qualcomm Stadium to capacity than the Padres, even if both have equally poor teams.

One might assume from this argument that Thomas would be happiest if the Bears could arrange to win all their games. You—and perhaps Thomas as

---

[14]The correlation coefficient for football is only 0.142, while the correlation coefficient for baseball is 0.556.

Table 2.2

NFL and MLB Winning Percentages and Home Attendance by Team

NFL Team	2001 Winning Percentage	2002 % of Capacity	MLB Team	2001 Winning Percentage	2002 % of Capacity
San Francisco 49ers	0.75	0.971	Arizona Diamondbacks	0.568	0.877
Chicago Bears	0.81	30.86	Anaheim Angels	0.463	0.632
Cincinnati Bengals	0.375	0.805	Baltimore Orioles	0.391	0.678
Buffalo Bills	0.188	0.926	Atlanta Braves	0.543	0.642
Denver Broncos	0.5	0.993	Tampa Bay Devil Rays	0.383	0.291
Cleveland Browns	0.438	1.001	Florida Marlins	0.469	0.236
Tampa Bay Buccaneers	0.563	1.01	Boston Red Sox	0.509	0.974
Phoenix Cardinals	0.438	0.56	Chicago Cubs	0.543	0.888
San Diego Chargers	0.313	0.884	Chicago White Sox	0.512	0.467
Kansas City Chiefs	0.375	0.984	Cincinnati Reds	0.407	0.58
Indianapolis Colts	0.375	1.01	Cleveland Indians	0.562	0.754
Dallas Cowboys	0.313	0.971	Colorado Rockies	0.451	0.673
Miami Dolphins	0.688	0.965	Detroit Tigers	0.407	0.47
Philadelphia Eagles	0.688	0.999	Kansas City Royals	0.401	0.42
Atlanta Falcons	0.438	0.967	Houston Astros	0.574	0.737
New York Giants	0.438	0.982	Minnesota Twins	0.525	0.488
Jacksonville Jaguars	0.375	0.771	Los Angeles Dodgers	0.531	0.69
New York Jets	0.625	0.982	New York Yankees	0.594	0.787
Detroit Lions	0.125	0.942	Milwaukee Brewers	0.42	0.572
Tennessee Titans (Oilers)	0.438	1.004	Oakland Athletics	0.63	0.614
Green Bay Packers	0.75	0.974	Montreal Expos	0.42	0.216
New England Patriots	0.688	1.006	Seattle Mariners	0.716	0.928
Carolina Panthers	0.063	0.976	New York Mets	0.506	0.645
Oakland Raiders	0.625	0.96	Philadelphia Phillies	0.531	0.328
St. Louis Rams	0.875	1.001	Texas Rangers	0.451	0.598
Baltimore Ravens	0.687	1.004	Pittsburgh Pirates	0.383	0.589
Washington Redskins	0.5	0.942	Toronto Blue Jays	0.494	0.4
New Orleans Saints	0.438	0.992	San Diego Padres	0.488	0.413
Seattle Seahawks	0.563	0.941	San Francisco Giants	0.556	0.984
Pittsburgh Steelers	0.813	0.943	St. Louis Cardinals	0.574	0.748
Minnesota Vikings	0.313	0.999			

Sources: NFL.com; MLB.com; individual team websites

well—may be surprised to know that fans are happiest if their favorite teams do not win all the time. The Cleveland Browns' dominance of the All American Football Conference in the late 1940s led to declining attendance at all games, including those played in front of Cleveland fans.[15] The predictability of the outcome made the game boring, even for the Browns fans.

---

[15]James Quirk and Rodney Fort, *Pay Dirt* (Princeton, N.J.: Princeton University Press, 1992), p. 240.

More recently the dangers of predictability led *Sports Illustrated* to ask whether the dominance of the Chicago Bulls in the 1990s was bad for the NBA.[16] As noted earlier, competitive balance is an important issue in any league, and thus, we devote an entire chapter to it in Part II (Chapter 5).

The desire to see games with playoff implications helps explain why fans who buy season tickets get a better price per game than do fans who buy tickets for individual games.[17] If Thomas knew that the game between the Raiders and the Bears would be a meaningful one between two contending teams, he would be much happier than if he knew that the game would be meaningless. If Thomas has to buy a season ticket before the season begins, he cannot be certain which type of game he will see. If he waits until the week of the game, he has a much better idea of how enjoyable the game will be. He can then decide whether buying the ticket is worthwhile. By selling Thomas the ticket before he knows how exciting the game will be, the Bears are getting Thomas to take the risk that the game might not be worth seeing. The odds are, however, that Thomas—like most of the rest of us—does not like risk, that he is **risk averse.**

People are risk averse if they are unwilling to accept a "fair bet" that gives them an equal chance of winning or losing a given amount. To see whether you are risk averse, ask yourself whether you would be willing to bet everything you own—double or nothing—on the flip of a coin. Almost all of you would immediately decline the bet, yet doing so seems to violate basic laws of probability. After all, you have an equal chance of winning and doubling your net worth and losing and ending up with nothing. Suppose your net worth is $1,000. There is no difference between standing pat at $1,000 and taking the bet, because the expected outcome of the bet is

$$0.5 \cdot \$2,000 + 0.5 \cdot \$0 = \$1,000.$$

Economists resolve this paradox by pointing out that people are more concerned about expected utility than about expected payoffs. The correct formulation of the value of the bet is

$$E(U) = 0.5 \cdot U(\$2,000) + 0.5 \cdot U(\$0).$$

We also know that the extra utility that one gets from additional wealth (or pizza or sweat socks) declines due to the principle of diminishing marginal utility. Figure 2.17 shows that the $1,000 one stands to lose in a bet—one's first $1,000 in income—brings greater utility than the additional $1,000 one gains from winning the bet. As a result, the expected utility from the fair bet is less than the expected utility from standing pat even though the expected payoffs are the same.[18] Because the uncertain outcome of the bet leaves one worse off, a risk averse person is willing to pay a **risk premium** to avoid the bet. (That is

---

[16]Jack McCallum, "A Cut Above," *Sports Illustrated* (March 10, 1997), pp. 24–29.

[17]Another important reason is that when fans buy tickets in advance, the team gets its revenue and can begin to earn interest earlier than if fans bought their tickets the day of the game.

[18]A **risk lover,** on the other hand, prefers the chance to make a big killing, since the additional $1,000 means more to him or her than the previous $1,000.

FIGURE 2.17

Risk Aversion

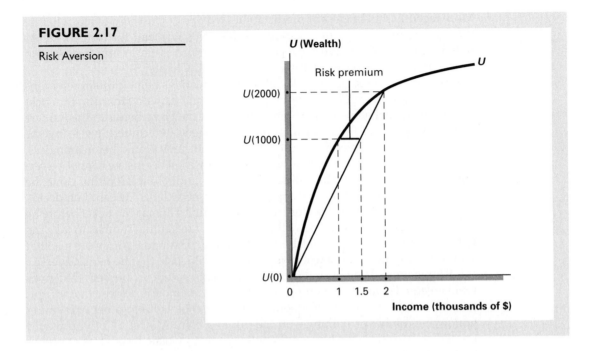

why people buy insurance.) Looked at the other way around, a risk averse person is willing to undertake the bet only if he or she is paid to do so.

In buying the season ticket, Thomas is betting that the Bears will be worth seeing in November and December. If Thomas is risk averse, however, he will not take this bet willingly. To get Thomas to assume the risk, the Bears have to offer him the inducement of lower ticket prices. As a result, season tickets will typically sell at a discount.

Thomas's willingness to take a "fair bet" becomes even more important if he also wants to place a wager on the outcome of the Bears–Raiders game. If Thomas is risk averse and if he regards each team as equally likely to win, then a $100 bet would give him the expected utility U_{bet} (Figure 2.18), which is lower than the utility he would have if he did not bet at all, U_0. This seems to imply that Thomas never accepts a fair bet. Paradoxically, many risk averse people who insure their health, homes, and cars also go to casinos where they place wagers at considerably less than fair odds. The solution to the paradox lies in the fact that Thomas may view his bet on the Bears as a form of entertainment rather than as a way to maximize his income. Still, even the entertainment value of the bet will not be enough to get Thomas to bet on the Bears if he thinks the Raiders are sure to win.

When betters agree on the outcome of an event—if, for example, everyone agrees that the Raiders will beat the Bears—bookies, the intermediaries between people who bet on different outcomes, face two problems. First, since bookies make their money by taking a percentage of every bet placed (what betters call the "vigorish"), they want to maximize the number of bets placed. When most

FIGURE 2.18

Expected Utility from a Bet

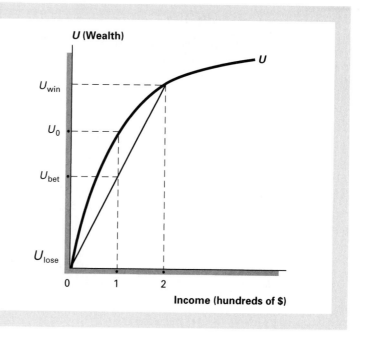

betters believe that the Raiders will win, then few people will bet on the Bears, and the bookies will make little money. Bookies also want to get a roughly equal number of people to bet on the different outcomes. If everyone bets on the Raiders and wins, the bookie can be driven out of business. A bookie in this situation is like an insurance agent whose clients all bet that an earthquake will occur by buying insurance and who all cash in at once. Bookies have developed two methods to maximize the number of bets placed and to ensure that the bets are relatively evenly spread.

Bookies can offset an unfavorable probability by offering an unbalanced payoff. Thomas may be unwilling to risk an even bet of $100 if he thinks the Bears will probably lose, but he may risk $100 if he can get $300 back should the Bears win. Figure 2.19 shows that the lower probability of winning pushes Thomas closer to U_L than to U_W, but the higher payoff increases U_W, so that Thomas may still be willing to bet.

Bookies can also attract betters by offering a "point spread," a predicted margin of victory for one of the teams. The favored team "covers the spread" if it wins by more than the predicted margin. A bookie will try to set the point spread on the Bears–Raiders game so that the amount bet by people who think the Raiders will cover the spread equals the amount bet by those who think the Raiders will fail to cover the spread. Point spreads thus allow Thomas to win the bet even if his beloved Bears lose the game.

FIGURE 2.19

Increasing the Payout Maintains Betting Interest in the Face of Poor Odds

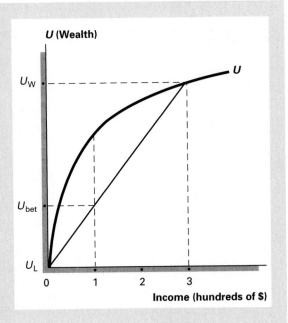

ADAM SMITH
BIOGRAPHICAL *Sketch*

It is not from the benevolence of the butcher, the brewer, or the baker that we expect our dinner, but from their regard to their self-interest.
— ADAM SMITH IN *THE WEALTH OF NATIONS*

Adam Smith never dunked a basketball, never moved a football franchise from one city to another, and never traded a baseball player from one team to another. In fact, the only exercise of any kind that he undertook with any regularity seems to have been long, absentminded walks. According to one account, one morning stroll through his garden turned into a 15-mile walk in his nightshirt. This book, however, owes as much to Adam Smith and to his ideas as to any figure from the sports pages. He represents the formal beginning of modern economic thought.

Western economic thought and the development of the world economy might have taken a very different turn had a group of gypsies traveling through Scotland moved a bit faster. A troupe going through Kirkaldy, the town where Smith had been born in 1723, kidnapped the four-year-old Smith. Pursued by Smith's family, the gypsies abandoned Smith by the side of the road. Thirteen years later, Smith again left Kirkaldy, this time willingly, to attend Oxford. Smith returned to Scotland in 1751 to take a position at the University of Glasgow. While at Glasgow, he produced the first of two works that were to establish his reputation. In *The Theory of Moral Sentiments*, published in 1759, Smith addressed how people could set aside their natural inclination toward pursuing their narrow self-interest and serve the common good.

Smith developed the answer to this question more completely in his masterpiece, *An Inquiry into the Wealth of Nations*, published in 1776. Much of what Smith said in *The Wealth of Nations* was not new, having been worked out by earlier philosophers and statesmen, but no one had seen how the individual insights could fit together into a broad theory of social organization. Smith's masterwork thus laid the groundwork for most of the Western economic tradition that was to follow, and much of the work done by economists in the intervening 225 years has been spent amplifying and refining the principles Smith set out in *The Wealth of Nations*.

The key insight of *The Wealth of Nations* was an answer to the question Smith raised in his *Theory of Moral Sentiments,* how selfish people could make for a harmonious society. In the earlier work, Smith had proposed that people could step outside their own skins and view their own actions from the dispassionate perspective of a third party. In *The Wealth of Nations,* Smith proposed a distinct third party that regulated people's actions—the disciplinary power of the competitive market. Thus, while individual merchants might wish to charge their customers outlandish prices, they were constrained to keep their prices low by the pressures of the marketplace. Producers were thus led to provide for the needs of society as if guided by an "invisible hand."

Smith, however, was no pro-business ideologue. While Smith's writings became the basis for *laissez-faire* policies, the idea that businesses best serve society if the government simply leaves them alone, he also saw that the invisible hand depended crucially on the forces of competition and not on the good wishes of proprietors. In *The Wealth of Nations,* Smith warns, "People of the same trade seldom meet together, but the conversation ends in a conspiracy against the public or in some diversion to raise prices."

Chapters 2 through 4 of this book thus owe much of their content to Smith's theories. Smith also wrote extensively about labor markets and occupational choice. He claimed that workers prospered only when they produced items that consumers desired. The

➡

same invisible hand that guided producers to make the items that consumers desired also guided workers to allocate (and propagate) themselves so as to satisfy the needs of employers. This helped Smith resolve the puzzle of why public executioners, who were reviled by society, received much greater pay than clergy, who were objects of veneration. Much of Chapter 8 thus also reflects Smith's theories.

Adam Smith died in 1790. Like Mozart's death just one year later, Smith's death attracted little attention. Also like Mozart, however, his work has lived on.

Source: Richard Heilbroner, *The Wordly Philosophers.* (New York: Clarion Book, 1967.)

SUMMARY

In this chapter, we reviewed the basic supply and demand model and discussed its power as an explanatory tool. In order to properly explain or understand most economic relationships, a solid understanding of this framework is needed. If you have a clear understanding of which external forces affect demand and which affect supply, then you can make accurate predictions regarding the direction of change in prices and output.

When markets are competitive, prices are lower and output is higher than if a firm has monopoly power; not all economic activity, though, occurs in competitive markets. Monopoly power gives the firm the ability to set prices rather than simply accept the price as determined by the market. In most sports markets, teams have some level of market power. By setting ticket prices, teams have the ability to control attendance, subject to the capacity of their building.

Costs and the distinction between fixed and variable costs play a vital role in the determination of output and prices. For professional sports teams, players' salaries are often best treated as fixed costs, because they are unrelated to the number of games played.

Uncertainty plays a dual role in the economics of sports. On the negative side, it prevents people from making advanced purchases and teams from paying advanced salaries with complete information about the value of those purchases. On the positive side, the uncertainty of outcome increases the utility derived from attending a game.

In the chapters that follow, we will extend our use of these tools and introduce new methods, based on these fundamentals, in order to further explain the economics of sports.

DISCUSSION QUESTIONS

1. Why do sports leagues sometimes guarantee teams that no new team will be placed within a certain geographic area surrounding existing teams?

2. Why do some cities have two teams in the same sport (e.g., the Cubs and the White Sox), while many other cities have no professional team?

3. Why do professional sports leagues not allow their teams to play against opponents who are not members of the league?

4. Discuss the assumptions of the perfectly competitive model as they relate to the National Collegiate Athletic Association (NCAA) and amateur sports.

5. Can players unions, such as the National Hockey League Players Association, be viewed as attempts to monopolize talent?

6. Would sports markets be more competitive if fans were only concerned about even contests rather than absolute quality?

7. From the league's perspective, what are the costs and benefits to increasing the number of teams?

8. Should ticket scalping be legalized? Who would benefit if it was?

9. Why do teams that win championships typically raise their prices the next season?

PROBLEMS

2.1 Show, using a graph with attendance on the horizontal axis, the effect on the NHL of the following changes:

  a. An increase in the quality of play due to increased use of international players

  b. A tax on each ticket sold

  c. A decrease in consumer income

  d. The start-up of a rival league

2.2 Suppose the market demand for tickets to a University of Tennessee basketball game is $Q^d = 40,000 - 1,000p$, and the supply is $Q^s = 20,000$. What is the equilibrium price of a ticket to the game? What would be the effect of an increase in consumer income on equilibrium price and quantity?

2.3 In Problem 2, what would be the effect on the market of a price ceiling set at $10? What about a ceiling set at $30?

2.4 Suppose the Jets raise ticket prices from $30 to $40 per seat and experience a 10-percent decline in tickets sold. What is the elasticity of demand for tickets?

2.5 A fan called a talk radio show and exclaimed, "I've had it with professional sports. The building is always sold out, and the tickets are too expensive!" Use supply and demand analysis, including graphs, to show that these claims cannot both be true simultaneously.

2.6 Suppose a monopoly team faces demand for a sporting event of $Q = 100 - p$. The associated marginal revenue function is $MR = 100 - 2Q$. If marginal cost is zero, what are the optimal quantity (of tickets) and price per ticket? If fixed costs are $500, what would the level of profit be?

2.7 Suppose that the Lakers did a study that showed that the demand for tickets was perfectly inelastic at the capacity of the building up to a price of

$500 per ticket, at which point it becomes perfectly elastic. Draw a supply and demand diagram assuming a building capacity of 20,000. What would this imply about their best pricing strategy?

2.8 Suppose that the demand for seats at a minor league baseball game in Trenton, N.J., is $Q^d = 6,000 - 10p$.

    a. How many fans would attend if tickets were free?

    b. At what price would no fans attend the game?

    c. If the building capacity (supply) is fixed at 4,000, what price would maximize revenue while ensuring a sellout?

2.9 Suppose the Chicago White Sox charge $10 for bleacher tickets and sell 250,000 of them over the course of the season. The next season, they raise the price to $12 and sell 200,000 tickets. What is the price elasticity of demand for bleacher tickets? Assuming the marginal cost of providing tickets is zero, is the price increase a good strategy?

2.10 Suppose the city of Anaheim places a tax on tickets to see the Mighty Ducks play. Use supply and demand curves to show that the fans and the team share the burden of the tax.

APPENDIX **2A**

Utility Functions, Indifference Curves, and Budget Constraints

This appendix reviews the basics of consumer theory. It contains an introduction to utility maximization, which involves the use of indifference curves and budget constraints.

2A.1 CONSTRAINED MAXIMIZATION

Sandy is a graduate student who loves to go to baseball games and read economics textbooks. In fact, tickets and books are the only things she buys.[19] Economists evaluate Sandy's feelings toward baseball and economics books by evaluating her **utility function.** Sandy's utility function tells us how much happiness (or utility) she gets from buying different amounts of baseball tickets and economics books. We can think of it as a mathematical representation of her preferences. In this example, Sandy's utility function contains only baseball tickets (T) and economics books (B), and so we can write her utility function as

$$U = u(B, T).$$

Since Sandy wants both books and tickets (they are "goods" as opposed to "bads" that she does *not* want), whenever the number of either books or tickets increases, Sandy's **total utility** increases as well.

In this framework, if Sandy's income were unlimited, she would make herself best off—she would **maximize her utility**—by buying an infinite number of tickets and books. In reality, no matter how wealthy, no one has limitless resources. These limits force us to make choices, to sacrifice some of one item in order to have more of another. Economists call the process by which people make themselves as happy as possible in light of limited resources **constrained maximization.**

Constrained maximization reflects the three basic principles of economic thought:

- People want to maximize their happiness.
- People cannot get everything they want.
- People make **rational choices** in order to be as happy as possible.

---

[19]Sandy surely buys more than just two items, but this simplification allows us to use two-dimensional pictures rather than multivariate calculus.

Economists, like Freudian psychologists, believe that people are motivated by a desire for pleasure. Freudians call the pleasure impulse "the id." Economists call it "utility maximization." Also like psychologists, economists see forces that hold the pleasure impulse in check. Rather than the internal, psychological barrier of Freud's superego, economists see external **constraints** in the limited resources that people have at their disposal. People have only so much money, time, and energy with which to satisfy their desires. As a result, they cannot have all things or engage in all activities that make them happy. Put simply, they have to make choices. They do not, however, choose randomly. Economists assume that people maximize their utility subject to constraint by making rational choices, the economic analogue to Freud's ego.

Many noneconomists have seized on the idea of rational choice to claim that economists view people as walking calculators who carefully weigh all options and have no room for emotions of any kind. Such a characterization is unfair. In fact, rationality need not connote careful decision making—or even sanity. To an economist, rational behavior is consistent, rather than reasonable, behavior. Actions that most people would regard as heinous or bizarre would still be rational to an economist as long as the person doing the actions did so consistently.

Indifference curves allow us to illustrate people's preferences in a world that contains two goods. Recall the case of Sandy, who likes to watch baseball games and buy economics texts. Sandy enjoys a certain amount of happiness from seeing 10 baseball games and buying four economics textbooks (a combination illustrated by point A in Figure 2A.1). If someone took away one of Sandy's books (moving her to point A'), she would not feel as happy as before.

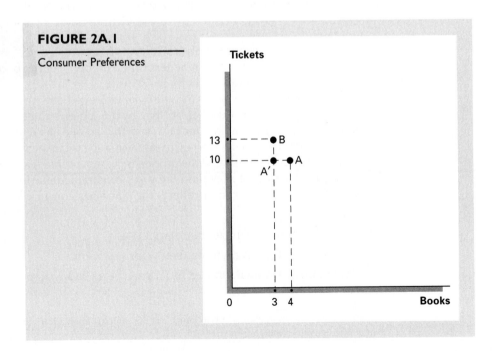

FIGURE 2A.1

Consumer Preferences

Sandy would not feel so bad, however, if the person who took away her book gave her a ticket to a ballgame in exchange. In fact, if the person gave her enough tickets (say three tickets, putting her at point B in Figure 2A.1), Sandy might feel just as happy as she did to begin with.

If Sandy feels exactly the same about the two combinations of ballgames and books, we say that she is **indifferent** between points A and B. There are typically many combinations of ballgames and books that make Sandy equally happy. Combining all these points yields an **indifference curve,** like the ones shown in Figure 2A.2.

Because every combination of ballgames and textbooks yields some level of utility, every point in Figure 2A.1 is on *some* indifference curve. As a result, drawing all of Sandy's indifference curves would require filling in the entire area of the graph as each successive curve was drawn infinitely close to the previous one. We therefore draw only a sampling of her indifference curves. While indifference curves can come in many different shapes, most look like those in Figure 2A.2: they are downward-sloping, convex, and cannot intersect.

Indifference curves slope downward any time we consider two products that the consumer likes. If we give Sandy more of a product that she likes, she is happier. To restore her initial utility level—and keep her on her original indifference curve—we have to take away some of something else that she values. More of one good means less of the other, and so the indifference curve slopes down. Having more of both goods would make Sandy happier, giving her a higher level of utility, shown by her being on a higher indifference curve in Figure 2A.2.

A convex indifference curve is typically very steep at first but becomes steadily flatter as one moves down and to the right. To see why, note that when

FIGURE 2A.2

Indifference Curves

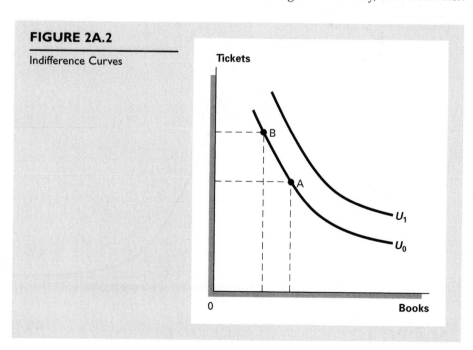

Sandy sees many ballgames and reads few books, she is willing to give up seeing a large number of ballgames in order to get only a few more books, as shown by the movement from point A to A' in Figure 2A.3. In this range, the indifference curve is steep. The same logic results in an almost flat indifference curve when Sandy has many books but sees only a few ballgames, as in the movement from B to B' in Figure 2A.3. Economists typically attribute Sandy's behavior to the principle of **diminishing marginal rate of substitution.** This principle asserts that as consumers give up each successive unit of one good, they need increasing quantities of the other good in order to maintain the same level of utility. It is closely related to **law of diminishing marginal utility,** which states that as a person consumes increasing quantities of one good, holding the consumption of all other goods constant, the marginal utility of the additional units consumed will eventually fall.

If indifference curves intersected, we would have to make some rather bizarre conclusions about how people behave. Figure 2A.4 shows what happens if two of Sandy's indifference curves, U_1 and U_2, cross at point A. Above point A, indifference curve U_2 lies to the right of indifference curve U_1. That means that Sandy can have more books without giving up any ballgames, leaving her better off. As a result, Sandy prefers all points on U_2 to all points on U_1. However, below point A, the positions of the indifference curves are reversed, meaning Sandy prefers all points on U_1 to all points on U_2. To make matters still more confusing, since the two curves have point A in common, Sandy must get the same level of utility from both curves.

FIGURE 2A.3

Diminishing Marginal Rate
of Substitution

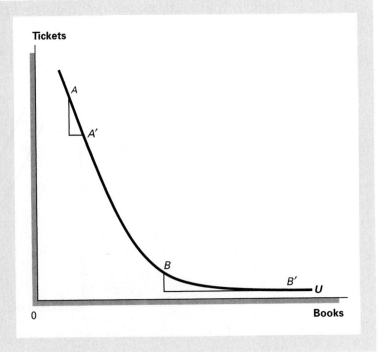

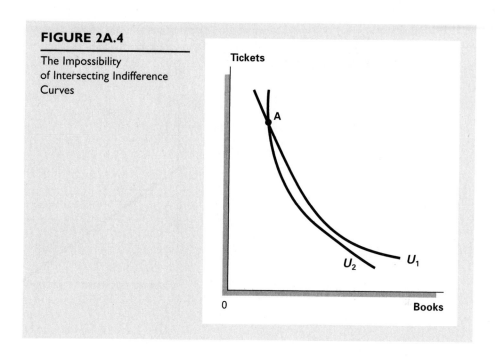

FIGURE 2A.4

The Impossibility
of Intersecting Indifference
Curves

To maximize her utility, Sandy wants to be on the highest possible indifference curve. She is limited, however, by the amount of time, energy, and income at her disposal. For simplicity, assume that Sandy is constrained only by her income (I) of $800 and that tickets to a ballgame cost $10 while economics texts cost $20. Figure 2A.5 shows that she can buy 80 tickets if she buys only tickets and 40 textbooks if she buys only books. Since books cost twice as much as tickets, Sandy must give up two tickets in order to buy one more book. As a result, her **budget constraint** is a straight line with slope −2 that connects the points corresponding to 80 games and zero books, and zero games and 40 books.

We can write Sandy's constraint algebraically as

$$20B + 10T = 800.$$

More generally, if p_b is the price of books and p_t is the price of tickets,

$$p_bB + p_tT = I.$$

To see how changes in income and prices affect the constraint, consider what happens when we change the two. If the price of a ballgame doubles to $20, Sandy's opportunities fall. She can now see only 40 games if she spends all her money on tickets. Figure 2A.6 shows that the vertical intercept slides down to 40 games, and the budget constraint becomes flatter. Since ballgames and textbooks now cost the same amount, Sandy can get one more book by sacrificing one ballgame, and the slope of the constraint becomes −1. If the price of a ballgame falls to $5, Sandy can see 160 games, her opportunities expand, and the slope of her constraint becomes −4.

FIGURE 2A.5

Budget Constraint

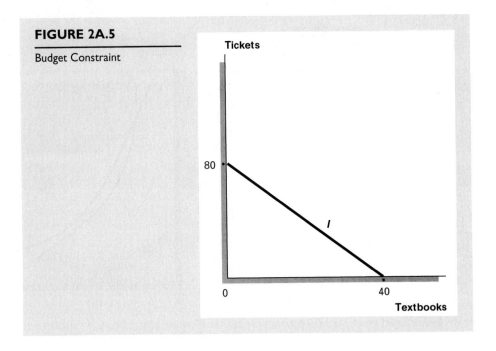

FIGURE 2A.6

The Effect of Changes in Price
on the Budget Constraint

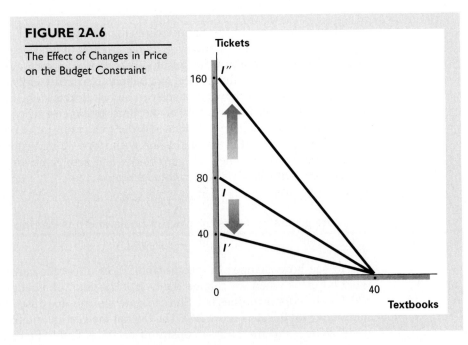

If Sandy gets a raise so that she now has $1,000 at her disposal (and all prices
stay at their original levels), her opportunities again expand. If she buys only
tickets, she can go to 100 games. If she buys only textbooks, she can buy 50 books.

Both intercepts in Figure 2A.7 increase, and the entire constraint shifts outward. Since the two prices have not changed, Sandy must still give up two ballgames to buy another book, and so the slope of her constraint remains –2.

Sandy's best possible choice of ballgames and economics texts comes on the highest indifference curve that still satisfies her budget constraint. This occurs where the indifference curve and the budget constraint are tangent, at point E in Figure 2A.8. To see that E is the best possible point, consider any other possible point on the budget constraint (we have chosen F in Figure 2A.8, but you can choose any other). One can draw a horizontal line from the combination of games and books represented by point F to combination G, which lies on the indifference curve. This means that Sandy can have more books without sacrificing any ballgames by moving from point F to point G, leaving her better off. We also know Sandy likes points G and E equally because they lie on the same indifference curve. Since we can do this for *any* other possible point, no other attainable combination of ballgames and textbooks provides as much utility as E. In addition, Sandy cannot afford a better combination of books and ballgames because any higher indifference curve lies outside her constraint.

2A.2 USING INDIFFERENCE CURVES AND BUDGET CONSTRAINTS: THE RISE OF SOCCER AND BASEBALL

For people to pursue a pastime as either a spectator or a participant, they must first have leisure time to devote to it. Labor economists have developed a model of leisure time in which people trade off leisure time against the goods

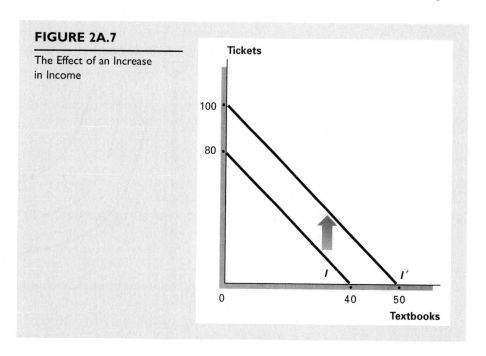

FIGURE 2A.7

The Effect of an Increase in Income

and services that they could buy from working. Figure 2A.9 illustrates Sandy's preferences over leisure time and consumption of goods and services.

FIGURE 2A.8

The Utility-Maximizing Bundle

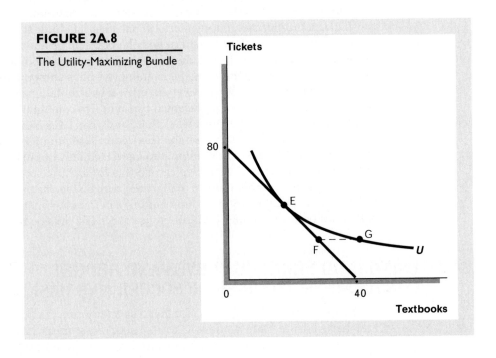

FIGURE 2A.9

The Trade-off Between Goods and Leisure

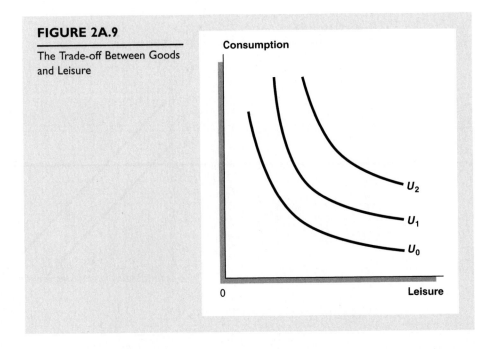

Sandy, however, has only so much time in a typical day, week, or month to allocate to either leisure or work.[20] To consume more, Sandy has to sacrifice leisure time. Sacrificing leisure time means that Sandy can earn more income and buy more goods and services. If, for example, Sandy earns $10 per hour, each hour of leisure that she sacrifices brings her $10 in added consumption. In this case, her budget constraint in Figure 2A.10 is a downward-sloping line connecting T hours, the maximum amount of leisure she can enjoy with $10 \cdot T$, the maximal amount of consumption she can enjoy. We next add a set of indifference curves that show Sandy's preferences regarding consumption and leisure. As before, Sandy is best off at the point of tangency between the indifference curve and her constraint.

As noted in the chapter, prior to the Industrial Revolution, most societies could be characterized as *subsistence economies* in which people had to spend all (or almost all) their time generating goods in order to survive. If Sandy must consume at least C_0 in order to survive, then she has an additional constraint. Her survival constraint is the horizontal line through C_0 in Figure 2A.11. Sandy cannot consume less and survive. If Sandy lives in a subsistence economy, she

---

FIGURE 2A.10

The Utility-Maximizing Combination of Goods and Leisure

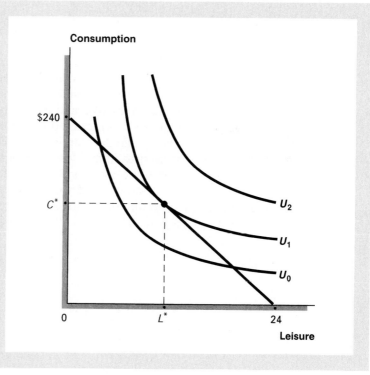

---

[20]Labor economists acknowledge that people can allocate their time in other ways. One example is "home production," the unpaid work that goes into cooking, cleaning, childrearing, and similar activities.

FIGURE 2A.11

Subsistence Level of Income
Allows No Leisure

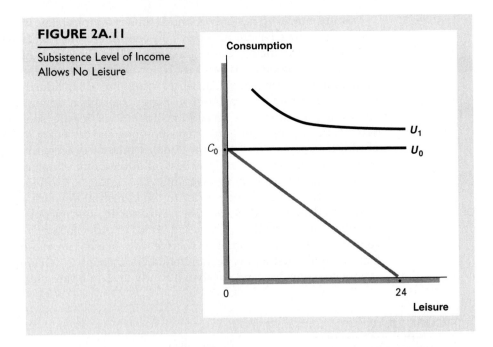

must spend all her time working in order to survive. This means that Sandy's budget constraint and her survival constraint meet at C_0.

As a society moves from a subsistence economy to an industrial economy, workers become more productive, and their wages rise. A higher wage allows Sandy to generate more consumption than before for every hour of leisure she sacrifices, so that her budget constraint swivels outward, and her maximum possible consumption rises from C_0 to C_1 in Figure 2A.12. Sandy now has several combinations of leisure and consumption that lie above her survival constraint. Sandy can now afford to consume both goods and services and leisure time. The advent of leisure time allows Sandy to pursue nonproductive activities such as the participation in and attendance at athletic events.

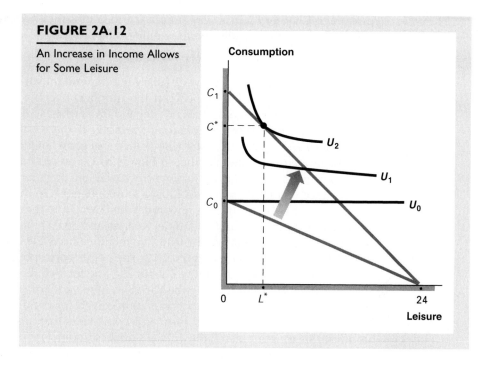

FIGURE 2A.12

An Increase in Income Allows
for Some Leisure

APPENDIX 2B

Regression Analysis in Brief

How many times have you and your friends debated whether a player is worth the money his team pays him? Economists are not content to debate the monetary value of a player over lunch. They estimate a player's value based on a sophisticated statistical technique known as regression.[21] While we cannot make you an expert in a few short pages, by the end of this appendix, you should have an appreciation of the concept of a regression, a general idea of how economists use regressions, and a basic grasp of how to interpret regression output.

Suppose you want to figure out how much Paul Kariya, a star forward with the Colorado Avalanche, is worth to his team. Presumably, the Avalanche pay him based on some measure of performance. (We shall discuss the precise

---

[21]See G. S. Thomas, "Surhoff Proves to be '99's Best Investment," in *Street & Smith's SportsBusiness Journal* (October 25–31, 1999), p. 1, for an article that uses a technique such as this.

measure in Chapter 8.) In a very simple world, teams may base the salaries of all players other than goalies on the number of goals they score:

$$\text{Salary} = f(\text{Goals}).$$

In the equation above a player's salary is a **dependent variable,** because its value depends on (is determined by) the number of goals a player scores. Because the number of goals does not depend on another variable in the equation above, we call it an **independent variable.** If the relationship between goals scored and a player's salary (the "functional form" of $f(x)$ in the equation above) was a straight line like that in Figure 2B.1, you would be able to compute how much Paul Kariya was worth based on the number of goals he scored. Since you know that Paul Kariya scored 44 goals in the 1999–2000 season, you could tell your friends how much he is worth to the team.

Unfortunately, life is not so simple. Salaries and goals scored do not line up perfectly along a straight line. Instead, the relationship is likely to be scattered around the line, as shown in Figure 2B.2. The points corresponding to players' goals and salaries may be scattered about the line for two reasons. First, there may be some error in measuring the variables involved. For example, Kariya's official salary may not include a bonus he received for making the NHL All-Star Team. If so, then the bonus resulted in payments that are not captured in his official salary. As a result, the official statistics understate Kariya's full compensation, and the point corresponding to Paul Kariya's goals and salary lies below the line.

Second, a player's salary and goals scored may not lie on the line because of some factor for which we have failed to account. For example, Kariya may also have many assists—plays that lead to goals scored by his teammates. If teams reward both players for both goals and assists, then Kariya's goal–salary

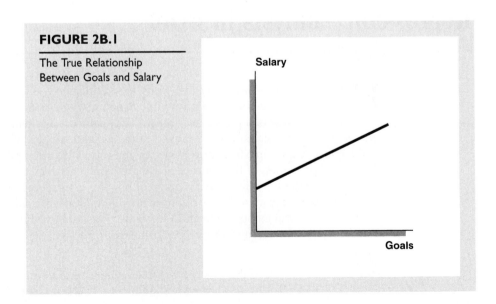

FIGURE 2B.1

The True Relationship
Between Goals and Salary

FIGURE 2B.2

Observations Scattered
Around the True Relationship

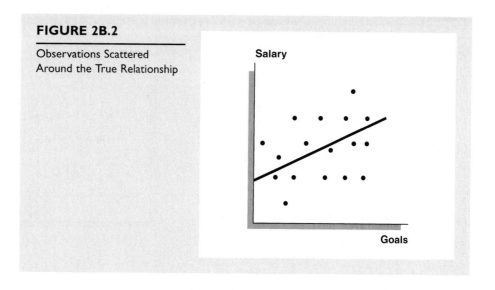

combination may lie above the line in Figure 2B.2 because his salary also reflects a factor that our goal–salary relationship ignores.

Making matters more difficult still, in real life, we do not observe the line in Figure 2B.2. All we see is the scatter of points. From this scatter of points, we must estimate the relationship between goals and salaries before making a statement about a given player.

An economist who wants to know the relationship between goals scored and salary in the NHL must first estimate the true relationship from the scatter of points that appear in Figure 2B.3. He or she does so through a process known as **ordinary least squares** (OLS). The name *ordinary least squares* indicates that the OLS process chooses the line that minimizes the sum of the *squared* distances between the points and the line. If e_i is the distance (measured as a vertical line) between each point (i = 1, . . . , n) scattered around the proposed line and the line itself, OLS minimizes the sum S, where

$$S = \sum_{i=1}^{n} e_i^2.$$

While we shall not bother with all the theory behind OLS estimation, it may help to see why economists prefer it to two alternative estimation methods. One possible alternative is to minimize the total error (Σe_i), in effect adding the signed distances of the points from the proposed line. Figure 2B.4 shows this method fails to distinguish between lines A and B, even though line A clearly gives the better fit. The problem is that the error for line B is also zero because the negative error offsets the positive error.

One can cure the problem of offsetting positive and negative misses by either squaring the errors or taking their absolute value ($\Sigma |e_i|$). The two methods, however, are not identical. If one added the absolute value of the error terms, one would conclude that either line C or line D in Figure 2B.5 fits the

FIGURE 2B.3

OLS Fits a Line to the
Scattering of Points

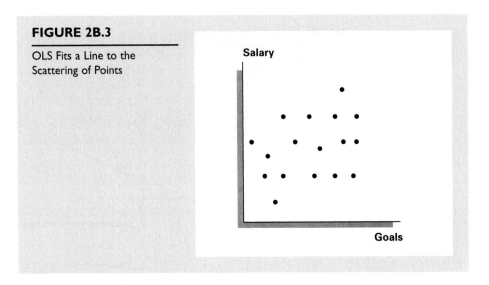

FIGURE 2B.4

Minimizing the Sum May Yield
a Poor Fit

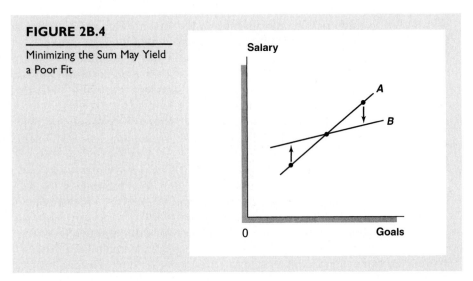

data equally well. By squaring the errors, OLS places greater weight on the large miss made by line D. OLS thus fits our intuitive notion that a line with several small misses fits the data better than a line than a few very large ones.

Economists call the OLS estimate of the line relating salary to goals a *simple regression,* because it assumes that there is a simple explanation for why some players make more than others: they score more goals. Using data from the 1998–99 season, the output from this simple regression would look like:

$$\text{Salary} = 643{,}416 + 93{,}183 \cdot \text{Goals}.$$

In this equation, the coefficient 643,416 is the *intercept term.* It is the salary a player receives if he does not score any goals (Goals = 0). The coefficient 93,183

FIGURE 2B.5

A Few Big Misses Are Better
Than Many Small Ones

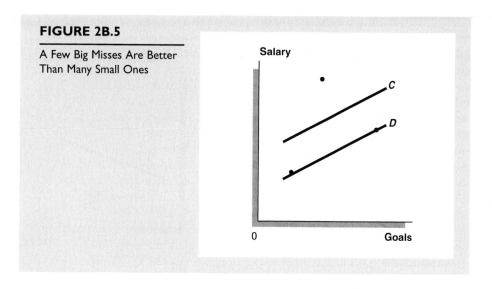

represents the *slope term*. It shows the impact that scoring an extra goal has on salary. It says that each goal scored adds a little over $93,000 to a player's salary. This model thus predicts that Paul Kariya will make roughly 643,416 + 93,183 · (44) = $4.74 million.

We cannot, however, be certain that a player's salary will actually rise by about $93,000 per goal scored. Figure 2B.6 shows two different sets of points that both lead to the same slope term. While the estimate is the same for each, we are far more confident of our results in Figure 2B.6a. Statisticians measure their confidence in their estimates with a measurement called the *standard error*. We shall not derive the formula for the standard error; we shall simply say that the closer the standard error of a coefficient is to zero, the more confident we are that our estimate accurately reflects the true value. A good rule of thumb is to look for a standard error that is no more than half the size of the coefficient. Sometimes computer programs compute the ratio of the coefficient to the standard error, a value called the *t-statistic*. Since we want the standard error to be no more than about half the value of the coefficient, we look for a *t-statistic* that is greater than 2.0. Most economics papers report both the coefficients and *t*-values like this:

$$\text{Salary} = 643,415 + 93,183 \cdot \text{Goals}$$
$$(9.135) \quad (13.308)$$

In this case, we can be confident that the true values of both the constant and the slope terms are not zero and that goals actually do have an impact on salary.

Multiple Regression and Dummy Variables

As noted earlier, we can probably make our measurement more accurate by including other variables that affect a player's salary. In fact, failing to include a

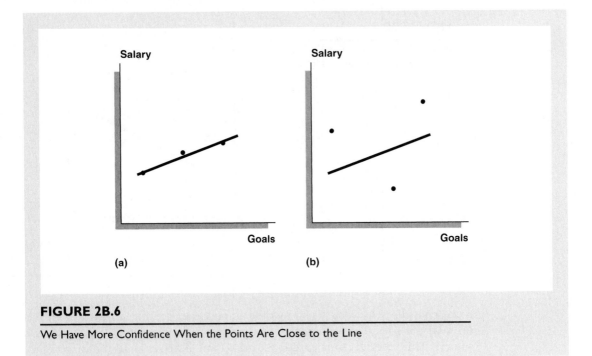

FIGURE 2B.6

We Have More Confidence When the Points Are Close to the Line

key variable such as assists may cause our coefficient on goals to be off target, a problem statisticians call *bias*. We call a regression that has several explanatory variables a *multiple regression,* reflecting the fact that a dependent variable (in our case, salaries) may be affected by multiple factors. The results of a multiple regressions look very much like those of a simple regression. In this case, we find

$$\text{Salary} = 566,498 + 71,928 \cdot \text{Goals} + 19,946 \cdot \text{Assists}$$
$$(7.826) \quad (8.159) \qquad\quad (3.895)$$

The interpretation of the coefficients becomes a bit more complex in a multiple regression. Now the coefficient on goals, 71,928, reflects the impact of an additional goal on a player's salary *holding the number of assists constant*. This statistical concept runs parallel to the economic concept of *ceteris paribus* that we outlined in this chapter. It allows us to say that if two players have the same number of assists (and any other factor one might include) but one of the players has 10 more goals than the other, we expect the player with more goals to earn about $720,000 per year more than the other.

While the standard errors and the *t*-statistics give a good idea as to how well specific variables explain the data, they do not tell how good a job the regression as a whole does. Fortunately, most regression packages provide several overall measures of the quality of the regression. The most intuitive measure of a regression's "quality of fit" is its R^2. The value of the R^2 tells us how much of the variation in the dependent variable can be explained by the explanatory variables in the regression. In the above regressions, for example, the R^2 rises from 0.222 to 0.241 when we add assists as an explanatory variable. This tells us that goals alone explain about 22 percent of the variation in salary, while goals and assists combined explain about 24 percent of the variation in salary. The quality of the regression rises as it explains a greater proportion of the differences in salary. Using both goals and assists improves the regression because the R^2 of the second regression is closer to 1, meaning it comes closer to explaining 100 percent of the variation in salary.

One additional variable we might want to include in our multiple regression is the player's position. Neither goals nor assists will be of as much importance to a defenseman, whose primary responsibility is to prevent scoring by the other team, as it is to an offensive player. One cannot add a player's position, however, in the same way that one would add the number of goals or assists he has. A player's position, like a worker's sex or race, is a *qualitative variable*; it does not have an obvious numerical value. To include position in our regression, we must first create an artificial numerical value—a *dummy variable*—to include in the regression. In this case, we let the dummy variable equal zero if the player was not a defenseman and one if the player was a defenseman. This changes the regression to

$$\text{Salary} = 261,128 + 91,569 \cdot \text{Goals} + 16,346 \cdot \text{Assists} + 585,560 \cdot \text{Defenseman.}$$
$$\quad (2.789) \quad (9.641) \qquad (3.301) \qquad\qquad (5.001)$$

Since the variable *Defenseman* equals zero for all players except those who play defense, the coefficient has no impact for them. We can think of the coefficient as the impact of playing defense, *ceteris paribus*—the impact of playing defense for a player who sco
res a given number of goals and who has a given number of assists. These results suggest that defensemen are paid a premium of over a half-million dollars. This does not mean that defensemen are more valuable to hockey teams. Defensemen are less likely to score goals or have assists than wings or centers. An offensive player who scores about six more goals than a defensive player makes up the half-million dollar difference of the dummy variable. As expected, adding a player's position to the analysis improves the quality of the regression—the R^2 rises to 0.270. We shall see in Chapter 8 that economists have used techniques like these to study players' value to their teams.

PART TWO

The Industrial Organization of Sports

CHAPTER 3

Sports Franchises as Profit-Maximizing Firms

*For almost twenty years I owned and ran a National Football League team,
the San Diego Chargers. When I bought the Chargers I believed I could apply
to professional football the same principles of good business management
that had enabled me to succeed in the corporate world. There was also a time
when I believed in Santa Claus, the Easter Bunny, and the Tooth Fairy.*

— GENE KLEIN[1]

INTRODUCTION

It would be an odd news conference where Richard Wagoner, Jr., the chairman of General Motors, stood up and said, "Our number one goal is to make the highest quality cars in the world, regardless of profit!" If you were a GM shareholder, such a statement would certainly give you cause for concern. We rightly expect corporate executives to maximize profit.

Sports fans, however, have a different attitude. They condemn team executives or owners whom they suspect of putting profit ahead of winning. Few owners are as popular as Mark Cuban, the owner of the Dallas Mavericks basketball team. In the 2001–2002 season, the Mavericks lost over $20 million, more than any other basketball franchise, [2] yet Cuban would probably say that it was worth every penny. Not only has he built a winning franchise, he is, in the words of one observer, "a *bona fide* sports star, better known and more popular than most of his players."[3] Cuban clearly views the Mavericks as a consumption good, a chance to have fun and to rub elbows with athletes, celebrities, and fans rather than as a source of income.

While many owners have nonfinancial motives for owning a sports franchise—a factor we explore in Section 3.1—few of them show as much disregard for profit as Mark Cuban. Instead, their behavior often seems consistent with

---

[1]Eugene Klein, *First Down and a Billion: The Funny Business of Pro Football* (New York: Morrow), p. 12.

[2]"NBA Team Valuations," *Forbes Magazine* online at www.Forbes.com.

[3]Chris Suellentrop, "Mark Cuban: How to Meddle with Your Sports Team—The Right Way," *Slate Magazine,* online at http://www.slate.com, December 4, 2002.

69

the standard principles of profit-maximizing behavior. [4] Teams that lose sight of the bottom line may share the fate of hockey's Ottawa Senators. The 2002–03 hockey season marked a dual culmination for the Senators. The team rose to among hockey's elite, amassing the best regular season record in the NHL. As this was happening, the team fell over $100 million in debt and slowly slid into bankruptcy. The financial failure in Canada's capital was an embarrassment for the team, the NHL, and the country that gave birth to ice hockey. For most of this chapter, we shall explore how teams and leagues maximize profit and what happens when they fail to do so. Along the way, we shall examine the following points:

- Why owners often pay more than a team is worth
- The role that gate revenue, media revenue, and venue revenue play in the profits of a franchise
- How owners can manipulate their costs to make profits look like losses
- The role that leagues play in the profits of individual teams.

3.1 SPORTS OWNERSHIP AND THE EGO PREMIUM

As noted above, owning a sports franchise also brings celebrity that even the very wealthy may not have. Table 3.1 shows that many sports owners are among the United States' wealthiest people. According to *Forbes Magazine*, 32 of the 400 wealthiest people in the United States own a controlling interest in some sports franchise. Jerry Jones was an obscure oilman from Arkansas until he bought the Dallas Cowboys, and George Steinbrenner was, in his own words, "just a shipbuilder from Tampa," before buying the New York Yankees.

Richard Sheehan notes that buying a sports franchise to raise one's profile or boost one's ego causes owners to pay tens of millions of dollars more for their franchises.[5] Figure 3.1 shows how this might occur. For simplicity, assume that a fixed number of teams are for sale, so the supply curve is perfectly inelastic (the vertical line S). If potential buyers consider only the financial gain from owning a franchise, the demand for teams is D_π. If ego gratification also plays a role in the desire to own a franchise, the taste for a team rises, and the demand curve shifts rightward to D_e. The increased demand results in a higher equilibrium price than if profits are the sole reason for owning a franchise, with the price differential (p_e^e-p_e^π) being the "ego premium."

Paying an inflated entry fee was the first of several mistakes that the Ottawa franchise made. Unable to afford the $50 million expansion fee, Senators' owner Rob Bryden went into debt to buy the rights for the team in 1991, putting the team in a hole it was never able to crawl out of. Throughout

---

[4]See, for example, D. W. Ferguson et al. in "The Pricing of Sports Events: Do Teams Maximize Profits?" *Journal of Industrial Economics*, v. 39 (March 1991), pp. 297–310.

[5]See Richard G. Sheehan, *Keeping Score: The Economics of Big-Time Sports* (South Bend, I.N.: Diamond Press, 1996), pp. 75, 90.

Table 3.1

Ownership of Professional Sports Teams by Selected Individuals

Name	Net Worth[a]	Teams	Source of Income
Paul Allen	$28,200	Seattle Seahawks (NFL) Portland Trail Blazers (NBA)	Microsoft
Phillip Anschutz[b]	$9,600	Los Angeles Kings (NHL)	Qwest
Alfred Lerner[c]	$4,900	Cleveland Browns (NFL)	Banking
Micky Arison	$4,600	Miami Heat (NBA)	Carnival Cruise Lines
Preston Tisch	$2,600	New York Giants (NFL)	Loews Corp.
William Davidson	$2,200	Detroit Pistons (NBA) Tampa Bay Lightning (NHL)	Glass manufacturing
William and Nancy Laurie	$2,100	St. Louis Blues (NHL)	Inheritance
Carl Pohlad	$2,000	Minnesota Twins (MLB)	Banking
H. Wayne Huizenga	$2,000	Miami Dolphins (NFL)	Investments
Glen Taylor	$1,800	Minnesota Timberwolves (NBA)	Printing
Richard DeVos	$1,700	Orlando Magic (NBA)	Amway
Arthur Blank	$1,600	Atlanta Falcons (NFL)	Home Depot
Mark Cuban	$1,400	Dallas Mavericks (NBA)	Broadcast.com
Billy Joe "Red" McCombs	$1,400	Minnesota Vikings (NFL)	Auto sales
William Clay Ford, Jr.	$1,200	Detroit Lions (NFL)	Ford Motor Co.
Stanley Kroenke	$1,100	Colorado Avalanche (NHL) Denver Nuggets (NBA)	Real estate
Robert McLane, Jr.	$1,100	Houston Astros (MLB)	Wal-Mart
Charles Wang	$925	New York Islanders (NHL)	Computer Associates
Alexander Spanos	$870	San Diego Chargers (NFL)	Real estate
Jerral "Jerry" Jones	$850	Dallas Cowboys (NFL)	Oil and natural gas

[a]In millions
[b]Coowner with Edward Roski, Jr. (net worth: $900 million)
[c]Died during 2002 season
Source: "The Forbes 400," at http://www.Forbes.com

the rest of this chapter, we shall see that, while the Senators made all the right moves to build a winning team on the ice, they consistently represent a worst-case scenario off the ice.

3.2 WHAT ARE PROFITS AND HOW ARE THEY MAXIMIZED?

Economists define profits as total revenue minus total cost:

$$\pi = TR - TC.$$

Total revenue is the sum of all revenues that the firm receives per period. In a typical market, total revenue is simply the price of the product times quantity

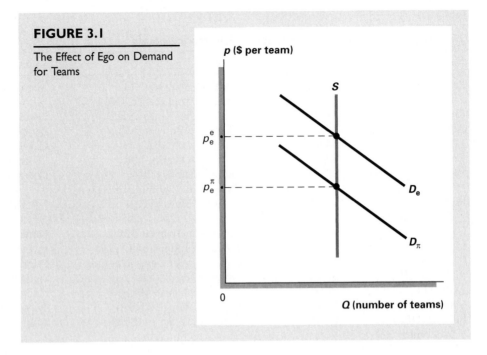

FIGURE 3.1

The Effect of Ego on Demand for Teams

sold. As we discussed in Chapter 2, though, there is no single, clear-cut definition of output in the professional sports market. Teams have numerous sources of revenue, not all of them directly related to attendance. Thus, total revenue in the above equation is the sum of several types of revenue: ticket sales, television rights, stadium revenues other than tickets (such as concessions and stadium-naming rights), licensing sales (jerseys, hats, etc.), shared or redistributed revenue from other teams, and subsidies from governments. An additional challenge for the study of team profits in professional sports is that profits—at least those profits reported using standard accounting rules—are easily manipulated. We discuss these difficulties in detail later in the chapter.

Like revenues, a firm's costs come in a variety of forms. Variable costs change with output. Most models of firm behavior consider the cost of labor to be a variable cost, since the firm must hire more labor in order to produce more output and can relatively easily change the number of workers that it hires. In professional sports, however, labor costs and most other costs are fixed (or variable over only a very narrow range) in a given season.

A Detailed Look at Revenue

Professional teams generate revenue from four principal sources: ticket sales or gate receipts (R_G), local and national broadcasting rights (R_B), licensing income (R_L), and other stadium-related revenues including luxury boxes, concessions, and stadium-naming rights (R_S):

$$TR = R_G + R_B + R_L + R_S.$$

The proportion of total revenue generated from each source varies substantially from sport to sport, and it is determined by the level of demand for each. The sources of revenue have also changed dramatically over time. Table 3.2 shows revenue and cost data compiled by *Forbes Magazine* for several teams in each of the four major sports.[6] While these revenue figures may seem large, a professional sports team is a relatively small firm within a large urban economy. For example, a professional sports team generates less annual revenue than a large department store.[7]

Table 3.2 shows *Forbes Magazine*'s estimates of the highest and lowest market value, revenue, player costs, and operating income (which, as we shall see, is closely related to profit) for each of the major North American sports leagues in the 2002 seasons (2001–02 for hockey and basketball). It also shows the median values for each league. The table shows that, on a league-wide level, football teams tend to be the most valuable. The median value of an NFL franchise is more than double that of the next most valuable sport. This difference largely reflects the greater **operating income** of NFL franchises. [8] Operating income is the difference between a team's revenue and the costs of its day-to-day operations. It excludes costs not related to daily operations, such as interest payments on loans or the wear and tear on the facility.

The market values of NHL franchises lag far behind those of the other three major U.S. sports. The typical NHL franchise is worth two-thirds that of a typical NBA franchise and just over one-fourth that of a typical NFL franchise.

Table 3.2 also shows differences in the dispersion of profitability and market value within the four sports leagues. For example, while the typical MLB franchise is worth less than half that of a typical NFL franchise, *Forbes* claims that the New York Yankees were the most valuable franchise in all of professional sports in 2001–02. With an estimated value of $849 million, the Yankees were worth about 3 times as much as the median baseball franchise and about 7.5 times as much as MLB's least valuable franchise, the Montreal Expos. By contrast, the most valuable NFL franchise, the Washington Redskins, were just 1.6 times more valuable than the median NFL franchise and 2.25 times more valuable than the NFL's least valuable franchise, the Arizona Cardinals. In addition, the NFL was the only sport in which no team lost money. *Forbes* estimates that 15 baseball teams, 10 hockey teams, and 9 basketball teams lost money in 2002.

In Chapter 2, we saw that a downward-sloping demand curve means that teams can charge higher prices for tickets only if they are willing to sell fewer tickets. If a team can increase the demand for its product, then it can sell more

---

[6]Data are from the 2002 and 2001–02 seasons. For the most up-to-date franchise valuation figures, go to http://www.forbes.com.

[7]Roger Noll, "The Economics of Sports Leagues," in *Law of Professional and Amateur Sports*, ed. by Gary A. Uberstine, K. R. Stratos, and R. J. Grad (Deerfield, I.L.: The West Group, 1989), p. 17-2.

[8]Our own computations show that the correlation between *Forbes*' estimates of operating income and market value is roughly 0.78.

Table 3.2

Major League Franchise Revenue, Cost, and Valuations for 2003 ($ Millions)

	Current Value		*Revenue*		*Player Expenses*		*Operating Income*	
MLB								
Highest	New York Yankees	$849	Yankees	$223	Yankees	$141	Seattle Mariners	$23.2
Lowest	Montreal Expos	$113	Expos	$66	Tampa Bay Devils Rays	$49	Los Angeles Dodgers	-$25
MLB Median		$254		$119.50		$75		-$0.20
NBA								
Highest	Los Angeles Lakers	$403	New York Knicks	$157	Portland Trail Blazers	$89.5	Chicago Bulls	$51.70
Lowest	Charlotte Hornets*	$135	Memphis Grizzlies	$53	Los Angeles Clippers	$32.6	Dallas Mavericks	-$23.4
NBA Median		$211		$81		$52.30		$3.80
NHL								
Highest	New York Rangers	$277	Rangers	$103	Rangers	$59.9	Toronto Maple Leafs	$15.4
Lowest	Phoenix Coyotes	$79	Coyotes	$39	Minnesota Wild	$18.4	Washington Capitals	-$15.5
NHL Median		$146.50		$61.50		$37.80		$3.50
NFL								
Highest	Washington Redskins	$845	Redskins	$204	Denver Broncos	$104	Redskins	$79.4
Lowest	Arizona Cardinals	$374	Cardinals	$110	Dallas Cowboys	$54.3	Green Bay Packers	$2.70
NFL Median		$518		$134		$76.90		$18.20

*Since moved to New Orleans

tickets and charge a higher price. Figure 3.2 shows the impact of a rightward shift in the demand for tickets.

To increase ticket sales from Q_0 to Q_1 along demand curve D, a team would have to lower its price from P_0 to P_1. If, however, the demand curve shifted rightward to D', the team could sell Q_1 tickets without lowering its price. Professional franchises are increasingly exploiting the fact that their fans' demand curve shifts right and left, depending upon the quality of the opposition. While teams used to charge a given price for a particular seat, regardless of the appeal of the opponent, they are now behaving in a manner shown in Figure 3.3.

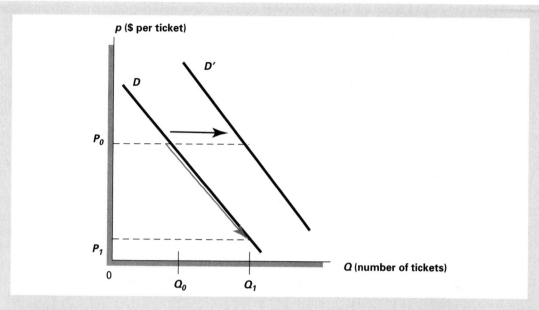

FIGURE 3.2

Rightward Shift of Demand

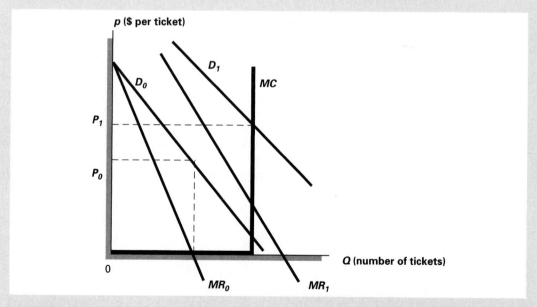

FIGURE 3.3

Fluctuating Demand Curve and Ticket Prices

In Figure 3.3, suppose D_0 is the demand for tickets to see the Chicago Cubs host the Milwaukee Brewers, a team that has had one of the worst records in baseball over the last decade. The equilibrium price for a Cubs–Brewers game, P_0, is very low. When the highly popular (or much despised) New York Yankees come to town, the demand shifts to D_1, and the equilibrium price rises to P_1. This helps to explain why the Cubs raised ticket prices for their games against the Yankees in the spring of 2003. More and more teams are following the Cubs' strategy and shifting to variable ticket prices.

Teams also try to shift their demand curve to the right through a variety of marketing techniques. However, even long-time baseball owner and master marketer Bill Veeck agreed, "You cannot draw people with a losing team by giving them bread and circuses."[9]

In the long term, a team will be able to increase the demand by it's fans to see it play only by building a successful team. Generally, this means obtaining or developing talented players, which, in turn, drives up the team's costs. Teams thus have two separate paths to short-term profitability: spending a lot of money with the hope of making even more revenue, or cutting costs and hoping that revenue does not fall even further. The NBA's Chicago Bulls have successfully followed both paths over the last 10 years. In the 1990s, the Bulls were a juggernaut both on and off the court, winning six NBA championships and serving as the marquee team of the NBA. Despite having one of the league's highest payrolls, topping out at over $61 million in their last championship year (1997–98), the Bulls were among the most profitable teams in the NBA. Since then, the Bulls have not been nearly as successful on the court, winning only 66 games combined from the 1998–99 season through the 2001–02 season, which is only 4 more wins than they had in the 1997–98 season. In spite of this, the Bulls remain a financial powerhouse. They may not generate as much revenue as they used to, but they decreased their 2001–02 payroll to under $33 million—only about half what it used to be. As a result, the Bulls were the NBA's third most valuable franchise in 2001–02 and made more than $50 million in operating income, which was more than any other team in the NBA and over $20 million more than the NBA champion, the Los Angeles Lakers.

Whether because they are more successful on the field or because they have a larger fan base, some teams prove to be more popular than others. Early in its history, the NFL saw the problems that such imbalances could create. If some teams were unable to draw large crowds, they might not generate enough revenue to stay in business. For the first 16 years of its existence, 1920 through 1935, the NFL did not field the same set of teams in two consecutive years. Faced with such extreme instability, the NFL instituted what remains the most generous revenue-sharing policy of all the major professional sports in the United States. Today, home teams in the NFL keep 60 percent of all gate revenue. The remaining 40 percent is put into a common pool that is distributed

[9]Bill Veeck and Ed Linn, *Veeck as in Wreck* (Chicago: University of Chicago Press, 2001), p. 118.

league-wide among all teams.[10] This sharing arrangement means that an NFL team's gate revenue is actually:

$$R_G = 0.6R_h + 0.4R_p$$

where R_h is a team's revenue from attendance at home games and R_p is the total amount of gate revenue generated by all the other NFL teams. This policy helped the league to survive its early lean years and helps to explain why operating incomes and market values are so much closer in the NFL than in the other major U.S. leagues. It also set the stage for other revenue-sharing policies that would help make the NFL the most profitable of all the major sports in the United States.

In contrast to the NFL, neither the NBA nor the NHL shares any gate revenue, so $R_G = R_h$. Because, as we shall see, NHL teams depend more heavily than any other sport on gate revenue, attendance can be crucial. In particular, making an extended run in the play-offs can make the difference between a profit and a loss. For example, the early exit of the Detroit Red Wings from the play-offs in 2003 may have cost them as much as $15 million. Because of their inability to advance far into the play-offs for most of their history, the Ottawa Senators lost out on a source of revenue that could have helped them pay off their debt.

In their most recent collective bargaining agreement, MLB teams agreed to increase the amount of gate revenue that they share. Starting with the 2003 season, MLB teams place 34 percent of their net local revenues, including gate revenues, in a common pool that is divided equally among all teams.

Television Revenue

Few events have changed the finances of professional sports as much as the advent of television. All four major sports currently enjoy huge revenue streams from both local and national broadcasting rights. Table 3.3 shows, however, that TV benefits some sports more than others. The prosperity of the NFL depends on its huge network contract, the revenue from which the teams split evenly. TV brings in almost half of the median team's revenue and almost two-thirds of the revenue of the NFL's least profitable team, the Arizona Cardinals. In the NBA, which also evenly shares TV revenue, the network contract is responsible for almost a third of the median team's total revenue and almost half the revenue of the NBA's least profitable team, the Memphis Grizzlies. The relative poverty of the NHL can be traced directly to its network contract, which is far less than for any of the other major U.S. sports and is worth less than one-third of NASCAR's TV contract. To see the difference TV can make, consider that the NFL's $17.6 billion dollar TV contract brings each team almost

---

[10]The NFL dates its founding from when the initial body, the "American Professional Football Association" took the name "National Football League" in 1922. See David Harris, *The League: The Rise and Decline of the NFL* (New York: Bantam Books, 1986), p. 12; and Eric M. Leifer, *Making the Majors: The Transformation of Team Sports in America* (Cambridge, M.A.: Harvard University Press, 1995), pp. 98–109.

Table 3.3

Revenue from Broadcast Rights Agreements

Sport	Years	Rights	Holders' Total Fees	Annual Average
NFL	1998–2005	ABC, Fox, CBS, ESPN	$17.6 billion	$2.2 billion
MLB (1)	2000–2005	ESPN	$851 million	$141.8 million
MLB (2)	2001–2006	Fox	$2.5 billion	$416.7 million
NBA	2002-2008	ABC/ESPN, AOL Time Warner	$4.6 billion	$766.7 million
NHL	1999–2004	ABC/ESPN	$600 million	$120 million
NASCAR	2001–2008	Fox/NBC, Turner	$2.4 billion	$400 million
PGA	2003–2006	ABC, CBS, NBC	$850 million	$212.5 million

Source: Street & Smith's SportsBusiness Journal

$71 million per year, while NHL teams get only $4 million a year from their contract. If these figures were reversed, the median revenue of an NHL franchise would be almost indistinguishable from that of an NFL franchise.

The fact that the NFL and NBA split their revenue from network contracts evenly is a major reason why revenues are relatively evenly balanced in the NFL and NBA. The influx of TV money probably keeps several of these franchises from going bankrupt.

Major League Baseball's network contract for national broadcasts is far less lucrative than basketball's or football's, but unlike the NBA and NFL, some baseball teams have another major source of TV revenue: *local* TV contracts. In 2002, individual baseball teams had local TV contracts worth a total of $692 million, of which about $494 million came from cable contracts. Unlike the network contract, however, local revenue is not evenly shared. While baseball teams started sharing roughly 34 percent of their local TV revenue in 2003 (as mentioned earlier, they are dividing all net local revenues), the inequality in the local TV revenues continues to separate MLB into *large market* teams and *small market* teams. The inequality in local TV revenues, shown in Table 3.4, created by the vast difference in the size of media markets, defines large- and small-market teams in baseball much more than the actual size of the city does. From 1987 to 1991, the Minnesota Twins drew almost exactly as many fans as the New York Yankees (11.1 million fans to 11.4 million fans), but they were never regarded as a large-market team. Similarly, baseball's Kansas City Royals often bemoan the woes of being a small-market team, whereas the Kansas City Chiefs of the NFL never make such complaints. Data that MLB provided to Congress revealed that in 2001, the New York Yankees made $57 million in local media revenue while the Kansas City Royals received only $6.5 million, which was less than all but two teams.[11] If the Kansas City Royals had the Yankees TV contract and spent the money on players, they would have had a payroll equal to the Los Angeles Dodgers and lower only than those of the Yankees and Boston Red Sox.

---

[11]The only teams to make less were the Milwaukee Brewers at $6.0 million and the Montreal Expos at a breathtakingly low $500,000. The Expos had no English language radio or TV, effectively ghettoizing them in Quebec.

Table 3.4

Local Television Revenue in Professional Baseball in 2001

Team	Local Media Money	Number of Free TV/Cable Games
New York Yankees	$56,750,000	50/100
New York Mets	46,251,000	50/100
Seattle Mariners	37,860,000	34/106
Boston Red Sox	33,353,000	67/85
Chicago White Sox	30,092,000	53/99
Los Angeles Dodgers	27,342,000	50/80
Texas Rangers	25,284,000	75/80
Chicago Cubs	23,559,000	78/72
Cleveland Indians	21,076,000	75/75
Baltimore Orioles	20,994,000	65/85
Atlanta Braves	19,988,000	90/59
Detroit Tigers	19,073,000	40/100
Philadelphia Phillies	18,940,000	45/113
Colorado Rockies	18,200,000	75/50
San Francisco Giants	17,197,000	62/60
Tampa Bay Devil Rays	15,511,000	65/64
Florida Marlins	15,353,000	55/95
Toronto Blue Jays	14,460,000	40/110
Arizona Diamondbacks	14,174,000	75/60
Houston Astros	13,722,000	62/75
San Diego Padres	12,436,000	25/115
St. Louis Cardinals	11,905,000	45/59
Anaheim Angels	10,927,000	40/50
Oakland Athletics	9,458,000	50/60
Pittsburgh Pirates	9,097,000	15/105
Cincinnati Reds	7,861,000	0/85
Minnesota Twins	7,273,000	25/105
Kansas City Royals	6,505,000	51/30
Milwaukee Brewers	5,918,000	50/80
Montreal Expos	536,000	0/48 (French)

Sources: TV/radio/cable money: MLB disclosures. Metropolitan populations: 2000 U.S. Census CMSA/MSA figures and StatCan 2000 estimates (Toronto and Montreal), adjusted for number of teams in market. Number of TV/cable games: 4/2/01 Broadcasting and Cable.

Because their network contract is so small, NHL teams also depend heavily on local media contracts. Again, Ottawa found itself in a bad situation. It has a population of less than 775,000, so Ottawa had a smaller media market than any other city. Because it has so few potential viewers, the Senators could not hope for media revenue close to that of Vancouver, let alone New York. With a minuscule network contract and a small local market, the Senators faced an uphill battle in paying off their debt.

One of the most important factors driving the divergence in local media revenues is the growth of cable broadcasting. As recently as 1996, almost 60 percent of all baseball broadcasts were still over-the-air telecasts. By 2003, almost 70 percent of the local telecasts were seen over cable. This switch occurred because cable is more lucrative to teams than over-the-air telecasts. When a network or a local station broadcasts a game, it receives no revenue from the viewers. The bulk of its revenue comes from advertisers. When a game is broadcast over a cable outlet such as ESPN, the station receives a monthly premium from the viewer in addition to advertising revenue. Neither broadcast allows the team to calculate a per-viewer charge. Payments to teams from broadcasters come from the fixed fees for **broadcast rights** that leagues and networks negotiate at the national level and individual teams and stations negotiate at the local level. Because of different revenue sources and because cable allows stations to extend their coverage to regional or national "superstations," the advent of cable television has exacerbated differences in local TV revenue.

Like fixed costs in a profit equation, fixed revenues such as broadcast fees have no impact on how revenues or costs change with output. Ignoring for the moment the possible impact of televising games on gate receipts, a fixed revenue payment for broadcast rights (R_B) enters the profit function as a constant.

Television and Gate Receipts—Exposure versus Substitution   Broadcasting games is a double-edged sword to teams. To the extent that fans prefer to watch games on television rather than go to the stadium, televising home games reduces gate receipts. The first instance of this effect occurred in 1948, when the Philadelphia Eagles saw attendance drop by 50 percent after they decided to televise all their home games. This is why the NFL "blacks out" (forbids networks from showing in the local market) games that are not sold out. Blacking out the home team's game may not be enough if a New England Patriots fan in Boston prefers watching a televised game between the Cowboys and Dolphins to shivering at Gillette Stadium on a cold December day. On the other hand, if television stimulates fans' interest in the game, more broadcasts may increase attendance at the gate. The NFL owes a good deal of its popularity to its focus on nationally broadcast games and the "Sunday doubleheader," which allows fans to watch popular teams from other cities.

Networks televise games when they profit from doing so. The demand by networks or local stations to televise games is a derived demand. The demand for a good or service is *derived* from the demand for another when the amount people are willing and able to buy depends on the market for a different product. For example, the demand for medical care depends on the demand for good health. In the case of broadcasting rights, the demand by TV networks for sporting events depends on—is derived from—the demand by sponsors for advertising time. A network's willingness to pay a league or team for the right to broadcast a game stems from its ability to sell advertising during the game. In the early 1980s, CBS paid $1 billion for the rights to broadcast the baseball "game of the week" largely due to a bidding war by the Anheuser-Busch and Miller Brewing Companies for advertising time.[12]

The exposure that broadcasts give a network and its advertisers explains why the NFL can charge so much more than the other sports. Table 3. 5 shows that football's viewership, as measured by the Nielsen Media Group ratings system, dwarfs all the other sports, while hockey lags badly. Hockey's poor Nielsen ratings have led some to speculate that hockey will have a hard time retaining even its small payment for broadcast rights. Hard times may also be ahead for the NBA and MLB. While basketball's ratings are still much higher than hockey's, they have plunged since Michael Jordan retired from the Chicago Bulls in 1998. The ratings for the NBA finals fell from 18.7 to 10.2 in 2002, and again to about 8.2 in 2003. Regular season ratings also fell, though only by about a third. Baseball's ratings have followed a similar, though slightly less severe, decline, with the ratings for the World Series declining from 17.4 in 1996 to 11.9 in 2002.

A network might pursue broadcast rights even though it knows that it will lose money as a result. The $17.6 billion contract that the NFL signed in 1998 with ABC, CBS, Fox, and ESPN is a case in point. The contract broke new ground in the amount that networks were willing to pay even though TV ratings and advertising revenue for the NFL had been stagnant for several years. The networks are willing to overpay because they view football as a "loss leader." The broadcast itself might lose money, but if it attracts viewers to other shows on the network, it may still be consistent with overall profit maximization. In the case of new entrants to the market, such as Fox, a contract with a major sport gives the network an air of credibility with sponsors and potential affiliates. Lucie Salhany, chairperson of Fox Broadcasting when Fox first began broadcasting NFL games, argued, "We had to have it and it didn't matter what we paid for it. It put us on the map. It got us more affiliates. . . . Sales-wise, there were people we could never call on that we could call on once we got football."[13]

Even Fox may have reached its limit with the latest set of contracts. In February 2002, it announced that it was *writing down*, officially announcing

Table 3.5

Over the Air Nielsen Ratings for the Four Major U.S. Sports, 2002

Sport	Regular Season	Playoff Finals*
MLB	2.5	11.9
NBA	3.1	10.2
NFL	10.1	40.4
NHL	1.4	3.7

*World Series, NBA finals, Super Bowl, and Stanley Cup finals
Source: *Street & Smith's SportsBusiness Journal: By the Numbers*

---

[12]John Helyar, *Lords of the Realm* (New York: Villard Books, 1994), pp. 392–393.

[13]Eric Schmuckler, "Is the NFL Still Worth It?" *Mediaweek* (September 28, 1998), pp. 26–32.

losses, of close to $1 billion on its rights to broadcast MLB ($225 million) and NFL ($387 million) games as well as NASCAR events ($297 million).[14] Disney, the owner of ABC and ESPN, and other networks have announced similar, though smaller losses. By contrast, NBC, which does not carry NFL games and recently replaced the NBA with Arena Football, reported a profit on its sport broadcasts over the same period, though it had lost $200 million in the previous year.

Television revenue has rivaled or surpassed gate revenue as the primary source of income for all major sports, and they have become so dependent on it that they have literally changed the way they play their games. Games are now interrupted by the infamous "TV time-out." Fans and players at the stadium wait while television viewers see advertisements, confident that play will not resume until the ads are over. Some sports, such as baseball, can easily accommodate such breaks. Other sports see stoppages in play extended for unnatural lengths. Football and basketball have gone so far as to introduce specific time-outs for no other purpose than to show commercials on TV. Fans at NHL games occasionally wait several minutes between face-offs to accommodate commercials. Football's two-minute warning came about as a concession to TV networks. The need to break for commercials represents a serious barrier to regular TV broadcasts of major league soccer, as play is continuous for long periods of time with no naturally occurring breaks.

In the case of television revenue, defining output is especially difficult, as contracts last for several seasons and national revenues are shared but local revenues are not. If profits were calculated on a per-season basis, broadcast revenues would simply enter as a fixed amount.

Stadium Agreements   The Dallas Cowboys are the third most valuable professional franchise in the United States. For most of the 1990s, they were *the* most valuable franchise. At first, it is hard to see why. While the Cowboys were one of the most successful teams in the NFL throughout the1990s, they could not capitalize very much on this success off the field. They play in a stadium that is no larger than the NFL average, and the NFL's 60–40 split of gate revenues limits what they earn when they play before sell-out crowds; in fact, 12 NFL teams make more in gate revenue. The Dallas media market is large, but it does not compare with those of New York, Los Angeles, and Chicago. Moreover, the Cowboys have to share all the revenue from their national telecasts equally with the other teams in the NFL. The key to the Cowboys' success lies in their extraordinarily profitable stadium agreement.

Venue revenues, or nonticket revenues from stadia (R_s), include revenue from parking and concessions, but, more importantly, they include revenue from luxury suites and other special seating, only a small portion of which counts as ticket revenue. That is why luxury seating has become particularly valuable in the NFL, because teams share a substantial portion of ticket revenue

---

[14]Peter S. Battin Media, *Television Sports Rights 2003*, at http://www.gouldmedia.com/nv_rpt_tsr03.php, June 18, 2003.

with each other (and with their players as part of the salary cap, discussed in Chapter 8). For example, suppose a luxury suite in Texas Stadium rents for $500,000 per year and has 20 seats in it. If the Cowboys claim the value of the seats to be $50 each, they must share only $3,200 ($0.4 \times 20 \times \$50 \times 8$ games). They can keep the remaining $496,800 for themselves. Again, much of this revenue enters as a lump sum per season, because luxury boxes are typically leased on a per-season basis. Other attendance-related revenue, such as parking and concession, is directly connected to how many people come to the games, so it is more variable.

One of the newest sources of revenue in professional sports comes from team's selling the name of their facility to the highest bidder. Stadium-naming rights are only one form of sponsorship. When you watch a NASCAR race, a European soccer match, or even a golf tournament, you can see the lengths to which companies go to associate their brands with a team, a player, or an event. Corporate names and logos adorn uniforms and equipment. One enterprising boxer even had an advertisement temporarily tattooed on his body.

Even against this background, naming rights stand apart. Rich Foods, Inc., was the first company to purchase naming rights to a stadium when it purchased the name of the Buffalo Bills' new stadium in 1973 for $1.5 million over 25 years. For the next 20 years, professional sports in America largely ignored the revenue possibilities of naming rights. In 1990, only a handful of teams had sold such rights. In the rest of that decade, however, the popularity of naming rights exploded. Today, more than half of all baseball and football stadiums and over three-fourths of all basketball and hockey arenas have corporate names. Naming rights have even filtered down to the college level. Table 3.6 shows some of the more prominent college venues with their corporate sponsors. Even at the college level, corporations have paid as much as $40 million for the right to have their names on stadiums.

Corporate executives and sports marketers clearly feel that naming rights are a great deal. In the words of Jeffrey Knapple, the president and CEO of Envision, "In a marketing landscape where corporations are continually striving to gain market share and 'share of mind' from their respective constituents, naming rights provides (sic) the ultimate opportunity to rise above the pack."[15]

Recent events and research, however, suggest that such optimism may be misplaced. Over the last several years, several companies have relinquished their naming rights due to financial distress. The large number of failures led one commentator to half-seriously refer to a "naming rights curse."[16]

In 2003, the NFL's Chicago Bears took naming rights a step further. Bank One, a financial institution headquartered in Chicago, paid the Bears $50 million to be the team's "presenting sponsor" for the next 12 years. In effect, Bank One has bought naming rights for the team itself, as Chicago fans will now be

---

[15]Jeffrey S. Knapple, "Naming Rights Industry" in *Naming Rights Deals* (Chicago: Team Marketing Report, 2001).

[16]Chris Isidore, "Stadium Curse Still Haunts Firms," *CNN Money,* at http://money.cnn.com/2003/01/03/commentary/column_sportsbiz/sponsor_stock_index/, January 3, 2003.

Table 3.6

College Naming Rights Agreements

University	Stadium / Arena	Year	Term	Corporate Sponsor	Funds ($)
Arizona State Univ.	Wells Fargo Arena	1998	10	Wells Fargo	5.0M
Fresno State Univ.	Save Mart Center	2003	20	Save Mart Co.	40.0M
Marquette Univ.	U.S. Cellular Arena	1999	6	U.S. Cellular Corp.	2.0M
North Dakota Univ.	First National Bank Center	N/A	20	First National Bank	7.2M
Ohio State Univ.	Value City Arena at the Schottenstein Center	1998	N/A	Value City	2.5M
Oregon State Univ.	Reser Stadium	1999	10	Al Reser	5.0M
San Diego State Univ.	Cox Pavilion	1997	10	Cox Communications	7.9 M
Syracuse Univ.	Carrier Dome	1980	N/A	Carrier Air-conditioning	2.75M
Texas Tech Univ.	United Spirit Arena	1999	N/A	United Airlines	10.0M
Univ. of Louisville	Papa John's Cardinal Stadium	1998	10	Papa John's Pizza	5.0M
Univ. of Maryland	Comcast Center	2002	25	Comcast Corp.	20.0 M
Univ. of Miami (FL)	Ryder Center	2002	N/A	Ryder Systems, Inc.	9.0 M
Univ. of Minn.-Mankato	Midwest Wireless Center at Mankato	N/A	20	Midwest Wireless	6.0M
Univ. of Washington	Seafirst Arena at Hec Edmundson Pavilion	2000	10	Seafirst Bank	9.0M

treated to "Bears football presented by Bank One," with the Bank One logo on everything except the entrance to the stadium.

While some regard this as a frighteningly commercial step for professional sports, the Bears' relationship with Bank One actually returns the team to its roots. The Bears were originally known as the Decatur Staleys, a reference to a starch manufacturer in Decatur, Illinois.[17] Nor was this practice limited to football. The Detroit Pistons' NBA franchise bears a name that seems to make sense in the original home of the U.S. auto industry. However, that is not the origin of their name. The Pistons were originally the Fort Wayne (Indiana) Zollner Pistons, named for the firm that sponsored the team.

Stadium-naming rights and advertising also provide teams with substantial fixed income. Naming rights to a new stadium generally sell for about $2 million per year. The Texans, playing in Reliant Stadium, have the most lucrative NFL deal, worth about $300 million over 32 years. In the most lucrative indoor-arena naming deal to date, the office supply superstore Staples is paying more than $100 million over a 20-year period to Phillip Anschutz, the

---

[17]ESPN News Services, "Bank One to be Bears' Presenting Sponsor," *ESPN Sports Business*, at http://espn.go.com/sportsbusiness/news/2003/0624/1572282.html; and Daniel Kaplan, "$50M Makes Bank One Presenting Sponsor of Bears," *Street & Smith's SportsBusiness Journal* (June 23–29, 2003), p. 1.

owner of the NHL's Los Angeles Kings. In exchange the building has been named the Staples Center. "The 160 suites in the building should generate $40 million a year. Advertising in the facility should bring in well over $5 million a year. . . . [M]ore than half of these revenues will be credited to Staples Center, owned by Anschutz, and not to the teams."[18]

Problems Created by Stadium Deals   In recent years, several NFL teams have moved away from their home cities to apparently illogical destinations. Both the Rams and Raiders left the Los Angeles market for far smaller markets in St. Louis and Oakland, respectively, leaving the nation's second largest market without a team. The Oilers abandoned the nation's 10th largest metropolitan area in Houston for the 40th largest market in Nashville. Even the Cleveland Browns' move to Baltimore was from a larger city to a smaller one. On the surface, all these moves seem unprofitable, as they limit both the fan base and the media exposure for the teams. Why, then, do the teams move?

The answer can be found in the peculiar interaction of revenue sharing and stadium deals. Because the teams in the NFL split their national TV contract equally and their gate receipts almost equally, the consequences of a team's moving to a smaller city are spread over all the other teams. In baseball, where teams depend so heavily on local media revenue, a team in a media market the size of Los Angeles would never leave for a much smaller city. The Yankees, for example, might threaten to move from the Bronx to Manhattan or northern New Jersey, but they would never threaten to leave the New York metropolitan area. The Rams, who did not depend heavily on local media revenue, had no such qualms about leaving Los Angeles. The moves to smaller cities, however, may hurt the NFL's ratings in the nation's second-largest media market. This, in turn, could lead to worse TV contracts for the NFL—and less revenue for all teams, including the teams that moved—in the future.

The damage that an individual team's behavior can do to the NFL as a whole results in what economists call the **tragedy of the commons**. The "tragedy" gets its name from the problem that cities faced long ago when farmers all put their livestock out to graze on the town common. Because no one property owner had a claim on—or responsibility for—the town common, no one had any incentive to limit the amount of grazing that went on. As a result, the commons were overgrazed and eventually became worthless. Similarly, NFL teams do not worry about the consequences of leaving major media markets uncovered if they can get a better individual deal elsewhere.

While the costs of the Rams' move from Los Angeles to St. Louis are spread over the entire NFL, the Rams get to keep the benefits for themselves. The stadium arrangement for the TransWorld Dome (since renamed the Edward–Jones Dome) granted the Rams all revenues from the 124 luxury suites. As noted earlier, this revenue is not shared with other teams. In addition, the NFL does not count luxury suite revenue as revenue that must be shared with its players as part of its salary cap agreement. As long as municipalities continue to try to

---

[18]Ozanian, "Selective Accounting" (1998), p. 126.

Advertisements have begun to appear in the oddest places.

outbid one another for the right to host an NFL franchise, the league may continue to see teams move to smaller markets in pursuit of better stadium arrangements. We discuss this problem in detail in Chapters 6 and 7.

The Effects of Revenue Sharing

There are two fundamental, interrelated reasons that teams might want to share revenue. The first is to promote financial stability. If some teams have access to large pools of revenue and others do not, league stability will be jeopardized as the "have not" teams struggle to survive financially. Throughout the history of professional sports, leagues in which some teams are highly unstable financially have fared poorly. The other reason leagues may want teams to share revenue is to promote competitive balance. In this chapter, we focus on the financial ramifications of revenue sharing. We discuss competitive balance extensively in Chapter 5.

All leagues share revenues to some extent. In the NHL and the NBA, revenue sharing does not extend beyond equally sharing licensing and national broadcast revenue. In the NBA, however, the size of each team's share of network revenue is so large that it smooths out the differences in gate and venue revenue. Because the NHL lacks a large TV contract, the differences in gate and venue revenue among the teams have more impact on the various teams' finances.

As mentioned earlier, with the collective bargaining agreement that took effect in the summer of 2003, MLB sought to imitate the NFL's generous revenue sharing. While the NFL teams share 40 percent of their gate revenue equally and split all network revenue equally, baseball teams now share 34 percent of all net revenue from home attendance and local TV broadcasts. The huge differences in local TV revenue, however, ensure that MLB will continue to have much greater imbalances in revenue than the NFL.

Some teams complain that revenue sharing is a tax on quality. They claim that—like any tax—a tax on quality reduces the incentive owners have to produce quality. They believe that revenue sharing punishes teams that try to give their fans a better product and rewards owners for fielding bad teams with low payrolls. The profit statements of teams seem to support such cynicism. We demonstrated earlier in the chapter how the Bulls made mediocrity pay. Sadly, they are not alone. In the NFL, the Cincinnati Bengals, the worst team in the league over the last decade, did not suffer the consequences of producing an inferior product. Thanks in part to shared gate and TV revenue, the Bengals' profit from day-to-day operations, their operating income, in 2002–03 was greater than that of than the Green Bay Packers, Atlanta Falcons, Miami Dolphins, and Oakland Raiders, all of whom went to the play-offs. In MLB, the transfers from wealthy teams to poor teams in 2002 meant that the Montreal Expos had higher operating income than seven other teams, despite drawing an average of only 10,000 fans per game, a figure exceeded by a few minor league teams, and having almost no local TV revenue. The Tampa Bay Devil Rays, perhaps the worst team in baseball, played in a stadium that was more than two-thirds empty, but they had higher operating income than the Boston Red Sox, who filled Fenway Park to 97 percent of capacity.

Cost

When considering the cost side of the profit equation, we again see substantial differences between what costs mean to a professional sports franchise and what they mean to most other industries. The data in Table 3.2 show that, not surprisingly, players' salaries figure prominently in the total costs of professional franchises. Salaries, which include deferred payments, bonuses, workers' compensation expenses, and pension contributions, make up over half a team's costs in every major sport. With a few exceptions, player costs are generally fixed from year to year.[19]

The remaining expenses include travel, marketing, administrative (both team and league), and venue expenses. For baseball and hockey, expenses also include player development. Travel expenses increase as the size of the team increases, with the number of away games, and with the distances traveled. Teams incur marketing and administrative costs at two levels. Each team does marketing specific to its own club and market, and each team has its own administrative costs, which include everything from office supplies to the salaries of the team executives.[20] Marketing and administrative costs are also incurred at the league level. These costs include broad-based marketing campaigns designed to

---

[19]The exceptions include trades, waiving a player in midseason, very short-term contracts such as the 10-day contract in the NBA, and "two-way" contracts that allow the team to pay a player one salary if he is in the major leagues and a lower salary if he is sent to the minor leagues.

[20]We return to this point in Section 3.5.

increase demand for the sport, and administrative costs such as the cost of paying a commissioner and maintaining league offices.

Total venue costs have fallen significantly in the 1990s with the recent flood of publicly funded venues in all major sports (Chapters 6 and 7 explore the relationship among teams, cities, and stadia in detail) and the highly favorable usage agreements that teams have negotiated. While a new, publicly financed facility is the route to prosperity for many franchises, Canadian cities, unlike U.S. cities, have been reluctant to pay for sports facilities. The failure of the Ottawa Senators to secure a publicly funded arena may have been the last straw in their financial undoing. Already in debt from paying the NHL entry fee, owner Bryden borrowed heavily to build the US$160 million Corel Centre himself. The Ottawa Senators have seen their venue revenue sag in recent years due to the bursting of the tech bubble in North America. With the relatively small Ottawa economy heavily dependent on the tech sector, luxury suite sales lagged in the Corel Centre. Unable to repay his debts, Bryden borrowed still further to pay his existing loans. This set off a vicious cycle of borrowing from which the Senators could not escape.

Both the NHL and MLB endure substantial player development costs because they maintain extensive minor league systems. In exchange for the minor league team's developing talent and providing players, the major league team subsidizes a major portion of the minor league team's labor and operating expenses. In sum, baseball's player development costs exceed $5 million per club per year.[21] These costs seem even greater when one considers that each minor league system generates only a few major league players per year. Thus, the development cost per major league player is well over $1 million.

Opportunity Cost—Teams on the Move

Opportunity cost is the one cost that never appears on a team's balance sheet, yet it figures vitally into the strategic decision making of all teams. When franchises move from one city to another, they are driven by the prospect of higher profits in the new city. Research has shown that the greater the fan loyalty in a city, the more likely that city is to provide public funding toward a new stadium.[22] The opportunity costs of staying in a given city are the profits forgone by not moving to the new city. When a team contemplates a move, its owner usually cites the need for more skyboxes, lower lease payments, and better practice facilities. The implied threat in such statements is that some other city is offering such facilities, as seen in two of the most infamous franchise moves, baseball's Dodgers and football's Colts. In order for teams to exert their market power over cities, the league should not place teams in every viable location. The size of the league relative to the number of cities that want to host teams plays a key role in the bargaining strength of the teams within that league. The bargaining power of teams over cities is explored in detail in Chapter 6.

---

[21]Andrew Zimbalist, *Baseball and Billions* (New York: Basic Books, 1992), p. 113.

[22]Craig A. Depken, "Fan Loyalty and Stadium Funding in Professional Baseball," *Journal of Sports Economics*, v. 1, no. 2 (May 2000), pp. 124–138.

While many teams move because they are suffering losses in their current city, not all teams that move are losing money. When the Dodgers moved to Los Angeles in 1957, they ended a remarkably profitable run in Brooklyn. In the decade before they moved West, the Dodgers were the most profitable team in baseball, accounting for 47 percent of the profits of the entire National League. Similarly, in their last season before sneaking off to Indianapolis, the Baltimore Colts had an operating profit of $5.1 million, the third highest in the NFL.[23]

3.3   TAXES, PROFIT, OWNER BEHAVIOR, AND VERTICAL INTEGRATION

Most people complain that owners such as Jerry Jones of the Dallas Cowboys or Jerry Reinsdorf of the Chicago Bulls and White Sox fail to measure up to the "sportsmen" of a bygone era. Fans of all sports look back fondly to owners who nurtured the game and viewed it as more than a profit center or ego boost. Unfortunately, that image is largely fiction. As early as the 19th century, commentators were complaining that the spirit of sport had been lost in the clamor for profit. The Toronto Blue Jays and the Colorado Rockies may owe their origins to their owners' desire to sell beer (Labatt's in Toronto and Coors in Colorado),[24] but these owners had a role model about a century earlier in Chris von der Ahe, a brewer and the founder of the original St. Louis Browns, who used the ball club to boost his own beer sales.

While most baseball teams rely heavily on the money from local broadcast rights, the Atlanta Braves and Chicago Cubs, each of which broadcasts its "local" games nationally over cable superstations TBS and WGN, reported surprisingly little local income. With revenue of $23.5 million, the Cubs made $6.5 less than their far less popular cross-town rivals, the Chicago White Sox. At only $20 million, the Braves trailed the Baltimore Orioles and barely beat out the Philadelphia Phillies and Detroit Tigers.

At first glance, these figures look completely unjustified. On closer examination, they make perfect economic sense. While the owners of the Tigers or the White Sox have a strong incentive to charge as much as possible for the right to broadcast their teams' games, neither Time Warner, the owner of the Braves and TBS, nor the Tribune Company, the owner of the Cubs and WGN, has an incentive to put broadcast rights up for competitive bidding. The Braves and the Cubs may not generate as much revenue this way as they could by selling the rights on the open market, but their parent companies are less interested in which subsidiary makes a profit than in their overall profits.

One change has occurred, however, in the pattern of sports ownership. As the prices of franchises have risen to stratospheric levels, they are beyond the

---

[23]Quirk and Fort, *Pay Dirt* (1992), p. 135; and Jon Morgan, *Glory for Sale: Fans, Dollars, and the New NFL* (Baltimore: Bancroft Press, 1997), p. 106.

[24]Some claim that the very name of the Blue Jays stems from the desire to promote one particular brand of beer, Labatt's Blue. See Helyar, *Lords of the Realm* (1994), p. 400.

means of most individual bidders. Media-related people such as Cablevision mogul Charles Dolan or corporations such as Fox and Disney now own more and more franchises. The joint ownership of sports franchises and media outlets for the teams suggests that businesses see efficiency gains from **vertical integration** and **cross subsidization** (the ability to move profits and expenses from one firm to another).

Whenever a media mogul—or a beer distributor—buys a franchise, the team's bottom line is affected. From the consumer's point of view, a media outlet's purchase of a sports franchise looks like a losing proposition. Alone, both the team and the broadcaster have monopoly power. Bringing the two together seems to create a "super monopoly" with even greater power to exploit consumers. Economic theory shows, however, that vertical integration of a team and a media outlet may actually improve the well-being of consumers.[25]

To see why, consider two firms, each with monopoly power in its own market. One firm produces an item that the other uses to produce a finished product for consumers. Imagine that the two firms are located along a river. The **upstream firm** produces its output and floats it down the river to the **downstream firm,** which then floats the final output down the river to consumers. If the upstream firm has monopoly power, it can charge a monopoly price to the downstream firm. The downstream firm regards the price it pays as part of its marginal cost of production. It uses this inflated marginal cost to determine the price it then charges to consumers.

Figure 3.4 illustrates the impact of upstream and downstream monopolies. For simplicity, we assume that the upstream firm's marginal costs are constant, so that its MC curve is a horizontal line. We also assume that the downstream firm has no other costs so that its MC curve is a horizontal line at the price it pays the upstream firm. Figure 3.4b shows that the consumer faces a double whammy of two monopolies. The higher price charged by the upstream monopolist raises the costs of the downstream monopolist, which then raises prices still higher in exercising its own monopoly power.

If the downstream firm vertically integrates by buying the upstream firm, it has no reason to charge itself a high monopolistic price.[26] The cost of the upstream product to the downstream firm is now simply the marginal cost of production. The double whammy of Figure 3.4 now falls to a single whammy in Figure 3.5. While two separate monopolies apply their monopoly power twice, a single, vertically integrated monopoly applies its monopoly power only once. The result is a lower price and higher quantity for the consumer. In this case, it means more Braves games at a lower cost to the cable subscriber than would otherwise be the case.[27]

---

[25]Horizontal integration combines two firms that produce the same item.

[26]In fact, we shall show in Chapter 4 that charging a high price would harm the firm by creating a deadweight loss.

[27]Although TBS is not a monopoly in the television broadcast market, it is a virtual monopolist in the market for broadcast of Braves games.

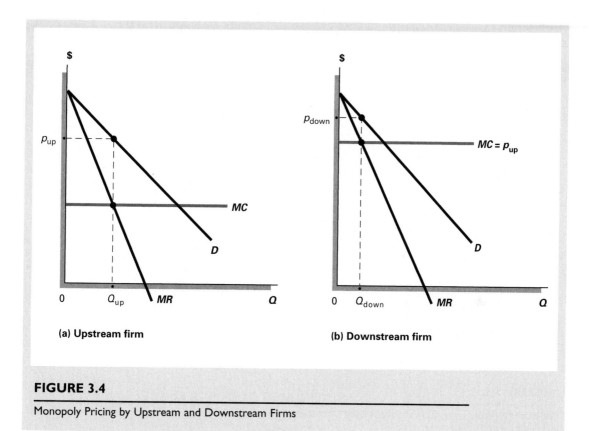

(a) Upstream firm

(b) Downstream firm

FIGURE 3.4

Monopoly Pricing by Upstream and Downstream Firms

　　From the owner's perspective, an individual or group that owns two vertically integrated firms will seek to maximize total profits of the two combined enterprises. From a purely financial standpoint, the owner does not worry whether one firm shows a larger profit than the other. The price at which the upstream firm sells to the downstream firm is called the **transfer price**. Changes in transfer prices change accounting profits (those reported to the IRS), but not the overall profitability of the combined enterprises. Thus, the joint owner of a franchise and the cable station that broadcasts the franchise's games will set a low transfer price (i.e., broadcast rights fee) if tax or political considerations make it advantageous to do so. For example, if a team did not want to show high profits while seeking a public subsidy, or if the players were entitled to a given percentage of team profits, then the owner could keep more of the profits by having them transferred to his cable company through a low broadcast rights fee. Conversely, if the profits of the cable company were regulated, the owner may want to minimize earnings by charging a high broadcast rights fee. The moral of the story is that when firms are vertically integrated, as is becoming more and more common in the sports industry, one must view accounting profits with a skeptical eye.

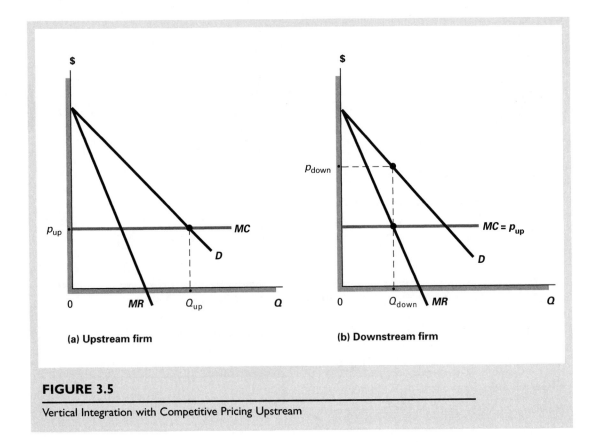

(a) Upstream firm

(b) Downstream firm

FIGURE 3.5

Vertical Integration with Competitive Pricing Upstream

The current direction of the relationship between the media and sports ownership is cloudy. On the one hand, some groups see the potential for greater profits by integrating vertically. For example, the NBA's New Jersey Nets and MLB's New York Yankees have recently joined forces to form the YES sports network, which will, of course, feature their own games as programming. On the other hand, some media giants no longer see any advantage in owning sports franchises. Disney, for example, has recently sold its baseball team, the Anaheim Angels, and is looking to sell its hockey team, the Mighty Ducks of Anaheim.

3.4   TURNING LOSSES INTO PROFITS: THE ACCOUNTING GAME

While teams worry about many different sources of revenues and costs, it still seems that one need only subtract the total cost from the various sources of revenue to calculate the profits. Unfortunately, nothing is simple in the finances of professional sports. Vertical integration is not the only tool that owners can use to manipulate profits. Paul Beeston, once the Toronto Blue Jays' vice president of business operations, put it best: "[A]nyone who quotes profits of a baseball club is missing the point. Under generally accepted accounting principles, I can turn a $4 million profit into a $2 million loss and get every national accounting firm to agree with me."[28] In this section, we explore how teams use the rules of accounting to manipulate their measures of profit.

Using Sports to Maximize Profits Elsewhere

Given Rupert Murdoch's reputation as a shrewd businessman, it is hard to explain the financial status of the Los Angeles Dodgers, which are owned by Murdoch's Fox News Corp. The Dodgers regularly draw over three million fans a year. They share the nation's second largest media market with the Anaheim Angels, a team that, until it won the 2002 World Series, was a clear second fiddle in the minds of Los Angelinos. They also own Dodger Stadium and over 300 acres of prime real estate adjacent to the stadium. Somehow, despite these advantages, *Forbes* claims that the Dodgers managed to lose over $25 million in 2002. [29] How did Murdoch manage to lose so much money?

Part of the answer lies in Section 3.3. As part of the Fox Sports empire, the Dodgers had little reason to seek the most lucrative media deal. As a result, according to MLB's own data, the Dodgers reported broadcast revenue of just over $27 million, less than half of what the Yankees received, and just 7 percent more than that received by the Texas Rangers, who play in a market about half the size of Los Angeles. [30]

Shuffling income from one subsidiary to another was only one of Murdoch's goals. The other goal helps to explain why Disney is unloading its sports teams in Anaheim and why Murdoch himself is looking to sell the Dodgers. Murdoch did not purchase the Dodgers because he was a baseball fan or because he saw synergies between the Dodgers and his regional Fox Sports network in Los Angeles. Instead, he bought them when he learned that Disney planned to establish a regional ESPN to compete with Fox. Murdoch's purchase of the Dodgers, which placed them firmly in the Fox camp, effectively blocked Disney's efforts. Once the threat to his media holdings had passed, the Dodgers had served their purpose and were no longer of much interest to Murdoch. The Dodgers were never anything more than a means to an end. While they may lose tens of millions of dollars a year, an unchallenged cable sports network is worth hundreds of millions.[31]

Operating Income, Book Profit, and Bill Veeck

To this point, we have been using operating profit, the net revenue from day-to-day operations, when discussing the profitability of sports franchises. When

---

[28]Quoted in Zimbalist, *Baseball and Billions* (1992), p. 62.

[29]The Dodgers dispute this figure. They claim to have lost about twice as much.

[30]Chris Isidore, "Baseball's Shell Game," *CNNMoney*, at http://cnnmoney.com, December 7, 2001.

[31]Bill Shaiken, "Fox Reaches Dodger Goals," *Los Angeles Times* (December 13, 2001), p. D8.

teams, or firms of any kind, report profits, however, they use **book profit**, the difference between total revenue and total cost. Book profit differs from operating income in that it nets out interest expenses and depreciation as well as the day-to-day costs of production. Since corporate profit taxes are based on book profits, firms can deduct interest payments from their corporate profit taxes, while they must pay taxes on the profits that make up dividend payments. The asymmetric treatment of interest and dividends has led economists to conclude that firms generally prefer to raise funds by issuing debt (in the form of bonds and loans on which they must pay interest) rather than stock, which results in dividend payments. Moreover, most borrowing, and hence most interest payments, stem from the initial purchase of the team. As noted in Section 3.1, most purchases entail a sizable "ego premium." If interest payments are tax deductible, then taxpayers are subsidizing the ego premium, allowing owners to overpay for their franchises.

Depreciation allowances permit firms to estimate how badly their plant and equipment have worn down as a result of the production process and to deduct this loss in value as an expense on their corporate taxes. Like other firms, sports franchises have often accounted for the decay of their physical plant. Unlike other firms, sports franchises have used this provision to write off the depreciation of their labor force by claiming that their players' skills erode just like machines wear out over time.

In 1949, Bill Veeck became the first owner to apply depreciation to his own players. Veeck's tenure as owner of the Cleveland Indians in the late 1940s was one of constant innovation. In 1947 he integrated the American League by signing Larry Doby. Not coincidentally, the Indians quickly became a contending team, winning pennants in 1948 and 1954, winning the World Series in 1948, and setting attendance records along the way. In his dealings with the Indians, Veeck introduced yet another innovation, a tax shelter that allowed an owner to make money by losing money.

The most flagrant use of this probably came in 1964, when a syndicate bought the Milwaukee Braves (and moved them to Atlanta a year later). The syndicate declared that only $50,000 of the $6.168 million it spent was for the team itself and that the remaining $6.118 million was embodied in the players. It also declared that the players were depreciable assets that wore out over a 10-year span, losing 10 percent of their original value each year. This method of estimating depreciation is called **straight-line depreciation** and is illustrated in Figure 3.6. The technique allowed the Braves to write off $611,800 as depreciation expenses each year. At a 52 percent tax rate, the team reduced its tax burden by over $300,000 per year for 10 years. The total tax savings meant in effect that the new owners of the Braves were able to foist almost half the purchase price of the team onto the American taxpayer.

A team with a single owner could take the process one step further. Upon purchasing the franchise, the owner could reorganize the team as a *subchapter S corporation*. In a subchapter S corporation, all of the firm's profits are treated as the personal income of the owner. The income is thus taxed at the personal tax rate rather than at the corporate rate. At first, this seems illogical, since personal tax rates for people wealthy enough to own a franchise are higher than

FIGURE 3.6
_____

Straight-Line Depreciation

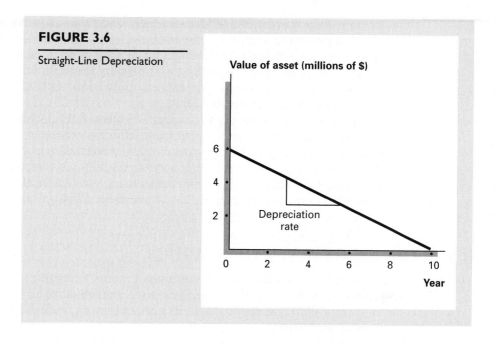

corporate rates.[32] If the depreciation write-off is high enough, however, the owner can create a book loss for his team even though it has a positive operating income. The $300,000 depreciation write-off allowed the Braves to transform an operating profit of $200,000 into a book loss of over $100,000. If the corporate tax rate were 52 percent, then the corporate tax write-off would have been $52,000. Since they were a subchapter S corporation, the Braves' losses were counted against the owner's personal taxes, allowing him to reduce his taxes at the higher personal tax rate. If the personal rate were 72 percent, then the write-off would have been $72,000.

Owners who follow a subchapter S strategy face a problem when they have fully depreciated their players, since they can no longer write off depreciation to create paper losses. The owners can escape the higher tax burden in one of two ways. They can sell the club, allowing the new owner to reorganize the corporation and begin the process all over again—even with the same players! Alternatively, they can take advantage of a one-time opportunity to revoke their subchapter S status.

---

[32]At the time Veeck introduced this shelter, the highest personal tax rate was 72 percent, while the corporate rate was a flat 52 percent. The attractiveness of this strategy has diminished over time due to the decrease in corporate tax rates and the refusal of courts to allow 90 percent of team value to be attributed to players. As part of the Tax Reform Act of 1976, the tax code was changed to create the presumption that no more than 50 percent of the value of a franchise be attributed to its players. For more details on this, see Paul Weiler and Gary Roberts, _Sports and the Law: Cases Materials and Problems_ (St. Paul, M.N.: West Publishing, 1993), pp. 412–414.

The reduction in tax rates since the 1950s and IRS rulings that reduced how much of the team's value could be attributed to the players from 90 percent to 50 percent have limited the profitability of subchapter S corporations. As a result, there is less of an incentive to use this tax loophole. Still several sports owners, including Vince McMahon, proprietor of World Wrestling Entertainment, have taken advantage of it.

The long-run desirability of owning a professional franchise in the face of ostensible losses can be seen in the fact that teams' market value has steadily increased over the years. Of the 34 teams that reported losses in the 2001–02 *Forbes* analyses (15 in MLB, 10 in the NHL, and 9 in the NBA), 21 increased in their estimated market value.[33] This suggests one of two possibilities: either the losses are overstated or owners have an additional motive for owning a sports franchise.

3.5 THE IMPORTANCE OF LEAGUES

All major professional team and individual sports are organized into leagues or associations. Forming a league appears to be a prerequisite for the financial stability of a sport, yet the arrival of leagues did not coincide with the advent of professional teams.[34]

Baseball's National League, the oldest existing professional league in the United States, did not appear until 1876, seven years after the Cincinnati Red Stockings, the first openly professional team, began to play in 1869. It took another 20 years for the National League to establish a stable set of teams. The NFL took even longer to establish itself. As noted earlier, the NFL formed in 1920, two generations after William Heffelfinger became the first professional football player in 1876, and did not field a stable set of teams until 1936.[35] Despite these delays, professional sports could not have survived without the formation of stable leagues.

Prior to the appearance of leagues, teams played each other on an informal, *ad hoc* basis. Until the latter part of the 19th century, most games involved teams from the same town. As transportation improved, matches were arranged between teams from different towns.[36] Informal trips to play teams in other towns, a practice known as barnstorming, became popular, but there was no guarantee that the opposition would show up or that the game would draw a sizable crowd. The experiences of the old Cincinnati Red Stockings illustrate this problem. During their grand tour of 1869, the Red Stockings drew large crowds from coast to coast while compiling a 56–0–1 record. The next year they lost only four games but disbanded when the season was over. The Red Stockings team resembled a strongman in a traveling carnival who offers to take on all comers.

---

[33]The 13 that did not increase in value consisted of 10 baseball franchises and 3 basketball franchises.

[34]Leifer, *Making the Majors* (1995), p. 15.

[35]Quirk and Fort, *Pay Dirt* (1992), pp. 333–334.

[36]See Michael Danielson, *Home Team: Professional Sport and the American Metropolis* (Princeton, N.J.: Princeton University Press, 1997), p. 20.

The sideshow may attract a crowd if it bills the strongman as "undefeated." A strongman who has won two-thirds of his matches (an enviable record for most teams today), however, would not generate much interest.

The typical fan regards a league as a collection of teams that agrees to play games against one another. This simple definition ignores the economic complexity of leagues. Leagues are by nature cooperative bodies. At one level, the teams are rivals that succeed at the expense of each other. At another level, each team's success depends on the success of the other teams in the league and on the success of the league as an institution. As Gerald Scully notes, the goal of the cooperative behavior is to maximize the combined wealth of the teams in the league.[37] Despite the existence of antitrust legislation in the United States (discussed at length in Chapter 4), teams try to limit their rivalry to the field of play and—to a limited extent—to the acquisition of talent. Off the field, team owners regard each other as colleagues rather than adversaries. Together, they try to maximize their wealth by maximizing revenues and controlling costs.

Leagues do much more than create a set of common opponents. Some of their activities include establishing a common set of rules, deciding on revenue-sharing arrangements, staging championship tournaments, creating a framework for the entry of new players and teams into the league, and conducting marketing campaigns.[38] In the next four sections, we focus on the following key activities:

- Setting the rules
- Limiting entry
- Competitive balance and revenue sharing
- Marketing at a league-wide level.

Setting the Rules

One of the most important—and most overlooked—ways that leagues maximize wealth is by establishing a set of commonly accepted rules. For example, the many different rules by which 19th-century English football clubs played created conflict between clubs and stymied the growth of the game. In 1863, many clubs joined to form the Football Association (FA) to establish a single set of rules.[39] In addition to standardizing rules, the FA gave football the nickname it now enjoys in England and the United States. The approved version of the game was dubbed "Association Football," later shortened to "Assoc. Football" or "soccer."

In the early years of soccer, teams did not play a fixed schedule, and attempts to stage a championship series often resulted in dull, one-sided games. Recognizing the need to provide stable competition between evenly matched

---

[37]Gerald Scully, *The Market Structure of Sports* (Chicago: University of Chicago Press, 1995), pp. 3–40.

[38]Groups such as the Professional Golfers' Association and the United States Tennis Association perform much the same function for these more individually based sports.

[39]Unhappy that the new rules did not allow their rougher version of football, devotees of the style developed at Rugby formed their own association, the Rugby Football Union, in 1871.

teams, 12 of the strongest clubs formed an elite grouping of teams in 1888 that called itself "the Football League" (FL). Despite the seeming conflict with the FA, the FL did not attempt to displace the FA to become the sole governing body of the elite teams. The members of the FL recognized that they were motivated by the interests of their individual clubs and not the welfare of the FL or the sport as a whole, and they chose to share power with the FA, allowing it to serve as an outside arbiter.[40]

Like soccer, baseball was played by different rules in different places. Two versions of the sport dominated, Massachusetts Rules and Knickerbocker Rules (also known as New York Rules). Knickerbocker Rules are the linear ancestor of modern baseball; Massachusetts Rules may seem bizarre to the modern observer. Under Massachusetts Rules, a team got an opposing player "out" by hitting him with a thrown ball, the bases were arranged in a square rather than a diamond, and winning a game required 100 runs or getting every member of the other team out, as in cricket. By the middle of the 19th century, the Knickerbocker Rules had become the norm.[41]

The earliest central authority in baseball, the National Association of Base Ball Players (NABBP), predates the FA, having formed in 1858. It did not arise out of a need to standardize rules, because the Knickerbocker Rules dominated the game played by the teams in the NABBP (largely in the New York area). Instead, it sought to combat professionalism and preserve the "gentlemanliness" of the game. The NABBP did not live up to expectations, and it succumbed to the growing professionalism of the sport. At first the growth was *sub rosa*, with individual players paid "under the table." In 1869 the Cincinnati Red Stockings cast aside all pretense and became an openly professional club. Teams in Chicago, Boston, and elsewhere soon followed suit.

Leagues establish and enforce a consistent set of rules off the field as well. Teams or players that do not obey the rules can be banished from the league. In its early years, the National League expelled teams for failing to meet their obligations to play out their schedule. Individual players were also banned from baseball for intentionally losing games, as was the case for eight of the Chicago "Black Sox" following the 1919 World Series, or for betting on baseball games, as Pete Rose was in 1989. The NFL suspended Alex Karras of the Detroit Lions and Paul Hornung of the Green Bay Packers for one year in 1963 for betting on league games. Players may also be suspended for engaging in activity that may reflect poorly on the league, as witnessed by the numerous suspensions in all sports for drug use and basketball player Latrell Sprewell's suspension by the NBA for choking his coach, P. J. Carlesimo, in 1997.

Leagues have also played a role in purging the crowds of "undesirable elements" that discouraged attendance. For example, Sunday beer sales at base-

---

[40]Wray Vamplew, *Pay Up and Play the Game: Professional Sport in Britain, 1875–1914* (Cambridge, U.K.: Cambridge University Press, 1988), p. 125.

[41]See Harold Seymour, *Baseball: The Early Years* (New York: Oxford University Press, 1960), pp. 23–30; and Robert Burk, *Never Just a Game: Players, Owners, and American Baseball to 1920* (Chapel Hill: University of North Carolina Press, 1994), p. 14.

ball games have only been allowed fairly recently. In the 1890s, the National League tried to present a wholesome image by expelling the Cincinnati Red Stockings for serving beer at all. Prior to the 1930s, games were not even played on Sundays in many cities. In the NHL, teams can be penalized during a game if fans repeatedly throw objects onto the ice and delay the game. In the NFL, the home team can be penalized if its fans are too noisy and prevent the opposing team from hearing its snap count.

Finally, rules have been manipulated to create more excitement and fan interest. The NFL has continually tried to "open up" the game by limiting how much contact defenders can have with quarterbacks or receivers. It has also made teams kick off from deeper and deeper in their own territory in an effort to generate longer and more exciting kickoff returns. In the NHL, the goals were moved farther from the end boards and the goal crease was reduced in size prior to the 1998–99 season to increase scoring. After seeing how popular it had been in the rival American Basketball Association (ABA) and American Basketball League (ABL),[42] the NBA added the three-point basket to increase scoring and restore the value of outside shooting; more recently, they permitted teams to play "zone" defense." Hockey has tried to widen its appeal by discouraging violent play. This policy may not be entirely successful. While TV interviews may be more appealing if the player being questioned has a full set of teeth, some research has found that violent games attract fans.[43] None of these changes was designed to increase the competitiveness or outcome of any specific contest. They were all made at the league level with the goal of making the game more spectator-friendly.

Limiting Entry

Suppose you are very wealthy and want to try your hand at owning a professional football team. You name your team the Vultures, create a sharp-looking logo, and design eye-catching new uniforms. Now all you need are opponents, players, and a venue. The only way to get them is to join the NFL, and the only way to join is to convince the other owners to admit you. Had you decided to open a shoe store, you would need only a storefront, a business license, a wholesale supplier, and a few employees. Can you imagine having to canvass the city, asking other shoe store owners for their permission to open? If you did, the retail shoe industry would certainly look quite different from how it does today.

In all professional sports leagues, such a restriction is accepted practice. Leagues not only limit the amount of entry, they dictate *where* entry can occur. With very few exceptions (such as Green Bay in Wisconsin), the NFL has placed all its teams in major metropolitan areas. These include almost all of the largest cities in the nation. Table 3.7 shows that, in 2000, each of the 15

---

[42]Terry Pluto, *Loose Balls: The Short, Wild Life of the American Basketball Association* (New York: Simon and Schuster, 1990), pp. 29–30.

[43]J. C. Jones, D. G. Ferguson, and K. G. Stewart, "Blood Sports and Cherry Pie: Some Economics of Violence in the National Hockey League," *American Journal of Sports and Sociology*, v. 52, no. 1 (January 1993), pp. 63–78.

Table 3.7

Fifteen Most Populous Metropolitan Areas and Their Sports Teams According to the 2000 Census

City	Population[a]	Sports Franchises
New York	21.2	MLB (2); NBA (2); NFL (2); NHL (3); MLS; WNBA(2)
Los Angeles	16.4	MLB (2); NBA (2); NHL; MLS; WNBA
Chicago	9.2	MLB (2); NBA; NFL; NHL; MLS
Washington/Baltimore	7.6	MLB; NBA; NFL (2); NHL; MLS; WNBA
San Francisco	7.0	MLB (2); NBA; NFL (2); NHL; MLS
Philadelphia	6.2	MLB; NBA; NFL; NHL
Boston	5.8	MLB; NBA; NFL; NHL; MLS
Detroit	5.5	MLB; NBA; NFL; NHL; WNBA
Dallas	5.2	MLB; NBA; NFL; NHL; MLS
Houston	4.7	MLB; NBA; NFL; WNBA
Atlanta	4.1	MLB; NBA; NFL; NHL
Miami	3.9	MLB; NBA; NFL; NHL
Seattle	3.6	MLB; NBA; NFL; WNBA
Phoenix	3.2	MLB; NBA; NFL; NHL; WNBA
Minneapolis	3.0	MLB; NBA; NFL; NHL; WNBA

[a]In millions

largest metropolitan areas had several professional franchises. As expected, New York, the largest market, had almost twice as many franchises as any other area, with 12 franchises. Los Angeles, San Francisco and Washington/Baltimore were tied for the second most franchises with seven, followed by Chicago with six. Each of these five metropolitan areas had multiple franchises in at least one sport, with New York, Los Angeles, and San Francisco having multiple franchises in several sports. MLB and the NBA had franchises in all of the 15 largest metropolitan areas. The NFL was in every area but Los Angeles, and the NHL was in every area except Houston and Seattle. Women's professional sports had entered fewer areas. Several cities hosted only one women's sports team, and Detroit and Miami had none.

Placing franchises in the largest cities ensures that each team will have a large fan base it can market to. For example, the Allentown/Bethlehem/Easton area of Pennsylvania is the state's third largest metropolitan region. Its efforts to obtain a MLB-affiliated minor league team have been complicated by the existence of major league and MLB-affiliated minor league teams in nearby areas. With the Philadelphia Phillies to the south, the class AAA Scranton/Wilkes Barre Red Barons to the north, the class A Trenton Thunder to the east, and the class AA Reading Phillies to the west, the league is not anxious to dilute the market further by adding yet another team. Adding teams to a market dissipates the monopoly power of the existing teams. To have an effective monopoly, a firm must produce a good with no close substitutes. As the number of available substitutes increases, the demand curve facing the incumbent firm becomes more elastic. In Figure 3.7, the addition of a new, near-by team shifts the demand curve from D_0 to D_1, reducing the profit-maximizing price from p_0 to p_1. The more teams that exist in any given area, the more vigorously they must compete with one another in all areas of revenue genera-tion, from luxury box sales to regular ticket sales to advertising. In terms of Figure 3.7, the more teams in the area, the more elastic the demand curve fac-ing any individual team, and the weaker its monopoly power.

If teams in a league are making large profits, new teams will want to enter. The ability of new firms to enter an industry where profits exceed the normal rate of return ensures that competitive markets respond to the desires of their consumers. The threat of new entry puts constant downward pressure on prices and profits. The desire to escape this pressure gives incumbent firms the incentive to prevent new firms from joining the industry.

If potential owners cannot join an existing league, they have an incentive to create a new one. The viability of a new league is much less certain, however, if all of the most profitable locations already have teams in the existing league. The lack of profitable markets dogged the ABA, a short-lived rival to the NBA that lasted from 1967 to 1976. Many of the ABA's former players, coaches, and owners claim that ABA basketball was more exciting than the NBA game at the time. As proof, they point to the adoption of several ABA rules by the NBA and the excellent performance of ABA teams and players after the NBA absorbed

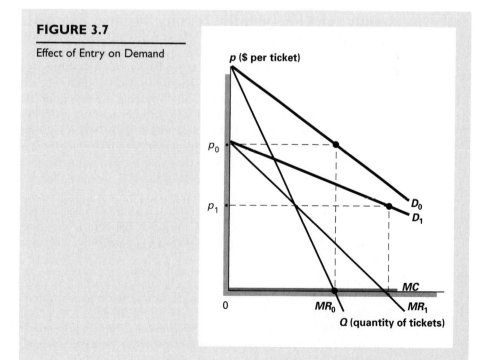

FIGURE 3.7

Effect of Entry on Demand

four ABA teams.[44] To avoid direct competition with the NBA, the ABA chose mostly midsized cities for its franchises. A better product in a weak location, however, is often doomed to fail. Such was the fate of the ABA. When the league folded, only the Denver, New Jersey, San Antonio, and Indiana franchises survived to join the NBA.

There have been several recent attempts to form rival leagues in both football and ice hockey. The World Hockey Association (WHA) played from 1972 through 1979. After the 1978–79 season, four teams from the WHA joined the NHL, two were compensated for not joining the NHL, and the remaining teams disbanded. All teams that attempted to compete head to head with NHL teams in the same large city market failed. The only teams to survive played in medium-sized markets where no other team already existed, and three of those teams (Winnipeg, Hartford, and Quebec) eventually moved to more profitable markets (Phoenix, Charlotte, and Denver, respectively). Many of the original owners of American Football League franchises in the 1960s were wealthy people who had been unable to buy NFL teams. Other leagues followed, including the World Football League (WFL), the United States Football League (USFL), and the Extreme Football League (XFL). The WFL lasted less than two seasons in the mid-1970s, failing largely because of its inability to maintain a television contract. The USFL played from 1983 to 1985 but also folded due to a lack of stable ownership and rapidly falling TV revenues.[45] The XFL, a combination of football and professional wrestling, lasted only the 2000–2001 season due to poor TV ratings.

Only the (Financially) Strong Survive: The ABL and the WNBA

In the 15 years that followed women's basketball becoming an Olympic event in 1976, six women's professional leagues reached the planning stage. Most of them never played a single game. The Women's Professional Basketball League (WPBL) began play in 1978 and lasted three seasons; even the most successful WPBL team lost over $700,000 before folding in 1981. The biggest problem was simply a lack of fans.[46] By 1991, it seemed that the idea of women's professional basketball was dead, but after a five-year hiatus, women's professional basketball came back strong. On the heels of the U.S. women's team winning the gold medal in the 1996 Olympics, two new leagues were organized and began play.

In the fall of 1996, the American Basketball League (ABL) fielded eight teams in mostly medium-sized markets. The following spring, the Women's National Basketball Association (WNBA) began play, with all eight of its teams

---

[44]Julius ("Dr. J") Erving notes that in the first all-star game after the ABA folded, essentially merging its most promising locations with the NBA, 10 of the 24 players selected had come from the ABA. Pluto, *Loose Balls* (1990), p. 35.

[45]Jim Byrne, *The $1 League: The Rise and Fall of the USFL* (New York: Prentice Hall, 1986), *passim.*

[46]Daniel Green, "Toss Up: Suddenly Women's Pro Sports Are Hot," *Working Woman* (April 1997), pp. 26–72.

in major NBA market cities. There is no doubt that the popularity of women's sports had increased significantly since the failure of the WPBL. In addition to the excitement generated by the Olympics, the TV ratings for the 1996 women's NCAA title game were nearly as high as the men's, and attendance at women's college games had tripled since 1985.[47] Still, experts in the fields of both economics and basketball wondered aloud if it was possible for both leagues to survive. The question was answered two and a half years later when the ABL permanently suspended play midway through its third season. The fact that the ABL and not the WNBA folded is a testament to the importance of league stability over quality of play.

The ABL was the brainchild of Gary Cavilli, Olympic gold medalist Anne Cribs, and investors Steve Hams and Bobby Johnson. Their goal was to have the league be a grassroots organization.[48] Players were given an incentive to help to market the product, and salaries were maintained at reasonable levels by making the players part owners. The league owned all eight teams and offered stock options to the players. In keeping with the grassroots theme, teams were located in relatively small markets (see Table 3.8) where women's basketball had been well received at the collegiate level.

Because the ABL was conceived before the WNBA and offered big-name players big-dollar contracts, most observers believed that the ABL had the better talent of the two leagues. It had star players such as Dawn Staley and 8 of the 12 players from the previous Olympic team, and the ABL's free throw percentage exceeded that of the (men's) NBA during its opening season. Probably the most striking evidence that the quality of play was better in the ABL was the WNBA's refusal to play an all-star game against the ABL. After the initial rebuff by the WNBA, Cavilli even offered to pay all expenses for the game, yet WNBA Commissioner Val Ackerman still rejected the offer.[49] With the advantage of being first to market and having a superior product, the ABL seemed to be in an excellent position to survive the battle of the rival leagues. Unfortunately for the ABL, the WNBA had a big brother with deep pockets—the NBA.

The challenge facing the ABL was the same as that for any new league— financial stability. With only $9 million in start-up capital, venues that held 4,000–15,000, and attendance averaging about 4,000 per game, finding sponsors and a television contract were critical. The only TV contract the ABL was able to land beyond the airing of two championship games on CBS, however, was a weekly broadcast on SportsChannel/Fox Sports Network and another on Black Entertainment Television. Lacking major network exposure, the games did not do well in the ratings, further discouraging sponsors. Even efforts to buy TV time during the 1998 NBA lockout failed.[50]

The WNBA overcame its late start and lack of advance planning thanks to its affiliation with the NBA. Until 2002, the NBA fully owned the WNBA, with

---

[47]"Two Leagues of Their Own?" *Business Week* (May 13, 1996), p. 52.

[48]"Hoop Dreams: New League Banks on Sisterhood," *Inc.* (June 1997), p. 23.

[49]"A Plucky Proposition," *Sports Illustrated* (February 16, 1998), p. 28.

[50]From sports "ticker," at http://bball.yahoo.com/nba/news/981222/ablbnkrpt.html.

Table 3.8

ABL and WNBA Franchise Locations

ABL	WNBA
Atlanta, GA	Charlotte, NC
Denver, CO	Cleveland, OH
Columbus, OH	Houston, TX
New England (Hartford)	New York, NY
Portland, OR	Los Angeles, CA
Richmond, VA	Phoenix, AZ
San Jose, CA	Sacramento, CA
Seattle, WA	Salt Lake City, UT

NBA franchises operating the WNBA teams in their cities. (After the 2002 season, the NBA teams were declared owners of the WNBA teams in their cities and were free to sell them to outside owners.) The NBA also provided the WNBA with corporate sponsors and a major TV deal. The WNBA's TV contract had a three-pronged approach, with games shown on NBC, ESPN (aimed at male fans), and Lifetime (aimed at female fans). Corporate sponsorship came from Sears, Nike, Spalding, Levi's, and Anheuser-Busch.

For fledgling leagues, money brings both stability and the chance to market their products. While the ABL spent only $1.5 million on marketing in its first year, the WNBA spent $15 million.[51] Much of the initial marketing push came in the form of heavy advertising during the NBA play-offs that immediately preceded the WNBA's inaugural season. Finally, while both leagues suffered the financial losses one would expect with any start-up venture, the NBA had an enormous capacity to absorb those losses, whereas the ABL had nothing to fall back on. When the ABL ran out of money in December of 1998, its only option was to cease operations. Some of the same factors that led the WNBA to outlast the ABL may now be working against it. After expanding to 14 teams in the wake of the ABL's demise, the WNBA has seen attendance and TV ratings steadily decline. In fact, the Nielsen rating of the WNBA's 2002 championship game was less than half that of the sole XFL championship game.[52] Alarmed by the WNBA's mounting losses, the NBA shut down two franchises after the 2002 season and began to dissociate itself from the WNBA. WNBA teams no longer need to partner with a NBA franchise and are increasingly assuming responsibility for their own finances. It remains to be seen whether the WNBA will be able to survive on its own.

---

[51]Steve Lopez, "They Got Next," *Sports Illustrated* (June 30, 1997), pp. 44–47.

[52]Stacey Pressman, "Slam Dunk," *The Weekly Standard,* online at http://www.theweeklystandard. com/Content/Public/Articles/000/000/002/515gdyfj.asp, April 8, 2003.

Controlling Entry as Cooperative Behavior

One way to analyze leagues is to think of them as a club.[53] The economic theory of clubs states that members in a "club" (i.e., teams in a league) act as semi-autonomous units that work together to maximize the consumption possibilities (or profits) of the group. According to this viewpoint, club behavior determines everything from play-off structure to restrictions on how, when, and where teams are allowed to move. For example, club theory concludes that there is a fundamental difference between the privately optimal number of teams in a league (the number that would maximize a monopoly league's profits), and the socially optimal number of teams (one where the marginal value of the last team added is zero). Admitting a new team to a league has both a positive and negative impact on existing members. On the positive side, the new entrant pays the league an admission fee and generates a new revenue stream in which the league can share. On the negative side, teams must share their revenues with yet another member. In addition, a new team reduces the geographic market of its closest neighbors and lessens the ability of existing members to use the threat of moving to that city as a bargaining chip when negotiating with their current home city. That gives the member teams the incentive to keep tight control over the location and number of franchises. The greater the revenue sharing between teams, the greater the economic gain of the group from preventing individual teams from making their own location decisions, and the more credible relocation threats will be. When the club members equally share the gains, they have the greatest incentive to ensure that the profits across all teams are maximized. (Chapter 4 explores the danger of keeping the size of the club small.)

Alternatively, one can consider the league as a multiplant monopoly. According to this view, a season of games is a "peculiar mixture: it comes in divisible parts, each of which can be sold separately, but it is also a joint and multiple yet divisible product."[54] For example, part of the excitement of attending a single game comes from how the outcome relates to league standings, which involves all teams in the league.

Leagues carefully coordinate the output (here measured as games played) and prices charged by member teams for the betterment of the league, even if such restrictions reduce the profits of some member teams. Major network television contracts are negotiated at the league level rather than by individual teams. Such cooperative behavior allows the most popular games to be aired on national television, and it prevents teams from competing with each other for broadcast rights, thereby keeping prices high. Such competition would

---

[53]The theory of clubs was developed in James Buchanan, "An Economic Theory of Clubs," *Economica*, v. 32, no. 125 (February 1965), pp. 1–14. It was explicitly applied to sports leagues by John Vrooman, "Franchise Free Agency in Professional Sports Leagues," *Southern Journal of Economics*, v. 64, no. 1 (July 1997), pp. 191–219.

[54]This view is expressed in W. Neale, "The Peculiar Economics of Professional Sports," *Quarterly Journal of Economics*, v. 78, no. 1 (February 1964), pp. 1–14. The quote is taken from p. 3.

inevitably lead to lower revenues for the league, because teams would have the incentive to reduce prices to networks for broadcast rights.

Restricting the number of teams (and the geographic locations they occupy) gives owners a guaranteed source of ticket and media revenue as well as a restricted market for apparel and other team-related enterprises. Leagues enforce territorial rights by setting a radius within which no other member of the league may locate. In the NFL, each team is given exclusive rights to an area with a radius measuring 75 miles from its home stadium. Territorial rights do not absolutely exclude other teams, but a team that moves into another's territory must compensate the existing team. For example, in the NBA, the Los Angeles Clippers had to pay the Los Angeles Lakers $6 million in 1984 for moving from San Diego into the Lakers territory without the league's permission.[55]

League Contraction

One of the central concerns facing a league is the appropriate number of teams. Admitting too many teams increases the likelihood that some teams will not be financially viable or competitive on the playing field. This happened, for example, during the early years of the NFL, when many teams failed, sometimes in midseason. Admitting too few teams, however, may leave markets open for rival leagues, which occurred in 1901 when the National League's policy of limiting itself to eight teams allowed the American League to compete as a rival "major" league.[56]

In the fall of 2001, MLB Commissioner Bud Selig announced that, after four decades of uninterrupted expansion, the sport had overextended itself and should contract. The blue-ribbon commission that he had appointed noted that the sport had become dangerously uncompetitive. When the commission divided the teams into four equal quartiles based on the size of the teams' payrolls, with Quartile I being the teams with the highest payrolls and Quartile IV being the teams with the lowest payrolls, it made a disturbing discovery. Over the 5-year period of 1995 to 1999, during which there were 158 postseason play-off and World Series games, "*no club* from Quartiles III or IV won a DS [Division Series] or LCS [League Championship Series] game and *no club* from payroll Quartiles II, III, or IV won a World Series game."[57] Selig went on to claim that two teams, later revealed to be the Minnesota Twins and the Montreal Expos, were no longer financially viable and should be folded. Perhaps as a consequence of overexpansion, half of all baseball teams lost money in 2002.[58]

[55]Scully, *The Market Structure of Sports* (1995), p. 22.

[56]The theoretical basis for this is Buchanan, "An Economic Theory of Clubs" (1965), pp. 1–1, and John Vrooman, "A General Theory of Professional Sports Leagues," *Southern Economic Journal*, v. 61, no. 4 (April 1995), pp. 971–990.

[57]Richard C. Levin, George J. Mitchell, Paul A. Volker, George F. Will, "The Report of the Independent Members of the Commissioner's Blue Ribbon Panel on Baseball Economics," July 2000, online at http://www.mlb.com/mlb/downloads/blue_ribbon.pdf, p.i.

[58]MLB Team Valuations," *Forbes Magazine*, online at http://www.forbes.com, April 28, 2003.

Some critics of contraction were quick to point out that the blue-ribbon commission claimed that there was no need to eliminate teams. Others noted that the Minnesota Twins were not one of the teams that *Forbes* reported as having negative operating income in 2002. They also brought out the fact that the Twins' owner was embroiled in a losing battle with the Minnesota legislature to get a new state-funded stadium and that baseball's owners were in the midst of contentious negotiations with the players' union. The threat of shutting down the Twins, these critics argued, could only strengthen team owners' hands in both disputes. Finally, the success of low payroll teams in the 2002 play-offs led some to question the conclusions of the blue-ribbon commission's report. In 2002, the World Series featured the Anaheim Angels and the San Francisco Giants, both teams with payrolls in Quartile II. The Giants got to the World Series by beating the St. Louis Cardinals, another Quartile II club, while the Angels defeated none other than the Minnesota Twins, which had the third lowest payroll in baseball. Even the downtrodden Montreal Expos managed to finish second in their division. In light of 2002's results, one must ask which was the anomaly: 2002 or the four years considered by the blue-ribbon commission.

While some firmly believe that baseball's calls for contraction were part of a bargaining ploy by the owners who were intent on driving a hard bargain with the players (which succeeded) and with the residents of Minnesota (which failed), the financial distress of the Expos, a team with virtually no gate or local media revenue, is indisputable. At this writing, MLB has taken over operation of the Expos and is seeking new owners in a new city.

Marketing

While one team's marketing efforts may increase the profits of other teams, such spillovers are likely to be small. First, a team will run the ads only in its home market.[59] The Houston Rockets will pay to advertise games that bring them substantial rewards. Because the NBA does not share gate or local media revenue, the Rockets have an incentive to pay for advertisements that encourage fans to attend Rockets home games and to watch or listen to local broadcasts of Rockets games. The rewards of fans attending games in other cities accrue to other teams and the rewards from national broadcasts are shared evenly, so the Rockets have little reason to pay for more broadly focused ads. Second, much marketing is aimed at increasing local media ratings. If all marketing were done in this way, analyzing its impact on demand and profit would be straightforward. Marketing expenditures would appear as a fixed cost, and, if effective, they would shift the demand curve for the event to the right. Each team would advertise up to the point where the marginal benefit (*MB*) from the last dollar spent on advertising was equal to the marginal cost (*MC*) of the ad, as shown in Figure 3.8.

---

[59]If a team broadcasts over a superstation, its "home" market may cover an extensive geographic area.

FIGURE 3.8

Determining the Optimal
Quantity of Advertisements

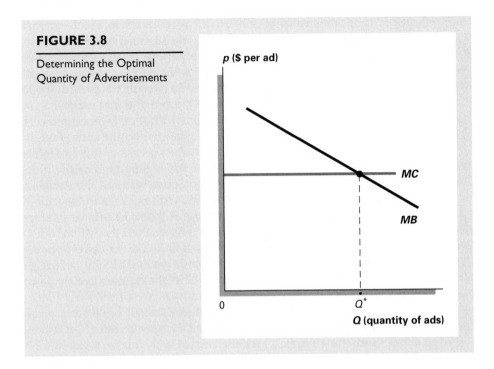

Leagues, in contrast, take a multilevel approach to marketing. As with tra-ditional franchises such as McDonald's, professional teams contribute to joint advertisements run at the league level. In turn, the leagues work to create a spe-cific image designed to increase demand for the sport as a whole. In its first year, the WNBA spent $15 million on marketing. The league developed a slo-gan ("We Got Next") and used it in a variety of ads designed to promote the league rather than any specific team.

Marketing at the league level promotes the welfare of all teams and thus is something of a **public good.** A public good is marked by **nonrivalry** in con-sumption. The benefit that one team receives from a league-wide marketing campaign does not diminish the benefit that any other team can receive from the same campaign. All teams receive equal amounts of the public good, even though they may value it differently. Public goods are also marked by **nonex-clusion**. One team cannot prevent another team from receiving the benefits of the campaign. Asking teams to contribute voluntarily, however, creates a **free rider** problem. Free riding is an attempt to pay less than one's marginal benefit from a public good and to exploit the production by others. Thus, there are two challenges when trying to determine the optimal provision of such a good. The first is to determine the marginal benefit of the good to society, and the second is to ensure that each consumer (team, in this case) pays his or her share.

In a market for a private good, such as the market for apples, we would arrive at the market demand by horizontally summing individual demand curves. If Amy would buy 4 apples at $1 per apple and Pat would buy 6 apples at $1 per apple, their combined demand would be 10 apples at $1. With public goods, because consumption is nonrival, demand or marginal benefit curves are summed *vertically* rather than horizontally. Suppose that 60-second advertising slots on network television are available at a constant marginal cost of $50,000. Alone, no team in the NBA (or any sports league) may be willing to pay for such an advertisement. However, if the first 60-second preseason commercial is worth $10,000 to 15 smaller-market teams such as the Sacramento Kings, and $20,000 to 15 larger-market teams such as the Los Angeles Lakers, the first commercial is worth $450,000 to the 30 teams combined. Assuming marginal benefits decline as usual, so that the demand curves slope downward, the optimal number of commercials in Figure 3.9 is seen to be 30.

The second challenge, getting those who benefit from the good to contribute toward its production, can be very complex. Once built, public goods such as parks and roads can be used by anyone, so identifying the beneficiaries can be difficult. Because leagues provide marketing for a limited clientele, they have a much easier time identifying exactly who benefits. As a result, each team contributes to the league-wide marketing fund.[60]

---

[60]Craig A. Depken, David R. Kamerschen, and Arthur Snow, "Generic Advertising of Intermediate Goods: Theory and Evidence," 1999, unpublished manuscript, showed that voluntary contributions to joint marketing of milk resulted in less than the profit-maximizing level of advertising in the milk industry.

FIGURE 3.9

Total Marginal Benefit when Consumption Is Nonrival

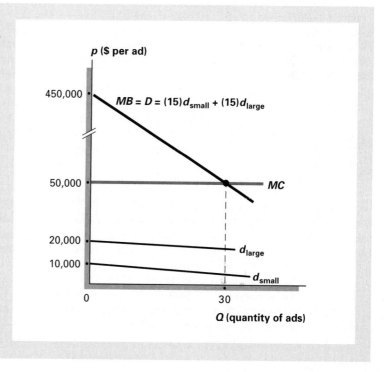

BILL VEECK
BIOGRAPHICAL Sketch

People need people (who else is there to take advantage of?)

— BILL VEECK[1]

Many owners have won more games than Bill Veeck did with the Cleveland Indians (1946–49), St. Louis Browns (1951–53), and Chicago White Sox (which he owned twice, 1959–61 and 1975–80). It is safe to say, however, that no owner in the history of the game had nearly as much fun. Veeck was literally born into baseball—his father was president of the Chicago Cubs—and he never left. In the 1920s, young Bill helped plant the ivy that now covers the wall at Wrigley Field.

A self-described hustler, Veeck was a showman *nonpareil* who gave baseball such attractions as bat day and the exploding scoreboard, and such disasters as "disco demolition night," at which a sellout Chicago crowd went out of control after thousands of disco records were blown up. Veeck also proposed many innovations that baseball adopted only after he had passed from the scene. In his 1969 memoir, *The Hustler's Handbook,* for example, Veeck proposed using the scoreboard to do a variety of things—to review disputed plays or to inform the fans about the type and speed of pitch that had just been thrown—that teams took decades to implement.

Bill Veeck had an innate sense of how the market and social justice come together. Between 1947 and 1964, only two American League teams other than the New York Yankees—the Cleveland Indians and the Chicago White Sox—won pennants, and only one won a World Series. Veeck was the owner of the Cleveland Indians when they won the 1948 World Series, and he built the team that appeared in the 1954 World Series. He was later the owner of the Chicago White Sox when they made it to the 1959 World Series, their only such appearance since the Black Sox

scandal of 1919. One other factor that distinguished these teams was that they were among the leaders in integrating the American League. Veeck brought Larry Doby to the Indians in 1947, a few weeks after Jackie Robinson broke the color line with the Brooklyn Dodgers. Veeck was also responsible for bringing the legendary Satchel Paige, regarded by most as the greatest pitcher in the history of the Negro Leagues, to the major leagues while he owned the Indians. In 1943, the Philadelphia Phillies were one of the worst teams in baseball and one of the least popular. Veeck tried to integrate baseball when he sought to buy the sad sack Phillies and stock the team with players from the Negro Leagues. Veeck had long opposed baseball's color line on moral grounds, but he also felt that integrating the game made good business sense. He thought that bringing in star players from the Negro Leagues would build a talented, exciting team that fans would want to see. According to Veeck, MLB Commissioner Kenesaw Mountain Landis stepped in at the last minute and found another buyer for the Phillies, preventing his purchase of the team.

Veeck also showed a sense of fairness as an outspoken critic of baseball's reserve clause, which effectively bound a player to a team for life. He went so far as to testify against the reserve clause in Curt Flood's lawsuit against baseball in the 1970s.[2]

Needless to say, Veeck's unorthodox beliefs and promotions did little to endear him to the other owners. They went so far as to block his attempt to move the Browns from St. Louis to Baltimore, allowing the move only after Veeck had sold the team. In St. Louis, the Browns were poor relations of the Cardinals. In an attempt to boost interest in his team, Veeck tried such

➡

stunts as sending 3'7"Eddie Gaedel to the plate as a pinch hitter—he walked—and holding "You Be the Manager Day," in which fans were given the opportunity to make substitutions and determine strategy. Predictably, some owners attempted to block Veeck's attempt to get back into baseball in the 1970s.

Veeck's last go-round as an owner—his second stint with the Chicago White Sox—was not as successful as his previous efforts. The advent of free agency and the growing importance of TV and venue revenue did not fit his limited means and hustler mentality. He was forced to sell the team after seven years. Fortunately, Bill's son Michael, the part owner of several minor league teams, has kept the Veeck

legacy alive. As owner of the St. Paul Saints, Michael Veeck staged such stunts as "Mime-O-Vision," in which mimes acted out the action on the field as a sort of living instant replay. The fans responded by pelting the mimes with hot dogs, a travesty trumpeted by headlines in all the local papers. Michael's father would have been proud.

[1] Bill Veeck, *The Hustler's Handbook*, p. 196.

[2]We discuss Flood's lawsuit in Chapter 4 and analyze the reserve clause in Chapter 8.

Sources: Bill Veeck, *The Hustler's Handbook* (Durham, N.C.: Baseball America Classic Books, 1996); and John Helyar, *Lords of the Realm* (New York: Ballantine Books, 1994).

SUMMARY

This chapter describes how professional sports teams go about maximizing profits. Teams derive their revenue from ticket sales, other venue-related income, the sale of broadcast rights, and licensing income. The degree to which revenues are shared among teams varies from league to league, with the most sharing occurring in the NFL. An interesting finding with respect to revenue sharing is that while it may promote league stability, it does not appear to improve the competitive balance in a league.

In the sports industry, most sources of cost are fixed over the period of a single season. Primary sources of costs are player salaries, stadium leases, and administrative costs. In the NHL and MLB, subsidies to minor league affiliates for player development also add significantly to team total cost.

In addition to individual actions, teams use leagues to stabilize revenues and control costs. In some cases, it is more useful to view the league as the monopoly and teams as producers of a joint product. In the next chapter, we look in detail at the monopoly aspects of professional sports.

DISCUSSION QUESTIONS

1. What do you predict about the popularity of PGA tour events if it was a virtual certainty that Tiger Woods would win every week?
2. How would professional leagues be different if teams only had corporate affiliation (e.g., the IBM Lions) rather than city or state affiliation?
3. Why aren't more teams separate, publicly traded corporations, as the Boston Celtics are, rather than held privately?
4. Why might a team not want to be too much better than its rivals?

5. Discuss the costs and benefits of expanding the NFL to include European teams.

6. Why do owners need to get the permission of the league to change cities?

7. What motivations lie behind the proposal that MLB contract by eliminating two teams?

PROBLEMS

3.1 Suppose that you were the owner of a professional baseball team in a major city. If the league decided to allow a second team in your city, as long as you were compensated for this infringement, on what basis could the appropriate compensation be determined?

3.2 Draw a graph that shows the demand for seats at an NFL stadium. Show how each demand would be affected if:

    a. The prices of parking and food at the games increase.

    b. Televised games switch from free TV to pay-per-view only.

    c. A new league forms with a team that plays nearby.

    d. The quality of the team decreases dramatically.

    e. The length of the season is increased.

3.3 True or false; explain your answer: "If all teams are of equal quality, it doesn't matter whether they share gate receipts or not—revenue will remain unchanged."

3.4 Some researchers argue that revenue sharing is like socialism in that it removes the incentive to outperform rivals. Do you agree with this statement? Why or why not?

3.5 Suppose that each team in a league has a demand curve for generic advertising (a league-wide, nonteam-specific campaign) equal to $Q = 1,000 - 5p$. If there are 20 teams in the league, and ads cost \$175 each, how many ads will the teams want to purchase as a group?

3.6 Many stadiums have restrictions that prohibit fans from bringing outside food and beverages into games. Under what circumstance will this be a profit-maximizing policy?

3.7 Would fans be better off if the government prevented media outlets such as Disney or local cable companies from owning pro sports teams?

3.8 Suppose an owner pays \$500 million to purchase a hockey team that earns operating profits of \$50 million per year. The new owner claims that \$200 million of this price is for the players, which he can depreciate using straight-line depreciation in five years. If the team pays corporate profit taxes of 40 percent, how much does the depreciation of the players save the owner?

3.9 How might the sale of the Dodgers by Fox News Corp. lead to an increase in the Dodgers' profits?

3.10 Why might a team owner prefer to raise funds by borrowing money to selling part ownership of the team to others?

CHAPTER 4

Monopoly and Antitrust

Gentlemen, we have the only legal monopoly in the country, and we're [messing] it up.

— ATLANTA BRAVES OWNER, TED TURNER[1]

INTRODUCTION

Major League Baseball's National League is the oldest professional sports league in the United States.[2] Founded in 1876, it rested on two basic principles:

1. The exclusive right of member clubs to their home territory
2. A reserve system that bound players to member ball clubs for as long as the team wanted them.

These rules proved so profitable that all succeeding sports leagues adopted them for themselves, often word for word. One need not look far to see why the system was so successful. The principle of "territorial rights" gave teams **monopoly power** in their host cities, as it precluded the entry of competing teams. The reserve system kept owners from bidding up salaries in order to lure away a rival team's players, giving each team **monopsony power** over its players. Baseball and all subsequent sports owe much of their early success to these two barriers.

While eliminating competition may be good for the teams, it imposes a cost on society. One of the themes of Chapter 2 was that competitive markets do a good job of allocating resources to their most appropriate use. Some segments of society may not like the resulting distribution of resources, but any attempt to override the forces of supply and demand typically leaves society worse off than before. The benefits of a free market, however, stem from the very competition that leagues have always sought to suppress. This chapter will explore the nature

---

[1]Quoted in John Helyar, *Lords of the Realm* (New York: Villard Books, 1994), p. 268.

[2]The fact that it predates the American League by about 25 years has led to its nickname, "the senior circuit."

and impact of monopoly and monopsony power in organized sports and how sports have frequently run afoul of our nation's attempts to rein in the power of monopolies and monopsonies. In the process, it will explain the following:

- Why teams sell personal seat licenses
- How the NFL was able to sign a TV deal worth $17.6 billion
- How the NCAA accidentally became a cartel, and why it was sued by its own members.

This chapter explains how leagues have obtained and maintained their monopoly power. To keep the focus on output markets, we save most of the discussion of the economics of monopsony (the market in which there is only one buyer) for Chapter 8. However, because the legal challenges to the monopoly power of professional sports leagues have often been bound up with challenges to their monopsony power, we shall briefly introduce the notion of monopsony and chart the legal challenges to monopsony as well as monopoly power.

4.1 WHAT'S WRONG WITH MONOPOLY?

As we saw in Chapter 2, monopolies operate where marginal revenue equals marginal cost, whereas perfectly competitive firms set price equal to marginal cost. Chapter 3 showed that one of the cornerstones of any professional league is the monopoly power it grants to each team over its home territory. Because of the NFL's monopoly power, consumers pay higher ticket prices and have the chance to see fewer games than they would if the NFL operated as part of a competitive industry. More broadly, the league's monopoly power leads it to provide fewer teams in fewer cities than if football were a competitive industry. Moreover, since the marginal cost of selling an additional ticket is virtually zero, almost the entire price of a ticket represents a return to the team's monopoly power. Figure 4.1 illustrates this setting with a marginal cost curve that coincides with the horizontal axis, and downward-sloping demand and marginal revenue curves. A competitive industry would operate at point C, where price equals marginal cost.[3] The NFL's monopoly power allows it to operate at point B, charging a higher price (say $20) and selling fewer tickets.

Monopolists and Deadweight Loss

Most noneconomists dislike monopolies because of the high prices they charge. High prices, however, are a two-edged sword. They may hurt the consumers who have to pay them, but they benefit the stockholders, employees, and other stakeholders in the firms that receive them. In Figure 4.1, consumers pay an amount equal to the area EFBG because they pay a price per unit equal to segment EF on EG units of output. While this exceeds the competitive price (zero

---

[3]Strictly speaking, the industry supply curve is the horizontal sum of all the individual marginal cost curves. For our purposes here, we ignore any complication raised by capacity constraints.

FIGURE 4.1

The Cost of a Monopoly
to Society

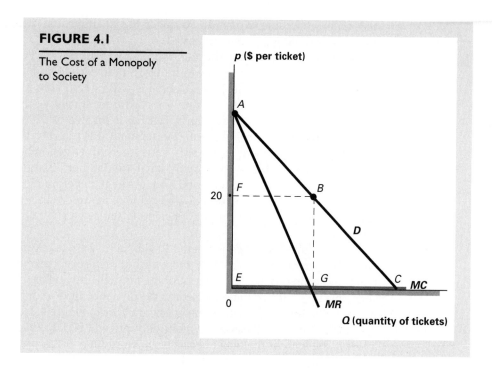

in this example), society—which consists of both consumers and producers—is not necessarily worst off, because producers receive EFBG more than before. Thus, higher prices reshuffle income without changing the total amount of income that society has. The higher price simply takes money from one pocket (the consumer's) and puts it in another (the monopolist's). Because one cannot say whether the higher prices that monopolies charge help or harm society, economists treat them as a **transfer** from consumers to producers, which brings no overall change in society's well-being.

Economists worry much more about the impact of the decline in output that accompanies monopoly. In particular, they worry about how monopoly affects the sum of **consumer surplus** and **producer surplus.** Consumer surplus stems from the fact that, despite our protestations to the contrary, we never would be satisfied "getting exactly what we paid for." In fact, if all we got out of an item was what we paid for it, we would be just as happy without it.[4]

To see how consumer surplus arises, consider the case of four football fans. Debbie loves the Carolina Panthers and is willing and able to pay $40 for a ticket to see them play. Bill also likes to go to Panther games, though not as much as Debbie; he is willing and able to pay $20. Jeff is still less enthusiastic;

---

[4]An explanation of producer surplus appears in Appendix 4B.

he is willing and able to pay $10. Kathleen has no interest in seeing the Panthers play; she is willing and able to pay $0.

If consumers must pay the competitive price of $0 from Figure 4.1, all four consumers buy tickets to see the Panthers, but none of them feels the same way about his or her purchase. Since Debbie is willing and able to pay $40 for the ticket but pays $0, she gets a bonus—or consumer surplus—of $40 (the vertical segment YY in Figure 4.2. Similarly, Bill has a surplus of $20 (the vertical segment ZZ), Jeff has a surplus of $10 (the segment WW), and Kathleen has no surplus whatever. Kathleen is the only consumer who "gets what she pays for." She is willing and able to pay exactly what the Panthers charge her. Purchasing the ticket leaves her no better—and no worse—than before. Economists refer to a person in Kathleen's position as a **marginal consumer,** since she is indifferent between buying and not buying. She could just as easily pass up the ticket as buy it.

In fact, thousands of consumers, all with their own desires and abilities to pay, want Panthers tickets. As a result, there are hundreds or thousands of vertical segments indicating consumer surplus for the fans who buy tickets. Eventually, these segments fill up the triangle formed by the demand curve and the horizontal line representing the market price (the horizontal axis in Figure 4.2.)

If the Panthers charged the monopoly price of $20, Kathleen would suffer a loss if she bought the ticket because she would pay $20 more than she is willing and able to pay. As a result, she no longer buys the ticket. Jeff, too, would

FIGURE 4.2

Consumer Surplus for Individual Consumers

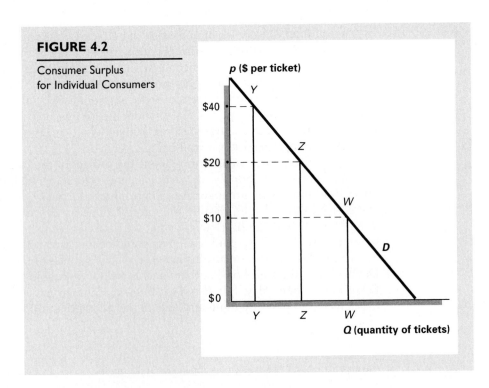

suffer a loss and would not buy the ticket. Bill would now be the marginal consumer, because he is paying exactly what the ticket is worth to him. Only Debbie would enjoy a consumer surplus, though her surplus is much smaller than it had been ($20 instead of $40). More generally, when a monopoly serves the market, consumers buy fewer tickets, and consumer surplus shrinks. In terms of Figure 4.1, consumer surplus would be ACE if the market for tickets were perfectly competitive. Because the equilibrium price in this example is zero, consumer surplus is the entire area under the demand curve. When the same market is a monopoly, consumers pay an amount equal to EFBG. As a result, consumer surplus shrinks to AFB. As we saw earlier, some of this lost consumer surplus is offset by increased revenue for the producer. In particular the added expenditure, EFBG, is transferred from consumers to the producer. In addition to the rectangle EFBG, consumers also lose the area of the triangle BCG. This loss occurs because consumers buy less and is not offset by gains elsewhere. Economists call losses that do not have offsetting gains elsewhere in the economy **deadweight losses.** The deadweight loss BCG that accompanies monopoly reduces the well-being of society.

Some economists, in particular those who belong to a particular school of thought known as **public choice,** believe that the social costs of monopoly far exceed the deadweight loss of triangle BCG in Figure 4.1. These economists regard the expenditure the monopolist makes to obtain and protect its market position—behavior they call **rent seeking**—as an unproductive expenditure that adds to society's deadweight loss. They would claim that the $1.2 million that baseball spent lobbying Congress in 2001 represents an effort by baseball to protect its monopoly power.[5] As such, it imposes an additional cost on society, since that money could have been spent in more productive ways. In the limit, the monopolist would be willing to spend up to the total gains from its monopoly position, the area of the rectangle EFBG.[6] As a result, the total cost to society is the original deadweight loss plus the revenue of the monopolist (BCG + EFBG).

Monopolists and Price Discrimination

The NFL could eliminate some or all the deadweight loss, though it would not make consumers any happier, by **price discriminating**. Unlike the common use of the word *discrimination*, price discrimination has nothing to do with dislike for a particular demographic group. Instead, a firm price discriminates when it charges more to customers who are willing and able to pay more. On the surface, charging wealthy consumers a higher price than poor consumers sounds

---

[5]"Commissioner Spent $1.2 Million on Lobbying Congress in 2001," ESPN.com, at http://espn.go.com/mlb/news/2002/0515/1382924.html, May 16, 2002.

[6]See, for example, Richard Posner, "The Social Costs of Monopoly and Regulation," *Journal of Political Economy,* v. 83, no. 4 (August 1975), pp. 807–827; Robert Tollison, "Rent Seeking," in *Perspectives on Public Choice: A Handbook,* ed. by Dennis Mueller (Cambridge, U.K.: Cambridge University Press, 1997); Associated Press, "Commissioner Spent $1.2 Million on Lobbying in 2001," ESPN.com, at http://www.espn.com, May 15, 2002.

like the fair thing to do. We shall see, however, that firms that price discriminate seldom have such altruistic motives and that price discrimination does not leave consumers any better off.

If the Panthers know exactly how much Debbie, Bill, Jeff, and Kathleen are willing and able to pay, they can extract their consumer surplus by charging each person exactly what he or she thinks the ticket is worth. By charging Debbie $40, Bill $20, and Jeff $10, the Panthers turn all their consumers into marginal consumers.[7] All the consumers are now just willing to pay for the tickets because what was once their consumer surplus is now additional profit for the Panthers.

By treating each additional consumer like the marginal consumer, the Panthers no longer charge a lower price to everyone when they want to sell more tickets. The process of charging each consumer the maximum that he or she is willing to pay is known as **first-degree price discrimination**. By perfectly (or first-degree) price discriminating, the Panthers' marginal revenue is the price of the last, cheapest ticket that it sells. The marginal revenue of selling a ticket to Bill is thus $20, while the marginal revenue of selling a ticket to Jeff is $10. In terms of Figure 4.1, if the Panthers can perfectly price discriminate, their MR curve coincides with their demand curve. The Panthers now sell the same number of tickets as a perfectly competitive industry, and total surplus grows to ACE. Social well-being is once again maximized, as the perfectly price-discriminating monopolist acts in an economically efficient manner. Consumers, however, do not receive any of the increase in social well-being. By charging all consumers exactly what the ticket is worth to them, the Panthers claim Debbie and Bill's consumer surplus for themselves. If the Panthers could perfectly price discriminate, they would charge all of the thousands of other fans exactly what they are willing and able to pay. This would enable the Panthers to capture all of the area ACE in Figure 4.1 as revenue.

Unfortunately for the Panthers, they have no way of perfectly discriminating among their consumers. They cannot figure out exactly how much each fan is willing and able to pay for a ticket to see them play. They can, however, make some reasonable guesses.

Even if the Panthers do not know how much Debbie, Bill, Jeff, and Kathleen are willing and able to pay, they can still practice **second-degree price discrmination** because they know that demand curves slope down. Second-degree price discrimination involves charging consumers different prices based on the quantity of the good they consume. The first form of second-degree price discrimination acknowledges that an *individual* demand curve slopes down. The Panthers know that the more games Debbie sees, the less she is willing or able to pay to see an additional game. They respond by charging Debbie less for season tickets than for separate tickets to each game.[8]

---

[7]Technically, the Panthers would have to charge $39.99, $19.99, and $9.99 to be sure that Debbie, Bill, and Jeff buy tickets. We round off for ease of exposition.

[8]Debbie pays $130 = $40 + 3 games · $30/game for the four-game plan, and she pays $210 = $40 + 3 games · $30/game + 4 games · $20/game for the season ticket.

Figure 4.3 shows Debbie's individual demand curve (for simplicity, we assume that all games are uniformly attractive to her) and the impact of second-degree price discrimination on Debbie's consumer surplus. If the Panthers operate where marginal revenue equals marginal cost (as shown in Figure 4.1), they charge Debbie $20 for each ticket. In this example, Debbie buys tickets to eight home games, pays $160 for tickets, and enjoys consumer surplus KFG. Alternatively, suppose the Panthers offer a plan that charges $40 for an individual ticket, $130 for a four-game ticket plan, and $210 for a season ticket. In that case, the first ticket costs Debbie $40, the next three tickets cost her $30 each, and the last four tickets cost her $20 each. The rectangles 0ABH, HMEI, and INGJ in Figure 4.3 show the cost of the incremental purchases as Debbie buys more tickets. They show that the Panthers can claim some of Debbie's consumer surplus if they charge her a price closer to her willingness and ability to pay. Some of Debbie's original consumer surplus (triangle KFG) is now taken up by the expenditure rectangles, reducing Debbie's consumer surplus to the three smaller triangles KAB, BME, and ENG.

The Panthers can also practice second-degree price discrimination by recognizing that *market* demand curves slope down. They may not know how much Debbie wants to pay, but they know that some members of her group are less willing or able to pay for tickets than others. The Panthers take advantage of this knowledge by offering group rates that are cheaper than tickets bought individually. Once a group is large enough, the individuals pay less for their tickets, inducing reluctant individuals to buy tickets.

FIGURE 4.3

Consumer Surplus in Second-Degree Price Discrimination

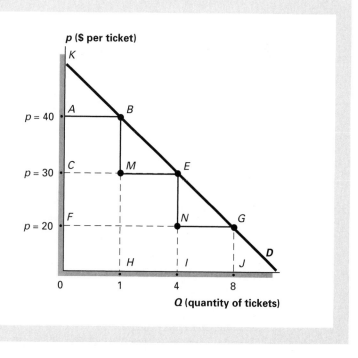

Sometimes, the Panthers may know nothing about individuals, but they may know that some groups are less willing or able to pay. For example, the Panthers may know that students on the whole have less disposable income and as a result are more sensitive to changes in price than are middle-aged adults.[9] If the Panthers can separate the student market from the adult market (e.g., by requiring students to show their university ID cards), then they can practice third-degree price discrimination by charging a higher price to adults than to students. **Third-degree price discrimination** occurs when a firm charges different prices for the same good in different segments of a market. Figure 4.4 shows what the Panthers can do if they can separate the demand by adults for Panthers tickets from the demand by students. Again ignoring capacity constraints, if the marginal cost of providing seats is approximately zero, the Panthers will maximize profit when the marginal revenue from selling to students and the marginal revenue from selling to adults both equal zero. Figure 4.4 shows that the $MR_s = MR_a = MC$ rule results in a lower price to students than to adults. In effect, the Panthers maximize profits by charging a lower price to those consumers whose demand is more elastic and a higher price to those with less elastic demand.

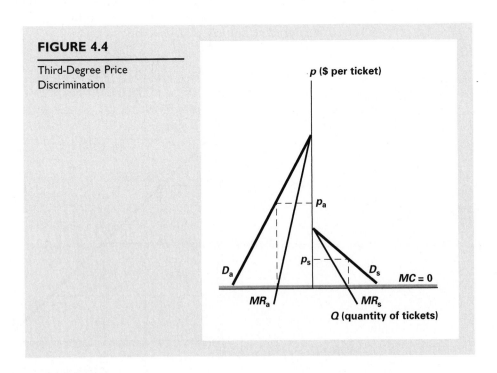

FIGURE 4.4

Third-Degree Price
Discrimination

---

[9]Senior citizens comprise another group that firms frequently feel is more sensitive to price.

Consumer Surplus and Personal Seat Licenses

Personal seat licenses (PSLs) are another way teams can extract consumer surplus and increase profits. PSLs became popular after the Carolina Panthers used them to help finance the construction of Ericsson Stadium in 1993. At first, the Panthers' use of PSLs had economists scratching their heads. The problem was that—on the surface—PSLs did not make much sense.[10]

The idea of a PSL is very simple. A person pays a fixed fee for the right to buy season tickets for a given period of time. One might naively conclude that the additional fee enables teams to raise more money. Such reasoning, however, ignores the fact that when people decide to purchase tickets, they weigh the benefits of seeing the ball games against the costs of seeing the games. The benefits include the pleasure of spending an afternoon or evening at the ballpark, rooting for one's favorite team, while the costs include the price of tickets, transportation, hot dogs, *and* PSLs. If teams charge an additional PSL fee, they must either provide additional benefits to offset the higher costs or charge lower prices for tickets. According to this argument, PSLs do not increase the revenue flowing to the team; they simply change the way the team collects money. Noll and Zimbalist justify the existence of PSLs by appealing to the incentives provided by tax laws that allow teams to deduct revenues raised by PSLs from their taxable income.

PSLs allow the Panthers to exert their monopoly power over consumers without sacrificing the deadweight loss that normally accompanies a monopoly. The Panthers eliminate the deadweight loss by charging the competitive price for season tickets and selling the competitive quantity. The lower price and higher quantity restore consumer and producer surplus to their competitive levels. The Panthers exert their monopoly power by charging the fixed PSL fee. The fee allows them to claim some of the consumer surplus that their fans enjoy. If the Panthers knew exactly how much consumer surplus the typical fan enjoyed, they could charge a PSL fee that extracted almost all of his or her surplus. This would leave the fan just willing to buy the season ticket. The Panthers could thus keep all the benefits of a competitive market for themselves. Consumer surplus would expand to triangle ACE in Figure 4.5, but it would be claimed entirely by producers.

Monopoly Stood on Its Head: A Brief Introduction to Monopsony

Monopsony is essentially the mirror image of monopoly. Monopolists derive their power from being the only seller and use this power to drive up the price of what they sell. Monopsonists derive their power from being the sole consumer and use their power to drive down the price of what they buy.

---

[10]The argument that follows is based on Roger Noll and Andrew Zimbalist, "Build the Stadium—Create the Jobs!" in *Sports, Jobs, and Taxes*, ed. by Roger Noll and Andrew Zimbalist (Washington, D.C.: Brookings Institution Press, 1997), pp. 20–25.

FIGURE 4.5

Consumer Surplus and Personal Seat Licenses

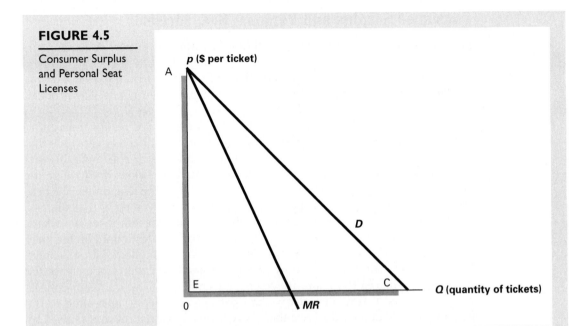

Until the 1970s, sports leagues held monopsony power through specific language in the standard player contract, called the **reserve clause.** The reserve clause effectively bound players to the team that held their contracts for as long as the teams desired their services. Thus, a player such as Otto Graham, who had a Hall of Fame career with the Cleveland Browns in the 1950s, could not sell his services to any NFL team except the Browns. For Graham, playing football in the NFL was indistinguishable from playing for the Browns. Facing no competition for Graham's services, the Browns could pay him a far lower salary than they would have if the Giants, Bears, or Rams could have bid for his services. We shall discuss the history and economics of the reserve clause in greater detail in Chapter 8. For now, we simply note that professional sports leagues were in the enviable position of having both monopoly power over fans *and* monopsony power over players, both of which increased profits and reduced economic efficiency.

4.2   WHAT'S RIGHT WITH MONOPOLY?

While monopolies often impose deadweight losses on society, the case against them is not always as easy as it may appear. First, it is not always so easy to identify a monopoly. For example, since Detroit has only one football team, the Lions, one might logically conclude that the Lions are a monopoly. The Lions, however, could plausibly claim that they are not a monopoly and that they actually operate in a very competitive environment. The key to this difference of opinion lies in the definition of the market in which the Lions operate. If the market is defined as one for an NFL team in the Detroit area, then the Lions are clearly a monopoly. The Lions could respond that such a definition is far too narrow. In the sports industry alone, the Lions must compete for attention with professional baseball, basketball, and hockey teams in and around Detroit. They also must contend with Division I-A football teams at the University of Michigan and Michigan State University. If the market is expanded still further to include all possible leisure and cultural activities in the area, the market becomes very crowded, and the Lions begin to look like very small cats in a large jungle.

Even if the Lions fail to convince you that they are not a monopoly, they may be able to persuade you that their monopoly power arose from the natural functioning of the marketplace, not from any immoral or illegal actions on their part. In short, the Lions may claim that they are a **natural monopoly.** Natural monopolies result when large firms operate more efficiently than small firms do. If the most efficient size of the firm is sufficiently large compared with the number of customers, there may be no room for competing firms to enter. **Large efficient size** generally results when firms face large start-up costs and low marginal costs.[11]

Figure 4.6a shows that a team such as the Lions may be a good example of a natural monopoly. As we illustrated in Chapter 2, a team's payroll can be thought of as a fixed cost, since the cost to the team will be the same regardless of its "output" as measured in tickets sold. Except for that part of rent that is tied to attendance, the expense of renting or building a stadium adds to fixed costs. Because the marginal cost of accommodating an additional fan is very small, the Lions' costs do not rise very much beyond this fixed amount until they reach the capacity of their stadium. Using these assumptions, we can approximate the **average cost,** or per-unit cost, of the Lions as

$$\text{Average cost} = \frac{\text{Total costs}}{\text{Quantity}} \sim \frac{\text{Fixed costs} + MC_0}{\text{Number of tickets sold}}$$

As the number of tickets the Lions sell rises, their average cost gets closer and closer to MC_0. As a result, "bigger is better" to the Lions, since they can charge a lower price as their output rises and still cover their costs. Figure 4.6b again shows the cost curves for the monopolist and adds the demand and marginal revenue curves. The monopolist produces Q^*, which is sold for price p^*. Note that if another firm entered the market, and output were divided equally, neither firm would be profitable, as price (p') is less than average cost (AC). In such cases, as the term implies, the market structure naturally evolves to a single seller.

---

[11]Robert Heintel, "The Need for an Alternative to Antitrust Regulation of the National Football League," *Case Western Reserve Law Review,* v. 46, no. 4 (Summer 1996), pp. 1033–1069 (from Blackboard Fulltext), has a good discussion of natural monopoly and the general issue of antitrust policy as it applies to the NFL.

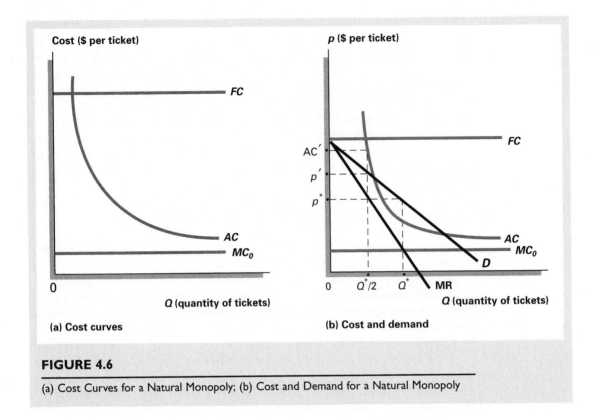

FIGURE 4.6

(a) Cost Curves for a Natural Monopoly; (b) Cost and Demand for a Natural Monopoly

If the Lions' claim that they are a natural monopoly leaves you unmoved, they may assert that their market power serves the public good. They may claim that their market power and the profits that it brings allow them to devote more resources to research and development (R&D) than would be possible in a competitive industry. The R&D provides future benefits to consumers by developing new, superior products and lowering costs to the consumer.[12] In professional sports, R&D takes the form of scouting staffs that locate talented prospects and coaching staffs that mold these prospects into accomplished players. In addition, the profits accruing to Major League Baseball and the National Hockey League help those teams support extensive "farm systems" that develop talent for the major league club. Krautmann and Oppenheimer demonstrated the extent of the investment in baseball. They showed that each MLB team spent approximately $6.2 million on player development in its minor league system in 1989. Each minor league system "graduated" only about four players per team per year, so that the average team invested roughly $1.6 million per player who was success-

---

[12]Robert Muglia, Microsoft's senior VP of Applications and Tools, testified that "Microsoft's enhancements and improvements to the Java technology have been pro-competition and good for software developers and consumers." Microsoft, "Testimony of Robert Muglia," online at http://www.microsoft.com/presspass/trial/feb99/02-25muglia.htm, February 1999.

fully developed.[13] Teams would be unlikely to make such an investment without some guarantee of recouping their investment. If players are free to move from team to team, owners will be less willing to make such an investment.

Leagues also claim that, while perfectly competitive markets increase the amount of the product and reduce its price, a league's monopoly power delivers other benefits to fans. One of the major benefits that MLB's monopoly power has conferred on baseball fans has been the relative stability of franchises. Owners who want to move their teams have traditionally had to seek the approval of the other owners. The failure of MLB's Pittsburgh Pirates and Chicago White Sox to secure approval was instrumental in preventing their moves to St. Petersburg. Leagues use these aborted moves as evidence that the monopoly power of leagues protects the interests of the hometown fans.

4.3   BARRIERS TO ENTRY

Not all monopolies stem from the natural working of the market or from explicit governmental policy. Some monopolies owe their existence to the barriers created by the monopolies themselves. Sports leagues have become experts at erecting barriers to entry, and—when the barriers have failed to keep out competitors—at coopting the opposition.

Not too long ago, the battle lines in professional football reflected network battle lines. Fans of the National Football League tuned in to CBS, while devotees of the American Football League watched their games on ABC and then NBC. Today the NFL licenses its broadcasts to an alphabet soup of networks (ABC, CBS, ESPN, and Fox). Broadcasting over so many networks is a great source of revenue for the NFL. The variety of networks also serves as a crucial barrier to entry. Since the early 1960s, rival football leagues have recognized that their livelihood depended on forming a lasting and profitable link with a television partner. The AFL owed much of the credit for its survival in the 1960s to the willingness of ABC and later NBC to pay for broadcast rights. The infusion of cash from network TV helped the AFL hang on through years of relatively low attendance. Much of the blame for the failure of the WFL in the 1970s and the USFL in the 1980s can be traced to their failure to get sufficient support from major television networks. The collapse of the XFL after only one season in 2002 stemmed largely from its steadily declining TV viewership.

As noted in Chapter 3, leagues can also forestall entry by locating franchises in the appropriate cities. In baseball, the American League found sufficient markets to enter thanks to the dogged refusal of the National League to admit more than eight franchises. The AFL tried to exploit a similar refusal to expand by the NFL in the late 1950s by planning flagship franchises for the rapidly growing cities of Dallas and Minneapolis. When the NFL got wind of these

---

[13]Anthony Krautmann and Margaret Oppenheimer, "Training in Minor League Baseball: Are Players Exploited?" in *Baseball Economics*, ed. by John Fizel, Elizabeth Gustafson, and Lawrence Hadley (Westport, C.T.: Praeger, 1996), pp. 85–98.

plans, it quickly convened an expansion meeting and awarded franchises to those same cities. This successfully prevented the AFL's entry into Minneapolis and doomed the Dallas entry to failure. The AFL sued, claiming that the NFL had awarded these franchises solely to monopolize professional football. Despite the admission by Redskins' owner George Preston Marshall that the NFL had awarded the franchises just to prevent the AFL from penetrating the markets, the AFL lost a bench verdict.[14]

While monopolies have the power to charge a higher price, they do not always exercise that power. Some monopolies operate in markets that have relatively low entry barriers. If potential competitors see the monopolist making high profits, they will enter the market and drive prices and profits down. Monopolists can discourage potential competitors by charging a lower price than their monopoly power would permit. This strategy of **limit pricing** brings the monopolist lower profits in the short run but preserves the firm's monopoly power and profits in the long run. Baseball has shown evidence of limit pricing by keeping the price of tickets relatively low.[15]

4.4   SOCIETY'S RESPONSE TO MONOPOLY AND MONOPSONY: ANTITRUST LAWS

In 1890 the nation made its first concerted effort to combat monopolies and monopsonies with the Sherman Antitrust Act. The Sherman Act was later supplemented by the Clayton Act, which allowed private lawsuits to recover damages (which would then be trebled by the court) caused by subversion of the free market. The Sherman Act has two main clauses aimed at limiting monopoly power:

1. Every contract, combination in the form of a trust or otherwise, or conspiracy, in restraint of trade or commerce among the several states, or with foreign nations is hereby declared to be illegal.

2. Every person who shall monopolize or attempt to monopolize any part of the trade or conspire with any other person or persons to monopolize any part of the trade or commerce among the several states or with foreign nations, shall be deemed guilty of a misdemeanor. . . .[16]

---

[14]The AFL's Dallas Texans moved to Kansas City in 1963 to achieve great success as the Chiefs. See Gary Roberts, "Antitrust Issues in Professional Sports," in *Law of Professional and Amateur Sports,* ed. by Gary Uberstine (Deerfield, I.L.: Clark, Boardman, and Callaghan, 1992), pp. 19-8; 19-9; and James Quirk and Rodney Fort, *Pay Dirt* (Princeton, N.J.: Princeton University Press, 1992), pp. 346–347.

[15]See Gerald Scully, *The Business of Major League Baseball* (Chicago: University of Chicago Press, 1989), pp. 105–106.

[16]William Shepherd, *The Economics of Industrial Organization* (Upper Saddle River, N.J.: Prentice Hall, 1997), pp. 355–361.

At first glance, the two clauses seem almost identical. The differences, while subtle, have been crucial in determining the course of antitrust suits against professional sports teams and leagues.

The first clause prohibits "independent entities that *ought* to be competing against one another from agreeing *not* to compete."[17] It prevents firms from joining together to form **cartels**, also known as *trusts* (hence the name of the act).

The second clause attacks monopolies themselves, regardless of how they are formed. It outlaws "conduct by a firm which creates, protects, or entrenches a dominant position in some relevant market."[18] Lawsuits brought under the second section, while well publicized, have generally had little impact on the sports industry.

The courts have vacillated between two competing interpretations of the Sherman Act, which place very different standards on the litigants. The first standard, the *per se* standard, follows from a literal reading of the Sherman Act. It states that all monopolies are inherently bad and should be broken up. One need only establish that monopoly power exists for the *per se* standard to apply. The alternative reading of the antitrust laws, the "rule of reason," takes a more nuanced view of monopolies. According to this standard, society should be willing to tolerate monopolies if they have failed to exercise their monopoly power or if the benefits that flow from them (such as returns to scale or R&D) outweigh the costs of higher prices and lower output.

On the surface, leagues of any kind appear to violate antitrust legislation. By their very nature, leagues coordinate the actions of their member teams. The coordination can be relatively innocent, as in the establishment and enforcement of a common set of playing rules or the arranging of a commonly respected schedule. The coordination can also result in **collusion,** in which teams cooperate and act like one big monopoly. Critics say the result has been higher prices for tickets and broadcast rights and a restricted quantity of franchises due to limits on the entry of new teams and broadcast coverage of individual teams.[19]

While leagues generally get their monopoly power from collusive agreements, some have operated as outright monopolies. In a successful effort to keep the individual franchises in line, Ban Johnson, the first president of MLB's American League, retained 51 percent of each team's ownership with the AL's central office in order to prevent the defections that sunk earlier rival leagues.[20] Another potential major league baseball rival, the Federal League, tried unsuccessfully to imitate this practice in 1914–15. Major League

---

[17]Roberts, "Antitrust Issues" (1992), p. 19-10.

[18]Roberts, "Antitrust Issues" (1992), p. 19-4.

[19]See, for example, Stephen Ross, "Should Congress Stop the Bidding War for Sports Franchises," Hearing Before the Subcommittee on Antitrust, Business Rights, and Compensation, Senate Committee on the Judiciary, v. 4, November 29, 1994, "Academics," *Heartland Policy,* at http://www.heartland.org/stadps4.html.

[20]Johnson was also not above manipulating rosters to ensure the success of teams that went head to head with National League teams in large cities such as Chicago and Philadelphia.

Lacrosse takes this concept to a still higher level, as all the teams in the league are centrally owned.[21]

4.5 AN IMPORTANT ANOMALY: BASEBALL'S ANTITRUST EXEMPTION

As noted in Section 4.2, breaking up a natural monopoly sacrifices the economic efficiency that its size brings. Little can be gained from antitrust action that creates many small, inefficient firms. Governments recognize this and try to retain the advantages that large size brings while limiting the ability of the natural monopoly to exploit its monopoly power. Governments try to **regulate** natural monopolies, prohibiting them from raising their prices without the approval of an oversight board. Those who feel that professional sports leagues are natural monopolies openly advocate regulating the sports industry to prevent it from earning monopoly profits.[22]

Sometimes governments allow monopolists to flex their muscle but limit the amount of time they have to do so. **Patents** give firms monopoly power over a specific process for 20 years (measured from the date the patent was filed). Similarly, copyright laws give monopoly power to those who produce intellectual property, such as movies or symphonies (or even catchphrases, such as when ex–Laker coach Pat Riley copyrighted the term "three-peat" when the Los Angeles Lakers seemed close to winning three consecutive NBA Championships in the 1980s).[23] When the patent or copyright expires, any firm may use the process or property free of charge. The government permits this limited monopoly to exist in order to promote innovation, experimentation, and creative expression. The promise of monopoly power provides artists with the incentive to create works of art and firms with an incentive to engage in costly and risky R&D.

Finally, the government explicitly rules out competition in some areas. For example, while competition may drive down costs, the United States government is unwilling to tolerate the existence of competing armies. At other times, the government may feel that other social aims merit granting a degree of monopoly power to producers. Most cities limit the number of vendors who may sell their wares outside. While this keeps prices higher than they would be if competing vendors could locate on city sidewalks, city governments are generally willing to tolerate the higher prices in order to improve the quality of urban life by avoiding congested sidewalks. In both cases, however, the government remains closely involved in the market. It carefully regulates licensed vendors and provides the military service itself.

---

[21]Ron Reid, "New League for Outdoor Lacrosse Keeping Favorable Eye on Philly," *Philadelphia Inquirer,* June 1, 1999.

[22]See, for example, Roberts, "Should Congress Stop the Bidding War for Sports Franchises" (1994), pp. 4–5.

[23]See Todd Kantorczyk, "How to Stop the Fast Break: An Evaluation of the 'Three-Peat' Trademark," *UCLA Entertainment Law Review,* v. 2 (1995), pp. 195–228.

Baseball occupies a unique place in the American economy. Unlike all other industries, it has long enjoyed an absolute exemption from all federal antitrust laws with no time limits, no governmental oversight, and no regulation of its pricing policies. Oddly, the courts and legislative branch recognized that baseball's exemption defies all legal and economic logic, yet they did nothing to terminate it for 75 years, and recent changes have been merely cosmetic, with no real effect.

Baseball owes its exemption to the last serious challenge to its monopoly position, the attempt by the Federal League to form a third "major" league in 1914 and 1915. The outlook for a third league seemed promising at the time. The successful entry by the American League to major league status after a "war" in 1901–02 showed that a rival league could succeed. The accommodation between the American and National Leagues prior to the 1903 season also caused considerable unrest among players, as salaries had been steadily falling since the leagues reached an agreement.[24]

As part of its assault on the two existing leagues, the Federal League filed an antitrust lawsuit against the 16 owners as well as the three members of the "National Commission" that oversaw the two major leagues. The lawsuit was based on both sections of the Sherman Act, as it charged the major leagues "with being a combination, conspiracy and monopoly."[25]

The Federal League filed its suit in the U.S. District Court of Northern Illinois before Judge Kenesaw Mountain Landis, specifically choosing to argue before Landis because he had acquired a reputation as a trustbuster. Unfortunately for the Federal League, he also proved to be a rabid baseball fan. Landis scolded the Federal League's lawyers, saying that attacks on baseball "would be regarded by this court as a blow to a national institution."[26] After hearing the arguments, Landis refused to issue a ruling for over a year, by which time the major leagues had reached an agreement with all but one of the Federal League owners, driving the Federal League out of business.[27]

The one holdout was Ned Hanlon, the owner of the Federal League's Baltimore Terrapins. Hanlon was upset that his buyout offer of $50,000 was well below that offered to owners whose teams competed in cities with major league franchises.[28] He was also offended because Charles Comiskey, the

---

[24]Roger Abrams, *Legal Bases: Baseball and the Law* (Philadelphia: Temple University Press, 1998), pp. 53–60.

[25]The commission consisted of Ban Johnson, the president of the American League; John Tener, the president of the National League; and August Hermann, the owner of the Cincinnati (NL) team, who had been instrumental in brokering the peace between the National and American Leagues. See Harold Seymour, *Baseball: The Early Years* (New York: Oxford University Press, 1960), p. 212.

[26]Harold Seymour, *Baseball: The Golden Age* (New York: Oxford University Press, 1971), p. 212; and Abrams, *Legal Bases* (1998), p. 55.

[27]Seymour, *The Golden Age* (1971), pp. 212–213; and Andrew Zimbalist, *Baseball and Billions* (New York: Basic Books, 1992), p. 9.

[28]Some Federal League owners bought the Major League teams with which they competed. Wrigley Field was originally built for the Federal League's Chicago Whales. See Seymour, *Baseball: The Golden Age* (1971), pp. 215–243; and Zimbalist, *Baseball and Billions* (1992), p. 9.

owner of the Chicago White Sox, had called Baltimore a "minor league city, and not a hell of a good one at that," and that Charles Ebbets, owner of the Brooklyn Dodgers, had said that Baltimore was unfit to have a team because "you have too many colored population. . . . " Hanlon filed his own antitrust suit—*Federal Baseball Club of Baltimore, Inc.* v. *National League of Professional Baseball Clubs* (hereafter *Federal Baseball*)—and won an $80,000 settlement (trebled under the provisions of the Clayton Act to $240,000) in a Washington, D.C., Federal District Court. The judgment was overturned on appeal, whereupon Hanlon took his suit to the Supreme Court.[29]

In 1922 the Supreme Court ruled unanimously that baseball was not subject to antitrust laws. In his opinion for the court, Justice Oliver Wendell Holmes Jr. wrote that baseball was a "public exhibition, not commerce and that the interstate travel," which would have made baseball subject to federal legislation, was purely incidental to staging these exhibitions.

The rationale for this ruling has never been clear. Some claim that the Court feared that ruling against MLB would do irreparable damage in the wake of the "Black Sox" scandal in which eight members of the Chicago White Sox had been accused of conspiring with gamblers to throw the 1919 World Series. Others point out that Chief Justice William Howard Taft had played third base for Yale and was related to Philip Wrigley, the owner of the Chicago Cubs.[30]

Subsequent court decisions made baseball's exemption increasingly difficult to justify. The Supreme Court consistently denied other industries, particularly other sports, the right to use the *Federal Baseball* ruling as a precedent. Somehow, the Court was able to see that other sports were commerce while it maintained the fiction that baseball was not.

In 1955, the Supreme Court undercut the idea that sports were not interstate commerce. The ruling came in an antitrust lawsuit that the U.S. government had brought against the International Boxing Club, a leading fight promoter. The Supreme Court ruled that, while boxing matches occurred in a specific place and did not involve moving across state lines, deals for TV, radio, and motion picture rights did cut across state boundaries. The Court acknowledged that this judgment contradicted previous rulings regarding baseball but declared that those rulings were "not authority for exempting other businesses merely because of the circumstance that they are also based on the performance of local exhibitions."[31]

Any question about the status of other sports was dispelled when the Supreme Court ruled on an antitrust lawsuit brought by George Radovich. Radovich challenged the right of the NFL to blacklist him for having played in

---

[29]Abrams, *Legal Bases* (1998), p. 56; Seymour, *The Golden Age* (1971), p. 243; and John Johnson, "When a Professional Sport Is Not a Business: Baseball's Infamous Antitrust Exemption," in *Sports and the Law*, ed. by Charles Quirk (New York: Garland Publishers, 1996), p. 151.

[30]Abrams, *Legal Bases* (1998), p. 57; and Johnson, "Baseball's Infamous Antitrust Exemption" (1996), p. 151.

[31]Earl Warren writing for the majority. Cited in *U.S. v. International Boxing Club of N.Y.* Available online at http://www.ripon.edu/faculty/bowenj/antitrust/ibcofny1.htm.

the All American Football Conference (AAFC). A lower court dismissed Radovich's suit on the basis of the *Federal Baseball* decision. Radovich appealed to the Supreme Court, which reversed the lower court ruling by a 6–3 vote in 1957. The decision explicitly denied any form of exemption to any sport except baseball and expressed disapproval of the *Federal Baseball* ruling, though it let that ruling stand, leaving baseball's exemption intact.

Lacking exemption from antitrust laws, the NFL could not withstand legal challenges to its version of baseball's reserve clause. Initially, players were kept in place by a "gentlemen's agreement" among the owners not to pursue one another's players. When the agreement began to break down in the early 1960s, NFL Commissioner Pete Rozelle imposed a compensation system that was so draconian that it effectively prevented players from switching teams. The "Rozelle rule" stipulated that a team that signed a free agent had to provide cash, draft choices, or players to the team whose player it signed. If the two teams could not reach an agreement on the appropriate compensation, the commissioner would impose an agreement. In 1972 John Mackey, the president of the National Football League Players Association (NFLPA) and star tight end for the Baltimore Colts, filed a lawsuit on behalf of himself and 31 other players.[32] The class action suit sought damages due to the Rozelle rule and other unfair labor practices. The U.S. District Court ruled that the Rozelle rule was a *per se* violation of the Sherman Act. An appeals court also ruled in favor of the NFLPA. Rather than file further appeals, the NFL chose to settle out of court with the NFLPA and to preserve a modified version of the reserve clause. Under the settlement, a team that signed a free agent now faced a fixed formula that dictated the cost of signing another team's player rather than submit to an uncertain ruling from the commissioner. While this removed the uncertainty associated with signing a free agent, the new rule continued to restrict player movement for over a decade.[33]

The tortured logic required to justify baseball's exemption from the antitrust laws was never more evident than in the early 1950s, when George Toolson, a player in the New York Yankees' system, resisted being sent back to the minor leagues by the Yankees. He then sued the Yankees, claiming that the reserve clause violated the antitrust laws. As Toolson's suit worked its way through the legal system, the House Subcommittee on the Study of Monopoly Power (chaired by Rep. Emmanuel Cellar and hence called the "Cellar Committee") began to hold hearings on baseball's antitrust exemption. When it became obvious that the Toolson case was going to the Supreme Court, the Cellar Committee postponed further action under the assumption that the courts would settle the matter. The Supreme Court seized upon this inaction,

---

[32]In a 1970 poll, Mackey was voted the best tight end of the NFL's first 50 years, but he was denied entrance to the Pro Football Hall of Fame until 1992, 20 years after he retired.

[33]See James Dworkin, *Owners Versus Players: Baseball and Collective Bargaining* (Boston: Auburn House, 1981), pp. 250–255; Quirk and Fort, *Paydirt* (1992), pp. 199–200; Roberts, "Antitrust Issues" (1992), pp. 19-31–19-33; and Richard Terry, "Tight End Mackey Blocks Commissioner Rozelle," in *Sports and the Law*, ed. by Charles Quirk (New York: Garland, 1996), pp. 187–189.

saying that Congress had signaled its approval of baseball's antitrust exemption by refusing to take any action to strip baseball of its privileged position. The "approval" granted by the Cellar Committee formed the basis of the Supreme Court's ruling in favor of the Yankees.[34]

Perhaps the most misunderstood legal case surrounding the reserve clause is Curt Flood's antitrust suit of the early 1970s. Most people incorrectly think of Flood as the man who single-handedly overthrew the reserve clause in baseball. In fact, Flood lost his case as well as his career. After the ruling against him, baseball players had to wait another four years before they were able to rid themselves of the reserve clause.

In the late 1960s, Curt Flood was a star outfielder for the St. Louis Cardinals. In 1968, after a particularly good season, Flood asked the team for a $30,000 raise. Not one inclined to tolerate such demands, Cardinals owner Augustus Busch traded Flood to the Philadelphia Phillies after the 1969 season. Curt Flood had many reasons for objecting to this trade. It sent him from a team that had won a World Series in 1967 and had come within one game of another championship in 1968 to a team that was a perennial also-ran. It also sent him to a town that had a history of bad relations with black ballplayers. Because of the reserve clause and baseball's exemption from antitrust regulations, however, Flood had no say in his own destiny. As a black man who had endured severe discrimination early in his career, Flood saw a parallel between his own position and that of enslaved blacks in America barely 100 years earlier. In asking Commissioner Bowie Kuhn to repeal the trade, Flood used words that Frederick Douglass might have used: "I do not feel I am a piece of property to be bought and sold irrespective of my wishes."[35]

In 1970, with the support of the Major League Baseball Players Association (MLBPA), Flood filed suit in U.S. Federal District Court against the commissioner's office, asking for $3 million (to be trebled) and for free agency. In language reminiscent of Kenesaw Landis's rhapsodies to baseball in the Federal League suit, the trial judge ruled in Kuhn's favor, arguing that baseball was on "higher ground" than mere commerce. An appeals court also ruled in Kuhn's favor, citing Congress's failure to act against the reserve clause, as the Supreme Court had argued almost 20 years earlier in its *Toolson* ruling.

The Supreme Court's decision, written by Harry Blackmun, was even more curious. Blackmun denied the basis for baseball's exemption by acknowledging that baseball was a business that engaged in interstate commerce. He called the exemption "an exception and an anomaly" and referred to the *Federal Baseball* and *Toolson* rulings as "aberration[s] confined to baseball." Despite these stinging condemnations of the reserve clause and of baseball's exemption from the

---

[34]See Abrams, *Legal Bases* (1998), p. 62; Quirk and Fort, *Pay Dirt* (1992), pp. 188–189; Roberts, "Antitrust Issues" (1992), pp. 19-33–19-36; and Zimbalist, *Baseball and Billions* (1992), pp. 12–15.

[35]While playing for a minor league town in the deep South early in his career, Flood was not allowed to mix his dirty laundry with that of his white teammates. White clubhouse attendants would not even handle his uniform. Flood's reference to slavery was not lost on Supreme Court Justice Thurgood Marshall, who also drew an analogy to slavery in his minority opinion.

antitrust laws, the Supreme Court ruled 6–2 (with one abstention) in Kuhn's favor in 1972 . The Court based its decision on the principle of *stare decisis* ("let the old decision stand"), effectively saying that the original antitrust ruling was wrong but that too much now rested on the original decision for the Court to overturn it.[36]

In 1998 Congress finally placed limits on baseball's antitrust exemption by passing the "Curt Flood Act." The legislation, however, does little to change the status quo. The legislation limits baseball's powers only in the area of labor relations, granting players the right to file antitrust suits to resolve labor disputes. The players' right to sue, however, is limited by the Supreme Court's 1996 *Brown v. Pro Football, Inc.* ruling, which effectively stated that the players association would have to decertify itself before a player could sue on antitrust grounds.[37]

The Economic Impact of the Antitrust Exemption

Baseball's exemption from the antitrust laws has given it a greater ability to protect both its monopoly power and its monopsony power in the marketplace. It is no coincidence that the Federal League, whose antitrust suit was the basis for the antitrust exemption, was the last league to pose a serious challenge to Major League Baseball. Since then, baseball has faced only the feeble attempt to form a rival Mexican League in the 1940s and the stillborn attempts to form the Continental League in the late 1950s and the Union League in the mid-1990s.

Unlike baseball, all the other major professional leagues have endured serious challenges to their monopoly power. In each case, the existing league has had to absorb teams from a rival league and—in one case—to merge with a rival entrant. In 1976 the NBA ended a costly 10-year war with the American Basketball Association by agreeing to allow the Denver Nuggets, the New Jersey Nets, and the San Antonio Spurs to join the NBA. Three years later, the NHL ended a costly war with the World Hockey Association in similar fashion.[38] The NHL stopped the bleeding by absorbing the surviving WHA teams: the Edmonton Oilers, the Hartford Whalers (now Carolina Hurricanes), the Quebec Nordiques (now Colorado Avalanche), and the Winnipeg Jets (now Phoenix Coyotes).

Perhaps because it was the most consistently profitable enterprise, the NFL faced the most frequent and the most successful challenges. In the midst of a war with the second of four challengers to call themselves the "American Football League," the NFL persuaded the Cleveland Rams to join the NFL as a

---

[36]Blackmun's decision included the poems "He Never Heard of Casey," by Grantland Rice, and "Baseball's Sad Lexicon," by Franklin Pierre Adams. See Abrams, *Legal Bases* (1998), p. 62; Quirk and Fort, *Pay Dirt* (1992), pp. 188–189; Roberts, "Antitrust Issues" (1992), pp. 19-33–19-36; and Zimbalist, *Baseball and Billions* (1992), pp. 12–15.

[37]Gary Roberts, "Brown v. Pro Football, Inc.: The Supreme Court Gets It Right for the Wrong Reasons," *Antitrust Bulletin*, v. 42, no. 3 (Fall 1997), pp. 595–639; and Sonya Ross, "Clinton Signs Bill Removing Baseball Antitrust Exemption for Labor Matters," Associated Press, October 28, 1998, at http://www.fl.milive.com/tigers/stories/19981028antitrust.html.

[38]Interestingly, one man, a lawyer named Gary Davidson, was instrumental in the formation of both the ABA and the WHA.

pseudo-expansion team in 1937. The AAFC, while it survived only from 1946 through 1949, had several lasting impacts on professional football. Of the four teams absorbed into the NFL in 1950—the Baltimore Colts, the Cleveland Browns, the New York Yankees, and the San Francisco 49ers—two (the Browns and the Colts) quickly went on to become the dominant teams of the 1950s. More importantly, by allowing teams to employ black players, the AAFC helped force an end to the NFL's short-lived color line. The most successful attack on the NFL's monopoly power came from the fourth and final iteration of the American Football League. After battling one another from 1960 through 1965, the two leagues agreed in 1966 to a full merger that was completed after the 1969 season.[39] Quirk and Fort note, "a full 40 of the 103 franchises operating in major league pro sports in 1991 began life as members of rival leagues, and 7 or 8 were created in direct response to the threats posed by rival leagues."[40]

In the 1980s, the USFL emerged as a threat to the dominance of the NFL. The failure of the USFL precipitated perhaps the oddest antitrust decision of all. This suit alleged that the NFL had denied rival leagues access to television by reaching agreements with all three major networks. A jury found the NFL guilty of violating the antitrust laws but assessed damages of only $1 (trebled, of course, to $3). Opinions regarding this ruling vary. Some say that the jury found the problems faced by the USFL to be largely self-inflicted, while others assert that the jury was confused and assessed the penalty under the—incorrect—assumption that the trial judge could later increase it.[41]

Supporters of baseball's exemption from the antitrust laws also point to the relative volatility of football franchises in recent years. While no baseball franchise has moved since the old Washington Senators moved to Arlington, Texas, to become the Rangers in 1972, football has seen seven moves since 1980.[42] The move that opened the floodgates in the NFL came in 1980 when the Raiders left Oakland for Los Angeles. When the other owners tried to block the move, Al Davis (the principal owner of the Raiders) and the Los Angeles Memorial Coliseum Commission brought a successful antitrust suit against the NFL. The logic to this ruling has eluded experts, leading some to conclude that the key to the ruling was that the jury was drawn from Los Angeles and so was biased in favor of the move.[43] Whatever the cause of the ruling, it has left the NFL powerless to block the movement of franchises from city to city. Some members of the

---

[39]One sidelight to the agreement was the institution of an AFL–NFL Championship Game, later renamed the Super Bowl.

[40]Quirk and Fort, *Pay Dirt* (1992), p. 297. The NFL's Yankees lasted for only a few years and played in Yankee Stadium.

[41]See Byrne, *The $1 League* (1986), p. 346; Roberts, "Antitrust Issues" (1992); and Leifer, *Making the Majors* (1995), p. 142.

[42]We do not include moves within a metropolitan area, such as the Patriots' move from Boston to Foxboro, Mass. The NFL teams that moved were the Raiders (twice), the Colts, the Cardinals, the Rams, the Oilers (now the Titans), and the Browns (now the Ravens). As of this writing, the Expos remain in Montreal.

[43]James Quirk and Rodney Fort, *Hardball* (Princeton, N.J.: Princeton University Press, 1999), pp. 119–121; and Roberts, "Antitrust Issues" (1992), pp. 19-17–19-20.

U.S. Senate have even proposed giving the NFL, the NBA, and the NHL *more* monopoly power in order to help them block the movement of franchises.[44]

Limited Exemptions: The NFL and Television

When Alvin "Pete" Rozelle became commissioner of the NFL following the death of longtime commissioner Bert Bell in 1959, professional football still lagged badly behind baseball and college football in the nation's consciousness. In the fall of 1998, the NFL signed the most lucrative TV deal in the history of professional sports, an agreement that will generate $17.6 billion in revenue over eight years. The NFL's ingenious use of television, which we detail in Chapter 3, could never have been implemented, however, were it not for the limited exemption that the NFL obtained for its broadcasts. While we all take "the NFL on Fox" or "the NBA on ABC" for granted, professional sports—and Rozelle in particular—had to overcome serious obstacles to obtaining a league-wide contract.

The most significant obstacle was that the courts had previously ruled that such contracts were illegal. The NFL had been under an injunction since 1953 that expressly prohibited a league-wide contract.[45] Faced with a legal system that would not permit such "restraint of trade," Rozelle actively lobbied Congress to extend a limited exemption from antitrust laws to football, basketball, and hockey. The exemption would apply solely to these leagues' ability to negotiate league-wide broadcast rights. In 1962, Congress granted the exemption.[46]

The exemption had an immediate impact on the market for broadcast rights. NFL teams no longer had to negotiate local contracts (often in markets that overlapped one another, further depressing prices). By 1969, a mere seven years after the exemption was granted, the revenue from broadcast rights had risen by a factor of 5 for the New York Giants. The Green Bay Packers, with their much smaller media market, saw their revenues rise by a factor of 13. The merger of the NFL with the rival AFL in the late 1960s further increased the monopoly power of professional football, giving yet another upward boost to prices.

4.6   THE NCAA: AN INCIDENTAL CARTEL

Supporters of the NCAA regard it as the guardian of integrity in collegiate athletics. Its foes see it as a money-grubbing cartel that ruthlessly exercises both monopoly and monopsony power. In fact, both views may be correct at the same time. Former Executive Director Walter Byers described his job as "keeping intercollegiate sports clean while generating millions of dollars each

---

[44]John Danforth, "Sports' Integral Role with a Community," *New York Times,* February 2, 1986, Section 5, p. 2.

[45]Due to its exemption from antitrust laws, baseball faced no such prohibition, though it did little in the 1950s to exploit this advantage.

[46]One of the concessions that the NFL had to grant Congress in order to get its limited exemption was a promise not to compete with college or high school football. As a result, the NFL does not play Saturday games until the high school and college seasons end in early December.

year as income for the colleges."[47] Many of the high-minded ideals, such as keeping professionalism out of collegiate sports and limiting the number of games schools can play, coincide with the goal of a monopsony to drive down labor costs and with the goal of a monopoly of limiting output to drive up prices. However, the NCAA is neither a monopoly nor a monopsony in the classic sense. Instead it is a collection of schools that have come together, for good or ill, to regulate intercollegiate athletics.

Economists call a group of firms that cooperate in order to exercise monopoly or monopsony power over a market a **cartel**. Members of cartels coordinate their activities so as to fix the market price, assign output levels to their members, divide profits, and erect barriers to entry by firms outside the cartel. The NCAA has—whatever its motives—done all these things, including erecting barriers to entry by driving out rival organizations. One example of the NCAA's predatory behavior came in the wake of federal legislation that vastly expanded funding for women's sports.[48] After first opposing any legislation that might drain resources away from its traditional interests, the NCAA changed strategy and sought to extend its authority to cover women's sports. The only problem was that an oversight body already existed, the Association of Intercollegiate Athletics for Women (AIAW). Over the course of the early 1980s, the NCAA used its power over men's sports to cajole and coerce member schools to switch their affiliation from the AIAW to the NCAA. The NCAA also used its control over men's sports to guarantee superior media access for those schools that participated in NCAA-sanctioned events. By 1982, the AIAW had folded.

While the NCAA acts like a cartel, it differs from the classic image of a cartel in two important ways. First, it was not formed in order to monopolize (or monopsonize) a market. In fact, the colleges and universities formed the organization that evolved into the NCAA under duress. Its initial goal was to formulate rules of play on the football gridiron. From regulating behavior on the field, it quickly moved into regulating behavior off the field, eventually morphing into a multimillion dollar organization that carefully protects its financial interests. This gradual evolution into a collusive structure has led economists to call the NCAA an **incidental cartel.**

In addition, unlike classic cartels, the NCAA does not seek to maximize the profits of its members. In fact, the members of the NCAA explicitly reject the profit motive. Eschewing profits does not mean, however, that academia is averse to money. As is the case for their explicitly professional brethren, colleges find ways to turn profits into expenses. Weight rooms with floor space that can be measured in acres, coaches whose salaries exceed those of their colleges' presidents, and subsidies to less profitable sports are all time-honored examples of ways to dissipate profit.[49]

---

[47]Walter Byers with Charles Hammer, *Unsportsmanlike Conduct: Exploiting College Athletes* (Ann Arbor: University of Michigan Press, 1995), p. 5.

[48]This legislation, known as Title IX, will be discussed more thoroughly in Chapter 10.

[49]See James Koch, "Intercollegiate Athletics: An Economic Explanation," *Social Science Quarterly*, v. 64, no. 2 (June 1983), pp. 360–374; and Arthur Fleisher et al., *The National Collegiate Athletic Association: A Study in Cartel Behavior* (Chicago: University of Chicago Press, 1992), pp. 73–94.

The origins of the NCAA are inextricably bound up with the development of football in America. At the start, American football resembled the rougher versions of football played in England. Football teams (and all other athletic clubs) were student-run organizations, so colleges often developed their own set of rules. The lack of consistent rules forced schools playing each other into negotiations that were sometimes comical. A game between Harvard and McGill in Montreal was played under Harvard's rules for one half and McGill's rules for the other.[50] The transaction costs of negotiating rules on a game-by-game basis thus continued to discourage the spread of football.[51] The lack of consistent rules also made it difficult to enforce any one set of rules. As a result, football became an alarmingly violent game.

Events came to a head after the 1905 season, during which 18 students were killed and 159 suffered relatively serious injuries. In the wake of this carnage, President Theodore Roosevelt summoned representatives of Harvard, Yale, and Princeton—three of the major football powers of the time—to the White House, where he warned them to regulate the game or see it outlawed. In response, representatives of 13 colleges met to adopt an explicit set of rules and to establish an enforcement mechanism. The resulting organization, the Intercollegiate Athletic Association of the United States (IAAUS)—renamed the National Collegiate Athletic Association in 1910—succeeded where prior organizations had failed. Within a year, it had established a common set of rules that a large number schools could accept.

For the first several years, the NCAA contented itself with standardizing rules in football and other intercollegiate sports. Soon, however, the NCAA turned its attention to rules for behavior off the field, passing numerous resolutions intended to discourage the professionalization of college sports. One can argue whether the NCAA's adherence to amateurism represented a high-minded stand in defense of the academic integrity of its members or an attempt to guarantee its members a cheap labor force. One cannot deny, however, that the NCAA was trying to serve as a coordinating body for its membership, urging them to coordinate on actions far beyond its initial mandate.

The NCAA quickly learned, however, that a successful cartel needs an enforcement mechanism by which it can coordinate the actions of its members and punish cheaters. In 1946 the NCAA finally tried to put an enforcement mechanism in place with the so-called **Sanity Code.** In the Sanity Code, the NCAA specified a set of principles designed to govern the behavior of member schools and recommended expulsion for members who failed to abide by its principles. However, seven schools—which came to be known as the "seven sinners"—announced that they would not abide by the Sanity Code's restrictions on financial aid.[52] In the first and only test of the Sanity Code, the NCAA

---

[50]See Leifer, *Making the Majors* (1995), pp. 40–42.

[51]The most serious early attempt, the Intercollegiate Football Association, however, ended in failure in 1894 after 18 years.

[52]The seven sinners were Boston College, the Citadel, the University of Maryland, the University of Virginia, Virginia Military Institute, Virginia Polytechnic Institute, and Villanova University.

membership failed to muster the necessary two-thirds majority it needed to expel the seven sinners. With no way to enforce coordinated action, the NCAA appeared dead as a cartel.

Ironically, the NCAA cartel was saved in the early 1950s by one of the most serious scandals in the history of collegiate athletics. In the postwar era, college basketball was enjoying an unprecedented surge in popularity. At the height of the boom, the sport was rocked by a series of point-shaving scandals. *Point shaving* was a way for unscrupulous gamblers to ensure that they beat point spreads.[53] Gamblers typically get players to shave points by paying them to win by a smaller margin than bookies predict. The gamblers then bet that the team will not cover the point spread.

The scandal destroyed the basketball programs of several schools in the New York area in 1952, including that of former national champion City College of New York.[54] It also implicated several members of the national champion University of Kentucky basketball squad. The ensuing investigation brought to light evidence that the Kentucky coach, Adolph Rupp, had associated with Ed Curd, a gambler with links to organized crime (and who may have abetted the point shaving), and that Rupp had flagrantly violated NCAA regulations regarding payments to athletes.

Lacking any real power to enforce its own guidelines, the NCAA was powerless to take action against Kentucky. The Southeastern Conference (SEC), the group of schools with which Kentucky was associated, however, was embarrassed and offended by Kentucky's actions. Bernie H. Moore, the SEC commissioner, suspended Kentucky from the SEC for the ensuing year. Since none of the other SEC schools had a program that matched its own, Kentucky retorted that it would simply play schools outside of the SEC. The NCAA then stepped in to back the SEC by writing to all its member schools and urging them to honor the boycott. Rather than fight the boycott, Kentucky's faculty representatives accepted their punishment, an action that ex–NCAA Commissioner Byers feels would be unthinkable in today's litigious climate.[55]

The "death penalty" levied on Kentucky gave the NCAA a new lease on life. By mobilizing its members into a boycott of Kentucky (not, as is popularly believed, closing the program), the NCAA had stumbled upon a weapon with which to penalize cheaters and had—almost accidentally—shown a willingness to use it. Schools now accept lesser punishments in part because of the fear that failure to do so will result in having their own program sentenced to death.[56]

---

[53]Recall our discussion of point spreads in Chapter 2.

[54]City College of New York is the only school ever to win the NCAA championship and the National Invitational Tournament (then the more prestigious event) in the same year. More recent point-shaving scandals have damaged programs from Boston College to Arizona State.

[55]See Murray Sperber, *Onward to Victory: The Crises that Shaped College Sports* (New York: Henry Holt and Co., 1998), pp. 330–343; Paul Lawrence, *Unsportsmanlike Conduct: The National Collegiate Athletic Association and the Business of College Football* (New York: Praeger, 1987), pp. 52–53; and Byers, *Unsportsmanlike Conduct* (1995), pp. 55–61.

[56]The most prominent recent imposition of the death penalty came against the football program at Southern Methodist University, which suspended its football program for the 1987 and 1988 seasons.

4.7 PRISONER'S DILEMMA: HOW RATIONAL ACTIONS LEAD TO IRRATIONAL OUTCOMES

As with many of the NCAA's anticompetitive actions, its restraint of trade in television began innocently. At a party in 1950, Dick Romney, the commissioner of the Mountain States Conference (now the Western Athletic Conference), approached University of Michigan coach Fritz Crisler and started discussing the TV package that the NCAA was then negotiating. He asked, half-seriously, if Crisler would be willing to set aside some games for the other schools so that schools such as Michigan would not get all the publicity and glory. To Romney's surprise, Crisler agreed and helped push through a limit on the number of games that each school could have on the network broadcast.[57]

As football became increasingly lucrative, the more powerful schools came to forget Crisler's spirit of fairness and wanted to increase their control over the flow of money. In 1976, 61 of the largest football powers in the NCAA formed the College Football Association (CFA), whose sole purpose was to lobby for greater control of television appearances and revenue. The NCAA responded in 1978 by recalculating its formula for dividing football programs. Previously, schools had been assigned to one of three divisions (Divisions I–III). These divisions were based on the size of their student populations in order to ensure competitive balance. In 1978 the NCAA split Division I, which consisted of the largest schools, into Division I-A and Division I-AA.

A tightening of the requirements for membership in Division I-A that went into effect in the fall of 2003 touched off a firestorm of criticism that may yet result in an antitrust litigation. The new requirements force colleges that wish to participate in Division I-A to sponsor at least 16 varsity teams (up from 14), play at least 5 home games against Division I-A opponents, average 15,000 paid attendance per game, and give at least 200 full athletic scholarships (at least 76.5 of them in football) or pay at least $4 million in scholarships.[58] At the time these requirements were implemented, about 30 of the 117 Division I-A schools failed to meet them. Many colleges were already angry that rules for postseason play heavily favored the six largest intercollegiate athletic conferences (ACC, Big East, Big 10, Big 12, Pacific 10, and Southeastern). Of the schools that have participated in the Bowl Championship Series (BCS) games, the most prestigious and most lucrative of the postseason contests, only one, Notre Dame, does not belong to one of these six conferences.[59] As a result, schools from the six "major" conferences have received more than $80 million annually from the bowls in the BCS, but schools from the other five Division I-A conferences (Mid-American, Mountain West, Conference USA, Sun Belt, and Western Athletic) have received only about $8 million. In response to what they perceive as one more power grab by the largest programs, the presidents of 44

---

[57]Anecdote related in Byers, *Unsportsmanlike Conduct* (1995), pp. 81–82. Schools were limited to three appearances over a two-year period. Each of 12 football conferences also had to be represented over this period.

[58]A half scholarship is one-half the dollar value of a full scholarship.

[59]The four BCS Bowls are the Tostitos Fiesta, FedEx Orange, Rose, and Nokia Sugar Bowls.

colleges formed the "Presidential Coalition for Athletic Reform," a group that has threatened to sue the other schools for what they perceive as an attempt to drive out competition and monopolize the big-time college football market.[60]

The new two-tiered Division I arrangement increased the share of income flowing to the big-time programs, though not enough to satisfy the schools that had formed the CFA. In 1982 two members of the CFA, the University of Georgia and Oklahoma University, brought an antitrust suit against the NCAA. The suit alleged that the NCAA had conspired to prevent its own members from engaging in free commerce. Federal District Court Judge Juan Burciaga ruled against the NCAA in no uncertain terms. He called the NCAA "a classic cartel" and claimed that "[c]onsumer demand and the free market are sacrificed to the interests of the NCAA administration. . . . It is clear that [the] NCAA is in violation of Section 1 of the Sherman [Antitrust] Act."[61]

After a series of appeals, the case went before the Supreme Court in 1984. The majority of the court ruled that the television contract was not a *per se* violation of antitrust laws, since the "industry" of college football needed some restrictions in order to operate. The court ruled instead that the NCAA failed to meet the rule of reason and upheld Burciaga's initial ruling by a 7–2 vote. The dissenting opinion, written by Byron ("Whizzer") White, a former All-American at the University of Colorado, claimed that the majority had misapplied the rule of reason by ignoring the noncommercial goals of the NCAA, a sentiment reminiscent of the *Federal Baseball* ruling.[62]

As expected, the ruling led to the flood of college games that we now see on television every fall. The separate deal cut by Notre Dame with NBC in 1991 even led some to say that the network's initials stood for "Notredame Broadcasting Corporation." Much to the surprise of the schools involved, their greater exposure did not make them any richer. In their haste to increase their TV exposure, the members of the CFA forgot that demand curves slope down. With more games on TV, the ratings for a typical broadcast fell by one-fourth. As a result, the fees schools could charge for broadcast rights plummeted. Four years after the decision, college football rights fees were only half of what they had been. In a crowning irony, Oklahoma, one of the plaintiffs in the case, saw its average revenue for a regional or national broadcast fall from over $425,000 the year before the Supreme Court ruling to less than $190,000 the season after.[63]

---

[60]See Tom Dienhart, "New NCAA Schools Make It Tough on Small Schools," *SportingNews.com*, at http://www.sportingnews.com/voices/tom_dienhart/20020603-p.html, June 3, 2002; and Josh Dubow, "Non-BCS Schools Allege Antitrust Violations," *CollegeSports.com*, at http://www.collegesports.com/sports/m-footbl/stories/072203aax.html, July 22, 2003.

[61]Quoted in Murray Sperber, *College Sports Inc.* (New York: Henry Holt and Co., 1990), p. 51.

[62]See Eric Seiken, "The NCAA and the Courts: College Football on Television," in *Sports and the Law*, ed. by Charles Quirk (New York: Garland, 1996), pp. 56–62; and Sperber, *College Sports Inc.* (1990), pp. 51–52.

[63]Sperber, *College Sports Inc.* (1990), p. 52; Francis Dealy, *Win at Any Cost: The Sell Out of College Athletics* (New York: Birch Lane Press, 1990), p. 150; and Roger Noll, "The Economics of Intercollegiate Sports," in *Rethinking College Athletics*, ed. by Judith Andre and David James (Philadelphia: Temple University Press, 1992), p. 202.

The members of the CFA seemed to defy one of the central tenets of economic theory by taking an action that made them all worse off. Earlier in their history, colleges had harmed themselves by failing to agree on a common set of rules. Outside of the sports world, there are many examples of seemingly self-destructive behavior, such as wasteful arms races or advertising campaigns that the participants would like to avoid but for some reason cannot. Economists call the broad set of seemingly optimal actions that lead to suboptimal outcomes a **prisoner's dilemma.** Prisoner's dilemma is a specific example of a broader tool of analysis called **game theory.** While one can use game theory to analyze athletic situations such as whether a pitcher should throw a curveball or whether a chess player should sacrifice a queen, it also has much wider applications. Game theory can shed light on any situation involving three elements: players (individuals, organizations, or nations), strategies, and outcomes.

With a few simplifications, one can use game theory to explain why Georgia and Oklahoma engaged in such seemingly self-destructive behavior. For simplicity, we shall consider only two "players," Florida State University (FSU) and the University of Miami, and assume that each faces two possible strategies: limiting its broadcasts in accordance with its agreement, or breaking the agreement and broadcasting many games. Two players each with two strategies results in four possible outcomes, or "payoffs," as illustrated in the **payoff matrix** in Table 4.1.

If both schools limit their appearances on TV, then both schools make high profits, as was the case under the NCAA-negotiated contract. The member schools that sued the NCAA thought that they could increase their profits by broadcasting unlimited games. In terms of Table 4.1, unlimited broadcasts are a **dominant strategy,** because each school finds it the best strategy regardless of what the other school does. If FSU limits its appearances, Miami will gain an advantage over FSU (moving from parity at $10 million to a $17 million advantage) by televising many games. If FSU televises many games, Miami protects itself (moving from a $17 million disadvantage to parity at $5 million) by televising many games as well. The "dilemma" of the prisoners' dilemma stems from the fact that, while broadcasting many games is optimal for each individual school, it results in a suboptimal outcome if all schools decide on the same strategy. As a result, broadcasting many games leaves both Miami and FSU worse off than they were initially.

Table 4.1

College Football Broadcasts as a Prisoner's Dilemma

	Miami Televises Many Games	*Miami Limits Appearances*
FSU Televises Many Games	Miami gets $5 million FSU gets $5 million	Miami gets $3 million FSU gets $20 million
FSU Limits Appearances	Miami gets $20 million FSU gets $3 million	Miami gets $10 million FSU gets $10 million

"PETE" ROZELLE

BIOGRAPHICAL Sketch

If he were in private business and accomplished what he had with the NFL, he'd be worth one hundred million dollars.

— ANONYMOUS CORPORATE EXECUTIVE[1]

Paul Tagliabue, the NFL's current commissioner, may have negotiated the NFL's recent $17.6 billion dollar mega-deal with the TV networks, and David Stern of the NBA may be professional sports' resident wizard, but none of the magic they worked would have been possible without the efforts of one man, Alvin Ray "Pete" Rozelle. As the NFL's commissioner from 1960 to 1989, Rozelle transformed football from an afterthought on the American sports scene to the most popular of our major team sports. In so doing, he also laid the groundwork on which the future success of other sports could be built.

Growing up just outside of Los Angeles, little about Rozelle's early life presaged a career in football. Like many young men his age, Rozelle entered the navy upon graduating from Compton High School in 1944. He returned in 1946 and entered Compton Junior College. In one of the remarkable coincidences that seemed to guide his career, the Cleveland Rams moved to Los Angeles that same year and selected Compton Junior College as their training base. Rozelle found part-time work in the Rams' publicity department to help support himself at college until he left to attend the University of San Francisco, which he chose after a chance meeting with USF's legendary basketball coach Pete Newell, who promised him a part-time job as athletic news director. When he graduated in 1950, Rozelle became USF's full-time news director. Thanks to the high profile of USF sports at that time (an undefeated football team and a basketball team that won the then-prestigious National Invitational Tournament), Rozelle had the opportunity to meet many prominent sports figures, including Tex Schramm, the general manager (GM) of

the Los Angeles Rams. When the Rams' public relations director abruptly left for another team in 1952, Schramm offered Rozelle the chance to come back to Los Angeles. Rozelle worked with the Rams until 1955, when he moved back to San Francisco to become a partner in a public relations firm.

Rozelle might never have had any further contact with football had it not been for the turmoil that engulfed the Los Angeles Rams in the late 1950s. Ownership of the team was equally divided between long-time owner Dan Reeves and two partners who shared a hatred for Reeves. The result was a paralysis that drove Tex Schramm to seek a job with CBS Sports and caused NFL Commissioner Bert Bell to seek a GM who could mediate between the two factions. Bell was a friend of Rozelle's partner in the firm and recalled Rozelle's previous attachment to the Rams as well as the work that he had done with the firm in marketing the 1956 Melbourne Olympic Games. In 1957, Rozelle once again headed south, to become GM of the Rams.

Two years later, fate again took a hand, when Bell died suddenly of a heart attack, leaving no clear successor. At their annual meetings the next January, the owners spent 10 fruitless days trying to agree on a new commissioner. Finally, during a break, Dan Reeves proposed his 33-year-old GM to Wellington Mara, the son of New York Giants' owner Tim Mara, as a compromise candidate. When Mara suggested the owners consider Rozelle, the ensuing discussion was almost comical.

"What do you know about him?" [Steelers owner] Art Rooney asked.

"Reeves says he's good," Mara answered. . . .

➡

"Rozelle?" Frank McNamee of the Philadelphia Eagles blurted out, "who's he?"[2]

Becoming "boy czar" of the NFL in 1960 was not the prize it would be today. The league had failed to capitalize on the popularity of its 1958 championship game between the Baltimore Colts and the New York Giants, and it remained a backwater. League offices were in the back room of a bank in Bell's hometown of Bala Cynwyd, Pa., and teams still struggled financially.

One of the main problems facing the NFL was the balkanized structure of its television dealings. With each team pursuing its own contracts, gross inequities in revenue resulted (the Baltimore Colts made $600,000 from television in 1959 while the Packers made only $80,000), though no team made very much. In the words of then-president of CBS Sports Bill McPhail, "Local stations made more money then by showing old movies than they did showing professional football games."[3]

Rozelle quickly responded to the challenge. To raise the profile and increase the marketability of the NFL, he immediately moved the league offices to Manhattan. He then set to work consolidating the league's television contracts. Rozelle faced two profound obstacles to his efforts. First, he had to instill a "league-think" mentality in owners who had previously had little ability or reason to look beyond their own survival. Using all the patience and marketing skills at his disposal, Rozelle finally convinced the owners of the big-city teams such as the Giants and the Chicago Bears to sacrifice their own short-term goals in favor of the long-term gains that would come from adopting a unified TV policy and sharing revenues equally.

Convincing the owners, however, was the easy part. Negotiating a league contract with the television networks was illegal for an entity that had lost any pretense of exemption from the antitrust laws with the *Radovich* decision of 1957. Rozelle spent the summer of 1961 lobbying Congress for a limited exemption that would allow the NFL to negotiate a single, league-wide TV contract. His efforts were rewarded that September with the Sports Antitrust Broadcast Act, which allowed football, hockey, and basketball leagues to pool their revenues from television.

Even then, Rozelle's work was not over. Unlike the lords of baseball, who steadily put obstacles in the way of television coverage, Rozelle actively courted the networks and their affiliates. The results of Rozelle's league-think mentality became readily apparent. In 1962–63, the NFL's first contract with CBS paid approximately $330,000 per franchise per year. By 1964–65, the payments had risen to about $1 million per franchise per year.

While such figures are far below current contracts, they broke new ground at the time and induced a sense of unity among the owners. This unity allowed Rozelle to create NFL Properties, which pooled the revenues from league licensing agreements. It also allowed the owners to withstand conflict with a restive players' union far better than the fractious lords of baseball.

In later years, Rozelle would see much of this unity of purpose fracture. The first major setback came with Al Davis's successful antitrust suit over the NFL's attempt to prevent his Oakland Raiders from moving to Los Angeles in 1980. The second came with the entry of a new breed of owners, best exemplified by the Cowboys' Jerry Jones, who—having paid huge sums for their franchises—were determined to maximize their own revenues, even if that meant scrapping the old league-think mentality. Still, the continued prosperity of the NFL and of all professional sports are a testament to the work of the one-time gofer for the Los Angeles Rams.

[1]David Harris, *The League: The Rise and Decline of the NFL* (New York: Bantam Books, 1986), p. 13.

[2]Quoted in Harris, *The League* (1986), p. 11.

[3]Quoted in Harris, *The League* (1986), p. 13.

Sources: David Harris, *The League: The Rise and Decline of the NFL* (New York: Bantam Books, 1986). John Hilyar, *Lords of the Realm* (New York: Villard Books, 1994).

SUMMARY

Monopolies maximize profit by raising prices and reducing output. Economists regard the higher prices as a transfer from consumers to producers that does not affect the overall well-being of society. The lower output, however, creates a deadweight loss that does reduce social well-being. Depending on how much information they have about consumers, monopolists may be able to capture some or the entire consumer surplus by engaging in different forms of price discrimination. Group discounts, season ticket plans, and personal seat licenses are three forms of price discrimination practiced by sports franchises.

Since the late 19th century, the U.S. government has opposed monopoly. The most famous antimonopoly legislation is the Sherman Antitrust Act, which has been applied against professional sports and the NCAA with varying degrees of success. Due to a series of bizarre court rulings early in the 20th century, baseball has enjoyed a blanket exemption from antitrust laws. It used the exemption to great effect, exerting monopsony power thanks to the reserve clause long after the clause was ruled illegal for other sports.

Some firms join together, forming cartels that exert monopoly power, almost accidentally. The NCAA is one example of an "incidental cartel." It was originally formed to establish rules of play for colleges. It soon learned, however, to cooperate for financial matters as well.

DISCUSSION QUESTIONS

1. Do you think that all professional sports should share baseball's exemption from antitrust laws or that baseball should lose its exemption?

2. In professional soccer, teams that signed another team's player had to pay a "transfer fee" to compensate the player's original team. How would this affect the market for soccer players?

3. Is society better off when monopolists can price discriminate or when they cannot?

4. Do you feel that leagues are better described as cartels made up of independent firms or as a single, multiplant firm?

5. What strategy would you follow if you were trying to create a rival basketball league?

6. Why do you think that antitrust lawsuits brought under the second clause of the Sherman Antitrust Act have generally been so unsuccessful?

7. Should major college sports powers be allowed to operate as cartels?

PROBLEMS

4.1 An athletic director was once quoted as saying that he felt his school spent too much on athletics but that it could not afford to stop. Use game theory to model his dilemma.

4.2 You are the commissioner of the National Hockey League. You have been called to testify at an antitrust case against the NHL. Argue that

a. The NHL is not a monopoly.

b. Even if it is a monopoly, it is a natural monopoly.

4.3 In one of the major upsets of the 2000 college football season, the University of Miami beat Florida State when the Miami quarterback threw a touchdown pass to a second-string tight end instead of All-American wide receiver Santana Moss. Use game theory to explain this action.

4.4 Are you better off with PSLs if you would not have bought a seat without them?

4.5 Suppose that the demand curve for tickets to see a football team is given by $Q = 100,000 - 100p$ and marginal cost is zero.

a. How many tickets would the team be able to sell (ignoring capacity constraints) if it behaved competitively and set $p = MC$?

b. How many tickets would it sell—and what price would it charge—if it behaved like a monopoly? (*Hint:* In this case the marginal revenue curve is given by $MR = 1,000 - .02Q$.)

4.6 Why was the limited exemption from antitrust laws so crucial to the development of the NFL?

4.7 Suppose the typical Buffalo Bills fan has the demand curve for Bills football games: $P = 120 - 10 \cdot G$, where G is the number games the fan attends.

a. If the Bills want to sell the fan a ticket to all eight home games, what price must they charge? What are their revenues?

b. Suppose the Bills have the chance to offer a season ticket that is good for all eight home games, a partial season ticket that is good for four home games, and tickets to individual games. What price should they charge? What is their revenue?

4.8 Suppose the Arizona Cardinals have fans who are much more sensitive to price than the fans in Buffalo as described in the previous question. Their demand curve for Cardinals football games is: $P = 120 - 15G$. What is true about the prices they are able to charge and their revenue if they try to practice second degree price discrimination as the Bills did? Why does this happen?

4.9 Suppose that, in order to protect David Beckham from his adoring fans, soccer teams that host Real Madrid must hire extra security, and security costs go up as the number of fans at the game goes up. When a team such as Arsenal hosts Real Madrid, how do these extra costs affect the price of a ticket for that game compared with the price of a ticket when they host any other team? Is this price discrimination by Arsenal? Why or why not?

4.10 If having more fans at the game improves a team's chance of winning, should the team reduce its ticket prices to increase attendance? (Hint: does it matter what the team is trying to maximize?)

An Alternative Application of Game Theory

The prisoner's dilemma is a particularly powerful and easily understood example of game theory and how it applies to economic settings. However, not all situations involving players, strategies, and payoffs result in a prisoner's dilemma, as the following example shows.[64]

You are playing at Centre Court at Wimbledon, down 6–5 in the third set of the Ladies' Finals. Serena Williams awaits your serve. You know from bitter experience that Serena has a devastating forehand. As a result, in this most important match of your life, you serve . . . directly to her forehand?

Playing to an opponent's strength may seem like the height of folly, but athletes, generals, and CEOs do it all the time. They recognize that sometimes no single strategy dominates another and that their best hope lies in being unpredictable, following a **mixed strategy.**

Your match with Serena Williams is a perfect example of just such a strategy. It seems obvious to all that you should avoid Serena's forehand at such an important point in the game. Of course, one of those to whom this strategy seems obvious is Serena herself. As a result, she prepares herself mentally and physically for a serve to her backhand, leaving her vulnerable to a serve to her strength. The payoff matrix in Table 4A.1 clarifies the wisdom of this strategy. You have two choices when you serve: going to Serena's forehand or backhand. Serena, in turn, has two possible strategies: anticipating a serve to her forehand or backhand. If she correctly guesses that you are serving to her forehand, she wins the point 60 percent of the time. If she correctly guesses backhand, she wins 50 percent of the time. If she guesses forehand but you serve to her backhand, she wins 40 percent of the time. If she incorrectly guesses backhand, she also wins 40 percent of the time.

Unlike the prisoner's dilemma example, this situation has no single equilibrium outcome. Suppose, for example, that you consistently serve to Serena's forehand. Serena sees this. By always preparing for a forehand serve, she wins 60 percent of the points (the upper left box). You realize that you can do better by fooling Serena, so you serve to her backhand and win 60 percent of the points (the lower left box). Serena quickly recognizes your new strategy and begins to expect a serve to her backhand, winning 50 percent of the points (the lower right box). You adjust again and now serve to

---

[64]For a more formal take on the game theoretic basis of tennis serves, see Mark Walker and John Wooders, "Minimax Play at Wimbledon," *American Economic Review*, v. 91, no. 5 (December 2001), pp. 1521–1538.

Table 4A.1

Mixed Strategies in Tennis

	Serena Guesses Forehand	*Serena Guesses Backhand*
You serve to her forehand	You win 40% Serena wins 60%	You win 60% Serena wins 40%
You serve to her backhand	You win 60% Serena wins 40%	You win 50% Serena wins 50%

Serena's strength. Because she still expects you to serve to her backhand, you manage to win 60 percent of the time (the upper right box). Serena again catches on, however, and correctly anticipates the serve to her forehand, bringing us back to our starting point (the upper left box), where you win 40 percent of the time.[65]

Since no strategy stays optimal for long, your greatest advantage comes from fooling Serena and hitting your serve "where she ain't." This means that you must follow a mixed strategy, serving sometimes to her forehand and sometimes to her backhand. When Serena guesses correctly, she may hit a devastating return. When she does not, you stand an excellent chance of winning the point. You must see to it that Serena does not guess correctly too often. Thus you must mix up your serves just often enough that Serena cannot gain any advantage by guessing that you will serve one way or the other.

Suppose your strategy is to serve to Serena's forehand with probability p (and hence to her backhand with probability $(1 - p)$). Suppose, further, that Serena's strategy is to anticipate a serve to her forehand with probability q (and a serve to her backhand with probability $(1 - q)$).[66] If Serena prepares for a serve to her forehand, then, from Table 4A.1, the probability that she wins the point is

$$Prob_{GF} = 0.6p + 0.4(1 - p),$$

because she wins 60 percent of the serves to her forehand and 40 percent of the serves to her backhand when she anticipates a serve to her forehand. By similar reasoning, the probability that she wins if she prepares for a serve to her backhand is

$$Prob_{GB} = 0.4p + 0.5(1 - p).$$

Your optimal strategy should be to serve to her forehand just often enough that Serena does not gain an advantage by guessing one way or the other. In other words, your best strategy is to choose p so that $Prob_{GF} = Prob_{GB}$. Setting these equations equal and solving for p, one finds that your optimal strategy

---

[65]To see this problem carried out to comic extremes, see the confrontation between Vizzini and the Dread Pirate Roberts in *The Princess Bride,* by William Goldman (1974).

[66]We assume that both decisions are random and that each player knows only the probabilities of her opponent's actions (e.g., from previous matches).

would be to serve to Serena's forehand one-third of the time ($p = 1/3$) and to her backhand two-thirds of the time. Then, no matter how she guesses, you will win 53.3 percent of the points.[67]

APPENDIX **4B**

Producer Surplus

Consumers are not alone in enjoying a surplus. Just as some consumers are willing and able to buy an item at different prices, producers are willing and able to sell that item at different prices. More efficient producers can produce profitably at lower prices than less efficient producers. Some producers cannot make a profit at the market price, and so they do not produce at all. Since all producers sell at a single price, p_m, the more efficient producers enjoy a greater profit, or surplus, than less efficient producers. The last, or marginal, producer enjoys no surplus at all. We measure producer surplus in Figure 4B.1 by drawing a segment between the supply curve, each point of which represents the price where some producers are just willing to produce and the market price (p_m). The segment is longest for the most efficient producer and disappears for the marginal producer.

As with consumers, as we consider more and more producers, we see more and more segments until the total producer surplus roughly equals the area of the triangle formed by the market price and the supply curve in Figure 4B.2.

Economists combine the surpluses enjoyed by producers and consumers to determine the total gain from exchange.

---

[67]Similar reasoning will tell Serena her optimal guessing strategy—that is, what percentage of the time (q) she should prepare for a serve to her forehand. If either you or Serena deviates from your optimal strategy, the other will see this (i.e., you can tell how often Serena prepares for a forehand serve [q] , and she can tell how often you serve to her forehand [p]). Then if, say, Serena sees you are not following the best strategy of serving to her forehand one-third of the time, she can adjust her strategy to reduce your winning percentage below .533.

FIGURE 4B.1

Producer Surplus to Individual
Producers

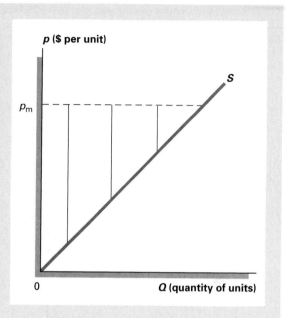

FIGURE 4B.2

Producer Surplus for Many
Producers

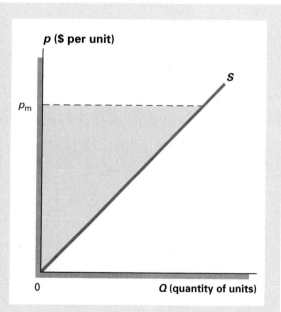

CHAPTER 5

Competitive Balance

Q. How many Cincinnati Bengals does it take to win a Super Bowl?
A. We may never find out![1]

One of the oldest adages in professional football is that on any given Sunday, each team has a chance to beat the other. But what if, year after year, some teams almost always lost while other teams almost always won? No doubt sports would be less interesting. As early as 1956, economists noted that successful leagues must be based on relatively even competition.[2] The degree of parity in a league is known as competitive balance. This chapter discusses competitive balance from the perspective of the fan and the owner. In addition, it explores the various ways in which economists measure competitive balance, how leagues may try to alter the competitive balance in a league, and why such efforts may not be successful. As we explain competitive balance, we will see the following:

- Concerns over competitive balance are not new
- Why some teams may win too often
- Why owners want competitive balance but not complete parity
- Why any single measure of competitive balance cannot capture all of its important dimensions
- Why the draft does not necessarily equalize talent across teams

---

[1]http://www.pasteeaters.com/funny_jokes/More_Cincinnati_Bengals_Jokes.asp
[2]Simon Rottenberg, "The Baseball Players Labor Market," *Journal of Political Economy*, v. 64, no. 3 (June, 1956), pp. 242–258.

5.1 THE FAN'S PERSPECTIVE

Suppose you are an exchange student to the United States, and your host family takes you to see your first baseball game; it's between the Detroit Tigers and the New York Yankees. The game quickly gets boring because the talent on the two teams is so uneven. The Yankees score on the hapless Tigers over and over again, and you notice that most fans leave well before the game is even close to being over. The final score is 11–0. "That's OK," your host says, "the Tigers lose all the time, and the Yankees always win." If that were your only exposure to baseball, you would probably leave America thinking baseball was a waste of time. If instead you had seen the Atlanta Braves beat the Arizona Diamondbacks in a wild 5–4 game after the catcher hit a home run in the bottom of the ninth, and you learned that almost all games are like this, you might become a lifelong fan.

From the fan's perspective, an uncertain outcome is much more interesting than a foregone conclusion. While some fans may argue that the degree of parity in the current NFL is too great, historically, fans have shown their displeasure with unbalanced competition, even when their own team did most of the winning. An often-cited example is the Cleveland Browns of the late 1940s; their continued dominance of the All-American Football Conference caused them to become less popular with their home fans. In baseball, the Yankees may have had the same kind of negative effect on attendance at their own games and across the American League when they won eight League pennants and six World Series between 1950 and 1958. Table 5.1 shows that between 1950 and 1958, a period generally marked by prosperity and growth, attendance at both Yankee games and those of the entire American League either stagnated or fell as the Yankees completely dominated professional baseball. The effect was especially pronounced in the late 1950s, as National League attendance grew substantially while American League attendance fell.

In fact, fans enjoy a contest with an uncertain outcome even though they root for their team to win every game. Recent research shows that fans are most

Table 5.1

New York Yankees' Success and American League and National League Attendance, 1950–58

Year	AL Champion	World Series Champion	Yankees Attendance	AL Attendance	NL Attendance
1950	Yankees	Yankees	2,081,380	9,142,361	8,320,616
1951	Yankees	Yankees	1,950,107	8,888,614	7,244,002
1952	Yankees	Yankees	1,629,665	8,293,896	6,339,148
1953	Yankees	Yankees	1,531,811	6,964,076	7,419,721
1954	Cleveland	NY Giants	1,475,171	7,922,364	8,013,519
1955	Yankees	Brooklyn	1,490,138	8,942,971	7,674,412
1956	Yankees	Yankees	1,491,784	7,893,683	8,649,567
1957	Yankees	Milwaukee	1,497,134	8,169,218	8,819,601
1958	Yankees	Yankees	1,428,438	7,296,034	10,164,596

Source: Attendance data are from Rodney Fort and James Quirk, *Pay Dirt* (1992). Performance data is from the official MLB website http://www.MLB.com.

interested in games when the home team has a 60 to 70 percent chance of winning.[3] This is not to say that fans want their teams to lose; they want them to have *a chance of losing*. If fans were certain that their team would win every week, it would take away a major source of excitement from the game. Economists call this the **uncertainty of outcome hypothesis (UOH).**

There is currently a great deal of research on UOH in sports economics, much of which is centered on baseball and the ongoing concern among both fans and team owners, who recently sponsored a blue ribbon commission to study the subject. A prominent fear is that the Yankees are so wealthy relative to other teams that they can "buy" championships year after year by offering salaries high enough to attract all of the best players. These concerns have been heightened by the fact that the Yankees now have their own television network, YES (Yankees Entertainment & Sports). If the Yankees can make tens of millions of dollars from selling YES broadcast rights to cable companies, they might use that revenue to purchase even more top players. Table 5.2 shows the great disparity in revenue earned from local television in professional baseball: The Yankees' local revenue is roughly 10 times that of the Milwaukee Brewers and 100 times that of the Montreal Expos. The fear among fans (and perhaps more importantly, among other owners) is that the dominance of the Yankees may become a never-ending cycle if revenue disparities create long-term performance disparities.

A similar concern was expressed during the Chicago Bulls' dominance of the NBA in the Michael Jordan era, when the Bulls won six out of eight

Table 5.2

Local Broadcasting Revenue in Major League Baseball for 2003

Team Local Broadcasting	Revenue	Team Local Broadcasting	Revenue
New York Yankees	$56,750,000	Tampa Bay Devil Rays	15,511,000
New York Mets	46,251,000	Florida Marlins	15,353,000
Seattle Mariners	37,860,000	Toronto Blue Jays	14,460,000
Boston Red Sox	33,353,000	Arizona Diamondbacks	14,174,000
Chicago White Sox	30,092,000	Houston Astros	13,722,000
Los Angeles Dodgers	27,342,000	San Diego Padres	12,436,000
Texas Rangers	25,284,000	St. Louis Cardinals	11,905,000
Chicago Cubs	23,559,000	Anaheim Angels	10,927,000
Cleveland Indians	21,076,000	Oakland Athletics	9,458,000
Baltimore Orioles	20,994,000	Pittsburgh Pirates	9,097,000
Atlanta Braves	19,988,000	Cincinnati Reds	7,861,000
Detroit Tigers	19,073,000	Minnesota Twins	7,273,000
Philadelphia Phillies	18,940,000	Kansas City Royals	6,505,000
Colorado Rockies	18,200,000	Milwaukee Brewers	5,918,000
San Francisco Giants	17,197,000	Montreal Expos	536,000

Source: Doug Pappas, "The Numbers (Part 2): Local Media Revenue," from *The Baseball Prospectus On-Line* at http://www.baseballprospectus.com/news/20011212pappas.html. December 12, 2001.

---

[3]Daniel Rascher, "A Test of Optimal Positive Production Network Externality in Major League Baseball," in *Sports Economics: Current Research,* ed. by John Fizel, Elizabeth Gustafson, and Larry Hadley (Westport, C.T.: Praeger Publishers, 1999), pp. 27–45.

New Jersey Devils' Captain Scott Stevens
holds aloft the Stanley Cup

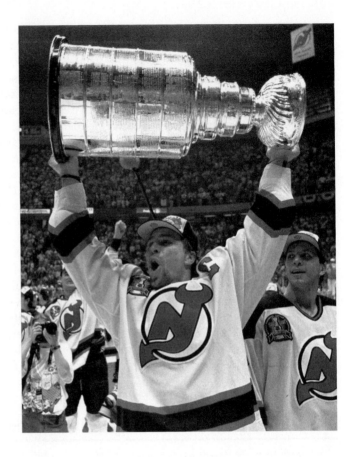

championships between 1991 and 1998, and about the Los Angeles Lakers, consistently a top team in the NBA in recent years. Perhaps the same concerns are now warranted in the NHL, as just three teams—the New Jersey Devils, the Colorado Avalanche, and the Detroit Red Wings—have won eight of the last nine Stanley Cups.

Part of the debate over competitive balance focuses on whether dynasties are good or bad for a sport. Do fans like dynasties? It depends on whether they support the team that is consistently winning championships or support the team that has little chance of winning one. Dynasties of the past do tend to be remembered more romantically by fans in all cities, in part because of the legendary players who made the teams so dominant.

Despite the flurry of recent research on the topic and activity at league meetings to "fix the problem," unbalanced competition is not a new issue. The dominance of the Yankees extends back to the 1920s, when the Yankees won six American League championships between 1921 (the year after they acquired Babe Ruth) and 1928. It was even more pronounced in the late 1940s and 1950s, when they won five straight World Series, eight in total between 1947 and 1958. Although there were fewer teams at the time—a fact that makes the current Yankees' success more impressive—the long history of championship dominance indicates that the current Yankees teams are no more, and may be less, dominant than past Yankees teams.

Two of the three other major sports have similar histories. The Boston Celtics won every NBA championship but one between 1959 and 1969. Between 1965 and 1979, the Montreal Canadiens won the NHL's Stanley Cup 10 times. The Canadiens' dynasty was followed by that of the New York Islanders, who won the Cup the next four years in a row. Only in the NFL has no team ever won the league championship—the Super Bowl—more than twice in a row, but even the NFL has several franchises that are historically uncompetitive, such as Cincinnati and Arizona.

Internationally, competitive balance in the elite European soccer leagues is even more skewed toward a few dominant teams. Manchester United has won the English Premier League eight times since the realignment of the league to create the Premier Division in 1992–93. During the same period, Real Madrid and FC Barcelona have won 8 of the last 11 championships in La Liga, the top Spanish League.

Changes in the relative importance of the various revenue sources and the growth of the sports industry in general have increased the concerns that the financial consequences of unbalanced competition are becoming more severe. Accordingly, we must consider the owners' perspective on equalizing competition.

5.2   THE OWNERS' PERSPECTIVE

As discussed in Chapters 2 and 3, leagues have long been aware that their success depends on staging games with an uncertain outcome. Whether it is a great boxing match between two undefeated rivals, a tennis championship between the first and second-ranked players in the world, or a baseball game in which the league's top two pitchers square off, fans' demand typically increases with the intensity of the contest. The more appealing the contest, the more fans will attend or watch the game on TV, and the more revenue will be generated.

If it is in the best interest of leagues to have relatively close competition between their member teams, they have an incentive to promote competitive balance. Leagues do not need to take specific action if they tend naturally toward equal strength. If, however, a few teams flourish while most teams languish, the league has an incentive to act. For instance, Chapters 3 and 4 explained how teams in larger, more populous markets generally have a larger fan base and higher gate and television revenues. They can thus afford to hire better players in a free market. In addition, successful teams are likely to have an advantage in attracting players, thereby creating self-perpetuating dynasties. Because all leagues now have free agency in one form or another, players can decide for whom they would most like to play. For example, veteran players near the end of their careers such as Karl Malone and Gary Payton in basketball, Dominik Hasek in hockey, or Roger Clemens in baseball, all made conscious decisions to play for top contending teams.

If dynasties are self-perpetuating, then leagues have an economic incentive to intervene in the market to ensure enough competitive balance to foster long-term profitability. Although a league's monopoly power affords it the ability to do so, a potential complication stems from the fact that, in the end, team owners control leagues. As a group, they would like to see balanced competition, but each individual owner would also like his or her team to be consistently successful, a point we return to later in the chapter.

One strictly economic force is present in all labor markets that mitigates the effects of unbalanced revenues across teams. The **law of diminishing marginal returns** (diminishing returns) reduces the incentive of any team to stockpile all of the top talent in a league, though this force may not be sufficient to prevent competitive imbalance. Diminishing returns to labor are found in every industry. In the short run, as a firm adds units of labor, the marginal product (the additional output) of the last unit of labor must eventually fall, even if the labor is homogeneous. The reason is straightforward: In the short run, capital is fixed. Thus, eventually, the additional workers have insufficient capital to work with, so they are not as productive.

In the context of sports, diminishing returns may set in very quickly, especially in basketball, where only five team members play at a time, substitution is relatively limited (i.e., the five starting players play the vast majority of the total minutes), and, as the saying goes, "there is only one ball." In most sports, players specialize in particular positions, and rules allow only a fixed number of players on the field at one time. For basketball, once a team has even two players who shoot frequently, adding a third shooter to the roster is likely to add very little to team quality, certainly less than the addition of the first two scorers. The Lakers would not dispute that Tim Duncan is a great player, but his value to the Lakers is surely less than the price another team without a top center would pay, given that the Lakers already have Shaquille O'Neal. Duncan's value will be greater to a team that does not already have a top scoring center or power forward. Therefore, while some baseball aficionados may claim that a team can never have too much pitching, a team with 15 pitchers certainly *would* have too much pitching, since rosters are fixed at 25 players, so that team would have almost no substitutes at other positions and some of those pitchers would rarely play.

Thus, teams have an incentive to allow talent to spread across their league—it simply doesn't make economic or strategic sense for a single team to have all or even most of the good players at any given position. Teams may benefit from stockpiling talent to prevent rivals from signing available stars, but with fixed roster sizes, the ability to do so is limited. The same type of restriction is imposed at the Division I level of collegiate football; the number of scholarships a team can offer is limited to 85.

The Effect of Market Size

Differences in market size across the league provide an additional challenge to team owners. If, as research shows, the dollar value of a win is greater to teams in large cities than to teams in smaller ones, maximizing competitive balance and maximizing total league profits may not be consistent goals.[4] Table 5.2 showed that large-market baseball teams (teams in big cities) have annual local broadcast revenues that are measured in the tens of millions of dollars, whereas the Montreal Expos, a small-market team, has a contract that is worth just $536,000. Even if fans desire some level of uncertainty, a profit-maximizing league may prefer to have the teams in the largest markets win more often than teams elsewhere. In a 30-team league, perfect parity would mean that the Yankees and Dodgers—teams in the two largest markets—would win the World Series only once every 30 years. If championships were allocated so that they were distributed equally on a per-fan basis, rather than a per-team basis, the large-market teams would win more frequently than once every 30 years because they have so many more fans than small-market teams. The tension here between individual team profits and overall league profits is similar to that of a cartel, which some accuse sports leagues of being. Each individual team can increase its profits by improving relative to the rest of the league, but from the league perspective, it is better if some teams are more successful than others.

To see why big-market teams benefit more from winning than small-market teams do, assume that each team gets its revenue only from tickets and local television revenue. Assume further that teams benefit from having a higher winning percentage, but the additional benefits of increasing the winning percentage become smaller as it approaches 1.000 (note that in this two-team example, the winning percentages must sum to 1). The logic here is that increasing a team's winning percentage from .470 to .500 increases revenues more than increasing it from .870 to .900. Thus, the marginal revenue curve from additional wins is positive but downward sloping. Because teams in larger cities enjoy greater increases in fan support (more marginal revenue) from an additional win than teams in small cities, the marginal revenue for a large city is greater at any given winning percentage. In Figure 5.1, the marginal revenue curve for a large-market team (MR_L) lies above the marginal revenue curve for the small-market team (MR_S).[5] Teams maximize profits by setting the marginal revenue from an additional win equal to the marginal cost of creating that win. To keep the focus on revenue, assume that the marginal cost of a win is constant and equal for all teams. This assumption is based on the implicit assumption that each team has equal access to player talent. Figure 5.1 shows that in equilibrium, when the teams maximize profits—rather than wins or championships—the marginal revenue of each team is set to marginal cost and teams in large cities will have more talent and higher winning percentages than teams in small markets.[6]

[4]For more on this topic, see Eric M. Leifer, *Making the Majors* (Cambridge, M.A.: Harvard University Press, 1995). See also John D. Burger and Stephen J.K. Walters, "Market Size, Pay, and Performance: A General Model and Application to Major League Baseball," *Journal of Sports Economics*, v. 4, no. 2 (May 2003), pp. 108–125, for research supporting the relationship between market size and performance.

[5]This model first appeared in Mohamed El-Hodiri and James Quirk, "An Economics Model of a Professional Sports League," *Journal of Political Economy*, v. 79, no. 6 (November/December 1971), pp. 1302–1319.

[6]Gerald W. Scully developed this approach in *The Business of Major League Baseball*, (Chicago: University of Chicago Press, 1989).

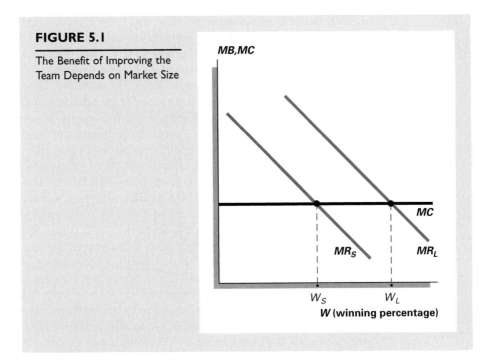

FIGURE 5.1

The Benefit of Improving the Team Depends on Market Size

5.3   HOW COMPETITIVE BALANCE CAN BE MEASURED

This section and those that follow focus primarily on the **analysis of competitive balance (ACB),** which centers on how to measure competitive balance and its importance to leagues. These sections also address how competitive balance might be, and whether it should be, altered by league rules and regulations.

There are three general approaches to measuring competitive balance.[7] Two focus on the dispersion of winning percentages and one on the concentration of championships won. The debate as to which approach is best is ongoing and may not have a single answer. The measure that reflects a fan's perspective may or may not be the same as the one that reflects an owner's perspective, and the method best suited to study short-run effects on demand may not be best suited to study the long-run impact. Moreover, more than one approach may be required to capture the various aspects of competitive balance that are important to fans and leagues. Each approach is described separately in the following pages.

Within-Season Variation

Undoubtedly, the **absolute quality** of play affects demand, as fans want to see the game played at the highest level possible. For example, the demand for

---

[7]For an excellent discussion of the technical merits of these measures, and more sophisticated variations of them, see Brad Humphreys, "Alternative Measures of Competitive Balance, " *Journal of Sports Economics,* v. 3, no. 2 (May 2002), pp. 133–148.

major league games is greater than the demand for minor league games. Within a league of a given quality, however, demand is also determined by **relative quality**, the quality of each team relative to the others in the league. Within-season measurement focuses on the relative quality of teams over a single season.

Measuring competitive balance for a given season is complicated by the fact that we must consider each team's winning percentage, not just an overall average. We cannot use the average winning percentage for the league because each game has one winner and one loser (ignoring ties). This means that the league-wide average winning percentage always equals .500. Thus we need to measure the dispersion of winning percentages—the variation around the average to measure the balance of competition.

To compute the dispersion of winning percentages (or of any variable), economists rely on the **standard deviation**. Standard deviation is a statistic that describes the average distance that observations lie from the mean of the observations in the data set. The formula for the standard deviation of winning percentages within a single season is

$$\sigma_{w,t} = \sqrt{\frac{\sum_{i=1}^{N}(WPCT_{i,t} - .500)^2}{N}},$$

where $WPCT_{i,t}$ is the winning percentage of the ith team in the league in year t, .500 is the average winning percentage of all teams for the year, and N is the number of teams in the league. The larger the standard deviation, the greater is the dispersion of the winning percentages. For example, consider the final standings for the NBA's 2002–03 season. Table 5.3 shows the final standing for the Atlantic division of the Eastern conference and the Midwest division of the Western conference. It is possible to get a first impression of how balanced the divisions were simply by looking at the winning percentages. In the Atlantic division, the two best teams (New Jersey and Philadelphia) won just under 60 percent of the time, and the worst team (Miami) won only about 30 percent of the time. The Midwest division seems less balanced, as the two best teams (San

Table 5.3

Winning Percentages for the Atlantic and Midwest Divisions for the 2002–03 NBA Season

Atlantic	*Winning Percentages*	*Midwest*	*Winning Percentages*
New Jersey	0.598	San Antonio	0.732
Philadelphia	0.585	Dallas	0.732
Boston	0.537	Minnesota	0.622
Orlando	0.512	Utah	0.573
Washington	0.451	Houston	0.524
New York	0.451	Memphis	0.341
Miami	0.305	Denver	0.207
σ	0.100	σ	0.197

Source: http://www.nba.com/standings/2002/by_division.html

Antonio and Dallas) won over 70 percent of their games, and the worst team (Denver) won only about 20 percent of its games.

Computing the standard deviations confirms our first impression about the competitive balance in the two divisions. The standard deviation was .100 in the Atlantic division and .197 in the Midwest division. Thus, the average winning percentage in the Midwest division was nearly twice as far from the division's mean than in the Atlantic division.[8] If all teams in the NBA for the 2002–03 season are included, the standard deviation of winning percentage is 0.144. Thus, the Atlantic division was more competitive than the league as a whole, and the Midwest division was less competitive than the league as a whole.

Although the standard deviation provides a more rigorous method for measuring competitive balance, it will be more useful when comparing different leagues and eras if we can define a common standard against which to measure them. What standard deviation is expected in a league in which each team has an equal chance of winning every game that it plays? This is equivalent to flipping a coin to see if the result is heads or tails. Try flipping a coin 10 times; the odds are that you will not come up with exactly 5 heads and 5 tails—which would translate to 2 teams with .500 winning percentages. As you flip the coin 100, 1,000, or 10,000 times, however, you will see that eventually, the number of heads and tails even out. Thus, for short seasons, all else being equal, teams are likely to have a greater spread of winning percentages, with some teams getting lucky breaks and other teams getting unlucky breaks. Only over a longer season would such breaks even out, just like a run of heads will eventually be offset by a run of tails when flipping a fair coin. If economists use the standard deviation to compare competitive balance across different sports, they must adjust for differences caused by differences in season length. Note that in the equation for within-season standard deviation, season length N appears in the denominator. As the season length, N, increases, the standard deviation falls, all else being equal.

The standard deviation that corresponds to the "ideal" competitive balance in which each team has a 0.5 chance of winning each game is $\sigma_I = .5/\sqrt{N}$, where .5 indicates that each team has a 0.5 probability of winning, and N is the number of games each team plays. In baseball, each team plays 162 games per season, so the ideal standard deviation is .039. In the NFL, the ideal standard deviation is much larger, .125, because teams play only 16 games, and a randomly occurring string of wins or losses has a greater impact on a team's final winning percentage. In the NHL and NBA, where teams play 80 and 82 games, the standard deviations are about .056.

To study competitive balance within a single season, we take the ratio (which we call R) of the actual standard deviation to the ideal standard deviation.[9]

$$R = \sigma_w / \sigma_I$$

---

[8]Because of interdivisional and interconference play, the mean winning percentages are not exactly .500 in this example.

[9]See Scully (1989) for an early use of this method as applied to professional baseball. We can also use the same idea to evaluate competitive balance over many seasons by calculating the average value of the standard deviation for a given year and using that value to create the ratio of actual to ideal standard deviation.

Thus, for the NBA in 2002–03,

$$R = 0.144/0.056 = 2.57.$$

Based on this result, we see that the standard deviation of winning percentages in the NBA is more than twice what it would be in a world with absolutely balanced teams. Again, this result is consistent with our casual observation that competition appears unbalanced in the NBA, as three teams (San Antonio, Dallas, Sacramento) had winning percentages of .700, while six teams (Miami, Toronto, Cleveland, Memphis, Denver, and the L.A. Clippers) had winning percentages of less than .350.

The NBA is not the only unbalanced sport. The dispersion of winning percentages is much greater than the "ideal" distribution in every league. Using data from the 2002 (2002–03 for NHL and NBA) seasons, Table 5.4 shows the actual standard deviation, the ideal standard deviation, and the ratio of the actual standard deviation to the ideal.

Historically, the measures of competitive balance for the four major sports are very similar to those from 2002–03. The average ratio of actual to ideal standard deviations is 2.20 for the baseball's National League and 2.12 for its American League (computed separately because there was no interleague play during these years); 2.43 in the NBA, 1.66 in the NFL, and 1.95 in the NHL.[10]

Between-Season Variation

For baseball fans everywhere, spring is a special time of year that brings with it the promise of a new baseball season and the chance that "this could be the year" that their team wins it all. Across seasons, competitive balance implies that each team has the opportunity to move up in the standings each year and compete for playoff berths. This type of competitive balance is called **turnover**, or team-specific variation. It is quite distinct from within-season variation in that it considers the change in the relative positions of the teams in the standings each year rather

Table 5.4

Dispersion of Winning Percentage for the 2002 or 2002–03 Season

League	Standard Deviation Actual	Ideal	Ratio
MLB	.075	.039	1.91
NFL	.184	.125	1.47
NBA	.160	.056	2.86
NHL	.121	.056	2.16

Source: Generated using standings from official websites and http://foxsports.com/nhl/history/standings/2000_standings_conference.sml. Note that in the NHL, ties are excluded.

---

[10]James Quirk and Rodney Fort, *Pay Dirt* (1992), p. 247. Samples used were 1901–90 for baseball, 1940–90 for basketball, 1920–90 for football, and 1910–90 for hockey.

than the distance between teams in a given season. Brad Humphreys (2002) defines team-specific variation for a team as

$$\sigma_{i,T} = \sqrt{\frac{\sum_{i=1}^{T} (WPCT_i - \overline{WPCT})^2}{T}},$$

where T is the number of seasons, and $\overline{WPCT}$ is the team's average winning percentage over the T seasons.[11] The larger σ_T becomes, the more a team's fortunes change from year to year. If a team always finished with the same record, σ_T would be zero. The more a team's fortunes change from year to year, the greater the standard deviation. If fans support a team only if it has a reasonable chance of winning its division or conference, variation across seasons is vital to maintaining fan interest over long stretches of time. If σ_T was zero for all teams, you would know how all teams would finish before the season even started. Such a situation would surely reduce demand for the weaker teams with below-average winning percentages, and over time it would probably hurt the stronger teams as well.

One frustrating aspect of using the variation between seasons is that, unlike the within-season standard deviation, there is no obvious standard of comparison. It is not possible to say whether fans or owners care more about how much their team's winning percentage varies across the years or how their team's position changes relative to other teams. For example, would Philadelphia Flyers' fans feel better if the Flyers had a very good record instead of a mediocre record but always finished second to the New Jersey Devils anyway? Though turnover is certainly important, the absence of an absolute standard means that σ_T is useful only as a relative measure of dispersion (when comparing one time period with another or one sport with another).

The Hirfindahl-Hirschman Index   Another measure that economists have used to measure turnover is the Hirfindahl-Hirschman Index (*HHI*), which was originally developed to measure the concentration of firms in an industry. In our case, we calculate the *HHI* by taking the number of times each team finished first, squaring it, adding these numbers together, and then dividing them by the number of years under consideration. A small *HHI* means that a large number of teams finish first, while a large *HHI* means that a small number of teams dominated the league.

$$HHI = \Sigma f^2 / N.$$

To see why, consider the championships won in a league with 5 teams over three 10-year periods. Suppose that in the 1960s, each team in the league finished first, twice. In the 1970s, competition was less balanced, and two teams

[11]If you are interested in reading about the debate over which measures are most appropriate, see the articles by Brad R. Humphreys and E.W. Eckard in *Journal of Sports Economics*, v. 4, no. 1 (February 2003).

each finished first, five times. Finally, in the 1980s, 1 team placed first all 10 times. The *HHI* for each decade would be

$$HHI_{60} = (2^2 + 2^2 + 2^2 + 2^2 + 2^2)/10 = 20/10 = 2.$$

$$HHI_{70} = (5^2 + 5^2 + 0^2 + 0^2 + 0^2)/10 = 50/10 = 5.$$

$$HHI_{80} = (10^2 + 0^2 + 0^2 + 0^2 + 0^2)/10 = 100/10 = 10.$$

As competition becomes less balanced, the value of *HHI* rises. An advantage of using the *HHI* instead of the standard deviation is that, for any given league, the *HHI* allows us to compute a benchmark against which we can compare results (as in the 1960s example above). A disadvantage, as with the other measures, is that the *HHI* still does not address the issue of optimal balance. A second disadvantage of this measure is the interpretation of the standard itself. According to this "ideal," fans in a league with *N* "perfectly balanced" teams will wait an average of *N* years for their team's "turn" to finish first to come around, after which they will wait another *N* years.

Frequency of Championships It is also possible to evaluate competitive balance by looking at the frequency with which teams win successive championships. On the one hand, if the Yankees win the World Series every year, then the winning percentages of the teams in the league do not matter as much, since the league is clearly unbalanced. On the other hand, if different teams win the American League and National League pennants every year, then it's possible to argue that competition in each league is balanced, regardless of how bad the worst teams are relative to the best teams. This criterion is similar to the turnover criterion discussed above, but it relates to championships rather than regular season standings. To focus strictly on championships, we can measure interseason balance by applying the *HHI* methodology to championships won instead of to first-place finishes. Another, more direct approach is to simply count the championships won by a team for a specific period of time.

When only championships are counted, Table 5.5 shows that the NBA again has the worst competitive balance problems. Just 3 teams won over 70 percent of the 24 championships from 1979–80 through 2002–03. Of these, many of the wins were in consecutive years. The Bulls won their six titles in just eight years, and more recently, the Lakers won three straight championships. Such domination makes it hard for a league to convince fans of other teams that they have much chance of seeing their team compete for a championship. As the table shows, this form of imbalance is not a uniquely American problem. Even the NBA does not rival European soccer when it comes to concentration of championships in the past decade. Manchester United may be the most dominant team in all of professional sports over the last 10 years.

In summary, there are many ways to measure competitive balance, and no single method should be regarded as most appropriate. To fully grasp the state of competitive balance in a league requires consideration of intraseason balance—the spread of winning percentages across teams—as well as interseason balance, the turnover of teams in the standings, and the frequency of

Table 5.5

Distribution of Championships, 1980 to 2002–03

NBA	NHL	NFL	MLB AL*	MLB NL*	English Premier**
Lakers—7	Oilers—5	49ers—5	Yankees—7	Braves—5	Manchester United—8
Bulls—6	Islanders—4	Cowboys—3	Athletics—3	Cardinals—3	Arsenal—2
Celtics—3	Devils—3	Redskins—3	Blue Jays—2	Phillies—3	Blackburn Rovers—1
Pistons—2	Red Wings—3	Broncos—2	Indians—2	Dodgers—2	
Rockets—2	Avalanche—2	Giants—2	Royals—2	Giants—2	
Spurs —2	Canadiens—2	Raiders—2	Twins—2	Marlins—2	
76ers—1	Penguins—2	Bears—1	Angels—1	Mets—2	
		Flames—1	Packers—1	Braves—1	
		Rangers—1	Patriots—1	Orioles—1	
		Stars—1	Pirates—1	Red Sox—1	
				Rams—1	
				Ravens—1	
				Padres—2	
				Diamondbacks—1	
				Reds—1	
				Tigers—1	

*No postseason play in 1994.
**European soccer. English Premier data begin in 1992–93.
Sources: Official league websites.

championships. Leagues must be concerned about all these forms of competitive balance because fan interest—and correspondingly attendance, television ratings, and league profits—is likely to be affected by each. The next section addresses how leagues may attempt to alter competitive balance.

5.4   ATTEMPTS TO ALTER COMPETITIVE BALANCE

Currently, both the popular press and the professional literature are discussing competitive balance in every major sport in the United States as well as in the European soccer leagues. The greatest concern in the United States is in baseball, in which most team owners and some economists believe that beginning in the 1990s, competitive balance has become substantially worse. Because a degree of parity is so important to the success of any league, all the major sports have developed processes designed to promote competitive balance. The most important of these are revenue sharing, salary caps, luxury taxes, and the draft. Leagues that have implemented these policies claim that they equalize access to talented players so that no one team or small number of teams can hoard an excessive number of talented players. The success of these policies depends to a large extent on two factors: whether a team's performance is strongly related to its payroll and whether making rules that limit payroll (such as salary caps and luxury taxes) increases competitive balance. The basics of each technique are described in following paragraphs, followed by a discussion of whether or not they are effective.

Revenue Sharing

As was discussed in Chapter 3, a primary outcome of revenue sharing is more equal profits. To the extent that revenue sharing also increases a financially weak team's ability to sign and retain players, it may also improve competitive balance. It is, however, only an indirect method of redistributing players and may not equalize talent. Two conditions must hold for revenue sharing to result in a more equal distribution of talent and thus improve competitive balance. First, if it is assumed that teams attempt to maximize profits, the teams that receive revenue must benefit financially from improving their performance. If these teams do not benefit sufficiently from spending the money on better players, they may simply keep the payment, and revenue sharing will have no effect on competitive balance. Second, revenue sharing can help a team acquire better players only if players can move—or be moved—easily from team to team. This presupposes the existence of either free agency or the ability to buy and sell the rights to players. Unfortunately, data from Commissioner Selig's blue ribbon commission show that some of the worst on-field teams in baseball were more profitable than other teams with much better records *and* were net receivers of shared revenue, a fact that seems to indicate that those teams that received revenue were inclined to keep it rather than spend it on better talent.

Salary Caps and Luxury Taxes

Salary caps stipulate the maximum that a team may spend on player salaries in a given year. Such a system is currently in place in the NBA and NFL. In 2003 (2003–04), each NFL team was not supposed to spend more than $75 million on player salaries, and no NBA team was supposed to spend more than $43.8 million. Teams that violate the cap are subject to fines from the league. Such stipulations have two primary effects. First, overall spending on players will decline, a topic covered further in Chapter 8. Second, and more importantly for competitive balance, no team will be able to pay to hire all of the best players, which should equalize talent across teams.

Luxury taxes, such as the one implemented in Major League Baseball, force teams to pay an additional fee to the league on any payroll expenditure above a certain amount. In 2003, any MLB team that spent more than $117 million on salaries for the year had to pay a tax of 17.5 percent of any overage into a league fund, which was then distributed to low-revenue teams as a form of revenue sharing. In subsequent years, the tax rate rises for second- and third-time offenders.[12] The luxury tax can be considered a weaker form of a salary cap. With a hard salary cap, no team is permitted to exceed the cap, regardless of its willingness to pay a penalty. With a luxury tax, teams may choose to exceed the tax threshold as long as they are willing to pay the tax. For example, in 2003, the Yankees' payroll of over $180 million exceeded the cap by over

---

[12]Three-time losers must pay a tax of 40 percent in 2005 and 2006. The luxury tax runs through the 2006 season. After that, MLB and the players association must renegotiate it. For more information, see "Summary of New 2002–2006 CBA," at http://www.roadsidephotos.com/baseball/laborstatus.htm.

$60 million. Based on the formula designed by Major League Baseball, the tax owed by the Yankees amounted to about $11 million. The high cost of obtaining a substantial percentage of the top players and the fact that low-revenue teams receive payments from the very high salary teams allows teams to have different profit-maximizing strategies with respect to the tax. As explained in Chapter 3, the benefits of fielding a high-quality team may be enormous for a large-market team such as the Yankees. Thus, it may be worthwhile for it to exceed the cap and pay the tax, whereas the cost of doing so would surely exceed the possible benefits for a small-market team.

The Reverse-Order Entry Draft

The reverse-order entry draft allows teams to choose incoming players in reverse order from their finish of the previous season. The team with the worst record is given the first choice, the second-worst team chooses second, and so on until the team that won the previous season's championship chooses last. The same procedure is followed through subsequent rounds. When the last round is complete, all remaining players who have not been chosen are free to try out for and sign contracts with any team.

The origin of the draft can be traced to 1934, when two NFL teams—the old Brooklyn Dodgers and the Philadelphia Eagles—bid against each other for the services of Stan Kostka, an all-American player at the University of Minnesota. The resulting bidding war drove salary offers to the then unbelievable level of $5,000 (what Bronko Nagurski—the greatest player of the era—made).

At the next league meeting, Bert Bell, the Philadelphia Eagles owner, proposed a unique way to avoid bidding wars over unsigned players in the future. Teams would select the rights to sign unsigned players, with the order of selection determined by each team's performance in the previous season. Ironically, the fact that the worst teams choose first in the draft—a feature that has led all leagues to cite the draft as a key to maintaining competitive balance—stems from the fact that Bell's Eagles were a last-place team at the time.[13] The implications for the power that this gave teams over the players' ability to negotiate for higher salaries are further discussed in Chapter 8. For now, we emphasize the fact that if the worst teams are always able to select the best players, it may help to equalize the talent across teams, because it prevents the teams with the most revenue from dominating the bidding for the most talented players.

Schedule Adjustments in the NFL

The NFL has a unique method for introducing an additional element of parity across seasons that is unrelated to the movement or acquisition of players. By rule, each team's schedule for the following season is determined in part by their performance in the previous season. The formula for opponents scheduled requires that each team play 14 of their 16 games against opponents that

---

[13]James Quirk and Rodney Fort, *Paydirt* (Princeton, N.J.: Princeton University Press, 1992), p. 187.

are common to all members of a division. Each team plays the other three teams in its own division twice, plus all four teams in one other division within the conference, plus all four teams from one division in the other conference for a total of 14 games. The relevant portion of the schedule for this discussion is that for each team, the remaining two games are played against opponents determined based on performance in the previous season. The first-place team in each division plays the first-place teams in the two divisions that the team is not scheduled to play; the second-place team plays the other two second-place teams, and so on. As a result, stronger teams play stronger schedules the following year, and weaker teams play weaker schedules the following year, creating a natural tendency towards parity.

5.5   THE EFFECTS OF ATTEMPTS TO ALTER COMPETITIVE BALANCE

Revenue sharing, drafts, salary caps, and luxury taxes can all help to increase the parity in a league. There are, however, a number of reasons why they might not. The most obvious is that player talent is intangible. Any given player may be dominant in one year and then perform very poorly in the next year. Similarly, no matter how highly regarded a player is in high school or college, his talent may not translate to the professional level. If players were robot-like in their consistency, it would be much easier to predict the best teams from season to season by comparing the quality of team rosters based on past performance. A logical extension of this argument is that if better players command higher salaries, whichever team spends the most on talent would always win.

Unfortunately for the owners, who must decide how much to pay each player, the relationship is not precise. Table 5.6 shows the correlation between payroll and winning percentage for each team in the four major sports in 2002. A correlation coefficient close to 1 would indicate that wins and payroll are very strongly related. A correlation coefficient close to zero would indicate that wins and payroll are not related. The table shows that although payroll and winning percentage are positively related, the relationship is far from perfect, especially in the NFL, where the correlation is essentially zero.

Table 5.6 also shows that, even if owners are willing to spend more to hire better players, success is not assured. The level of uncertainty is even higher

Table 5.6

The Correlation Between Payroll and Winning Percentage

Sport	Correlation Coefficient	Sport	Correlation Coefficient
MLB	.415	NBA	.228
NFL	.024	NHL	.311

Source: Baseball data are for 2003. All other sports are seasons ending in 2002. Performance data are from official league sites. Salary data for football are from http://espn.go.com/nfl/columns/pasquarelli_len/1422828.html. All other salary data are from http://www.Forbes.com.

when trying to select players who are entering the league for the first time. There are countless stories of highly drafted players who end up never playing a down in the NFL, never swinging at a MLB pitch, never taking a shift in an NHL game, and never playing a minute in the NBA. Even for those who do make the teams that choose them, success is not precisely related to draft order.

There are many examples of the tenuous relationship between expenditure or draft order and performance. Michael Jordan, perhaps the greatest basketball player ever, was chosen third in the NBA draft by the Chicago Bulls, behind Hakeem Olajuwon and Sam Bowie. While Olajuwon went on to have an outstanding career, Bowie played just five lackluster seasons in the league before injuries forced him to retire. In the NHL, the Flyers traded away the rights to Peter Forsberg, Ron Hextall, and 4 other players *plus* $15 million to acquire the rights to Eric Lindros. Forsberg went on to become one of the most dominant forwards in the game for the Colorado Avalanche (who were the Quebec Nordiques at the time of this deal), leading them to the Stanley Cup in 1996 and 2001. Unfortunately for the Flyers, Lindros was plagued by concussions and had a falling out with team management, leading to one of the unhappiest chapters in the team's history.

In summary, the uncertainty that surrounds talent and the relatively weak relationship between expenditure and team quality cast doubt on the effectiveness of policies that equalize expenditure and limit opportunities to select new players. The next section discusses another powerful force that may serve to undo any efforts by the league to enhance competitive balance.

The Coase Theorem and Competitive Balance

In order for any attempt to equalize talent to be effective, there must be some institutional mechanism to move players from one team to another. Chapter 4 described how for much of the 20th century, professional sports leagues controlled player movement through a reserve system that essentially gave the teams the "rights" to a player for his entire career. More recently, players in baseball, basketball, and football have won the right to sell their services to the highest bidder through free agency. Owners have long argued that free agency is bad for competitive balance because it allows the teams with the most resources to purchase the best talent and dominate the league. As it turns out, economists argue that it does not matter which system is in place. Neither system affects competitive balance because the owners' reasoning flies in the face of a theory of resource markets known as the **Coase Theorem**. The central finding of the Coase Theorem is that the initial allocation of property rights (whether a player has the right to sell his services to any team or the owner has the right to hold a player's contract for his entire career) does not matter.[14] As long as property rights are clearly established (as long as someone owns the

---

[14]The theorem was largely responsible for Ronald Coase's receiving the 1991 Nobel Memorial Prize. See Ronald Coase, "The Problem of Social Cost," *Journal of Law and Economics*, v. 3 (October 1960), pp. 1–44.

resource in the first place) and bargaining costs are low, the resource will be put to use by the person or firm that benefits from it most. If a player owns the rights to his services, that is, if he has the right to sell his services to the highest bidder, the team that values him the most will offer the best contract and sign him. If profit-maximizing teams hold the property rights to player services and are able to buy and sell the rights to players, the best players again end up on the teams that value their services the most, because those teams will make the highest offers. Thus, the Coase Theorem predicts that free agency has no impact on the distribution of talent. Economists commonly refer to this as the **invariance hypothesis.**

The allocation of property rights should not affect the final distribution of talent. Regardless of who owns the rights, players end up on the teams that value their services the most. The only difference between the two systems is that if the players own the rights to their services (as in free agency), they keep the gains from their movement from one team to another, whereas if the owners reserve the players' rights, the benefits from the payments flow to the owner who sells the player. Chapter 8 covers this last point in more detail. This section focuses only on what the Coase Theorem predicts about the distribution of talent.

Suppose that a star shooting guard adds $5 million per year to the revenue of the Indiana Pacers. Largely because of the difference in market size, the value of that same player would be $7 million if he played for the Los Angeles Lakers. Under complete free agency, the Lakers would outbid the Pacers, and the player would play in Los Angeles for between $5 million and $7 million. If instead there were no free agency but teams could "sell" players for cash or payment in kind, the Lakers would pay the Pacers more than the $5 million that the player contributes to the Pacers but less than the $7 million that the player is worth to the Lakers, and both teams are better off. In either case, the player ends up playing for the team that values his services the most. Although some leagues have placed restrictions on the outright sale of players, as long as teams can trade draft picks and players, the same result holds. The Coase Theorem thus predicts that free agency alone does not distribute playing talent less equally than a reserve system. A recent study of Major League Baseball shows that the advent of free agency in 1976 did not lessen competitive balance and may actually have improved it. The study found that the distribution of winning percentages did not change significantly after 1976 and that the correlation of winning percentages (turnover) from one year to the next actually fell after 1976.[15]

Salary Caps

Salary caps can even out the talent across a league, at least in principle. There are two types of salary caps, soft and hard. A soft cap, such as was in place from 1983 until 1999 in the NBA, does very little to promote balance. Under this system, NBA teams were allowed to sign new players up to the value of the cap and

---

[15]Michael R. Butler, "Competitive Balance in Major League Baseball," *American Economist*, v. 39, no. 2 (Fall 1995), pp. 46–50.

then re-sign their own free agents in excess of the cap figure, a provision that became known as the "Larry Bird exemption," as it was first used by the Boston Celtics in order to re-sign their star player in 1983. At that time, the Celtics were loaded with stars, and a hard cap would have meant that the Celtics would have had to break up this very popular team in order to re-sign Larry Bird. To avoid this, the league softened the cap, permitting the Celtics to keep their team intact. The result was that teams routinely spent much more than the salary cap, and competitive balance was not improved. In fact, the within-season standard deviation of winning percentages actually rose consistently through the soft-cap era, indicating a decrease in competitive balance.[16]

A hard salary cap, such as the one currently in force in the NFL, limits any one team's ability to sign a large number of free agents because it provides only a few exceptions (such as for injuries) to the salary limit. Going back to the earlier example about the Pacers' star guard, if the Lakers are already at their salary cap limit, the value they place on the Pacers' guard is irrelevant. They cannot offer him a contract unless they drop other players from the roster. If strictly enforced, these payroll limits would prevent wealthy teams from stockpiling talent. Enforcement is not a trivial component here, as the players union reported that in 1995, as many as 26 teams used loopholes in the salary cap language to spend in excess of the cap in the NFL. Although some research supports the idea that a hard salary cap improves competitive balance, the lack of a hard salary cap in baseball, English soccer, and ice hockey, and strategic maneuvering to circumvent the letter or spirit of the salary cap make empirical testing difficult.

In addition to exceeding salary caps, teams frequently undermine their effectiveness by restructuring their players' contracts (e.g., deferring bonus payments) in order to obey the letter of the salary cap regulations while violating them in spirit. For example, some NBA teams that were close to the salary cap exploited the Larry Bird exemption to attract free agents by signing them to a low salary for one year and then re-signing them to a much higher salary a year later. The Portland Trailblazers were the first to use this provision—over the protests of the NBA commissioner's office—in 1993, when they signed Chris Dudley away from the New Jersey Nets. The Miami Heat later used the same tactic to lure Alonzo Mourning away from the Charlotte Hornets. The NBA owners tried unsuccessfully to curb this practice in the 1995 collective bargaining agreement. Although they failed to institute a hard salary cap covering all players in the 1995 agreement, the owners were able to institute a rookie salary cap. The larger problem of the loophole in the overall team cap remained (under which Michael Jordan alone virtually exhausted the Chicago Bulls' salary cap) and was a major factor in the hard line taken by the NBA in the 1998 contract negotiations. The impact of the more restrictive 1999 collective bargaining agreement on the NBA will not be fully felt for several years. Most players in the NBA have multiyear contracts that are "grandfathered" (exempt from) the new agreement. Until the new provisions that set individual salary caps cover all players, it will be impossible to measure their

---

[16]Andrew Zimbalist, "Competitive Balance in Sports Leagues: An Introduction," *Journal of Sports Economics*, v. 3, no. 2 (May 2002), pp. 111–121.

full impact. Anecdotally, there is evidence that it will cause salaries to fall. For example, Juwan Howard signed a contract with the Orlando Magic worth approximately $5.9 million per year, a dramatic decrease from his prior contract with the Washington Wizards, which was valued at approximately $15 million per year, despite no decrease in his productivity.

The Draft

Despite its curious origins, all leagues claim that the reverse-order draft is vital to preserve competitive balance. In theory, teams that finish last choose the best available players and have the best chance to improve. Unfortunately, several factors limit the effectiveness of drafts. The biggest obstacle is the uncertainty over whether and when a player will make significant contributions to the team. Thus, the draft highlights the managerial skill of the team. Some teams consistently finish last because their management and coaching staff do a poor job of identifying or developing talented players. High draft picks do such teams little good.[17] In some sports, such as baseball, players chosen in the draft are usually several years away from being ready to play in the major leagues. For some positions in football, the players in them undergo extensive training before it is apparent how well they will perform. Thus, even if they choose the right players, the weakest teams may see improvement only with a significant lag.

Managerial skill also plays a role in whether the team ever uses the draft picks to which it is entitled. Skillful trading of draft picks may garner teams more talent than it could have obtained through the draft, while missteps may doom it to years of mediocrity. The NBA has attempted to reduce the problems caused by bad managerial decision making by restricting the number of first-round picks that teams can trade. An added problem is that even if a team selects the "right" player, that player may be unwilling to play for the team that picked him. This happened when Steve Francis, a star guard for the University of Maryland, refused to play for the Vancouver Grizzlies, who had selected him in the 1999 NBA draft. Unable to force Francis to sign, the Grizzlies traded him to the Houston Rockets for players that most observers agree provided the Grizzlies with less than equal value.

In a related problem, draft rules may not square with league-wide profit maximization. If players are chosen based on their productivity so that the most productive players are chosen first, then players chosen later in the draft should be worth less to the teams that choose them. The problem with this reasoning is that value of a player to his team is the combination of marginal productivity and the value of that added output to the team. Because a player's marginal revenue product is determined by both the player's marginal product and the marginal revenue of his output, players are generally not assigned (drafted) in a profit-maximizing way. For example, a player who is drafted by a small-market team may have a lower market value than a player selected later in the draft by a large-market team even though the player drafted by the small-market team is more productive. If the league assigned players to teams in a profit-maximizing way instead of

---

[17]See, for example, R. Hoffer, "The Loss Generation," *Sports Illustrated*, April 17, 2000, pp. 56–59.

through a reverse-order draft, it would begin by matching the player–team combination that creates the highest marginal revenue product, and then the second highest, and so on. Although this may be profit-maximizing, it is likely that it would be so politically unpopular with fans and small-market owners that it could never become policy (even though according to the Coase Theorem, players will end up distributed this way anyway).

Finally, the reverse-order draft gives teams an incentive to lose late in the season with the hope of improving their draft position.[18] The NBA lottery system, wherein the last-place finishing team is no longer guaranteed the first choice, was created specifically to prevent teams from intentionally losing games near the end of the season to ensure a good draft position.

Revenue Sharing and Luxury Taxes

As was discussed in Chapters 3 and 4, professional sports share revenue in a variety of ways. To equalize teams' ability to pay for talent, leagues can stipulate that national television contract revenue, gate revenue (in some sports), and licensing revenue are shared. They can also tax teams that overspend and distribute those funds to low-revenue teams (as in baseball and basketball). Previous chapters have shown that the primary motivation for such revenue sharing is league-wide economic stability, not competitive balance. Revenue sharing can affect competitive balance if the teams that are net recipients of funds (that receive more funds than without revenue sharing) use the additional money to improve the quality of their teams. If those teams simply pocket the additional revenues they receive, revenue sharing cannot improve competitive balance. To date, there is no strong empirical evidence that revenue sharing does equalize competition. It remains to be seen whether the new, more generous sharing formulas in baseball will increase competitive balance.

---

[18]For more information on this phenomenon, see Beck A. Taylor and Justin G. Trogdon, "Losing to Win: Tournament Incentives in the National Basketball Association," *Journal of Labor Economics,* v. 20, no. 1 (January 2002), pp. 23–41.

BUD SELIG

BIOGRAPHICAL *Sketch*

Selig listened and questioned and murmured empathetically, all of the things he did best.

—JOHN HELYAR[1]

Perhaps no person symbolizes the struggle over competitive balance more than baseball Commissioner Alan H. ("Bud") Selig. To his supporters, Selig is a hero of the underdog. To his detractors, Selig is simply out of his depth. Whether admiring him or hating him, however, no one disagrees that Selig is motivated by a devotion to his home state of Wisconsin with a deep love of baseball.

Selig's Wisconsin roots run deep. Born in Milwaukee, he graduated from the University of Wisconsin at Madison in 1956 and, after serving in the military for two years, joined his father's automobile business. Business proved so good that, when major league baseball came to Milwaukee, Selig was able to act on his love of baseball by becoming a stockholder in the Milwaukee Braves. Selig's ties, however, were to the *Milwaukee* Braves. When the team moved to Atlanta in 1965, Selig promptly sold his stock and formed a group dedicated to bringing a new team to Milwaukee. His efforts bore fruit when the Seattle Pilots, a badly financed expansion team, went bankrupt after the 1970 season. Selig immediately bought the team for $10.8 million and moved it to Milwaukee.

With Selig as their president, the Brewers gained a reputation as an exemplary organization, and the team came within a game of winning the 1982 World Series. The Brewers' performance on and off the field led Selig to play a growing role in the governance of Major League Baseball's affairs. When the owners forced Fay Vincent to resign as commissioner in 1992, Selig, as chairman of the owners' executive council, effectively took over the duties of commissioner. For the next six years, Selig walked a tightrope, serving the interests of all of baseball while working to advance the interests of his own Milwaukee Brewers. Finally, in July 1998, Selig's fellow owners elected him as commissioner. Selig then put his holdings in the Brewers into a blind trust and turned operations of the Brewers to his daughter Wendy Selig-Preib.

Selig's popularity with his fellow owners and his insistence on consensus among the team owners has brought unprecedented tranquility among the owners and a cohesion that has enabled him to introduce a variety of innovations designed to bring greater excitement to the game. Under his tenure, baseball raised the number of divisions per league from two to three, increasing the number of teams entering the postseason. The number was further increased by the introduction of a "wildcard" playoff team (which won both the 2002 and 2003 World Series). He also oversaw a greater consolidation of the American and National Leagues, whose war of the early 1900s did not fully end until Selig brought both leagues under the authority of the commissioner's office in 2000.

Most importantly, by bringing the often-fractious owners together, Selig reversed a trend of over 20 years. Under previous commissioners, all labor stoppages had effectively ended with the owners' capitulating. The 1994–95 strike effectively ended in a draw, with neither side achieving its aims. In the near strike of 2002, the ownership actually succeeded in forcing the players association to blink and to approve a revenue-sharing plan and luxury tax that it had bitterly opposed. This marked ownership's first outright victory in negotiations since the first dispute in 1972.

Despite these successes, Selig's tenure has not been without controversy. Some critics have accused him of unduly favoring small-market teams in general

➡

and his own Milwaukee Brewers in particular. They cite, for example, his refusal to enforce limits on the amount of debt a team could carry as long as the Brewers were deeply in debt (up to 97 percent of the team's value by some estimates) and reversing himself only after the Brewers had secured a new ballpark and significantly reduced their debt burden.

Critics also point to Selig's threat in the winter of 2001 to "contract" two teams, generally assumed to be the Montreal Expos and Minnesota Twins. While the Expos were in genuinely dire straits, many saw darker motives behind the threat against the Twins. Some claimed that contraction was nothing more than a heavy-handed attempt to secure public financing for a new ballpark in Minneapolis and to intimidate the players association while the owners and players were negotiating a new contract. Some also construed it as a way to improve the finances of the Milwaukee franchise by eliminating a significant geographic rival. Finally, some felt that if the league bought out the Twins at more than market value and then shut them down, it would represent a payback of a secret loan that the Twins' owner had made to the Brewers in 1995, a loan that apparently violated League Rule 20(c), which prohibits loans among owners without the express consent of the commissioner and the other owners. Former Commissioner Vincent has called the loan "treacherous," while

Drayton McLane, the owner of the Houston Astros has claimed that it was "honest and ethical."

Even Selig's victories over the players association came at a large cost. In particular, the 1994–95 stoppage caused the cancellation of the 1994 World Series, something that two world wars had failed to do. Selig's awkward declaration that the 2002 All-Star Game was a tie (due to both leagues' having exhausted their bullpens) created further embarrassment at what should have been a celebration of baseball.

Because of his controversial record, some see Bud Selig as a man who saved the game. Others feel that he was ill suited to be anything other than the owner of a small-market team. Whatever one's opinion of him, few can deny that he has had a greater impact on the game than almost all his predecessors as commissioner.

[1]John Helyar, *Lords of the Realm* (1994), p. 505.

Sources: Associated Press, "MLB Official Says 'Nothing Improper' About 1995 Loan," ESPN Baseball at http://espn.go.com/mlb/news/2002/0108/1307601.html, January 9, 2002; Anonymous, "Bud Selig," BaseballLibrary.com at http://www.baseballlibrary.com/baseballlibrary/ballplayers/S/ Selig_Bud.stm; Anonymous, "Alan H. 'Bud' Selig" Commissioners at http://mlb.mlb.com/NASApp/mlb/mlb/history/mlb_history_people_profile.jsp?section=bio&persontype=com&personid=9

SUMMARY

In order for a league to be financially successful in the long run, there must be a semblance of even competition among teams. That said, it is unlikely, given that the value of a win is much greater in large cities, that leagues would maximize revenue from perfect parity across teams and would likely do better to have better teams in cities where demand for the sport is greatest.

There are a variety of methods to measure and analyze competitive balance both within a single season and across seasons. Within-season measures focus on the dispersion of winning percentages across the league between the best and worst teams. Across-season measures tend to focus on turnover of standings. Because fans are concerned about both types of balance, it is not possible to choose a single measure of competitive balance, and instead a measure based on the type of balance under study must be considered.

Attempts to alter competitive balance using systems such as revenue sharing, salary caps, and drafts are currently in place in all American professional sports. They do not appear to have a major impact in most cases, although the

NFL is the most balanced league in terms of competition and shares revenue the most aggressively across teams.

DISCUSSION QUESTIONS

1. Why might owners not want perfect parity in a league?
2. How would competitive balance in the American and National Leagues change if baseball owners forced the Yankees to move to Albuquerque, New Mexico?
3. What do you believe means more to fans, having a chance to win the championship once in a while or being competitive every year?
4. Should leagues have hard salary caps that teams cannot exceed under any circumstances?
5. Why might the players unions not want owners to enact competitive-balance enhancing measures?
6. Most leagues have about 30 teams. As a fan, would you be willing to endure 29 losing seasons if you were guaranteed a championship in the 30th?

PROBLEMS

5.1 Suppose, as an owner, you could leave the highly competitive league (in terms of closeness of contests) that you currently play in and enter a league that assured that your team would never lose again. Would you want to do so? Why or why not?

5.2 Explain how the law of diminishing returns provides a natural tendency toward competitive balance.

5.3 Suppose in a six-team league, the winning percentages were as follows at the end of the season. Team A: .750, Team B: .600, Team C: .500, Team D: .500, Team E: .400, Team F: .250. Compute the standard deviation of winning percentages.

5.4 In question 3, suppose each team plays a 50-game schedule. Compute the "ideal" benchmark standard deviation based on equal playing strength, and the ratio of the actual to the ideal.

5.5 If the NFL increased its schedule from 16 games to 30, what would the new benchmark ideal standard deviation be (assuming equal playing strength)?

5.6 What is the main prediction of the Coase Theorem with respect to free agency and competitive balance?

5.7 Which would be more effective for increasing the level of competitive balance in baseball, a hard salary cap, or a 50-50 gate revenue-sharing plan? Why?

5.8 Suppose that over five seasons, the order of finish for five teams in the West League and the East League are as follows. Use the HHI to determine which league has better competitive balance across seasons.

West League Season						East League Season				
1	**2**	**3**	**4**	**5**		**1**	**2**	**3**	**4**	**5**
A	A	A	E	E		A	B	C	D	E
B	B	D	D	D		E	A	A	A	A
C	C	C	C	C		C	B	D	E	D
D	D	B	B	B		B	D	B	B	B
E	E	E	A	A		D	E	E	C	C

5.9 If you were a fan of team A, which set of distributions shown in the previous question (West or East) would you prefer? Why?

5.10 If, as commissioner of professional baseball, you could make one change in the current league rules with the goal of increasing competitive balance as much as possible, what change would you make and why?

5.11 Go to the official MLB website (http://www.mlb.com) and check the order of finish in the American League East for the 1997–2003 seasons. What is the between-season variation for this league over this time span?

APPENDIX 5A

Two Additional Ways to Measure Competitive Balance: The Lorenz Curve and the Markov Chain Method

In the body of the chapter, we introduced several ways to measure competitive balance. Depending on the literature that you read on competitive balance, you may encounter others. In this Appendix, we cover two additional methods for measuring competitive balance: the Lorenz curve and the Markov chain.

The Lorenz curve is most often found in studies of income inequality, as it was originally designed for this purpose and can be used to easily summarize how close a group of people (such as the citizens of a nation) are to perfect income equality. In Chapter 8, we will see an application of the Lorenz curve to athlete salaries in individual sports. Here, we apply the Lorenz curve concept to team success over a fixed time period. The Lorenz curve is a cumulative distribution of observations as measured against a variable of interest. Sports economists have adapted the Lorenz curve to show how near or far a league is from perfectly balanced competition over a given period of time by measuring the percentage of teams that have won championships over a given number of years.

To see how the Lorenz curve works, suppose that a league has five teams. With perfectly equal competition, we would expect each team to win 5 championships each over a 25-year period. Put in cumulative terms, 20 percent of the teams (1 team in this case) would win 20 percent of the titles (5). Continuing, 40 percent of teams (2) would win 40 percent of the titles, and so on, until we reach 100 percent of the teams have won 100 percent of the titles. Such a distribution of winning would result in the Lorenz curve in Figure 5A.1. In this case, the curve is not a curve at all but a straight 45-degree line that now serves as the benchmark for perfect equality.

If we change the distribution of wins in our hypothetical league, we can see how the curve shifts. When all teams were equally successful, it did not matter in what order we recorded the teams' performance. When championship titles are not distributed equally, we form the cumulative distribution by arranging the observations such that we begin with the team that won the fewest and continue to the team that won the most. Suppose instead of perfect equality that the number of wins over the 25 years under consideration were as shown in Table 5A.1. The far-left column shows the cumulative distributions we would expect under perfect equality.

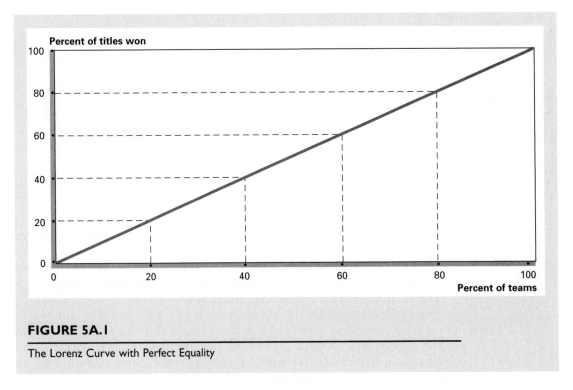

FIGURE 5A.1

The Lorenz Curve with Perfect Equality

Figure 5A.2 shows the distribution of titles from Table 5A.1 as well as the line of perfect equality. As you can see, when competition is unbalanced, the line bows downwards, away from the line of perfect equality. The more unequal is competition, the more the line will be bowed downwards. Thus, the Lorenz curve is useful to compare relative equality of competition from one time period to another or from one sport to another.[19]

Table 5A.1

Distribution of Championships Over 25 Years

Team	Number of Titles	Cum. Percentage	Perfect Equality
A	1	4.0 = (1/25)*100	20
B	2	12.0 = (3/25)*100	40
C	5	32.0 = (8/25)*100	60
D	7	60.0 = (15/25)*100	80
E	10	100 = (25/25)*100	100

[19]A more quantitative basis of comparison from the same data would be to construct a statistic known as the GINI coefficient, which measures the ratio of the area between the line of perfect equality and the Lorenz curve, and the area under the lower triangle. The closer the GINI coefficient is to zero, the closer the league is to perfect equality. A GINI coefficient of 1.0 would indicate perfect inequality (one team wins all of the championships).

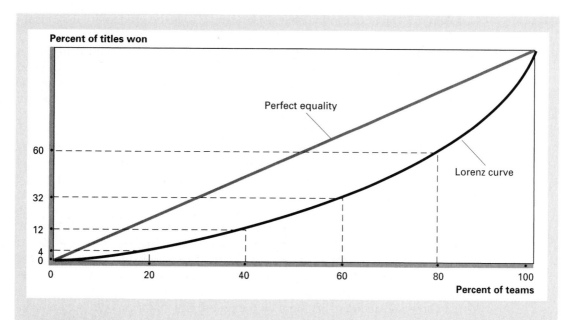

FIGURE 5A.2

The Lorenz Curve with an Unequal Distribution of Wins

A relatively new measure of interseason balance is a new application of an existing technique known as the **Markov process**. A Markov process shows the probability that a person or group changes in some particular way from one period to the next. Hadley, Ciecka, and Krautmann (2003) have applied this technique to baseball to evaluate competitive balance in the 1990s. They use the Markov process to measure the probability that a given team's performance in one season depends on its performance in the previous season. Their model is structured such that a team can be in one of three "states": winner, contender (within six games of qualifying for the playoffs), and loser (a team that finishes more than six games out of the playoffs).[20] At the end of each season, every team must be in one of these three states. The appeal of this model is it is very simple to compute and interpret results, yet it is highly revealing.

From a competitive balance standpoint, we are most interested in the probability that a team's quality changes (i.e., it moves from one state to another over time). We can calculate a set of three "transitional probabilities" for each group (winners, contenders, and losers). For example, P_{WW} is the probability that a team will go from being a winner in one season to a winner in the next season, P_{WC} is the probability that a team will go from being a winner in one

---

[20]Larry Hadley, James Ciecka, and Anthony Krautmann, "Competitive Balance in the Aftermath of the 1994 Players' Strike," presented at the 2003 meetings of the Western Economic Association, Denver, C.O. The authors acknowledge that the choice of six games back at the breakpoint between contender and loser is somewhat arbitrary, but it indicates that a contending team had a chance to be a winner up until the last week of the season.

season to a contender in the next season, and P_{WL} is the probability that a team will go from being a winner in one season to a loser in the next season.

If team quality is highly variable from year to year, teams would change from one state to a different state more frequently than if some teams were usually good while others were usually bad. As a benchmark for competitive balance, the authors choose a world where a team's finish in one year has no impact on how it will do the next year. For example, a team that was a winner this year has a probability of one third, or .33, of being a winner, a contender, or a loser the next year. Table 5A.2 shows the states and probabilities that exist for the three-state baseball model. With perfect balance, each of these probabilities would equal .33.

To see how transitional probabilities are calculated, let's assume that we are interested in the competitive balance for a 3-team league over a 10-year period. If, in 5 of the 10 years, the winner repeated the following year, $P_{WW} = 5/10 = .50$. If in 3 of the 10 years, the winner dropped to being a contender, $P_{WC} = 3/10 = .30$. In the other two years, the contender transitioned to loser, $P_{WL} = 2/10 = .20$.

Table 5A.3 shows the changes in the transitional probabilities that occurred in the aftermath of the 1994 players' strike, a period widely cited as being characterized by a marked decline in competitive balance.

These probabilities shed light on the probability that teams can become winners at some time over a period of seasons and whether those probabilities have changed over time. The table shows that very few of the state probabilities are close to 0.33. It also shows that P_{WW} increases markedly in the post–1994 strike era, from 0.20 to 0.55 while P_{WL} decreases from 0.61 to 0.34. Both of these statistics indicate a decrease in interseason competitive balance in the poststrike era.

Table 5A.2

Conditional Probabilities for a Model with Three States

Winners	Contenders	Losers
P_{WW}	P_{CW}	P_{LW}
P_{WC}	P_{CC}	P_{LC}
P_{WL}	P_{CL}	P_{LL}

Table 5A.3

Markov Conditional Probabilities for Major League Baseball in the 1994 and 1994 Era

Transitional Probabilities	Pre–1994	Post–1994
P_{WW}	0.20	0.55
P_{WC}	0.18	0.11
P_{WL}	0.61	0.34
P_{CW}	0.27	0.33
P_{CC}	0.14	0.11
P_{CL}	0.59	0.56
P_{LW}	0.12	0.14
P_{LC}	0.12	0.08
P_{LL}	0.76	0.78

Source: Hadley, Ciecka, and Krautmann, "Competitive Balance in the Aftermath of the 1994 Players' Strike" (2003).

PART THREE

Public Finance and Sports

CHAPTER 6

The Public Finance of Sports: The Market for Sports Franchises

[T]hey ain't going nowhere 'cause they're the **Brooklyn** Dodgers.
—USHER AT EBBETS FIELD[1]

In sports today the Phoenix Cardinals, who used to be the St. Louis Cardinals, took a seemingly insurmountable three-touchdown lead into the fourth quarter of their game against the Indianapolis Colts, who used to be the Baltimore Colts—not to be confused with the Baltimore Ravens, who used to be the Cleveland Browns—only to see the game slip from their grasp when, with three seconds left in the game, the Colts announced that they were moving to Albuquerque to become a professional hockey team.
—DAVE BARRY[2]

INTRODUCTION: HOW WALTER O'MALLEY CHANGED THE LANDSCAPE OF SPORTS

One day in the late 1950s, Jack Newfield and Pete Hamill, both reporters for New York newspapers, discussed writing an article called "The Ten Worst Human Beings Who Ever Lived." On a whim, each wrote the names of the three people he regarded as "the all-time worst" on a napkin. To their amazement, they listed the same three names: Adolf Hitler, Joseph Stalin, and Walter O'Malley.[3]

---

[1]Quoted in Michael Danielson, *Home Team: Professional Sport and the American Metropolis* (Princeton, N.J.: Princeton University Press, 1997), p. xvii.

[2]Dave Barry, *Dave Barry Turns 50* (New York: Random House, 1999), p. 62.

[3]Geoffrey Ward and Kenneth Burns, *Baseball: An Illustrated History* (New York: Alfred A. Knopf, 1994), pp. 351–352.

Since Newfield and Hamill lived in a nation with fresh memories of the Second World War and new worries over the Cold War, their inclusion of Hitler and Stalin was not what caused their surprise. Instead, it was their mutual summoning of the third name. Unlike his companions on the list, O'Malley's crime against humanity did not involve mass murder or show trials. Instead, he changed the landscape of professional sports forever by moving the Dodgers from Brooklyn to Los Angeles.

While their move was the most notorious, the Dodgers were not the first team to change cities. Teams entered, exited, and moved so frequently in the early years of all professional leagues that they were reluctant to erect permanent facilities. As a general rule, the moves were from small towns to large ones. The NFL likes to reminisce about its small-town, midwestern origins, but professional football did not become financially stable until teams in major cities such as Detroit, Chicago, and Washington, D.C., replaced teams in small towns such as Portsmouth, Ohio; Decatur, and Duluth.[4] Sports leagues generally achieved financial stability only after they located franchises in the nation's largest cities. In fact, unfavorable demographics proved the undoing of entire leagues, as seen by the demise of baseball's American Association in the 1890s, the National Basketball League in the 1940s, and the American Basketball League in the 1990s.

The "Golden Age" of baseball marked the longest such period of franchise stability. Between 1903, when the Baltimore Orioles left for New York to become the Highlanders (and later the Yankees), and 1953, when the Braves left Boston for Milwaukee, no Major League Baseball team entered, left, or changed cities. Baseball's growing prosperity led to the construction of its historic ballparks, starting with Shibe Park in Philadelphia and Forbes Field in Pittsburgh in 1909 and followed a year later by Comiskey Park in Chicago. The construction boom effectively ended with Yankee Stadium in 1923. Between the 1920s and the 1950s, only one new baseball stadium was built.

The Braves' move to Milwaukee led few to believe that this golden era was at an end. The Boston Braves; the Philadelphia Athletics, who moved to Kansas City in 1954 (and then to Oakland in 1968); and the St. Louis Browns, who moved to Baltimore and were rechristened the Orioles in 1953, were all neglected stepsisters in cities whose hearts belonged to the Red Sox, Phillies, and Cardinals, respectively. When the Braves left Boston, few fans noticed and fewer still mourned their loss. In their first nine games in Milwaukee, the Braves drew as many fans as they had attracted in the entire preceding year.[5]

Unlike the franchises that moved in the early 1950s, the Brooklyn Dodgers played second fiddle to no one. In the 11 years prior to their move, from 1947 to 1957, the Dodgers were the most successful and most profitable team in the National League. The value of the Dodgers, however, could not be measured

---

[4]See Danielson, *Home Team* (1997), pp. 20–24; and Charles Euchner, *Playing the Field* (Baltimore: Johns Hopkins University Press, 1993), p. 4. The NFL Hall of Fame is in Canton, Ohio, home of the long-defunct Canton Bulldogs.

[5]Neil J. Sullivan, *The Dodgers Move West* (New York: Oxford University Press, 1987), p. 42.

solely in dollars and cents. They were "a cultural totem" for the residents of Brooklyn, a rallying point for those who felt scorned by the wealthier, more sophisticated Manhattanites.[6] It was this sense of loss—and the sense of powerlessness that accompanied it—that prompted the sportswriters to elevate O'Malley to the elite company of Stalin and Hitler.

To O'Malley, the issue was a simple matter of economics. While the Dodgers did well in Brooklyn, he realized that the Dodgers would earn even more if they had Los Angeles (and, at the time, all of Southern California) to themselves. In effect, O'Malley recognized the difference between accounting and economic profits that we emphasized in Chapter 2. Although extremely profitable, the Dodgers averaged somewhat over 1.5 million fans in their last decade in Brooklyn. After moving to Los Angeles, they set new standards in attendance, frequently drawing more than 3 million fans in a season.

Even when teams do not move, they have frequently used the threat of a move to coerce their home cities to subsidize or build new facilities. Public funds often go to people who have little need for financial support. In Chapter 3, we showed how many team owners are extraordinarily wealthy. Their wealth, however, does not stop them from relying on public funds for their facilities. Table 6.1 shows how much public money went to provide facilities for owners who were included in the *Forbes 400* list of the wealthiest people in America.

Moreover, cities that appear to have far more pressing needs have spent considerable sums on sports facilities. Over the course of the 1990s, Cleveland—a city whose school system had gone into receivership—committed itself to spending over a billion dollars financing facilities for its baseball, basketball, and football teams.[7] Even when the electorate turns down funding in referenda, public officials sometimes go to extraordinary lengths to subvert the electoral process in order to get the funding approved. After the residents of Phoenix voted against public funding for a new stadium, the Arizona State Legislature approved a bill that gave authority to raise money for a new facility to the Maricopa County Board of Supervisors.[8] Such maneuvering suggests that the public sector will be underwriting sports franchises for a long time to come.

In this chapter, we explore the power that team owners have held over cities and the impact of that power on the decisions cities and franchises make. Along the way, we consider the following:

- That teams have profited from stadium deals, though these profits seem to be falling for baseball

---

[6]See Sullivan, *The Dodgers Move West* (1987), p. 15; and Danielson, *Home Team* (1997), p. 9. Manhattan was the home of the Dodgers' archrivals, the New York Giants, who, ironically, moved to San Francisco when the Dodgers left for Los Angeles.

[7]In the fall of 2000, Philadelphia committed itself to a $1 billion project for new facilities for the Phillies and Eagles.

[8]For details on the birth of the Arizona Diamondbacks, see Len Sherman, *Big League, Big Time* (New York: Pocket Books, 1998).

Table 6.1

Owners' Net Worth and Public Funding of Facilities

Name	Net Worth[a]	Facility	% Public Funding
Paul Allen	$28,200	Seahawks Stadium	70%
		Rose Garden	13%
Philip Anschutz[b]	$9,600	Staples Center	22%
Alfred Lerner[c]	$4,900	Cleveland Browns Stadium	70%
Micky Arison	$4,600	American Airlines Arena	59%
Preston Tisch	$2,600	Giants Stadium	100%
William Davidson	$2,200	Palace at Auburn Hills	0%
		St. Pete Times Forum	62%
William and Nancy Laurie	$2,100	Savvis Center	15%
Carl Pohlad	$2,000	Metrodome	91%
H. Wayne Huizenga	$2,000	Pro Player Stadium	10%
Glen Taylor	$1,800	Target Center	100%
Richard DeVos	$1,700	T.D. Waterhouse Centre	100%
Arthur Blank	$1,600	Georgia Dome	100%
Mark Cuban	$1,400	American Airlines Center	42%
Billy Joe "Red" McCombs	$1,400	Metrodome	91%
William Clay Ford, Jr.	$1,200	Ford Field	35%
Stanley Kroenke	$1,100	Pepsi Center	3%
Robert McLane, Jr.	$1,100	Minute Maid Park	68%
Charles Wang	$925	Nassau Veterans Coliseum	100%
Alexander Spanos	$870	Qualcomm Stadium	100%
Jerral "Jerry" Jones	$850	Texas Stadium	83%

[a]In millions
[b]Co-owner with Edward Roski, Jr. (Net worth: $900 million)
[c]Died during 2002 season
Source: "The Forbes 400" at http://www.Forbes.com; National Sports Law Institute, "Facility Update Charts," Sports Facility Reports, v. 3, no. 2, at http://law.marquette.edu/cgi-bin/site.pl?2130pageID=470.

- That market forces give sports leagues the power to command financial support from cities
- That when cities bid for the Olympics or other special events, they often overspend
- How the market for sports franchises has affected the character and location of sports facilities.

6.1   THE COMPETITION FOR TEAMS AND THE VALUE OF A NEW STADIUM

In Chapter 4, we demonstrated how professional sports teams and leagues exert monopoly power over fans and the media. Here, we show that they hold similar monopoly positions over entire cities. Unlike fans and the media, who compete in markets for access to teams, cities compete over the right to host a franchise.

Many municipal government officials believe that playing host to a professional franchise will generate economic growth in their city. Their demand for a franchise stems from the perceived financial benefits of hosting a team as well as intangible benefits, such as the pride in being considered a "big league" city.

If the politicians are correct, and cities do benefit from hosting a franchise, then they might be better off buying a franchise outright. As owners, cities would not have to worry about whether the team would move as soon as its lease was up. Professional leagues, however, have gone to considerable lengths to prevent cities from owning franchises. Major League Baseball owners, for example, blocked Joan Kroc's attempt to give the Padres to San Diego after she inherited the team from her late husband. The NFL's bylaws specifically require that teams have an individual owner. The Green Bay Packers are an often-cited exception to this rule. Contrary to popular opinion, however, the Packers are not municipally owned. They are a publicly held corporation. As such, they recently threatened to leave Green Bay if the city did not accede to their demands for stadium improvements.[9]

Cities also differ from consumers in that they do not participate in a formal market in which they pay directly for a good or service. Instead, they pay for the right to host teams by building them facilities, providing them with revenue guarantees, and allowing them to capture revenue from such sources as parking, concessions, and luxury boxes.

Cities could provide the same inducements with the more traditional market transaction of paying a fixed sum directly to the franchise. While such behavior might prove more efficient, city officials do not find such payments politically feasible. Instead, the city may garner political support for the project by employing local contractors and construction workers in constructing the facility. (We explore such political behavior in Chapter 7.) Moreover, city officials seem to be subject to an "edifice complex," a bias for "high visibility projects with political payoff, such as sites and structures."[10]

During the 1990s, a wave of "retro" stadiums seemed to bring a new source of prosperity to baseball franchises. The first two franchises to tap this trend, the Baltimore Orioles and the Cleveland Indians, continue to serve as examples to other teams, though, as we shall see, the example of the 1990s may be misleading.

Eli Jacobs bought the Orioles in 1988 for $70 million. Oriole Park at Camden Yards opened 4 years later at a cost of over $200 million.[11] The stadium features

---

[9]They are, however, the only team that does not have a single managing partner. See Joanna Cagan and Neil deMause, *Field of Schemes* (Monroe, M.E.: Common Courage Press, 1998), pp. 93–94 and 191–192; and Richard Jones and Don Walker, "Packer Boss Warns of Move if Stadium Doesn't Get Upgrade," *Milwaukee Sentinel Journal,* March 1, 2000, at http://www.jsonline.com/packer/news/feb00/lambeau01022900.asp; and Barry Lorge, "Kroc Wanted to Give Padres to City," *San Diego Union-Tribune,* July 29, 1990, p. H1.

[10]Arthur Johnson, *Minor League Baseball and Local Economic Development* (Urbana: University of Illinois Press, 1995), p. 2. For additional motivations, see John Siegfried and Andrew Zimbalist, "The Economics of Sports Facilities and Their Construction," *Journal of Economic Perspectives,* v. 14, no. 3 (Summer 2000), pp. 95–114.

[11]Maryland spent $99 million for the land and $105.4 million for the stadium itself.

72 luxury boxes that lease for up to $175,000. The Orioles' 30-year lease is so favorable that, when Jacobs went bankrupt due to the failure of other business ventures and was forced to auction off the team in 1994, he was able to sell it for $173 million, almost a 150 percent profit. Moreover, the single most valuable asset listed at the auction was the team's lease.[12]

The Cleveland Indians provide an even more extreme example. In 1993, the year before Jacobs Field opened, the Indians were among the least valuable franchises in baseball, worth an estimated $81 million. By 1996, the team's value had risen 54 percent to $125 million.[13] The growth in value continued through the 1990s, culminating in the sale of the Indians for a then-record $323 million in early 2000.

While Jacobs Field clearly contributed to the increase in the Indians' value, the impact of the new stadium is clouded by the upturn in the Indians' fortunes in the mid-1990s, highlighted by their appearances in the 1995 and 1997 World Series. One could reasonably attribute some of the franchise's increased value to its improved performance on the field, an upturn that began in 1993, the year before Jacobs Field opened, when attendance rose from 1.22 million to 2.18 million. More recently, as the Indians' performance on the field has declined, so have attendance and revenue. In 2002, attendance at Jacobs Field had fallen to 2.62 million, down from a high of 3.47 million in 1998.

The link between a new stadium and prosperity has become more tenuous in general in recent years. Since the initial success of the Orioles and Indians, the impact of a new stadium on attendance has steadily declined. Table 6.2 shows that only 2 of the 12 franchises that have built new facilities since the Baltimore Orioles touched off the building craze in 1992 had higher average attendance in 2003 than they did during their last year in their previous ballpark. In most cases, the percentage decline has been in double figures, and in five cases, it has been over 20 percent.[14]

In addition, the two teams that experienced increases can be considered special cases. The San Francisco Giants went to the World Series in 2002. Such a performance is almost certain to improve attendance regardless of where the team plays. The other team, the Cincinnati Reds, in its first year in Great American Ballpark, drew less than 2.36 million fans. This was "the lowest total for any team playing its first full season in a new ballpark since Toronto . . . in 1989."[15] While disappointing, the lower attendance may not translate into lower revenue, however, as extras such as luxury boxes may still increase team revenue.

---

[12]The Orioles pay the Maryland Sports Authority (MSA) rent of 7 percent of net admission revenues. MSA also receives 7.5 percent of concession revenues, 50 percent of parking receipts, 25 percent of net ballpark advertising revenues, 10 percent of net luxury suite revenues, and 7.5 percent of revenues from club level licenses or membership fees. Data from D. Todd Gruen, ed. *Inside the Ownership of Professional Sports Teams* (Chicago: Team Marketing Report, 2001), p. 70.

[13]Cagan and deMause, *Field of Schemes* (1998), p. 5.

[14]The comparison may be somewhat unfair for the Colorado Rockies, as they previously played at Mile High Stadium, a football facility that held over 76,000 fans.

[15]Eric Fisher, "Reds' Ballpark Honeymoon Cut Short," *Washington Times*, August 3, 2003, p. C3.

Table 6.2

Declining Attendance for Baseball Teams in New Facilities

Team	Year New Stadium Built	Change in Attendance[a]
Baltimore Orioles	1992	-18.6%
Cleveland Indians	1994	-28.1%
Texas Rangers	1994	-4.0%
Colorado Rockies	1995	-50.7%
Atlanta Braves	1997	-30.3%
Houston Astros	2000	-19.8%
San Francisco Giants	2000	+50.5%
Seattle Mariners	2000	-0.2%
Detroit Tigers	2000	-38.5%
Milwaukee Brewers	2001	-13.0%
Pittsburgh Pirates	2001	-22.1%
Cincinnati Reds	2003	+12.2%

[a]Compares 2002 season attendance with season before new stadium was built. Cincinnati figure estimated for 2003 based on partial season attendance.
Source: Bill King, "New Ballparks Sport Old Look: Empty Seats," *Street & Smith's SportsBusiness Journal*, May 26–June 1, 2003, p. 37.

Team values also reflect the declining impact of a new stadium on baseball teams. In 1999, *Forbes* reported that six of the seven most valuable baseball franchises played in facilities built since 1992. That year, the Baltimore Orioles, Cleveland Indians, (Denver) Colorado Rockies, and Seattle Mariners were all more valuable than the Los Angeles Dodgers, Chicago Cubs, or Chicago White Sox. Only the New York Yankees, with their immense media deal, managed to be in this group despite playing in an old stadium. Just three years later, the picture had changed considerably. In 2002, the 4 most valuable franchises (the Yankees, New York Mets, Boston Red Sox, and Dodgers)—and 5 of the most valuable 10 franchises—played in facilities built before 1965.

In contrast, *Forbes* finds that 8 of the 10 most valuable NFL franchises played in facilities built since 1996. Only the Dallas Cowboys, with their 379 luxury boxes, and the Miami Dolphins managed to crack the top 10 despite playing in older facilities. In fact, the value of a new stadium has become so great in the NFL that it threatens to undo the balance in revenues that the league has been so careful to maintain over the years.[16] As we noted in Chapter 3, with the bulk of media revenue shared equally, and gate revenue split 60–40 with the rest of the league, venue revenue is one of the few ways football teams have to add to their own revenue.

While stadium deals no longer ensure riches in all sports, the lack of facilities has been a factor in condemning the NHL to second-rate status. Much of

---

[16]Daniel Kaplan, "Stadiums Tilt NFL's Economic Playing Field," *Street & Smith's SportsBusiness Journal*, May 26–June 1, 2003, p. 1.

the NHL's financial instability is due to its poor TV ratings and resulting low TV revenue, but NHL teams have also suffered from their role as secondary tenants in facilities that cater to NBA teams. That the NHL finds itself in this second-class position is an ironic twist, given that in its early years, the owners of hockey teams invited basketball teams to play in arenas they owned as a way to generate extra revenue on off-nights. Their position today as secondary tenants means that hockey teams frequently face worse financial arrangements than do the basketball teams with whom they often share arenas.[17] It is no surprise that the most profitable hockey teams in the NHL—the New York Rangers, Philadelphia Flyers, Boston Bruins, and Detroit Red Wings—are all primary tenants in their facilities. The Rangers, Bruins, and Flyers have arrangements with Madison Square Garden, the Fleet Center, and the Wachovia Center that are equal or superior to those of their cotenants, the NBA's Knicks, Celtics, and 76ers, while the Red Wings do not share their venue—the Joe Louis Arena—with the NBA's Pistons.

The benefits of a new stadium would not amount to much if the team had to pay rent that was commensurate with the value of the facility. As we see later in the chapter, cities do not charge market rates to their tenants. As a result, much of the impact that new facilities have on teams' profit streams stems from the teams' getting something for nothing. Table 6.3 shows that the burden of financing new facilities abruptly shifted from teams to cities about 50 years ago. Even teams that have supposedly paid for their facilities often benefited from substantial government funding. Pacific Bell Ballpark in San Francisco was widely touted as the first privately funded baseball stadium since the O'Malley family built Dodger Stadium almost 40 years earlier, though the comparison may not be appropriate. Those who cite Dodger Stadium as an example of a privately built ballpark ignore the fact that Los Angeles agreed to almost $5 million in road construction and improvements and donated 300 acres of prime real estate in Chavez Ravine to Walter O'Malley as the site of the new stadium. By contrast, the city of San Francisco paid only $10 million, though it did guarantee a $145 million loan to the team.[18]

Such subsidies are not limited to baseball. The Philadelphia Flyers and 76ers also received substantial implicit subsidies from Philadelphia and Pennsylvania for the construction of the Wachovia Center (originally called the CoreStates Center). Their contributions included the land on which the Center was built, a $6.5 million dollar low-interest loan (originally to have been an outright grant), and $12 million to demolish JFK Stadium, which had stood on the site of the new facility as well as funding to construct a parking lot. Parking also played a role in Boston, where the "privately built" Fleet Center rests atop a

---

[17]See Robert La Franco, "Profits on Ice," *Forbes*, May 5, 1997, pp. 86–89.

[18]Andrew Zimbalist, *Baseball and Billions* (New York: Basic Books, 1992), pp. 125–128; Matthew Freedman, ed., *2000: Inside the Ownership of Professional Sports Teams* (Chicago: Team Marketing Report, 2000), pp. 118–119; and Sullivan, *The Dodgers Move West* (1987), pp. 99–104.

[19]Kenneth Shropshire, *The Sports Franchise Game* (Philadelphia: University of Pennsylvania, 1995), pp. 20–26.

Table 6.3

Patterns in Stadium Expenses 1887–1976

Stadium	Year Opened	Construction Cost	Public Expense
Baker Bowl	1887	$ 1.87	$ 0
Shibe Park	1909	5.84	0
Forbes Field	1909	37.07	0
Comiskey Park	1910	12.53	0
Polo Grounds	1911	4.47	0
Tiger Stadium	1912	8.65	0
Fenway Park	1912	6.31	0
Crosley Field	1912	6.92	0
Ebbets Field	1913	12.56	0
Wrigley Field	1914	4.12	0
Yankee Stadium	1923	30.36	0
County Stadium	1953	31.65	31.65
Metropolitan Stadium	1956	27.64	27.64
Candlestick Park	1960	180.52	180.52
RFK Stadium	1962	119.81	119.81
Dodger Stadium	1962	153.16	26.17
Colt Stadium	1962	11.04	0.00
Shea Stadium	1964	129.08	129.08
Atlanta–Fulton Stadium	1964	99.50	99.50
Astrodome	1965	201.24	201.24
Oakland–Alameda Stadium	1966	132.40	132.40
Busch Memorial Stadium	1966	123.33	123.33
Anaheim Stadium	1966	128.46	128.46
Jack Murphy Stadium	1967	138.48	138.48
Riverfront Stadium	1970	233.76	233.76
Three Rivers Stadium	1970	235.91	235.91
Veterans Stadium	1971	203.89	203.89
Kauffman Stadium	1973	189.05	176.12
Kingdome	1976	195.90	195.90

Figures are for initial construction costs only.
All figures are in millions of 1999 dollars. The table does not include facilities built earlier and later retrofitted to attract a team.
*$100 million in cost overruns are still in dispute.
Sources: Raymond Keating, "Sports Pork," *Policy Analysis,* no. 339 (Washington D.C.: Cato Institute, 1999). Paul Munsey and Corey Suppes, "Ballparks," at http://www.ballparks.com., Mark Rosentraub *Major League Losers,* (New York: Basic Books, 1997).

$100 million publicly built parking lot.[19] In the next section, we explore why teams have been able to extract such large sums from the cities that host them.

6.2 HOW TEAMS EXPLOIT MARKET FORCES

Three market forces play into the hands of professional sports franchises, each of which gives them an advantage in their dealings with cities. We have already encountered one of the forces at work, monopoly power. In Chapters 3 and 4, we explained how professional sports leagues and amateur sports associations exercise the market power that comes with being the only provider of their sport and the only buyer of athletic talent for that sport. We now look more closely at how teams and leagues use their monopoly power to extract the best deal they can from cities.

The second market force also stems from a familiar source. In Chapter 4, we demonstrated how most fans enjoy a consumer surplus when they attend a sporting event and that teams can use price discrimination or personal seat licenses to claim a portion of this surplus for themselves. Like fans, cities can enjoy a surplus from hosting a franchise or event. Leagues and event coordinators have learned to extract the surplus that cities gain from hosting a franchise. They do so by forcing cities to spend more than they would ideally choose to by confronting them with the all-or-nothing choice of either hosting a team full-time or not at all.

The third market force is that under certain circumstances, monopolists can induce consumers to spend more than the good or service is worth to them. Leagues can exploit the uncertainty of cities that bid to host franchises and charge the "winning" city a price that exceeds the value of the franchise. Economists call this paradox—in which the "winning" city is actually worse off than it would have been had it lost the bid—the **winner's curse**.

Leagues, Cities, and Monopoly Power

Leagues have several reasons for wanting to limit the number of teams. Leagues that overexpand become unwieldy and unprofitable. The fear of uncompetitive—and hence unprofitable—teams motivated the National League to set a strict limit of eight teams once it attained monopoly status in the 1890s. Fiscal instability also kept the NFL, NHL, and NBA from expanding until the 1960s. With the moves of franchises in the 1950s—especially those of the Giants and Dodgers to California—leagues discovered a new reason for limiting size. Limiting the number of franchises enables a league to act as a **franchise monopolist** and maximize its members' monopoly profits. By restricting the number of franchises that are available, they can drive up the price cities pay to attract a franchise or to retain one they already have. Donald Fehr, the executive director of the MLBPA, summed up this point of view when he explained the White Sox threat to move to Tampa if Chicago did not build the team a new stadium: "[I]f you put a team in Tampa, [owners such as the Chicago White Sox Jerry] Reinsdorf can't extort money from the city of Chicago by threatening to move to Tampa."[20] In the summer of 2003, MLB felt the impact of overexpansion as it sought a new home for the Montreal Expos. With only two serious candidates—Portland, O.R., and Washington, D.C.—and a weak economy, the bidding war that had marked previous expansions never developed.

---

[20]Quoted in Euchner, *Playing the Field* (1993), p. 24.

Even before World War II, both MLB and the NFL recognized that declining transportation costs and changing population patterns were undermining the traditional location of teams. By the 1940s, it made little economic sense for Los Angeles to have no major league franchises while Boston had two baseball teams and a hockey team. San Francisco had a half million more people in its metropolitan area than St. Louis, but it had no major league sports teams while St. Louis had two baseball teams.[21]

After the war, both MLB and the NFL put franchises on the West Coast, but neither sport did so by expanding the number of franchises. The NFL's Rams moved to Los Angeles from Cleveland in 1946, a departure prompted by the arrival of the Cleveland Browns of the new All-American Football Conference.[22] Baseball had an explicit offer to expand westward when the Pacific Coast League (PCL), a high minor league that had sent stars such as Joe DiMaggio and Ted Williams to MLB, broached the idea of becoming a third major league. The negotiations fell through, however, when MLB, which regarded its own reserve clause as sacrosanct, refused to honor the PCL's contracts with its own players. Instead, MLB chose to allow the Giants and Dodgers to move west, establishing a beachhead on the West Coast and reducing the PCL to truly minor league status.[23]

MLB seemed perfectly content to respond to demographic pressures by rearranging franchises until it undertook the first systematic expansion by a professional sports league in 1961. The new policy, however, did not reflect a change of heart. Instead, it was a direct response to pressure from Congress. Faced with the highly unpopular moves of the Dodgers and Giants and aghast at the impending loss of the Washington Senators to Minneapolis–St. Paul (where they became the Twins), Congress had once again begun to investigate baseball's antitrust exemption. In addition, Branch Rickey, the man who built the great Cardinal teams of the 1930s and Dodger teams of the late 1940s and 1950s, was looking into forming a new league, with two of the flagship teams planned for Houston and New York. Not surprisingly, three of MLB's first four expansion teams were located in Houston, New York, and Washington, D.C.[24] The fourth team, the Los Angeles (later Anaheim) Angels, gave the American League the West Coast presence that it had long coveted.

The NFL's first several expansions also came under duress. As noted in Chapter 4, the NFL had no intention of expanding in the early 1960s until it learned that the fledgling AFL planned to put teams in Dallas and Minneapolis. The AFL also spurred the NFL's second expansion in 1967. This time, however, the motive was peace, not war. The NFL and AFL recognized that their impending

---

[21]See Danielson, *Home Team* (1997), p. 25.

[22]The Rams feared the popularity of a new team headed by the legendary Ohio State coach Paul Brown, who gave his name to the new team. See Jon Morgan, *Glory for Sale: Fans, Dollars, and the New NFL* (Baltimore: Bancroft Press, 1997), p. 59.

[23]See Sullivan, *The Dodgers Move West* (1987), pp. 90–94.

[24]See Zimbalist, *Baseball and Billions* (1992), pp. 16–17; and James Miller, *The Baseball Business: Pursuing Pennants and Profits in Baltimore* (Chapel Hill: University of North Carolina Press, 1990), pp. 78–84.

merger would run afoul of the antitrust laws and requested special legislation that would allow them to merge. In their path stood two powerful legislators from Louisiana, Representative Hale Boggs and Senator Russell Long, who could have delayed or derailed the legislation. Fortunately for the NFL, both men were keen to have an NFL franchise in New Orleans. Not surprisingly, less than two weeks after Congress passed the legislation granting the NFL and AFL the right to merge, the NFL approved the creation of the New Orleans Saints.[25]

Cities sometimes contribute to the monopoly power of teams by committing themselves to projects despite having no corresponding guarantee from the franchise. For example, in May 1990, the residents of Cuyahoga County, which includes Cleveland, voted to approve the construction of a new baseball stadium for the Indians and a new basketball arena for the Cavaliers, who were playing in the Richfield Coliseum in a nearby suburb. Unfortunately for Cuyahoga County, the Indians did not agree to lease terms until December and the Cavaliers did not agree until even later. Worse still, the teams had not even agreed on architectural plans for the new facilities. Having committed themselves to new facilities, the civic leaders forfeited any bargaining power with the franchises. The teams were able to insist on such added features as stadium suites, office complexes, and restaurants, all at no extra charge to them. These add-ons led Jacobs Field to cost about $48 million more than estimated and Gund Arena to cost $73 million more, almost double the arena's estimated cost.

The All-Or-Nothing Demand Curve

While a monopoly has the power to set the price it charges or the quantity that it sells, it generally cannot do both simultaneously. For example, if a monopolist sets the price of its product, consumers' responses determine quantity. They respond to the monopoly price by buying as much of the good or service as they want. The monopoly's power is thus limited by the demand curve that it faces. If, as in Figure 6.1, the monopoly raises its price from p_0 to p_1, it must accept the fact that its sales fall from Q_0 to Q_1. Even the most powerful monopolist generally cannot tell consumers how much to pay *and* how much to buy.

Under certain circumstances, a monopolist can dictate both price and quantity. Foot-long hot dogs at the ballpark or one-pound boxes of Milk Duds at the movie theater may have become something of a tradition, but they are also far bigger than most consumers want to buy. They are, instead, part of an attempt by producers to extract consumer surplus by getting consumers to buy more than they would choose. By not allowing consumers to bring in their own candy, the theaters establish local monopoly power over the sale of candy.[26] Similarly, sports leagues—or individual team owners—exploit their monopoly

---

[25]Morgan, *Glory for Sale* (1997), p. 89; and David Harris, *The League: The Rise and Decline of the NFL* (New York: Bantam Books, 1986), p. 17.

[26]For an alternative interpretation of the behavior of vendors at theaters or arenas, see Steven Landsburg, *The Armchair Economist: Economics and Everyday Life* (New York: Free Press, 1993), pp. 157–167.

FIGURE 6.1

To Sell More, Most Monopolists Must Reduce Price

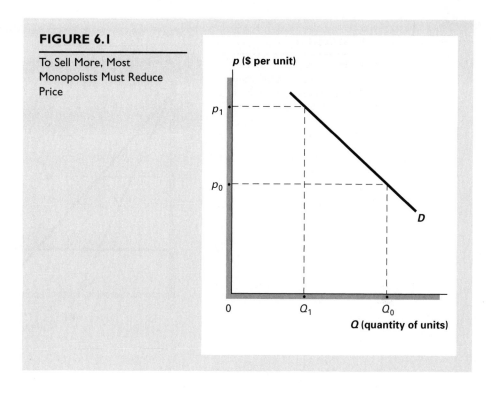

power by auctioning off teams to an array of eager cities. Teams confront cities with an all-or-nothing choice. Since the city cannot choose to host a franchise for a smaller part of a season at a lower overall cost, it must pay the full price or have no franchise at all.

If a sports franchise acted like a typical monopolist, it would charge the city the monopoly price of p_1 per game and let the city "buy" all the games it wanted. As seen in Figure 6.2, the city would choose to "buy" Q_1 games, and the city's residents would enjoy the consumer surplus ACE. Figure 6.2 shows that the team can take some of this surplus by telling the city that if it wants to host any games at all, it must host all Q_2. Buying more games than it wants at the price p_1 imposes a "consumer loss" equal to EFG, because residents of the city must pay more than the additional games are worth to them. The city will accept this loss as long as the surplus that residents enjoy on the first Q_1 games is greater than the loss residents suffer on the next $Q_2 - Q_1$. That is, as long as consuming "too many" games is preferable to consuming nothing, the city will choose to consume too much. The franchise can push the city to host more games until the size of the loss (EFG) catches up with the size of the surplus (ACE).

The Winner's Curse

Even the pressures created by the all-or-nothing demand curve understate the power of sports leagues or teams to extract consumer surplus. They often can

FIGURE 6.2

A Monopolist Can Extract
Consumer Surplus by Setting
Price *and* Quantity

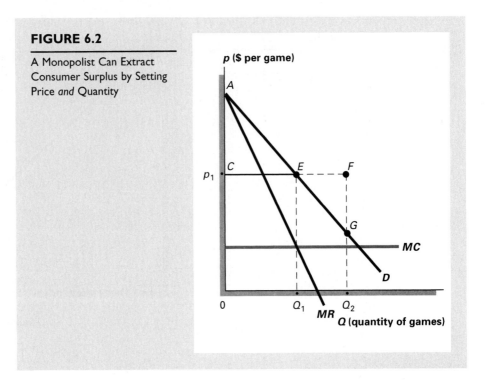

solicit bids that exceed the value of the franchise to the winning city. In any auction in which the bidders do not know the value of the prize with absolute certainty, the winner may well overpay for what has been won, falling victim to the "winner's curse." The winner's curse was first applied to oil leases, when researchers sought to explain why investments by oil companies in the oil-rich Gulf of Mexico "paid off at something less than the local credit union." Since then, it has been applied to contexts as diverse as advances paid to authors and the salaries paid to baseball players.[27]

To see how the winner's curse works, consider what happens if Memphis and several other cities bid to host the Grizzlies basketball team. To win the auction, Memphis must outbid the other potential host cities. Each competitor bases its bid on how much it expects the Grizzlies to be worth.[28] The competing cities hire experts to evaluate the benefits of a new franchise. Based on these estimates, each submits bids to the NBA. Memphis wins the auction by bidding

---

[27]Richard Thaler, "The Winner's Curse," *Journal of Economic Perspectives,* v. 2, no. 1 (Winter 1988), pp. 191–202. For an application to sports, see James Cassing and Richard Douglas, "Implications of the Auction Mechanism in Baseball's Free Agent Draft," *Southern Economic Journal,* v. 47, no. 1 (July 1980), pp. 110–121.

[28]Since cities have much greater access to capital than individuals do, we ignore the question of the city's ability to pay.

more than any other city. It may do so for any of three reasons. First, it can make more profitable use of the franchise than other cities can. For example, a basketball franchise may allow Memphis to exploit synergies with other attractions that do not exist elsewhere.[29] Second, if Memphis overestimates the benefits that the Grizzlies will bring, it may overbid for the franchise and win the auction even though it would have been better off losing. And third, the auction process itself may lead Memphis to bid more than the Grizzlies are worth even when it correctly estimates the team's value.

At first glance, the chance of Memphis's overbidding for the Grizzlies seems unlikely. As we saw in Chapter 2, if Memphis recognizes that the Grizzlies pose an uncertain payoff and Memphis is risk averse, then its expected utility from winning the auction falls. Figure 6.3 shows that a risk-averse city has lower expected utility from a project that pays $200 million or $0 with equal probability than it does from a project that pays $100 million with certainty. In Figure 6.3, the city will bid no more than $40 million for a project with an expected value of $100 million, much less than they would pay for the project that returns a sure $100 million. Based on this reasoning, uncertainty should cause cities to underbid rather than overbid for franchises.

FIGURE 6.3

Cities Prefer Sure Payoffs to Risky Ones

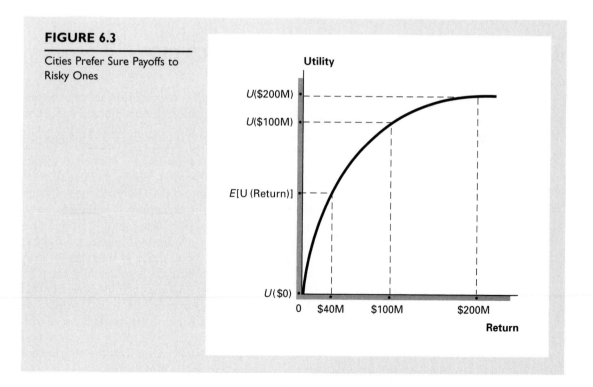

[29]For example, Montreal and Atlanta converted their main stadiums to baseball stadiums after the Olympics.

The key to the winner's curse lies in the fact that not all cities have the same expectations and that only the most optimistic bidder wins the prize. In addition to any objective advantages it may have over other cities, Memphis's winning bid also reflects its optimism about the uncertain value of the Grizzlies. If Memphis is more optimistic than other cities about its ability to turn a profit, it is also more likely to overstate the value of the Grizzlies and hence more likely to submit a bid that is higher than the true return to hosting the Grizzlies. In the context of Figure 6.3, Memphis feels that it has a much higher probability of success than any other city, leading the expected profit from the games to move upward toward $200 million.

Finally, Memphis may simply get caught up in trying to win the right to host the Grizzlies, independent of expected benefits. Empirical studies and clinical experiments of bidding behavior have shown that, on average, bidders accurately assess the value of uncertain prizes. The winning bid, however, consistently overstates the value of the prize. Moreover, the degree to which a winner overbids, and hence the degree of loss, generally rises with the number of bidders. This has led some economists to conclude that participants get caught up in the action and begin to set winning the auction as a goal in itself. As a result, bids by cities and individuals alike may reflect both the value of the prize and the desire to win the prize regardless of its inherent worth.

6.3   HOW THE OLYMPICS AND THE WORLD CUP INDUCE OVERSPENDING

The International Olympic Committee (IOC) and soccer World Cup organizers, the Federation Internationale de Football Association (International Federation of Association Football, better known as FIFA) may be the ultimate franchise monopolists. With one Summer Olympics, one Winter Olympics, and one World Cup held every four years, cities see each event as a chance to attract hordes of tourists and generate international attention. The high price of staging these events and the corruption that has tainted the Olympic site selection process in recent years form a case study of the three forces outlined above. Cities that wish to host one of these events must purchase the right from a producer with little direct competition. Cities that consider bidding for the right to host the Olympics or World Cup also face the constraint that they cannot purchase part of an event and thus face an all-or-nothing decision. Finally, the winning city may be overly optimistic about the benefits that being a host city will bring or may be led by the auction process to overbid. In this example, we explore how the IOC and FIFA have exploited each of the market forces outlined earlier in this chapter.

Over the years, there have been numerous entrants into the market for multisport athletic competition, making for about 40 Olympic-style events. These generally consist of regional competitions, such as the Pan American Games, or events focused on specific sets of competitors, such as the Commonwealth or World University Games. The Goodwill Games were the only events in recent history that attempted to rival the Olympics in offering broad-based competitions among the world's athletes. The failure of the Goodwill Games suggests that the audience may not be large enough to justify the large fixed cost of staging competing games. FIFA also faces no direct competition. The only other global soccer competition is sponsored by the Olympics. That event, however, carefully avoids direct competition with the World Cup by limiting the age of competitors to 21 years or younger. The limited market for competitions such as the Olympics or the World Cup suggest that each might be a natural monopoly.

While they may be natural monopolies, neither the IOC nor FIFA has relied solely on market forces to protect its monopoly power. Both have ferociously defended their brand name. The IOC, for example, has repeatedly gone to court to protect its trademark rights over the term "Olympics."[30] In addition, one could view the shift from holding winter and summer Games in the same year as an attempt to flood the market in order to forestall entry by competitors.

Massive spending by cities seeking to host the Olympics has long been a part of its history. Los Angeles spent about $1 million to build the Coliseum in an unsuccessful attempt to attract the 1924 Games and spent almost another $1 million (for a total of about $22.5 million in 2002 dollars) to refurbish the Coliseum in its successful bid for the 1932 Games. Cleveland spent even more, roughly $3 million (almost $39 million in 2002 dollars), to build the mammoth Municipal Stadium—when completed, it had the largest seating capacity of any outdoor arena in the world—in its unsuccessful bid to host the 1932 Games. Germany spent huge sums as part of its successful effort to outdo the 1932 "Hollywood Olympics" and to present the world with a positive image of the Nazi regime during the 1936 Berlin Games. One of the cities Berlin beat out was Barcelona, which housed much of the 1992 Games in the stadium it built in 1929 in an attempt to host the 1936 Games.[31]

In more recent years, the cost of attracting and staging the Games has reached truly Olympian heights. In 1976, Montreal spent roughly C$1.6 billion on its Summer Games. Lacking a significant tax base, Montreal was left with a debt burden of about C$1 billion (about US$750 million) that would be paid in part by residents who had not been born when the torch was lit.[32] At the time, Montreal's expenditure seemed the height of folly. Eight years later, however, the stakes rose dramatically.

---

[30]See, for example, James Grimaldi, "Olympics File Suit Over Web Domain," *Washington Post,* July 14, 2000, p. E4, at http://washingtonpost.com/wp-dyn/articles/A40476-2000July13.html.

[31]Raymond Keating, "Sports Pork: The Costly Relationship Between Major League Sports and Government," *Policy Analysis,* no. 339 (Washington, D.C.: Cato Institute, 1999), p. 4; Mark Rosentraub, *Major League Losers* (New York: Basic Books, 1997), pp. 253–254. The propaganda value of the 1936 Olympics and the elaborate preparations for the Games are described in Duff Hart-Davis, *Hitler's Games* (London: Century, 1986); and R. Mundell, *The Nazi Olympics* (New York: Ballantine Books, 1972).

[32]Ed Zotti, "Hosting the Olympics—Not All Fund and Games," *Advertising Age,* v. 54, no. 6 (February 7, 1983) (from ProQuest); and M. Lawson, "Going for Gold," *Accountancy,* v. 117, no. 1234 (June 1996), pp. 30–32.

In staging the 1984 Summer Games, the Los Angeles Olympics Organizing Committee, headed by Peter Ueberroth, showed that cities could work with private sponsors to stage a highly profitable Olympics. It was not long, however, before the costs caught up with revenues. In order to host the 2004 Olympics, the Greek government is spending over $5 billion. When added to the expenditures of the Olympic Committee itself, the total expenditures come to about $7.5 billion. While Greece is spending more than four times as much as Canada spent on the Montreal Games, its expenditures are dwarfed by those of the People's Republic of China on the 2008 Games. The Chinese government estimates that the cost of the Beijing Games will rise to almost $35 billion, a figure that surpasses even the then-unthinkable $13 to $14 billion that Japan spent on the 1998 Nagano Games.[33]

In order to host the 2002 World Cup, Japan and Korea spent huge amounts to build and upgrade facilities. Japan spent about $4.5 billion on constructing 7 new stadiums and refurbishing 3 others for the World Cup finals, while South Korea spent $2 billion on 10 new facilities. Most of these are now white elephants for the communities that had them built. The Japanese district of Saitama built a 64,000-seat stadium for the preliminary rounds of the World Cup at a cost of $667 million. Saitama must now spend $6 million per year to maintain the facility for a local professional team that draws barely 20,000 fans.[34]

Officials in Japan and Korea vastly overstated the benefits of hosting the World Cup finals. Prior to the tournament, a Japanese research group predicted benefits of over $26 billion to the Japanese economy. The Korean organizing committee was also very optimistic, predicting benefits of over $5 billion. However, in their study of the actual impact of the World Cup on the Japanese and Korean economies, Robert Baade and Victor Matheson found that hosting the games actually *cost* the two countries a combined total of $5.5 billion.[35]

The IOC's monopoly position explains only a part of its power over cities. The profits shown by the 1984 Los Angeles Games dramatically increased the number of cities bidding to be a host site. In effect, the Games became an asset that the IOC could auction off to the highest bidder, much like a valuable painting on auction at Sotheby's or a firm that is the target of competing takeover bids. As the number of competing bidders rises, the bidders drive the price of the asset upward. In the limit, the price of the asset approaches the expected profits (or utility) that the asset can provide. The original owner of the asset—

---

[33]Figures taken from Alan Abrahamson, "Athens Makes Security 'Priority No. 1'" *Los Angeles Times*, August 13, 2003, Part 4, p. 8; Kieran Daley, "Olympic Games: Beijing to Boost Security Budget by Up to Pounds $280M," *The Independent (London)*, July 19, 2003, p. 9; Anonymous, "Asia: Downhill All the Way," *The Economist*, February 7, 1998, p. 44; SportZone, "Nagano Olympics Has $32 Million Surplus," at http://espn.go.com/olympics98/news/980709/00765455.html, January 12, 1998; and Douglas Robson, "Sydney Finds Its Facilities Formula in Blend of Public–Private Financing," *Street & Smith's SportsBusiness Journal*, v. 2, no. 27 (October 25–31, 1999), p. 33.

[34]Doug Struck, "Hosts Left to Foot World Cup Bill," *Washington Post*, June 29, 2002, p. A1; and Robert A. Baade and Victor A. Matheson, "The Quest for the Cup: Assessing the Economic Impact of the World Cup," forthcoming in *Regional Science*.

[35]Struck (2002) and Baade and Matheson (forthcoming).

in this case, the IOC—captures all the value of the asset, just as the monopolist can extract all consumer surplus through the all-or-nothing demand curve.

To see how much a city would be willing to bid, we make three simplifying assumptions. First, suppose that all costs are paid the moment the city wins the bid. Second, suppose that the revenue the city receives from the Games (e.g., revenue from the Games themselves and from future use of the facilities built for the Games) comes in annual lump sums. Third, assume that cities know exactly how much they must spend and exactly how much revenue they will receive, so that expected revenue always equals actual revenue. The first two assumptions make our analysis much neater without straying too far from reality. We shall eventually replace the third assumption with a less restrictive one. Under these assumptions, if the city receives benefits of B_t for each of T years after it wins the bid, then it is willing to pay the price P, where P equals V, the value of the future stream of returns.

One might expect V to equal the sum of payments the city receives $(B_1 + B_2 + B_3 + \ldots)$, but reality is a bit more complicated. The city must compare a *present* cost with a *future* stream of benefits. Because one can save the dollar that one receives today and earn the market rate of interest, r, a dollar today actually equals $1 + r$ dollars a year from today, $(1 + r)^2$ dollars two years from today, and so on. The **future value** that \$1 today will have in t years is thus $\$(1 + r)^t$, while the **present value** of \$1 that one will receive t years from today equals $\$1/(1 + r)^t$. The present value of the stream of benefits to the city equals

$$V = \frac{B_1}{(1+r)} + \frac{B_2}{(1+r)^2} + \frac{B_3}{(1+r)^3} + \cdots + \frac{B_T}{(1+r)^T}.$$

When the stream of benefits from hosting an Olympics increased in the wake of the 1984 Los Angeles Games, the IOC was able to extract greater payments from cities. These payments took the form of increasingly elaborate facilities, increasingly luxurious accommodations for IOC members, and finally, outright payments to members of the IOC site selection committee.

The revenue stream that the host city will receive, however, is far from certain. As we saw in our discussion of the winner's curse, the winning city is likely to overstate the value of the Games to the city and wind up paying a price that exceeds the actual value of the Games ($P > V$).

Finally, cities may just want to win. The competition among the cities hoping to host the 2008 Summer Olympics—Beijing, Paris, Istanbul, and Osaka—exemplified the pressure on the cities to win the auction. From the outset, the rival sites viewed the bidding process as "a high-level competition between cities and countries."[36] Consciously or not, the IOC structures the selection process as a tournament, with cities advancing from preliminary rounds to "the

---

[36]Beijing's Vice-Mayor Liu Jingmin, deputy director of the Chinese Olympics Bidding Committee, quoted in "Bejing Enters Play-offs to Be Olympics Host," *People's Daily Online*, March 24, 2000, at http://english.peopledaily.com.cn/200003/24/eng20000324S101.html.

finals," with the ante rising at each stage. Even the terminology used by journalists and bid officials resembled that of the athletic competition they hoped to stage. The official Chinese news source pictured Beijing as being in a "neck-in-neck [*sic*] competition" to host the 2008 Games, while Osaka officials cited the need to catch their breath before moving forward. Toronto officials were even more explicit, saying, "We've made the play-offs . . . [b]ut there are a bunch of rounds coming up and we've got to make sure that we're the last survivor at the end of the day." The emotion and self-esteem invested in such competition makes winning the competition an end in itself, beyond the financial merits of the actual prize.[37]

In sum, the Olympics represent a very challenging problem for potential host cities. Those that would like to host the Games face a monopolist offering an all-or-nothing demand curve in an environment in which costs and benefits are both highly uncertain. More broadly, the resources that cities expend simply in an effort to win the right to stage the Games reduce efficiency in the overall economy.

6.4   THE FORM AND FUNCTION OF STADIUMS AND ARENAS

The ability of leagues and event organizers to exploit their market power has had a major impact on the nature of the facilities themselves. Facilities have changed names, location, and even size and shape over the years as the source of funding has shifted from the owners to the public sector. In this section, we examine how the growing involvement of the public sector in the 1960s gave rise to the large, multipurpose stadium. Along the way, we encounter the economic theory of location and why the skyline in Crookston, MN, does not resemble the skyline in Manhattan and why central business districts are indeed central.

What's in a Name?

At the risk of some oversimplification, one can divide the history of sports facilities into three broad eras. Like a paleontologist identifying dinosaur bones, one can discern one era from another by looking for certain telltale signs in each facility. The first era consisted of baseball stadiums with names such as Forbes Field, Wrigley Field, or Shibe Park. The second era was marked by multipurpose facilities with names such as the Texas Stadium, Oakland–Alameda County Stadium, or Atlanta–Fulton County Stadium. The third era consists of sport-specific venues with names such as Bank One Ballpark, the Wachovia

---

[37]See *People's Daily Online* (2000); Channel Sports, "Beijing Welcomes Inclusion on Shortlist to Hold 2008 Olympics," *China Daily Information,* August 29, 2000, at http://www.chinadaily.net/cover/storydb/2000/08/29/sp-beiji.829.html; Reuters, "Osaka Vows to Battle On to Host 2008 Olympics," August 28, 2000, at http://web4.sportsline.com/u/wire/stories/0,1169,2712403_15,00.html; and Dan Ralph, "Toronto Among Finalists to Host 2008 Olympics," *Canadian Press,* August 29, 2000, at http://www.herald.ns.ca/stories/2000/08/29/f161.raw.html.

Center, or the National Car Rental Arena. Sometimes a given facility reflects the transition from one era to another, as when Riverfront Stadium in Cincinnati was renamed Cynergy Field.

The first era covered the first two decades or so of the 20th century. All of the facilities built during this era have two things in common. First, none has the word "Stadium" in its title. The universal use of the word "Park" or "Field" reflects the pastoral origins of baseball. In baseball's formative years, prior to the enclosure of games in private structures, games were played in open fields or parks. The term "stadium" was not used until Jacob Ruppert applied the name to his new "Yankee Stadium" in 1923 in a deliberate attempt to recall the grandeur of classical architecture. (*Stadium* comes from the Greek word *stadion*, which originally referred to a specific distance, later referred to a race of that distance, and eventually came to mean the seats for spectators who watched the race.) Second, all of the ballparks, with the exception of Fenway Park, bear the name of the owner of the baseball team for which the stadium was built.[38] During this era, teams typically built their own ballparks because the point of enclosing the field was to prevent bystanders from seeing ballgames for free.[39]

The unparalleled stability that baseball enjoyed during its "Golden Age" brought no need for new construction. Prior to 1950, Cleveland's Municipal Stadium and the Los Angeles Coliseum were the only major publicly built facilities, and—as noted earlier in this chapter—they were built with the Olympics in mind and not baseball or football. Since that time, the aging of the facilities, the changing face of American cities, and the growing ability and willingness of franchises to utilize the market forces described earlier in this chapter led to the gradual disappearance of facilities built in the first era. Of these ballparks, only Wrigley Field, Fenway Park, and Yankee Stadium still exist, and recent attempts have been made to replace the latter two parks.

While there were some antecedents in the 1950s—such as Milwaukee's County Stadium and Baltimore's Memorial Stadium—the second era of stadium construction ran roughly from 1962 to 1991. The first stadium in this new era, Dodger Stadium in Los Angeles, was one of the key lures that brought the Dodgers west. While "Dodger Stadium" is a relatively neutral name, most of the new stadiums of this era have names that reflect the fact that municipalities were now paying for the new ballparks. Most municipalities chose to name the facilities for themselves; for local geographical features, such as Three Rivers Stadium in Pittsburgh; or for patriotic causes, such as Veterans Stadium in Philadelphia.

The third set of names represents the newest trend in facilities, the sale of naming rights to private sponsors. As shown in Chapter 3, naming rights form a significant, though often overstated, source of income for teams. Bank One Ballpark, the TransWorld Dome, and National Car Rental Arena were all built largely with public funding. Even the Wachovia Center and Ericsson Stadium,

---

[38]Wrigley Field was originally named Weghman Field for the owner of the Chicago Whales of the Federal League. When Philip Wrigley bought the team and the stadium, he renamed it for himself.

[39]In 1936 Connie Mack went so far as to erect a "spite fence" behind right field of Shibe Park to prevent fans from viewing the game from the roofs of nearby apartment buildings.

which were ostensibly privately built, received substantial implicit subsidies from state and local governments.[40]

The Size and Shape of Facilities

In Chapter 2, we pointed out that the Philadelphia Phillies seldom sold out because they played in a stadium that is too big for them. Most baseball teams fail to sell out a significant amount of the time. The only teams that reported sell outs for one-third of their games in 2003 were the Boston Red Sox and Chicago Cubs, who play in relatively old ballparks, and the San Francisco Giants, who play in a new, baseball-only stadium and played in the 2002 World Series. During the second era of sports facilities (1962–1991), stadiums grew significantly and assumed the "cookie-cutter" shape that has since been so reviled. In this section, we examine why the size and shape of stadiums changed so dramatically.

Multipurpose Facilities: Size Does Matter   The trend toward publicly funded facilities was accompanied by a trend toward larger arenas. Until the 1960s, baseball team owners built ballparks specifically to house the teams they owned. Like the hockey owners who rented their arenas to basketball teams, baseball owners allowed football teams to rent the facilities in the off-season for an additional source of revenue. Football teams jumped at this arrangement, since they could not afford to build their own facilities and were often anxious to capture some of the reflected glory of the baseball teams.[41]

By the 1960s, as cities became more involved in funding and designing facilities, football had begun to overtake baseball in popularity. Previously, football teams were forced to play in baseball stadiums that failed to provide proper sight lines for watching a football game. In addition, the size of the old ballparks was beginning to prove inadequate. Playing only eight regular season home games a year, usually on Sunday afternoons, professional football teams began to draw far more fans than baseball teams for a typical game. In conjunction with Pete Rozelle's "league-think" leadership style, football teams were enjoying their own era of stability in the 1960s and 1970s. Lacking a credible threat to leave town, NFL franchises were not yet in a position to demand their own ballparks. However, their growing prominence on the American sports scene was reflected in the design of the new facilities. The new, multipurpose stadiums had to accommodate the larger fan base for football teams, leaving the capacity far larger than a baseball team could fill for most games. As a result, baseball teams whose home fields

---

[40]"The city [of Charlotte] put in about $30 million of work prior to the announcement [that the Charlotte ownership group had been selected for an NFL franchise]." Catherine McHugh, "Ericsson Stadium," *TCI*, v. 31, no. 4 (May 1997), pp. 32–35 (from ProQuest).

[41]NFL teams even adopted variants of the names of MLB teams whose facilities they used (e.g., the Chicago Bears, who rented Wrigley Field from the Cubs) or took on the names of the teams themselves (e.g., the New York Giants of the NFL, who rented the Polo Grounds from MLB's Giants). Ironically, college football enjoyed a building spree during the early decades of the century, when classic facilities such as Michigan Stadium and the Yale Bowl were built.

were built during the second era of facilities rarely sell out their games. Football teams that play in the same facilities are far more likely to draw capacity crowds.

Shape Matters, Too A camel has often been called "a horse designed by committee." Like the camel, the circular, multipurpose stadiums that were built during the second era reflected a compromise of interests that in the end satisfied no one. Cities that constructed multipurpose facilities now had to take the popularity of football into consideration. Unfortunately, the ideal football stadium and the ideal baseball stadium look nothing alike.

Football teams play on a standardized, rectangular field. Teams score by going to one end of the field or the other, but the bulk of the action takes place in the middle of the field. A football stadium's least desirable seats are therefore located in either end zone. Such seats give little perspective on the action and provide a poor view of what is happening on much of the field. They are typically the cheapest and last to sell. Figure 6.4 shows the design of a new football-only facility, Lincoln Financial Field in Philadelphia. It maximizes the number of fans who can sit along either sideline and has relatively few seats far from the action.

By contrast, most of the action on a baseball field takes place within the diamond that forms the infield. Early baseball stadiums thus consisted of grandstands that extended outward from home plate around the foul lines and did not encompass the outfield. The new "fan friendly" ballparks have returned to this pattern. One of the newest ballparks, Bank One Ballpark, has only 15 percent of its seats in the outfield.[42] Figure 6.5 shows the design of Philadelphia's baseball-only facility, Citizens Bank Park. Like the older ballparks whose memory it seeks to evoke, Citizens Bank Park maximizes the number of seats near home plate and the infield, where most of the fans focus their attention, and has relatively few seats in the outfield, far from the action.

The circular shape of the cookie-cutter stadiums struck a middle ground between the two ideal shapes, providing fans with a good view of neither sport. Figures 6.6 and 6.7 show Veterans Stadium in Philadelphia when it was configured for baseball and football games, respectively. In both cases the stadium had a relatively large number of seats in the least desirable locations. When arranged for football, Veterans Stadium had a large number of seats in the end zone, and many of the seats near midfield were far from the field of play. When arranged for baseball, it had a large number of seats in the outfield, far from the action. As a result, a substantial number of both baseball fans and football fans had inferior views of the action. Not surprisingly, the teams had trouble selling tickets in these areas.

The cookie-cutter shape of the second era's facilities also imposed uniformity on baseball, which had previously been characterized by idiosyncratically shaped ballparks. While the size and shape of a football field and a baseball infield are carefully specified, the shape of a baseball outfield has few restrictions. As a result, the first era of facilities contained stadiums in a dizzying array of

---

[42]Sherman, *Big League, Big Time* (1998), p. 218.

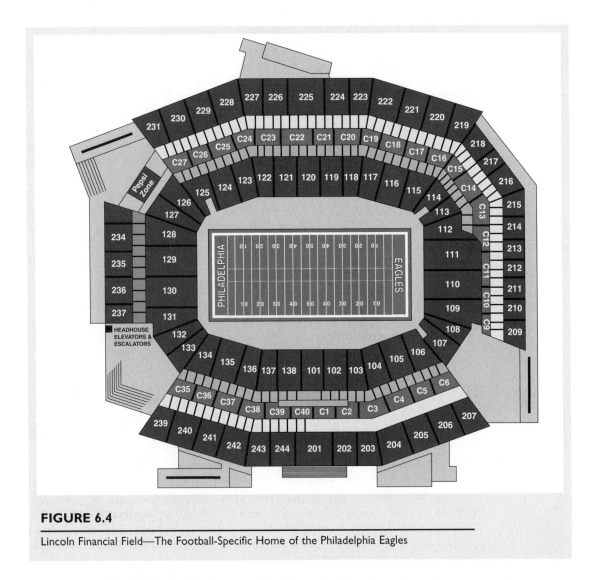

FIGURE 6.4

Lincoln Financial Field—The Football-Specific Home of the Philadelphia Eagles

sizes and shapes. Some were shaped around the particular strengths or weaknesses of the home team. Yankee Stadium may have been the "house that Ruth built," but it was also built to order for Babe Ruth, a left-handed batter who hit prodigious home runs. Yankee Stadium accommodated Ruth with a short right field fence and left-center field so deep that it came to be known as "Death Valley." The old Baker Bowl in Philadelphia so favored left-handed hitters that Red Smith, the famed columnist, was moved to comment, "It might be exaggerating to say the outfield wall casts a shadow across the infield. But if the right fielder had eaten onions at lunch, the second baseman knew it."[43]

---

[43]Quoted in Rich Westcott, *Philadelphia's Old Ballparks* (Philadelphia: Temple University Press, 1996), p. 32.

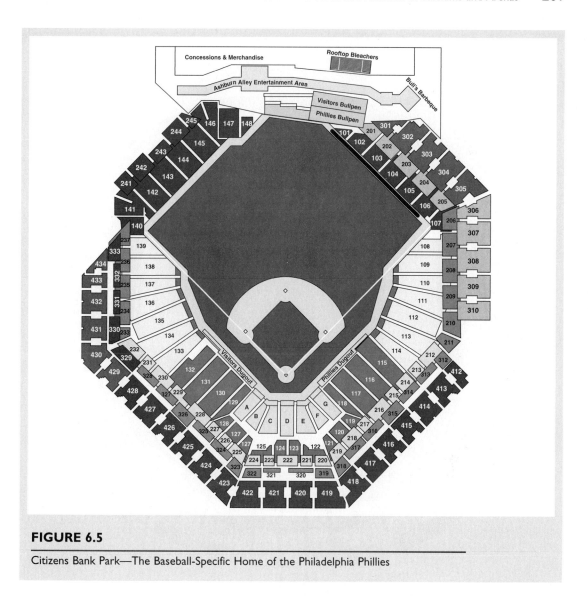

FIGURE 6.5

Citizens Bank Park—The Baseball-Specific Home of the Philadelphia Phillies

Other fields were shaped to fit into a preexisting city plan. Center field in Philadelphia's Shibe Park came to a distinctive point 515 feet from home plate so that the stadium could fit in the square block grid. Two of the most dramatic plays in baseball history—Bobby Thompson's "shot heard round the world," a dramatic ninth-inning home run that beat the Dodgers in a 1951 playoff game, and Willie Mays's miraculous catch of a mammoth drive by the Cleveland Indians' Vic Wertz in the 1954 World Series—had as much to do with the configuration of the Polo Grounds as with the talents of the two players. With one of the oddest shapes of any baseball stadium, the Polo Grounds, named for an area north of Central Park that the New York Giants shared with polo teams

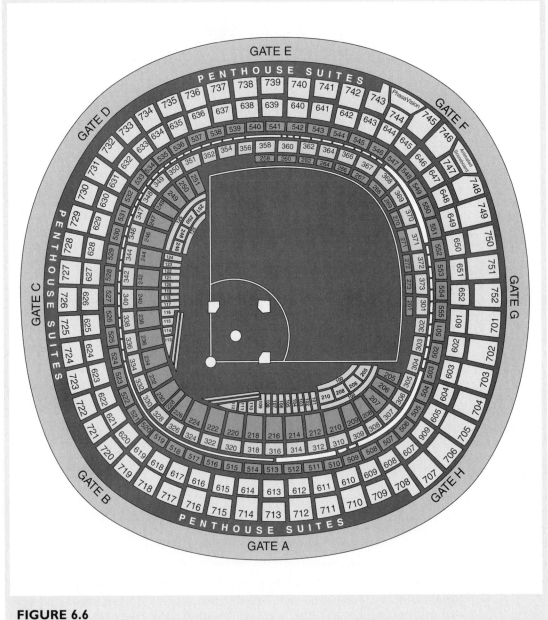

FIGURE 6.6

Veterans Stadium—A Multipurpose Venue Configured for the Philadelphia Phillies

before moving to their home in upper Manhattan, could be a very easy place or an incredibly difficult place in which to hit a home run, depending on where one hit the ball. The left field wall was only 258 feet away, with an overhang

FIGURE 6.7

Veterans Stadium—A Multipurpose Venue Configured for the Philadelphia Eagles

that reduced the effective distance of the left field seats—where Thompson hit his home run—to only 250 feet. Center field was a different story. The stands in left-center field and right-center field were about 450 feet away, with a cutout in dead center field that extended the distance to about 480 feet.[44] In almost any other stadium, Willie Mays would have been staring at the ball Vic Wertz hit as it sailed out of the park.

One can generally identify venues belonging to the current era of sports facilities by the corporate names they bear. Even facilities that ostentatiously rejected corporate naming rights, such as Cleveland Browns Stadium, built in 1999 for the new franchise that replaced the team that moved to Baltimore, could not resist selling the naming rights to the four entrances to the stadium. Baseball and football fields built during the latest era have also generally returned to the single-purpose facilities of the first era.

Starting with Oriole Park at Camden Yards, the latest generation of baseball fields has striven to recapture the feel of these old ballparks. The new ballparks, however, have been built with far looser budget constraints than the old ballparks on which they are modeled. With cities picking up most of or the entire bill, team owners are now able to build on a far grander scale. The supposedly intimate Ballpark at Arlington (home of the Texas Rangers) takes up 13.6 acres, about 2.5 times the space occupied by Ebbets Field and 50 percent more than the supposedly impersonal Kingdome did in Seattle.

The larger "footprint" of the modern stadiums allows teams to fill them with a wider array of accommodations than ever before, from food courts to restrooms. Most importantly, they allow teams to fill stadiums with luxury suites and other special seating. Because these seats occupy prime sight lines, the general admission seats above them must be pushed up and back. In the past, upper-deck seats—such as the overhang at the Polo Grounds—were close to the action, supported by columns that obstructed the view of some. Modern architecture allows the upper deck to be supported without obtrusive pillars, and modern aesthetics rebel against obstructed seats. The result has been seats that, while not obstructed, are much farther from the action than in the ballparks they have replaced. According to one advocate, the last row of the upper decks of Tiger Stadium and the old Comiskey Park were closer to the field than the first row of the upper decks of their replacements.[45] Upper-deck seats in supposed throwback parks such as Jacobs Field in Cleveland, Coors Field in Denver, and the Ballpark in Arlington are even more distant from the action.[46] Ironically, while the new stadiums may no longer have views obstructed by pillars, the average fan may have a worse view of the action on the field than ever.

Location, Location, Location

Nostalgia buffs and urban planners delight in the fact that all the ballparks built since the early 1990s, starting with Baltimore's Oriole Park at Camden

---

[44]The precise distance varied over the years. See Paul Munsey and Corey Suppes, *Ballparks*, 1999, at http://www.ballparks.com.

[45]Cagan and deMause, *Field of Schemes* (1998), p. 135; and http://www.fieldofschemes.com/comerica.jpg.

[46]Phillip Bess, "Urban Ballparks and the Future of Cities," *Real Estate Issues*, v. 21, no. 3 (December 1996), pp. 27–30.

Yards, have a "retro" feel. Not only are they built to look like the old ballparks (both Miller Field in Milwaukee and the proposed new stadium for the New York Mets deliberately evoke memories of the Brooklyn Dodgers' old Ebbets Field), but they also are frequently in downtown areas, reminiscent of the old parks' locations.

The warm and fuzzy feeling associated with the downtown location of many of the newest stadiums is proof that nostalgia is not what it used to be. When they were first built, the old ballparks were no more urban than the multipurpose facilities of the 1960s and 1970s. When Shibe Park (later renamed Connie Mack Stadium) was built at 21st and Lehigh Streets in North Philadelphia in 1909, it stood near the site of a recently demolished hospital for communicable diseases. Given the state of medical knowledge at the turn of the 20th century, society tended to deal with communicable diseases by locating the patients as far from town as possible. For several years after Shibe Park was built, Philadelphians complained about the distance they had to travel to reach it.[47] Similarly, Yankee Stadium in the South Bronx was not always associated with urban devastation. It was built on an empty 10-acre lot, bordered by unpaved roads, in a part of town known as "Goatville," hardly a metropolitan setting.[48] Brooklyn's Ebbets Field was not much different. By the mid-1950s, it may have come to epitomize the urban ballpark, but in 1913, the neighborhood in which it was built bore the nickname "Pigtown . . . where poor Italian immigrants lived in miserable shanties amidst goats and dandelions."[49]

As time went on, urban areas developed and then decayed around many of the old ballparks. As the old stadiums began to decay themselves, team owners and cities turned their attention to the outskirts of town and the suburbs for sociological, technological, and economic reasons. An increasingly suburbanized fan base was more and more reluctant to attend games in the crumbling inner city.

The movement to the suburbs also brought a need to accommodate fans who drove to the game. Any new ballpark would have to come packaged with acres of parking lots, and this vastly increased the space required for a stadium. Space, however, costs money and becomes increasingly expensive as one moves toward the center of town. Consider, for example, the case of two bookstores, Barnes and Noble and Borders, that are trying to figure out where to locate in the circular city shown in Figure 6.8. If the population is evenly spread over the city, then the best place for the stores to locate is in the very center of the circle. To see why, assume that the stores initially consider locating at the edge of town, along the diameter AA in Figure 6.8. Since the stores are identical in every way but convenience, customers base their purchases on how close they are to each store. In this case, half the city's population is closer to Barnes and Noble and half is closer to Border's. As a result, each store gets an equal share of the city's

[47]See Bruce Kuklick, *To Everything a Season: Shibe Park and Urban Philadelphia, 1909–1976* (Princeton, N.J.: Princeton University Press, 1991), pp. 21–25; and Westcott, *Philadelphia's Old Ballparks* (1996), pp. 104–105.

[48]W. Nack, "This Old House," *Sports Illustrated*, June 7, 1999, pp. 100–116.

[49]Harold Seymour, *Baseball: The Golden Years* (New York: Oxford University Press, 1971), p. 52.

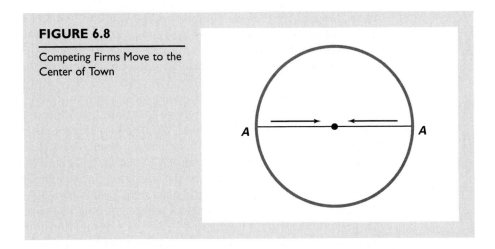

FIGURE 6.8

Competing Firms Move to the Center of Town

business. The managers of the Barnes and Noble quickly learn how customers decide to shop and recognize that they can capture some of Borders' business by moving to a more convenient location. They can do so by moving along the diameter toward the center of the circular town. The managers at Borders also recognize this and try to do Barnes and Noble one better by moving still closer to the center of the circle. The process continues until both stores compete for space in the center of town. The tendency of businesses to locate in the center of a city has given rise to the term **central business district**.

The competition for space also explains why property values are so much higher toward the center of town. Urban economists call the movement in property values the **rent gradient.** Figure 6.9 shows a typical rent gradient. As one moves toward the center of town, the value of property rises. The increasing price of land leads people to economize on their use of land, and buildings become taller. Since expanding horizontally becomes more expensive closer to the center of town, developers start to expand vertically. Figure 6.9 could measure the height of buildings as well as the cost of land, since both rise as one moves inward. A stadium with its surrounding parking facilities requires so much space that the cost of land can make locating in the center of town prohibitively expensive.

The move away from the center of town and the creation of large parking areas has made stadiums virtual islands in "seas of asphalt or concrete."[50] Fans drive to these isolated stadiums on highways designed to take them to the stadium from their suburban enclaves with minimal contact with the center of town and its attendant traffic jams. Largely built with public funds in order to attract consumer spending and income, the cookie-cutter stadiums of the 1960s, 1970s, and 1980s were designed in a way that minimized any spillover of consumer spending into the surrounding community. Since fans have found it inconvenient to go into town to enjoy restaurants, taverns, and other forms of entertainment,

---

[50]Robert Baade and Allen Sanderson, "Field of Fantasies," *Intellectual Ammunition*, March/April 1996, at http://www.heartland.org/01maap96.htm, p. 2.

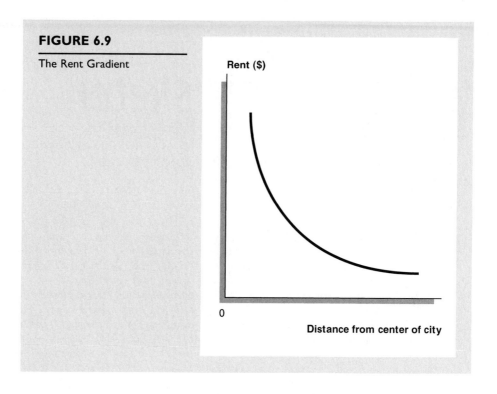

FIGURE 6.9

The Rent Gradient

the stadium has taken on many of those functions itself, further isolating the stadium and its income flows from the host area. In the words of Robert Baade, "[I]n many cases the modern sports facility resembles a small walled city."[51] In moving stadiums back to the center of town, cities are expressing a willingness to spend more in order to generate greater spillovers for the community.

[51]Robert Baade, "Should Congress Stop the Bidding War for Sports Franchises?" Hearing Before the Subcommittee on Antitrust, Business Rights, and Compensation, Senate Committee on the Judiciary, v. 4, November 29, 1995, "Academics," *Heartland Policy,* at http://www.heartland.org/stadps4.html, p. 16.

AL DAVIS

BIOGRAPHICAL Sketch

To me, professional football is a business and an avocation. I never wanted to hurt anybody. To Davis, it is a war.

—GENE KLEIN[1]

In the history of professional football, few owners have been so completely identified with their teams as Al Davis is with the Oakland Raiders. He has been the Raiders' head coach, their general manager, and even the commissioner of the old American Football League. However, in a sport that prides itself on its working-class, midwestern roots, Al Davis cuts a most unlikely figure. A fast-talking Brooklynite from an upper-middle class family, Davis originally preferred the "city game" of basketball. Unable to play varsity basketball at a major program, he wandered from college to college—attending Wittenburg College, Hartwick College, and Syracuse University—searching for a way to fit into the sports world.

Davis discovered his niche when Syracuse hired Ben Schwartzwalder as head football coach. Enthralled with Schwartzwalder's innovative offensive schemes, Davis became a fixture at strategy classes and team practices, even though he had no official position with the team. Never one to let the lack of credentials get in his way, Davis talked his way into a job as an assistant coach at Adelphi University immediately after graduating from Syracuse. Later stops at the Citadel and the University of Southern California confirmed Davis as a first-rate offensive mind and a brilliant recruiter. These qualities, however, also had a downside, as Davis could not fit into the hierarchy of a coaching staff. He constantly battled with fellow assistant coaches and never hid his desire to become a head coach. To make matters worse, his aggressive recruiting practices often ran afoul of NCAA regulations.

Tainted by scandal and unable to move up to a head coaching position, Davis found himself adrift in 1960. Fortunately for him, that was the year that the fledgling AFL opened up a realm of new opportunities, and he soon found a position on the staff of the Los Angeles (later San Diego) Chargers. Under the tutelage of head coach Sid Gillman, a widely acclaimed offensive genius, Davis refined the concept of an attacking, pass-oriented offense. He also applied his marketing skills to stealing players from the NFL and rival AFL clubs. The Chargers' dominance of the AFL put Davis in position to grab the chance of a lifetime—though it hardly seemed such at the time.

For the first three years of its existence, the Oakland Raiders was the laughingstock of the nascent AFL. They were, in fact, something of an accidental franchise. As noted in Chapter 4, the AFL had originally hoped to locate a flagship franchise in Minneapolis. Caught unprepared when the NFL hastily expanded to Minneapolis, the AFL awarded the Minnesota franchise to Oakland even though no one in Oakland had expressed an interest in owning a franchise. A group led by developer Wayne Valley eventually stepped forward, but the Raiders reflected their slapdash origins, compiling an appalling record in front of minuscule crowds. In 1963, desperate for a respectable team, the Raiders hired Davis as head coach. Within a year, Davis made the Raiders competitive, and within five years, they were playing in the Super Bowl. By that time, however, Davis had already moved beyond the coaching ranks.

In 1966, the AFL's owners narrowly approved Davis as the league's second commissioner. Six months later, they negotiated a merger with the NFL behind his back. This experience confirmed Davis's low opinion of football's owners and inculcated a deep dislike of NFL Commissioner Pete Rozelle, whom Davis—

➡

Rozelle's opposite in upbringing and temperament—felt had undermined him during the merger talks. Some even believe that Davis felt that *he* should have been named commissioner of the expanded league.

His term as commissioner quickly over, Davis again was a man without a team until Wayne Valley agreed to bring Davis back in 1966 as a "managing general partner" with a one-tenth interest in the team. Valley's move came as a surprise to many who had seen the growing friction between Valley and Davis. Valley soon regretted bringing Davis back to Oakland. In 1972 Davis masterminded a coup that reduced Valley to a figurehead position and—after four years of bitter legal battles—gave Davis control of the team.

As effective owner of the Raiders, Davis quickly became a pariah among the other owners, who were deeply committed to the "league-think" approach of Commissioner Rozelle. Whether out of principle or personal animosity, Davis repeatedly challenged the rest of the league. Unlike his peers, he welcomed free agency, declaring, "Just cut all the players and make everybody a free agent." He testified on behalf of the USFL in its antitrust suit against the NFL. (In return, the USFL pointedly sued only 27 of the existing 28 teams in the NFL.) He even refused to sign over the Raiders' share of profits from NFL Properties to the NFL Charities Foundation, claiming that the Raiders did their charity work locally.

Davis's biggest challenge to Rozelle and the NFL came in March 1980, when he sought to move the Raiders to Los Angeles. Davis had long coveted a larger stage than Oakland afforded, and he was among the first owners to see that favorable stadium deals would affect the balance of power in the NFL. The other owners, however, forbade him from moving the team, citing the league's constitution, which barred a team from moving into another's home territory without the league's unanimous consent. Davis responded by filing an antitrust suit against the NFL. After a series of

trials that were finally settled in 1989, the NFL dropped its objections to the move and agreed to pay the Raiders $18 million. The impact of the judgment, however, went far beyond the courtroom. Never again would the NFL invoke its bylaws to block a franchise from moving. This opened the door for later moves by the Colts, Rams, Browns (now Ravens), Oilers (now Titans), and the Raiders themselves—back to Oakland—in 1995. Davis had quickly become disenchanted with his agreement with the authorities in Los Angeles. The rush to an agreement had left much of the language open to multiple interpretations, and Davis soon saw that his move would not bring the financial benefits that he had anticipated.

The return to Oakland has not been the joyous homecoming that one might have expected. Davis has recently won a $34 million judgment against the Oakland–Alameda County Coliseum for allegedly misleading him as to the potential profits from moving back to Oakland. This may well pave the way for yet another move back to Los Angeles. Perhaps because of these many moves, the Raiders have not been the dominant team that they were in the 1970s and 1980s. Almost constant litigation since the mid-1970s has absorbed much of Davis's time and energy. In addition, the rest of the league has finally caught on to Davis's tactics. Perhaps even worse for Davis, the new breed of owner—best personified by Cowboys' owner Jerry Jones—has come to imitate his persona. No longer the rebel, Davis is now the role model, a position he cannot relish.

[1]Eugene Klein, *First Down and a Billion: The Funny Business of Professional Football* (New York: Morrow, 1987).

Sources: Glenn Dickey, *Just Win, Baby: Al Davis and His Raiders* (New York: Harcourt, Brace and Jovanovich, 1991); David Harris, *The League: The Rise and Decline of the NFL* (New York: Bantam Books, 1986); and Mark Ribowsky, *Slick: The Silver and Black Life of Al Davis* (New York: Macmillan, 1991).

SUMMARY

Since the 1950s, the burden of financing facilities has shifted from franchises to the cities that host them. Several characteristics of the market in which sports leagues and cities operate help to explain the large expenditures cities have made to attract or keep franchises. Monopoly power explains why leagues have limited the number of franchises and have been so reluctant to expand.

All-or-nothing demand curves and the winner's curse have allowed leagues to extract whatever consumer surplus may have remained. The growing involvement of cities has had significant effects on the size, shape, and location of facilities. From the 1960s through the 1980s, cities favored large, circular, multipurpose facilities that could accommodate both baseball and football teams. These facilities were often built on the edge of cities or in the suburbs. Recently, teams have begun to build facilities downtown, as cities have come to recognize that they have not benefited from locating facilities far from the center of town. Whatever its other effects, the growing involvement of cities has had a significant positive effect on the bottom line of the teams they host.

DISCUSSION QUESTIONS

1. How would you explain the fact that the Oakland Raiders moved back to Oakland from Los Angeles?

2. Have teams that have moved in the past 20 years become uniformly better off?

3. What is it about new facilities that makes the teams that occupy them more valuable?

4. Not long ago, the NFL dissuaded the owner of the Seattle Seahawks from moving to Los Angeles. Why would it do this?

5. Suppose your city (or the nearest large city) is trying to decide where to build a new facility. Think of two or three alternative sites and explain the pros and cons of each.

6. Studies have shown that the winner's curse is more severe in large groups than in small groups. Why do you think this is so?

PROBLEMS

6.1 Show that a monopolist that uses an all-or-nothing demand curve is more efficient (in the sense of minimizing deadweight loss) than a standard monopolist.

6.2 Show why New York is not likely to build a new stadium for the Yankees in midtown Manhattan.

6.3 Critics of referenda often complain that this method of determining expenditure often results in the community spending more than it really wants to. Do they have a point? Explain your answer.

6.4 What happens to a city's bid to host an Olympics if:

   a. Stadium construction costs rise?

   b. The city's NFL franchise offers to buy the Olympic stadium after the Games?

   c. Interest rates rise from 5 percent to 10 percent?

6.5 While football and baseball teams have gone from multipurpose to football- and baseball-only facilities, basketball and hockey teams continue to share arenas. Why?

6.6 Suppose that New Orleans wants to host the Super Bowl. Arrange the following in order of their impact on the price that New Orleans is likely to pay:

    a. The monopoly power of the NFL

    b. The NFL's use of the all-or-nothing demand curve

    c. The winner's curse.

6.7 Why does the fact that the NFL does not have a franchise in Los Angeles give its teams greater leverage with their host cities than teams in the other sports have?

6.8 If a new baseball stadium has only a very short-term impact on a team's attendance, why do MLB teams still pursue them?

6.9 Suppose the International Olympic Committee announced that it would hold all of its Summer Games in Athens and all of its Winter Games in Osaka. What is the likely impact on the monopoly power of the IOC, the IOC's ability to exploit an all-or-nothing demand curve, and the winner's curse?

6.10 Suppose a city is laid out along a major highway, so the city is shaped like a straight-line segment rather than a circle. If the city wants to build a sports arena, where along the segment should the city build the arena? Why?

CHAPTER 7

The Costs and Benefits of a Franchise to a City

The pride and the presence of a professional football team is far more important than 30 libraries.
— Art Modell, owner of the Baltimore Ravens[1]

INTRODUCTION

"Build it, and they will come." The mantra worked such wonders for Kevin Costner in *Field of Dreams* that cities adopted it as their own. Many state and local officials see sports facilities as the anchors around which their cities can revive their decaying downtown areas.[2] They have visions of tourists drawn to their towns to attend sporting events, of residents staying in downtown areas for entertainment and shopping rather than heading for the suburbs, and of local merchants relocating to prosperous downtown sites. When they propose building sports facilities based on these projections, however, state and local officials enter a political minefield. Like any other economic entity, municipalities face constraints. They cannot do everything and must choose among alternatives. Thus, citizens may eventually ask why their tax dollars go toward building playgrounds for millionaires rather than improving inner-city schools or repairing local roads. The decision to build these facilities is inextricably bound up with the decision of how to finance their construction.

This chapter explores the pros and cons of the public sector's involvement in subsidizing facilities for professional sports franchises. It then considers what the most economically efficient method of financing a facility would be

---

[1]Quoted in Joanna Cagan and Neil deMause, *Field of Schemes* (Monroe, M.E.: Common Cause Press, 1998), p. 137.

[2]Mark Rosentraub, "Stadiums and Urban Space," in *Sports, Jobs, and Taxes,* ed. by Roger Noll and Andrew Zimbalist (Washington, D.C.: Brookings Institution Press, 1997), pp. 178–180.

and compares the ideal with what states and municipalities have actually done. Along the way the chapter also discusses the following:

- Why governments exist
- Why governments sometimes aid the few at the expense of the majority
- How a dollar of expenditure creates "ripple effects" in a local economy
- What an optimal tax system should look like.

After briefly summarizing the experiences of several cities, this chapter shows that the reality of building and then possessing facilities may not justify the enthusiasm with which local officials embraced the concept of doing so. Chapter 6 explained how professional franchises have benefited tremendously from public sector involvement; however, the public sector itself seems to have little financial gain to show for its investment in professional sports.

7.1 WHY DO CITIES DO IT? THE BENEFITS OF A FRANCHISE

Critics of stadium projects often complain that if a new stadium is such a good idea, then the team should pay for it. In fact, under certain circumstances, substantial public funding for a stadium may be justified. By their very nature, governments evaluate projects by different criteria than do private firms. The private sector's pursuit of profit generally does a good job of allocating resources, but the private sector sometimes fails to provide the socially desired amount of a good or service. The market may fail because the firm does not account for the full costs or benefits of the good or service it provides. Economists often justify the existence of government by appealing to its role in correcting such **market failure.**

This section explores two commonly accepted sources of market failure: **public goods** and **externalities.** The rationale for public funding of a stadium or arena stems from the belief that sports franchises are public goods and that they have positive externalities for the community. Examining why cities subsidize sports facilities gets at the heart of the difference between the motives and actions of the private and public sectors.

Privately Built Facilities

A team will build a new facility if it expects the project to generate positive economic profits. That occurs if the net expenditures by fans on tickets and on related activities at the facility exceed the cost of building and maintaining it. The pressure to maximize profit and the difference between revenue and cost will tend to keep the expenditures on the facility in check. Foxboro (originally Schaefer) Stadium, home of the NFL's New England Patriots from 1971 to 2001, is one example of how economic pressures can keep the cost of a facility down. With no one to bankroll them, the Sullivan family—who owned the Patriots at the time—found a number of creative ways to minimize cost, including exchanging free advertising for a scoreboard and acquiring free artificial turf from a firm that was seeking to break into the industry. All told, they built the stadium for only $6.7 million, roughly $1/_8$ of what Kansas City spent on its municipally funded football stadium a year later and about $1/_{50}$ of what the Patriots' new home, the publicly funded Gillette Stadium, cost in 2002. When team owners do not spend their own money, it seems that they are less likely to seek low-cost solutions.[3]

When owners do not keep their impulses in check, they often face severe consequences. Constructed in 1913, Ebbets Field was a wonder of its day. Fans entered through an 80-foot rotunda enveloped in Italian marble and walked under a chandelier with 12 baseball-bat arms that held 12 globes shaped like baseballs. The cost of the stadium put Charles Ebbets so badly into debt that he had to offer half his interest in the team to two local contractors.[4] This split the ownership of the team into two warring factions, which doomed the Dodgers to mediocrity for three decades.

Is a Stadium a Worthwhile Investment for a City?

While building a stadium might be good business for a franchise, having a city build a stadium for it is better still. Since the 1950s, professional franchises have exploited the forces outlined in Chapter 6 to shift the burden of building and maintaining facilities onto cities. While most teams pay rent on their facilities, cities generally do not charge enough rent to make a profit. This need not imply that cities should not subsidize new sports facilities. Just as the benefits a TV network realizes from putting sporting events on the air go beyond the advertising revenue the broadcasts generate, the benefits a city realizes from hosting a franchise go beyond its financial dealings with the team. Still, the more a city pays for the privilege of hosting a franchise, the smaller the net benefits will be.

A city's revenue from a publicly built stadium consists of any rental payments made by the team (these can be a percentage of the gross or a flat fee) as well as the city's share of revenue from sources such as parking, concessions, and luxury boxes. The city's profit from the facility is the difference between these revenues and the cost of building and operating it.

Some costs, such as utility bills and the salaries paid to construction workers, are obvious. Other expenses, such as depreciation, are easily accounted for in theory but hard to measure in practice. As noted in Chapter 3, depreciation is largely an accounting fiction designed to provide tax incentives for firms to invest. The actual wear and tear on a firm's assets is seldom consistent with the simplistic depreciation rules that a firm follows.

---

[3]Raymond Keating, "Sports Pork," *Policy Analysis,* no. 339 (Washington, D.C.: Cato Institute, 1999), pp. 6, 13; and James Quirk and Rodney Fort, *Pay Dirt* (Princeton, N.J.: Princeton University Press, 1992), p. 158.

[4]Harold Seymour, *Baseball: The Golden Years* (New York: Oxford University Press, 1971), p. 52; and P. Munsey and C. Suppes, *Ballparks,* 1999, at http://www.ballparks.com.

In contrast, a city faces a very real cost when it helps to pay for a new facility. If it must borrow money, the city must pay interest. If it uses funds on hand, it sacrifices the return it could earn on those funds. To illustrate this cost, suppose that Sacramento is considering spending $150 million on a new basketball arena for the Kings, the local NBA franchise. It expects the facility to last 30 years and to be worthless thereafter. Sacramento raises the money by issuing 30-year municipal bonds that pay a real return of 3.5 percent. If it is assumed that Sacramento makes equal annual interest payments on the bond, it is possible to calculate the annual payment according to the equation:

$$P = \frac{V}{\dfrac{1 - (1 + r)^{-t}}{r}}$$

where V is the value of the bond issue ($150 million), r is the interest rate (0.035), t is the length of the loan (30 years), and P is the annual payment. In this example, Sacramento's annual payment to finance a new arena is $8.16 million. Thus, even if Sacramento has no other expenses associated with the arena, it must receive annual revenues of $8.16 million just to break even.

Stadium Rents: What Do Teams Pay?

Subsidies to professional franchises also stem from a more obvious source: highly favorable lease agreements. The NFL's Baltimore Ravens pay no rent at all, and MLB's Chicago White Sox pay a token rent of $1 per year. The Phoenix Suns and the Milwaukee Bucks also pay no rent; on top of that, they share a portion of the revenue from concessions, signage, and parking. In sum, teams generally pay bargain-basement rates for the facilities they occupy.

However, most franchises do make more than token payments to the civic authority that runs the facility. Some cities receive a percentage of the parking and signage fees as well as a fraction of the revenue from luxury boxes. Others receive just a rental fee. Still others receive a mixture of rent payments and revenue sharing. Frequently, a team's rent payment is linked to the attendance it draws. In particular, many leases contain attendance guarantees, which can significantly reduce the rent that the team pays. The Cleveland Indians, for example, pay rent to the Gateway Economic Development Corporation, a quasi-governmental agency that oversees Cleveland's facilities for the Browns, Cavaliers, and Indians. The Indians pay Gateway a fee of $1.25 per ticket when they draw more than 2.5 million fans. If attendance falls below 2.5 million, the fee also drops, to $1 per ticket. If the Indians do not draw 1.85 million fans, they pay nothing. While this looked like a good deal for the city when the Indians drew over 3 million fans from 1996 through 2001, the recent slide in attendance that has accompanied the team's declining fortunes on the field has greatly diminished the Gateway Corporation's revenues. In 2003, the team drew only 1.7 million fans, so it owed no rent.

The NFL's San Diego Chargers have had a deal with the city of San Diego since 1995 that actually pays them more for not selling tickets than for selling them. As part of their lease agreement with Qualcomm Stadium, the Chargers keep 90 percent of all ticket revenue (40 percent of which they then share with the rest of the NFL). San Diego agreed, however, to reimburse the Chargers for 100 percent of the value of all tickets that the team failed to sell. The Chargers thus stand to gain $27 from the sale of a $50 ticket, while they gain $50 if they do not sell that same ticket. As of 2001, San Diego had paid the Chargers over $25 million for unused seats.[5] To make matters worse, the lease gives the Chargers an incentive to lose football games, which drives away fans but increases revenue.[6]

The Cleveland Cavaliers of the NBA benefited from a civic oversight that seems to combine the deals negotiated by the Indians and the Chargers. The Cavaliers pay rent to Cleveland based on a sliding scale similar to that faced by the Indians. However, no one seemed to notice that the Cavaliers play in a facility that holds only 20,562 people for 41 regular season games, rather than the 43,368 capacity for 81 home games at Jacobs Field. As a result, the Cavaliers have not paid any rent at all during their stay in Gund Arena.[7] Partly as a result of these miscues, Gateway Corporation has faced chronic financial distress.

Why Governments Subsidize Sports Franchises

Cities justify arrangements such as those made in Baltimore, Chicago, Cleveland, and San Diego by correctly claiming that local governments consider a much more complex set of benefits and costs than do firms in the private sector.

First, the benefits. The city must account for a variety of indirect benefits in addition to the direct benefit derived from the revenues it receives. Even if the facility itself is unprofitable, the city will still want it if it generates spillovers into the local economy that more than make up for the venue losses and associated costs. The spillovers come in two parts: the direct impact of the team on incomes in the local community, and the indirect, ripple effect that the higher incomes set off. Finally, governments must somehow add intangible benefits, such as the sense of identity that a team provides residents, to the revenue stream a team provides. While difficult to measure, all residents can feel this bond and enjoy following the hometown team regardless of whether they actually attend a game. The sections below explore the direct and indirect benefits of a team on the local economy.

Direct Benefits   In 2003, the New York state comptroller released a report on the impact of the Buffalo Sabres hockey team on the Buffalo–Niagara region that asserted that the Sabres brought direct benefits of $43.6 million to the region. This figure consists of "$31 million in gate receipts, $8.6 million in concessions

[5]Darren Rovell, "What's the Lease You Can Do?" *ESPN: Sports Business,* September 20, 2002, at http://ESPN.com.

[6]Cagan and deMause, *Field of Schemes* (1998), pp. 59–60; and Caitlin Rother, "Tab Climbs in Charger Ticket Deal with City," *San Diego Union-Tribune,* September 12, 2000, p. B1.

[7]They have made other payments to the city out of luxury box and club seat revenue. Mark Rosentraub, *Major League Losers* (New York: Basic Books, 1997), pp. 267–275.

revenue, and $4 million in broadcast and advertising revenue."[8] However, these figures vastly overstated those direct benefits. The direct benefits a franchise brings a city stem from the new spending it generates. New spending can take one of two forms. First, a franchise may cause the residents to spend more—and save less—of their incomes; this increases their **average propensity to consume** (APC). A person's APC is the ratio of his or her expenditure on consumption goods to his or her total income. Thus, if Rachel earns $40,000 and spends $30,000, her APC is $30,000/$40,000 = 0.75.

Second, and more significantly, a franchise can stimulate **net exports** by the city. International trade economists define net exports as the difference between the value of goods and services a nation exports and the value of goods and services it imports. While Buffalo and Detroit are not separate countries, they resemble separate countries in that they buy and sell goods from one another and other cities. Buffalo exports the services of its hockey team, the Sabres, to the surrounding region if the team attracts fans from the surrounding area to its games in Buffalo. The Sabres also increases Buffalo's net exports by reducing the city's imports from other cities. Buffalo's imports fall if residents attend Sabres games in Buffalo rather than spend their money in the surrounding area.

Accounting only for the expenditures of Sabres fans, however, overstates the impact the Sabres have on Buffalo's net exports. One must look at the Sabres' expenditures as well, because they may stimulate imports as well as exports. Athletes or coaches who play for the Sabres but live outside of Buffalo count as inputs that must be imported. Unfortunately for Buffalo, most of the full-time jobs and most of the income generated by the Sabres go to the team's athletes, coaches, front-office staff, executives, and owners, relatively few of whom live year-round in Buffalo. The Sabres thus serve as a conduit, transferring money from one set of out-of-town residents to another set of out-of-towners.

Even if all the personnel associated with the Sabres lived in Buffalo, counting all the expenditures that they generate as new revenues would still overstate their direct impact on Buffalo. If it is true, as Baade and Sanderson claim, that "Hollywood enjoyed its best September ever during the [1994 baseball] players' strike,"[9] then the money fans spend on hockey games could just as easily have gone to some other form of local entertainment without increasing overall expenditure, and the impact of the Sabres was highly overstated.

Substitution may also occur on the supply side. If Buffalo's economy is close to full employment, then expanding one sector of the economy comes at the expense of another sector of the city's economy. The **production possibilities frontier** (PPF) in Figure 7.1 shows the impact of expanding expenditure on a sports franchise. The PPF shows the combinations of sports facilities and other goods that Buffalo can offer. It can provide any combination of sports facilities and other goods inside (point A) or on (point B) the frontier. Buffalo

---

[8]Figures taken from Gene Warner, "Hockey Team Has $65 million Impact, Hevesi Says," *Buffalo News,* online, February 26, 2003, at http://www.Buffalo.com

[9]Robert Baade and Allen Sanderson, "The Employment Effect of Teams and Sports Facilities," in *Sports, Jobs, and Taxes,* ed. by Roger Noll and Andrew Zimbalist (Washington, D.C.: Brookings Institution Press, 1997), p. 97.

FIGURE 7.1

Points A and B Are Feasible,
but C Is Preferred

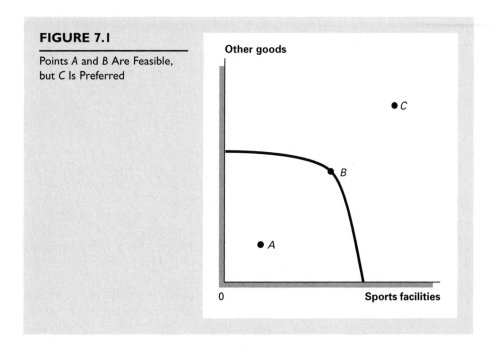

does not have enough resources, however, to produce at a point outside the frontier (point C). If Buffalo is not at full employment—at point A—then expanding the sports sector can increase the total level of spending and production. If, however, resources are already fully employed, as at point B on the PPF, then Buffalo can expand the sports sector only by reducing the output of the other goods.

Finally, despite their high profile, sports franchises are really a rather small business. For example, "the sales revenue of Fruit of the Loom exceeds that for all of Major League Baseball."[10] In Chicago, which has five major professional franchises within the city limits, commercial sports account for only about 0.25 percent of the total payroll and 0.08 percent of overall personal income.[11] Nor is this pattern peculiar to Chicago. Sports account for no more than 0.75 percent of private sector payrolls in all 161 counties in the United States that have populations over 300,000.[12] The impact of sports franchises on specific cities is thus very small.

To put these numbers in perspective, *Forbes* listed the gross revenues of the Buffalo Sabres in 2002 as about $56 million. Compare this with the revenues of

[10]Robert Baade, "Should Congress Stop the Bidding War for Sports Franchises?" Hearing Before the Subcommittee on Antitrust, Business Rights, and Compensation, Senate Committee on the Judiciary, November 29, 1995, v. 4, "Academics," *Heartland Policy,* at http://www.heartland.org/stadps4.html, p. 19.

[11]Robert Baade, "Professional Sports as Catalysts for Metropolitan Economic Development," *Journal of Urban Affairs,* v. 18, no. 1 (1996), p. 5; and Baade, "Should Congress Stop the Bidding War" (1995), p. 19.

[12]Rosentraub, *Major League Losers* (1997), p. 141.

Haverford and Bryn Mawr, two small Quaker-affiliated colleges in suburban Philadelphia. The total revenues of the two colleges from tuition alone (disregarding, for example, research grants or consulting revenue earned by the faculty) accounted for $74.4 million. By this reasoning, Buffalo would generate substantially more income if it let the Sabres move but induced the two colleges to move to town.[13] The evening news, however, has no reports of cities trying to lure colleges to town.[14]

Indirect Costs and Benefits Clearly, the direct benefits that cities enjoy from having franchises do not come close to justifying the millions of dollars that they have spent luring or retaining the teams. Unlike directors of a private firm, however, public officials must account for costs and benefits that accrue to residents who do not attend home games. Unlike payments to athletes or revenues from fans, these costs and benefits are indirect, that is, external to the profit maximization decision described in Chapter 3. A private firm such as the franchise has no reason to account for these indirect costs and benefits. It may even be unaware that such costs and benefits exist. Economists call the benefits conferred on third parties **positive externalities**. They call the costs that producers impose on third parties who do not buy from or sell to the firm **negative externalities.** One of the major justifications for the existence of government is to account for the benefit or harm done by positive or negative externalities.

Like monopoly and monopsony power, positive and negative externalities interfere with the market's ability to allocate resources. Consider, for example, the negative externalities the Buffalo Sabres would create if there were no government. In addition to whatever direct costs and benefits the Sabres convey on the residents of Buffalo, they also create negative externalities such as congestion, noise, and crime each time they play a game. In deciding how much to produce, the Sabres and the NHL as a whole worry about how much they must spend on salaries, travel, and a host of other inputs. They do not, however, consider—and may not even be aware of—the health problems and inconvenience they create for people affected by the congestion, pollution, and crime. The private costs that form the basis of the Sabres' and NHL's profit maximization decisions understate the full social costs, which include both private costs and the costs imposed on third parties.[15] If the Sabres or any firm considered all costs, the net rewards associated with any given price—and the incentive to produce—would be lower. As a result the "private" supply curve (S_p) in Figure 7.2, which includes only private

---

[13]The Sabres' revenue comes from NHL team valuations online at http://www.forbes.com. The tuition revenue for Haverford and Bryn Mawr were simulated assuming each school had 1,200 students and charged the stated tuition of $31,000.

[14]There is at least one example of cities competing for colleges. In the mid-1950s, Winston-Salem, N.C., paid for Wake Forest University to move from its original site to help create a middle class in town.

[15]Some teams have tried to reduce or eliminate negative externalities. The Chicago Cubs provide shuttle buses to reduce traffic and cleanup crews to reduce litter in the surrounding community. See Christopher Hepp, "Near Fabled Park, Ambience a Lure," *Philadelphia Inquirer* (September 29, 1999), pp. A1, A6.

costs experienced directly by the firm, lies to the right of the "social" supply curve (S_s), which includes all private and social costs.

The market equilibrium that results from the private decisions of producers and consumers in Figure 7.2 is Q_p, while the "social equilibrium" is only Q_s games. The difference ($Q_p - Q_s$) shows that the negative externality causes the Sabres to schedule too many games when left to their own devices. Similarly, the difference between the price that the Sabres charge and the price that society would like them to charge ($p_p - p_s$) shows that a negative externality causes the Sabres to charge their fans too little.

The Sabres benefit from the negative externality because they do not have to pay for the damage that crime, noise, and congestion impose on third parties. Fans who attend Sabres games benefit because they can see a game more cheaply, since the Sabres need not account for all the costs of production. Buffalo as a whole suffers, however, because costs more appropriately borne by the Sabres and the NHL are imposed on city residents.

Surprisingly, Buffalo generally would not want to eliminate the negative externalities that the Sabres impose on it. The only way to ensure that the Sabres impose no negative externalities on Buffalo would be for the Sabres to play no games there. Negative externalities, however, are not bad; they are negative by-products of a process that gives people something they want. In general, people would be worse off without the output even if it meant a cleaner, safer environment. In this example, the people of Buffalo want to see the number of games reduced to Q_s, where the benefits and social costs of one more hockey game are equal, but they do not want to eliminate the games entirely.

FIGURE 7.2

Negative Externalities Shift the Supply Curve Inward

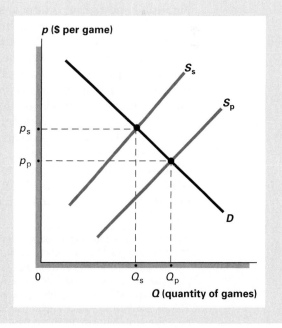

Oddly, the negative externalities associated with sports facilities seem to apply most to newly proposed facilities. Although residents of neighborhoods where a structure will be built often complain bitterly about the problems it will bring, residents are almost rhapsodic about many existing structures. In the words of baseball historian Harold Seymour, a ballpark is "a landmark, an asset to city life—especially to the lives of those who live in the neighborhood."[16]

One major reason for the difference in attitudes comes from the fact that most of the costs that an old ballpark such as Wrigley Field imposes on its neighbors have already been internalized, so fans who live near Wrigley Field have been compensated for any inconvenience the Cubs may impose in the form of lower housing costs. To the extent that proximity to Wrigley imposes costs on residents of the neighborhood, newcomers will pay less for homes or apartments. The prices and rents compensate residents for any costs imposed on them by the Cubs, thereby internalizing the externality. The only ones to be hurt would be the original homeowners and landlords, few, if any, of whom are still alive. By contrast, the negative externalities generated by newer facilities, such as Chicago's United Center, which was built in 1994, have yet to be fully internalized. People who own nearby housing may see the value of their property decline. Unlike the residents near Wrigley Field, they paid a higher price for their property.

Most local politicians believe that the negative externalities associated with franchises are dwarfed by the positive externalities they convey. They believe that professional sports franchises bring benefits to the city for which the team is not rewarded. Just as the costs that a negative externality imposes cause the supply curve to be too far out in Figure 7.2, the benefits a positive externality conveys cause the demand curve to be too far to the left. Figure 7.3 shows that, in the absence of government intervention, a positive externality would cause the Sabres to play too few games. Buffalo would like the Sabres to play Q_s games, but the Sabres would play only Q_p. Because the Sabres' revenues understate the total benefit to the residents of Buffalo, the city must provide an additional incentive for the Sabres to play games in Buffalo rather than elsewhere. In the case of professional sports franchises, these incentives often take the form of public funding of sports facilities.

The impact of a professional sports franchise on a city or region goes far beyond a strict dollars and cents accounting. As noted above, states, cities, or neighborhoods can derive a sense of identity from having a professional franchise in their midst.[17] A successful team, in particular, may contribute to a city's self-image. As Bill Veeck said of his 1948 Cleveland Indians, "[T]here is that feeling of reflected glory in a successful baseball team. Cleveland is winning the

---

[16]See the Foreword to Michael Betzold and Ethan Casey, *Queen of Diamonds: The Tiger Stadium Story* (West Bloomfield, M.I.: Northfield Publishing, 1992).

[17]Michael Danielson, *Home Team: Professional Sport and the American Metropolis* (Princeton, N.J.: Princeton University Press, 1997); Rosentraub, *Major League Losers* (1997), pp. 30–73; and David Swindell and Mark Rosentraub, "Who Benefits from the Presence of Professional Sports Teams? The Implications for Public Funding of Stadiums and Arenas," *Public Administration Review*, v. 58, no. 1 (January/February 1998), pp. 11–20.

FIGURE 7.3

Positive Externalities Shift the
Demand Curve Outward

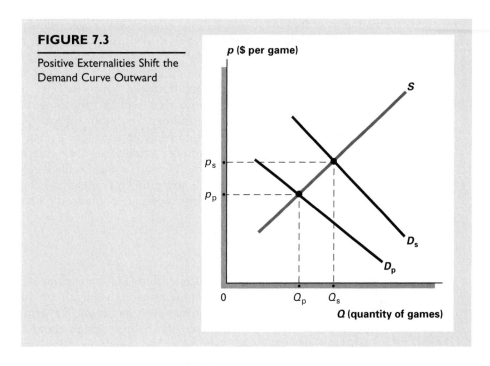

pennant. The eyes of the whole country are upon Cleveland, upon us, upon me
and you. *We're looking pretty good, aren't we, Mac?*"[18] All the residents of a community can share in the reflected glory of their hometown team without having
to pay for the privilege. A franchise thus has aspects of a public good in that
those who consume it do not prevent others from enjoying the team's presence,
further justifying a role for government in providing it. The nonrivalry and
nonexclusion allow people to free ride by passively following the team rather
than buying tickets. The free rider problem means that fans do not compensate
teams fully for the benefits they provide. This, in turn, reduces the incentive
teams have to provide their services, causing them to provide too little of the
good. Chapter 3 showed that teams solve their own free rider problem by forming a larger collective known as a league. The league resolves the free rider
problem by forcing teams to contribute to activities that benefit all teams.
Society deals with the free rider problem by forming a larger collective known
as government. The government forces people to contribute to collectively consumed public goods by imposing taxes and providing the good.

Small to midsized cities, in particular, generate a sense of being a "big-
time" city from having a major league franchise. Indianapolis may not be able
to compete with New York in terms of economic or cultural clout, but it derives
a sense of superiority to New York whenever *our* Indiana Pacers defeat *their*
New York Knicks. It may therefore come as no surprise that a recent survey of

---

[18]Bill Veeck and Ed Linn, *Veeck as in Wreck* (Chicago: University of Chicago Press, 1962), p. 121.

residents of Indianapolis found that the Indiana Pacers were a close second to the city's museums as a source of civic pride, with the Indianapolis Colts placing third.[19]

City officials often claim that, in addition to improving the self-esteem of residents, having a professional franchise gives the city a higher profile, which in turn attracts business that would otherwise not locate there. However, this is disproved by the experts. From the pathbreaking work of Robert Baade and Richard Dye to more recent work by Ian Hudson and by Dennis Coates and Brad Humphreys, economists have consistently found no evidence that facilities and teams have an impact on the level of employment, incomes, or wages in a city.[20] They uniformly conclude that neither sports franchises nor new facilities bring appreciable financial gain to the communities where they are located.

Multiplier Effects

While the New York state comptroller finds that fans spend $43.6 million on the Buffalo Sabres, he concludes that the team has a $65 million impact on the local economy. Where does the extra money come from? The difference lies in the fact that any new spending that the Sabres brings about in Buffalo has a **multiplier effect.** That is, each new dollar spent on the Sabres generates additional expenditures, increasing the overall impact of the Sabres on spending and incomes in Buffalo.

To envision the multiplier process, think of Buffalo's economy as a still pond. Attracting the Sabres to town is like throwing a pebble into the pond. The direct impact of the Sabres is the splash caused by the pebble's hitting the water. A series of ripples quickly spreads out from the initial point of impact. As they spread out, the ripples become fainter and fainter, until they are indistinguishable from the flat pond. The multiplier effect is like those ripples, spreading the direct impact that the Sabres has on Buffalo throughout the entire city. To illustrate this, the income that Donna, a Buffalo resident, earns from working as an accountant for the Sabres is part of the direct impact the Sabres have on income in Buffalo. Her salary is thus part of the initial splash the pebble makes in the pond. Donna saves some of her income and spends some, perhaps on a new condominium in town. Her expenditure on the condo becomes part of the first ripple. Her purchase, in turn, increases the income of the local

---

[19]Mark Rosentraub, "Stadiums and Urban Space" (1997), pp. 189–190; and Swindell and Rosentraub, "Who Benefits from the Presence of Professional Sports Teams?" (1998), pp. 11–20.

[20]Robert Baade and Richard Dye, "The Impact of Stadiums and Professional Sports on Metropolitan Area Development," *Growth and Change,* v. 21, no. 2 (Spring 1990), pp. 1–14; Ian Hudson, "Bright Lights, Big City: Do Professional Sports Teams Increase Employment?" *Journal of Urban Affairs,* v. 21, no. 4 (1999), pp. 397–407; and Dennis Coates and Brad Humphreys, "The Effect of Professional Sports on Earnings and Employment in U.S. Cities," *Regional Science and Urban Economics,* v. 33, no. 2 (March 2003), pp. 175–198.

builder (and realtor and others). The builder then saves some of his additional income and spends some, perhaps buying a new computer from a local computer outlet, forming yet another ripple, and so on.

The ripples get smaller because people do not spend all their additional income. Economists call the fraction of an additional dollar of income that consumers spend the **marginal propensity to consume** (MPC). They call the fraction of an additional dollar that they save the **marginal propensity to save** (MPS). Consumers must spend or save that entire additional dollar, so

$$MPC + MPS = 1.$$

Most economists believe that Americans spend more than nine-tenths of each additional dollar that they earn. Assuming for simplicity that the $MPC = 0.9$; if Donna earned $100,000, then she would spend

$$(0.9)(\$100,000) = \$90,000.$$

The $90,000 that Donna spends is additional income to other people, who then spend nine-tenths of that income, or

$$(0.9)[(0.9)(\$100,000)] = \$81,000.$$

The process continues in steadily decreasing ripples until the additional expenditure becomes indistinguishable from zero and the ripples effectively disappear.

The total impact of Donna's $100,000 income on the Buffalo economy is

$$T = \$100,000 + \$90,000 + \$81,000 + \$72,900 + \cdots.$$

While the numbers in this sum decline steadily to zero, it is not clear what the total impact is. To see the total impact, rewrite the sum as the product of the initial salary payment and successive MPCs:

$$T = \$100,000 + (0.9)(\$100,000) + (0.9)[(0.9)(\$100,000)] + (0.9)\{(0.9)[(0.9)(\$100,000)]\} + \cdots$$

Combining the MPCs and expressing them as exponents yields

$$T = \$100,000 + (0.9)(\$100,000) + (0.9)^2(\$100,000) + (0.9)^3(\$100,000) + \cdots$$

Factoring out the $100,000 simplifies the expression to

$$T = (\$100,000)[1 + 0.9 + (0.9)^2 + (0.9)^3 + (0.9)^4 + \cdots] = (\$100,000)(S)$$

where

$$S = [1 + 0.9 + (0.9)^2 + (0.9)^3 + (0.9)^4 + \cdots]$$

The individual terms in the brackets get closer to zero as the exponent rises. Eventually the exponent gets so large—and the terms get so small—that in effect, zero is added. The fact that the terms in S approach zero allows the use of a simple mathematical trick. Start by multiplying S by 0.9, and then subtract this product from the original S:

$$S = 1 + 0.9 + (0.9)^2 + (0.9)^3 + (0.9)^4 + (0.9)^5 + \cdots$$
$$S' = -(0.9)S = -0.9 - (0.9)^2 - (0.9)^3 - (0.9)^4 - (0.9)^5 - \cdots$$

All the terms in the two sums line up—and thus cancel each other out—except for the very first term of S and the very last term of S'. The last term of S' is effectively zero since it equals 0.9 to a very high power. As a result, the difference $S - S'$ can be approximated as:

$$S - (0.9)\,S \approx 1.$$

Rearranging terms yields an approximate value of the infinite sum S:

$$S \approx \frac{1}{1-0.9} = \frac{1}{0.1} = 10.$$

More generally, the **simple multiplier** equals:

$$M = \frac{1}{1-MPC} = \frac{1}{MPS}.$$

In this example, Donna's $100,000 salary creates $1 million in extra income for Buffalo, 10 times the initial impact.

Clearly, the size of the multiplier has major implications for the value of a franchise to a city. A relatively small direct impact can lead to a huge increase in incomes and the well-being of the city. There is, however, reason to believe that the simple multiplier derived above grossly overstates the true multiplier. The most important reason concerns leakages from the system. It was shown above that Donna's $100,000 salary has no direct impact on incomes in Buffalo if she lives and shops in the suburbs and commutes to the city. The derivation of the simple multiplier was also based on the assumption that Donna—and all subsequent beneficiaries—spent all their money in Buffalo. If instead of a condo Donna bought a car from an auto dealer in Orchard Park, then that portion of her income leaks out of the system and reduces the size of all future ripples. Since a substantial amount of income goes to people who spend a considerable amount of their time and money outside of Buffalo, the size of the multiplier is likely to be much smaller than 10, even if the MPC equals 0.9. The leakages are likely to be larger—and the multiplier effect smaller—for smaller cities, since residents are more likely to spend a portion of their incomes elsewhere.

The multiplier falls still further because most professional teams pay more than half of their revenues to their athletes (and a substantial portion of the rest to highly paid executives). Even if the athletes live in the town in which they play, the peculiar nature of their earnings stream reduces the multiplier effect. Most elite professional athletes make unusually high incomes for relatively short periods of time. Their high incomes put athletes in relatively high tax brackets, meaning that they pay a higher proportion of their income in taxes. The greater bite that taxes take out of their incomes reduces the amount of money they have available to spend, thereby reducing subsequent ripple effects. In addition, because they earn the bulk of their incomes over a relatively short time span, professional athletes have an incentive to save more than people whose peak earnings are spread over a longer period of time. Professional athletes thus have a lower MPC and higher MPS, which further reduces the ripple effects of their high earnings. Finally, since the wealthy have already met most of their immediate needs, they tend to save more of an additional dollar and spend less. The MPS is thus higher (and the MPC lower) for wealthy people.[21]

Noll and Zimbalist provide a modified multiplier that takes account of the unique factors facing a municipality that hosts a professional sports franchise:

$$M_{\text{local}} = \frac{1}{(1 - MPC \cdot f)}.$$

where f is the fraction of local consumption expenditures that causes local incomes to rise.[22] They claim that the factors mentioned above reduce the relevant MPC from 0.9 to about 0.67 and that f equals about 0.5. These parameters yield a multiplier of only 1.5, far less than the simple value of 10. Because a large city with a diversified economy is likely to capture more expenditure, the multiplier for a team in a large city is likely to be larger than 1.5. Similarly, expenditures generated by a franchise in a smaller city are more likely to leak out to surrounding communities. As a result, the multiplier will probably be smaller than 1.5. By predicting a total impact of $65 million when direct expenditures are only $43.6 million, the New York state comptroller implicitly assumes that the multiplier for Buffalo is 1.5.

Even with the multiplier, the overall financial impact of a franchise seems small. A study by Deloitte and Touche of the economic impact of the Arizona Diamondbacks on the state's economy found that the state gained about 340 full-time jobs at a cost of $240 million.[23] While $706,000 per job created may be higher than for most cities, it is not extraordinarily high for the cost of jobs created by a sports facility. In its analysis of the new stadium it was building for the Baltimore Ravens, the Maryland Department of Business and Economic Development projected economic benefits of $111 million and 1,394 new jobs from the Ravens. Other analysts claim that these estimates are too high and put the true impacts at $33 million and 534 jobs. As a result, the estimates of the cost to the state of Maryland per job created range from $127,000 to $331,000. While this figure is better than for Arizona, it is still far higher than other job-creation projects. Compared with the 5,200 full-time jobs created by Maryland's Sunny Day Fund for economic development, which cost taxpayers only $6,250 per job, the Ravens seem like a poor choice as a spur for economic development.[24]

The simple truth is that a professional franchise cannot be an engine for regional or local growth when its facility is empty more than 200 days a year.

---

[21]See, for example, Noll and Zimbalist, "The Economic Impact of Sports Teams and Facilities" (1997), p. 72.

[22]Noll and Zimbalist, "The Economic Impact of Sports Teams and Facilities" (1997), p. 75.

[23]Baade and Sanderson, "The Employment Effect of Teams and Sports Facilities" (1997), p. 101.

[24]Dennis Zimmerman, "Subsidizing Stadiums: Who Benefits, Who Pays?" in *Sports, Jobs, and Taxes,* ed. by Roger Noll and Andrew Zimbalist (Washington, D.C.: Brookings Institution Press, 1997), p. 122. These figures agree with the finding that the jobs created by the new basketball and baseball facilities in Cleveland cost $231,000 per job. See Ziona Austrian and Mark Rosentraub, "Cleveland's Gateway to the Future," also in *Sports, Jobs, and Taxes,* p. 382.

Because their main tenants do not use football stadiums more than 350 days per year, football in particular is a poor vehicle for growth. In fact, some studies find that, because a sports franchise often drains resources from more productive expenditures, spending money to attract or retain a team can actually inhibit municipal growth.

Although there is little evidence that a team or a facility brings financial benefits, a city may still be willing to go to the expense of hosting it. As Bill Veeck and others have suggested, the main benefits a sports franchise brings a city are intangible feelings of well-being.[25] In a recent study, Rappoport and Wilkerson claim that such benefits could make a sports franchise worthwhile for a city even if it does not bring financial gain. Because they are intangible, however, these benefits are difficult to measure. Coates and Humphreys attempt to capture the intangible value of a franchise by looking at the impact of a team on property values, holding housing and other community characteristics constant.[26] All else equal, they find that housing located within a half-mile of the team does have higher value, though the effect quickly declines at greater distances. They conclude that a professional sports franchise makes the immediate community more attractive to potential homebuyers but that it has little effect on the city as a whole.

Can Anyone Win at This Game?

Although the consensus among economists is that cities do not come out ahead in what Shropshire calls "the sports franchise game,"[27] some cities clearly do better than others. Some of the determinants of success have more to do with accidents of geography and history. The difficulties experienced by midsized American cities such as Hartford, which lost its NHL team in 1997 and more recently tried unsuccessfully to attract an NFL team, as well as the "skate drain" that is slowly drawing hockey franchises out of Canada demonstrate the problems some cities face. Still, by carefully incorporating sports franchises in a broader economic development plan, local politicians can increase the benefits a franchise brings to their city.

Larger cities have a natural advantage at attracting and retaining franchises. As noted in Chapter 3, leagues that placed franchises in midsized cities all lost out to leagues that placed teams in larger cities. Larger cities have more people who benefit, directly or indirectly, from having a team in town. While their fans may be more rabid and more knowledgeable, towns such as Winnipeg or Quebec cannot generate the same fan base or media market as a team in Phoenix or Denver can. Bigger cities also have larger

[25]Others include Danielson (1997) and Swindell and Rosentraub (1998).

[26]Jordan Rappoport and Chad Wilkerson, "What Are the Benefits of Hosting a Major League Sports Franchise?" *Federal Reserve Bank of Kansas City Economic Review*, First Quarter, 2001, pp. 55–85; Dennis Coates and Brad R. Humphreys, "Professional Sports Facilities, Franchises and Urban Economic Development," *UMBC Working Paper 03–103*, 2003.

[27]Kenneth Shropshire, *The Sports Franchise Game* (Philadelphia: University of Pennsylvania Press, 1995).

multiplier effects because their employees are more likely to live in town or in surrounding communities.

While franchises benefit greatly from locating in a large local market, larger cities do not necessarily benefit more from hosting them. The size and diversity of the local economy has an ambiguous effect on the value of a franchise to a city. Larger, more diverse economies give residents more opportunities to spend their money with local proprietors. If the local economy can capture more of the ripple effect, the multiplier effect rises, making a franchise more valuable to a city. A more diverse economy also increases the substitution effect, since people are likely to spend their money on more types of other local activities if they do not have a local sporting event to attend.[28] This, in turn, makes a franchise less valuable.

In sum, cities such as Denver have a big advantage over cities such as Hartford when it comes to attracting franchises. Denver is a large city surrounded by smaller cities that offer little competition for entertainment dollars. It can therefore draw fans from a sizeable geographic area. Hartford, by contrast, is a midsized city that is squeezed between New York and Boston. As a result, Hartford had a much harder time creating a fan base and capturing the direct and indirect benefits of a professional franchise. Local politicans can try to offset this disadvantage, but they cannot eliminate it.

Similarly, Canadian cities have struggled mightily to retain franchises for their national game. In the 1990s, teams left Quebec for Denver and Winnipeg for Phoenix. In the decade ahead, the Calgary Flames, Edmonton Oilers, and Ottawa Senators all may leave for the United States.

Quebec and Winnipeg were doomed by their small size, their small fan base and limited gate revenue, and local media revenue. Although the NFL can support small-market cities such as Green Bay, thanks to generous gate revenue sharing and a large national TV contract (which is shared equally among all teams), the NHL has a minimal safety net: it does not share gate revenue at all and gets much less revenue from its network contract than does the NFL.

In addition, the Canadian franchises have been badly stung by the relatively high tax rates in Canada. Because high tax rates reduce the disposable income available to hockey players on Canadian teams, Canadian teams and cities are less attractive to play for. As players have won more control over where they can play and as the NHL increasingly draws players from around the globe who lack personal ties to Canada, players are choosing to leave Canadian teams and play on American teams. High tax rates also reduce the after-tax profits of Canadian franchises relative to franchises in the United States, making it more difficult for franchises to offer attractive salaries and compete for players in free agent markets.

Finally, the steady erosion of the Canadian dollar relative to the U.S. dollar has seriously damaged the ability of Canadian teams to compete with their U.S. rivals because Canadian teams' revenue streams are largely in Canadian dollars, but they must pay salaries that match those paid by teams in the

---

[28]See Noll and Zimbalist, "The Economic Impact of Sports Teams and Facilities" (1997), pp. 79–80.

United States. Local and provincial governments have attempted to subsidize their hockey franchises to prevent them from moving. Canadian voters, however, have been reluctant to approve taxes that would be earmarked for privately owned sports teams. A more recent attempt to establish a wage tax on visiting hockey players has been opposed by other teams and by the NHL Players Association.

To show the impact of exchange rates on Canadian franchises, we make the simplifying assumption that a Canadian team pays its team in U.S. dollars. Since its revenues are all in Canadian dollars, the team must buy U.S. dollars before it can pay its players. It does so by buying dollars on a **currency market.** Currency markets treat dollars, yen, or francs like any other commodity. Figure 7. 4 shows the market for U.S. dollars. The "price" of U.S. dollars is the number of Canadian dollars it takes to buy US$1. This price is called the **exchange rate,** because it determines how many Canadian dollars must be exchanged to get US$1. It takes about C$1.50 to buy US$1, so the exchange rate for U.S. dollars is about 1.5.

The Canadian hockey teams' expenses are thus magnified 50 percent by the exchange rate with the U.S. dollar. This has created an "exchange rate deficit" of up to C$8 million for some teams, despite tax breaks of up to C$4 million given by some Canadian provinces. Team owners can escape this burden—and lessen their tax burden as well—by moving south of the border. When players are discouraged from choosing to sign with Canadian franchises, this, in turn, discourages attendance and puts further economic pressure on Canadian franchises to relocate. The flow of teams from Canada to the United States has some speculating that Canada may eventually be left with only the Toronto Maple Leafs and the Montreal Canadiens.[29]

So what can local officials do to maximize the benefits of hosting a sports franchise? Some experts claim that a city gains more from attracting or retaining a franchise—and hence can afford to make a more attractive offer to a franchise—if it has integrated the facilities into the urban fabric.[30] According to these analysts, many cities waste their chance to benefit from hosting a franchise by making their decisions at the last minute under threats by teams to move if their demands are not satisfied. Members of the Illinois legislature literally had to stop the clock to prevent the White Sox from leaving Chicago for St. Petersburg.[31] Chicago's lack of planning showed in the decision to locate the "New Comiskey Park" (now U.S. Cellular Field) across the street from the old one with little attention paid to incorporating the stadium into broader plans for economic development.

---

[29]Michael Farber, "Giant Sucking Sound," *Sports Illustrated* (March 20, 1995), p. 104; and Tim Panaccio "Senators Owner Bryden Got Tired of Fighting Exchange-Rate Deficit," *Philadelphia Inquirer* (December 5, 1999), p. C5.

[30]Thomas Chema, "When Professional Sports Justify the Subsidy," *Journal of Urban Affairs,* v. 18, no. 1 (1996), p. 20; and Baade and Sanderson, "The Employment Effect of Teams and Sports Facilities" (1997), pp. 94–95.

[31]Shropshire, *The Sports Franchise Game* (1995), p. 11.

FIGURE 7.4

At Equilibrium, US$1.00 Costs C$1.50

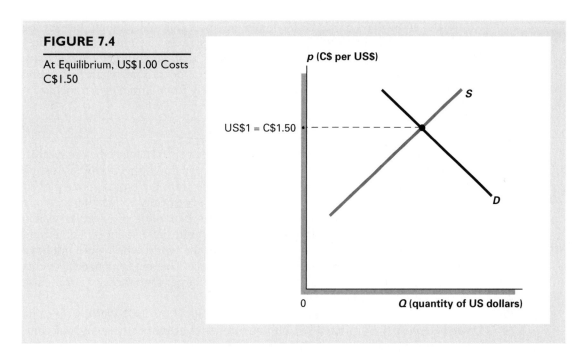

By contrast, Baltimore, Cleveland, and Indianapolis all undertook extensive efforts to incorporate the new facilities into their plans for urban revival. Baltimore sought to capitalize on the success of its efforts in the Inner Harbor, anchored by the Baltimore Aquarium, by building Oriole Park at Camden Yards and M&T Bank Stadium (home of the Ravens) close by. In Cleveland, Jacobs Field, which kept the Indians in town, and the Gund Arena, which brought the Cavaliers back to Cleveland from suburban Richfield, were all part of a broader Gateway Project designed to revitalize downtown Cleveland. In the 1980s, Indianapolis also decided to redevelop its downtown by extensive construction of a wide array of athletic facilities, including the Hoosier (later RCA) Dome. It linked this construction to the expansion of nonsports facilities such as the campus of Indiana University–Purdue University at Indianapolis.

All three projects have been loudly proclaimed as successes in creating jobs and revitalizing downtown areas. A closer look suggests that even a carefully planned sports complex may not have much of an impact. Indianapolis had only moderate, short-term success in retarding the relocation of employment to the suburbs.[32] While Cleveland did experience job growth following the construction of the sports facilities, the growth was actually lower downtown than elsewhere in the region and was slower than in the years immediately preceding the project.[33] Despite the fanfare surrounding the "best case" scenario of Camden Yards,

---

[32]Rosentraub, "Stadiums and Urban Space" (1997), pp. 178–207.
[33]Austrian and Rosentraub, "Cleveland's Gateway to the Future" (1997), pp. 355–384.

estimates show that Orioles Park has created fewer than 600 jobs and has left the typical household roughly $12 poorer through the taxes they must pay to support the construction. Preliminary estimates show that, if anything, M&T Bank Stadium does an even worse job.[34] In sum, it appears that regardless of the approach they take, cities do not gain significantly from attracting a franchise.

The Impact of Special Events

Even if cities do not gain much from hosting a sports franchise, they may profit from hosting a special event, such as the Super Bowl, the Olympics, or the World Cup finals. Special events like these differ from the typical game played by local franchises in that they do not appeal specifically to local fans. While much of the money spent by local fans on a baseball game or a regular season football game may just replace money they would have spent on something else, special events attract people from all over the world who would not have come to the host city had the event not taken place. The impact of special events would therefore be expected to be significantly larger than those of a franchise over a similar period of time.

As shown in Chapter 6, however, the benefits of the 2002 World Cup came nowhere near the projected $31 billion. Similar overoptimism seems to accompany the Super Bowl. Here, though, even the findings after the fact are subject to dispute. In his study of the economic impact of the Super Bowl, Philip Porter notes that studies conducted by host committees or the NFL on the Super Bowls held in Tampa (1991), Miami (1995), and Phoenix (1996) show an impact ranging from almost $120 million to over $160 million.[35]

Porter examined the impact of the Super Bowl on Miami, Tampa, and Phoenix by estimating the impact of the Super Bowl on the dollar value of sales in each city's county (Dade, Hillsborough, and Maricopa Counties, respectively) for the 1979, 1984, 1989, 1991, 1995, and 1996 Super Bowls. He found little evidence that the Super Bowl had a major financial impact on the local economies. He found a statistically significant impact only for the 1984 Super Bowl in Tampa, and even this indicated that local sales increased by only $1.3 million during the month of the Super Bowl.

How can one reconcile Porter's findings with the huge returns detected by the NFL and the host committees? The key seems to be analogous to our finding that spending by city residents on local sports franchises crowds out other local spending. In this case, the NFL and host committees seem to have assumed that all spending on the Super Bowl was new expenditure by additional tourists. Porter concluded that spending on a Super Bowl largely displaces spending by tourists who would have gone to these cities but could not do so because of the influx of football fans. The net impact of a Super Bowl in such a situation is essentially zero.

---

[34]Bruce Hamilton and Peter Kahn, "Baltimore's Camden Yards Ballparks," in *Sports, Jobs, and Taxes,* ed. by Roger Noll and Andrew Zimbalist (Washington, D.C.: Brookings Institution Press, 1997), pp. 245–281.

[35]Philip Porter, "Mega-Sporting Events as Municipal Investments: A Critique of Impact Analysis," in *Sports Economics: Current Research,* ed. by John Fizel, Elizabeth Gustafson, and Larry Hadley (Westport, C.T.: Praeger Publishers, 1999).

7.2 A PUBLIC CHOICE PERSPECTIVE

If cities do not gain significantly from sports franchises, then their spending millions of dollars on facilities for these franchises seems to defy all economic logic. A relatively new area of economic thought—known as **public choice theory**—provides an economic framework that makes it possible to understand why cities do what they do.

Public choice theory stems from the work of Nobel laureate James Buchanan, Gordon Tullock, William Niskanen, and others in the 1960s. The basic premise rests on the notion that decision makers in the public sector do not automatically act to resolve the market failures of public goods and externalities. Instead, public officials are subject to many of the same temptations and constraints facing consumers and producers in the private sector.

According to the public choice perspective, the interests of politicians and the owners of sports franchises come together very neatly. Politicians have an interest in attaining, maintaining, and advancing their political standing. They therefore undertake actions that they feel will ensure their reelection or get them elected to higher office. To do so, they respond to the interests of the electorate. Since it is costly to determine the specific interests of large numbers of disparate voters, politicians are most responsive to organized group interests; the more highly organized the group, the more influence it wields over officeholders.[36]

Team owners, often in alliance with business and labor interests, have sought to use their organized influence over the political process. At times, the groups may actually improve the efficiency of the political process. By expressing the intensity of their desires, interest groups may—through a process known as **logrolling**—induce politicians to pass legislation that the electoral process would deny. To see this, suppose a legislature consists of three equal groups, each representing one-third of the state (i.e., East, Central, and West). The state is considering building two stadiums, one each in the East and West of the state. Suppose each new stadium would greatly benefit the region in which it is located but mildly hurt—through higher taxes that everyone in the state must pay to fund the stadiums—the other two portions of the state, as seen in Table 7.1. If the representatives voted according to the impact of the stadium on their constituents, they would defeat both stadium proposals, because each proposal hurts two-thirds of the state. According to the payoffs in Table 7.1, however, the benefits of each proposal benefit the constituency so much that majority rule leaves the state worse off. By expressing the intensity of their desires, group interests may induce legislators from the East and West to vote for each other's proposals and improve social well-being by passing both proposals. The proposal would therefore pass by a 2–1 margin, despite the fact that each facility benefits only one region.[37]

---

[36]See, for example, Arthur Seldon, "Public Choice and the Choices of the Public," in *Democracy and Public Choice*, ed. by Charles Rowley (London: Basil Blackwell, 1987), pp. 122–134. In Chapter 10 we explore the role played by bureaucrats who are not directly answerable to voters.

[37]See, for example, Thomas Stratmann, "Logrolling," in *Perspectives on Public Choice: A Handbook*, ed. by Dennis Mueller (Cambridge, U.K.: Cambridge University Press, 1997), pp. 322–341.

Table 7.1

How Logrolling Can Improve Social Well-Being

Region	Payoff to Proposal #1	Payoff to Proposal #2
East	+$10 million	–$2 million
Central	–$2 million	–$2 million
West	–$2 million	+$10 million
Overall impact	+$6 million	+$6 million

Generally speaking, group interests do not have such a positive impact on society. This is particularly true when groups use their political influence to pursue rents. Chapter 4 explained how rent-seeking behavior by firms in the private sector may increase the deadweight loss due to monopoly. In the public sphere, rents result from the monopoly right to provide an output. Rent-seeking behavior in the public sector thus consists of a two-step process. First, the rent seeker must control the political process that determines the distribution of rights or output. Second, once in control of the political process, the rent seeker then exploits his or her monopoly position.

It's possible to see such a two-stage process in the expenditures well-organized interests make to pursue their political ends. Pro-stadium forces in Cleveland raised over $1 million to pay for their 1990 referendum effort; this included payments of over $300,000 from the Indians and Cavaliers. In a more extreme example, Paul Allen, who used some of the fortune he made from Microsoft to purchase the Seattle Seahawks football team, paid the state of Washington $4.2 million to cover the costs of the referendum on financing a new football stadium. This move neatly sidestepped the state's requirement that the team demonstrate sufficient support for a publicly funded referendum by gathering petitions. Allen also spent $5 million during the campaign to convince voters to support the proposal to spend $300 million on the new Seahawks stadium. The effort proved successful, as Washington voters narrowly approved the proposal. The $300 million return on a $9.2 million investment proved to be one of Allen's most profitable moves since joining with Bill Gates to form Microsoft.[38]

7.3 FINANCING FACILITIES

Section 7.1 showed that state and local governments can—at least in theory—justify subsidizing franchises, if the city or state benefits from the public good aspect of the franchise or from the positive externalities it conveys upon the city. Because the local team is not rewarded for all the benefits it provides to the community, it may not have enough of an incentive to locate in the city without a public subsidy. The subsidy, however, has to come from somewhere. State

---

[38]Cagan and deMause, *Field of Schemes* (1998), pp. 16, 44, 166–168.

and local governments have two basic sources of revenue: taxes and debt. Both sources have their advantages and disadvantages. Even if the community borrows, however, it eventually will have to raise taxes in order to repay the loan. Since governments cannot escape imposing a tax, they should pay careful attention to the form of tax they impose, as different taxes have significantly different impacts on subgroups in the population. In the first part of this section, we present several criteria by which economists evaluate tax plans. In the next three subsections, we then use these criteria to evaluate methods that cities have chosen to finance new facilities. In the final part of this section, we look at why governments prefer using debt to finance new facilities.

An Economic View of Taxes: Who Should Pay?

We have seen that negative externalities cause society to produce and consume too much of a good and that positive externalities cause it to produce and consume too little. Governments typically try to resolve the problems that externalities cause by *internalizing* them. In the case of negative externalities, taxes raise the cost of production, causing firms to produce less. In the case of positive externalities, subsidies increase the rewards from production and encourage firms to produce more.

Using a subsidy to eliminate a positive externality raises a crucial question: where does the government get the money to provide the subsidy? Economic theory explains that governments maximize the well-being of their residents, if they finance the subsidy by imposing taxes or fees based on the benefits each person receives from the positive externality. Unfortunately, the nature of positive externalities often makes it difficult to identify exactly who benefits. Fortunately, it is possible to establish some general principles for determining who should pay how much for a sports franchise.

One such principle—known as the **Ramsey rule**—dictates that sales taxes should be levied in inverse proportion to the price elasticity of demand for the good or service on which the government places the tax. Such a tax is efficient in the sense that it minimizes the deadweight loss imposed by the tax.

Suppose Miami wishes to raise money to fund a new baseball stadium for the Florida Marlins and is considering two possible sources of tax revenue: cruise passengers and kidney dialysis patients. Assume, for simplicity, that the city feels it can raise all the revenue it needs by imposing a $4 tax on either. Figure 7.5 shows the impact of a tax on cruises. As shown in Chapter 2, a $4 sales tax causes consumers to see a supply curve that is $4 higher than the true supply curve.

Since the equilibrium number of days spent on cruises falls from Q_0 to Q_1, the deadweight loss imposed by the tax equals the area of the triangle ECH. This burden consists of lost consumer surplus for cruise takers (EGH) and lost producer surplus for cruise operators (CGH). The implications of this shared burden are explored later in the chapter.

Contrast the deadweight loss from a cruise tax with the deadweight loss from a tax on kidney dialysis, as seen in Figure 7.6. A $4 tax on dialysis shifts

FIGURE 7.5

The Impact of a $4/Day Tax on Cruises

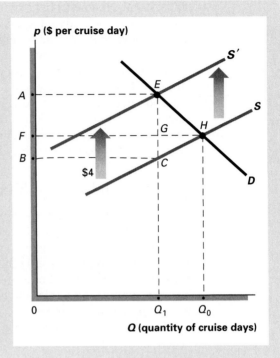

FIGURE 7.6

A Tax on Dialysis Causes Very Little Deadweight Loss

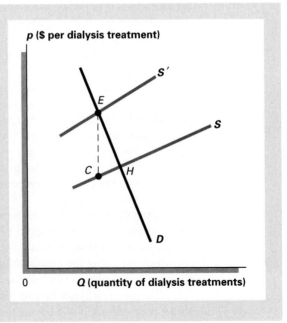

the supply curve (which, for simplicity, we assume to be identical to the supply curve in Figure 7.5) up by $4, just like before. Unlike cruises, kidney dialysis has no good substitutes. The demand for dialysis is therefore much less sensitive to changes in price than the demand for cruises. Since the demand curve is so inelastic, the quantity of dialysis hardly changes and the price increases by almost the full amount of the tax. Because the tax on dialysis causes little loss of output, there is very little deadweight loss (the area of the triangle ECH).

If Miami wants to impose a tax that minimizes deadweight loss, then a tax on dialysis may be just the thing. Most people, however, would not choose to impose a greater burden on people who are unfortunate enough to require dialysis.

Society must often choose between policies that are efficient and policies that satisfy some notion of fairness or *equity*. Tax analyses frequently apply two forms of equity: **horizontal equity** and **vertical equity.** Economists say that a policy satisfies vertical equity if it takes account of people's ability to pay. More generally, one can say that a vertically equitable tax does not fall particularly heavily on those with an already low level of income. Since cruises are pleasure trips typically taken by the well-to-do while dialysis is an undesired burden borne by people from a variety of income groups, a cruise tax is more vertically equitable than a dialysis tax.

While vertical equity applies across income or utility levels, horizontal equity refers to fairness at a given level. A tax is horizontally equitable if it treats equals equally. Since public expenditure often confers unequal benefits on the population, the pursuit of horizontal equity leads governments to levy taxes in proportion to the benefits received from the expenditure. In this example, the cruise and dialysis tax appear to do equally well by this criterion.[39]

Some economists feel that governments should rely on **user fees** rather than public taxation to fund facilities. They believe that the public good aspects of a professional franchise are dwarfed by the private consumption that takes place. The emphasis that teams now place on luxury boxes and prime seating has made it difficult for middle- or low-income fans to attend the major professional sports games on a regular basis. In 1994, the median income of fans who attended sports events in the United States was almost double the median income level of the country as a whole. Whether a cause or a result of this trend, new facilities have tended to emphasize revenue from luxury boxes and special seating at the expense of affordable seating for the general public.[40]

The growing reliance of many teams on cable television has also made it increasingly difficult for low- and middle-income fans to follow the team at home. While all the citizens of New York may take pride in the success of the Yankees, much of the city benefits only from having something to talk and feel

---

[39]For more on these—and other—criteria for evaluating taxes, see, for example, Harvey Rosen, *Public Finance* (Chicago: Irwin, 1995).

[40]Figures from John Pastier, "Diamonds in the Rough: Two Cheers for the New Baseball Palaces," *Slate Magazine,* July 31, 1996, at http://slate.msn.com/feature2/96-07-31/feature2.asp; and John Siegfried and Andrew Zimbalist, "The Economics of Sports Facilities and Their Construction," *Journal of Economic Perspectives,* v. 14, no. 3 (Summer 2000), pp. 95–114.

proud about since they can afford neither tickets nor cable fees. Poor and minority residents, in particular, must content themselves with radio broadcasts or newspaper accounts of their home team.[41]

In fact, many of the consumption benefits of a major league franchise flow out of the city to the residents of the relatively wealthy suburban ring. The suburbs disproportionately house the people who can most afford tickets to sporting events. They also disproportionately house corporate executives who use the luxury boxes and other premium seating that now account for so much of the cost of a facility. In addition, as explained earlier, most cities got only a small fraction of the revenue from luxury boxes. Taxes that fall on residents of the city that houses the team therefore allow suburbanites to free ride, while those who pay the most may enjoy the least consumption value from the team.

Sales Taxes

In addition to creating a deadweight loss, sales taxes often place a burden on groups that the government does not wish to target. Depending on the products subject to tax, the burden may fall upon people who do not benefit from the new facility, thereby violating horizontal equity. The merits of sales taxes on items directly related to sports facilities are considered later in the chapter. This section explores the problem posed when the burden of a sales tax does not fall solely on the people who ostensibly pay the tax. The tax burden shifts because people respond to the world around them. Governments that impose a tax expecting people to behave the same way they did before the tax was levied are in for a rude awakening.

The Florida Marlins stirred up a major controversy in south Florida when they proposed raising the $300 million for a new stadium with a $4 per-day sales tax on people who take cruises out of the Port of Miami. One might think that such a tax would be a very popular way to fund a new stadium. Since 85 percent of the people who take cruises are from out of state, such a tax seems like a natural way to export the burden of paying for a new stadium to taxpayers from other states. The tax, however, generated virulent opposition among cruise operators even though the tax was not imposed on them.[42]

To see why, consider the impact of a $4 tax on the roughly 1 million people who take cruises from the Port of Miami. If the typical tourist takes a 5-day cruise, then it's possible that the the tax will raise $20 million per year ($4 per day × 5 days per tourist × 1 million tourists per year). However, this ignores the fact that consumers respond to higher cruise prices.

---

[41]See, for example, Roger Thurow, "Thrown for a Curve," *Wall Street Journal* (August 28, 1998), pp. A1, A6.

[42]For accounts of this debate, see Linda Kleindienst, "Broward Opposes Bill Levying Cruise Tax to Help Pay for Marlins Stadium," *Fort Lauderdale Sun Sentinel,* March 22, 2000; and Charles Savage, "Panel OKs Cruise Tax; Broward Is Exempt," *Miami Herald,* March 29, 2000, at http://www.herald.com/content/today/docs/013838.htm.

Recall from Figure 7.5 that the tax causes the price of a day on a cruise to rise—though by less than $4—and the number of days spent on cruise ships to fall. The higher price that people pay per day on a cruise (segment AF in Figure 7.5) is the portion of the $4 daily tax that they bear. Since the government has imposed a $4 tax but the price of a cruise rises by less than $4 per day, cruise operators receive a lower price per day than they did before the tax was imposed. The lower price that cruise operators receive (segment FB in Figure 7.5) is the portion of the $4 tax that tourists have passed on to the local cruise industry.

The total tax burden equals the $4 per day tax (segment AB in Figure 7.5) times the number of rooms rented (segment AE). This product, the total tax revenue, equals the area of the rectangle ABCE in Figure 7.5. The portion of this rectangle that lies above the original price of the room (the rectangle AFGE in Figure 7.5) is the burden on people who take cruises. The rectangle below the original price (FGCB in Figure 7.5) is the burden on cruise lines. Since visitors respond to the higher price of cruises from the Port of Miami by taking fewer or shorter cruises, the tax revenue falls short of the $20 million target. The fall in visits also imposes a new cost on both those who take cruises and cruise operators.

Cleveland applied a different kind of sales tax to help fund the facilities it built. It imposed a 15-year **sin tax** on residents of Cuyahoga County. Like most sin taxes, these taxes consisted of sales taxes on tobacco products and alcohol. They are popular with many citizens because they impose a burden on people who engage in or cater to "sinful" behavior. Much of the public thus views sin taxes as a way to raise revenue by taxing other people and as a way to discourage undesirable activity. Unfortunately, sin taxes cannot achieve both of these ends. As shown in Figure 7.5, if a tax discourages behavior, it creates a large deadweight loss and fails to raise the anticipated amount of revenue. To the extent that drinking and smoking are addictive behaviors, the demand for them is highly price inelastic. Figure 7.6 showed that taxes on goods for which demand is inelastic create very little deadweight loss and come much closer to raising the desired revenue. However, they do so because they fail to discourage the sinful behavior.

Public choice theory helps to explain why Cleveland's sin taxes stirred less organized opposition than south Florida's proposed cruise tax. The deadweight loss of a tax adds to the burden on the group that pays the tax and hence subsidizes the publicly funded facility. A larger burden makes that group more likely to organize opposition to the tax. Since the demand for cigarettes and alcohol are far less own-price elastic than the demand for cruises, a smaller deadweight loss and less opposition arose to the sin tax. Since the tax falls most heavily on the poor and minorities, who are less likely to enjoy the benefits of the new ballpark, the tax and stadium policies fail on grounds of both vertical and horizontal equity.[43]

Lotteries as an Alternative Revenue Source

On the face of things, Baltimore seems to have found a better way to finance M&T Bank Stadium and Oriole Park at Camden Yards than either Miami or

---

[43]See Gary Becker, "A Theory of Competition Among Pressure Groups for Political Influence," *Quarterly Journal of Economics*, v. 98, no. 3 (August 1983), pp. 371–400.

Cleveland. Both of Baltimore's facilities were built with funds from a state lottery. Since a lottery is a voluntary purchase rather than an involuntary payment, it seems like an ideal source of revenue. The growing reliance of states on lotteries seems to support this view.

However, state lotteries do not stand up to closer scrutiny. First, they are highly inefficient revenue sources. Only about a third of the revenue they raise goes into state coffers. A substantial portion of the remainder is spent trying to induce people who do not otherwise gamble to spend money on lottery tickets. Evidence also indicates that lotteries are **regressive,** meaning that wealthy people spend a smaller proportion of their incomes on lottery tickets than do poor people (sin taxes are also generally regressive taxes). A California survey in the mid-1980s showed that a household making $10,000 per year spent roughly the same amount of money on lottery tickets as a household making $60,000 per year. In fact, the purchase of lottery tickets is inversely related to several measures of socioeconomic status. For example, studies have shown that people with more formal education are less likely to play the lottery and that laborers are the most likely to play the lottery while professionals are the least likely. This led Milton Friedman and Leonard J. Savage to claim in their classic work on risk and uncertainty that low-income people take such risks in a desperate attempt to improve their social standing. The poor and uneducated are precisely the people who benefit the least from the presence of a professional franchise. It is a small wonder that lotteries are often termed taxes on this socioeconomic class.[44]

From a public choice perspective, lotteries are a logical choice, because the poor and uneducated are far less likely to form political pressure groups—or even to vote—than are the wealthy and highly educated. Like the sin tax, however, it fails on grounds of both vertical and horizontal equity.

Two Superior Funding Mechanisms

None of the above funding mechanisms does a particularly good job of meeting the criteria set out at the beginning of this section. Some are inefficient; others fail on equity grounds. We now turn to two funding sources that, while flawed, do a better job of meeting the criteria. Each tries explicitly to allocate burdens more equitably, though they do so in different manners.

The first mechanism is exemplified in the way that the Milwaukee Brewers' has funded the new stadium, Miller Park, by thinking big. They instituted a sales tax on Milwaukee and the surrounding five-county region. The broader geographic reach of this tax accounts for the regional impact of a stadium and thus reduces the vertical and horizontal inequities that result when inner-city taxpayers finance a facility that benefits wealthy suburbanites. While the regional tax reduces inequities, it does not eliminate them entirely. In addition, while the sales

---

[44]See Zimmerman, "Subsidizing Stadiums: Who Benefits, Who Pays?" (1997), pp. 125–126; Robyn Gearey, "The Numbers Game," *New Republic* (May 19, 1997), pp. 19–24; Charles Clotfelter and Phillip Cook, "On the Economics of State Lotteries," *Journal of Economic Perspectives*, v. 4, no. 1 (Fall 1990), pp. 105–119; and Milton Friedman and Leonard J. Savage, "The Utility Analysis of Choices Involving Risk," *Journal of Political Economy*, v. 56, no. 4 (August 1948), pp. 279–304.

tax does a better job of targeting the beneficiaries of the stadium, it remains a rather broad brush, as it is based on a person's purchases of goods and services and not on a person's benefits from having the Brewers in town.[45]

The second mechanism is demonstrated by the way that Seattle and the state of Washington are funding the Mariners' new home, Safeco Field, by thinking small. They have tried to target the funding of the new ballpark directly at the beneficiaries of the public expenditure with a special sales tax of 0.5 percent on restaurants, bars, and taverns in King County and a tax of up to 5 percent on admissions to Safeco Field. They have also sought to export some of the burden with a 2 percent tax on rental cars. This sales tax does the best job of matching burdens to benefits in order to impose the tax burden on those who benefit from having the Mariners in town, though it does not get things quite right. By charging a five-star French restaurant at the opposite end of the county the same tax that it charges a bar across the street from the stadium, the government does not match costs to benefits particularly well. Their tax on admissions does a far better job of matching costs and benefits. The tax on car rentals has the same imperfect impact as the cruise tax example discussed earlier.[46]

Despite each mechanism's drawbacks, these plans appear to do the best job of minimizing deadweight loss while averting horizontal and vertical inequities.

Taxes or Debt?

State and local governments can finance stadium construction by borrowing as well as by taxing their residents. Since David Ricardo first stated his famous "equivalence theorem," economists have known that borrowing and taxation have the same impact on residents, at least in theory.[47] State and local governments, however, face several institutional factors that lead them to prefer debt funding to direct taxation.

While people and small firms typically borrow money by taking out a loan at a bank, large corporations and governments often want to borrow more money than a single lender is willing to provide. As a result, they typically borrow by issuing **bonds.** A bond is a promise to pay the person who owns the bond a fixed amount—the **face value** of the bond—at some future point in time. Few people are willing to lend money without some form of additional compensation, and so bonds also promise to make periodic **interest** payments as well.[48] Consumers can compare two bonds with different face values and interest payments by computing the **interest rate.** The interest rate equals the ratio of the interest payment to

---

[45]See Zimmerman, "Subsidizing Stadiums: Who Benefits, Who Pays?" (1997), p. 137.

[46]MSC Sports, "New Park Financing: How the Deals Got Done," 1999, at http://www.wcco.com/sports/stadiums.html.

[47]For a more complete treatment, see N. Gregory Mankiw, *Macroeconomics* (New York: Worth, 2000), pp. 419–424.

[48]Lenders demand interest because they are sacrificing the chance to use that money by letting someone else have it. The interest payment is compensation for that lost consumption.

the price of the bond. This provides a common yardstick for comparing the value of two different bonds to lenders and the cost to borrowers.

Bonds issued by state or local governments have an advantage over otherwise identical bonds offered by corporations. Tax laws allow bondholders to deduct the interest they earn from state and local bonds from their federal taxes. The higher preference for municipal government bonds drives up the demand for them and causes their price to rise from p_0 to p_1, as shown in Figure 7.7.

If the price of the municipal bond rises, then the interest rate falls. Bonds offered by state and local governments are then cheaper to the state and local governments because of federal tax laws. The lower tax revenues mean that taxpayers elsewhere will have to pay higher taxes, that federal programs will have to be cut, or that the federal government will have to borrow more and drive up interest rates. No matter what, the deductibility of municipal bonds imposes costs on the rest of the nation. Municipalities thus like the idea of debt finance because it imposes some of the cost of a stadium on residents of other municipalities.

Even if debt did not export the burden geographically, it could export the burden intertemporally. If future generations enjoy the benefits of the new facility, then economic theory says that society is better off if they pay some of the burden. Debt financing allows a city to impose some of the burden of a new facility on future generations. Unfortunately, one result of the increasing exercise of monopoly outlined in Chapter 6 has been the steady decreasing of a facility's economic life. Structures that could stand for 40 to 50 years now become economically obsolete in only 10 or 20. Future generations may therefore be stuck with the bill for a facility that their teams have already abandoned.

FIGURE 7.7

Tax Breaks Favor Municipal
Bonds

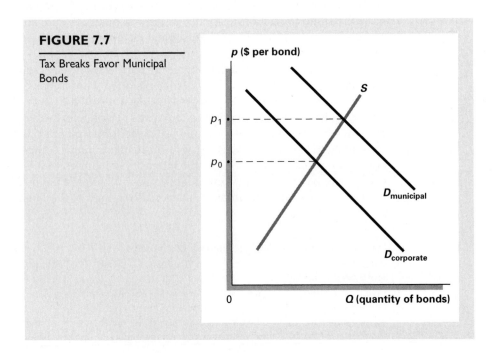

"MITT" ROMNEY
BIOGRAPHICAL *Sketch*

"He felt like he was walking into an empty elevator shaft."
—Fraser Bullock, describing Romney's reaction to learning the
financial state of the Salt Lake Organizing Committee[1]

Seldom have politics and sports been more intertwined than in the recent career of Willard ("Mitt") Romney. Mitt Romney was born and raised in Michigan; his father, the late George Romney, had served as the state's governor and had once been a presidential candidate. A practicing Mormon, Romney graduated with highest honors from Brigham Young University in 1971, and in 1974, he received both a JD and an MBA. from Harvard. After spending two years on a Mormon mission to France, Romney went to work at Bain and Co., a Boston management consulting firm. In 1984, he founded Bain Capital, a venture capital firm that invested in hundreds of companies, including Staples, Domino's Pizza, and The Sports Authority.

In 1994, Romney entered the political arena by challenging Senator Edward Kennedy's reelection bid. The election's outcome was a foregone conclusion. Kennedy soundly defeated Romney, garnering 60 percent of the vote. This may have been the end of Romney's political career were it not for a surprising move he made five years later.

In late 1998, the Salt Lake Organizing Committee (SLOC), the body charged with organizing and financing the 2002 Winter Olympics, was facing a severe crisis. With the Olympics just three years off, the SLOC was almost $400 million in debt, having badly underestimated the costs of the Games. To make matters worse, fundraising was at a standstill, with no new sponsors secured in over a year. Voluntarism was also lagging, and the leadership of SLOC was under investigation by the U.S. Justice Department for giving alleged bribes exceeding $1 million to International Olympic Committee officials in order to secure the

Games for Salt Lake City. SLOC was in desperate need of a person who could combine business connections and savvy with unquestioned integrity *and* who would not mind moving to Utah for the next three years. The job requirements seemed to fit Romney perfectly, and he soon showed why.

In February 1999, Romney took over as CEO and president of the SLOC and quickly began putting his personal stamp on the process. Recognizing that the allegations of corruption had demoralized workers and frightened off donors, Romney insisted on strict ethical standards in all SLOC's activities. He opened all meetings and records to the public. He also demanded that all employees and board members report any possible conflicts of interest and complete annual surveys of ethical conduct.

Ethics would help, but morality alone would not balance the budget. Romney cut the Games' budget by about $200 million and vigorously pursued his political and business connections. The results were impressive. Romney's governmental contacts helped secure an estimated $1.5 billion from the federal government. That total is almost ten times more than the amount of federal support per athlete provided at the 1996 Summer Olympics Games in Atlanta. Between the government support and private sponsorships, the SLOC managed to dig out of its financial hole and wind up slightly in the black. The citizens of Utah were also energized, as 67,000 people volunteered for 23,000 volunteer positions.

Although the Games did little to revive the flagging business community in Salt Lake City, they were a public relations triumph. As head of the Games, Romney had become a celebrity. Less than six weeks after the Olympic flame had been extinguished, Romney had become the Republican standard bearer in the race for governor of Massachusetts, despite his having spent most of the previous three years across the country. In November of 2002, Romney was elected governor.

Some day, Romney may well turn his Olympic experience into a springboard for a presidential run. If he does, he will not be the first person to use sports that way. After all, President George W. Bush first entered the public eye as a member of the ownership group of the Texas Rangers baseball team.

[1]Cathy Harasta, "Romney Shows his Mettle," *Dallas Morning News*, February 17, 2002, online at http://olympics. belointer-active.com/otherstories/0217olyromney.218e4.html.

Sources: Donald Bartlett and James Steele, "Snow Job," *Sports Illustrated*, December 10, 2001, pp. 79–97; Paul Foy, "Romney Just Glad Olympics Worked," *2002 Winter Olympic Games* online at http://olympics.hiasys.com/ olympics_main/news/ap_olynewsscene02252002. htm; "Governor Mitt Romney," *Massachusetts Office of the Governor* online at http://www.mass. gov/portal/index. jsp?pageID=agccagid=govagca=biographiesagcc= mittromneybio; Paula Parrish, "Leap of Faith: Mitt Romney Embraces Challenges, and This Might Be His Biggest One," *Rocky Mountain News*, February 4, 2002, p. 8S; Lewis Rice, "Games Saver," *Harvard Law Bulletin*, Spring 2002, online at http://www.law.harvard.edu/alumni/bulletin/ 2002/spring/ feature_1-1.html.

SUMMARY

In this chapter, we examined why cities might be willing to make such huge payments to help build facilities for sports teams. Cities do not—and should not—operate with the same goals as a private firm. Building and maintaining a stadium may not be profitable for the city, but it may generate enough positive externalities to justify the expense. The externalities reflect benefits to people or businesses that have no direct contact with the franchise. Many of these perceived benefits come from the argument that a substantial multiplier effect is operating on spending in the local economy. However, most evidence shows that the financial benefits of a facility do not outweigh the costs.

Cities must also find the appropriate funding mechanism for a facility. Economic theory indicates that the tax burden should reflect the benefits that a person or business receives from the expenditure. Most cities, however, do not adhere to this principle when they fund their facilities.

DISCUSSION QUESTIONS

1. What kinds of promises might a city ask a team to make about a stadium-funding deal to increase the size of the indirect benefits that the facility yields?

2. Which is better for a city, a stadium right in the downtown area or one on the outskirts of town? Which is better for the team?

3. Describe the externalities associated with a football stadium compared with an amusement park. Which would have greater positive externalities? Negative externalities?

4. Think of some taxes that would be highly progressive. Why are such taxes difficult to pass?

5. If an urban municipality decides to assist in the funding of a baseball stadium, what other types of public spending will likely need to be increased as well?

6. Which do you believe is more important in taxing the public to provide funds for stadiums—horizontal equity or vertical equity? Why?

7. Would the opportunity cost of constructing a stadium in a relatively poor city be greater or less than the opportunity cost for a relatively wealthy city? Why?

PROBLEMS

7.1 Evaluate the following taxes from the standpoint of vertical and horizontal equity:

   a. A 25-cent per-gallon tax on milk

   b. A tax on stock market transactions

   c. A sales tax on men's clothing

   d. A tax on cigarettes.

7.2 Suppose the demand for toothbrushes is perfectly inelastic, at $Q_d = 3,000$. The market supply curve is perfectly elastic and is equal to $p = 2.00$. What would be the deadweight loss associated with a \$0.20 tax on toothbrushes? Based on the Ramsey rule, would this be a good product to tax or not?

7.3 If the marginal propensity to consume in a municipality is 0.8, what is the value of the simple multiplier? If a new stadium that adds \$30 million in new consumption expenditures is built, what is the impact on the economy based on this multiplier?

7.4 In Problem 3, how would your answer change if the people who receive the initial \$30 million live in that municipality only six months of each year? (*Hint:* Start with the Noll and Zimbalist multiplier.)

7.5 True or False; explain your answer. "The new stadium was entirely privately funded because all the city contributed was a 50-acre site on which to build it."

7.6 You own a team in San Francisco. What does public choice theory say about what you will do if Los Angeles presses the California legislature to underwrite a new stadium in Los Angeles?

7.7 Why is the multiplier effect for the Los Angeles Lakers likely to be greater than the multiplier effect for the Sacramento Kings when they are both teams in the NBA?

7.8 Your city is committed to raising \$100 million for a new arena. The mayor suggests putting a tax on taxicab rides since out-of-towners disproportionately use taxicabs. Is this a good policy decision?

7.9 Why might a city want to go into debt as a way to fund a new stadium?

7.10 Why would a Super Bowl played in Detroit probably have more of an impact than a Super Bowl played in Miami, even if both were to draw the same amount of fans? Why would a Super Bowl at Ford Field in Detroit have more of an impact on Detroit than a regular season Detroit Lions game that draws the same number of fans?

PART FOUR

The Labor Economics of Sports

CHAPTER 8

An Introduction to Labor Markets in Professional Sports

Show me the money!

—CUBA GOODING, JR., AS ROD TIDWELL IN *JERRY MAGUIRE*

INTRODUCTION

Not many topics within sports generate as much controversy as why athletes make so much money relative to people in other, more "worthwhile" professions. A typical professional basketball player earns more in one week than the average American earns in a year. Even journeyman players earn salaries many times greater than workers in most other industries. Yet surprisingly, some research indicates that, from an economic standpoint, many of today's top athletes are paid much less than they are worth to their teams.

Table 8.1 shows average salaries in the four major team sports from 1970 through 2002. It indicates that athletes in each sport have extraordinarily high salaries and that these salaries are growing at an equally extraordinary rate. Salaries in baseball, football, and basketball more than doubled in the 1990s, though for baseball, this represents a slowdown from the 500 percent growth of the 1970s and early 1980s. The most impressive growth in the 1990s came in hockey, where salaries increased by over 400 percent. This chapter explores how labor markets operate in professional sports. Along the way, we explain these seemingly unbelievable salary increases and discuss such topics as:

- Why some players leave the game even though they could earn millions by staying
- Why Michael Jordan was a bargain for the Bulls at $30 million per year
- The potential benefits to Lebron James of skipping college.

Table 8.1

Average Player Salaries 1970–2002

Year	MLB	NFL	NHL	NBA
1970	29,303	41,000	25,000	—
1972	34,092	45,000	45,000*	—
1974	40,839	56,000	65,000*	—
1976	51,501	78,000	86,000	—
1978	99,876	100,000	92,000	139,000
1980	143,756	117,000	108,000	170,000
1982	241,497	157,000	120,000	212,000
1984	329,408	279,000	118,000	275,000
1986	412,520	288,000	144,000	375,000
1988	438,729	307,000	172,000	510,000
1990	597,537	430,000	211,000	750,000
1992	1,082,667	551,000	368,000	1,100,000
1994	1,168,263	674,000	562,000	1,700,000
1996	1,119,981	807,000	892,000	2,000,000
1998	1,398,831	1,000,000	1,167,713	2,297,000
2000	1,895,630	1,116,100	1,642,590	4,200,000
2002	2,295,694	1,300,000	1,790,000	4,500,000

*Estimates.
Salary figures are estimates based on information reported by major news services such as Slam! Sports at http://www.slam.ca/ BaseballMoneyMatters/salaries_by_sport.html. These estimates vary slightly from source to source based on the method used amortize salary, bonuses, and benefits.

8.1   OVERVIEW OF LABOR SUPPLY AND DEMAND

This section looks at both sides of the labor market. On the supply side, individual players offer their services to professional sports teams in order to maximize their utility. Teams demand labor in order to maximize profits. Chapter 3 showed that profit maximization may lead to a variety of personnel decisions, including fielding a low-quality team. Unless we state otherwise, for the remainder of this chapter we assume that team quality and profits are directly related. The interaction of supply and demand determines the labor market for professional athletes.

Labor Supply[1]

In many ways, the labor supply decision resembles the firm's supply decision, and the labor supply curve is similar to the supply curve for a product. Several important differences, however, require some explanation. People decide how much labor to supply based on their preferences and wage rates. Suppose, for example, that basketball players are paid by the game at the wage rate w/game. When the wage increases, the player is expected to work more (play

---

[1]For a more complete treatment of the labor supply curve and the labor–leisure choice model, see Appendix 8A.

more games) in order to increase income. If this is so, the individual labor supply curve is upward-sloping like most supply curves, as shown in Figure 8.1a. If all workers feel the same, they have identical supply curves, and the market labor supply curve, which is the sum of all of the individual supply curves, is also positively sloped, as shown in Figure 8.1b.

The individual labor supply curve rests on the notion that people choose how much to work based on the wage and the alternative to work—leisure. At first, such a model might seem ill-suited to professional sports, an industry in which the personnel are referred to as *players* rather than workers. This distinction, however, suggests that professional athletics is a leisure activity rather than a way to make a living. While most, if not all, professional players might still play "for fun" if they could not play professionally, playing professionally requires a level of dedication from the players that goes well beyond what they would choose for pure recreation.

To understand the shape of the individual labor supply curve, consider a person's options at various wages. When wages are low, the opportunity cost of not working is low. As wages increase, the cost of not working rises, because workers must sacrifice higher earnings when they choose to "purchase" leisure. As Chapter 2 explained, the substitution effect causes workers to shift away from the now more expensive leisure and to work more when wages rise, creating the positively sloped supply curve.

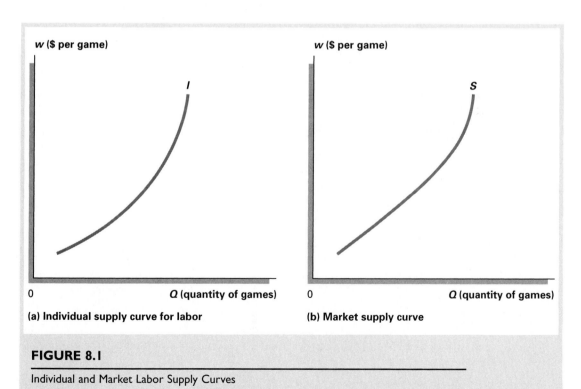

(a) Individual supply curve for labor

(b) Market supply curve

FIGURE 8.1

Individual and Market Labor Supply Curves

Changes in the wage also affect a worker's income, touching off an income effect as well. If leisure is a normal good, then the worker buys more leisure—and works less—as his or her income rises. In this case, the income effect counteracts, rather than reinforces, the substitution effect.

The combined force of the income and substitution effects generates the change in hours (or games, in this case) that results from a change in the wage rate. At low wage rates, the substitution effect is typically greater than the income effect, and the labor supply curve slopes upward. At very high wage rates, the income effect may dominate. In Figure 8.2, at wages up to $1,000 per game, the substitution effect is stronger than the income effect, and *ll* has a positive slope (slopes upward). At wages above $1,000 per game, the income effect is dominant, and *ll* is negatively sloped.

The labor–leisure model can also be applied to lifetime labor supply decisions. Michael Jordan is an example of an athlete who for a time chose leisure over work. He retired from the Chicago Bulls after the 1997–98 season while still one of the top players in the NBA. Although he could have continued to earn tens of millions of dollars per year, he decided to leave, in part to concentrate on his golf game. (He returned to the NBA from 2000–03 as president of basketball operations and an active player for the Washington Wizards.) Many people would like to retire while still young and concentrate on golf, but most cannot afford to. The extraordinary level of income that Jordan generated early in his career allows him the option of working very little or not at all. His case is certainly not an isolated one. Almost every year, a player or coach decides to retire to "spend more time with my family." While it may be another way of saying, "I've been fired and have nowhere

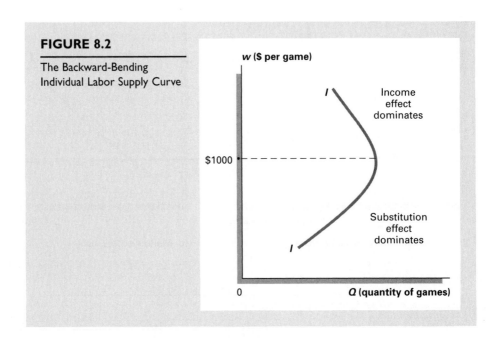

FIGURE 8.2

The Backward-Bending Individual Labor Supply Curve

else to go," it also reflects the labor–leisure choice and the dominance of the income effect.

Labor Demand

Much of the confusion regarding athletes' salaries stems from a failure to understand the demand for labor. Armchair quarterbacks may spend the afternoon yelling at their televisions, calling different players "worthless," but in reality, many professional athletes are underpaid. To show why, we begin by assuming that both the labor market and the output market are perfectly competitive. We then extend the analysis to show what happens when players, teams, or both have the power to affect wages.

We start with a short-run framework in which capital is fixed and labor is the only variable input. Firms cannot set the price of their output in a competitive output market, but they can decide how much to produce. Since firms can change output (Q) only by varying the amount of labor they use, they maximize profit by choosing the amount of labor that maximizes the difference between revenue and cost. When making such a decision, the firm compares the marginal cost of an additional worker with the marginal revenue earned from employing that worker. If the labor market is perfectly competitive (and we ignore all forms of compensation other than the worker's wage), the marginal cost of the worker is that worker's wage, w.

The benefit of adding a worker is the extra revenue that he or she brings in. This extra revenue is determined by the additional output the worker produces—his or her **marginal product**—and the price of that additional output. Marginal product is the change in output that results from a one-unit change in labor:

$$MP_L = \frac{\Delta Q}{\Delta L}.$$

If a football manufacturer increases its workforce from 9 to 10 employees, and output increases from 100 to 120 balls, the marginal product of the 10th worker is 20 balls. In the short run, the marginal product of labor declines and the marginal product curve (see Figure 8.3) is downward-sloping because of **the law of diminishing returns.** This law states that the marginal product of any variable input eventually declines as more of it is added to a fixed amount of other inputs.

Economists call the extra revenue generated by an additional worker the **marginal revenue product.** Since marginal revenue equals price in a competitive industry, marginal revenue is simply the price per unit of output times the additional output produced:

$$MRP_L = MR \cdot MP_L = p\left(\frac{\Delta Q}{\Delta L}\right).$$

If, for example, the 10th worker produces an additional 20 balls that can be sold for $5 each, the value of the 10th worker to the firm is $100 = \$5 \times 20$.

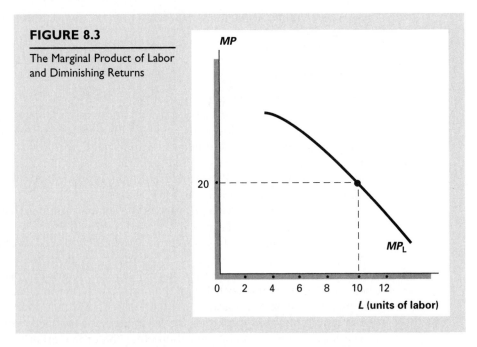

FIGURE 8.3

The Marginal Product of Labor
and Diminishing Returns

As outlined in Chapter 2, the profit-maximizing firm balances marginal benefits and marginal costs. This means that it hires just enough workers so that the marginal cost, w, equals the marginal benefit, MRP_L:

$$MRP_L = w.$$

If the wage rises, marginal costs exceed marginal benefits, and the firm responds by hiring fewer workers. When the firm hires fewer workers, the MP_L rises and marginal benefits again equal marginal costs. This yields the downward-sloping short-run demand curve for labor shown in Figure 8.4.

A star player's marginal revenue product can be extraordinary. For example, economists felt that Michael Jordan, who was paid over $30 million by the Chicago Bulls for each of his last two seasons, was a terrific bargain for the Bulls and the NBA. Before Jordan arrived, the Bulls were a mediocre team that averaged fewer than 7,000 paying fans per game. In his last year, the Bulls averaged 24,000 fans per game, 17,000 more than before Jordan joined the team. The added attendance generated revenues of $25.5 million, not including increased concession, parking, advertising, playoff, and skybox revenues. Most of this increase was attributable to Jordan. Estimates of Jordan's value to the Bulls for 1997–98 come to about $40 million per year.[2]

Jordan also created a positive externality for the rest of the NBA, since his $40 million value to the Bulls did not include his impact on the attendance of teams throughout the league.[3] Jordan and the Bulls were a prime cause of the

[2]E. M. Swift, "The $40 Million Man," *Sports Illustrated* (June 10, 1996), pp. 44–45.

[3]Recall that NBA teams do not share home revenue.

FIGURE 8.4

The Short-Run Profit-Maximizing Demand for Labor for the Firm

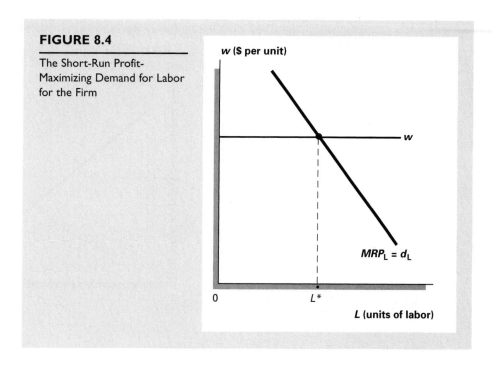

skyrocketing TV and merchandising revenues that the NBA experienced in the 1990s, and his retirement sent the league as well as its primary network, NBC, reeling. When Jordan played for the Bulls, their national telecast ratings were 102 percent higher than telecasts that did not feature the Bulls, and NBA-licensed apparel sales fell by 30 percent when he left the game.[4] The effect that superstars such as Michael Jordan have on leagues is analyzed later in the chapter.

Market Demand and Equilibrium

Recall from Chapter 2 that the market demand for labor is the sum of all of the individual demand curves. Initially, we assume that markets are competitive. Later in this chapter, we will see how the results of the model change when players or teams have some ability to control price. In the NBA, the market demand for players equals the sum of the teams' demand curves. The market supply is the sum of the players' supply curves. Combining the market demand and supply curves yields the equilibrium wage, as shown in Figure 8.5.

Using this model, we can predict what happens to players' wages when market conditions change. Suppose, for example, that basketball becomes much more popular with fans, as what happened in the 1980s. With more fan interest,

---

[4]Richard Sandomir, "NBC Confronts the Departure of Its Must-See N.B.A. Star," *New York Times* (January 13, 1999), p. D3.

FIGURE 8.5

The Equilibrium Wage and
Quantity in the Labor Market

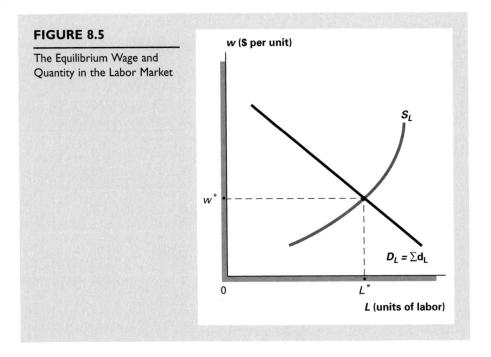

the marginal revenue product of the players increases—not because their productivity increases but because the additional fans increase marginal revenue—resulting in an increase in demand for labor. When the demand curve shifts right, wages rise. As shown in Table 8.1, average pay in the NBA increased from $375,000 in 1986 to $4.5 million in 1996. A similar increase in demand between 1996 and 2006 like that shown in Figure 8.6 would lead to a further increase in average salaries.

Imperfect Competition and the Demand for Labor

While the competitive model forms a useful baseline, professional sports markets frequently violate its underlying assumptions. Recall from Chapters 3 and 4 that a monopoly sets a price that exceeds marginal revenue because the marginal revenue curve lies below and to the left of the demand curve. As a result, the MRP_L curve for the profit-maximizing monopolies lies to the left of the MRP_L curve of the competitive industry, and the monopolist hires fewer workers and pays lower wages than it would if the industry were competitive. Figure 8.7 shows that if demand were based on competitive markets, teams would pay salaries of w_c and hire L_c players. However, because demand is based on a monopoly in the output (games) market, MRP is below and to the left of the competitive market labor demand curve. As a result, only L_m players are hired, and wages fall to w_m.

FIGURE 8.6

Wages Increase in the NBA Due to Increases in Demand

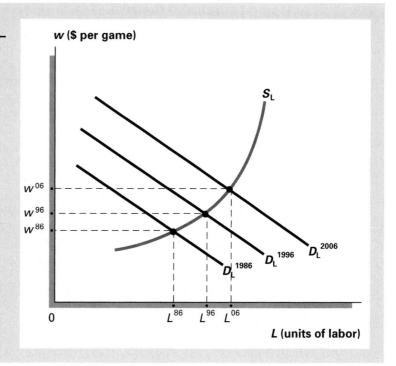

FIGURE 8.7

The Monopolist's Marginal Revenue Product Curve

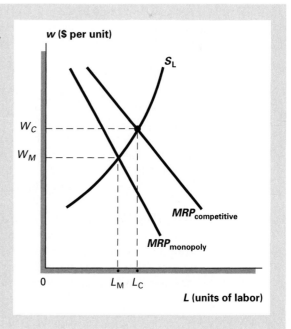

Human Capital Theory

If workers are more productive, the MP_L and MRP (which is also the demand for labor) rise, and hence wages rise as well. It follows that if people can increase their productivity, they can increase their earnings. **Human capital** is the set of skills that contribute to a person's productivity. The term implies that each person has a *stock* of skills and knowledge that can be increased through *investment*.

Nobel laureate Gary Becker developed the theory of human capital in the 1960s.[5] According to Becker, a business investing in human capital is similar to a firm investing in physical capital. When a firm purchases a drill press, it makes a one-time expenditure in return for an expected stream of benefits over the life span of the equipment. Similarly, a hockey player who spends four years in the minor leagues developing his skills benefits from his investment because he can use these skills for his entire career.

Unlike physical capital, human capital tends to depreciate with age or disuse rather than with use. Many of the skills an athlete acquires, such as learning the basic rules of play, will not depreciate until long after retirement. Although physical abilities depreciate with age, an athlete's knowledge of the game may increase throughout his or her career. An important difference between human and physical capital is that one firm can generally transfer physical capital to another simply by selling the asset. Human capital, however, is embodied in the worker and thus cannot be transferred.

Human capital theory divides training into two types: **general** and **specific.** General training increases the worker's productivity regardless of the setting. For example, learning to read increases one's productivity no matter where one works. General training in football includes learning the rules of football, how to make an open field tackle, or how to avoid a blocker. The better a football player can master any of these skills, the more valuable he is to all football teams.

Specific training increases a person's MRP only at the firm that provides the training. For example, learning the plays in a team's playbook helps a person only as long as he or she is part of that team. Many forms of training provide both general and specific skills. A soccer team typically provides training that improves individual skills such as passing, shooting, or tackling. Players can apply such skills for any soccer team. The team also teaches the player how to work within a specific system, coordinating the player's individual skills with those of his or her teammates. If the player moves to a different team with different players, his or her investment in learning this system will largely be wasted.

Who Pays for Training? Becker concluded that the nature of the training a worker receives determines who pays for it. When a player receives specific training, the team can capture at least some of the returns to that training because it must pay the player only enough to prevent him or her from moving to another team. Thus, the team and the player typically share the cost of specific

---

[5]Gary S. Becker, *Human Capital*, 3d ed. (Chicago: University of Chicago Press, 1993).

training, and the player's pay plus the cost of training is no larger than the team's reward in the form of increased productivity.

When a person receives general training, his or her productivity rises at all firms. If the team has no way to restrict player mobility, such as with the reserve clause, it is unwilling to pay for the training. Suppose, for example, the Toronto Maple Leafs of the NHL pays for a player's training costs by hiring coaches and providing training facilities while the player plays for the Maple Leafs' minor league team. With no restrictions in place, the player could simply leave the Leafs for another team when his contract expires, taking his human capital with him. The Maple Leafs would end up paying for the training without receiving the benefit of the player's increased productivity. Because all teams recognize this potential loss of investment, they force players to pay for general training in the form of low minor league salaries. We can formalize the model a bit to see why this is so.

For simplicity, assume that a player's career lasts only two seasons. A player's value to his team over the two seasons is his value in the current season (MRP) plus the present discounted value of his productivity from season two (MRP_2).[6] As Chapter 6 showed, if r equals the interest rate, the player is worth $MRP_2/(1 + r)$ in the second season. The total benefit of a player to any team is[7]

$$B = MRP_1 + \frac{MRP_2}{1 + r}.$$

In a competitive labor market with two-year contracts, the team is willing to pay up to the point where the present discounted value of the worker over his career equals his total cost to the team. If wages are the only cost in each period, then the cost of the player is $w_1 + w_2/(1 + r)$, and the team structures its wage offer (w_1, w_2) so that

$$MRP_1 + \frac{MRP_2}{1 + r} = w_1 + \frac{w_2}{1 + r}.$$

If the costs to the team also include training costs T, the equation becomes

$$MRP_1 + \frac{MRP_2}{1 + r} = w_1 + \frac{w_2}{1 + r} + T.$$

The team must somehow reduce the player's wages so that the equality still holds. If the training increases the player's productivity and value for all

---

[6]We discount their value in the second season due to the time value of money. Benefits (B) in the future are not worth as much as benefits received in the current season, because benefits received now could be invested at the current interest rate r and would be worth $B(1 + r)$ in the next season.

[7]Appendix 8B provides a brief primer on the time value of money and the importance of the discount rate.

teams—if it is general training—then the team has to pay the competitive wage ($MRP_2 = w_2$) in the second period. It will therefore provide training only if the player pays the training costs (usually in the form of reduced wages) in the first period ($MRP_1 = w_1 - T$).

In baseball, minor league salaries are extremely low compared with major league salaries. As of 1992, minor league players typically earned less than $2,000 per month.[8] Owners claim that by accepting very low salaries, players are paying the cost of the training they need to reach the major leagues.

Experience is one of an athlete's most valued characteristics. Commentators frequently contrast the guile of a veteran player with the energy and power of a younger player. The human capital model predicts that experience increases productivity through on-the-job training. To the extent that veterans are more knowledgeable, they should be more productive than a rookie with the same physical skills. The value of experience is apparent in the NFL, because most quarterbacks, no matter how physically gifted, typically spend at least one year as understudies, often to aging veterans with less physical talent.[9]

8.2 MONOPSONY AND OTHER RESTRICTIONS OF COMPETITIVE MARKETS

In all professional team sports, there are important deviations from the assumptions of the competitive model. This section examines the deviations that most significantly shape labor markets in sports, including monopsony, restrictions on free agency, salary caps, and the draft. The final part of the section includes a discussion of how the effects of such deviations can be investigated empirically and the findings of a few well-known studies.

Monopsony

Like a monopolist, a **monopsonist** does not have any competition. A monopsonist is the sole buyer of a good or service. Firms that sell their goods or services in a monopsonistic market can sell them to no one except the monopsonist. Monopsonistic exert their market power like monopolists, though their impact is the mirror image of the monopolist's. While a monopolist uses its power to drive up the price it can charge consumers, a monopsonist uses its market power to drive down the prices it must pay producers or workers. A monopsonist and a monopolist are identical in one respect. Both restrict the quantity of transactions compared with a perfectly competitive industry. The resulting reductions in output and consumption impose a deadweight loss on society.

---

[8]Andrew Zimbalist, *Baseball and Billions* (New York: Basic Books, 1992), p. 106.

[9]Some research indicates that experience is such a prized attribute in professional sports that it becomes more important in salary determination than actual performance and thus contradicts human capital theory. See Asher C. Blass, "Does the Baseball Labor Market Contradict the Human Capital Model of Investment?" *Review of Economics and Statistics*, v. 71, no. 2 (May 1992), pp. 261–268.

Figure 8.8 shows that, since the monopsonist is the only buyer in a market, its supply curve is the same as the market supply curve (just as the monopolist's demand curve is the market demand curve). The upward-sloping supply curve reflects the fact that the monopsonist can buy more only if it is willing and able to pay more. Since a monopsonist usually cannot tell exactly which seller is willing to sell for how much, it generally must pay a higher price for all the items it buys—not just for the additional items. The cost of buying a little more, the **marginal expenditure,** is thus greater than the cost of the additional purchases, because the monopsonist must spend more on the marginal unit as well as on all preceding units. As a result, the monopsonist's **marginal expenditure curve** lies above and to the left of the supply curve (just as the monopolist's marginal revenue curve lies below the demand curve). The monopsonist maximizes its profits when it buys just enough so that its marginal benefit equals its marginal expenditure.

In Figure 8.8 the demand curve shows the monopsonist's marginal benefit (recall that the demand curve for labor is derived from the additional revenue it generates for the firm). The monopsonist hires workers until marginal benefit equals marginal expenditure. The monopsonist has market power over the input market, and so it can pay lower wages if it hires fewer workers. Just as the monopolist determines its price by looking up to the demand curve, the monopsonist determines its price by looking down to the supply curve. Thus, the monopsony price in Figure 8.8 is w_m, not the competitive wage w_c. In the graph, the marginal expenditure curve cuts the marginal benefit curve at point r. Employment is L_m, and the wage is w_m. If the labor market were competitive,

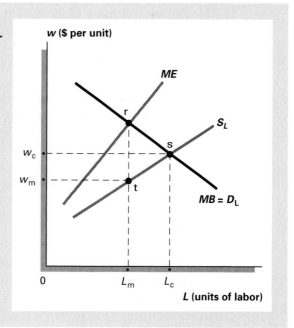

FIGURE 8.8

Employment and Wage Level for a Monopsonist

firms would hire workers until the marginal benefit of the last worker equaled the wage (w_c, L_c). Thus, monopsony results in lower wages and lower employment than in a competitive market. It also results in a deadweight loss (the area rst). **Monopsonistic exploitation** is the difference between the value of the labor to the firm and the wage paid to the worker (the vertical segment rt).

Monopsony power was once one of the cornerstones of professional leagues. As noted in Chapter 4, the formation of the National League in baseball can be traced directly to professional sports' most famous exercise of monopsony power, the creation of the **reserve clause.**

The Reserve Clause

In the early years of professional baseball, players went from team to team, sometimes jumping contracts in the middle of the season.[10] All this changed in 1876. Envious of the success of the Boston club, William Hulbert, the financial backer of the Chicago White Stockings, lured away four of Boston's star players (and one from Philadelphia) late in the 1875 season. In a remarkable display of chutzpah, Hulbert then appealed to the other backers to create a new system that would—among other things—stop the bidding war for players. This coup d'état overthrew baseball's existing structure, the National Association of Professional Base Ball Players. The name of the new organization—the National League of Professional Baseball Clubs—was highly significant. Prior to Hulbert's coup, players' associations had run baseball. Now the clubs—and their owners—reigned supreme, and the players occupied a secondary position.[11]

Just how secondary became apparent in 1887, when the owners unveiled what had been an implicit "gentlemen's agreement" for the previous decade. With the formation of the National League, each owner reserved the rights to five players' services for as long as he wanted them.[12] By 1889 the system of reserving players had expanded to the entire roster and had been installed as a clause in the standard player's contract:

> [I]f, prior to March 1, . . . the player and the club have not agreed upon the terms of such contract [for the next playing season], then on or before ten days after said March 1, the club shall have the right to renew this contract for the period of one year on the same terms except that the amount payable to the player shall be such as the club shall fix in said notice.[13]

On the surface, the clause seems fairly innocuous. It restricted a player to a team for the length of the contract plus, if the team renewed the existing contract by March 1, one additional year of service. The catch lies in the fact that the owners interpreted the right to "renew this contract . . . on the same terms"

---

[10]One of the institutional weaknesses of the Negro Leagues was the inability of teams to maintain stable rosters. See Robert Peterson, *Only the Ball Was White* (New York: Gramercy Books, 1970), pp. 95–98.

[11]Harold Seymour, *Baseball: The Early Years* (New York: Oxford University Press, 1960), p. 80.

[12]Perhaps not surprisingly, this was exactly the number that Hulbert had signed away in 1875.

[13]Quoted from James Quirk and Rodney Fort, *Pay Dirt* (Princeton, N.J.: Princeton University Press, 1992), p. 185.

as renewing all the terms of the contract, including the reserve clause, thus binding the player to the team for yet another year. Using this recursive system, a team could restrict a player from selling his services for as long as it wanted to keep him. Leagues in other sports saw the value of the reserve clause in keeping down costs and copied this clause almost word for word in their standard contracts.

With no alternative employer able to bid away the services of their players, teams drove down their players' salaries to levels that just kept them in the sport. While players today can afford to support small entourages, even stars of an earlier time had to hold second jobs. Imagine walking into an appliance store and buying a washing machine from Allen Iverson. In 1951 you could have done just that from Jackie Robinson.[14]

Free Agency

From the beginning, players have opposed the reserve clause as a restrictive device that reduces freedom of movement and salaries. Starting in the 1970s, players in the four major sports began to win the right to move freely by either weakening the reserve clause or overthrowing it entirely. All four major sports now have some form of free agency.

Team owners in these sports have complained loudly that free agency causes them to overbid for players, paying salaries greater than the players' *MRP*. They claim that this has tilted the competitive balance in professional sports in favor of the wealthy teams that can afford to bid away other teams' most talented players.[15] Players counter that the only way to eliminate monopsonistic exploitation is to give them the right to "test the market" to determine the competitive value of their services. These differing perspectives have caused free agency guidelines to be the most contentious issues in labor negotiations in professional sports.

The limits placed on free agency vary from sport to sport. A player cannot become a free agent until after six years of service in MLB, four years in the NFL, five years in the NBA, and four years the NHL.[16] In basketball, football, and hockey, players obtain free agency in stages, with players first qualifying as **restricted free agents.**

In the NHL, players fall into one of five groups depending on their age and level of experience. A player's movement between teams becomes easier at each stage. Group II free agents, for example, may not switch teams if their current team matches another team's offer. The player's new team may have to compensate his former team with as many as five first-round draft choices. An extreme example came in 1997, when the Philadelphia Flyers had to give the

---

[14]John Helyar, *Lords of the Realm* (New York: Villard Books, 1994), p. 12.

[15]We shall deal with this claim in some detail in Chapter 9.

[16]These length-of-service requirements are subject to a variety of exceptions, such as waived players and further restrictions, such as age minimums and compensation to the team that loses the free agent player under certain conditions, such as in the NHL.

Tampa Bay Lightning four first-round draft choices as compensation for signing center Chris Gratton.[17] This compensation scheme creates an enormous roadblock to player movement.

Final Offer Arbitration

In 1972, the baseball owners entered their negotiations with the Major League Baseball Players Association wary of the implications of Curt Flood's antitrust suit. Though he had lost the suit, Flood had energized the union, and the owners feared a direct challenge to the reserve clause. The owners sought to mollify the players by making an offer that would give the appearance of a concession without changing the structure of the monopsonistic labor market. In this case, the actions of the owners proved to be highly beneficial to the players. Their "minor" concession to the players was **final offer arbitration** (FOA). FOA has arguably had a greater impact on salaries than the free agency the owners so feared. With FOA, if a player and his team cannot agree to a contract, each side submits its final offer to an independent arbitration panel that selects either one final offer or the other. No compromise is allowed.

FOA is one of a number of tools negotiators have developed to resolve disagreements without resorting to conflict. In **mediation,** for example, a neutral third party facilitates compromise by meeting separately with both parties to the disagreement and seeking some middle ground. The mediator allows each side to discuss its position without revealing weakness to the other side and thus promotes compromise.

Sometimes the parties cannot come to an agreement on their own and need a third party—called an **arbitrator**—to suggest or impose a settlement after hearing both sides present their cases.[18] **Arbitration** can take one of two forms: **binding** or **nonbinding.** In nonbinding arbitration, the two sides hope that the moral authority of the arbitrator's ruling will force both parties to adhere to the agreement. In binding arbitration, both sides formally agree ahead of time to abide by the arbitrator's ruling. Binding arbitration is particularly popular in the public sector. Fearful of the consequences of a strike by police or firefighters, municipal officials have often offered binding arbitration in exchange for the unions' acquiescence in laws that outlaw strikes by some public unions.

While arbitration may resolve disagreement without conflict, it creates a new set of problems: arbitrators may have their own agenda. In particular, arbitrators *like* being arbitrators; it is a lucrative and prestigious occupation. If an arbitrator rules in favor of labor or management too often, he or she could acquire a reputation of favoring one side or the other—even if the arbitrator's judgments are perfectly in accordance with the evidence before him or her. Arbitrators thus may prefer to "split the difference" of any two offers put before them. If, as seen in Figure 8.9, an arbitrator sees the union propose w_L

---

[17]The Flyers then traded Mikael Renberg and Karl Dykhaus to Tampa to get their picks back.

[18]The popular TV shows *The People's Court* and *Judge Judy* are actually arbitration hearings rather than trials.

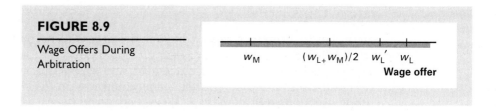

FIGURE 8.9

Wage Offers During
Arbitration

w_M $(w_{L}+w_M)/2$ w_L' w_L

Wage offer

and management propose w_M, he or she will feel pressured to rule that the settlement should be $(w_L + w_M)/2$. That way, neither the union nor management can accuse the arbitrator of being prejudiced. If both the union and management recognize the predilection to choose middle ground, they lose all incentive to compromise on their own. The union, for example, fears that if it moderates its position to w_L', the arbitrator will choose a new midpoint that is closer to w_M. Thus, the two parties stay far apart, forcing themselves into arbitration after arbitration. The arbitration process thus becomes addictive.[19]

Final offer arbitration eliminates the addictive nature of arbitration by forcing the arbitrator to choose between the parties' two final offers. Since the arbitrator cannot choose a middle ground, he or she can safely choose one side or the other.[20] Each side now has an incentive to moderate its proposals so as to convince the arbitrator to choose its proposal. Ideally, both parties continue to moderate their positions until they reach a settlement without having recourse to arbitration.

The major problem with FOA as it has been applied to MLB lies in the ground rules facing the arbitrator. Arbitrators must base their rulings on information regarding the performance of the player who has filed for arbitration and the performance and salaries of comparable players. The arbitrator cannot consider the financial position of the team or whether it is willing to pay such a salary. The arbitration process thus considers only the supply side of the labor market, explicitly ignoring the demand side. As a result, FOA tends to promulgate unwise decisions. If the Mets overpaid Mo Vaughn when they signed him as a free agent in 2001, other players can use his salary to argue that they are underpaid. The arbitrator cannot rule that Vaughn's contract was a mistake and thus should be discounted; he or she can rule only on whether the player at hand is paid on a par with his peers. FOA may thus impose a greater burden on teams than free agency, because teams can always continue negotiating with a free agent who demands too much, but they cannot ignore an arbitrator's ruling. A team that is unhappy with an arbitrator's ruling can only release the player (if his contract is not guaranteed) or try to trade him.

---

[19]See Ronald Ehrenberg and Robert Smith, *Modern Labor Economics* (Reading, M.A..: Addison Wesley Longman, 2000), pp. 500–503.

[20]David M. Frederick, William H. Kaempfer, and Richard L. Wobbekind, "Salary Arbitration as a Market Substitute," in *Diamonds Are Forever: The Business of Baseball*, ed. by Paul M. Sommers (Washington, D.C.: The Brookings Institution, 1992), pp. 29–49; note that arbitrators in FOA may try to rule alternately in favor of labor and management so as to appear fair.

Salary Caps

Salary caps first emerged as a counterbalance to free agency in the NBA in the early 1980s.[21] Salary caps set maximum payroll figures for each team. Prior to the 1999 collective bargaining agreement, the salary cap in the NBA was referred to as a "soft cap" because teams could re-sign their own free agents without regard to the salary cap. This exception to the cap arose in the 1983 agreement when the Boston Celtics pointed out that the salary cap would force them to break up an outstanding, popular team since most of their allotted salary would have to go to re-sign their superstar, Larry Bird. As a result, the amendment to the salary cap became known as the "Larry Bird exception." After a lockout that canceled almost half of the 1998–99 season, players agreed to a new salary cap that set both team limits and maximum salaries for all individual players based on years of service. It is too early to tell how much the new salary cap rules will affect players' attempt to use the market to obtain competitive salaries.

The NFL has a system of free agency with a salary cap that resembles the NBA's system.[22] At first, the NFL had a reserve clause almost identical to baseball's. When the *Radovich* decision established that the NFL's reserve clause violated the Sherman Act (as described in Chapter 4), owners engaged in a "gentlemen's agreement" not to pursue each other's players. This agreement broke down in 1963 when the Baltimore Colts signed away another team's player. Commissioner Pete Rozelle immediately responded by imposing what became known as the "Rozelle rule." The Rozelle rule permitted a player to sign with any other team at the end of his contract. However, the team that lost the player was entitled to compensation from the team that signed the player, typically in the form of draft picks. If the teams could not agree on compensation, then the commissioner would impose the "appropriate" level of compensation. Typically, the compensation was so severe that it effectively killed free agency for all but marginal players for whom compensation was relatively low.[23]

The current NFL system went into effect for the 1994 season. For 2002, the cap was set at $71.1 million per team. Chapter 5 showed how strictly enforced salary caps can equalize talent across teams. Although the NFL does have a reputation for a high degree of parity, there are other, perhaps unanticipated effects of the current salary cap system. It appears to have created a two-class system, where star players make extraordinary salaries while journeyman veterans are frequently offered only the league minimum for a player with that many years of service. Such division is exacerbated by a provision added to the salary cap language that allows teams to count only 50 percent of a veteran's salary against their cap if the player signs for the league minimum. The provision was added as a result of fears that too many veterans were being released.

---

[21]Paul D. Stoudohar, "Salary Caps in Professional Team Sports," in *Compensation and Working Conditions* (Washington, D.C.: U.S. Department of Labor, Spring 1998), pp. 3–11.

[22]Details of collective bargaining agreements appear in Chapter 9.

[23]See David Harris, *The League: The Rise and Decline of the NFL* (New York: Bantam Books, 1986), p. 182.

Unfortunately for these players, it creates a strong incentive for teams to offer the league minimum, as any offer over the minimum means that the entire salary counts against the cap instead of only half. Thus, when Brian Mitchell, perhaps the greatest kick return specialist of all time, was informed by the Philadelphia Eagles in 2003 that he would be offered only the league minimum, he elected to leave the team and sign with the Giants instead. Around the same time, Donovan McNabb, the Eagles quarterback, signed an extension worth over $100 million; this is a perfect example of a team implenting the two-class strategy toward the salary cap. Given this uneven distribution of revenue across players, further changes seem likely.

The WNBA, as initially structured, and some other fledgling professional leagues present the players with a pure monopsony. When the WNBA was founded, the league owned all of the teams, and so the concept of free agency was meaningless. No matter how long the players stayed in the league or what team they played for, they always worked for the same employer. In such a case, the only opportunity to establish a competitive market for labor is through rival leagues. Unfortunately for the players, the demand for sports such as women's professional basketball and professional lacrosse is not high enough to support multiple leagues. The WNBA is now moving to a structure of independent team ownership. It remains to be seen how this organizational change will affect player salaries.

The Draft

Prior to the 1930s, the reserve clause bound players under contract to their teams forever but players who had not yet signed a contract remained free agents. The competition for unsigned players gave them their one chance to operate in a free market. Leagues eventually closed even this loophole by instituting an annual draft in which teams selected eligible amateurs, thereby extending their monopsony power over athletes who had never played professional ball.

As noted in Chapter 5, the origin of the draft can be traced to 1934, when two NFL teams—the old Brooklyn Dodgers and the Philadelphia Eagles—bid against each other for the services of Stan Kostka, an All-American player at the University of Minnesota. The resulting bidding war drove salary offers to the then unbelievable level of $5,000 (what Bronko Nagurski—the greatest player of the era—made).

Perhaps the most restrictive labor practices for players not yet under contract was the system once in place in professional hockey. NHL teams used to be able to restrict players by placing their names on a "negotiation list" that prohibited other teams from dealing with them. Teams did not have to sign the player to a contract, select players in a formal draft, or even inform the players that their names were on the list. They simply had to send a telegram to the NHL office to ascertain that the players were not on someone else's list. Bobby Hull, the great "Golden Jet" of the Chicago Blackhawk team of the 1960s and 1970s, was placed on such a list when he was 11 years old after a Blackhawk coach saw him warm up before a junior league game. Hull did not even learn that he had been placed on the list until two years later.[24]

While owners argue that they need the draft to maintain competitive balance, players see it as a further restriction on their freedom to choose employers. As a fan, you may take the draft for granted or even look forward to it. Imagine, though, how you would feel if a firm chose you in an entering-worker draft when you graduated from college. Once selected, your choices were to work for that firm or not work at all. Most of you would not care for such a system. Athletes would rather sell their services to the highest bidder than face a monopsony upon entering the league. Although no players association has succeeded in eliminating the draft altogether, the NBA did reduce the draft from 7 rounds to just 2, and the NFL reduced its draft from 12 rounds to 7. This reduction gives all players who would have been lower-round draft choices the freedom to try out with any team they choose.

Empirical Evidence on Restricted Player Movement and Player Salaries

Most research on salary determination and monopsonistic practices in professional sports stems from the pioneering work by Gerald Scully on baseball.[25] In his original model, Scully estimated players' marginal revenue products and then compared his estimates with the wages they earned. In baseball, as in all professional sports, the marginal revenue product of a player is the revenue generated as a result of the skills and abilities of that player. The revenues, in turn, stem from the increased gate receipts and television revenues that result from that player's contribution to team performance. (Note that in this case, teams are rewarded for producing wins, so here the relevant measure of output is wins rather than games played or attendance.)

The foregoing analysis relies on being able to estimate how much a Barry Bonds home run is worth to the San Francisco Giants or an Eddie George touchdown to the Tennessee Titans. Unfortunately, marginal product is not directly observable in the world of sports. It is possible, however, to create a set of causal linkages for evaluating a player's *MRP*.

Suppose, for simplicity, that teams have only two sources of revenue, gate receipts and television revenues. A greater number of wins increases both revenue streams, and the number of wins is determined by the players' abilities and managerial skill. All else being equal, the more productive the players, the more the team will win and the more revenue the team will earn. Thus, the basic model has only two equations: one that relates the players' productivity to winning percentage and another that relates winning percentage to revenue:

[24]Scott Young, *100 Years of Dropping the Puck: A History of the OHA* (Toronto: McClelland and Stewart, 1989), pp. 239–240.

[25]Gerald W. Scully, "Pay and Performance in Major League Baseball," *American Economic Review,* v. 64, no. 5 (December 1974), pp. 915–930.

$$PCTWIN = f(PRODUCTIVITY)$$

$$REVENUE = g(PCTWIN).$$

Following the original work by Scully, there have been many attempts to estimate the marginal revenue product of professional athletes. We first summarize Scully's basic model and then discuss two refinements. All of these models use regression analysis to determine the relationships between variables. (If you are not familiar with this statistical technique, review Appendix 2B.)

Scully envisioned a two-stage process in which he estimated the impact of wins on revenue and the impact of players' characteristics on team performance. In the revenue equation, Scully looked at the impact of winning percentage ($PCTWIN$) while controlling for population size in the home city ($SMSA$), differences in fan interest across locations ($MARGA$), differences in quality of leagues (NL), stadium quality as measured by its age (STD), and possible discrimination against black players ($BBPCT$). In the winning percentage equation, Scully measured a hitter's contribution with slugging average (total bases per at bat) and a pitcher's contribution with his strikeout–walk ratio. Because wins and losses occur at the team rather than individual level, Scully included the team slugging average (TSA) and team strikeout–walk ratio (TSW) in the equation, along with a National League indicator (NL) and two measures of team quality: one for contenders ($CONT$) and one for teams that are out of contention (OUT). Estimates for the two equations based on data from the 1968 and 1969 seasons are

$$PCTWIN = 37.24 + 0.92\ TSA + 0.90\ TSW - 38.57\ NL +$$
$$43.78\ CONT - 75.64\ OUT$$

$$REVENUE = -1{,}735{,}890 + 10{,}330\ PCTWIN + 494{,}585\ SMSA + 512$$
$$MARGA + 580{,}913\ NL - 762{,}248\ STD - 58{,}523\ BBPCT$$

The first equation shows that an increase in a team's slugging average of 1 point increases its winning percentage by .92 points (e.g., from 50.00 to 50.92). Thus, the marginal product of hitters (as measured by their slugging percentage) is .92. The marginal revenue associated with the production of raising the winning percentage by 1 point is $10,330, the coefficient of the $PCTWIN$ variable in the second equation. The product of these two coefficients, then, is $MP \times MR = MRP = \$9{,}504$. The same calculation for pitchers yielded an MRP of $9,727. Since an average hitter has a slugging average of about .340, and each hitter makes up about $1/12$, or .0833, of his team's offense, Scully calculates that an average hitter adds about 28.3 points to the TSA, implying a marginal revenue product of about $270,000. Even after subtracting the costs of other inputs required to produce games (for example, administrative and training costs) to obtain a measure of net marginal revenue product, his results indicated that marginal revenue products were much greater than salaries prior to free agency, when $100,000 was the unofficial ceiling facing even star players.

Table 8.2 shows a portion of Scully's results. It clearly shows that players were typically paid only 10 to 20 percent of their MRP.

Table 8.2

Estimated Marginal Revenue Products and Salaries

	Performance (SA or SW)	MRP	Salary
Hitters	270	213,000	31,700
	330	261,400	39,300
	370	292,700	44,400
	410	325,000	49,600
	450	356,400	54,800
	490	387,800	60,000
	530	420,100	65,300
	570	451,400	70,600
Pitchers	1.60	185,900	31,100
	2.00	209,200	37,200
	2.40	278,900	43,100
	2.80	325,400	48,800
	3.20	371,900	54,400
	3.60	418,400	58,800

Source: Gerald W. Scully, "Pay and Performance in Major League Baseball," *American Economic Review,* v. 64, no. 5 (December 1974), p. 923. Excerpted from Table 1.

Andrew Zimbalist estimated a more complex (and complete) model of marginal revenue product and monopsonistic exploitation using more recent data. His findings indicate that between 1986 and 1989, "apprentice" players, who were not yet eligible for free agency, were highly exploited; "journeyman" players, who were eligible for arbitration but not free agency, were somewhat exploited; and free agents were actually paid in excess of their marginal revenue products.[26] As players move from new entrant status, bound by the reserve clause, to free agent status, able to sell their talents to the highest bidder, market power shifts from team to player.

MacDonald and Reynolds also used data from 1986–87 to test the difference between career *MRP*s and salaries.[27] They divided players into three groups: rookies (players with less than three years' experience), arbitration-eligible players (three to six years), and free agents (six or more years). Their results indicate that players eligible for final offer arbitration and free agency are paid in accordance with their marginal products. They also found that inexperienced players (who have no mobility) were paid less than their *MRP* and thus were exploited by the owners.

Citing the inconsistent results of *MRP* estimates using the Scully method, another economist, Anthony Krautmann, developed a simple yet intuitively

---

[26]Andrew Zimbalist, "Salaries and Performance: Beyond the Scully Model," in *Diamonds Are Forever: The Business of Baseball,* ed. by Paul M. Sommers (Washington, D.C.: The Brookings Institution, 1992), pp. 109–133.

[27]Don N. MacDonald and Morgan O. Reynolds, "Are Baseball Players Paid Their Marginal Products?" *Managerial and Decision Economics,* v. 15 (September/October 1994), pp. 443–457.

appealing approach.[28] Krautmann hypothesized that free agents are paid their marginal revenue product because of the competitive bidding that takes place for their services. Recall that in the competitive model, players' wages (w) equal their MRP because teams bid up a player's wage until his pay equals his contribution to the team (assuming, of course, that there is no winner's curse, as described in Chapter 6). The beauty of this approach lies in its simplicity. Assuming that free agents are paid their marginal revenue products, Krautmann proposes a wage equation that relates free agents' performances to their wages. He then uses the same equation to predict the wages, and thus the MRPs, of players restricted by the reserve clause (apprentices) and those eligible only for final offer arbitration (journeymen) by inserting their statistics into the equation and comparing the predicted salary with the actual. Using data from the early 1990s, Krautmann finds that journeymen are paid approximately 85 percent of their MRPs, while apprentices are paid about 27 percent of their MRPs.

While estimates of the degree of exploitation differ from economist to economist, research on the labor market in baseball consistently shows that players who are not free to test the market receive less than their marginal revenue products. All the above findings suggest that players were exploited during the 100 years that the reserve clause was in effect.[29]

Some economists suggest an alternative explanation for the difference between a player's MRP and his salary. Krautmann and Oppenheimer have argued that the apparent exploitation of players in their first few years of service is actually a payment for general training received while playing in the minors.[30]

Using this model for sports such as basketball, football, and hockey poses some statistical difficulties, because players' productivity levels are much more interdependent. In addition, many of the performance measures make sense only for specific positions. This is particularly true for a highly specialized sport such as football.[31]

The Impact of Rival Leagues

While the reserve clause prevented teams in a league from bidding away each other's players, rival leagues can and have done so. Competition for players reduces the monopsony powers of existing leagues. For example, the salaries of baseball players rose dramatically in 1901, when the American League sought to become a "major league," and declined when the American and National

---

[28]Anthony C. Krautmann, "What's Wrong with Scully Estimates of a Player's Marginal Revenue Product," *Economic Inquiry,* v. 37, no. 2 (April 1999), pp. 369–381.

[29]We return to the issue of the impact of free agency on player salaries in Chapter 9.

[30]Anthony C. Krautmann and Margaret Oppenheimer, "Training in Major League Baseball: Are Players Exploited?" in *Baseball Economics,* ed. by John Fizel, Elizabeth Gustafson, and Lawrence Hadley (Westport, C.T.: Praeger, 1996), pp. 85–98.

[31]Sandy Kowalewski and Michael Leeds, "Winner-Take-All in the NFL," unpublished manuscript, 2000.

Leagues agreed to respect each other's reserved players. The fear of higher salaries attending the entry of the Federal League led Connie Mack to sell off the star players from a powerful Philadelphia Athletics baseball club in 1915. Similar "wars" drove up salaries when the American Basketball Association challenged the NBA in the 1960s and 1970s and when the World Hockey Association went head to head with the NHL in the 1970s. The salary data in Table 8.1 indicate that salaries in the NHL more than tripled in just six years between 1970 and 1976, the time period in which the WHA actively competed against the NHL for players. Figure 8.10 indicates how a rival league drives up salaries in the existing league by undercutting its monopsony power. Initially, the monopsonist hires L_m and pays the monopsony wage w_m. When the rival league enters, the teams must compete for players. Even if the increase in demand is relatively small, total employment increases to L_c, and competition for players forces the wage up to w_c.

Over the 1970s and 1980s, the NFL faced two rival leagues: the World Football League, which operated in 1974 and 1975, and the United States Football League, which operated from 1983 through 1985. Especially in the 1980s, the existence of the rival league resulted in significant increases in player salaries. Average NFL salaries increased over 83 percent in the four years between 1982 and 1986 (see Table 8.1).

As noted, salaries in the NHL increased dramatically while the WHA was competing for players' services, although team revenues did not grow signifi-

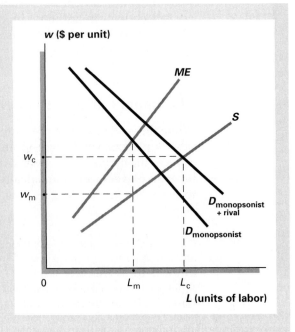

FIGURE 8.10

The Effect of a Rival Entering a Monopsony Market on Wages

cantly. One study showed that by the time the WHA folded, monopsonistic exploitation in the NHL was zero or even negative, meaning players were paid more than their marginal revenue product.[32] By stimulating competition for players, the rival leagues reduced the monopsonistic exploitation by the NFL and the NHL.

The owners' bidding for free agents resembles their own efforts to get cities to bid for their franchises described in Chapter 6. The winner's curse—the misfortune of winning a bidding war—applies just as well to the owners who vie for players as it does to cities that vie for teams.

The fear of the winner's curse and of free agency in general led the owners in baseball to seek extreme measures to reestablish their monopsony power. From 1985 through 1987, for example, baseball owners colluded with one another, agreeing not to bid for each other's free agents. The strategy proved highly successful, because only two players who were still desired by their original teams signed with another team. One of these players, Andre Dawson, who played for the Montreal Expos, so wanted to play with the Chicago Cubs that he adopted a unique strategy that shamed the Cubs into signing him. Dawson submitted a contract to the Cubs that left the salary blank and asked the Cubs to fill it in. The Cubs reluctantly did so, though only after writing in a salary substantially below the Expos' offer.

While successful, the owners' actions were also illegal. When the players found evidence of collusion, they submitted a series of grievances in 1986, 1987, and 1988. The owners were found to have violated the terms of their collective bargaining agreement, and they lost all three arbitration hearings. They were fined $280 million, were forced to allow all the players who were affected by the collusion a "second look" at free agency, and were forbidden from cooperating with each other regarding the labor market.[33]

In sum, part of the profit-maximizing strategy of teams in a league is to use monopsony power to reduce player salaries. The existence of institutional constraints such as the reserve clause and the entry draft significantly enhance this power, because they prevent players from selling their services to the highest bidding team. For this reason, players have fought with varying degrees of success for free agency in all four major sports. Perhaps the most effective force for reducing monopsonistic exploitation is the existence of a rival league. The section that follows shifts focus to the earnings of athletes in individual sports and explores cases where players have been able to extract what seem like extraordinary fees for their services.

---

[32]J. C. H. Jones and W. D. Walsh, "The World Hockey Association and Player Exploitation in the National Hockey League," *Quarterly Review of Economics and Business*, v. 27, no. 2 (Summer 1987), pp. 87–101.

[33]MacDonald and Reynolds, "Are Baseball Players Paid Their Marginal Products?" (1994), pp. 443–457.

8.3   THE ECONOMICS OF TOURNAMENTS AND SUPERSTARS

Mike Weir won the 2003 PGA Masters by a single stroke over Len Mattiace. After four rounds of golf plus one playoff hole covering four days and 73 holes, Weir had played 286 shots, Mattiace 287. The match could not have been closer. For his first-place finish, Weir received a check for $1,080,000. Mattiace received $648,000 for second, a difference of $432,000. With productivity so similar, one would expect their pay to be similar as well. The huge difference in payoffs seems even more drastic when one considers that in the same tournament, the two players who finished 48th and 49th were also just one stroke apart, yet they received $21,000 and $19,000, a difference of only $2,000. This disparity in prize winnings is typical of all professional tournaments. In the PGA, about 18 percent of the total prize money is awarded to the winner, about 10.8 percent to the second-place finisher, and 6.8 percent to the third-place finisher. Below the top 10 finishers, the prize money is much smaller and varies less between positions. The difference between finishing 22nd versus 23rd means a difference of only 0.1 percent of the prize money.[34] Productivity in golf may be measured in strokes, but some strokes are clearly worth more than others. The same holds true for tennis, bowling, figure skating, and most other individual sports.

In such cases, *relative* productivity, rather than absolute productivity, matters. The winner of a golf tournament receives the same prize no matter what his or her final score is. The only objective is to have a lower score than any other player.[35] Because the order of finish is the only performance criterion, such contests are known as **rank-order tournaments.**

Why would the organizers of a tournament set prizes based on rank order rather than absolute quality of performance? In all individual sports, the quality of any single performance depends on a long list of factors that have nothing to do with individual ability, such as the quality of the playing surface, the weather conditions, and in sports such as tennis, the ability of the opponent.[36] To determine the absolute level of a player's marginal product, judges would have to account for all these factors, a difficult and expensive task. And without the *MRP*, it is not possible to use the standard model of wage determination. If tournament organizers cannot measure marginal product, they cannot provide a wage based on the players' *MRP*. They must devise a new way to distribute prize money and provide appropriate incentives for participants. Fortunately, relative performance is more readily measured. The highly uneven distribution of the purses appeals to the most basic of economic tenets: self-interest.

---

[34]Ronald G. Ehrenberg and Michael Bognanno, "Do Tournaments Have Incentive Effects?" *Journal of Political Economy*, v. 98, no. 6 (December 1990), pp. 1307–1324.

[35]Two men were being chased by a grizzly bear when one of them stopped and began to put on track shoes. The other stopped and said, "You don't think track shoes are going to help you outrun a grizzly, do you?" The first man looked up and replied, "It's not the grizzly I'm trying to outrun."

[36]In one famous example, the course of the 1960 World Series was changed when a ground ball to the Yankee shortstop hit a pebble, took an unexpected bounce, and sustained a key Pirate rally in the seventh and deciding game.

We start by assuming that participants maximize utility and that their utility increases with income and leisure and, hence, decreases with effort. We also assume that the organizers of the tournament want players to give their maximum effort. If all players are paid the same regardless of performance, then players do not have an incentive to work as hard as they can to win. Because effort is not perfectly observable, the organizers must award prize money so that players have the incentive to play their best.

Figure 8.11 shows how a player determines how much effort to expend in a tournament. Casual observation is enough to show that the marginal cost of effort is positive, implying that there are costs associated with trying harder to win (more hours of practice, learning to handle pressure situations, and extra effort in the contest itself). Thus, the marginal cost curve slopes upward in Figure 8.11. The marginal cost curve also becomes steeper (increases at an increasing rate) as the amount of effort rises. The increasing slope means that changes in effort level become costlier as effort level rises. For example, moving from E_0 to E_1 adds little to the player's cost. In contrast, increasing effort from an already high level, such as from E_2 to an even higher level, E_3, comes at a great cost.

If the tournament's organizers (reflecting the desires of the fans who buy tickets and the advertisers who sponsor broadcasts) want to see the players try their hardest, they must make sure that the differences between the prizes increases for players who reach the top of the rankings. Figure 8.12 shows why. In a contest with one winner and one loser, such as the finals of a tennis match, and with contestants who are roughly equal in ability, the difference between

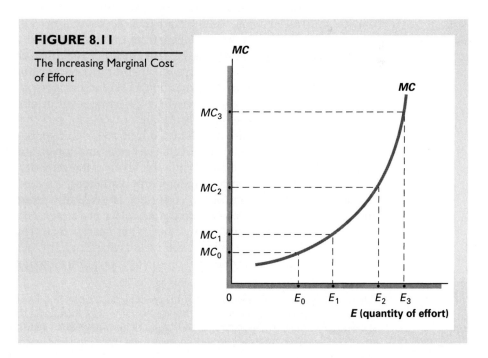

FIGURE 8.11

The Increasing Marginal Cost of Effort

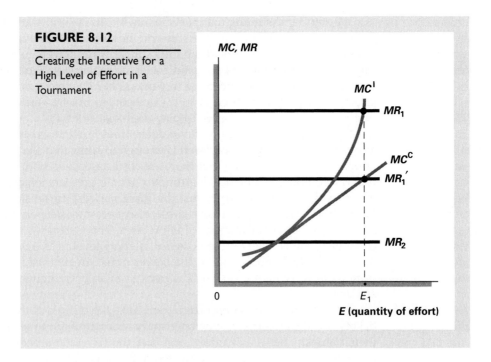

FIGURE 8.12

Creating the Incentive for a
High Level of Effort in a
Tournament

winning and losing may come down to random factors such as playing conditions.[37] The increasing marginal cost of effort is MC^I. Organizers want to stage the most exciting (and thus marketable) possible contest, and so they want the players to give their maximum effort (E_1). A player's marginal benefit is the additional (marginal) revenue he gets from moving up one position (e.g., from second to first). By creating a large difference between first and second prize, MR_1, the players have an incentive to expend much more effort than if the difference were small (MR_2). If the marginal cost of effort is constant, as shown by the line MC^C, the organizers can elicit the same level of effort with a much smaller difference between prizes (MR'_1).

Economic contests are not restricted to the world of sports. Table 8.3 shows the compensation levels for the top 10 celebrities and top 10 athletes for 2002, as compiled by *Forbes* magazine. While the level of the celebrity salaries is quite impressive, the *increase* in pay received upon attaining the top spot is of greater interest. The salary scales of top celebrities are typically structured as tournaments. The same is true for executives. The salary of a top executive in a large corporation is likely to be twice that of his or her nearest rival. This does not mean that the *MRP* of the top-ranked executive is twice that of his or her nearest rival. In fact, the value of their marginal product is very difficult to determine, because

---

[37]If the contestants are not equal in ability, the resulting tournament may be poor entertainment. If the weaker opponent knows he or she has no chance to win, there is no incentive to try. For a detailed discussion of this point, see Michael Leeds, "Rank-Order Tournaments and Worker Incentives," *Atlantic Economic Journal*, v. 16, no. 2 (June 1988), pp. 74–77.

Table 8.3

The Ten Highest-Paid Celebrities and Ten Highest-Paid Athletes in 2002

Rank/Individual	Industry/Occupation	2002 Earnings (in millions)
Celebrities		
1. Stephen Spielberg	Filmmaker	$200
2. George Lucas	Filmmaker	$183
3. Oprah Winfrey	Television/publishing	$180
4. J. K. Rowling	Author	$131.4
5. Tiger Woods	Golf	$78
6. Michael Schumaker	Formula 1 racing	$75
7. The Rolling Stones	Music	$66.5
8. Will Smith	Actor	$60
9. Paul McCartney	Music	$59
10. Tom Hanks	Actor	$55
(tie) David Copperfield	Magician	$55
Athletes		
1. Tiger Woods	Golf	$78
2. Michael Schumaker	Formula 1 racing	$75
3. Michael Jordan	Basketball	$35
4. Shaquille O'Neal	Basketball	$30.5
5. Oscar de la Hoya	Boxing	$30
6. Kevin Garnett	Basketball	$28
7. Alex Rodriguez	Baseball	$26
8. Grant Hill	Basketball	$25.5
9. Andre Agassi	Tennis	$24
10. Jaques Villeneuve	Indy racing	$23

"The Celebrity 100," Forbes online at http://www.Forbes.com/static_html/celebs/index.shtml, June 19, 2003.

they do not produce output that can be readily measured. To ensure that second-tier executives give their best effort, tournament-style wages create disproportionately large rewards for increases in rank.

Evidence on the Potential Inefficiency of Tournaments

Tournaments can also have negative effects on athletes' behavior in both individual and team sports. When teams compete in tournaments, competition for awards given to one player, such as Most Valuable Player or scoring titles, can lead to selfish play and damage the chemistry a team needs to succeed. Perhaps the most vivid evidence of the pressures a tournament creates comes from the case of Tonya Harding, a former national champion figure skater who admitted to "hindering prosecution" in the plot to injure fellow skater Nancy Kerrigan prior to the 1994 Winter Olympics. Kerrigan was attacked during the National Championships, the competition at which the Olympic team was to be chosen. Harding's ex-husband and an accomplice confessed to carrying out the attack and claimed that Harding herself was involved in planning it.[38] Harding's primary motivation behind the attack was to remove Kerrigan as the preeminent U.S. woman figure skater so that Harding could assume that role, thus providing her "ticket to fame and fortune."[39]

Possibly the most frightening example of the potential for undesirable outcomes in tournaments comes from a surprising yet familiar source. Imagine a country in which selected children are put to work full-time. School, friends, a normal childhood are all denied them as they perform hours of backbreaking work. When they try to get away, they are subjected to physical and emotional abuse, sometimes at the hands of their own parents. By the time they reach adulthood, many of them are physically broken—some even killed—by the arduous demands of their supervisors. Still others bear permanent emotional scars. Unable to form normal relationships with their peers, some take solace in drugs and others in self-abusive behavior. The country is the United States, and the abused children are the same ones we cheer on at events such as the Olympics, Wimbledon, and the NCAA championships.[40]

These youths are victims of a reward system in which first place counts for everything and second place for next to nothing. Adolescent girls take to the ice for the Olympic figure skating championship with greater individual rewards at stake than for any single event except, perhaps, a heavyweight boxing championship.[41] A gold medalist such as Sarah Hughes may get TV specials and starring roles in skating exhibitions. Her name will be entered in record books, and fans will remember her performance fondly for years to come. In contrast, all but a few relatives and friends will soon forget the performance of the fourth-place finisher.

As a result of the highly skewed reward structure, young girls are willing to work extremely long hours, some in excess of 45 hours per week. Their coaches and gyms, which stand to benefit mightily from the publicity these girls bring them, would be violating child labor laws if they paid the girls for their efforts. The long hours of training can bring permanent physical and psychological damage. Hoping to please their parents and coaches and yearning for a chance to stand on the Olympic podium, young gymnasts suffer through severe injuries that they do not allow to heal for fear of missing a championship or an Olympics before they become too old. One elite coach discouraged girls from having casts put on fractured limbs because "he feared it would hurt their muscle tone."[42] Some take an array of "laxatives, thyroid pills, and diuretics to lose the weight brought on by puberty."[43] The obsession with weight can

---

[38]Sonja Steptoe and E. M. Swift, "A Done Deal," *Sports Illustrated* (March 28, 1994), pp. 32–36.

[39]E. M. Swift, "Anatomy of a Plot: The Kerrigan Assault," *Sports Illustrated* (February 14, 1994), pp. 28–38.

[40]Joan Ryan, *Little Girls in Pretty Boxes* (New York: Doubleday, 1995), catalogs the horrors confronting many young female gymnasts and figure skaters.

[41]Ryan, *Little Girls in Pretty Boxes* (1995), p. 193.

[42]Merrell Noden, "Dying to Win," *Sports Illustrated* (August 8, 1994), pp. 52–59.

[43]Robert Frank and Phillip Cook, *The Winner-Take-All Society* (New York: The Free Press, 1995), p. 132.

become so serious that eating disorders can develop. Surveys show that almost a third of female college athletes—and up to two-thirds of the female gymnasts surveyed—admit to some sort of eating disorder. One young gymnast, Christy Henrich, literally starved herself to death. The eating disorders can have long-term effects, leading to menstrual dysfunction and osteoporosis.[44] The athletes are caught in a prisoner's dilemma like that outlined in Chapter 4. They feel pressured into taking dangerous—and potentially life-threatening—drugs, because they fear that others who do take the drugs will outperform them and feel that they can gain a much-needed edge by taking performance-enhancing drugs if the others do not. Little wonder that a survey of almost 200 sprinters, swimmers, powerlifters, and other athletes, most of them U.S. Olympians or aspiring Olympians, delivered such startling results. The survey confronted the athletes with a hypothetical situation:

> You are offered a banned performance-enhancing substance that comes with two guarantees:
> 1. You will not be caught.
> 2. You will win every competition you enter for the next five years, and then you will die from the side effects of the substances.
>
> Would you take it?

"More than half the athletes surveyed said they would accept such an offer."[45]

What Is a Gold Medal Worth?

The extreme behavior described above may seem absurd given that the Olympics are supposed to be an "amateur" event. Ideally, fans want athletes to give their best performance out of pride in their country and the thrill of being the best in the world, but from the athlete's perspective, much more than medals are at stake. The commercial endorsement value of a gold medal in some events is more than $1 million. The reward comes in the form of pictures on cereal boxes, sneaker endorsements, speaking engagements, and appearance fees. Since the endorsement value of a bronze medal is less than half that of a gold, the incentive structure of a rank-order tournament exists in the absence of explicit wages. Tara Lipinski, who retired from amateur skating at the age of 15, is an example of just how valuable a gold medal can be. After winning her medal, Lipinski agreed to participate in the Campbell Soup Champions on Ice Tour for several million dollars per tour. Though impressive, for skaters such as Lipinski, the income earned from touring ice shows typically represents only about 50 percent of total earnings. An additional 22 percent

---

[44]See S. Gilbert, "The Smallest Olympians Pay the Biggest Price," *New York Times* (July 28, 1996), p. E4; Noden, "Dying to Win" (1994), pp. 52–59; Ryan, *Little Girls in Pretty Boxes* (1995), pp. 17–54; Ian Tofler, Barri Katz Stryer, Lyle Micheli, and Lisa Herman, "Physical and Emotional Problems of Elite Female Gymnasts," *New England Journal of Medicine*, v. 335, no. 4 (July 25, 1996), pp. 281–283.

[45]Michael Bamberger and Don Yaeger, "Over the Edge," *Sports Illustrated* (April 14, 1997), pp. 61–70.

comes from personal appearances, 22 percent from professional competitions, and 6 percent from endorsements.[46]

An Exception to the Rule: NASCAR

The reward scheme used in NASCAR racing is an interesting exception to both the standard model of wage determination and the highly nonlinear rewards used in golf and tennis.[47] Although stock car racing appears to satisfy the basic conditions for a rank-order tournament, the reward scheme on a per-race basis is nearly horizontal. Figure 8.13 shows the NASCAR prize money for a single race and, for comparison, the prize structure for a single PGA tournament. The 21st-place finisher in either event receives roughly the same prize (around $35,000). Moving down 20 spots to 41st in the golf tournament reduces the prize to $11,250.

FIGURE 8.13

Comparison of the Rewards in the PGA Championship Versus the Food City 500

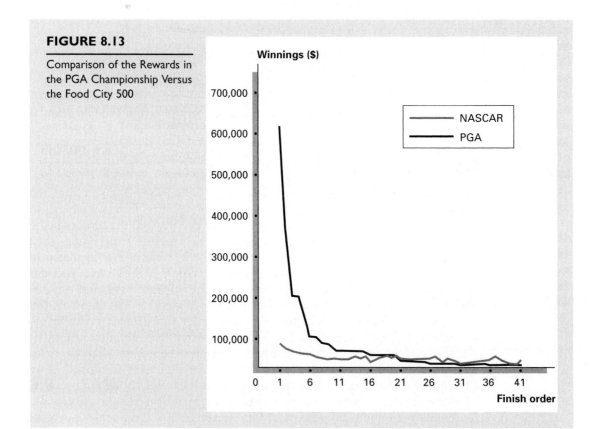

[46]See Sheryl Berk, "Golden Girl," *McCalls* (December 1998), pp. 18–24; and "How They Bring in the Gold," *U.S. News and World Report* (January 31, 1994), p. 16.

[47]This section is based on Peter von Allmen, "Is the Reward System in NASCAR Efficient?" *Journal of Sports Economics*, v. 2, no.1 (February 2000), pp. 62–79.

The Duralube 500 at
Phoenix International
Raceway

In the race, however, drivers who finished as low as 43rd earned as much as $32,000. Finishing first increases the payout in the golf tournament to $630,000 but only to $92,435 in the race. While one might initially expect the same winner-take-all pressure in NASCAR as in figure skating or gymnastics, several unique features of racing work against the use of tournament-style rewards.

As noted on the previous page, in most individual sports, the competitors have no way to prevent their opponent from succeeding. In racing, however, where drivers all compete on the same track at the same time, tournament-style wages may lead to reckless driving—with catastrophic results. The risk of a severe accident raises the probability that high social costs may exist with a win-at-all-cost strategy that would not be present in other individual sports. In addition, in NASCAR racing, teams that sponsor cars have relatively complex revenue and profit functions that include revenue from sponsors, year-end prize money, and a wide variety of bonuses that drivers can win during races. The accumulation of on-air time for sponsors and season championship points give drivers a powerful incentive to remain on the track for the entire race rather than risk crashing in order to achieve a greater share of the purse for that race. Thus, highly nonlinear reward schemes for individual races would likely do more harm than good.

The Distribution of Income

Because financial rewards for individual victories are so heavily weighted in favor of the highest-place finishers, and top performers consistently place highly throughout the season, the distribution of income in professional individual sports is highly skewed. A **Lorenz curve** shows how equally income is distributed.

The Lorenz curve measures inequality by graphing the percentage of people in a country (or other demographic or economic group) against the percentage of total income (or other measure of well-being) that they account for. We could, for example, sort all people in the United States according to their incomes, from lowest to highest, and draw a graph with the percentage of people on the horizontal axis and the percentage of the nation's income on the vertical axis. If everyone had the same income (perfect equality), counting 5 percent more of the population would account for 5 percent more of the nation's income. In such a case the Lorenz curve is a straight line, as shown in Figure 8.14. If income is not equally distributed, the poorest people (those we count first) have a disproportionately small share of total income while the richest people have a disproportionately large share. As a result, the Lorenz curve is flat at first and becomes steeper as one moves to the right. This causes the Lorenz curve to bow downward.

In practice, one cannot easily count each person in the United States or even in a much smaller group. As a result, researchers typically divide the relevant population into groups, such as deciles (equal divisions of 10 percent). One then compares the share of total income for each decile with the total income of the population. Figure 8.15 shows a Lorenz curve for the top 50 money winners in the 2002 Women's Tennis Association (WTA). The population deciles appear across the horizontal axis, from "poorest" on the left to the "richest" on the right. The vertical axis shows the percentage of total income earned by that group and all lower groups (the "cumulative distribution"). As before, if each player on the WTA had the same income, then each decile would

FIGURE 8.14

The Lorenz Curve

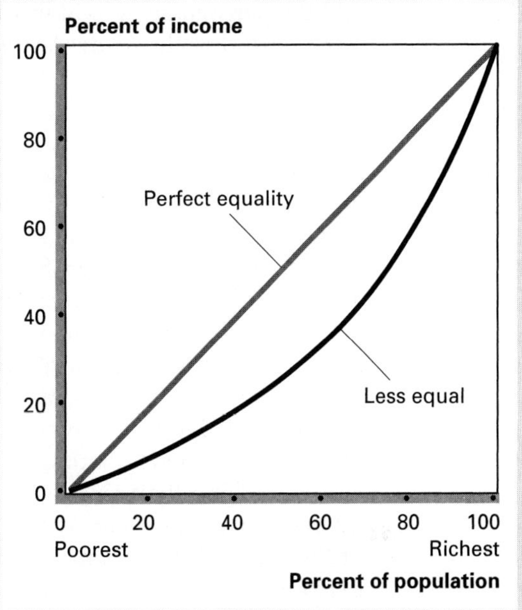

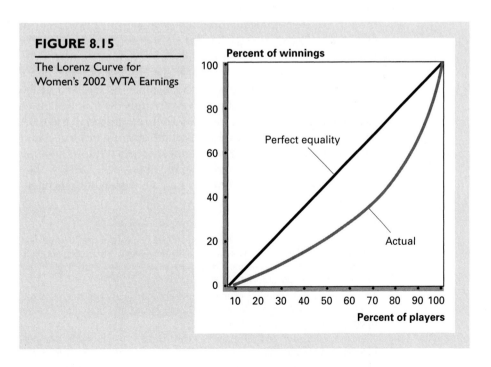

FIGURE 8.15

The Lorenz Curve for Women's 2002 WTA Earnings

account for 10 percent of the total income. The percentage of the population and the percentage of total income would rise at the same rate, and the Lorenz curve would be the 45-degree line labeled "perfect equality." The actual Lorenz curve is bowed downward because the lowest 10 percent of the players earned only 3 percent of the income in the WTA, and the top 10 percent earned over 34 percent.[48] In fact, the top two players, Serena and Venus Williams, won more than the entire bottom 3 deciles, over 30 percent of players, combined. Season earning totals in other sports show similar inequalities.[49]

The salary structure in all sports is highly uneven due to the earnings of superstars. Even at the professional level, relatively few players have abilities and charisma that set them apart from the rest.[50] Players such as Wayne Gretzky, Babe Ruth, Michael Jordan, and Walter Payton stood at the extreme right tail of the talent distribution. The extraordinary performances of which such athletes are capable vastly increased the demand to see games in which they played. Most fans would rather see one San Francisco Giants game in which Barry Bonds continues his quest to catch Hank Aaron as the all-time home run king than five games played by two teams stocked with mediocre hitters. Thus, the demand by fans and sponsors is greatest for the smallest part of the talent distribution. The very high demand for a very small number of performances disproportionately increases the salaries of top players.

Research on superstars in the NBA has shown that their presence increases TV ratings and merchandise sales.[51] For example, the television ratings for the 1993 NBA finals between the Phoenix Suns and the Chicago Bulls featuring Michael Jordan were 5.5 percentage points higher than the 1994 finals between the New York Knicks and the Houston Rockets. The decline occurred even though the 1994 finals featured teams in significantly larger media markets. In fact, NBA playoff ratings have declined every year since the breakup of the Jordan-era Bulls. Because they increase attendance and TV ratings whenever they play, superstars do more than just create value for their own teams. They create positive externalities, because other teams benefit from higher attendance and local media ratings even though they do not pay the visiting stars' salaries. The externality is particularly pronounced in the NBA and NHL, since these leagues do not share home-ticket revenue or local broadcasting revenue. Even when a league shares revenues, teams without superstars still free ride because the pool of shared revenue increases. During the 1989–90 season, games featuring Magic Johnson had television ratings that were 31 percent

---

[48] http://sportsillustrated.cnn.com/tennis/stats/2002/womoney/

[49]See Quirk and Fort, *Pay Dirt* (1992), pp. 235–239; and Sandra Kowalewski and Michael Leeds, "The Impact of the Salary Caps and Free Agency on the Structure and Distribution of Salaries in the NFL," in *Sports Economics: Current Research*, ed. by John Fizel, Elizabeth Gustafson, and Lawrence Hadley (Westport, C.T.: Praeger, 1999), pp. 213–226.

[50]For a detailed description of the phenomenon of nonlinear returns, see Sherwin Rosen, "The Economics of Superstars," *American Economic Review*, v. 71, no. 5 (December 1981), pp. 845–858, upon which this section is based.

[51]Jerry A. Hausman and Gregory K. Leonard, "Superstars in the National Basketball League: Economic Value and Policy," *Journal of Labor Economics*, v. 15, no. 4 (1997), pp. 586–624.

higher than games without him.[52] In the 1991–92 season, Michael Jordan's total value to the NBA, including the positive externalities he generated for other teams, was $53 million.[53]

When to Turn Pro, or a Tale of Two High School Stars With superstars' annual incomes now measured in the tens of millions, deciding when to leave the ranks of amateur competition looms large for top prospects. Such was the case in 2003 for high school basketball phenom Lebron James. From an economic perspective, the young athletes face the question of how to maximize lifetime wealth. Their problem resembles that of a logging company deciding when it should cut down a tree. The longer the company allows the tree to grow, the greater the value of the tree when it is harvested, but the longer the tree sits unharvested, the greater the company's opportunity cost. Just as trees or wine increase in value as they age, so does a potential superstar. When making his decision, Lebron James no doubt considered the cases of Kobe Bryant and Korleone Young. When Bryant and Young decided to go straight from high school to the NBA, each weighed the value of the experience he could gain by playing one or more years in college against the income he expected to receive from entering the draft.

We can use a simple economic model to formalize the decision processes. We simplify the problem facing Lebron James by assuming that he knows with certainty what his lifetime earnings will be in the NBA if he turns pro. We also assume that each year staying in school increases a player's skills (e.g., developing a better jump shot or playing better defense), thereby increasing his lifetime earnings by a given factor, g_s, where s is the number of years of college, and that additional years in school add decreasing amounts to his skills and earnings (i.e., $g_1 > g_2 > g_3 > g_4$). Finally, we assume that the athlete will have a career of a given length, so that spending one more year in college does not shorten his professional career. Letting V equal the lifetime value of a player's earnings if he turns pro immediately after high school, going to college for one year increases the lifetime value of earnings to $(1 + g_1)V$, staying in school for two years increases lifetime earnings to $(1 + g_2)(1 + g_1)V$, and so on. Staying in school, however, also comes at a cost, as it delays his earnings. By waiting a year, the athlete gives up use of his salary for that year. Economists typically assume that the lost income from saving or investing—or the lost pleasure from spending that money—is given by the rate of interest, so that earning V in one year is equivalent to earning $V/(1 + r)$ today, where r denotes the rate of interest. Going to college for one year is thus worthwhile if it adds more to earnings than the waiting takes away, just like a vintner ages his wine until the added value of a more mature wine is offset by the cost of waiting.[54] That occurs if

---

[52]Larry Bird and Magic Johnson are frequently cited as having "saved" the NBA from lackluster ratings and poor attendance in the 1980s.

[53]Hausman and Leonard, "Superstars in the National Basketball Association" (1997), pp. 586–624.

[54]To see how this was first applied to the maturing of a wine, see Knute Wicksell, "On the Theory of Interest," in *Selected Essays in Economics: Volume I*, ed. by Bo Sandelin (London: Routledge, 1997), pp. 41–53.

$$\frac{(1+g_1)}{(1+r)} V > V$$

or, more simply, if $g_1 > r$. He will stay for two years if

$$\frac{(1+g_1)(1+g_2)}{(1+r)^2} > V$$

or if $g_2 > r$, and so on, until he finally graduates or $g_i < r$ for some $i < 4$.

In reality, players do not know how quickly their skills and earnings will grow with an extra year in college. A young player may be able to use scouts' projections to get a good idea of what his salary would be if he entered the draft that year. However, there is no guarantee that g will be the same next year as it was this year. On the one hand, the player may lose out by staying in school if he is injured or fails to develop at the same rate. On the other hand, turning pro too early may cause him to miss out on a significant improvement in his skills.

Salary cap restrictions further complicate the player's decision. If rookie salaries face salary limits (salary caps) as described in Section 8.2 and the marginal revenue product of the potential entrant exceeds the cap, he will receive the maximum allowable salary whenever he decides to turn pro. The NBA had hoped that installing a rookie salary cap would give young stars more incentive to stay in college, because the lower salaries would be less of a temptation. Unfortunately for the league, this effect is offset by the impact of free agency. The sooner a player enters the draft, the younger he will be when he becomes a free agent.

Kobe Bryant and Korleone Young had careers that took decidedly different turns after they left high school. The Charlotte Hornets selected Bryant with the 13th overall pick in the first round of the 1996 draft. The Hornets immediately traded his rights to the Lakers, where he has become one of the league's most exciting players. He has earned millions of dollars in salary and endorsement deals. In Bryant's case, the value added of a college playing career would probably have been minimal, and his decision appears to have been a good one.

Korleone Young's decision to turn pro seems to have been a mistake. Like Bryant, Young was considered one of the top high school players in the country during his senior year. Rather than play college basketball, he declared himself eligible for the 1998 NBA draft. Unfortunately for Young, he was not chosen until the 40th pick overall (the middle of the second round) and did not receive a guaranteed contract. After playing only 15 minutes in the NBA in 1999, he was released, a "poster child for players who turned pro too soon."[55] He spent the 1999–2000 season with the Richmond Rhythm of the International Basketball League, working on his game and hoping to get another shot at the NBA. Although Lebron James has already profited enormously from endorsement contracts with Nike and Upper Deck, his success in the NBA as a player will only be revealed over time.

---

[55]Stephen A. Smith, "Phenom Works to Capture His Lost Dream," *Philadelphia Inquirer* (January 14, 2000), pp. D1–D2.

BABE DIDRICKSON ZAHARIAS
BIOGRAPHICAL Sketch

I knew exactly what I wanted to be when I grew up. My goal was to be the greatest athlete that ever lived.

— BABE DIDRICKSON ZAHARIAS[1]

One of the consequences of rank-order tournaments and superstar effects is a tendency for athletes to specialize. The highly skewed winner-take-all reward system discourages athletes from pursuing any outside distractions. "Two-way" football players have become a rarity, and crossover athletes who play more than one sport have all but disappeared. It is thus unlikely that the athletic world will ever see another Babe Didrickson Zaharias. Zaharias dominated the athletic world like no athlete before or since, achieving star status in the disparate worlds of basketball, track and field, and golf. In so doing, she experienced perhaps the greatest single day an athlete has ever known.

Mildred Ella Didrickson was born in 1911 to impoverished Norwegian immigrants in Port Arthur, Texas. The sixth of seven children and the youngest girl, Mildred got the nickname "Babe" while a young girl and still the "baby" of the family, though she later attributed the nickname to comparisons with baseball hero Babe Ruth. Her last name was changed to "Didrickson" as a result of a spelling error in her school records.

Growing up in Port Arthur and later in Beaumont, Zaharias was drawn to sports at a time when sexual stereotypes still discouraged women from participating in "manly" sports. In this case, however, Zaharias' lower-class upbringing freed her from many of the restrictions that otherwise would have constrained her development as an athlete. She did not take an active part in organized sports, however, until she left high school in 1930 to play basketball for the Employers Casualty Insurance Company.

It may seem odd today for an athlete to advance her career by taking a day job as a secretary for $75 a month with an insurance company, but at that time, many colleges did not offer athletic programs for women, and the fledging NCAA was openly disdainful of women's athletics. Employers Casualty played in the 45-member Women's National Basketball League, which played under the auspices of the Amateur Athletic Union (AAU). The AAU was then the dominant athletic body; it oversaw competitions by a few schools and by companies that sponsored teams. Like firms that offer part-time employment for Olympic athletes today, companies found that athletes were generally very productive employees who generated favorable publicity.

In joining the Employers Casualty "Golden Cyclones," Zaharias was joining one of the very best amateur teams in the nation. When the first All-American women's basketball team was announced in 1929, Employers Casualty had eight All-Americans on its roster. She quickly established herself as a star among stars, being named an All-American for three straight years.

As good as she was on the basketball court, Zaharias found her greatest success in track and field. It was here that she recorded the greatest single performance in the history of track and field and perhaps of any athletic competition. The 1932 National Track and Field Competition served as the trials for the 1932 Olympic Games to be played in Los Angeles. Zaharias arrived at the competition as the sole representative of the Employers Casualty team. In one afternoon, she ensured that Employers Casualty won the team championship by winning the competition in the shot put, the baseball throw, the javelin throw, the 80-meter hurdles, and the broad jump. She also tied

➡

for first in the high jump and finished fourth in the discus, an event in which she normally did not compete. In all, she won six gold medals and broke four world records in about three hours.

Zaharias hardly skipped a beat in the Olympics, setting world records in the javelin throw and the 80-meter hurdles. She also tied for first in the high jump, though her then-unorthodox style (the so-called Western Roll that soon became the dominant style) caused a controversy among some of the judges who thought it illegal. As a compromise, she was declared the second-place finisher and given the only half-gold-half-silver medal in the history of the modern Olympics.

As the dominant performer and personality of the 1932 "Hollywood Games," Zaharias quickly became a national celebrity. Her publicity, however, came at a considerable cost. The public did not know what to make of a woman who defied sexual stereotypes, hailing her accomplishments but never truly embracing her. She seemed destined to fade from public view when the AAU stripped her of her amateur status for being featured in an automobile advertisement (even though, apparently, she had not given permission for the firm to use her likeness). After a year or so of stunts and exhibition tours, she returned to work for Employers Casualty.

Over the next several years, Zaharias reconstructed her personal and athletic lives. Stung by her treatment in the press, she strove to develop a more feminine image, playing up her role as a wife following her marriage to professional wrestler (and later sports promoter) George Zaharias in 1938. She was anything but a typical housewife. Having picked up golf as a teenager, Zaharias threw herself into her new, more socially accepted sport. In 1935, she won the Texas State Women's Golf Championship and was ready to enter full-time competition when the United States Golf Association banned her from amateur competition because of her appearance in the automobile advertisement. She responded by explicitly turning pro, but she quickly realized that professional golf provided neither adequate competition nor adequate remuneration. She succeeded in having her amateur status reinstated in 1943, though she would have to wait until the end of World War II to enter the next stage of her athletic career; it was worth the wait.

Zaharias burst onto the women's golf tour in 1945, winning the Texas Women's Open and the Western Open, and being named "Woman Athlete of the Year" by the Associated Press (an award she had won 13 years earlier for her Olympic exploits). This proved merely a warm-up for 1946, when she won 14 straight tournaments (a figure she later inflated to 17). In 1947, Zaharias became the first American woman to win the British Women's Amateur golf championship in the 55-year history of the event.

After her victory in the British Amateur event, Zaharias again turned pro and a year later signed on as a charter member of the newly formed Ladies Professional Golf Association (LPGA—it chose the term "Ladies" to avoid conflict with the unsuccessful *Women's* PGA). Her talents led her to be a dominant figure in the LPGA—she won about two of every three events she entered for 1950 and 1951—and her showmanship, while not always appreciated by her competitors, helped market the new tour.

In 1953, Zaharias was diagnosed with rectal and colonic cancer. During the surgery, doctors found that the cancer had spread to the surrounding lymph nodes and told her family and friends (but not Zaharias herself) that she had less than a year to live. Within four months, however, she was back on the tour, finishing as the sixth-highest money winner for 1953. She did even better in 1954, winning five tournaments and having the lowest average on the tour. The cancer finally reappeared in 1955, and Babe Didrickson Zaharias, arguably the greatest athlete of the century, died in 1956.

[1]Susan Cayleff, *Babe: The Life and Legend of Babe Didrikson Zaharias* (Urbana: University of Illinois Press, 1995), p. 46.

Source: Susan Cayleff, *Babe: The Life and Legend of Babe Didrikson Zaharias* (Urbana: University of Illinois Press, 1995).

SUMMARY

In this chapter, we considered theories of labor economics that are used to determine a player's value, or marginal revenue product. Monopoly leagues that also function as monopsony employers reduce the bargaining power of employees in favor of employers. Because monopsonies have the ability to reduce wages, professional leagues have fought to maintain versions of the reserve clause, which binds players to teams. Players' organizations, however, have fought to reduce monopsony power through free agency. The minor leagues in the NHL and MLB serve as general training grounds, where players receive very low wages that may reflect both monopsony power due to the reserve clause and a payment by the player for general training costs.

The distribution of income in professional sports is highly skewed toward those with the most talent. In individual sports, tournament-style wages create powerful incentives to perform at the highest levels of effort. Superstar wages also exist in team sports, and these can be attributed to the small number of superstars relative to the demand to see them play. In the next chapter on unions, we turn our attention to the world of player associations, agents, and collective bargaining.

DISCUSSION QUESTIONS

1. Describe how you might determine the marginal product of
   a. A running back
   b. A quarterback
   c. A lineman
   d. A linebacker.

2. For a hockey player, what types of skills could be improved through general training? Specific training?

3. Where do NFL players receive most of their general training? Is the same true for baseball players? Why or why not?

4. In a football draft, comment on the strategy of choosing the "best available player" regardless of position from the standpoint of marginal revenue product. Is this always the best strategy?

5. Why might tournament-style wages be ineffective at maximizing player effort in a team sport such as baseball?

6. Under what circumstances do individual awards for achievements in team sports, such as batting titles and stolen bases, distort incentives?

PROBLEMS

8.1 Suppose that the market demand for baseball players is perfectly inelastic (vertical) at 750 players. If the market supply increases due to an increase in the number of available international players, show using a graph how wages will change as a result.

8.2 Suppose that there are two types of players, good and medium. The team demand curve for top-quality players is $Q = 27 - 5w$, and the market supply of top players is $Q = 4w$, where w is the wage in millions of dollars. How many top-quality players will the team hire? What will they be paid?

8.3 Use a graph similar to Figure 8.5 to show the effect on league salaries of

    a. An increase in the number of players available

    b. A decrease in television revenues due to fan preferences for drama shows

    c. A minimum salary set above the equilibrium wage.

8.4 Log on to the Economics of Sports website at http://www.aw.com/ leeds_vonallmen, and download the data from the icon marked "hockey salary data." Use regression analysis to estimate a wage equation. If players are paid their marginal product, how much is an extra goal worth to the team? What performance indicators matter most? Least?

8.5 Explain and show using a graph why, at any given wage, a monopoly firm will hire less labor than the total employment if the industry were competitive.

8.6 Explain how reverse-order entry drafts and the reserve clause create monopsony power for teams within a league.

8.7 European soccer players are free to sell their services to any team in any league. How would it affect the profitability of these teams if instead players were bound by a reserve clause? Use a graph to show how wage rates would differ under the two scenarios.

8.8 Using a graph, show what happens to player effort in a tournament if the marginal cost-of-effort curve shifts upward.

8.9 Suppose a college junior could earn a salary of $500,000 by declaring himself eligible for the draft. If he waits until after his senior year, his salary will be $600,000. If the interest rate is 8 percent, should he stay for his senior year or not?

8.10 In Problem 9, what should the player do if there is a 50 percent chance that the league will institute a rookie salary cap next year set at $500,000?

APPENDIX 8A

The Labor–Leisure Choice Model of Indifference Curves

L ike all decisions in economics, the decision to work is one of choosing among alternatives. In the simple labor–leisure choice model, a person chooses between working for pay and not working (consuming leisure). Each person possesses a **utility function** as defined in Appendix 2A. Labor economists typically assume that utility results from consuming goods (X) and leisure (Z), both of which are normal goods, as shown in the following equation:

$$U = u(X, Z).$$

We can illustrate the utility function using indifference curves, as shown in Figure 8A.1. Each curve represents a specific level of utility, and utility increases as we move northeast, away from the origin (i.e., $U_2 > U_1$). The slope of an indifference curve, also called the **marginal rate of substitution,** represents the rate at which the person is willing to exchange one good for the other, holding utility constant. Recall that the negative slope of an indifference curve

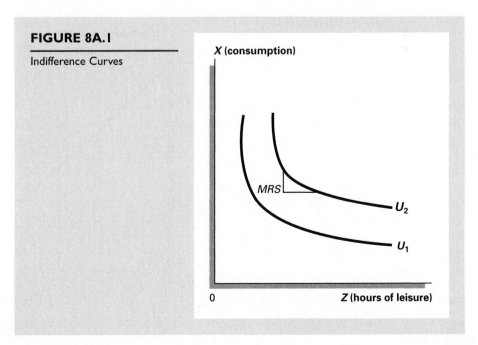

FIGURE 8A.1

Indifference Curves

X (consumption)

MRS

U_2

U_1

0

Z (hours of leisure)

implies a trade-off: the person must receive more of one good if he or she receives less of the other in order to hold utility constant. The convex shape of the indifference curves reflects the diminishing marginal utility associated with consuming more and more of any single commodity.

Consumption is limited by an **income constraint** and a **time constraint.** A person's income consists of his or her earnings from working h hours at wage w, and exogenous income V, which consists of all nonlabor income such as dividends, inheritances, and so on:

$$X = wh + V$$

The time constraint reflects the fact that there are only so many hours in a day (T) and that the hours must be allocated to either work or leisure. The time constraint implies that the opportunity cost of consuming one additional hour of leisure equals the hourly wage:

$$T = h + Z$$

In Figure 8A.2, the time constraint mandates that a person cannot spend less than zero hours working and more than T hours at leisure (and vice versa). Because the person receives some exogenous income even if he or she does not work, the budget constraint begins from a point $\$V$ directly above T. The constraint has a slope equal to $-w$ since the person must give up $\$w$ for every hour of leisure he or she consumes.

We can combine the person's utility function with his or her budget constraint to determine the person's utility-maximizing choice. Suppose a local

FIGURE 8A.2

The Income and Time Constraints

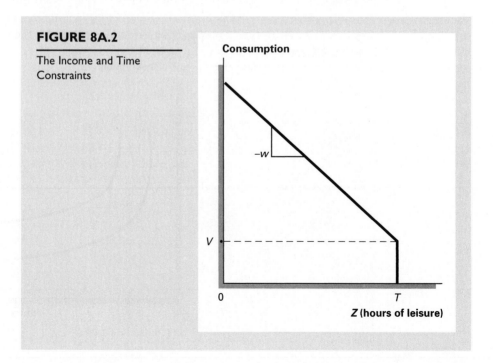

golf pro, Bill, can earn income by giving golf lessons for $20 per hour. In addition, he receives $100 per day in dividend income. His constraints are

$$X = 20h + 100$$
$$24 = h + Z$$

Bill can teach all the lessons he wants, but each hour that he spends teaching requires that he give up one hour of leisure. Conversely, the opportunity cost of consuming an extra hour of leisure is $20. Bill's utility maximizing solution is shown in Figure 8A.3. He maximizes his utility by teaching 8 hours per day and consuming 16 hours of leisure.[56] His total daily income is $260, and his utility level is U_2. At the utility-maximizing point, S, the marginal rate of substitution (the slope of the indifference curve) equals the wage rate, the slope of the budget constraint:

$$MRS = w$$

If Bill had a strong preference for leisure, we could illustrate his preferences with the dashed indifference curve U_1. In this example, Bill does not want to work at all. The indifference curve U_1 touches the budget line at Z, which means that $h = 0$, and all time is devoted to leisure. Economists refer to such an outcome as a **corner** solution.

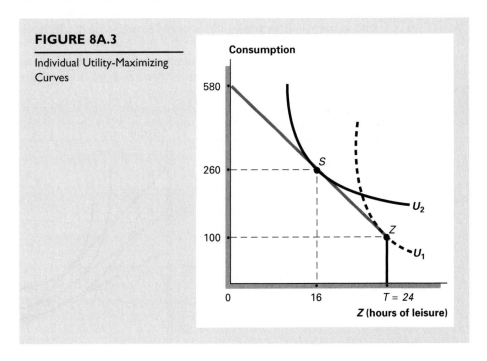

FIGURE 8A.3

Individual Utility-Maximizing Curves

---

[56]We could alter the model by assuming that Bill needs to devote a certain portion of each day to personal needs such as sleeping and eating, but the framework would be the same. With such an allowance, T would simply shift to the left by the amount of personal time, p, per period $(T - p = h + Z)$.

By varying Bill's wage rate, we can derive his labor supply curve. Figure 8A.4 shows Bill's initial optimal point from Figure 8A.3 and the effect of a decrease in his hourly wage to $10 per hour. When Bill's wage rate falls to $10 per hour, his budget line becomes flatter (ZB') and his utility level falls to U_1 at point R. At the new, lower wage, Bill works 6 hours per day and consumes 18 hours per day of leisure. His total income is now $160 per day. Finally, Bill responds to an increase in his wage to $30 per hour (which shifts the budget line to ZB'') by choosing the consumption–leisure combination labeled T on the indifference curve U_3. Again Bill decides to work 6 hours per day, giving him an income of $280, and he consumes 18 hours per day of leisure.

From Figure 8A.4 we can easily derive Bill's labor supply curve. Like any supply curve, a labor supply curve shows the quantity (of hours in this case) that Bill supplies at various prices. In Figure 8A.5, points R', S', and T' correspond to the tangencies R, S, and T in Figure 8A.4. The line ll that connects these points is Bill's labor supply curve. The difference between this supply curve and a typical product supply curve is that it bends backward at wages above $20. To see why, we must look further into the labor–leisure decision.

Labor supply curves bend backward because of the *income* and *substitution effects* we described in Appendix 2A. The substitution effect causes a person to shift his or her consumption away from goods that have become more expensive. Because the opportunity cost of leisure is the wage rate, when Bill's wage rate increases, it increases the cost of leisure, which will lead him to consume less leisure and work more.

If leisure is a normal good, then an increase in income results in an increase in the demand for leisure. When Bill's wage rises, his ability to obtain income

FIGURE 8A.4

Changes in Labor Supply Due to Wage Changes

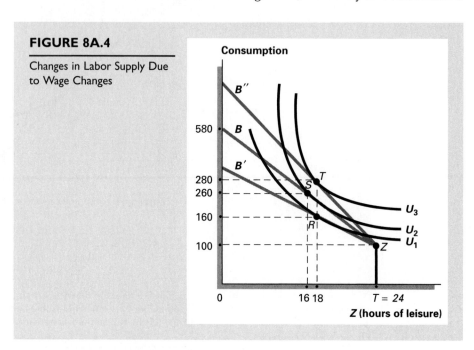

FIGURE 8A.5

The Individual Labor Supply Curve

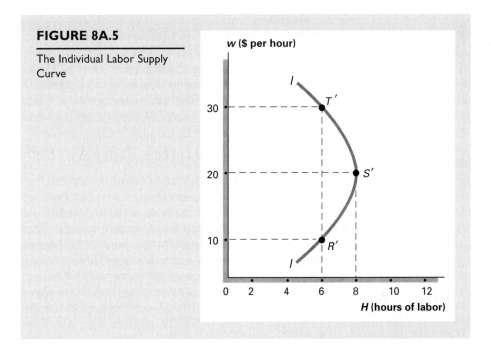

increases as well, which increases his demand for leisure, leading him to work fewer hours. In effect, he "buys" time away from work with his increased earning power. The substitution and income effects work in opposite directions in this case. Whether Bill's labor supply curve slopes upward or backward at any given point depends on which effect is stronger. When the substitution effect is larger than the income effect, Bill works more as his wage increases. When the income effect dominates, he works less in response to a wage increase. Figure 8A.5 shows that Bill's substitution effect dominates at wages below $20 per hour, but his income effect dominates at wages above $20 per hour.

Because of the intense level of training and dedication required at the professional level, a player or a coach will sometimes walk away from the game despite still being able to compete at the highest level in order to pursue other activities, such as spending more time with his or her family. Dick Vermeil, coach of the 2000 Super Bowl champion St. Louis Rams, had become a classic case of burnout almost two decades earlier. While coaching the Philadelphia Eagles from 1976 to 1983, Vermeil worked so many hours that he noticed a growth spurt of his second oldest son only while watching game film with his assistant coaches and seeing his son standing on the sidelines.[57] He left coaching at the end of the 1982–83 season after working himself to the point of complete physical exhaustion. Although he worked after that as a broadcaster and motivational speaker, he did not return to coaching again until 1997, when he took over as head coach of the Rams. For Vermeil, a change in his preferences away from work toward leisure led him to leave the game.

---

[57]Gary Smith, "A New Life," *Sports Illustrated* (March 28, 1983), pp. 60–67.

We can also show how an increase in wealth affects the decision to work using the labor–leisure model. Consider the example of Michael Jordan described in the text. In the case of Jordan and other highly paid athletes, the vertical portion of the income constraint becomes very large over time due to endorsement and accumulated past income. As the exogenous income segment increases, so does the income effect, because a person can achieve greater and greater utility levels without working, as shown in Figure 8A.6.

The Labor–Leisure Model when Hours Are Fixed

The labor supply model assumes that a person can choose the number of hours that he or she would like to work. In many occupations, people cannot choose the number of hours they work. For example, some production workers may prefer to work part-time but must work a full 40-hour week in order to keep their jobs. The same is true in sports. Athletes face two possible constraints when they play in a professional league: the season may be either shorter or longer than they prefer. For example, Nikki McCray originally chose to play in the ABL because she preferred to play a longer season.[58] At the time, the ABL played a 40-game season, while the WNBA played only a 28-game season. When the ABL folded and her only option was the WNBA, her hours were set at a level below the level she

FIGURE 8A.6

Increases in Wealth that
Result in No Labor Supplied

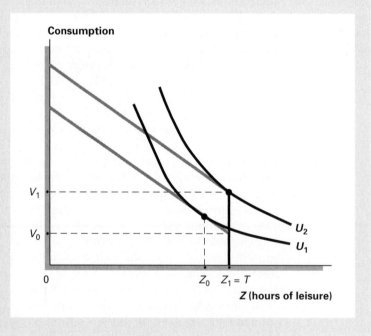

[58]Steve Lopez, "They Got Next," *Sports Illustrated* (June 30, 1997), pp. 44–47.

would have chosen. We illustrate the effects of the shorter season on her utility maximization problem in Figure 8A.7 by imposing another constraint, fixing hours (or games in this case) along the vertical line set at Z_0. In the absence of this constraint, McCray maximizes her utility on U_1 by playing 40 games. In the presence of the games constraint, however, she cannot play more than 28 games (WNBA players are contractually forbidden to play in other leagues or for other teams). Thus, she maximizes her utility by playing only 28 games and consuming more leisure than she would like. While some leisure is a good thing, when a person consumes very large quantities of any good, leisure included, the marginal utility received from the last hour becomes very small.

Athletes who play individual sports typically do not face such stringent quantity constraints. For example, a professional golfer with a newborn child may elect to take several weeks away from the tour.[59] For athletes involved in team sports, part-time play is generally not an option. For them, when family needs dictate time away from the game, retirement may be the only option. Such was the case with Mark Rypien, who retired from the Atlanta Falcons in order to care for his terminally ill son. In other cases, players leave the labor force temporarily. For example, Buffalo Bills linebacker Chris Spielman left the team for a full season to care for his critically ill wife.

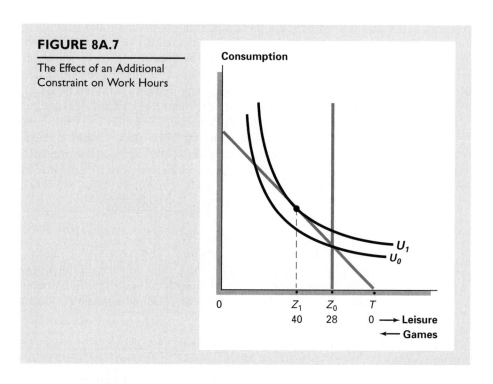

FIGURE 8A.7

The Effect of an Additional Constraint on Work Hours

---

[59]The LPGA now maintains a day care center that travels with the tour, allowing golfers to keep their small children with them rather than be forced to choose between playing and staying home.

The Time Value of Money

The future is now.

—ATTRIBUTED TO GEORGE ALLEN

When sports fans read about the huge multiyear contracts that players sign, they have difficulty understanding how teams can afford such expenses. How the Texas Rangers can spend $250 million on Alex Rodriguez or the Minnesota Timberwolves can spend $126 million on Kevin Garnett seems beyond all imagining. While the sums are indeed staggering, they are not quite so unaffordable as they first appear. The passage of time means that Garnett's $126 million contract does not really cost the Timberwolves quite this much.

In Garnett's contract, the Timberwolves pay him $126 million over 7 years. To pay Garnett, however, the Timberwolves do not have to set aside $126 million today. Suppose, for simplicity, that Garnett's contract consists of equal payments of $18 million at the beginning of each season for 7 years. The Timberwolves make the first payment today, the second in one year, and so on, until they make the final payment six years from today.

The first payment costs the team $18 million. The second payment, however, does not cost the Timberwolves $18 million. In order to spend $18 million a year from today, the team needs to set aside enough money today so its savings plus interest equal $18 million. We compute the **present value** of $18 million in one year by dividing this dollar amount by one plus the interest rate:

$$PV_1 = \frac{\$18,000,000}{(1+r)}.$$

where r is the rate of interest they receive on their savings. If the Timberwolves earn a 10 percent return on their savings, they must set aside "only" $16.4 million today in order to have $18 million in one year. The **future value** of $16.4 million in one year at 10 percent interest rates is therefore $18 million. More generally:

$$FV_1 = PV_1(1+r).$$

Because the last expenditure on Garnett's contract does not take place for six years, the burden of the last payment is still lighter. The team can **discount** the last expenditure six times:

$$PV_6 = \frac{\$18,000,000}{(1+r)^6}.$$

because we apply the discount factor $1 + r$ once for each year. The burden of the last expenditure is thus about $10.2 million, a little more than half the cost of the initial payment. The present value of Garnett's entire contract is

$$PV_{\text{contract}} = \sum_{t=0}^{6} \frac{\$18,000,000}{(1.10)^t} \approx \$97,700,000.$$

While still a huge contract, the passage of time makes the contract far more affordable than it first appears.

On a smaller scale, the impact of time on the value of payments provides an additional reason that teams sell season tickets at a discount. When the Chicago Bears sells Thomas a season ticket, they do more than just transfer risk to him (as we saw in Chapter 2). By selling Thomas a ticket in March or April for a game that will not take place until November or December, the Bears has use of his money for about eight months longer than it would if they sold the ticket on the day of the game. The Bears is willing to charge less for the ticket because the future value of the ticket purchase is greater than its face value.

We justified discounting future cash flows by saying that the team does not need to set aside the full amount of the payment today because it could save a lesser amount and accumulate interest. This justification begs the question of why interest exists to begin with. It also places the notion of discounting in a more limited setting—cash transactions—than need be the case. We can both justify the existence of interest and broaden the scope of our analysis by appealing to the problem facing a general manager.

In trying to build and maintain winning teams, general managers frequently have the opportunity to obtain veteran players who can help their teams win now in exchange for prospects who will help the team win in the future. Consider the late-season trade between the Boston Bruins and the Colorado Avalanche in the spring of 2000. The Avalanche obtained Ray Borque, a future Hall of Fame defenseman who was near the end of his career, in exchange for several young prospects, including Sami Pahlsson. In making the trade, the Avalanche made an explicit choice to try to win a Stanley Cup in 2000 at the cost of having access to players who may help them win in the future. Colorado was willing to make the deal because they placed a higher value on winning right away than on the prospect of winning down the road. Even if Colorado expected their prospects to have the same eventual impact on their team that Borque did, they were still willing to make the trade. There are several reasons that this might be so.

First, a lot can happen in, say, three or four years that will prevent a team from benefiting from its prospects. The team may have to trade them for financial reasons. In addition, prospects such as Pahlsson represent potential quality, whereas Borque proved over the course of a long career that he was a top player. The Colorado general manager and coach may be fired before the prospects reach their potential. Waiting for three or four years deprives the team and its management of the goodwill that winning today provides. Winning in a few years will be nice, but winning today is better.

The uncertainty and the lost opportunities of delaying the pleasure of winning hockey games cause general managers to demand superior prospects in exchange for seasoned veterans. Like general managers who have traded established talent for prospects, lenders face uncertainty that they will ever get their money back and the lost opportunity to benefit from their money. To compensate them for their loss, they insist on an additional payment for their loan, called **interest.** To determine the cost of the loan, we must look at the ratio of the interest payment to the size of the loan—called the **principal.** We call this ratio the **interest rate.**

Finally, we can use the concept of discounting to show why owners and players squabble over the timing of payments in multiyear contracts. If payments received are unequal over time, as they often are in professional athletes' salaries, the present value of a multiyear contract must reflect the fact that cash flows (CF) of varying magnitudes must be discounted to the present:

$$PV_0 = CF_0 + CF_1 \frac{1}{1+r} + CF_2 \frac{1}{(1+r)^2} + \cdots + CF_n \frac{1}{(1+r)^n}$$

We can now use these concepts to show that, all else being equal, players prefer up-front payments in the form of signing bonuses rather than balloon payments (large payments that occur at the end of a contract). When players are drafted, they must negotiate a contract with the drafting team before they can begin their official participation with that team. Negotiations over compensation tend to be relatively drawn out and at times seem enormously complex. In fact, there are three principal issues that both sides must agree on: how much, over how many years, and how the total value of the contract will be paid over the life of the contract. To maintain our focus on the topic at hand, we assume that the team and the player have agreed that the player should receive a total of $5 million guaranteed over four years, thus resolving the first two issues.[60] What remains is to decide how the payments will be spread over the life of the contract. The player's agent first proposes that the player be paid $4.4 million now as a signing bonus and first-year salary and $200,000 for the 3 remaining years. Using the equation below, and assuming a discount rate of 5 percent, the present value of this contract is

$$PV_0 = \$4,400,000 + \frac{200,000}{1+0.05} + \frac{200,000}{(1+0.05)^2} + \frac{200,000}{(1+0.05)^3}$$
$$= \$4,400,000 + 190,476.19 + 181,405.90 + 172,767.52$$
$$= \$4,944,649.61.$$

---

[60]By assuming that the contract is guaranteed, we avoid issues of uncertainty. If the money were not guaranteed, as is usually the case in the NFL, the player must make the team every year or be injured while playing in order to receive payment.

The owners, unhappy with the idea of paying so much money so early in the contract, counter with an offer of $1.25 million each year for 4 years. The present value of this contract offer is

$$PV_0 = \$1,250,000 + \frac{1,250,000}{1+0.05} + \frac{1,250,000}{(1+0.05)^2} + \frac{1,250,000}{(1+0.05)^3}$$
$$= \$1,250,000 + 1,190,476.19 + 1,133,786.85 + 1,079,797.00$$
$$= \$4,654,060.04.$$

Thus, although it seemed that the two sides agreed on the value of the player to the team, they are in fact almost $300,000 apart. The difference lies in the time value of the money.

CHAPTER 9

Labor Unions and Labor Relations

When Nick Kypreos of the New York Rangers, returning from Canada after the lockout, was asked by customs officials if he had anything to declare, [he] replied, "No, the owners took it all."

—PAUL STAUDOHAR[1]

We have met the enemy, and he is us.

—POGO

INTRODUCTION

For the last 50 years, unions have occupied a steadily decreasing role in the private sector of the American economy. In the late 1940s and early 1950s, unions represented more than a third of the civilian nonfarm labor force. Today, barely 10 percent of the private sector's nonfarm labor force belongs to a union. The unionization rate of public sector employees continued to increase over the 1960s and 1970s with the growing recognition of public employees' right to organize. Since then, however, even public sector unions have been on the defensive, barely managing to hold onto earlier gains. By contrast, unions in professional sports have continued to thrive. Union representation of the major sports remains much higher than for other sectors of the economy.

This chapter examines why professional sports have been so strongly unionized. In doing so, it explores the following:

- What type of union represents professional athletes
- How unions in professional sports differ from any other form of union
- What factors lead to labor conflict and how they apply to each major sport
- How effective each union has been in pursuing the well-being of its members.

---

[1]Paul Staudohar, *Playing for Dollars: Labor Relations and the Sports Business* (Ithaca, N.Y.: ILR Press, 1996), p. 151.

9.1 A BRIEF INTRODUCTION TO THE ECONOMICS OF UNIONS

Unions typically fall into one of two categories: **craft unions** and **industrial unions.** Craft unions are by far the older of the two. Their origins can be traced back to the medieval guilds, groups of skilled artisans who joined together to prevent others from entering the city to undercut their prices. Modern craft unions consist of workers who share a common skill. One can typically discern this skill from the name of the union. For example, it is easy to guess what sort of job the members of the International Brotherhood of Electrical Workers or the Screen Actors Guild perform. Early in the 20th century, a number of craft unions joined forces to form the American Federation of Labor (AFL).

In contrast, industrial unions are a relatively recent creation. They represent a response by workers to the harsh conditions that they confronted as a result of the rise of large employers during the Industrial Revolution. Partly because they opposed the entrenched interests of their employers, organizers of industrial unions faced greater hostility. As a result, they grew in importance much later than craft unions. Industrial unions take their names from the types of product they produce, such as the United Auto Workers or the United Steel Workers. In the 1930s, a number of industrial unions joined to form the Congress of Industrial Organizations (CIO). After many years of sometimes violent conflict, the two labor organizations joined together to form the single umbrella organization, the AFL–CIO.

The different organizational structures of the two types of unions cause them to use different tactics to improve the well-being of their members.[2] Craft unions increase wages by limiting access to the union and to skills. In effect, they attempt to shift the supply curve of labor back from what it would be in a competitive labor market, as seen in Figure 9.1. The result is a union wage (w^u) greater than the competitive wage (w^{nu}) and a deadweight loss equal to the shaded area.

Industrial unions represent workers with many different skills. Unlike craft unions, which assign workers to employers through "hiring halls," industrial unions do not hire or fire workers. They try to push up the wage through the institution of collective bargaining, in which the union induces employers to increase pay above the competitive level by threatening to strike. This again raises the wage (w^u) above the competitive level and creates a deadweight loss, as seen in Figure 9.2.

The need to stage or threaten a damaging strike means that industrial unions derive their strength from being inclusive. They cannot succeed unless the firms' employees remain loyal to the union during a job action. This stands

---

[2]While workers and unions worry about many different aspects of the job, we shall simplify the analysis that follows by focusing solely on wages.

FIGURE 9.1

Effect of a Craft Union on
Wages and Social Well-Being

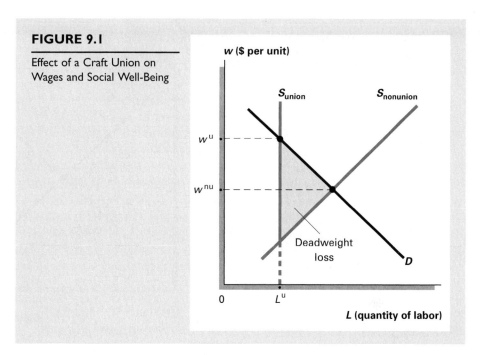

in stark contrast to the craft unions, whose strength comes from being exclusive and keeping out potential competitors.[3]

The viewpoint presented thus far presumes that unions create inefficiency in the economy. It says that unions limit employment and production, thereby harming society as a whole. The opponents of unions claim that when unions push the wage above free-market levels, they put domestic producers at a disadvantage and encourage relocation abroad.

Some economists feel that the opponents of unions paint an unnecessarily harsh picture. They claim that unions provide an important outlet for workers that improves efficiency. They point out that unions formalize grievance procedures by workers, giving them a way to express their concerns to employers and allowing employers to respond to the needs of their workforce, thereby reducing conflict in the workplace. They also point out that studies have failed to show that unions either reduce productivity or slow productivity growth. Finally, some economists suggest that unions may serve as a countervailing force against the monopsony power of employers, forcing employers to pay workers their marginal revenue product and—perhaps—making the labor market more closely resemble a competitive market.

---

[3]Cynthia Gramm and John Schnell, "Difficult Choices, Crossing the Picket Line During the 1987 National Football League Strike," *Journal of Labor Economics*, v. 12, no. 1 (January 1994), pp. 41–71, point out that the NFL Players Association had difficulty maintaining unity during its most recent strike due to racial divisions among the players.

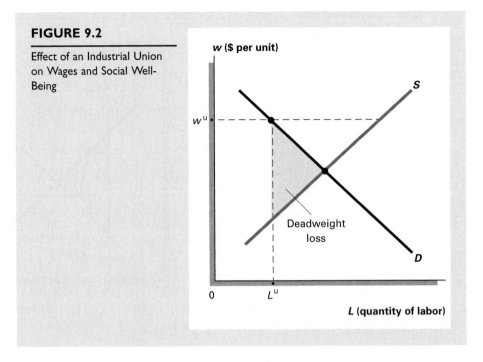

FIGURE 9.2

Effect of an Industrial Union on Wages and Social Well-Being

Figure 9.3 shows that a monopsony drives down the wage from the competitive level, w^c, to the monopsony level, w^m. It also drives down employment from L^c to L^m, creating a deadweight loss. By setting a wage above w^m, a union may actually increase employment and reduce or eliminate the deadweight loss. For example, setting the wage at w^c makes the marginal expenditure curve a horizontal line at that level and forces the monopsony to act like a competitive industry.[4]

When a monopoly union confronts a monopsony employer—a situation that economists call **bilateral monopoly**—the wage falls into an indeterminate range between the monopoly wage (what the union wants) and the monopsony wage (what the firm wants). In Figure 9.4, the union would like to set its wage where the marginal revenue of union members (MR) equals the supply of labor (S). The monopoly wage w^u is determined by looking up from this intersection to the demand curve for labor. The monopsonist would like to set the quantity of labor where the marginal expense of the last worker (ME) equals the marginal revenue product ($MRP = D$) of the last worker. The monopsony wage w^m comes from looking down to the supply curve of labor. The precise settlement lies somewhere between w^u and w^m in Figure 9.4 and depends on the bargaining strength of the two sides.

In 1950, Nobel laureate John Nash developed a model to solve these types of bargaining problems that has served as the basis for much of the work on bargaining since. One of the Nash model's central findings was that a group's

---

[4]See Richard Freeman and James Medoff, *What Do Unions Do?* (New York, Basic Books, 1984), for a good example of this more positive view of unions.

FIGURE 9.3

A Union Facing a Monopsony
Employer

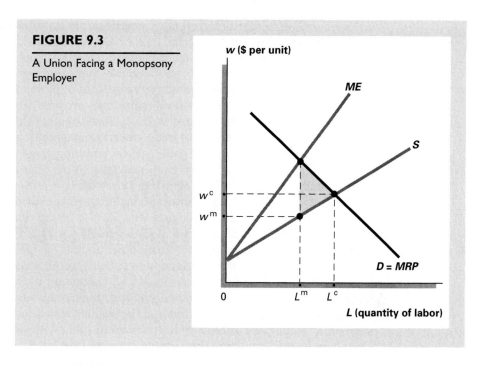

FIGURE 9.4

Bilateral Monopoly

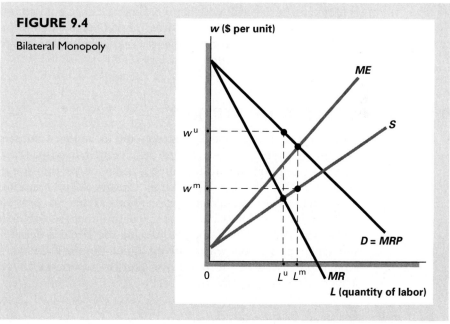

bargaining power—and hence its ability to reach a favorable settlement—stems
from its ability to walk away from the bargaining table. Nash calls the value of
the opportunities that one side or the other has outside the current contractual

arrangement (its opportunity costs of entering into an agreement) the bargainer's **threat point.** The higher the threat point for either side, the greater its bargaining power and the more favorable a solution it can achieve.

If, for example, the employer has a readily available source of labor (perhaps due to high unemployment rates), the benefits of permanently dissolving its relationship with the union—its threat point—may be very high. All else being equal, this will allow the firm to drive a harder bargain and reach a lower wage settlement. Alternatively, if union workers have high-paying jobs awaiting them elsewhere, their threat point and the resulting wage both rise.

Unions in professional sports do not readily fit into one of the neat categories outlined above. On the one hand, they clearly represent workers with similar and distinct skills, like a craft union. On the other hand, they engage in collective bargaining with employers who do the hiring and firing, like an industrial union. In addition, they do something—or rather they do *not* do something—that sets them apart from all other unions: the major sports unions do not directly engage in negotiations over the specific wages of individual players.[5] Instead, they restrict themselves to bargaining over the general climate within which individual players and their agents can bargain with teams. In addition, the major sports unions and the leagues with which they negotiate sometimes argue for positions that put them at odds with their counterparts elsewhere in the economy. The dispute between the NBA and the National Basketball Players Association (NBPA) that took place in 1998–99, for example, centered on the issue of whether workers would be paid according to a more or less fixed scale or whether the free market would determine salaries. Here, however, the union advocated the free market while the otherwise free-market oriented owners advocated the salary scale.

9.2 AN OVERVIEW OF STRIKES

From an economic perspective, strikes and lockouts do not seem to make sense because they typically harm both sides. As such, they seem to violate basic economic assumptions regarding rational behavior, yet they are a fact of life in the labor market. Over the last quarter century, labor relations in professional sports have been particularly contentious. Table 9.1 provides a timeline of union activity in professional sports. It shows that each of the four major sports has experienced a work stoppage during the 1990s, a decade when the union movement as a whole was relatively quiet. By one estimate, unions in professional sports were about 50 times as likely to experience a work stoppage from 1987 to 1996 as other unions.[6]

---

[5]The NFLPA actually reserved the right to do this in its collective bargaining agreement, but it has never exercised this right. Staudohar, *Playing for Dollars* (1996), p. 67.

[6]Had other sectors of the U.S. economy had the same labor relations as professional sports, there would have been 20,000 work stoppages instead of only 403. See James Quirk and Rodney Fort, *Hardball* (Princeton, N.J.: Princeton University Press, 1999), p. 68.

Table 9.1

Summary of Union Events and Activities in Professional Sports

Date	Strike or Lockout	Event/Outcome
(a) Football		
1956		NFLPA formed
1957		NFL loses *Radovich* antitrust case
1968	10-day strike and lockout of training camp	First CBA: 2-year agreement
1971	20-day strike and lockout of training camp	5-year CBA backdated to 1970; Ed Garvey becomes NFLPA executive director
1974	42-day strike of training camp	
1977		Third CBA signed 2 years after second agreement expires (5-year agreement)
1982	57-day strike	
1983		Gene Upshaw replaces Ed Garvey as executive director
1987	24-day strike	Owners employ replacement players
1988		NFLPA decertifies
1992		*McNeil* decision brings free agency
1993		New CBA creates salary cap
(b) Baseball		
1885		National Brotherhood of Professional Ball Players founded
1890		Players League founded
1900		League Protective Players Association founded
1912	1-day strike by Detroit Tigers	Baseball Players Fraternity founded
1946		American Baseball Guild founded
1954		Major League Baseball Players Association founded
1966		Marvin Miller becomes executive director
1972	13-day strike over pensions	
1975		Jim "Catfish" Hunter declared a free agent
1976		*McNally–Messersmith* case brings free agency
1976	Owners lock players out of training camp	
1981	50-day strike	
1985	2-day strike	
1987		Arbitrators find owners colluded in 1985; Later found for 1986 and 1987 as well
1989		32-day lockout in spring training
1994–95	232-day strike (includes 52 days of 1994 season and 25 days of 1995 season)	

Table 9.1

(continued)

Date	Strike or Lockout	Event/Outcome
(c) Hockey		
1947		Pension plan established
1958		NHL recognizes NHLPA; Alan Eagleson becomes head
1992	10-day strike prior to playoffs	Bob Goodenow succeeds Eagleson at NHLPA; Gary Bettman succeeds John Siegler as commissioner
1994–95	103-day lockout	
(d) Basketball		
1954		NBPA formed
1957		NBA recognizes NBPA
1962		Lawrence Fleisher becomes general council for NBPA
1964		Pension plan created when players threaten to boycott All-Star game
1967		NBA and NBPA sign first CBA in pro sports
1976		Settlement of *Robertson v. NBA* brings eventual free agency to NBA
1983		Salary cap agreement; David Stern becomes commissioner
1988		Charles Grantham succeeds Fleisher; named executive director of the NBPA
1994		Simon Gourdine succeeds Grantham
1995	Lockout by owners (season unaffected)	Billy Hunter replaces Gourdine
1998–99	191-day lockout by owners	

Like war or costly litigation, a strike or a lockout is a two-edged sword. A union, for example, will go on strike to gain greater concessions from management than it otherwise might. It hopes that lost sales and revenue will persuade the firm to adopt a more conciliatory posture in negotiations. The strike also imposes costs on the union, because its members lose wages and benefits. In going out on strike, the union seeks to gain a greater share of the pie, but it does so at the cost of throwing away some of that pie.[7]

Economists reconcile strikes with rational behavior by recognizing the important role uncertainty plays in the analysis. Uncertainty affects negotiations in one of two ways. If one side is overly pessimistic—either because it underestimates its own bargaining power or because it overstates the power of

---

[7]Economists have applied similar reasoning to economic theories of why nations go to war or why people resort to litigation. See, for example, William Landes and Richard Posner, "Adjudication as a Private Good," *Journal of Legal Studies*, v. 8, no. 235 (July 1979), pp. 77–94.

its opposition—it may settle for a less favorable agreement than it could have reached. If the participant errs on the side of optimism—overestimating its own bargaining power or understating the power of its opposition—a strike may occur. Unduly optimistic perceptions of reality lead one or both parties to refuse to make the necessary concessions in time to prevent conflict.

A bargainer's uncertainty may be aggravated by a mistrust of the other side. If one party has reason to mistrust its counterpart, then it runs the risk of discounting a truthful position. Many of the strikes that have occurred in professional sports—particularly in baseball and football—have been accompanied by deep mistrust and personal animosities between the chief negotiators. As Colorado Rockies owner Jerry McMorris noted during the failed negotiations that led to the 1994 baseball strike, "I never would have believed the level of mistrust and lack of confidence in each other. . . . It made it very difficult for people to compromise or experiment."[8]

If both labor and management know exactly how far they can push the other side, they can typically reach a settlement without resorting to conflict. Figure 9.5 illustrates how this might come about. In the figure, the union wants to push wages higher while the employer wants to drive wages lower. Unless labor and the employer are better off separating permanently, each side will be willing to accept a range of wages or salaries that is also acceptable to the other side. We have labeled this range of wages the **contract zone.**

The precise position of the contract zone depends on the two sides' threat points. If the union has strong alternative opportunities, then its threat point corresponds to a higher wage and the lower end of the contract zone moves to a higher wage, as shown in Figure 9.6a. If the firm has better alternatives, the upper end of the contract zone moves to a lower wage, as shown in Figure 9.6b.

The precise settlement depends on the bargaining strength of the two parties. The problem comes when workers, firms, or both do not know how far

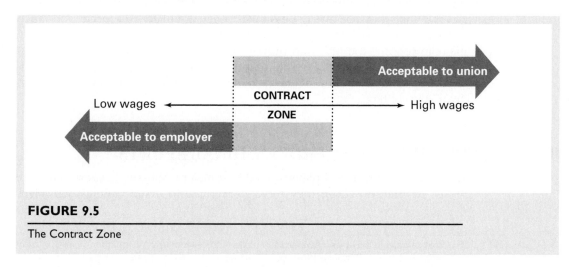

FIGURE 9.5

The Contract Zone

[8]John Helyar, *Lords of the Realm* (New York: Villard Books, 1994), p. 602.

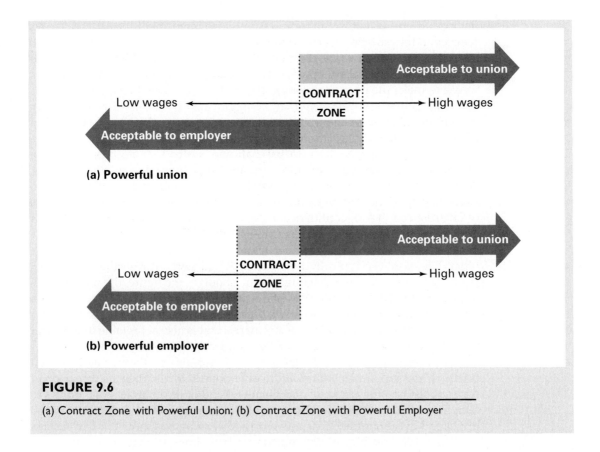

FIGURE 9.6

(a) Contract Zone with Powerful Union; (b) Contract Zone with Powerful Employer

they can push the other side—or even how far they are willing to go themselves. When they are overly pessimistic, they are likely to concede too much and reach an unfavorable settlement. When they are overly optimistic, they are likely to concede too little and provoke conflict.[9] Each of the case studies that follow show how uncertainty led to either a strike or a lockout; they are followed by an examination of the factors that caused one side or the other to "win" the conflict.

9.3 LABOR CONFLICT IN PROFESSIONAL SPORTS

Unions have represented players in all four major professional sports since the 1950s. At first, however, they took great pains to avoid calling themselves

---

[9]See, for example, Beth Hayes, "Unions and Strikes with Asymmetric Information," *Journal of Labor Economics*, v. 2, no. 1 (January 1984), pp. 57–84; and Michael A. Leeds, "Bargaining as Search Behavior Under Mutual Uncertainty," *Southern Economic Journal*, v. 53, no. 3 (January 1987), pp. 677–684, for two different perspectives on the role uncertainty may play.

unions,[10] using the term "association" instead. Baseball players belong to the Major League Baseball Players Association; football players, the National Football League Players Association (NFLPA); basketball players, the National Basketball Players Association; and hockey players, the National Hockey League Players Association (NHLPA).

This section contrasts the state of labor relations in the four major sports by examining one conflict in each. The conflicts represent a variety of time settings, ranging from the very first strike by professional athletes in 1972 to the 1998–99 NBA lockout. Two sets of strikes are considered—one in baseball and one in football—and two sets of lockouts—one in hockey and one in basketball. These conflicts stemmed from a variety of circumstances and yielded differing outcomes. According to most observers, the baseball players won their strike in 1972, whereas it is generally agreed that the owners came out on top in the other situations. The section concludes with a case in which the league and the union narrowly avoided conflict: baseball's 2002 collective bargaining agreement.

Strike One: The Baseball Strike of 1972

The baseball strike of 1972 marked a turning point in the relations between players and owners in professional sports. The job actions prior to this did not have the same impact. In 1912 the players on the Detroit Tigers struck when their star, Ty Cobb, was suspended for attacking a fan. The strike dissolved after one day when the Tigers franchise played its next game with replacements drawn from the Philadelphia area, where the Tigers were opening a series with the Athletics. Baseball endured another job action of sorts in 1969, when the MLBPA's executive director, Marvin Miller, convinced the players to refuse to sign contracts prior to the start of training camp to show displeasure with the lack of progress in negotiations over the pension fund. This crisis was defused before it could affect the regular season when newly selected Commissioner Bowie Kuhn intervened at the last moment to get the owners to soften their position. The NFL and the NFLPA had already engaged in two sets of strikes and lockouts prior to 1972, but both occurred during training camp, and neither directly affected the regular season.

Thus, the 1972 strike was the first to affect regular season games. It marked the maturation of the MLBPA, as measured by its willingness to challenge the owners. It was also the beginning of a new, more contentious era of labor relations in Major League Baseball. Not until 2002 would baseball's union and owners be able to agree on a new collective bargaining agreement without recourse to a strike or lockout.

Ostensibly the 1972 strike was over the players' pension and health benefits plans. Marvin Miller, however, believes that the owners simply used the

---

[10]For example, Allie Reynolds, one of the founders of the baseball union, said of the MLBPA, "[I]f I had any suspicion that we in baseball were moving towards a union, I would not have anything to do with the enterprise." Quoted in Charles Korr, "Marvin Miller and the New Unionism in Baseball," *The Business of Professional Sports*, ed. by Paul Staudohar and James Mangan (Urbana, I.L.: University of Illinois Press, 1991), p. 116.

pension disagreement to provoke a strike. He claims that the owners felt they could crush the union by provoking a short-lived strike. As evidence, Miller points to the reluctance of the owners to negotiate and their retraction of an offer late in the negotiations.[11]

If the owners did provoke the 1972 strike, they could not have picked a worse issue. For a union that was still feeling its way and an executive director who could still not count on his membership to stay out on strike, no other issue could have sparked such solidarity. Pensions were the one item that all the membership recognized as important. Indeed, the MLBPA came into being in order to create the pension fund, and, prior to its hiring Marvin Miller, it had devoted almost all of its energy toward protecting the pension fund.[12]

In addition to choosing a highly incendiary issue, the owners seemed to choose an unnecessary one. The owners could have easily met the players' demand for higher pension benefits, thanks to an $800,000 surplus that the pension fund had accrued. Moreover, the temperament of the owners and the organizational structure of their bargaining team seemed designed to promote, rather than resolve, conflict. According to Miller, no owner on the Player Relations Committee, the group of owners that dealt with player grievances and negotiations, ever attended a negotiation meeting during his tenure (between 1967 and 1985). As a result, the players could never be sure that the owners' chief negotiator truly spoke for the owners, and the owners never gained any firsthand knowledge about the players' attitudes.[13]

The owners, the self-proclaimed "magnates" of baseball, had ruled the sport with an iron fist for almost 100 years. Having successfully quashed any attempt by players to challenge their authority, they failed to realize that Miller had changed the terms of engagement. As a result, the owners grossly underestimated the militancy and solidarity of the players. Despite evidence to the contrary, they firmly believed that the union would quickly collapse and made no provision for extended conflict.[14] Figure 9. 7 shows one way to illustrate this misperception. The owners felt that the players had a much weaker threat point than they really had. As a result, the owners felt that they were negotiating over a contract zone *A* when in fact, they were negotiating over contract zone *B*. Their overconfidence in their own strength helped ensure the strike that followed.

The MLBPA also had reason to be optimistic. In 1969, Bowie Kuhn established a precedent of undercutting the owners' negotiating position (Kuhn would again undercut the owners in 1976, and Commissioners Peter Ueberroth and Fay Vincent would do the same later). The commissioners' distaste for conflict would

---

[11]The owners and the MLBPA hold separate negotiations over the benefits plan and the collective bargaining agreement. See Marvin Miller, *A Whole Different Ballgame* (New York: Carol Publishing Group, 1991), p. 204, for his perspective on the reason for the conflict.

[12]See, for example, Helyar, *Lords of the Realm* (1994), pp. 13, 25; Miller, *A Whole Different Ballgame* (1991), pp. 7, 99; and Korr, "Marvin Miller and the New Unionism in Baseball" (1991), p. 121.

[13]Helyar, *Lords of the Realm* (1994), p. 116; and Miller, *A Whole Different Ballgame* (1991), p. 204.

[14]See Helyar, *Lords of the Realm* (1994), p. 116; Miller, *A Whole Different Ballgame* (1991), pp. 123, 203; and Korr, "Marvin Miller and the New Unionism in Baseball" (1991), p. 131.

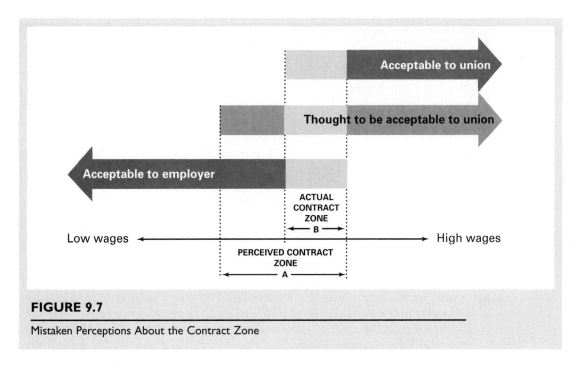

FIGURE 9.7

Mistaken Perceptions About the Contract Zone

lead the owners to go without a permanent commissioner from 1992 to 1998 and then to appoint Bud Selig, who had been the owner of the Milwaukee Brewers.[15]

In the end, the owners capitulated. After a 13-day strike (including 9 days at the start of the 1972 season), which saw 86 regular season games canceled, the owners realized that they could give the union what it wanted at no significant cost. Unfortunately for them, the strike had cost them over $5 million in lost revenue and showed the players that they could stand up to the owners and win.[16] That knowledge would strengthen the players' resolve in future conflicts with the owners so that, with the exception of the ambiguous end to the 1994–95 strike and the conflict in 2002 that was averted at the last minute, the MLBPA has "won" every conflict with the owners.

Strike Two: The NFL Strike of 1987

While baseball is usually considered to be the most contentious of all the major sports, football matched baseball job action for job action through the 1970s and 1980s. Prior to 1994, the NFL and NFLPA had never reached a collective bargaining agreement without conflict of some kind.[17] In 1987,

---

[15]See Helyar, *Lords of the Realm* (1994), pp. 118–119, 350–351, 443–447; and Miller, *A Whole Different Ballgame* (1991), pp. 161–162.

[16]Helyar, *Lords of the Realm* (1994), pp. 124–129; and Miller, *A Whole Different Ballgame* (1991), pp. 218–222.

[17]Staudohar, *Playing for Dollars* (1996), p. 73; and Paul Staudohar, "The Football Strike of 1987: The Question of Free Agency," *Monthly Labor Review*, v. 111, no. 8 (August 1988), p. 27.

however, there was reason to hope that the two sides would resolve their differences peacefully. NFLPA Executive Director Ed Garvey, whose leadership had been marked by a confrontational style, had stepped down after the bitter failure of the NFLPA's strike in 1982, and most observers regarded the new director, Gene Upshaw, formerly a star offensive lineman for the Oakland Raiders, to be more moderate. Upshaw also seemed to get along on a personal level with Jack Donlan, the owners' chief negotiator, reducing the personal animosity that had marked earlier negotiations. Finally, unlike 1982, the NFL and the NFLPA sought to conduct negotiations out of the public eye, reducing the temptation to harden their positions and use the media to put pressure on the opposition.[18]

Unfortunately, any hopes of concluding negotiations peacefully were doomed by a number of factors. Upshaw's newness to negotiations created a degree of uncertainty in his mind and in the owners' minds. The owners, in particular, may have felt unduly optimistic due to Upshaw's close relations with Los Angeles (now Oakland) Raiders owner, Al Davis, for whom Upshaw once played. Adding to the uncertainty was the demise of the USFL the previous year. While never a serious threat to the popularity of the NFL, the USFL had caused the average salary to rise substantially (see Table 8.1). The upward pressure had added to the militancy of the owners' intent on keeping costs under control, while the loss of a rival league spread fear among players that the restoration of monopsony power would allow owners to put downward pressure on salaries.[19]

The owners had taken pains to prepare for major conflict in 1987. They had carefully built up a strike fund since the last strike. They also had readied themselves to continue the season despite a strike by signing replacement players in about two-thirds of the teams who agreed to play in the event of a player walkout. In short, the NFL owners were loaded for bear and Upshaw, who was anxious not to appear too soft on the owners in his first set of negotiations, was not in a position to back down.

On the players' side, the situation was made more difficult because the NFLPA has had a history of having more trouble communicating with its membership than do the other unions in professional sports. NFL squads are more than twice as large as baseball teams and three to five times as large as hockey and basketball teams. As a result, Upshaw found himself having to negotiate with the people he represented as well as with the people he opposed.[20]

When the players decided to strike, the owners' preparations paid off. With replacement players who cost them only $1,000 per game, teams' profits actually rose by more than $100,000 per game (from about $800,000 to about

---

[18]David Harris, *The League: The Rise and Decline of the NFL* (New York: Bantam Books, 1986), details Garvey's rocky relations with the owners. See also Staudohar, *Playing for Dollars* (1996), pp. 68, 73, 152; and Staudohar, "The Football Strike of 1987" (1988), p. 27.

[19]Harris, *The League* (1986), pp. 247–248; and Staudohar, "The Football Strike of 1987" (1988), p. 26.

[20]Staudohar, *Playing for Dollars* (1996), p. 149; Staudohar, "The Football Strike of 1987" (1988), pp. 26–27, 29; and Paul Staudohar, "Professional Football and the Great Salary Dispute," *Personnel Journal*, v. 61, no. 9 (September 1982), p. 675.

Washington Redskin players picket during the 1987 NFL strike.

$921,000).[21] By contrast, the union had secured neither a strike fund nor a line of credit for strikers.

The continuing profits and the continued "league-think" mentality kept owners solidly in line with the official bargaining policy. While the NFLPA generally supported the strike (about 84 percent of the players remained out for the duration of the strike), the union was driven to settle by the imminent collapse of the strike. The striking players, having lost about $80 million in salary, returned to work without making any progress on their central goal of free agency. Clearly, they had underestimated the bargaining strength of the owners.

Strike Three: The NHL Lockout of 1994–95

The 1994–95 NHL lockout may have been the most self-destructive of all labor disputes. The year before, the 1993–94 season had given badly needed publicity

---

[21]The higher revenues were later offset by the need to reimburse the TV networks about $60 million for one lost weekend and for lower ratings overall. See Staudohar, "The Football Strike of 1987" (1988), p. 29; and Staudohar, *Playing for Dollars* (1996), pp. 74–75.

to a league that had long been the 98-pound weakling of the major sports. Stirring playoffs had brought the New York Rangers their first Stanley Cup since 1940 and generated an upsurge of interest in hockey in the nation's largest media market. With baseball's labor strife shutting down the last month and a half of the 1994 season and canceling the World Series for the first time since 1904, hockey seemed poised for a breakout year. Instead, it lost half a season due to a disagreement of its own.

The seeds of this disagreement were sown in 1989 when a group of current and former NHL players hired former NFLPA Executive Director Ed Garvey to look into irregularities in the NHLPA pension fund. The investigation found that the owners had misappropriated funds from international exhibitions such as the Canada Cup that had been earmarked for the players' pension fund (players agreed to forego salaries for appearing in these exhibitions with the understanding that they were helping the pension fund). The investigation led to a successful lawsuit against the NHL in which Canadian courts awarded $50 million to the NHLPA. The courts also rebuked Alan Eagleson, the long-time director of the NHLPA and director of the foundation that oversaw the international exhibitions, for knowing about the owners' misdeeds but taking no action to prevent or protest them. Eagleson resigned as director of the NHLPA in 1992, and he was eventually fined and imprisoned on fraud and mail fraud charges.[22]

Eagleson's resignation brought Bob Goodenow to power as head of the NHLPA. Goodenow proved far more militant than his predecessor, in part because he did not have Eagleson's conflict of interest. Marty McSorley, a player on the association's negotiating committee noted, "The players don't look at Mr. Goodenow as being the same as Mr. Eagleson. . . . They see Mr. Goodenow sitting on our side of the table this time."[23] After years of what they now perceived as exploitation, the players were not about to trust owners, who complained about skyrocketing costs. Once again, the two sides perceived contract zones that failed to overlap.

It took Goodenow little time to show the players just how combative he could be, as he led the players in a 10-day strike on the eve of the 1992 playoffs. While the outcome of the strike proved inconclusive, giving both the union and the league something to point to as a victory, it clearly signaled a new relationship between the two sides.

The 1992 strike might have been a one-time occurrence, attributable to anger over Eagleson's "betrayal" and to the unexpectedly hard line taken by his successor. However, soon after the 1992 strike, the NHL introduced further uncertainty to the mix by replacing Commissioner John Ziegler with Gary Bettman. Having previously served as David Stern's third in command at the NBA, Bettman brought an upscale, New York-oriented business sense to a league that had long reflected the slower pace of Montreal or Toronto. Moreover, the own-

---

[22]Jane O'Hara, "In the Name of Greed," *Maclean's* (January 19, 1998), pp. 22–24; and Staudohar, *Playing for Dollars* (1996), pp. 140–141.

[23]Quote taken from Stanley Fischler, *Cracked Ice: An Insider's Look at the NHL* (Chicago: Master's Press, 1999), p. 116. See also Staudohar, *Playing for Dollars* (1996), pp. 148–150.

ers saw Bettman as a man who could bring costs under control.[24] While at the NBA, Bettman had received much of the credit for the creation and implementation of that league's salary cap.[25]

The negotiations thus brought together a union leader still anxious to prove his militancy and a commissioner used to dealing with a more passive union who wanted to prove to the owners he could control costs. To make matters worse, the transition from Ziegler to Bettman delayed the formation of a joint NHL–NHLPA study committee that might have addressed the league's proposed salary cap and revenue sharing in a timely fashion.

The NHL prepared to enter the 1994–95 season without having signed a new collective bargaining agreement with the NHLPA. Fearful of another stoppage at playoff time, the league owners staged a preemptive **lockout.** A lockout is the flip side of a strike. While a strike consists of workers refusing to report for work, a lockout consists of management refusing to let its workers work.

The NHL's owners chose to lock out the players at the beginning of the season because the timing of a lockout—as with a strike—can be crucial. In professional sports, players have the incentive to strike near the end of the season, when fan interest is high and network coverage is most intense. Because any stoppage of play at this time would have a significant impact on both gate revenue and media revenue, the owners are highly vulnerable to a strike. In addition, the players are best able to withstand a strike at the end of the season because they have already received most of their salaries. Owners understand this, and they have the incentive to lock players out early in the season, minimizing the costs to them and maximizing the costs to the players.

In the 1994–95 NHL lockout, the two leaders were eager to put their stamp on the negotiations, which caused the lockout to drag on far longer than anyone anticipated. After a 103-day strike that ended only when the season itself seemed on the verge of cancellation, the union blinked and signed a new, 6-year agreement. While the owners did not get an overall salary cap, they did get a salary cap for rookies and tighter restrictions on the eligibility for free agency. Perhaps no one at that time could have predicted the dramatic increase in player salaries that would follow, since the average NHL salary reached almost $1.8 million in 2002. This dramatic increase in player salaries sets the stage for renewed conflict in 2004, when the 1994–95 agreement expires.

Strike Four: The 1998–99 NBA Lockout

For years, observers who were disgusted with the state of labor relations in other sports would point to basketball as the shining exception. In basketball a militant union seemed capable of providing for its members without the animosity that marked the other major sports. The cooperation between labor and management

---

[24]Salaries had grown from 42 percent of NHL revenues in 1989–90 to 61 percent in 1993–94. Staudohar, *Playing for Dollars* (1996), p. 151.

[25]Fischler, *Cracked Ice* (1999), pp. 77–87; and Staudohar, *Playing for Dollars* (1996), pp. 144–146.

seemed to reach its peak in 1983 when the NBA and the NBPA agreed to a salary cap that guaranteed players 53 percent of designated league revenue.[26]

In the mid-1990s, the cooperative spirit began to unravel. Players wanted to share in the growing prosperity of the league and the growing reliance of teams on "nondesignated" sources of revenue, such as luxury boxes, by eliminating the salary cap and other restrictions on movement, such as the collegiate draft. The players attempted to impose their demands through the courts, playing the 1994–95 season without a contract and filing an antitrust suit against the NBA. The court ruled against the players, however, claiming that the NBA was covered by the labor exemption from antitrust laws. As Chapter 4 showed, the labor exemption removes labor issues from the purview of the antitrust laws. In 1994 the courts ruled that the NBPA's suit was groundless since it had freely agreed to the features over which it now sued in its collective bargaining agreement (CBA) with the league.[27]

Denied a legal remedy, the NBPA tried to achieve its goals at the bargaining table. The players also moderated their demands, dropping their outright opposition to the salary cap and seeking instead to expand the definition of "designated" revenues. Negotiations, however, were complicated by the abrupt resignation of the union's executive director, Charles Grantham. Grantham's resignation was symptomatic of a deeper problem facing the union. Divisions had begun to appear among the players, prompted in part by the agents of star players. Agents' objections to limits on salary growth subverted a tentative agreement reached between the league and the union's new executive director, Simon Gourdine, after the 1994–95 season. Under the agents' direction, star players such as Michael Jordan and Patrick Ewing called for the union to decertify itself, thereby avoiding the labor exemption.[28]

The call for decertification prompted the league to provide the union both with a carrot and a stick. On the one hand, the league proposed raising the cap from 53 to 57 percent of designated revenue and including some luxury box revenue and additional sponsorship revenue under the cap. On the other hand, it imposed a lockout on the players. The league wisely declared the lockout in June, allowing plenty of time for players to respond to the new proposal before training camp opened. The union accepted the new proposal and soundly defeated the decertification move. However, the seeds for future conflict had been sown.

Subsequent actions by both sides further destabilized future negotiations. First, Billy Hunter replaced Simon Gourdine as the union's executive director. As seen with the NFL and NHL, a new negotiator, especially one brought in to replace a negotiator who had been perceived as too soft, will show a bias

---

[26]Paul Staudohar, "Labor Relations in Basketball: The Lockout of 1998–99," *Monthly Labor Review*, v. 122, no. 4 (April 1999), pp. 3–9; and Staudohar, *Playing for Dollars* (1996), pp. 117–120, 152–157.

[27]See, for example, Gary Roberts, "*Brown v. Pro Football, Inc.*: The Supreme Court Gets It Right for the Wrong Reasons," *Antitrust Bulletin*, v. 42, no. 3 (Fall 1997), pp. 595–639; and Paul Weiler and Gary Roberts, *Sports and the Law: Cases, Materials and Problems* (St. Paul, M.N.: West Publishing Co., 1993), pp. 164–168.

[28]Staudohar, "The Lockout of 1998–99" (1999), pp. 3–9.

toward a hard-line position. The growing influence of agents added to the uncertainty and the militancy. Hunter had to sell any position he took to a variety of constituencies, not all of whom made their influence known.

For its part, the league was fearful that it had reached a turning point in its fortunes. For over a decade, the NBA had hitched its ever-improving fortunes to its stars. The departure of charismatic stars such as Larry Bird and Magic Johnson, the impending departure of Michael Jordan, and the failure of a new generation of stars to make their mark all left teams wondering whether revenues would continue to rise. As it was, the dominance of the Chicago Bulls was beginning to impose a burden on other teams. Attendance was down by as much as 20 percent in some cities in 1997–98. Apparel sales were slumping, and—according to the league—almost half the teams were losing money. Despite this bad news, salaries continued to rise. Many observers point to the $126 million, 7-year contract the Minnesota Timberwolves gave to the 21-year-old Kevin Garnett as the final straw. The 1995 agreement had given owners the right to reopen the contract for negotiation after three years if salaries exceeded 51.8 percent of revenues. With salaries accounting for more than 57 percent of revenues, the league voted 27–2 in March 1998 to reopen negotiations on the terms of the collective bargaining agreement.[29]

Their confidence bolstered by the success of their 1994 lockout, the NBA owners again declared a lockout in the fall of 1998. This time, however, the two sides did not come to an agreement until 191 days later. Like the NFL and the NHL before it, the NBA managed to maintain unity among the owners. In part, this probably stemmed from the owners' faith in Commissioner David Stern, who cast aside any pretense of impartiality and represented the interests of the owners. It was also due to the preparations that Stern had made for an eventual showdown with the NBPA. As part of its negotiations over broadcast rights, the NBA had ensured that payments from TV networks would continue even if no games were played. While it would have to repay the networks eventually, the league maintained its cash flow and effectively received a three-year, interest-free line of credit.

On its side, the NBPA could not even secure payment on guaranteed contracts. Lacking the credit that the league had secured, it was only a matter of time before the union folded. On January 6, 1999, despite Commissioner Stern's claims that no one had won the lockout, the NBA owners clinched an unprecedented victory over the players' union when the NBPA agreed to a contract that provided the first pay scale in a major professional sport. Table 9.2 shows that under the new agreement, player salaries are capped at much lower levels than top stars had earned before the lockout.

The agreement also lowered the overall team salary cap to 55 percent of revenues, which would rise back to 57 percent only in the seventh year of the deal. Finally, it severely restricted the "Larry Bird exemption," limiting re-signing raises to no more than 12 percent per year. It is no wonder that Marvin Miller disparaged

---

[29]Staudohar, "The Lockout of 1998–99" (1999), pp. 3–9; and Leigh Montville, "Howlin' Wolf," *Sports Illustrated* (May 3, 1999), pp. 40–51.

Table 9.2

The New NBA Pay Scale

Years of Experience	Maximum Pay per Year
Up to 5	$9 million
6–9	$11 million
More than 10	$14 million

Source: Paul Staudohar, "Labor Relations in Basketball: The Lockout of 1998–9," *Monthly Labor Review,* v. 122, no. 4 (April 1999), p. 3–9.

this agreement, saying, "The players association has agreed to provisions that will provide a lower salary scale than if there were no union at all."[30]

Balk: The 2002 Agreement in Baseball

On August 30, 2002, after countless hours of negotiations that were punctuated by offers, counter-offers, threats of work stoppages, claims of unscrupulous accounting, and much of the animosity that has typified virtually all union-management negotiations in baseball, the owners and players reached a 4-year agreement on a new contract without a strike or lockout for the first time in over 30 years. It certainly was close. The players had set a strike date of August 30. All games played on August 29 had been completed, and many players literally waited in airports to see if they would be flying home to begin a strike or if they would be flying on to the next city to continue their road trips. Planes were delayed, buses were held. When the agreement finally came, it included major changes from the previous contract. In addition to being notable for avoiding a work stoppage, these were the first negotiations in over 30 years at which the owners did not wind up capitulating. According to many observers, the owners actually "won" this round of negotiations.

The two most contentious issues throughout the negotiations were the league's proposal to eliminate what it claimed to be two nonviable franchises—the Montreal Expos and the Minnesota Twins, and a system of luxury taxes that would limit salary increases by penalizing teams whose payrolls exceeded more than an agreed upon maximum. A third significant issue was a local revenue-sharing plan that most owners believed would improve competitive balance and financial stability by increasing the percentage of local television revenue that is shared.

Owners had argued all along that contraction was needed to increase the level of competitive balance in the league. They had sent shock waves throughout the league by voting 28–2 the previous November to eliminate the Twins and Expos

---

[30]Roy Johnson, "We Got Game (Finally)," *Fortune,* v. 139, no. 2 (February 1, 1999), pp. 28–29; Sarah Smith et al., "The Miller's Tale," *Village Voice* (January 19, 1999), p. 189; Staudohar, "The Lockout of 1998–99" (1999), pp. 3–9; and Phil Taylor, "To the Victor the Spoils," *Sports Illustrated* (January 18, 1999), pp. 48–52.

at the end of the 2002 season. While eliminating two weak teams would almost by definition reduce the gap between the best and worst teams, players saw this as distinctly antilabor, because it would reduce the number of major league players as well as the minor league systems that served the two clubs. In addition, there were questions about the choice of teams to eliminate (many analysts thought the Brewers, a team once owned by the current Commissioner Bud Selig were a much better candidate for elimination than the Twins). The owners' efforts to shrink the league were dealt a serious blow when the Minnesota courts issued an injunction preventing the Twins from being eliminated on the grounds that contraction would violate the team's lease with the Metrodome. After the appeal to the Minnesota State Supreme Court was denied, the contraction movement lost its sense of urgency, because the owners were effectively locked into continuing the Twins at least through 2003. This turn of events was ironic in that, as shown in Chapters 6 and 7, stadium deals typically work against cities in favor of the team and league. In this case, the contractual obligation created by the Twins lease worked in the city's favor as it struggled desperately to hold onto its team.

Negotiations over the luxury tax stalled over most of the negotiating sessions. Because the players believed that the luxury tax was a form of a salary cap, they staunchly resisted taxing high-paying teams. Owners, however, saw the luxury tax as a competitive balance tax (or as some called it, the "Yankee tax")—one that would harshly penalize teams for spending freely on players. In what observers have called the most significant victory for owners since the 1970s, the players relented at the last minute, agreeing to a formula for taxing high-payroll teams that went into effect in 2003 and would last until 2005 (the tax reverts to zero in 2006). In 2003 teams that spend over $117 million are subjected to the first-time offenders tax rate of 17.5 percent (the rate increases to 22.5 percent in 2004 and 2005). Although the maximum allowable salary increases over the life on the contract, repeat offenders are taxed much more severely: 30 percent for second-time offenders, and 40 percent for third-time offenders.[31] While the league tax on overspending teams may reduce player salaries and increase competitive balance, it does not tax the actual source of the problem. The disparity in revenues that sets the stage for disparate spending on salaries is rooted in differences in market size. As such, a more efficient method of taxation would be to tax revenues that differ based on market size. However, because such a tax would not restrict payrolls, the luxury tax most likely created a better mechanism to limit players' salaries, especially those with free-spending owners.

The new contract also increased local revenue sharing from 20 percent to 34 percent of local net revenue, which is then redistributed equally across all 30 teams. Although the players would have preferred that less local revenue be shared, they succeeded in their efforts to increase mimimum salaries from $200,000 to $300,000.

Thus the new agreement was historic on many fronts. It increased local revenue sharing to a level much beyond that specified in any previous agreement,

---

[31]For a summary of the 2002 agreement, see http://theolympian.com/home/specialsections/Mariners2002/20020831/41339.shtml.

it put in place a luxury tax system that creates a strong incentive for teams to remain within specified maximum limits, and perhaps most significantly, it was reached without a work stoppage. Whether this agreement serves as a new era in owner–player relations will likely be revealed when the next round of bargaining begins in 2006.

9.4 COMPARING THE MAJOR UNIONS: HOW THEY ATTACKED THE RESERVE CLAUSE

The preceding section showed the mixed success that unions have had in their conflicts with professional sports leagues. Those cases, however, covered a variety of issues and spanned a generation in time. This section compares the different unions by examining how each dealt with a specific issue, free agency. Here, too, the unions attacked their leagues' monopsony power in a variety of ways with differing results.

Mighty Oaks from Little Acorns Grow: The MLBPA and the Reserve Clause

While baseball was not the first sport to gain free agency, it was the first to use free agency effectively. The MLBPA was also the only union to achieve free agency without the help of the judicial system. Chapter 8 showed that baseball's unique exemption from the nation's antitrust laws ensured that it could withstand any direct legal assault by the MLBPA on the reserve clause.

The power of baseball's magnates and their relentless use of that power since the National League was formed in 1876 ensured two things. First, as Table 9.1b demonstrates, players frequently organized challenges to the owners' authority. Second, as is implicit in Table 9.1b, these challenges invariably failed. By the mid-1960s, the players were represented by the equivalent of a "company union." As was mentioned in the previous section, the MLBPA had been founded in 1954 for a sole purpose: to ensure adequate funding of the players' pension fund. Any vigor with which the MLBPA's first executive director, retired Judge Robert Cannon, might have pursued the players' interests was undercut by two factors. First, the owners, in violation of the nation's labor laws, underwrote his position, making him effectively their employee. Second, Judge Cannon hoped one day to be the commissioner of baseball, an ambition that meant staying on the good side of the owners.

All this came to an end in 1966 when Marvin Miller was chosen as the first full-time director of the MLBPA. Miller became the paragon that all future union heads sought to emulate and all future owners learned to regard with a mixture of awe and hatred. Starting from a position of abject weakness—when he took over, the union consisted of a battered filing cabinet and a $5,400 bank account—Miller made the MLBPA the strongest of all the unions in professional sports and did what all had thought impossible: destroy the reserve clause.[32]

---

[32]Helyar, *Lords of the Realm* (1994), p. 25; and Miller, *A Whole Different Ballgame* (1991), p. 7.

From the very beginning of his tenure, Miller believed that the reserve clause bound a player for only one year. He realized, however, that he could not challenge the reserve clause without changing the beliefs of players, who still viewed unions with suspicion, and without changing the decision-making process of baseball.

When Miller took office, players who had grievances against owners could appeal only to the commissioner. Miller, however, firmly believed that the commissioner was a tool of the owners, a perception strongly reinforced by the fact that, before becoming commissioner in 1969, Bowie Kuhn had been the assistant legal counsel of the National League.

Miller chose not to attack the commissioner's power directly. Instead, he used baseball's first collective bargaining agreement to establish a formal grievance procedure in 1968. (The union also secured some relatively minor financial concessions, such as an increase in the minimum salary from $6,000 to $10,000—the first such increase in over 30 years!—and some improvements in travel conditions.) The owners saw little to fear in granting arbitration to the players. After all, the arbitrator was Kuhn himself, whom the owners trusted to look after their interests.

Miller's next step was to take the arbitration procedure out of Kuhn's hands. In the 1970 negotiations, he pressed for an independent, three-person arbitration panel to replace the commissioner. In reality, only one person on this panel mattered, since one member represented the interests of the owners and a second represented the interests of the players, so they consistently canceled each other out. Miller managed to push the panel through for two reasons. First, with the *Flood v. Kuhn* ruling still pending, the owners wanted to show that they did not use their antitrust exemption to exploit the players. Second, Miller promised Kuhn that the arbitration panel's powers would be restricted to monetary matters. Overarching rulings that affected the "integrity of the game" would remain securely in the commissioner's hands. At first, the complaints before the panel were relatively trifling matters. However, in 1975, the panel received a case that was to open the first crack in the reserve clause.

Before the start of the 1975 season, Jim "Catfish" Hunter signed an unusual two-year contract with Oakland Athletics owner, Charles O. Finley. Hunter would receive half of his $100,000 salary (the unofficial ceiling paid to star players) as a regular salary. The remainder was to be invested in a tax-deferred annuity of Hunter's choosing. When Finley realized that he could not write off the $50,000 cost of the annuity on his taxes, he neglected to purchase the annuity. When Hunter and the union learned that Finley had not made the deposit, they notified him that unless he made a deposit within 10 days, the contract would be invalidated. Finley responded by offering Hunter a $50,000 check in lieu of the annuity, but Hunter refused payment and filed a grievance with the arbitration panel.

A few years earlier, Hunter could have appealed to no one but Bowie Kuhn, who was already on record as supporting Finley. Now, his appeal would be judged by the professional arbitrator, Peter Seitz (Marvin Miller voted for Hunter and John Gaherin, the owners' chief negotiator, voted against him).

Seitz recognized the obvious when he ruled that the $50,000 check was not the same as payment into an annuity:

> Obviously, payment in 1974 to Mr. Hunter would have completely thwarted the objective of the Special Covenant, which was to defer payment to the employee in order to avoid taxes on current income, as Mr. Hunter testified and I find, that the deferral was an important consideration in his agreeing to play with the Club at the salary stipulated in the Player's Contract. A payment of the $50,000 to Hunter in the tax year 1974 would mean that he would have to pay income taxes on that amount and the particular purpose of the Special Covenant will have been defeated.[33]

Having ruled that Finley had defaulted on the contract, Seitz had no alternative but to rule Hunter's contract with the A's null and void. Jim Hunter thus became baseball's first free agent in almost 100 years. He soon signed a 5-year guaranteed contract worth $3.5 million with the New York Yankees.[34]

Jim Hunter's new contract showed the riches that could come with free agency, but it was a special case that did not directly challenge the reserve clause. Miller now needed a test case that would. The reserve clause had long been held in place by the owners' refusal to allow players to play without a signed contract. Table 9.3 shows, however, that the players were coming ever closer to playing a complete year without a signed contract.

In 1975, Andy Messersmith, a star pitcher for the Los Angeles Dodgers, presented another possible challenge to the reserve clause. With the Dodgers unwilling to offer a contract with a no-trade clause, Messersmith entered August without a signed contract. Only at that point did Miller and the MLBPA approach him about the implications of his holdout. Recognizing that the owners had prevented previous challenges by sweetening the offers they made, Miller found insurance in the form of Dave McNally, a star pitcher with the Baltimore Orioles in the 1960s and early 1970s who had hurt his wrist while pitching for the Montreal Expos and retired early in the 1975 season without signing a contract. McNally guaranteed that the case would go to arbitration because he was still subject to the reserve clause, but with a bad wrist, an abiding loyalty to the union, and

Table 9.3

Close Calls for the Reserve Clause

Year	Player	Action
1969	Al Downing	Signed contract during spring training
1972	Ted Simmons	Signed contract at mid-season
1973	Sparky Lyle	Signed contract two weeks before end of season
1974	Bobby Tolan	Signed contract on last day of season

Source: John Helyar, *Lords of the Realm* (New York: Villard Books, 1994).

---

[33]Quoted in Miller, *A Whole Different Ballgame* (1991), p. 228.

[34]The Yankees did not make the highest offer. Both the Kansas City Royals and the San Diego Padres offered Hunter more money. Helyar, *Lords of the Realm* (1994), pp. 141–158; Miller, *A Whole Different Ballgame* (1991), pp. 111–112, 226–234; and James Dworkin, *Owners Versus Players: Baseball and Collective Bargaining* (Boston: Auburn House, 1981), pp. 71–72.

no desire to return to the game, no amount of money could induce him to sign another contract with the Expos. Recognizing that the union could use McNally to challenge the reserve clause even if Messersmith signed with the Expos, the Dodgers hardened their position, and neither player signed a contract. As a result, shortly before Thanksgiving, the same panel that had declared Jim Hunter a free agent a year earlier met to consider the much broader question of whether the reserve clause actually bound a player to his team for life.

As before, Miller and Gaherin's votes were predictable, and the decision came down to Peter Seitz. Perhaps sensing the importance of the decision, Seitz sought to have the two sides reach a compromise at the bargaining table. The owners, however, believed that no one could take away the power they had wielded for a century and refused to negotiate. Seitz's own ambivalence about the forces he was unleashing and the skill with which Miller and the union had framed the issue are apparent in this passage from Seitz's opinion:

> It would be a mistake to read this Opinion as a statement of the views of the writer either for or against a reserve system or, for that matter, the Reserve System presently in force. It is not my function to do so! . . . [T]his decision . . . does no more than seek to interpret and apply provisions that are in the agreements of the parties.[35]

Seitz went on to conclude that the reserve clause did what it said, binding the player for one year beyond his contract.[36]

The owners' response was immediate and futile. The ink was not yet dry on the ruling when they dismissed Seitz. They then filed an appeal in federal court, which was quickly denied. Finally, they tried to coerce the players to give back their newly won free agency with a lockout the following spring. The owners may well have succeeded in outwaiting the players except for the fact that Bowie Kuhn abruptly ordered an end to the lockout without consulting the owners' Player Relations Council. Most attribute Kuhn's move to backstage manipulation by Walter O'Malley, who—as owner of the top-drawing Dodgers—was reluctant to lose a single regular season date.[37] The end of the lockout marked the end of the owners' attempt to restore the reserve clause. Future disagreements took place over the form and limits of free agency, but free agency itself had become an unquestioned part of the landscape.

Snatching Defeat from the Jaws of Victory: The NFLPA and the Reserve Clause

The NFLPA has enjoyed several significant advantages over its baseball counterpart. As noted in Chapter 4, the 1957 *Radovich* decision established that the NFL did not share baseball's antitrust exemption. As a result, the first official free agent of the modern era in professional sports was R. C. Owens, who moved from the San Francisco 49ers to the Baltimore Colts in 1962. To stanch

---

[35]Quoted in Dworkin, *Owners Versus Players* (1981), p. 80.

[36]Helyar, *Lords of the Realm* (1994), pp. 170–179; Miller, *A Whole Different Ballgame* (1991), pp. 239–243; and Dworkin, *Owners Versus Players* (1981), pp. 72–82.

[37]Helyar, *Lords of the Realm* (1994), pp. 183–187.

the movement of players, Commissioner Pete Rozelle instituted a compensation system that came to be known as the "Rozelle rule":

> Whenever a player, becoming a free agent in such manner thereafter signed a contract with a different club in the league, then unless mutually satisfactory arrangements have been concluded between the two League clubs, the Commissioner may name and then award to the former club one or more players from the Active, Reserve, or Selection List (including future selection choices of the acquiring club as the Commissioner in his sole discretion deems fair and equitable); any such decisions by the Commissioner shall be final and conclusive.[38]

At the same time that Curt Flood was fighting the reserve clause in baseball, Joe Kapp challenged the Rozelle rule in football. Kapp had been a star quarterback for the Minnesota Vikings and led the team to the 1970 Super Bowl while playing without a contract. He then signed as a free agent with the New England Patriots, though the two teams avoided the Rozelle rule by agreeing on compensation. The problem came when Kapp insisted that his contract with the Patriots not contain the Rozelle rule. The NFL voided Kapp's contract, and Kapp sued the league for violation of antitrust laws. In a bizarre split decision, the court ruled that the NFL had violated antitrust laws but refused to award damages.

The players got another chance in 1976 when the NFL finally dropped its appeal of John Mackey's lawsuit. The final ruling of the *Mackey v. National Football League* lawsuit struck down the Rozelle rule. The NFLPA fumbled away this chance, however, when it bargained away free agency in order to restore the automatic payment of union dues. Because the union had no collective bargaining agreement that allowed it to collect dues automatically, the union was effectively bankrupt by the time of the *Mackey* decision. Executive Director Garvey was worried about the financial health of the union and concerned that free agency would aggravate the star system prevalent in the NFL. The owners played on these fears to get Garvey to allow them to retain a modified version of the Rozelle rule in exchange for greater benefits and automatic dues payment with a new collective bargaining agreement.[39]

The *Mackey* decision proved to be the NFLPA's last shot at free agency for almost a generation. The players soon came to realize that the revised Rozelle rule—which simply replaced the whim of the commissioner with a formula that defined the compensation—was no less restrictive than the old rule. Between 1977 and 1988, an average of more than 125 players per year filed for free agency. Only two of those players changed teams. The owners' unwillingness to bid for players is perhaps best exemplified by Walter Payton's situation. In 1981, Payton was soon to become the NFL's all-time leading rusher, yet he found no takers except for his old team, the Chicago Bears.[40]

---

[38]Quoted from the standard player contract in Dworkin, *Owners Versus Players* (1981), p. 250.

[39]Unlike Miller, who felt that high salaries for stars would filter down to all players, Garvey felt that the NFLPA was "for the guards and tackles. The quarterbacks can take care of themselves." Quoted from Helyar, *Lords of the Realm* (1994), p. 311. See Harris, *The League* (1986), pp. 181–257, for an account of the *Mackey* decision's aftermath.

[40]James Quirk and Rodney Fort, *Pay Dirt* (Princeton, N.J.: Princeton University Press, 1992), p. 201.

Unable to win back free agency through the unsuccessful strikes in 1982 and 1987, the NFLPA again sought remediation in the courts immediately after the 1987 strike was settled. While sympathetic on the issues, the courts no longer applied the same standard as in 1976. In 1976, the courts found that the original Rozelle rule had been imposed on the players, but now they found that the revised rules had been reached at the negotiating table through what the court calls "arm's-length bargaining." As a result, the new Rozelle rule was subject to the labor exemption to the antitrust laws. The only way around the exemption was for the NFLPA to disband, thereby dissolving the collective bargaining agreement it had reached with the league. In 1988, it did just that, allowing individual players to file antitrust suits against the NFL. This policy paid off in the 1992 *McNeil v. Pro Football, Inc.* decision, in which running back Freeman McNeil and seven other litigants were declared free agents.

In the wake of the ruling, the NFLPA quickly recertified and negotiated a new agreement with the league in 1993. Astonishingly, this agreement placed severe limits on free agency. It allowed players to become free agents only if they had at least five years of experience. It also permitted each team to designate one "franchise player" whom it can "reserve" as long as it pays him no less than the average of the top five salaries at his position.

Most significantly, the agreement instituted a salary cap. The salary cap agreement guaranteed players at least 58 percent of designated revenue (estimates have put designated revenue at about 95 percent of total revenue) in 1994. While this forced a few low-budget teams to increase their payrolls, it actually reduced the share of revenue going to labor. In 1993 the players had received 67 percent. Labor's share declined to 64 percent in 1994, 63 percent in 1995, and 62 percent in 1996. Moreover, the NFL's cap is a hard cap that does not allow any "Larry Bird"-type exemptions.[41] As a result, despite the presence of the rival WFL in the 1970s and USFL in the 1980s and despite being the most profitable of the major sports over the last two decades, average salaries in the NFL have lagged badly behind those in baseball and basketball, and each year dozens of players are cut simply to create salary cap room.

The NFLPA's weakness stemmed in part from the nature of the sport and in part from the perceptions of the leadership at the time. Having the shortest expected career (slightly over three years), football players did not see the same benefits to eventual free agency. It also meant that the union continually had to reinvent itself. While Marvin Miller took great pains to educate the baseball players, long-time NFLPA head Ed Garvey's style was much more autocratic. As such, he was the sole source of the NFLPA's positions. The long, Socratic MLBPA meetings stood in stark contrast to the NFLPA's meetings at which Garvey "had his ducks lined up in a row." Perhaps in part due to difficulty in communicating with players discussed earlier, Garvey consulted with his players much less than Miller did. While Garvey's method might be more efficient than Miller's, it did not build the same degree of loyalty to the union.[42]

---

[41]Staudohar, *Playing for Dollars* (1996), p. 88.

[42]Harris, *The League* (1992), pp. 165–166.

Garvey's tendency to dominate meetings also led him to make one of the most serious of all errors for a negotiator: he got too far out in front of his membership. Economists have frequently noted that unions are political entities in which the leadership cannot afford to be either too far behind the membership or too far in front. In this case, Garvey got too far out in front of members by staging a battle that they were not prepared to fight. Unlike Miller, who worked incrementally toward his challenge of the reserve clause, Garvey sought to build the union by destroying the reserve clause, making it the highest priority issue before creating a sense of solidarity among the players. However, while the reserve clause proved a rallying point for the NFLPA union leaders, it did not resonate with the rank and file. One reason for the indifference of so many players may have stemmed from the very nature of football. The violence of the sport leads naturally to a preference for insurance, health, and pension benefits. About half of all players eventually suffer from a permanent disability, and some estimates put the life expectancy of an NFL veteran at 55 years, more than 15 years shorter than the average American male. In the end, Garvey's insistence on attacking the reserve clause was simply out of touch with the priorities of the players, which made them unwilling to bear a heavy burden in lost wages to support his views.[43]

The NBPA and the Reserve Clause: Pioneering a Partnership

Like the NFLPA, the NBPA used the courts as its main weapon against restrictions on player movement. Unlike the NFLPA, the NBPA exploited the presence of another league to attain its ends.

As with football, antitrust laws forced basketball to replace a formal reserve clause with a compensation mechanism overseen by the commissioner of the NBA.[44] This compensation mechanism effectively prevented players from moving freely between teams. As a result, in 1967, player salaries amounted to only about 30 percent of the NBA's gross revenue.

The late 1960s, however, brought the last serious challenge by a rival basketball league, the American Basketball Association. The league disappeared after about 10 years, leaving as its legacy four teams that were absorbed by the NBA and the end of basketball's reserve clause.

The first chink in the reserve clause came in 1967, when Rick Barry sued the NBA after it tried to block his jumping from the NBA's San Francisco (later

[43]Contrast Garvey's saying, "You had to break the Rozelle Rule to have an effective union" (quoted in Harris, *The League* [1986], p. 200) with the careful building by Miller shown in Korr, "Marvin Miller and the New Unionism in Baseball" (1991). Orley Ashenfelter and George Johnson, "Bargaining Theory: Trade Unions and Industrial Strike Activity," *American Economic Review,* v. 59, no. 1 (March 1969), pp. 35–49; and Henry Farber, "Bargaining Theory, Wage Outcomes, and the Occurrence of Strikes: An Econometric Analysis," *American Economic Review,* v. 68, no. 3 (June 1978), pp. 262–271, discuss the union as a political entity. See also Staudohar, "The Football Strike of 1987" (1988), p. 27, and *Playing for Dollars* (1996), p. 69.

[44]Dworkin, *Owners Versus Players* (1981), p. 235.

Golden State) Warriors for the Oakland Oaks of the ABA. As later proved to be the case in other sports, the court ruled that San Francisco could renew Barry's contract for only one year; after this, he was free to negotiate with any ABA team. Barry's victory, however, was limited to movement between leagues. The court's ruling did not strike down the compensation mechanism in place for intraleague movement.[45]

As early as 1969, the NBA and the ABA had begun to talk about merging and actually reached a tentative agreement by 1970, subject to the same sort of congressional approval that the NFL and AFL required for their merger. A major reason for seeking a merger was the dramatic increase in player salaries that the rivalry had unleashed. The war between the two leagues had driven the average salary from $20,000 to over $140,000.

Fearful that a merger would restore the monopsony power of the NBA, Oscar Robertson, the president of the NBPA, led an antitrust lawsuit against the NBA in 1970. The NBPA hoped that the lawsuit would bring free agency to the NBA. It also hoped that the lawsuit would scuttle the merger with the ABA. The NBPA felt that if it could show that the NBA was violating antitrust laws, then legislation permitting a merger that further reduced competition would stand little chance of passage. After five years of litigation, the court found the NBA guilty of violating the Sherman Act. In 1976 the NBA and the NBPA reached an out-of-court settlement before the court determined damages. In addition to a substantial financial settlement, the NBA agreed to eliminate compensation for teams losing free agents by the end of the 1980–81 season and to phase in free agency by the 1987–88 season.[46]

By 1983, the financial strains of even limited free agency had become apparent. Players' salaries accounted for almost three-fourths of team revenues. According to the league, over two-thirds of the teams lost money in the 1981–82 season and the average losses in 1983 averaged $700,000. There was speculation that the league was ready to drop as many as five teams. To make matters worse, the owners were unable to agree on a revenue-sharing package.

With the owners unable to reach agreement among themselves, Commissioner Lawrence O'Brien and his assistant, future Commissioner David Stern, reached an agreement with NBPA Executive Director Lawrence Fleisher and the union president, Bob Lanier, on a formula that put a cap on team salaries. The agreement guaranteed players 53 percent of revenues—far below the levels it had enjoyed—and allowed teams to reduce their active rosters from 13 players to 12.

The reduction in the union's slice of the pie did not restrict salaries as one might expect, because at about the same time, the league entered an era of unprecedented growth. The NBA's TV revenues alone rose from less than $50 million in 1983 to over $600 million in 1996. Thus, while the players' share of the pie shrunk, the pie itself grew so rapidly that the average salary continued

---

[45]Staudohar, *Playing for Dollars* (1996), pp. 110–111; Dworkin, *Owners Versus Players* (1981), p. 236.

[46]Until then, teams could retain free agents by exercising a "right of first refusal" in which they matched a bona fide offer from another team. Staudohar, *Playing for Dollars* (1996), pp. 108–115.

to grow.[47] Although the current collective bargaining agreement does not contain the reserve clause, the caps on individual player salaries as well as team caps will likely reduce the movement of players between teams.

Bringing Up the Rear: Free Agency in the NHL

Of all the major professional sports, hockey has the greatest limits on free agency. The experiences of the NHLPA combine the opportunities faced by the NBPA with the missteps of the NFLPA.

As in the NBA, the first major challenge to the reserve system came with the entry of a rival league, the World Hockey Association in 1972. Like the NBA, the NHL tried to prevent players from jumping to the WHA by claiming that the reserve clause bound players to their original teams. A series of lawsuits culminated in 1972 in the *Philadelphia World Hockey Club* v. *Philadelphia Hockey Club* case, which struck down the NHL's reserve clause because it did not result from arm's-length negotiations and hence did not qualify under the labor exemption.

The NHL responded to this setback by inserting the "equalization clause" in the 1975 collective bargaining agreement. This clause required compensation by teams that signed another team's free agent. If the clubs could not agree on the appropriate compensation, the dispute went to an outside arbitrator. The arbitrator then decided on the appropriate compensation through final offer arbitration. Like the Rozelle rule in the NFL, the equalization rule effectively destroyed the impact of free agency.

Dale McCourt, a star player with the Detroit Red Wings, challenged equalization in a 1979 court case after he was "awarded" to the Los Angeles Kings as compensation for the Red Wings' signing the goaltender Rogatien Vachon. He was unsuccessful because the equalization principle had been approved by the NHLPA in its collective bargaining agreement.[48]

The NHLPA tried to correct matters in the next round of negotiations. In 1982 it managed to make the degree of compensation more predictable by basing compensation on the salary of a player who changed teams. Players could become unrestricted free agents when they were 33 years old. While this greatly increased the number of free agents, it did little to pry star players loose from their teams, as many of the players changing teams were at the low end of the pay scale, frequently unwanted by their original team. The 1987 agreement left the basic structure intact, though it liberalized the compensation slightly by raising the pay levels corresponding to each compensation level. The 1989 agreement again reduced the degree of compensation that teams had to pay for signing a free agent and lowered the age at which a player could become an unrestricted free agent to 30.

---

[47]Quirk and Fort, *Hardball* (1999), pp. 64–67; and Staudohar, *Playing for Dollars* (1996), pp. 108, 116–120.

[48]Staudohar, *Playing for Dollars* (1996), pp. 154–155; and Weiler and Roberts, *Sports and the Law* (1993), pp. 175–179, 458–47.

Despite the heavy restrictions on free agency, average salaries grew rapidly, from less than $150,000 in 1984–85 to more than $600,000 in 1994–95. The rapid salary growth motivated the owners to adopt the hard line that eventually led to the 1994–95 lockout. The settlement significantly restricted the players' right to change teams. In particular, players who have finished the terms of their first contract can no longer file for free agency. Table 9.4 shows the compensation required for signing a free agent under the current contract.[49]

Of all the major sports unions, the NHLPA has thus made the least progress. Much of this can be attributed to hockey's weaker overall financial health as well as the problems stemming from the close relationship of the union's former executive director with the owners. By contrast, the MLBPA has made the most progress. It started from a far weaker legal position than any other sports union and has succeeded better than any of them in withstanding efforts to impose a salary cap. The success of the recent NHL and NBA lockouts suggest a growing willingness of the owners to stand against the unions in order to impose limits on player salaries. Upcoming negotiations in football and baseball will show if that determination has spread to the other two sports.

Table 9.4

Compensation Schedule under the 1994–95 Contract

Salary of Player Changing Teams	Compensation Required
<$400,000	No compensation
$401–550,000	3rd round pick
$551–650,000	2nd round pick
$651–80,000	1st round pick
$801,000–1 million	1st and 3rd round picks
$1.0–1.2 million	1st and 2nd round picks
$1.2–1.4 million	Two 1st round picks
$1.4–1.7 million	Two 1st round picks and one 2nd round pick
>$1.7 million	Three 1st round picks, with one additional pick for each $1 million up to five picks

Source: Paul Staudohar, *Playing for Dollars: Labor Relations in the Sports Business* (Ithaca, N.Y.: ILR Press, 1996).

---

[49]Staudohar, *Playing for Dollars* (1996), pp. 155–157.

MARVIN MILLER

BIOGRAPHICAL Sketch

*Man, don't the owners know that there's going to be a whole genera-
tion of ballplayers' sons who grow up with the middle name Marvin?*

—New York Yankees pitcher Rudy May[1]

When reporters first asked Marvin Miller why he had gone from being chief economist of the United Steelworkers (USW), one of the nation's foremost unions, to heading a ragtag players association that did not even have a permanent office, he had a simple response for them: "'I grew up in Brooklyn,' I said, 'not far from Ebbets Fields.' . . . Heads nodded. No further explanation was required."[2] Further explanation *is* required, however, of a man who almost single-handedly overthrew the powers of one of the most powerful monopolies in America and transformed the face of professional sports. In so doing, Marvin Miller evolved from a man who might be the subject of an occasional dissertation on the history of unions to one of the towering figures in professional sports.

Miller did grow up in the shadow of Ebbets Field, the son of a storekeeper and a teacher in the New York public school system. He got his first taste of labor relations during World War II when he worked at the National War Labor Board, which adjudicated union–management disputes as part of labor's pledge not to impede the war effort by going on strike.

After the war, Miller worked at a variety of jobs with little clear direction when, in 1950, Otis Brubaker, the research director at the United Steelworkers and an acquaintance from the National War Labor Board, asked Miller to join his staff at the USW. Miller found a home at the USW and worked his way up to becoming the USW's chief economist and assistant to the union's president, David J. McDonald. Ironically, Miller's most notable accomplishment at USW was the creation of a "productivity sharing plan" at Kaiser Steel that became a model for promoting good union–management relations and preventing conflict.

In 1965, however, I. W. Abel defeated McDonald in a hotly contested union election that centered on McDonald's reliance on "technicians," such as Miller, rather than elected officials. With his future at USW uncertain, Miller was intrigued when several player representatives approached him about becoming the first full-time executive director of the Major League Baseball Players Association.

The road to becoming director, however, was not smooth. In a full vote, the player representatives chose their part-time director, Robert W. Cannon, instead. When Cannon attached additional conditions to becoming full-time director, refusing, for example, to move from his office in Milwaukee to New York, the players turned to Miller as their second choice. Even then, Miller's selection was far from certain, as he had to secure the approval of the full membership. Egged on by owners who viewed him as a rabble-rousing union boss, the players were skeptical. The Cleveland Indians' manager, Birdie Tebbetts, openly asked Miller, "How can the players be sure you're not a Communist?" After a rocky start—Miller was voted down by the players at the Arizona spring training facilities 102–17 before being approved overwhelmingly by the players at the Florida camps—Miller quickly earned the players' approval and then their fierce devotion.

Miller viewed the MLBPA as a chance to practice principles of democratic unionism that would have been so hard to implement in a huge union such as the USW. He won the players' confidence not by using the sophisticated arguments that Ed Garvey used with the football players or by intimidating the players like Alan Eagleson did in hockey but by listening. He made a point of meeting every player during spring training and meeting every team's player representative at least four

➡

times a year. These meetings, moreover, were not intended to rubber stamp prearranged positions. The meetings were often lengthy, untidy affairs with players arguing with Miller and each other at great length. The one rule that Miller imposed was that the players had to leave the meeting unified. "'Anything less than 100 percent is unacceptable,' was his unshakable motto."[3] The result was a union that managed to do what many thought impossible, overturn the reserve clause when it lacked any legal standing to do so.

[1] Quoted in Helyar, *Lords of the Realm* (New York: Villard Books, 1994), p. 239.

[2] Quoted in Miller, *A Whole Different Ballgame* (1991), pp. 11–12.

[3] Helyar, *Lords of the Realm* (1994), p. 84.

Sources: Dworkin, *Owners Versus Players* (1981); Korr, "Marvin Miller and the New Unionism in Baseball" (1991); Miller, *A Whole Different Ballgame* (1991); and Helyar, *Lords of the Realm* (1994).

SUMMARY

Unlike unions elsewhere in the economy, unions in professional sports have proven remarkably successful at organizing their workforce. The sports industry has also experienced far more labor conflict than have other labor markets. Economists have difficulty explaining conflict, as it seems to defy rational behavior. When one accounts for uncertainty and excessive optimism, however, one can explain strikes as a mistake by one or both of the negotiating parties.

Baseball has concluded only one collective bargaining agreement without either a strike or a lockout since the early 1970s. Labor relations in football have been almost as contentious. In recent years, the relatively peaceful relations in hockey and basketball have also deteriorated. These conflicts have not been uniformly successful for the unions. The Major League Baseball Players Association has enjoyed the greatest success, starting with its successful strike in 1972. The National Football League Players Association has been uniformly unsuccessful in its job actions, as seen by the failure of its 1987 strike. Both the NHL and the NBA were successful in imposing their will on the players in lockouts in the 1990s.

The relative success or failure of the unions can be seen in how they approached the reserve clause, which once dominated labor relations in all sports. The MLBPA was able to overthrow the reserve clause despite baseball's exemption from the antitrust laws. The other major sports had to rely on court rulings in order to achieve their ends. Even then, the NFLPA gave up free agency the first time it got it, the NBPA had to agree to increasingly stringent salary caps as a price of free agency, and the NHLPA has never been able to achieve the degree of free agency enjoyed by the other sports.

DISCUSSION QUESTIONS

1. How would the ability of professional sports unions to reach agreements be affected if they adopted a strategy of bargaining for wages as well as benefits?

2. Suppose the NHL goaltenders decided to break away from the NHLPA and form their own union. Would owners welcome this change or try to fight it? Why?

3. Does Becker's theory of human capital, discussed in Chapter 8, argue against or for the existence of a reserve clause? Why?

4. If the media is a source of information, and more information is beneficial to preventing strikes and lockouts, why would both parties agree to negotiate under conditions of a media blackout?

5. Should the government get involved in the settlement of strikes in professional sports?

6. Why is it unlikely that NCAA Division I football players will organize a union?

7. Why do unions bargain over roster sizes? Why would they want larger rosters if it results in less playing time per player?

PROBLEMS

9.1 Draw a graph similar to Figure 9.1 to show the effect of a union advertising campaign designed to increase demand for the product.

9.2 What happens to the magnitude of the deadweight loss in Figure 9.2 if after the wage is agreed upon, demand for the sport falls?

9.3 Would a craft union or an industrial union be more inclined to argue against the designated hitter? Why?

9.4 Show the impact of the *McNeil* decision on the contract zone between the NFLPA and the NFL. Justify your answer.

9.5 Using the Internet, log on to the official sites of each of the leagues and the official sites of the respective players associations. Describe any differences you see in how players associations depict the game compared with the leagues' depictions. Are there any significant differences across sports?

9.6 What effect might the dramatic increase in players from European countries have on the NHLPA's ability to negotiate a collective bargaining agreement?

9.7 Is it likely that professional golfers will unionize? Why or why not?

9.8 Why do unions advertise the sports (not just the players) that they represent?

9.9 Under what circumstances would a union favor the once-proposed contraction of Major League Baseball?

9.10 Assume that players bargain for only two things: wages and pensions. Use indifference curves to show that the more diverse a player's tastes and preferences are, the more difficult the players will be to represent.

CHAPTER 10

Discrimination

The biggest thing I don't like about New York are the foreigners. I'm not a very big fan of foreigners. How the hell did they get in this country? I'm not a racist or prejudiced person, but certain people bother me.

—John Rocker, Former Major League Pitcher[1]

I was raised on the beliefs of my father, my uncle, and Dr. Martin Luther King which, in essence, are "Don't do me any favors. Let's agree on what the rules are, and then judge me fairly."

—Arthur Ashe[2]

INTRODUCTION

On April 18, 1946, in a minor league game between the Montreal Royals and the Jersey City Little Giants, Jackie Robinson crossed the color line and became the first African American baseball player since the 1880s to play professional baseball in the "major leagues." His first at bat, a ground ball to the Jersey City shortstop, ended more than 50 years of segregated professional baseball in the United States.[3] Almost exactly one year later, on April 15, 1947, he took the field as a Brooklyn Dodger. Over the objections of many fans, players, and owners, Dodgers' president Branch Rickey had reintegrated baseball. Three months after Robinson broke the color barrier in the National League, Larry Doby became the first black to play in the American League when Bill Veeck signed him to a contract with the Cleveland Indians. Doby

---

[1]Jeff Pearlman, "At Full Blast," *Sports Illustrated* (December 27, 1999–January 3, 2000), pp. 62–64.

[2]Francis Dealey, *Win at Any Cost: The Sell Out of College Athletics* (New York: Birch Lane Press, 1990), p. 101.

[3]He did, however, hit a home run later in the same game. From Robert Peterson, *Only the Ball Was White: A History of Legendary Black Players and All-Black Professional Teams* (New York: Gramercy Books, 1970), p. 194.

suffered much of the same treatment as Robinson did, including endless streams of insults from fans and players alike, death threats, and segregated hotels and restaurants that prevented him from staying and eating with his teammates. It is remarkable that Robinson and Doby flourished despite the tense atmosphere in which they were forced to play. While baseball's history of discrimination against black players is surely the most widely known case of discrimination in sports, it is by no means the only one. Just as discrimination has long been a source of concern in almost every walk of life, it has been an issue in virtually every sport. The purpose of this chapter is to show how economists study and measure discrimination and to discuss a few instances when those methods have uncovered significant evidence that discrimination exists in the sports industry. Thus, there is a chance you may come away from this material with the perception that discrimination in professional sports is widespread. In fact, most current research finds that players' opportunities are remarkably free from discrimination.[4] For example, the 2003 *Racial and Gender Report Card,* which is published annually by the Institute for Diversity and Ethics in Sport at the University of Central Florida, gives the NFL, NBA, MLS (Major League Soccer), WNBA, and MLB straight A+'s for their performance in racial equity among players (the report did not include the NHL). [5] Although the report generally graded the leagues lower in areas such as coaching and management, it determined that widespread systemic discrimination against players is largely a thing of the past.

As we explore discrimination in professional and college sports, we need to distinguish between prejudice, which is a feeling or emotion, and discrimination, which is an action. A simple, economic definition of discrimination is the "unequal treatment of equals."[6] This chapter focuses solely on the economic effects of discrimination in the labor market. Thus, we use human capital theory and productivity data to discuss the existence, measurement, and changes in discrimination over time. The underlying question for all studies in this area is whether people of different demographic groups are evaluated and rewarded solely on the basis of their productivity.

Economists who study discrimination usually focus on two areas of inquiry. The first is whether equally qualified people have equal access to labor markets. This issue can be summarized as *equal access to work.* For example, if only whites are allowed to play quarterback in the NFL, or if only men are allowed to work as referees in the NBA, we would say that blacks and women do not have equal access to these labor markets. The second issue, *equal pay for equal work,* asks whether equally qualified workers in identical positions are paid equally. For example, if French-Canadian hockey players were paid less

---

[4]A good overview of studies of discrimination in sports can be found in Lawrence M. Kahn, "The Sports Business as a Labor Market Laboratory," *Journal of Economic Perspectives,* v. 14, no. 3 (Summer 2000), pp. 75–94.

[5]Richard E. Lapchick, *Racial and Gender Report Card* (2003 edition). Available at http://www.bus.ucf.edu/sport/public/downloads/media/ides/release_report.pdf.

[6]*MIT Dictionary of Economics,* 3rd edition, ed. by David W. Pearce (Cambridge, M.A.: The MIT Press, 1986), p. 109.

than English-speaking Canadian players of equal ability, our second criterion would be violated.

This chapter explains the following:

- Why an owner who discriminates against black players suffers economically for his actions

- Discrimination in sports may stem from owners, players, fans, or all three at once

- How black players in the NBA can be the victims of discrimination even though they earn more than white players

- How new laws protect and encourage women's sports at the collegiate and scholastic level.

Nobel Prize–winning economist Gary Becker, whose work on human capital is discussed in Chapter 8, also made major contributions to the way economists view discrimination. We focus much of our attention on his model. The next section describes how Becker's model approaches and measures discrimination. Section 10.2 applies the Becker model to discrimination in professional sports, introduces a method by which economists measure discrimination, and reviews some of the important empirical studies. Section 10.3 discusses discrimination at the collegiate level and recent legislation designed to increase athletic opportunities for women.

10.1 BECKER'S THEORY OF LABOR DISCRIMINATION

Before focusing on the economics of discrimination, we should acknowledge that economics is not the only lens through which one can view discrimination. The economic approach to discrimination is relatively new. In fact, before Gary Becker introduced the neoclassical theory of discrimination in his ground-breaking book, *The Economics of Discrimination* in 1957, economists had generally left the field to other disciplines.[7] Psychologists and sociologists have spent a great deal of time studying discrimination and its roots. From the perspective of social psychology, discrimination is the result of a three-part process that begins with prejudice. Prejudice is a form of group identification, based on an attitude not supported by facts. It is the *affective* component, meaning that it is based on feeling or emotions—an irrational feeling of negativity toward another group. To say that you are part of one group, say African Americans, and someone else is not, makes them somehow different from you. The irrational component is the assumption that "different" is "inferior." The second part, the *cognitive* component, is the assignment of a single set of characteristics to all members of a group, creating a stereotype. To say, for example, that all blondes are dumb is a stereotype. The third part is the *behavioral* component that translates prejudices

---

[7]Gary S. Becker, *The Economics of Discrimination,* 2nd edition (Chicago: University of Chicago Press, 1971).

based on stereotypes into actions. To disallow all Jews membership in a club is a discriminatory action.[8] The economic approach to the study of discrimination is consistent with this three-part approach. However, economists focus much more on the outcome of discrimination than its origin. A more radical political–economic theory is the Marxian view, which regards discrimination as a tool used by capitalists to divide the working class.

The theory Becker developed is different from the social–psychological approach or the Marxist approach in that he saw neither irrationality nor plots. Instead, he introduced the concept of a **taste for discrimination.** Tastes are one of the basic building blocks of economic theory. As such, they are generally not questioned. It is possible, however, to alter people's decisions regardless of their tastes.[9] To see the futility of challenging tastes, ask a friend what his favorite flavor of ice cream is. When he responds, ask him why he chose that flavor (say, peach). He will probably say something like, "Because peach tastes good." Now try asking him why peach tastes better than chocolate chip. Odds are he will shrug his shoulders and say he does not know why, or he will offer a variant on "because it tastes good."

Your friend's inability to explain the reasons behind his tastes does not, however, mean that you cannot alter his actions. If you offer your friend a large enough cash payment along with the chocolate chip ice cream or charge a high enough price for the peach ice cream, you may convince him to eat the flavor that he does not prefer. Becker's central insight was that people could have a taste for discrimination just like they can have a taste for a specific flavor of ice cream. People have a taste for discrimination if they act as if they are willing to pay something in order to associate with one group rather than another.

Thus, rather than wrestle with the complexity of the roots and mechanics of prejudice, Becker's theory allows economists to focus directly on behavior. It uses money to measure a person's taste for discrimination, avoiding problems associated with finding the reasons why someone discriminates. With this definition, testing for the presence of, and measuring the results of, discrimination are fairly straightforward. In addition, it makes it possible to predict how discrimination affects people who practice it and who are victimized by it.

In labor markets, the payment a discriminator makes in order to avoid associating with another group can take many forms, such as lower profits, higher prices, or lower wages. We distinguish between these forms of payment because the source of discrimination and the nature of the payment depends on which party (if any) gains and which party loses.

---

[8]For a more complete introduction to discrimination and prejudice from the perspective of social psychology, see, for example, Eliot Aronson, Timothy D. Wilson, and Robin M. Akert, *Social Psychology: The Heart and Mind* (New York: HarperCollins, 1994).

[9]A classic treatment of tastes and how economists regard them can be found in George Stigler and Gary Becker, "De Gustibus Non Est Disputandum," *American Economic Review*, v. 67, no. 1 (March 1977), pp. 76–90.

10.2 DIFFERENT FORMS OF DISCRIMINATION IN PROFESSIONAL SPORTS

This section describes how employers, employees, and consumers practice discrimination. Although in each case we use money to measure discrimination, we shall see that the Becker model is based on utility maximization. As people with a taste for discrimination maximize their utility, their willingness to pay in order to indulge their tastes has a variety of effects on the market. In addition, the structure of the market has important implications for both the discriminator and the groups that are discriminated against.

Employer Discrimination

Because it is based on utility maximization, Becker's model takes a broader view of the firm than simple profit maximization. For example, an employer may be willing to sacrifice profits in order to avoid associating with a group of people that reduces his or her utility. Because a firm may be willing to sacrifice profits in order to satisfy the owner's taste for discrimination, we can make specific predictions regarding firms that discriminate in both competitive and monopoly or monopsony markets. We discuss this outcome below in greater detail, as it has a significant bearing on the persistence of discrimination in the marketplace.

Most people associate labor market discrimination with employers who refuse to hire women or minorities or who do not pay them wages commensurate with their abilities. In this case, employers have a set of preferences regarding employees with whom they do and do not want to associate. For example, there is an ongoing debate in the sports economics literature regarding discrimination against French-speaking hockey players (Francophones).[10] Many studies claim that whether a team discriminates depends in part on the players' positions—whether they are forwards or defensemen—and where the team is located. One study found evidence of employer discrimination against French-speaking defensemen but not forwards.[11] Another study found evidence of discrimination only by teams based in the English-speaking provinces of Canada.[12]

---

[10]A recent study is Neil Longley, "The Underrepresentation of French Canadians on English Canadian Teams," *Journal of Sports Economics,* v. 1, no. 3 (August 2000), pp. 236–256. Marc Lavoie, Gilles Grenier, and Serge Columbe have written several papers that support the hypothesis of discrimination. Several appeared in the journal *Canadian Public Policy—Analyse de Politiques:* issues v. 13, no. 4 (December 1987), pp. 407–422; v. 15, no. 1 (1989); and v. 18, no. 4 (December 1992), pp. 461–469.

[11]J. C. H. Jones and W. D. Walsh, "Salary Determination in the National Hockey League: The Effects of Skills, Franchise Characteristics, and Discrimination," *Industrial and Labor Relations Review,* v. 44, no. 4 (July 1988), pp. 592–604.

[12]Neil Longley, "Salary Discrimination in the National Hockey League: The Effects of Location," *Canadian Public Policy—Analyse de Politiques,* v. 21, no. 4 (December 1995), pp. 413–422. Others dispute these claims, criticizing the statistical analysis. See William D. Walsh, "The Entry Problem of Francophones in the National Hockey League: A Systematic Interpretation," *Canadian Public Policy—Analyse de Politiques,* v. 18, no. 4 (December 1992), pp. 443–460, for a critique of Lavoie, Grenier, and Columbe. See Michael Krashinsky and Harry D. Krashinsky, "Do English Canadian Hockey Teams Discriminate Against French Canadian Players?" *Canadian Public Policy—Analyse de Politiques,* v. 23, no. 2 (June 1997), pp. 212–216, and Longley's reply that immediately follows in the same issue (pp. 217–220).

French Canadian Vincent Damphousse moves the puck against the Red Wings.

There is general agreement among researchers that French-speaking Canadians have a different style of play than English-speaking Canadians. Many believe that French-speaking Canadians are more offense-oriented and are less likely to engage in fights during the game than their English-speaking Canadian counterparts. The disagreement over whether teams discriminate stems from differences in the samples chosen and the measurement of defensive ability.

To simplify matters, assume that there are only two groups of players, English speaking (E) and French speaking (F). To keep the focus on discrimination, assume for the moment that although the players' styles may be different, they are equally productive. This way, in the absence of discrimination, demand for the two types of players would be equal. Becker measures the distaste that owners have for French-speaking players with a **discrimination coefficient** (d_F). The discrimination coefficient stems from the owners' feeling that they pay an emotional (or *psychic*) cost in addition to the wage when they employ a French-speaking player. When hiring, they act as if the wage were w for all E workers and $w(1 + d_F)$ for all F's. If NHL owners do have a taste for discrimination and prefer hiring English-speaking Canadians to hiring French-speaking Canadians, the demand for English-speaking Canadians (D_E) will be greater than that for French-speaking Canadians (D_F). In Figure 10.1a, we assume that there is an equal supply of each type of player ($S_E = S_F$). The difference in demand based on employer preferences, however, leads to a difference in wages as well as a difference in the number of players hired.

If the supply of English-speaking Canadians is greater than that of French-speaking Canadians, or the taste for discrimination (that creates the differences in demand) is great enough, teams may hire no French-speaking Canadians. That is, there would be unequal access to work. To use an example from other sports, the NFL and the National and American Leagues in baseball hired no blacks at all between 1890 and 1947. Alternatively, if there were no discrimination at all, we could simply add the two supply curves in Figure 10.1a to arrive at the market supply and add the two demand curves (which would be identical) to get the market demand, and players would be hired from the market supply without regard to race, as in Figure 10.1b.

Suppose that Jake, the owner of an NHL club, is evaluating, drafting, and signing players. Two players, Eddie and François, perform identically on every skill test, play the same position, and have identical past experience. From a productivity standpoint, they are perfect substitutes. Either player would sign a contract for $500,000 per season. However, during the interview process, Jake discovers that, although François has no trouble communicating with his English-speaking teammates, his primary language is French. Jake now separates the prospects into two groups: Eddie is an E, and François is an F. Because he has a taste for discrimination against all F's, Jake's discrimination coefficient is a positive number, say 0.2. Thus, when making his final decision, Jake feels as if he were paying Eddie $w_E = \$500,000$, and François $w_F = \$500,000(1 + 0.2) = \$600,000$. Jake does not actually pay the

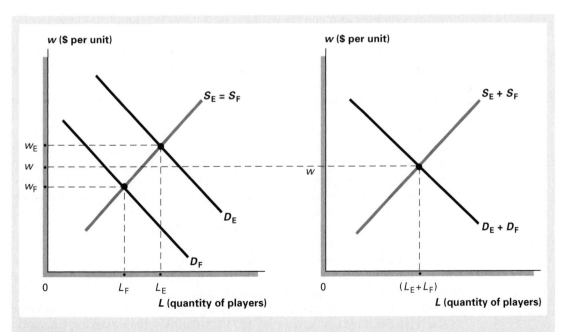

FIGURE 10.1

(a) Equilibrium wages with discrimination (b) Equilibrium wages with no discrimination

extra $100,000, but his desire to not be associated with French-speaking players makes him feel as though he were paying the extra, psychic cost.[13]

Jake does incur additional cost, however, if the increase in demand for E's increases their wages above $500,000. If enough owners have a taste for discrimination against F's, the market for players will be similar to that shown in Figure 10.1a, and owners with a taste for discrimination will pay higher wages than those without.

Discriminating clearly makes the team owner worse off economically. If Jake's taste for discrimination against F players makes the psychic and monetary wage of group F players greater than w_E, he will not hire any players from group F. Jake is happier paying w_E to fill his roster with English speakers than he is paying a mixed team the competitive wage w. The economic cost of employing only English speakers depends on the elasticities of supply and demand, or more simply, the relative slopes of the supply and demand curves. For example, if the supply of E players is perfectly elastic (a horizontal line), then owners will not have to increase w_E at all when they hire more of them.

However, even prejudiced owners may employ F players if the players are willing to work for wages that are low enough. For example, in the previous example, Jake's discrimination coefficient makes him feel that he is paying a wage premium of 20 percent. If the F's are willing to work for 20 percent less than E's, Jake would be willing to hire them. In this case, the situation would be unequal pay for equal work.

If the market for players is not competitive because players are not homogeneous, Jake may also end up with a mixed team. For simplicity, suppose E's and F's consist of good players (E_g and F_g) and bad players (E_b and F_b). If the E_g's are relatively scarce, Jake may exhaust the supply of E_g's, and he must choose between the less productive E_b's and the more productive F_g's. In such a case, Jake may maximize his utility by hiring some F_g's.

Discrimination clearly makes players in group F worse off. F's receive no offers as long as employers feel they pay F's more than the wage of players in group E. Even if F's are hired, they receive lower offers than equally productive E's. E players are better off as a group because their chances of making the team and their pay if they do both increase. Although owners avoid associating with group F players, they pay for the privilege in the form of reduced profits. We stress that owners are worse off *economically* and not that they are worse off overall. Owners who discriminate do so in order to maximize utility. In this case, utility maximization comes at the cost of reduced income.

Statistical Discrimination   It is also necessary to admit that differences in average performance across groups may exist. For example, it may be the case that on *average,* French-speaking Canadian players have better offensive statistics and lesser defensive statistics in college or junior hockey (the stepping stone to the NHL for most Canadian players) than their English-speaking Canadian

---

[13]As noted above, the Becker model does not address the issue of *why* the owner feels this way. We discuss later the question of why people might develop tastes for discrimination.

counterparts. The problem is that group averages are just that. They mask the individual variation *within* groups. Thus, each player must be judged on his own merits, rather than those of the group to which he belongs. The use of group averages to judge individual productivity levels is called **statistical discrimination.**[14] Statistical discrimination differs from discrimination that stems from tastes and preferences, because it is based on incomplete information rather than on the utility-maximizing choices of people with accurate information.

Statistical discrimination is troublesome for two reasons. First, it may be profit-maximizing behavior on the part of firms. Even though assuming that each French-speaking Canadian player is weaker defensively than each English-speaking Canadian is not always accurate, teams may be correct on average if they always use this assumption when choosing players. Thus they may feel justified in acting as discriminators. Second, statistical discrimination can become a self-fulfilling prophecy. If offensive-minded French-speaking Canadian forwards are drafted and defensive-minded ones are not, over time, league statistics will reflect that French-speaking Canadians are offensive-minded. Unfortunately, this means that statistical discrimination and its fallout can occur even if the initial difference in offensive versus defensive ability stemmed from inaccurate perceptions.

Does Anyone Win with Employer Discrimination?

As noted above, one group that certainly loses from the presence of discrimination is the employees who are the victims of discrimination. Employers lose profits but do so willingly in order to maximize utility. To see if any groups benefit economically from the employers' taste for discrimination, consider the case of racial discrimination in Major League Baseball. Blacks were effectively barred from organized baseball from 1898 to 1947 by a "gentlemen's agreement." Many black players who were good enough to play in the major leagues—some of them good enough to be admitted to baseball's Hall of Fame—were relegated to the Negro Leagues; these leagues lasted until the late 1950s.[15] Such players were certainly worse off.

One group that benefited from discrimination was white players of that era. Because blacks were excluded, more white players played in the major leagues than would have been possible otherwise. For purposes of illustration, we begin by assuming that all players are equally productive (homogeneous) and subsequently consider the more realistic case of variation in player quality. If all labor was homogeneous from a productivity standpoint, and 30

---

[14]In the case of ethnicity, players are not able to switch groups. In some cases, however, employees may be able to switch from a less preferred group to a more preferred group in an attempt to signal to potential employers that they are highly productive. For example, a college degree may signal to employers that a person is highly productive. Employers would want potential employees to send this signal if it is costly to find out the truth about whether they are highly productive. For a detailed explanation of signaling, see Michael A. Spence, "Job Market Signaling," *Quarterly Journal of Economics*, v. 87, no. 3 (August 1973), pp. 355–374.

[15]For an excellent history of the Negro Leagues, see Peterson, *Only the Ball was White: A History of Legendary Black Players and All-Black Professional Teams* (1970).

percent of the available labor force was black, in the absence of discrimination, 30 percent of the players would be black. If there was a very large pool of available labor, the market supply curve of players would have been a horizontal line, as shown in Figure 10.2. Players' wages will be set at the market level at w. In this case, the labor force is so large relative to demand that the labor supply curve for white players only (S_w) still results in the same wage. Because employers have a taste for discrimination, no blacks will be hired and employment of whites will be much greater than if there were no discrimination.

In practice, of course, players are not homogeneous. Players vary greatly in ability. When employers have a taste for discrimination and the quality of players of both races varies, teams will choose marginal white players over blacks of greater ability to fill out their rosters. White players of marginal ability were the beneficiaries of the owners' taste for discrimination. Even with no formal or informal color line, as long as the decrease in marginal revenue product that results from hiring a less-skilled white player is less than the wage premium an owner would feel that he or she is paying a black player based on his or her taste for discrimination, the white player would be hired.

While white players would be expected to benefit and black players to be hurt by the color line, one set of beneficiaries may come as a surprise. The color line allowed owners of Negro League baseball teams—themselves largely African American—to draw on a large pool of captive talent.[16] In addition, demand for Negro League baseball was much greater than it would have been

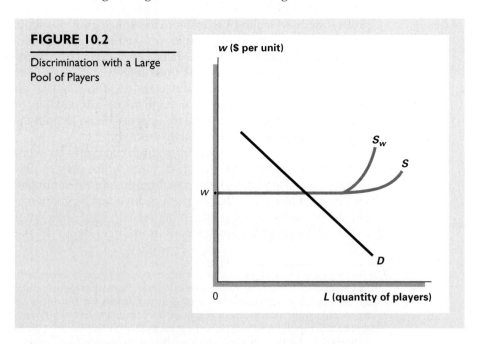

FIGURE 10.2

Discrimination with a Large Pool of Players

---

[16]While the word "Negro" is no longer used to describe African Americans, historians and economists still use the term "Negro Leagues" to describe the collection of all-black teams that competed in the era when baseball was segregated.

with integrated major leagues. Figures 10.3 and 10.4 show that black fans' desire to see black players reduced their demand for major league baseball and increased their demand for Negro League baseball. In each case, D_S represents the level of demand for tickets when the leagues were segregated, and D_I represents the demand for tickets when leagues were integrated. If each league plays a set schedule, the supply curve is a vertical line. Integration brings higher prices in the major leagues and lower prices in the Negro Leagues.

To see the Negro Leagues' reliance on segregation, one need look no further than the demise of the Negro Leagues after Robinson and other Negro League stars jumped leagues. Attendance dropped sharply, and in 1947, nearly every team lost money. By 1950, all but five major league teams had integrated. As Negro League teams lost increasing numbers of talented young players to the major leagues, gate receipts dwindled, teams folded, and a chief source of revenue became the sale of rights to their players to the major leagues. Player salaries for those that remained in the Negro Leagues dropped by about 50 percent, to as low as $200 per month. Despite valiant efforts to keep the league going, it finally folded in 1960.[17]

How Competition Can Eliminate Discrimination   Becker's theory implies that less discriminatory employers will be more successful than highly discriminatory employers. Suppose, for example, that because of their taste for discrimination, discriminatory employers are willing to pay blacks $10 per hour

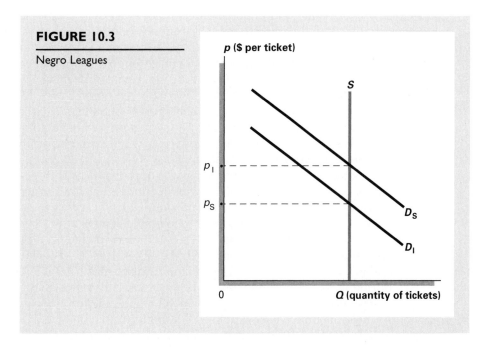

FIGURE 10.3

Negro Leagues

---

[17]Peterson, *A History of Legendary Black Players and All-Black Professional Teams* (1970), pp. 203–204.

FIGURE 10.4

Major Leagues

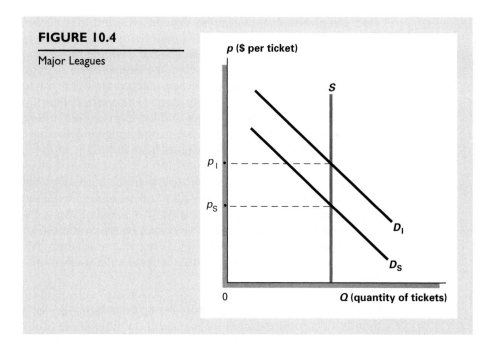

and whites $15 per hour. A potential employer who does not have any prejudice ($d = 0$) can enter and undercut any employer who uses white labor by hiring only blacks and paying them $11 per hour. Continued entry by unprejudiced employers increases the wage paid to black workers, driving down the profits available to potential entrants. If there are enough unprejudiced employers, black workers' wages rise until the wages of blacks and whites are equal. At this point, all prejudiced employers either stop acting on their prejudices or are driven from the market. In professional sports, although the markets are not perfectly competitive, the competition to win games and championships can be viewed as a powerful motivating force for owners to overcome their prejudices in order to maximize team quality.

A quick review of baseball's history supports the hypothesis that discriminators pay a price measured in wins for indulging their tastes. Historically, employers that integrated their teams more quickly have generally won more games than those that were slower to integrate. For example, the Dodgers, who led the way to racial integration of the National League, won NL pennants in 1947 and 1949, and five pennants in the 1950s. The Giants, which ranked second in their use of blacks, won pennants in 1951 and 1954. Table 10.1 shows that during 1952–56, the five Major League Baseball teams that employed the largest number of black players were all among the top six teams in baseball. At the same time, the Boston Red Sox (ironically, the first major league team to give Jackie Robinson a tryout) maintained a white-only roster until 1959 and languished from 1952 to 1956 with a record of just over .500. The Detroit Tigers and Philadelphia Phillies, the only other two teams with all-white rosters in the

1952–56 period, also struggled in the standings. Only the Yankees stood among the top teams in the 1950s with a relatively low percentage of black players.

While most owners were aware of the large pool of talent in the Negro Leagues before the color line was broken, only a few were willing to act on this knowledge. Bill Veeck attempted to purchase the Philadelphia Phillies in 1943 and planned to stock the team with stars from the Negro Leagues (for more information on Veeck, see his biographical sketch in Chapter 3 on pages 110–111). Major league owners blocked him by selling the team to someone else for much less than Veeck was willing to pay.[18]

When Markets Are Not Competitive Becker's theory can also be used to predict outcomes when workers are not homogeneous—and hence not perfect substitutes for one another—and when markets are not competitive, as is the case in professional sports. As in competitive markets, monopsonistic employers with a taste for discrimination treat the wage of the less-preferred group as though it were the wage $\times (1 + d_i)$. Unlike competitive markets, however, where there

Table 10.1

Cumulative Number of Black Player Years and Won–Lost Record of Major League Baseball Teams 1952–56

Team	1947–56	1952–56	Games Won 1952–56 (%)	W/L Ranking 1952–56
Brooklyn Dodgers (N)	37	22	.630	2
New York Giants (N)	25	18	.527	6
Cleveland Indians A)	20	12	.619	3
Boston Braves (N)	18	18	.548	5
Chicago White Sox (A)	14	12	.571	4
Chicago Cubs (N)	12	12	.439	12
Cincinnati Reds (N)	8	8	.489	10
Philadelphia Athletics (A)	8	8	.394	14
Pittsburgh Pirates (N)	3	3	.351	15
Saint Louis Browns (A)	3	3	.387	16
Saint Louis Cardinals (N)	2	2	.502	9
New York Yankees (A)	2	2	.638	1
Washington Senators (A)	1	1	.432	13
Philadelphia Phillies (N)	0	0	.509	8
Boston Red Sox (A)	0	0	.516	7
Detroit Tigers (A)	0	0	.440	11

(N) Indicates National League; (A) indicates American League.
Source: James A. Gwartney and Charles Haworth, "Employer Costs and Discrimination: The Case of Baseball," *Journal of Political Economy*, v. 82, no. 4 (July/August 1974), p. 875.

---

[18]James A. Gwartney and Charles Haworth, "Employer Costs and Discrimination: The Case of Baseball," *Journal of Political Economy*, v. 82, no. 4 (July/August 1974), pp. 873–881.

are many employers, monopsonistic employers will not be driven from the market if workers have nowhere else to sell their services. If employers discriminate, players with lesser abilities can end up making more than players with greater abilities. Perhaps more difficult to see, a discriminatory monopsonist may end up paying the "victims" of his prejudice more than players he ostensibly favors. For example, suppose that E's value to the team is $1,000 per game, and F's value to the team is $1,500. The employer has no taste for discrimination against E and thus sets the monopsony wage at $w = \$800$ in Figure 10.5. Note that in Figure 10.5, the demand curve is also labeled as the marginal revenue product (MRP). Recall from Chapter 8 that the MRP is the value of an additional unit of labor to the firm. By setting the ME equal to MRP, the firm equates the marginal benefit and cost of additional labor.

Figure 10.6 shows the wages paid to F players by both a nondiscriminating employer and one with a taste for discrimination. For the nondiscriminating employer, the relevant demand curve is D, which, again, is also MRP. As in Figure 10.5, the nondiscriminating monopsonist sets ME equal to the MRP and then takes the wage of $1,200 from the supply curve for the more productive F workers. The discriminating employer has a taste for discrimination against F players that is 0.2. This reduces the employer's demand curve from D to D' in Figure 10.6. Because the employer is a monopsonist, he forces F to accept $w/(1 + d_i) = \$960$ per game or be excluded from the market. As F's cannot earn more than $960 in any other labor market, they accept the offer. Thus, despite earning 20 percent more than E, who earns $800, F is discriminated against. The actual MRP of F's is $1,800, and they receive only $960 because of the combined forces of monopsonistic exploitation and discrimination. As such, they are paid $840 less than their contribution to

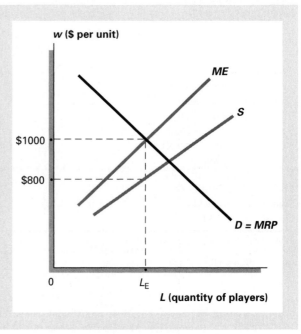

FIGURE 10.5

Monopsony Market for E
Players

FIGURE 10.6

Monopsony Market for *F* Players

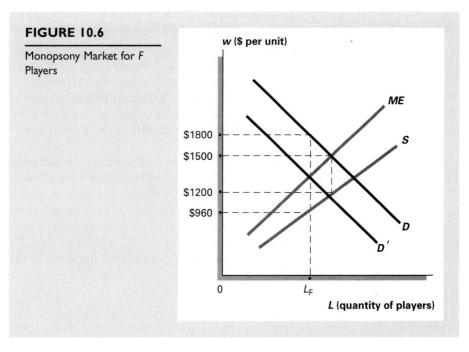

the team, whereas *E*'s are paid only $200 less than their contribution to the team. Thus, *F*'s are paid more but also are exploited to a much greater extent than *E*'s.

In addition, unlike the competitive firm, a monopsonist who discriminates is not necessarily driven from the market. If players are bound to a team by a reserve clause, they cannot use the force of the market to increase their wage. If they have no employment opportunity outside the league that can offer the same wage or greater, they will stay, and the employer will profit from the players' inability to change teams.

Employee Discrimination

Discrimination is not limited to employers. Prejudiced employees can also discriminate against their coworkers. Employees with a taste for discrimination regard their wage *w* as $w(1 - d_j)$ if they must work with members of a group they do not like. As before, d_j represents the coefficient of discrimination.

In the 1880s, a small number of black players played in the American Association, then a "major" league. The first was Moses Fleetwood Walker, who played for Toledo in 1884. Fleetwood's brother Weldy also played part of one season with Toledo. A somewhat larger number of blacks played in the International League, which was a minor league. Some white players refused to play for teams that also hired blacks. Others played only grudgingly. In 1887, Douglas Crothers was suspended from the Syracuse Stars of the International League for refusing to appear in a team photo with Bob Higgins, a black pitcher on the team. Cap Anson, a star white player of the same era with a well-known dislike for black players, gained much notoriety from his refusal to play against blacks (though he did play when he learned he would not be paid otherwise) and his opposition to the New York Giants' desire to sign black pitcher George Stovey.[19] Such behavior persisted even though the few blacks who were in the game, such as Fleetwood Walker and Frank Grant, were among the top players in their leagues. It is a sad footnote on baseball history that the origin of the feet-first slide was from attempts of white players to spike Grant, a second baseman; he eventually invented the shinguard to protect himself from their spikes. Discriminatory behavior toward blacks continued when the major leagues were reintegrated in 1947.

During their first season, Larry Doby and Jackie Robinson were subjected to employee discrimination by several opposing teams and even by their own teammates. When Doby was introduced to his new team, several players refused to shake his hand. When the other Dodger players learned that Robinson was to begin the season with their club, several of his teammates, including such prominent players as Dixie Walker, Carl Furillo, and Eddie Stankey, circulated a petition opposing the decision. Dodger manager Leo Durocher's response was to call team meeting at 1:00 in the morning in which he told his players, in part:

> Boys, I hear that some of you don't want to play with Robinson. Some of you have drawn up a petition. Well you know what you can use that petition for. . . . I'm the manager and I'm paid to win and I'd play an elephant if he could win for me and this fellow Robinson is no elephant. You can't throw him out on the bases and you can't get him out at the plate. This fellow is a great player. He's gonna win pennants. He's gonna put money in your pockets and mine. . . . Unless you wake up, these colored ball players are gonna run you right outa the park. I don't want to see your petition. . . . The meeting is over. Go back to bed.[20]

Ironically, Pee Wee Reese, a Kentucky native and shortstop who ran the risk of losing his position to Robinson, refused to sign.[21] Early in the 1947 season, both the Philadelphia Phillies and St. Louis Cardinals threatened to strike rather than play against Robinson when he came to town.[22] They relented only when faced with forfeiture and suspensions for not playing. In Robinson's first game in Philadelphia, however, the Phillies, led by their manager, Ben Chapman, hurled such savage abuse and obscenities at Robinson throughout the game that even those Dodgers who had opposed Robinson rallied around him.

The extent of the economic harm prejudiced workers do to others and themselves depends on the nature of the labor market. If players are perfect substitutes for one another and the labor market is competitive, the Becker model predicts that prejudiced employees would never accept employment on a team that is integrated because they perceive the market wage, w (that is offered to all employees), to be $w/(1 + d_j)$. Thus, they require a wage of $w/(1 + d_j)$ in order to feel as though

---

[19]Peterson, *Only the Ball was White: A History of Legendary Black Players and All-Black Professional Teams* (1970), p. 28.

[20]From Roger Kahn, *The Era: 1947–1957* (New York: Ticknor and Fields, 1993), p. 36.

[21]Ken Burns, *Baseball* series, "Bottom of the Sixth" episode.

[22]Peterson, *Only the Ball was White: A History of Legendary Black Players and All-Black Professional Teams* (1970), p. 199. Neither strike occurred after the league threatened suspensions.

they have received the market wage. However, no such offers exist in a market with a perfectly elastic supply of players (horizontal supply curve). Crothers and others who refused to play alongside black players were simply replaced by those who would. If a prejudiced player with a taste for discrimination was traded to an all-white team, he would no longer require a wage premium. Thus, one possible outcome of employee discrimination is segregation. Although segregation is usually considered to be employer driven, in this case, the taste for discrimination by employees creates the segregated market.[23]

As with employee discrimination, the results of the model are different when markets are not competitive. If players have different playing abilities, more than one market wage will exist, and prejudiced employees may end up as teammates of players they dislike. For example, an owner may be willing to pay the wage differential demanded by a top player with a taste for discrimination because there are no viable substitutes of equal quality.

If markets cannot be segregated, and players of different groups are perfect substitutes for one another, those with a taste for discrimination will be driven from the market. The players who discriminate, not the players discriminated against, end up suffering the most. Becker argued that this should eliminate employee discrimination from the market in the long run. Although employer and/or employee discrimination may have significantly depressed salaries of minorities as recently as the mid-1980s, most recent studies find that in the NFL, NBA, and MLB, wage differentials based on race have been eliminated.[24] If Becker's theory is correct, there are two possibilities of why this has happened. The competition between teams could have driven discriminatory owners or players from the market. Alternatively, the utility derived from the economic gains could be so much greater than the utility derived from discriminating that those with a taste for discrimination choose to stay in the market and bear the disutility of playing with groups they do not like.

Consumer Discrimination

Recent research on salary differentials among black, white, and Latino baseball players indicates that neither race nor ethnic background affects salaries.[25]

---

[23]Becker, *The Economics of Discrimination* (1971), p. 56.

[24]Orn B. Bovarsson, "A Test of Employer Discrimination in the NBA," *Contemporary Economic Policy*, v. 17, no. 2 (April 1999), pp. 243–256, cites several recent studies that find no statistical evidence of employer discrimination. In addition, Jeffrey A. Jenkins, "A Reexamination of Salary Determination in Professional Basketball," *Social Science Quarterly*, v. 77, no. 3 (September 1996), pp. 594–608; and Matthew S. Dey, "Racial Differences in National Basketball Association Salaries: A New Look," *American Economist*, v. 41, no. 2 (Fall 1997), pp. 84–90, find no significant differences in NBA salaries by race. Lawrence M. Kahn, "The Effects of Race on Professional Football Players' Compensation," *Industrial Labor Relations Review*, v. 45, no. 2 (January 1992), pp. 295–310, finds that as early as 1989 racial differences between blacks and whites were no more than 4 percent. In a survey article, Kahn also discusses his own work using 1989 data that show no significant discrimination against blacks or Latinos in major league baseball. See Lawrence M. Kahn, "Discrimination in Professional Sports: A Survey of the Literature," *Industrial and Labor Relations Review*, v. 44, no. 3 (April 1991), pp. 395–418.

[25]For more study results and discussion on this point, see Kahn, "Discrimination in Professional Sports" (1991).

However, evidence from both baseball and basketball indicates that discrimination still exists among consumers in the sports industry.

Consumers have a taste for discrimination if they prefer to not purchase goods or services from members of a specific group. For example, if a basketball fan has a taste for discrimination against black players, he or she perceives the price of admission to a game involving only white players to be p and the price of admission to a game in which blacks also play to be $p(1 + d_k)$.

Consumer discrimination can be difficult to isolate in a typical product market because product characteristics, particularly product quality, can cause variations in demand that are not the result of discrimination. One study did find that Nielson television ratings of basketball games are higher when white players play more.[26] On a more anecdotal level, the Boston Celtics of the 1980s are a frequently cited example of consumer discrimination. They were a very good team, and white fans may have followed the Celtics for only that reason. But 8 of 12 players on the 1985–86 Celtics roster were white, including stars Larry Bird, Kevin McHale, Danny Ainge, and Bill Walton. The mix of black and white players was so different from the rest of the league that it drew significant attention from members of the media, some of whom claimed that the Celtics were in danger of not having "enough" black players, given that 80 percent of players in the NBA were black. The Celtics management denied using race as a criterion for selecting players. K. C. Jones, an African American who coached the Celtics during the 1980s, put it this way: "I think it has a lot to do with identification. A lot of blacks identify with Magic Johnson. The white population identifies with Larry Bird. It's not a question of race, it's a question of identification with someone who has something in common with you. So who fills the stands? Ninety-five percent white."[27]

To conclude that consumers discriminate, one must confirm that race or ethnicity affects consumers' demand. To isolate consumers' preferences regarding specific players, researchers have turned to trading cards to study customer discrimination in Major League Baseball.[28] Unlike attendance figures, card prices allow researchers to look at fans' attitudes toward individual players by eliminating the impact of a player's teammates and opponents. Some research has shown that white players' baseball cards did sell for more than those of black players of equal ability. Nardinelli and Simon, for example, tested for consumer discrimination in baseball by comparing player productivity with card prices.[29] They divided a sample of players into pitchers and hitters in order to control for different attitudes toward pitchers and everyday players. They found that nonwhite hitters' cards sold for about 10 percent less than white hitters of compara-

---

[26]Mark T. Kanazawa and Jonas P. Funk, "Racial Discrimination in Professional Basketball: Evidence from Nielson Ratings," *Economic Inquiry,* v. 39, no. 4 (October 2001), pp. 599–608.

[27]Dan Shaughnessy, *Evergreen: The Boston Celtics* (New York: St. Martins Press, 1990), p. 147.

[28]For a different approach to consumer discrimination, see Daraius Irani, "Estimating Consumer Discrimination Using Panel Data: 1972–1991," in *Baseball Economics: Current Research,* ed. by John Fizel, Elizabeth Gustafson, and Lawrence Hadley (Westport, C.T.: Praeger, 1996).

[29]Curtis Nardinelli and Clark Simon, "Customer Discrimination in the Market for Memorabilia: The Case of Baseball," *Quarterly Journal of Economics,* v. 105, no. 3 (August 1990), pp. 575–595.

ble ability and that differences were especially large for Latinos. They also found that prices for nonwhite pitchers were about 13 percent lower than for white pitchers. Another study used data from 1960 and 1977 and found that fans discriminated against blacks but not Latinos in the 1977 sample and that discrimination against blacks increased between 1960 and 1977, especially for star pitchers.[30] Greater discrimination against superstars is consistent with Becker's theory, as he predicted that the most visible members of a group suffer the greatest discrimination because the discriminator encounters them more frequently.

In a more recent attempt to create a continuous measure of race and ethnicity, Fort and Gill had a group of people rate "how black" and "how Hispanic" individual players were by having the group members look at pictures on baseball cards. In this process, players with darker skin or more obvious Latino surnames were rated as "more black" or "more Hispanic." Fort and Gill then compared these ratings with current market prices of the cards. Although the magnitude of the discrimination differed from previous results, they did find evidence of discrimination against black and Latino hitters and against black pitchers.[31] Moreover, their results showed that race and ethnicity are continuous, not binary, variables. This, in turn, raises the question of whether social class and other nonrace characteristics contribute to how players are perceived and how much discrimination they face.

Consumer discrimination can affect attendance in several ways. First, consumers could show their taste for discrimination by supporting teams that have fewer players from the group that they dislike. Second, consumers could follow teams that are integrated but do so with less intensity—going to fewer games, buying fewer jerseys, watching the team less on television. Perhaps most extreme, they could stop following the sport altogether if too many players come from the group they dislike.

Consumer discrimination is also reflected in advertising firms' choices of athletes as sponsors. Demand for athletes as endorsers is driven by consumers' desire to emulate people they admire. If audiences are predominantly white, and consumers have a taste for discrimination, firms may in turn discriminate against black athletes.

Evidence suggests that consumer discrimination still existed in the NBA until the early 1990s. Wage differentials between blacks and whites persisted in professional basketball, and discriminating consumers seemed to be the source of the differential.[32] A major study by Kahn and Sherer found that in the mid-1980s, blacks in the NBA earned about 20 percent less than equally productive

[30]Torben Anderson and Sumner J. La Croix, "Customer Discrimination in Major League Baseball," *Economic Inquiry*, v. 29, no. 4 (October 1991), pp. 665–677.

[31]Rodney Fort and Andrew Gill, "Race and Ethnicity Assessment in Baseball Card Markets," *Journal of Sports Economics*, v. 1, no. 1 (February 2000), pp. 21–38.

[32]Lawrence M. Kahn and Peter Sherer, "Racial Differences in Professional Basketball Players' Compensation," *Journal of Labor Economics*, v. 6, no. 1 (January 1988), pp. 40–61; and Barton H. Hamilton, "Racial Discrimination and Professional Basketball Salaries in the 1990s," *Applied Economics*, v. 29, no. 3 (March 1997), pp. 287–296.

white players.[33] A follow-up study by Hamilton found that the average salaries of black and white players had become virtually identical by the 1994–95 season. However, Hamilton also found large differences between blacks and whites at both very high incomes and very low incomes.[34] Hamilton controlled for differences in attendance that resulted from the quality of the team, population and average income in the metropolitan area, and the fraction of the population in the local area that was black. Once all the variation that could be explained by these factors was removed, he was able to zero in on the variation in attendance that could be attributed to the number of players on the team that were white. His results indicate that at the bottom end of the pay scale, near what was then the league minimum of $150,000, there were many more whites than blacks. This appeared to indicate discrimination against whites. However, in contrast to the lower end of the distribution, in the upper ranges of NBA salaries, whites earned 19 percent more than equally productive blacks. Thus, even though blacks earned more than whites on average, it was the black players who were discriminated against overall. Again, evidence supports the prediction that the more contact the consumer has with the athlete, the more intense the discrimination will be. In this case, highly paid stars are much more visible than bench players who earn the NBA minimum.

Evidence of consumer discrimination also exists in the men's college Division I basketball market. Regression techniques similar to those described above show that fans spend an additional $121,000 (as measured by home-gate revenues) if an additional white player is added to the team.[35] It is encouraging to note that research on consumer discrimination using the results of fan voting for all-stars in baseball shows that this type of discrimination has declined sharply since the 1970s and that a study on wages of NBA players using data from the 1995–96 season found no evidence of discrimination, contradicting Hamilton's findings from just one year earlier. The lack of clear evidence of the presence of discrimination is itself a good indication that it is less prevalent than in the past.[36]

Unfortunately, consumer discrimination differs from other types of discrimination in one important regard: market forces do not eliminate it over time. In fact, if consumers have a taste for discrimination against a particular group, and employers maximize profit, the employers will not hire any members of that group. It is the only form of discrimination that harms the group that is discriminated against without in turn damaging those with the taste for discrimination.

In MLS, consumer discrimination and a concern for competitive balance have led to an interesting form of discrimination regarding the use of non-Americans.

---

[33]Kahn and Sherer, "Racial Differences in Professional Basketball Players' Compensation" (1988), p. 51.

[34]Hamilton, "Racial Discrimination and Professional Basketball Salaries in the 1990s" (1997).

[35]Robert W. Brown and R. Todd Jewell, "Is There Customer Discrimination in College Basketball? The Premium Fans Pay for White Players," *Social Science Quarterly,* v. 75, no. 2 (June 1994), pp. 401–412.

[36]Andrew F. Hanssen and Torben Anderson, "Has Discrimination Lessened over Time? A Test Using Baseball's All-Star Vote," *Economic Inquiry,* v. 37, no. 2 (April 1999), pp. 326–352; and Mark Gius and Donn Johnson, "An Empirical Investigation of Wage Discrimination in Professional Basketball," *Applied Economics Letters,* v. 5, no. 11 (November 1998), pp. 703–705.

Because soccer is so much more a part of the culture in Europe and South American than it is in the United States, male players from these areas are generally recognized as superior to American male players. The problem for MLS is that in an American league, fans want to see American players. To prevent MLS from becoming an American league with very few American players, MLS teams may not have more than three foreign players per team, excluding developmental players. From an economic standpoint, this quota represents a form of consumer discrimination. If consumers only wanted to see the best soccer, MLS officials would allow anyone who could earn a roster spot to play.

Positional Discrimination or Hiring Discrimination[37]

Given the high percentage of athletes of differing races and ethnic groups in the major leagues and the results of recent research, such as Hamilton's study of the NBA, there is little evidence of discrimination that affects access to professional leagues. However, this ignores the question of whether minorities have equal access to all positions. For example, since about 65 percent of the players in the NFL are black, one would expect about 65 percent of the players at each position to be black. One would also expect the racial balance of the coaches in the league to be similar to that of the players. As it turns out, however, these expectations are not realized.

Historically, positional discrimination, also known as **stacking**, has been an issue in both the NFL and MLB. As recently as 1998, only 9 percent of NFL quarterbacks were black. In contrast, only 9 percent of the safeties were white and only 1 white player started at cornerback (Jason Sehorn of the Giants). Since that time, stacking in the NFL has become less of a concern at the quarterback position. In 2002, although 98 percent of cornerbacks and 88 percent of receivers were black, 24 percent of the league's quarterbacks were black, an all-time high.

Economists call the systematic steering of minorities to specific positions on the field and within the coaching ranks **role discrimination.** For example, if a player must have a strong arm and quick reactions in order to be a quarterback and if coaches erroneously assume that blacks do not possess these attributes at the same level as whites, then coaches will discourage young black players from investing in the skills required to play quarterback.[38]

Table 10.2 shows the racial and ethnic breakdown of major league players for 2002. It shows that although Latinos make up 28 percent of the league overall, 60 percent of shortstops and 43 percent of second basemen are Latino. In contrast, blacks are much more likely to be outfielders than their overall percentage would suggest, and whites are much more likely to be pitchers.

---

[37]Data in this section, unless otherwise noted, are from Richard E. Lapchick, *Racial and Gender Report Card* (2003 edition), available at http://www.bus.ucf.edu/sport/public/downloads/media/ides/release_report.pdf.

[38]The same argument is frequently used to explain why women are overrepresented in certain occupations and underrepresented in others.

Table 10.2

Racial and Ethnic Breakdown of MLB Players in 2002 at Selected Positions (%)

	Total	*Pitchers*	*Catchers*	*First Base*	*Second Base*	*Third Base*	*Shortstop*	*Outfield*
White	60	72	61	61	36	71	29	41
Black	10	3	14	14	21	0	11	31
Latino	28	22	23	23	44	29	60	25
Asian Americans	2	3	1	1	0	0	0	2

Source: Richard E. Lapchick, *Racial and Gender Report Card* (2003).

There is simply not enough evidence to discuss race and positional segregation in hockey, as whites made up 98 percent of the players in the NHL in 2000–02. An early survey of the evidence of positional stacking of Anglophones versus Francophones was inconclusive, whereas a more recent study using data from the 1980s showed that French Canadian players made up about 10 percent of forwards and 7 percent of defensemen. In contrast, they made up over 28 percent of goalies. The unusually large representation of Francophone goalies, however, seems to reflect the lack of goalies from Europe or the United States rather than a displacement of Anglophone Canadians.[39] The most significant change in the makeup of hockey personnel in recent years is the large influx of European—particularly Eastern European—players since the fall of the Berlin Wall in 1989. As of 2002, 27 percent of the league's players were international (non–North American). The large influx of star players such as Peter Forsberg, Teemu Selanne, and others improved the quality of play in the NHL. Although not all European players have enjoyed immediate success in the NHL due to the differences in the size of the ice surface and style of play, in some cases, teams have thrived after successfully signing top players from former Eastern Bloc countries such as Russia and the Czech Republic. The Detroit Red Wings are the best example of the impact of accepting foreign players. The Red Wings' "Russian Five" were a key element in their success in the 1990s, capped by their 1997 and 1998 Stanley Cup victories.

Role discrimination is a form of statistical discrimination. For example, if on average women do not know as much as men about sports, they could be systematically discouraged from pursuing roles as officials or broadcasters. The problem is that uncertainty causes the employer to attribute the characteristics of the average person in the group to each member of the group. There is no way to determine without testing whether a specific woman has the knowledge to officiate a game. Unfortunately for women, if the discrimination occurs early in the application screening process, they may never get the opportunity to reveal their skills. The same is true in positional discrimination. If, for example, potential black quarterbacks are never given the opportunity to try out, they

---

[39]J. E. Curtis and J. W. Loy, "Race/Ethnicity and Relative Centrality of Playing Positions in Team Sports," *Exercise and Sport Science Reviews*, v. 6 (1978), pp. 285–313; and Marc Lavoie, Gilles Grenier, and Serge Columbe, "Discrimination and Performance Differentials in the National Hockey League," *Canadian Public Policy—Analyse de Politiques*, v. 13, no. 4 (December 1987), pp. 407–422.

cannot demonstrate their skills to coaches and prove they are capable of playing the position.

Discrimination in Coaching and Administrative Ranks   If blacks had only recently entered professional sports in significant numbers, one might not expect to find many black head coaches. However, the racial composition of the NFL has been relatively constant for the last 10 years (as mentioned above, it is roughly 35 percent white, 65 percent black). Since most coaches are former players, one might expect 65 percent of the coaches to be black as well. However, in 2002, 94 percent of head coaches in the NFL were white and only 6 percent were black. The numbers were only slightly more balanced for assistant coaches (71 percent white, 28 percent black, 7 percent other).[40]

Black baseball players are also less likely to become coaches than whites, although the percentage of blacks that go into coaching is increasing over time.[41] The data in Table 10.3 show that the percentage of MLB managers that are black has increased substantially in the last few years. It is also encouraging to see the upward trend in minority head coaches in the NBA, especially given that it has the highest percentage of black players of any of the major professional sports leagues.

One possible explanation for the slow growth in minority baseball coaches and managers is that in baseball, players that go on to become managers are predominantly infielders.[42] As was noted earlier, a disproportionate number of black baseball players play outfield. If playing an infield position gives a person valuable training for becoming a successful manager, then the positional discrimination creates the imbalance at managerial positions. Thus, premarket factors and not discrimination at the managerial level might have created the imbalance. Such an argument cannot, however, explain the lack of significant representation of Latinos among managers, as they frequently play infield positions.

While women have had little more than a token role in the NBA and NHL and have not appeared at all as players in MLB or the NFL, they do work in

[40]The extent of the discrimination is difficult to measure precisely, as the racial makeup of the applicants is not known.

[41]Larry Singell, Jr., "Baseball-Specific Human Capital: Why Good but Not Great Players Are More Likely to Coach in the Major Leagues," *Southern Economic Journal*, v. 58, no. 1 (July 1991), pp. 77–86.

[42]Gerald W. Scully, *The Business of Major League Baseball* (Chicago: University of Chicago Press, 1989), pp. 179–181.

Table 10.3

Percentage of Black Head Coaches and Managers in the NBA, NFL, and MLB in the 1990s

	1989–90	*91–92*	*93–94*	*95–96*	*97–98*	*99–2000*	*2001–02*
NBA	22	7	19	19	17	21	48
NFL	4	7	7	10	10	6	6
MLB	4	7	14	11	10	13	26

Source: Richard E. Lapchick, *Racial and Gender Report Card* (2003). Available at http://www.bus.ucf.edu/sport/public/downloads/media/ides/release_report.pdf.

administrative positions in all sports. The obstacles facing women in such positions vary with the nature of the jobs they hold. The value of having previously played the game is different for different jobs. General managers, for example, evaluate talent and work with the coach, so people who have played the game have a significant advantage in obtaining these positions.[43] Thus, one would not expect to find many women filling these roles. In fact, the only record of a female general manager in a male sport is Lynne Meterparel of the MLS San Jose Clash, appointed for the 1999 season.[44]

One would, however, expect to find a significant number of women in other administrative positions, where playing experience does not provide a meaningful advantage. Women are most frequently found as community relations directors; in the NHL, as many as 79 percent of these positions are staffed by women. In 2001–02, women filled between 0 percent (NFL) and 50 percent (MLS) of public relations director positions, and between 30 percent (NHL and NBA) and 43 percent (MLS) of chief financial officer positions. At the highest levels, almost all of the key front office executives in the major professional sports are male and white. The NBA is a notable exception; 17 percent of those in charge of day-to-day operations were black in the 2001–02 season, though this represents a decline since the mid-1990s, when roughly 30 percent were black.

The hiring records at the collegiate level are very similar to those at the professional level. In both coaching and administrative positions, Division I athletic programs are dominated by white males. Between 77 and 97 percent of Division I football, basketball, and baseball coaches are white. Roughly 42 percent of Division I women's sports teams have male head coaches, a figure that has not improved in the last six years. Perhaps more disappointing is that even in Division II and III, the percentages of minorities and women are similar, and in some cases worse. In fact, blacks are so underrepresented as head coaches in Division II male sports that they are outnumbered by women head coaches of male sports. Given these figures, it should not come as a surprise that at the highest administrative level, 88 percent of Division I athletic directors are white males.

We will return to the question of discrimination in collegiate athletics in Section 10.3. For now, we simply note that the imbalance at the collegiate level is likely to slow changes at the professional level, because top-level collegiate programs often serve as training grounds for future professional coaches. Thus, the argument that the absence of minority professional coaches is simply a "pipeline" problem (that is, that the data will improve over time as more top-level candidates become available) seems misguided. If increases in the number of black NFL head coaches must be preceded by increases in Division I minority representation, it appears that the status quo will continue for some time. In addition, recent research by Janice Madden shows that between 1990 and 2001, those minority coaches who have reached the level of head coach in the NFL have been signifi-

---

[43]It may also be the case, however, that having prior playing experience does not yield any significant advantage. For example, it seems likely that a top caliber women's basketball player would also be an effective evaluator of male basketball talent. If this is the case, then the absence of women as general managers in basketball would also represent role discrimination.

[44]Richard Lapchick, *Racial and Gender Report Card* (2003).

cantly more successful than their white counterparts, raising the question of whether a double standard is in force in which blacks must have higher qualifications to reach the level of head coach than whites.[45]

Gender Equity—A Special Case?

Women rarely attempt to enter traditionally male professional or college sports leagues such as football. Gender differences in size, weight, and strength make such occurrences unlikely in the future as well. Annika Sorenstam provided a rare exception when she competed in the men's 2003 PGA Bank of America Colonial tournament. The only sports where men and women routinely compete against one another at the professional level are mixed doubles in tennis, auto racing, and as jockeys in horse racing. Mixed doubles (with one man and one woman per team) is a somewhat contrived event at major professional tournaments. Only in auto racing and thoroughbred horse racing do men and women compete against one another under a common set of rules. Thus, they provide a unique opportunity to test for the existence of gender discrimination. A 1993 study by Ray and Grimes of thoroughbred racing showed that, holding performance and experience constant, female jockeys receive significantly fewer racing opportunities. As a result, they have significantly fewer winnings than similarly qualified male jockeys.[46]

No systematic research has been done to investigate the economics of gender discrimination in auto racing. Even though Shirley Muldowney is one of the most successful drag racers of all time, she is only one of six women to ever win an NHRA national title event in the professional category.[47] The relatively small number of successful female race drivers raises the question of whether so few women are found in the sport because of low demand or low supply. If no evidence exists that women are inferior race drivers or that they lack the human capital needed to become professional drivers, a lack of demand for women drivers represents employer discrimination. If the small number of drivers is the result of a lack of supply (not many women pursue this career), it could be caused by role discrimination or not be discrimination at all.

Recall from Chapter 3 that television rights are a derived demand, driven by the demand of advertisers that are in turn determined by ratings. If the demand for women's sports is as high as that for men's matches, and no other cost differences exist, then in the absence of discrimination, there should be equal prize money.[48] Sponsors should have the same willingness to pay for advertising time regardless of gender.

---

[45]Janice Fanning Madden, "A Study of Racial Differences in the Records of NFL Coaches 1986–2001," available at http://www.findjustice.com/ms/nfl/frameIndex.htm.

[46]Margaret A. Ray and Paul W. Grimes, "Jockeying for Position: Winnings and Gender Discrimination on the Thoroughbred Track," *Social Science Quarterly*, v. 74, no. 1 (March 1993), pp. 46–61.

[47]"Shirley Muldowney: 2000 Star Tracks Archive," at http://www.nhra.com/drivers/driver. asp?driverid=976.

[48]It should be noted that men and women do not produce equivalent output in tennis matches, because men's matches are typically best of five sets and women's are best of three.

Unfortunately for the players, owners, and fans of women's sports, it appears that there are significant differences in the public demand for professional teams across gender. The recent demise of the U.S. women's professional soccer league (the WUSA) serves as a case in point. Although the league was unquestionably the preeminent league in the world, employed top stars from the Women's World Cup team such as Mia Hamm, and had benefited from over $100 million in initial investments, there simply was not enough demand from fans and sponsors to keep the league from folding in 2003.

In individual sports, women have fared better. A striking example of how players can raise not only awareness but also wages comes from the world of tennis. Open tennis tournaments began in the late 1960s. Today, both amateurs and professionals can qualify to play in an open tournament through a series of local and regional competitions. Initially, men's prize money was approximately 10 times that of women. In November 1972, the women's U.S. Open champion, Billie Jean King, threatened to lead a boycott of the 1973 Open unless the prize money was equalized. Her protest was successful, and prize money was eventually equalized. Gender-based differences in prize money persist, however, in other major tournaments, such as Wimbledon and the French Open. As noted, prize differences in and of themselves are not sufficient for most economists to conclude that discrimination exists. However, in 1998, HBO television ratings went up by over 18 percent after increasing its coverage of women's play at Wimbledon, yet women still receive 11 percent less than men for winning the singles title.[49]

10.3 TITLE IX AND DISCRIMINATION IN COLLEGE SPORTS

Title IX has been the most important measure ever undertaken to promote gender equity in sports. It has completely changed the face of scholastic and collegiate opportunities for women. Some even ascribe the success of the WNBA and the U.S. Women's World Cup soccer team directly to Title IX. It has not, however, been universally praised. Many claim that Title IX has denied opportunities to as many people as it has helped.

Title IX reached its 30th anniversary in 2002. Though it stands as a lightning rod for both proponents and detractors of women's athletic rights, it is a seemingly innocuous section of the 1972 Educational Amendments to the 1964 Civil Rights Act. For such an important piece of legislation, Title IX itself is remarkably unimposing, measuring only one sentence in length. It reads:

---

[49]"Not About Money: HBO Declines to Renew Wimbledon Contract After 25 Years," CNN/SI at www.cnnsi.com/tennis/1999/wimbledon/news/1999/06/28/hbo_wimbledon/index.html. Another frequently cited example of women's sports eclipsing men's in popularity is that ratings from television broadcasts of the Olympics show that women's figure skating and gymnastics are consistently among the most watched events.

No Person in the United States shall, on the basis of sex, be excluded from participation in, be denied the benefits of, or be subjected to discrimination under any
educational program or activity receiving federal financial assistance.[50]

Three years later, the Department of Health, Education, and Welfare established three areas of regulatory jurisdiction:

1. Financial aid
2. Other benefits and opportunities
3. Participation in athletics.

The third of these areas is directed at accommodating men and women in
their efforts to participate in intercollegiate athletics. Congress established compliance guidelines for athletics in a 1979 amendment to the original legislation.
Compliance can be achieved in one of three ways: proportionality, program
expansion, or accommodating the interests and abilities of the student body.

Proportionality means that the percentage of women who participate in
sports at a university should approximate the percentage of female undergrad-
uates enrolled at the school. For example, if women make up 55 percent of a
school's undergraduate enrollment, approximately 55 percent of the athletes
participating on the school's teams would have to be female. The Office of Civil
Rights of the Department of Education oversees the enforcement of Title IX and
uses a ± 5 percentage point rule in its interpretation of this test (e.g., if a
school's enrollment is 50 percent female and 45 percent of women are on school
teams, the school would be in compliance).

To show program expansion, the college must demonstrate that it has
increased and continues to increase opportunities for the underrepresented sex.
This criterion is open to interpretation. Depending on how one interprets the
word *expansion*, women's sports could achieve proportionality with men in
very short order, or it could take an almost infinitely long time to reach equal
or proportional programming levels for men and women.

Finally, colleges may show that they have fully accommodated the interests
and abilities of the underrepresented sex. It is also difficult to use this criterion
to challenge a school, because the school itself can be the judge of a student's
ability to participate.

Each of these criteria leaves room for interpretation. Perhaps because it is a
numerical measure and thus most easily checked, challenges to schools' compliance with Title IX have generally been based on the proportionality standard.[51]

Like most legislation, Title IX has had both intended and unintended effects.
Unless a program can generate enough revenue to support itself, it can gain funding only if the university increases funding to athletics or if another program is
cut. The balanced-budget approach to changes in athletic funding has greatly contributed to the controversy over the implementation of Title IX guidelines, as
men's sports have at times paid the ultimate price—cancellation of their program—in order to accommodate new women's programs. According to the

---

[50]"A Basic Title IX Presentation," at http://bailiwick.lib.uiowa.edu/CHBGrant/Present.html.

[51]Andrew Zimbalist, *Unpaid Professionals* (Princeton, N.J.: Princeton University Press, 1999), p. 63.

Independent Women's Forum, which documents the effect of Title IX quotas, over 350 men's programs were discontinued between 1992 and 1997.[52] Though not all were the result of Title IX, it is likely that many were. Among Division I schools, in 54 percent of cases, schools that dropped men's teams cited gender equity as a "great or very great" influence on their decisions.[53] Schools thus claim that, by forcing them to cut opportunities for men in order to open opportunities for women, Title IX has imposed a **zero-sum game** on them.

When analyzing the effects of Title IX on specific programs, it is useful to divide athletic teams into three categories.[54] The first group includes only two men's sports—Division I-A football and Division I basketball, commonly known as **revenue sports.** "Revenue sports" is actually a misnomer, as the term does not mean that they generate revenue but that they generate revenue in excess of their costs. The term is also misleading, as many Division I-A football and basketball teams do not earn positive net revenue on a regular basis—a topic that is discussed in detail in Chapter 11. Sports in the second group— women's sports—and the third group—men's sports such as golf, tennis, wrestling, and gymnastics—generate little, if any, net revenue.

When a college tries to increase women's sports relative to men's in order to comply with Title IX, it can increase women's athletics, cut men's athletics, or do a combination of both. From the early 1980s to the mid-1990s, women's athletics at the Division I level grew dramatically. Between 1981–82 and 1994–95, the number of Division I women's teams increased by 28 percent, from 2,011 to 2,576. Over the same period, the number of men's Division I teams was nearly stagnant, at about 2,850. Thus, Title IX has increased the opportunity for women to participate in Division I athletics. On the men's side, however, the nearly constant total number of teams does not adequately reflect the turmoil that has occurred. As noted, from 1992 to 1999, more than 350 men's programs were cut while a nearly equal number of programs were either started or raised to the Division I level.[55] A typical example of such cuts is the elimination of soc- cer, tennis, and wrestling at Miami University of Ohio.[56] With a few exceptions (such as baseball at Providence and the University of Wisconsin), the men's programs that were cut came in low-profile, nonrevenue sports.

Proponents of Title IX argue that such tough choices are necessary in order to advance women's athletics. As evidence that the demand for girls' sports was not being served, they point to the dramatic increase in participation in sports by high school girls (which are also covered by Title IX), from 294,000 in 1971 to 2.8 million in 2002.[57] Those who believe that men's sports are being sac-

---

[52]Jessica Gavora, *Tilting the Playing Field* (San Francisco: Encounter Books, 2002), p.53.

[53]"'Open to All' Title IX at Thirty," Report of the Secretary of Education's Commission on Opportunity in Athletics, p.19.

[54]We return to this discussion in Chapter 11 in the context of the NCAA as an institution.

[55]Pete Du Pont, "Men's Athletic Programs Cut to Satisfy Quotas," *Human Events*, v. 55, no. 33 (September 3, 1999), p. 14.

[56]*Sports Illustrated,* Scorecard (April 26, 1999), p. 22.

[57]"'Open to All': Title IX at Thirty," Report of the Secretary of Education's Commission on Opportunity in Athletics, p. 13.

rificed to satisfy destructive quotas point to surveys such as the one done at the University of Wisconsin–Lacrosse showing that women are less interested in watching and participating in sports than men, and that women rarely cite lack of opportunity as the reason that they do not play a sport.[58]

In 1992, a landmark Supreme Court decision in the case of *Franklin v. Gwinnet County Public Schools* allowed plaintiffs to recover monetary damages in Title IX suits. As a result, some schools have paid dearly for their resistance to Title IX. Perhaps the highest-profile Title IX case was filed in 1992 by the women's gymnastics and volleyball teams at Brown University. After five years of litigation, Brown agreed to establish and maintain compliance after the Supreme Court refused to hear its appeal in 1997. Its five-year battle cost Brown an estimated $2 million in legal expenses for itself and the plaintiff. Brown also bore the cost of the negative publicity that it received for taking such an unpopular stance in its effort to cut just $63,000 from its budget.[59] Those who sided with Brown noted that at the time of the suit, Brown already had more women's sports than men's and more women's sports than any other school in the country except Harvard.[60]

Most appellate courts have supported the reasonableness of the regulations for compliance. However, the cancellation of men's sports that often accompanies the increase in women's offerings has led to a spate of countersuits, such as *Chalenor v. University of North Dakota* over the cancellation of its wrestling program. In general, such suits (including this one) have been unsuccessful in convincing the courts that the damage done to boys and men's opportunities more than outweighs the benefit to girls' and women's programs.

Although Title IX is almost certain to remain a source of ongoing debate, it seems clear that it will remain. After much contentious debate, the Secretary of Education's Commission on Opportunity in Athletics concluded in its study of Title IX that it had resulted in 30 years of great progress for women and girls and that it should remain, with the goals of continuing this progress while retaining the opportunities for boys and men. In the words of U.S. Secretary of Education Rod Paige, "Without a doubt, Title IX has opened the doors of opportunity for generations of women and girls to compete, to achieve and pursue their American Dreams. This Administration is committed to building on those successes."[61]

---

[58]Paul Dubois, "Title IX: A Critique from the Underclass," *Physical Educator,* v. 56, no. 3 (Fall 1999), pp. 159–167.

[59]Zimbalist, *Unpaid Professionals* (1999), pp. 56–58.

[60]Jessica Gavora, *Tilting the Playing Field,* pp. 45, 72.

[61]"'Open to All' Title IX at Thirty," Report of the Secretary of Education's Commission on Opportunity in Athletics, p. 2.

BRANCH RICKEY

BIOGRAPHICAL Sketch

The greatest proof of Rickey's genius was that you always knew what he was doing—except when he was doing it to you.

—BILL VEECK[1]

Even if Branch Rickey had never broken baseball's color line, he would still be remembered as one of baseball's greatest innovators. In fact, by the time Rickey first joined the Dodgers at the age of 62, he had already experienced a full career in baseball.

Born in 1881, Wesley Branch Rickey was raised in a staunch Methodist family. A budding baseball career pretty much ended one day in 1903 when he refused to play on a Sunday. For the rest of his life—with the exception of a special war bonds drive during World War II—Rickey never attended a ballgame on a Sunday, though—some were quick to point out—that did not stop him from calling the ballpark to check on the day's gate receipts.

Rickey's preoccupation with money probably stemmed from an impoverished upbringing. Rickey was so poor that he had to delay going to college for several years after he graduated from high school. He later recalled that when he finally went to Ohio Wesleyan University, "[d]uring my first term . . . I had only one pair of pants, and nobody saw me wear anything else."[2]

Rickey's frugality was to follow him when he assumed a front office job with the St. Louis Cardinals, who had hired him away from their crosstown rivals, the Browns, in 1916. Frustrated that his scouts would frequently identify talented minor league players only to lose them to wealthier teams such as the New York Giants, Rickey began to buy minor league teams so as to keep players within the fold. This was the beginning of baseball's first "farm system." The Cardinals' system became so extensive and so laden with talent (the products of that system included Hall of Famers Dizzy Dean, Joe Medwick, and Stan Musial) that the Cardinals displaced the Giants as the National

League's dominant team in the 1930s. Rickey's spending on the team, however, eventually ran afoul of the team's ownership, and in 1943, at the age of 62, he headed east to Brooklyn to become president and 25 percent owner of the Dodgers.

While rebuilding the Dodgers' farm system in the early and mid-1940s, Rickey also introduced a number of other innovations that are now taken for granted. He was the first to use a pitching machine and to have players practice their slides in sliding pits. Inspired by Dwight Eisenhower's account of preparations for D-Day, Rickey borrowed the philosophy to create "Dodgertown," in Vero Beach, F. L. Dodgertown was a vast complex where the entire Dodger system, minor leaguers and major leaguers alike, could receive instruction at one time.

Rickey became a well-known figure to New York sportswriters, who dubbed him "The Mahatma" because they saw Rickey's image in John Gunther's description of Mohandas "Mahatma" Gandhi as "a combination of God, your father and Tammany Hall."[3] His double-talk was so renowned that his office in Brooklyn became know as "The House of Winds." One thing about which Rickey was absolutely silent was his plan to break baseball's color line.

One can only speculate about Rickey's motivation for seeking to integrate the Dodgers. Publicly, he spoke of the added fans and higher gate receipts an integrated team would attract. Privately, however, he recounted a different motivation that stemmed from his days at Ohio Wesleyan. While with the baseball team there, he roomed with a black teammate. On one road trip, the team was denied admission to a hotel because of the black player. After making arrangements at another hotel that involved sneaking

➡

the player in through the kitchen, Rickey found his roommate in tears, scratching at his hands and asking himself why the color couldn't rub off.

Whatever his reasons, Rickey took great care in finding the right player to integrate the major leagues. With a stealth that befitted a Cold War spy novel, Dodger scouts fanned the nation, ostensibly looking to recruit players for a new Negro League team to be called the "Brooklyn Brown Dodgers." Ruling out established stars such as Satchel Paige or Buck O'Neill as being too old to be able to establish careers in a new league and young stars such as Roy Campanella or Don Newcombe as being too young to withstand the pressures of being the first player to cross the color line, Rickey settled on Jackie Robinson, a rising star with the Kansas City Monarchs.

On October 23, 1945, the Brooklyn Dodgers revealed that they had signed Robinson to a contract with their top farm club, the Montreal Royals. Rickey had carefully chosen both the signing date and the ball club to which he assigned Robinson. The date was early enough that other players would know that they were likely to play with a black ballplayer and could arrange for a trade if they objected to doing so. The Montreal club was far enough out of the limelight and from America's overheated racial environment to allow Robinson some chance of a normal environment. (Even so, he recalled being close to a nervous breakdown by the end of the season.)

Soon after signing Robinson, Rickey had to withstand pressure from other owners—among them the legendary Connie Mack—who called to complain that he was about to ruin the game; they arranged a vote on the Dodgers' move in which Rickey cast the only approving vote. Far from being discouraged at the attitudes of the other owners, Rickey quickly became the one to sign the second, third, fourth, and fifth black baseball players to contracts.

Rickey also had to deal with on-the-field problems. At first he had to reassure the manager in Montreal, a Mississippian named Clay Hopper, who asked, "Mister Rickey, tell me—do you really think a nigra's a human being?"[4] Rickey was so reassuring and Robinson's play and demeanor so exemplary that Hopper eventually became one of Robinson's biggest backers. After Robinson's outstanding year in Montreal, Rickey then had to convince the Dodgers' manager, Leo Durocher, and the team's Mississippi-born broadcaster, Red Barber, to support his move.

In 1950 Walter O'Malley, who also owned 25 percent of the Dodgers and was Rickey's rival for control of the club, gained control of another 25 percent of the Dodgers and forced Rickey out as president. Rickey quickly landed a position as vice president and general manager of the Pittsburgh Pirates. Although he did not have the same success there as he did in St. Louis or Brooklyn, Rickey did build the foundation of a team that would win the 1960 World Series, bringing pitchers Vernon Law and Bob Friend to the team and stealing a young prospect named Roberto Clemente from the Dodger organization.

Rickey continued to affect baseball well into the 1960s. His attempt to create a rival Continental League forced the National League into its first expansion of the century and led the National League to replace the departed Dodgers and Giants with the New York Mets. In 1963, Rickey returned to the Cardinals as a consultant. He helped oversee the 1964 Cardinals as they appeared in and won the World Series, their first win since the 1946 team, which Rickey also built. Branch Rickey died in 1965, after spending almost 70 years in baseball and living long enough to share the podium at the Baseball Hall of Fame induction of his good friend, Jackie Robinson.

[1]Bill Veeck, *The Hustler's Handbook* (Dunham, N.C.: Baseball America Classic Books, 1996), p. 100.

[2]Harvey Frommer, *Rickey and Robinson* (New York: Macmillan, 1982), p. 38.

[3]From Harvey Frommer, *Rickey and Robinson* (New York: Macmillan, 1982), p. 87. Tammany Hall was where New York City's notorious political machine had been headquartered, so that any political boss in New York was dubbed "a Tammany Hall politician."

[4]Harvey Frommer, *Rickey and Robinson*, p. 120.

Sources: John Helyar, *Lords of the Realm* (New York: Ballantine Books, 1994); Harvey Frommer, *Rickey and Robinson* (New York: Macmillan, 1982); and Bill Veeck, *The Hustler's Handbook* (Dunham, N.C.: Baseball America Classic Books, 1996).

SUMMARY

This chapter introduced economic theories of discrimination and used them to describe how the tastes and preferences of employers, employees, and consumers can affect wages of athletes. Evidence shows that, although discrimination was overt in the 1940s, it has diminished over time. Examples from baseball in the 1950s support the hypothesis that discriminators will suffer lower profits or at least lower success rates, as measured in wins. There is evidence that some discrimination on the part of consumers still creates wage differentials in sports such as basketball. There is also substantial evidence that positional discrimination still exists in the NFL and in other sports on the playing field as well as in the coaching ranks. The implementation of Title IX in the 1970s stands as a watershed event in the effort to achieve gender equity in college sports.

DISCUSSION QUESTIONS

1. Think of recent events from the sports industry that show a taste for discrimination. Do they represent consumer, employer, or employee discrimination?

2. Discuss the role of the media in shaping perceptions about racial and ethnic diversity in professional and amateur sports.

3. How might the development of the NFL and MLB have been different if blacks had not been excluded from these leagues during the years that spanned World War II?

4. Try to identify specific economic concepts and theories about discrimination in Leo Durocher's statement about Jackie Robinson on page 358.

5. If implementing Title IX means that men's sports must experience a reduction in funding, should it be eliminated?

6. Discuss the implications of a government policy that any network that intends to cover the Olympics must devote equal air time to men's and women's events.

7. What men's and women's sports have recently been added to your school? Have any been discontinued? Is the discontinuation worthwhile?

PROBLEMS

10.1 Suppose that the competitive wage in minor league baseball is $20,000 per season. A minor league owner has a taste for discrimination against all nonwhite players. Her coefficient of discrimination against Latinos is 0.20, and her coefficient of discrimination against blacks is 0.18. What would she consider the wages of people who are members of these two groups to be? If the supply of players were perfectly elastic, how many of each group would be hired?

10.2 How can you determine if a running back in the NFL is suffering from wage discrimination? Would the process be the same for a lineman?

10.3 Under what circumstances would an owner be able to practice employer discrimination over a long period of time?

10.4 Why is it difficult to isolate gender discrimination in professional leagues of team sports?

10.5 Use Becker's model to explain why sponsors who discriminate will likely experience lower profits for doing so.

10.6 Using supply and demand graphs, show how positional segregation can occur even if only the players (including potential future players) believe that such discrimination exists.

10.7 True, false, or uncertain: Title IX compliance requires equal expenditures on men's and women's sports. Explain your answer.

10.8 For each type of Title IX compliance, give an example of a situation that would result in a violation.

10.9 Would it be possible to have legislation similar to Title IX that governed professional sports? Why or why not?

10.10 Draw a set of indifference curves (as described in Appendix 2A) depicting an owner with a taste for discrimination against Francophones. Put Anglophones on the horizontal axis.

PART FIVE

Sports in the Not-For-Profit Sector

CHAPTER 11
The Economics of Amateurism and College Sports

The Economics of Amateurism and College Sports

The American sportswriter defines an amateur as a guy who won't take a check.
—Paul Gallico[1]

Not everyone comes to college to be in college.
—Damon Moore, defensive back, Ohio State University[2]

INTRODUCTION

The preceding chapters discussed a variety of economic theories as they are applied to the sports world, including the following concepts:

- How and whether teams are profitable—and the difficulty in measuring profits
- How monopolies create barriers to entry by potential competitors
- How sports leagues have used their monopsony power to minimize labor costs
- How cities have based economic development on sports franchises.

All these factors apply as well to the relationship between colleges and their athletic programs, for it is impossible to deny that college sports are a very big business. The finances of college athletic departments sometimes rival those of professional franchises in both size and complexity. Observers claim that the two profit centers—football and men's basketball—of the most profitable athletic programs

---

[1]Paul Gallico, *Farewell to Sports* (New York: Alfred A. Knopf, 1938), p. 109.

[2]Quoted in Mike Freeman, "Pursuit of Victories Presses on Colleges," *New York Times,* July 13, 2003, pp. 8–4.

compare favorably with the market values of their professional counterparts.[3] At the other end of the scale, some major college programs resemble unprofitable professional franchises in their struggle to keep their heads above water both competitively and financially. The TV contract for the NCAA men's basketball tournament exemplifies the stakes involved. The current contract with CBS is worth $6 billion over 11 years. With each win in the tournament worth $780,000 to the victorious college, huge sums rest on the performance of young men who are not permitted to accept money for playing basketball.

Chapter 4 explained how the NCAA can be regarded as an "incidental cartel," and Chapter 7 showed how cities have attempted to use sports as a vehicle for economic growth. This chapter combines these two forces and demonstrates how they affect colleges. Colleges—like cities—have used athletics in an effort to improve their prestige and bottom line. We also explore how the monopsony power that colleges can exercise over their athletes has depressed the returns to the participants. Since much of the economics in this chapter deals with organizations such as the NCAA and attitudes such as the Olympic ideal, we place the analysis in the appropriate historical and institutional context and explain the following points:

- How profit-maximizing cartels allocate output among their members
- The role of an enforcer in a cartel
- The economic theory of how bureaucracies operate.

11.1 THE TROUBLESOME CONCEPT OF AMATEURISM

Much of the controversy surrounding college sports and the NCAA centers on the role of amateurism in college sports. In its otherwise critical report on the state of college sports, the Knight Commission claimed in 2001, "At one time . . . [a]mateurism was a cherished ideal. In such a context, it made sense to regard athletics as an educational undertaking. Young people were taught values ranging from fitness, cooperation, teamwork and perseverance to sportsmanship as moral endeavor."[4] Many of the regulations that colleges routinely place upon themselves—and just as routinely violate—stem from their acting as if they are upholding the notion that student-athletes are students first and athletes second. The idealized image of the past, however, is an illusion. Big-time college athletics long ago abandoned any such ideals, and the term "student-athlete" itself has a checkered history.

---

[3]See, for example, Richard Sheehan, *Keeping Score* (South Bend, I.N.: Diamond Press, 1996), pp. 70–74, 101, and 272–274.

[4]Knight Foundation Commission on Intercollegiate Athletics, *A Call to Action: Reconnecting College Sports and Higher Education,* John S. and James L. Knight Foundation, June 2001, p. 13.

A Brief History of Amateurism and "the Olympic Ideal"

Long after the Olympics themselves abandoned amateurism as a condition for competing, American colleges and universities remain wedded to the concept that their athletic teams should consist of students who engage in sports as a pastime rather than as a profession. Those who call for the "deprofessionalization" of college athletics often evoke the image of Olympic purity and sometimes explicitly urge colleges to "return to the Greek notion of amateur competition."[5] However, the historical record shows that the modern view of amateurism has less to do with the Greek Olympic ideal than with 19th-century British class divisions.

The Original Olympic Games   The Olympic Games were actually one of four sets of Greek athletic contests, the other three being the Pythian, Nemean, and Isthmian Games. The Olympics were first held in 776 B.C. and continued every four years to honor the Greek god Zeus. These athletic competitions had a deeper, more spiritual role in the lives of the ancient Greeks than sporting events have in the lives of people today. Athletic contests were an integral part of religious festivals, not a sideshow like the modern Thanksgiving Day football game or the Fourth of July doubleheader. The ancient Olympic Games came about "because Olympia was already an established sacred site, not the other way round."[6]

In the worldview of the ancient Greeks, people could rise above the limits of their mortality by defying death and performing heroic deeds in war. When they had no war to fight, the Greeks replaced the battlefield with the athletic field. In their struggles against one another and against adversity, the participants came to resemble the gods they worshipped. Indeed, the word *athlete* comes from the Greek word *athlos,* which means "conflict," or "struggle." Initially, the rewards for success at the Games were crowns of olive sprigs. This practice (which was the original reward even when the modern Olympic Games were revived) was supposed to symbolize the pure motives of the competitors, who sought only the joy and glory of competition as their reward.

---

[5]The University of Colorado's president, Gordon Gee, quoted in Shannon Brownlee and Nancy Linnon, "The Myth of the Student-Athlete," *U.S. News and World Report,* January 8, 1990, p. 50 (from Lexis-Nexis). See also Welch Suggs, "The Demise of the 'Amateur Ideal,'" *Chronicle of Higher Education,* October 29, 1999, pp. A75–A76. The earliest known reference to an athletic contest was the funeral games that Achilles staged for his friend Patroclus in *The Iliad.*

[6]Quotation taken from Moses Finley and H. W. Pleket, *The Olympic Games: The First Thousand Years* (New York: Viking Press, 1976), p. 15. The other games honored Apollo, Herakles, and Poseidon. See Finley and Pleket, *The Olympic Games* (1976), pp. 23–25; Lynn Poole and Gray Poole, *History of Ancient Greek Olympic Games* (New York: Ivan Obolensky, Inc, 1963); B. Kidd, "The Myth of the Ancient Games," in *Five Ring Circus: Money, Power and Politics at the Olympic Games,* ed. by Alan Tomlinson and Garry Whannel (London: Pluto Press, 1984), p. 73; Francis Dealy, *Win at Any Cost: The Sell Out of College Athletics* (New York: Birch Lane Press, 1990), pp. 31–32 and 60; and Lawrence Hatab, "The Greeks and the Meaning of Athletics," in *Rethinking College Athletics,* ed. by Judith Andre and David James (Philadelphia: Temple University Press, 1991), pp. 32–35.

Even then, however, the symbol of amateurism had little to do with reality. The practice of awarding an olive crown stems from the same legend that surrounds the origins of the Games. It states that in order to win the hand of the daughter of King Oenomaus and hence inherit the kingdom, Pelops, a young Greek hero, first had to beat Oenomaus in a chariot race. Having won the race—and in the process killing the king—by sabotaging his chariot, Pelops wished to dispel the impression that he sought personal gain. He thus turned down the gold that was part of his prize for winning the race and asked instead to mark his victory with a crown made of a branch from a wild olive tree.

Following in this tradition, the olive crown given to the winners of the Olympic Games masked an array of greater rewards. Those selected to compete in the Games were regarded as heroes in their home cities. Honors, favorable marriages, and cash awaited them, especially if they returned victorious. According to Plutarch, Athenian winners at the Olympic Games were awarded 500 drachmai by their grateful city as early as 600 B.C. An Athenian inscription from the fifth century B.C. notes that Athens rewarded citizens who won an Olympic event with a free meal every day for the rest of their lives.[7] As a result of the ever-increasing prizes for victors at the Games, participants became increasingly professional, training full time for the Games. They also began to specialize in certain events, further detaching the Games from their original connection to warfare.[8] After the Romans conquered Greece in the second century B.C., taking over their customs in the process, the Games turned into flagrant competitions between professional athletes, and they slowly degenerated until Christian Emperor Theodosius stopped them in A.D. 393, when he banned all pagan practices.[9]

The British Ethic and the Rise of the Modern Olympics   By the 19th century, the Olympic Games of ancient Greece had been forgotten by all but a few historians and archaeologists. However, as the British came to dominate the economics, politics, and culture of Europe, their particular brand of "muscular Christianity" assumed increasing importance in the minds of friends and foes alike. The British, more than any country, took Juvenal's claim *mens sana in copore sano* ("a sound mind in a sound body") to heart. The Duke of Wellington found a practical application of this admonition when he attributed his victory over Napoleon at Waterloo to the sports his soldiers played at British public schools.[10]

---

[7]Finley and Pleket, *The Olympic Games* (1976), pp. 77–78; and University of Pennsylvania Museum of Anthropology and Archeology, "The Real Story of the Ancient Olympic Games," at http://www.upenn.edu/museum/Olympics/olympicathletes.html, 1996.

[8]Finley and Pleket, *The Olympic Games* (1976), pp. 70–71; Dealy, *Win at Any Cost* (1990), p. 60; and Hatab, "The Greeks and the Meaning of Athletics" (1991), pp. 31–35.

[9]Hatab, "The Greeks and the Meaning of Athletics" (1991), p. 35; Richard Mandell, *The Nazi Olympics* (New York: Ballantine Books, 1972), pp. 4–5; Poole and Poole, *History of Ancient Greek Olympic Games* (1963), pp. 24–25 and 33; and Kidd, "The Myth of the Ancient Games" (1984), pp. 72–80.

[10]"The Battle of Waterloo was won on the playing fields of Eton." See Mandell, *The Nazi Olympics* (1972), pp. 8–9.

For the rest of Europe, the impetus to develop sports programs seems to have sprung from defeat on the battlefield. Humiliated by Napoleon, the German states found a way to express their national sentiments and to combat the popular perception that they were physically inferior to the French through a mass gymnastics program known as the *Turnverein,* or Turner Movement.[11]

When the newly formed German nation turned the tables on the French in the Franco-Prussian War of 1870–71, the French sought a model for national revival. A wealthy young Frenchman named Pierre de Coubertin looked to England to find a way to restore French youth to the moral and physical vigor associated with the days of Napoleonic glory. Two particular items captured de Coubertin's attention: the British educational system and its emphasis on athletics (probably a result of his lifelong fascination with the book *Tom Brown's School Days*) and the "Wenlock Olympic Games," a festival staged in the town of Wenlock by a physician and fitness advocate named William P. Brookes.

De Coubertin's 1892 proposal to revive the "Olympic" Games thus stems from an attempt to shame and inspire French youth to follow the example of superior athletes from elsewhere in the world, especially from England and the United States. In fact, de Coubertin's choice of the name "Olympic Games" was a mix of public relations gimmickry and his happening upon Dr. Brookes and his festival. De Coubertin found the name of Brookes's contest "more festive and potentially inspiring than any other at hand."[12]

De Coubertin's aristocratic upbringing, his indifference to the reality of the original Olympic Games, and his worship of the English system of education explain the central part that amateurism plays in the modern Olympic ideal. Since the English schools that de Coubertin visited drew from the upper strata of British society, when he began to develop the foundation for the Olympic Games, he focused largely on attitudes held by the British upper class. As the next section describes, however, the British aristocracy was beginning to feel threatened by and to react to the encroachments made by working-class athletes on the "gentlemen's" sporting world.

11.2 AMATEURISM, PROFITS, AND THE NCAA

This section shows how the concept of amateurism is applied to the contemporary American university, revealing the dual nature of many restrictions placed on the collegiate athlete. Depending on one's viewpoint, the restrictions can be seen as either a moral stance in favor of academic ideals or as an exercise of monopsony power. The discussion builds upon the monopsony model described

---

[11]Mandell, *The Nazi Olympics* (1972), pp. 12–13. Mass gymnastics survive to this day, as in the Czech *Sokol* movement.

[12]Mandell, *The Nazi Olympics* (1972), pp. 12–24; Alan Tomlinson, "De Coubertin and the Modern Olympics," in *Five Ring Circus: Money, Power and Politics at the Olympic Games,* ed. by Alan Tomlinson and Garry Whannel (London: Pluto Press, 1984), pp. 88–90; and David Young, *The Modern Olympics: A Struggle for Revival* (Baltimore: Johns Hopkins University Press, 1996), pp. 24–80.

earlier and provides further insights into the relationship between marginal and average costs.

Chapter 2 showed that organized sports first took root among the well-to-do in the United States and England, spreading to other nations as they developed economically. As it expanded geographically, sports also expanded economically, coming within reach of the working class in the United States and England as the benefits of industrialization spread across all segments of these societies. The upper classes viewed the increasing participation—and then dominance—by the working-class teams with alarm. They felt that losing to teams drawn from "lesser" classes upset the natural order of society. In his classic *Theory of the Leisure Class*, Thorstein Veblen singled out sports as one of the "occupations" of a leisure class that studiously abstained from productive behavior. Their defeat at the hands of their social inferiors set dangerous social and political precedents, much as the competition between all-black and all-white teams would in generations to come.[13]

The responses of the upper classes to this challenge varied. Harvard and Yale responded to losses in rowing competitions against "lesser" colleges—such as Massachusetts Agricultural College (later renamed the University of Massachusetts)—by withdrawing from intercollegiate competition in 1875. This effectively ended crew's two-decade dominance of intercollegiate athletics in the United States.[14]

Crew teams in England—where Oxford and Cambridge Universities had been competing since 1829—took a more proactive approach to restricting competition by lower classes.[15] The British Rowing Association restricted competition to amateurs and defined an "amateur" as one who had never been "by trade or employment for wages a mechanic, artisan, or labourer or engaged in any menial duty."[16] This definition diverged dramatically from the notion held by the ancient Greeks, for whom "professional . . . meant a man who received proper training and devoted himself more or less full-time to an activity."[17] It also effectively excluded all competitors who were not independently wealthy.

---

[13]William Baker, *Sports in the Western World* (Totowa, N.J.: Rowman&Littlefield, 1982), p. 125; Robert Burk, *Never Just a Game: Players, Owners, and American Baseball to 1920* (Chapel Hill: University of North Carolina Press, 1994); and Thorstein Veblen, *Theory of the Leisure Class* (New York: The Viking Press, 1967), particularly Chapter 3, "Conspicuous Leisure."

[14]Ronald Smith, *Sports and Freedom: The Rise of Big-Time College Athletics* (New York: Oxford University Press, 1988), pp. 38–51.

[15]Allen Guttman, "The Anomaly of Intercollegiate Athletics," in *Rethinking College Athletics*, ed. by Judith Andre and David James (Philadelphia: Temple University Press, 1991), p. 18; and Ronald Smith, *Sports and Freedom* (1988), pp. 26–29.

[16]Quoted in Dealy, *Win at Any Cost* (1990), p. 60; and Smith, *Sports and Freedom* (1988), p. 166. Baker, *Sports in the Western World* (1982), p. 125, cites similar attitudes in the British Football Association. The class snobbery and ethnic prejudice that accompanied the code of amateurism is eloquently expressed in the 1981 film *Chariots of Fire*.

[17]Finley and Pleket, *The Olympic Games* (1976), p. 71.

The Code of Amateurism: Academic Ideals or Monopsony Power?

The British attitudes toward education and athletics took easy root in American universities, since "[n]ot only was the structure of educational instruction patterned after the English but the form of collegiate living, the collegiate way[,] was borrowed from the English."[18] Central to the "collegiate way" was a preoccupation with building the character of the students. The emphasis on character, which initially took the form of rigidly enforced religious devotions, often competed with intellectual concerns for primacy in American colleges.

While American society steadily moved away from strict religious adherence, colleges' preoccupation with character did not cease but was slowly replaced by the character-building force of athletics, epitomized in the 1940 film *Knute Rockne—All American*, a semibiographical film about the man who, as football coach at Notre Dame from 1918–31 first brought the team to prominance. In the film, Rockne proclaims, "We [coaches] believe the finest work of man is building the character of man. We have tried to build courage and initiative, tolerance and persistence—without which the most educated brain in the head of man is not worth very much."[19]

Amateurism today is enshrined in the NCAA manual, which states:

> Student athletes shall be amateurs in an intercollegiate sport, and their participation should be motivated primarily by education and the physical, mental, and social benefits to be derived. Student participation in intercollegiate athletics is an avocation, and student-athletes should be protected from exploitation by professional and commercial enterprises.[20]

The manual goes on to define what aid a college athlete may receive:

> A grant-in-aid administered by an educational institution is not considered to be pay or the promise of pay for athletics skill provided it does not exceed the financial aid limitations set by the association's membership.[21]

The NCAA itself has found, however, that a full athletic scholarship fails to cover the full cost of attending college. Athletic scholarships are limited to tuition, room and board, and necessary expenses such as required textbooks. Once incidentals, such as trips home—which the NCAA does not allow schools to finance—are added up, the NCAA has concluded that students fall short by as much as $2,400 per year. Minority athletes, who are more likely to come from impoverished households and to play in sports that generate large revenue streams for their schools, are hit particularly hard. One NCAA study estimated

---

[18]Smith, *Sports and Freedom* (1988), p. 11.

[19]Quoted in Murray Sperber, *Onward to Victory: The Crises that Shaped College Sports* (New York: Henry Holt and Co., 1998), p. 18. Sperber makes an intriguing case for claiming that this movie is the most significant American film of the 20th century.

[20]NCAA, *1997–1998 NCAA—Division I Manual* (Indianapolis: NCAA, 1997), p. 5.

[21]NCAA, *Division I Manual* (1997), p. 69.

that even full scholarships leave black football and basketball players with an average of $25 or less each month for personal expenses.[22]

These restrictions—like much of the NCAA's legislation surrounding student-athletes—can be viewed in two fundamentally different ways. On the one hand, the NCAA can be seen as vigorously defending the academic mission of the university. According to this view, students who participate in athletics should not receive any privileges not accorded to the general student body.

On the other hand, it's possible to conclude that the NCAA—meaning the member schools that make up the NCAA—has subverted the market for athletic talent. Colleges have strict limits on what they can pay to attract a star quarterback or point guard. This restriction has led some to conclude that the NCAA is effectively acting like the enforcer in a cartel.[23] An enforcer can help a cartel to avert prisoner's dilemma problems like the one discussed in Chapter 4, in which some colleges overturned TV restrictions that had proved highly profitable for all colleges in favor of a less restrictive—and less profitable—arrangement. Table 11.1 shows that the same forces could lead colleges to compete for athletes by offering to pay them their market value, an action that some observers forcefully advocate.[24]

Table 11.1 shows a simplified version of the problem facing colleges that want to win but do not want to break the bank doing so. Both schools—Darwin and Huxley—are evenly matched if neither spends money to attract athletes. Each school realizes, however, that it can dominate the other by spending heavily on its athletes. Each school also realizes that it cannot compete with the other school if it fails to match that school's spending. Both schools wind up spending large sums of money to attract students (the upper-left payoff cell in Table 11.1), though they would be better off not spending so much money (the lower-right payoff cell).

An enforcer can help Darwin and Huxley avoid the prisoner's dilemma by enforcing cooperation. This is accomplished by monitoring the schools' behavior and punishing anyone who deviates from the strategy that maximizes the

---

[22]Dealy, *Win at Any Cost* (1990), pp. 102–103; Steve Rushin, "Inside the Moat," *Sports Illustrated*, March 3, 1997, p. 74; and Sheehan, *Keeping Score* (1996), p. 291.

[23]This view is forcefully expressed in Robert W. Brown, "An Estimate of the Rent Generated by a Premium College Football Player," *Economic Inquiry*, v. 21, no. 4 (October 1993), pp. 671–684; Robert W. Brown, "Measuring Cartel Rents in the College Basketball Player Recruitment Market," *Applied Economics*, v. 26, no. 1 (January 1994), pp. 27–34; Walter Byers with Charles Hammer, *Unsportsmanlike Conduct: Exploiting College Athletes* (Ann Arbor: University of Michigan Press, 1995); Arthur Fleisher, Brian Goff, and Robert Tollison, *The National Collegiate Athletic Association: A Study in Cartel Behavior* (Chicago: University of Chicago Press, 1992); and Paul Lawrence, *Unsportsmanlike Conduct: The National Collegiate Athletic Association and the Business of College Football* (New York: Praeger, 1987). While we focus on the exploitation of athletes, the NCAA also depressed the pay of assistant coaches, for which it was successfully sued for $54.5 million (see, for example, Welch Suggs, "NCAA to Pay $55-Million to Settle Lawsuit by Assistant Coaches," *Chronicle of Higher Education*, March 19, 1999, p. A47) .

[24]See, for example, Gary S. Becker, "College Athletes Should Get Paid What They're Worth," *Business Week*, September 30, 1985, p. 38; and Rick Telander, *The Hundred Yard Lie: The Corruption of College Football and What We Can Do to Stop It* (New York: Simon and Schuster, 1989) .

Table 11.1

The Prisoner's Dilemma Leads Colleges to Spend Heavily

	Darwin Spends Heavily	*Darwin Doesn't Spend*
Huxley Spends Heavily	Schools recruit evenly High recruiting costs	Huxley dominates rivalry
Huxley Doesn't Spend	Darwin dominates rivalry	Schools recruit evenly Low recruiting costs

group's well-being. In a cartel such as OPEC, an enforcer can be a large oil producer that threatens to increase production and drive down prices if the members do not obey their quotas. In college athletics, the NCAA can limit TV appearances, cut scholarships, or impose the "death penalty" described in Chapter 4 to keep schools from stepping out of line.

The goal of the cartel in this case would be to act like a monopsonist and minimize expenditures on athletes. This occurs where marginal expenditure on labor equals the marginal benefit of the last worker employed. Figure 11.1 shows the impact of a typical monopsony. The employer reduces both the number of workers and the level of pay below the competitive level, and a deadweight loss occurs.

The owners of professional teams relied on the reserve clause to ensure their monopsony power, and college athletes face similar types of rules that

FIGURE 11.1

The Monopsonist Drives Down the Wage It Pays

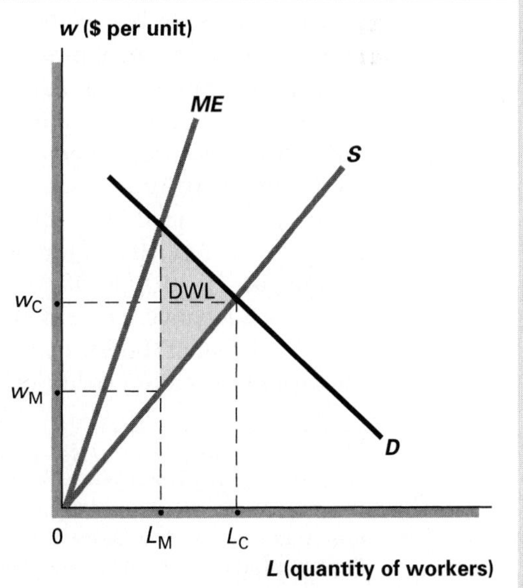

bind them to the colleges they initially commit to play for. NCAA regulations require that collegiate athletes who have made a written commitment to a school must sit out a year and lose a year of eligibility when they attempt to play for another school. For example, when basketball player Jonathan Haynes sought to transfer to Villanova University after spending only a few weeks at Temple University in the 1990–91 academic year, he had to sacrifice two years, losing his eligibility for the year that he had briefly attended Temple and for the next year as well.

Again, these restrictions can be viewed in a more benign light. Restrictions on movement may help prevent the excesses of the "tramp athlete" of the early 20th century. Like the baseball players who jumped contracts in the days before the reserve clause, the tramp athlete was a mercenary who traveled from school to school, looking for the best deal. Carl Johanson, who spent eight years playing football at Williams, Harvard, and Cornell, may have set the record for such activity in the late 19th century. Some players never even bothered to enroll, as was the case for seven players on the 1893 University of Michigan football team.[25] The restrictions may thus have reinforced the academic mission of the university as well as its monopsony power.

Pay for Play: The Grant-In-Aid

Today, when sports fans across the country anxiously scan the newspapers to find out what blue-chip prospect has accepted a scholarship to play for old State U., it is hard to imagine that athletic scholarships were ever a subject of controversy. As recently as the late 1950s, however, many colleges refused to offer such payments for nonacademic talent.

While some schools openly offered athletic scholarships as early as 1900 (when Penn State began the practice) and a great many more offered money under the table, such practices were largely frowned upon.[26] In 1929, the Carnegie Commission on Education reported with some horror that a "system of recruiting and subsidizing has grown up, under which boys are offered pecuniary and other inducements to enter a particular college." Prior to 1956, the NCAA officially forbade schools from making any distinction in the aid it offered athletes and nonathletes, though the Carnegie Commission reported that as many as three-fourths of the NCAA's members disobeyed the rules they helped promulgate.[27] Officially, if not in practice, all students drew from the same pool of funds, which were awarded on the basis of a uniform set of criteria.

The defeat of the Sanity Code (detailed in Chapter 4) spelled the end of the attempt to treat athletes like other students. Indeed, the Code's defeat stemmed

---

[25]Smith, *Sports and Freedom* (1988), p. 177; and Lee Sigelman, "It's Academic—or Is It? Admissions Standards and Big-Time College Football," *Social Science Quarterly*, v. 76, no. 2 (June 1995), p. 247.

[26]Smith, *Sports and Freedom* (1988), p. 171. In the 1880s Yale supposedly had a secret $100,000 fund to pay its athletes. See Dealy, *Win at Any Cost* (1990), p. 69; and Andrew Zimbalist, *Unpaid Professionals* (Princeton, N.J.: Princeton University Press, 1999), p. 7.

[27]Quote from Guttman, "The Anomaly of Intercollegiate Athletics" (1991), p. 20. See also Zimbalist, *Unpaid Professionals* (1999), p. 8.

largely from its attempts to formalize the limits on financial aid and on the rampant unofficial support given to athletes by alumni and other boosters. In 1956, the NCAA membership voted to allow schools to provide scholarships to athletes regardless of their financial need or academic merit. The justification for athletic grants-in-aid had a similar flavor to that for legalizing drugs or prostitution: "Everyone is doing it anyway," went the general argument, "so we may as well keep it all out in the open where we can regulate things." In fact, the Big 10 conference tried for several years to hold athletes and nonathletes to the same standard for financial aid. Other schools questioned the sincerity of the Big 10's stance and pointed out that, while the schools did not give outright athletic scholarships, they did provide ample compensation for questionable on-campus employment.[28]

What's In a Name? The Lot of the "Student-Athlete"

While the advent of grants-in-aid specifically targeted for athletes may have eliminated hypocrisy in recruiting, it also created a number of philosophical and legal problems for colleges. Philosophically, schools now had to reconcile themselves with their provision of financial assistance to students for participating in activities that often forced them to miss classes. In the 1999–2000 season, West Virginia University's basketball team sought to cope with an asbestos problem in its home arena by scheduling "home games" in Wheeling (75 miles away) and Charleston (155 miles away). Futhermore, the West Virginia coach wanted to practice at the arena the day before a game, meaning that the West Virginia team was on the road for 52 days from December 1999 through February 2000.[29]

More practically, schools had placed themselves in the position of being considered the athletes' employers. This relationship left colleges open to claims for workers' compensation insurance by athletes who were injured "on the job." NCAA Executive Director Walter Byers first coined the term "student-athlete" in an attempt to avoid such claims. In a Kafkaesque twist, athletes who wish to receive an athletic scholarship must now sign an agreement that explicitly rejects the notion that they are being paid for their performance as athletes.[30]

Measuring the Net Value of Athletes to Colleges

By depressing what they pay their athletes, colleges can generate considerable net revenues. These "rents" equal the difference between the marginal revenue product (*MRP*) of the athlete and the payment for tuition and fees. Robert

---

[28]See, for example, Byers, *Unsportsmanlike Conduct* (1995), pp. 67–72; and Sperber, *Onward to Victory* (1998), pp. 177–185 and 227–242.

[29]See Seth Davis, "A Blight on the Mountaineers," *Sports Illustrated,* December 6, 1999, pp. 80–81. See also Byers, *Unsportsmanlike Conduct* (1995), p. 103.

[30]Zimbalist, *Unpaid Professionals* (1999), p. 37; and Byers, *Unsportsmanlike Conduct* (1995), pp. 67–70.

Brown has measured the rents that a college generates as a result of attracting a premium athlete to its program.

Brown estimated the *MRP* of premium players by first assuming that a professional franchise drafts a player only if it regards that player as having the potential to be a professional. He then estimated how the number of players the college teams have sent to the professional draft (controlling for overall team quality) affects the teams' revenues.

Brown found that a player with the potential to play in the NFL brought a college football team between $539,000 and $646,000 per year, more than $2 million over a 4-year career. The premium for attracting a blue-chip basketball player was even greater, as he generated between $871,000 and $1 million annually.[31] In both cases, the colleges appear to profit handsomely from an annual commitment of perhaps $30,000 in scholarship money.

Dividing the Profits: The NCAA as an Efficient Cartel

As we showed in Chapter 4, the NCAA has also tried to use its power as an incidental cartel to act as a monopolist. Our simple model of monopoly behavior, however, is inadequate for analyzing how cartels behave. Unlike a monopoly, a cartel is not monolithic. In addition to determining what level of output maximizes profit, a cartel must allocate output and profit among its members. To see how a cartel operates, consider a cartel with only two members (the general conclusions hold for a cartel of any size).

The problem facing a cartel with two members is identical to the problem facing a monopoly that must decide how to allocate its output between two plants. If the plants are identical in every way, the decision is easy: just allow each plant to produce half the output. This corresponds to an equal division of the monopoly profit between the two members of the cartel.

Generally, however, cartels consist of firms that are not identical. Figure 11.2 shows the marginal cost curves for two heterogeneous firms, A and B. Since the marginal cost curve for Firm A lies below that for Firm B, it is cheaper for Firm A to increase its output a little bit than it is for Firm B if both firms are producing the same level of output. Given the marginal cost curves for the individual firms, we can construct the marginal cost curve for the monopoly by computing the horizontal sum, just as we computed the market demand curve from individual demand curves in Chapter 2. At very low levels of output, the joint marginal cost curve corresponds to the marginal cost curve for Firm A alone (MC_A), since Firm B can produce nothing at such low marginal cost. Until Firm A's output reaches Q_1, the cartel as a whole can increase output most cheaply by letting Firm A produce everything. When Firm A reaches output level Q_1, the cost of increasing its output by one unit is the same as Firm B's cost

---

[31]Brown, "An Estimate of the Rent Generated by a Premium College Football Player" (1993), p. 679; and Brown, "Measuring Cartel Rents in the College Basketball Recruitment Market" (1994), p. 32. Brown's actual estimation is more complex than shown here.

FIGURE 11.2

The Cartel's *MC* Curve Is the Horizontal Sum of the Individual *MC* Curves

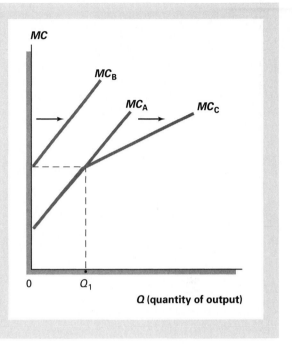

for producing its first unit of output. At this point, it pays for both firms to produce, and the marginal cost curve of the cartel (MC_C) is the horizontal sum of the individual firms' curves.

If the two firms act like a single firm, then they face a single market demand curve. This effectively says that consumers do not care whether they make their purchases from Firm A or Firm B. As a result, the two firms also face a common marginal revenue curve, as seen in Figure 11.3.

The optimal level of output for the cartel occurs where the cartel's marginal cost curve (MC_C) meets the marginal revenue curve (MR). The overall output of the cartel is thus Q_C^*, where $MR^* = MC_C^*$. The division of output that maximizes overall profit allocates production according to the individual firms' marginal costs so that $MC_A = MC_B = MR^*$. In Figure 11.3, this occurs at Q_A^* for Firm A and Q_B^* for Firm B. Because the marginal cost curve for the cartel is the horizontal sum of the individual marginal cost curves, $Q_A^* + Q_B^* = Q_C^*$.

To see why this division of output maximizes the overall profit of the cartel, consider any other allocation, for example, one that allocates less output to Firm A and more to Firm B, as seen in Figure 11.4. At the allocation (Q'_A, Q'_B), $MC_A < MR^*$ and $MC_B > MR^*$. This means that if the cartel reduces its output at Firm B by one unit, it will reduce its costs by more than its revenue. Similarly, if it increases its output at Firm A by one unit, it will add more to revenue than it does to costs. The cartel can thus increase its profits by reallocating its output from Firm B to Firm A. It will continue to reallocate output until it can no longer increase its profits by doing so. This occurs where $MC_A = MC_B = MR^*$.

FIGURE 11.3

Optimal Division of Output by a Cartel

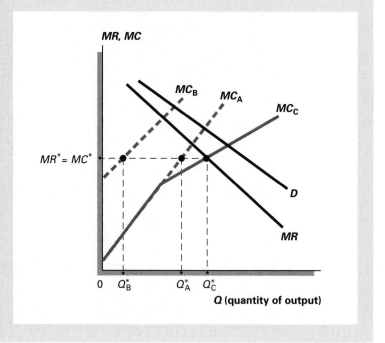

FIGURE 11.4

Reallocating Output Means Firm A Produces Too Much and Firm B Produces Too Little

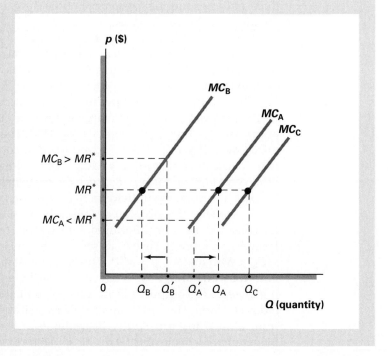

A standard cartel therefore allocates the lion's share of output and profit to its most efficient members. In this case, it would reward colleges that generate the greatest net revenue. Colleges cannot allocate resources quite this easily. Athletic conferences and the NCAA itself have traditionally required that schools share their revenues with less profitable members. The need to share revenues means that the NCAA and collegiate conferences may more closely resemble clubs than cartels. Recall that, according to the theory of clubs, a league determines its optimal size by weighing the additional revenue from admitting a new member against the cost of sharing revenue with an additional member. In effect, when a league adds a new member, it increases the size of its pie, but it also increases the number of slices into which the pie must be sliced. Leagues therefore seek out those members who contribute the most revenue and weed out members that are a drag on net revenues. This has led to several recent controversies in college sports.

College football's Division I-A level was created because the most profitable football programs wanted to stop sharing TV revenue with less profitable programs. The conflict lay behind the antitrust suit by the Universities of Georgia and Oklahoma discussed in Chapter 4. After losing the lawsuit, the NCAA recognized that it had to accommodate the major football powers. Before the lawsuit, the NCAA had sorted all athletic programs into Divisions I, II, and III according to the number of sports they sponsored and the size and number of athletic scholarships they offered. The NCAA now subdivides Division I into Division I-A and I-AA. While there are a number of criteria for Division I-A status, the most controversial criterion relates to a school's profitability rather than a school's size. Specifically, a Division I-A school must have an average home attendance at its football games of at least 15,000.[32]

Recently, Division I-A has subdivided still further. In the 1990s, the commissioners of the major football conferences and representatives of the major TV networks created the Bowl Championship Series (BCS). The avowed aim of the BCS is to bring order to the mass of postseason bowl games (totaling 28 in 2002–03) and to create a clear "national champion" collegiate football team. An additional effect of the consortium has been to restrict participation in the major bowl games largely to teams from the major football conferences. Since the BCS bowl games generate larger TV ratings and, as a result, are far more lucrative than the non–BCS bowl games, the effect has been to increase the disparity between the major football conferences and the lesser conferences. Table 11.2 shows the difference in net revenue that now exists between conferences whose champions automatically qualify for the BCS and conferences without guaranteed access to the BCS. The football programs in BCS conferences average net revenue of $8.25 million, while those in non–BCS Division I-A conferences average losses of $1.25 million. This has led a coalition of non–BCS schools to threaten an antitrust lawsuit against the BCS coalition.[33]

---

[32]Until 2003, schools had to sell an average of 17,000 tickets. The new requirement refers to actual attendance.

[33]See, for example, Alan Schmadtke, "Money Divides Colleges," *Orlando Sentinel*, February 9, 2003, online at http://www.orlandosentinel.com.

Table 11.2

Net Revenue from Football for BCS and Non–BCS Conferences

Conference	BCS Conference?	Average Net Revenue from Football
Atlantic Coast	Yes	$4.32 million
Big East	Yes	$2.80 million
Big 10	Yes	$12.80 million
Big 12	Yes	$8.30 million
Conference USA	No	−$260,878
Mid-American	No	−$1.20 million
Mountain West	No	−$52,166
Pacific 10	Yes	$6.84 million
Southeastern	Yes	$18.44 million
Sun Belt	No	−$904,959
Western Athletic	No	−$3.81 million

Source: Alan Schmadtke, *"Money Divides Colleges,"* Orlando Sentinel, February 9, 2003, online at http://www.orlandosentinel.com

The competition for profitable members has also led conferences to raid members from other conferences. Four schools from the Big East Conference are currently suing the University of Miami and Boston College for abandoning them to join the Atlantic Coast Conference (ACC).[34] The ACC invited Miami, Virginia Tech, and Boston College, which presently have the most powerful football programs in the Big East, in an attempt to raise its profile in, and profits from, football. Conveniently forgotten in the litigation are the facts that the Big East lured Virginia Tech and Rutgers away from the Atlantic 10 Conference several years earlier and that it has replaced the teams it has lost with teams lured away from other conferences: University of Cincinnati, DePaul University, University of Louisville, Marquette University, and University of South Florida.

11.3 COLLEGE AS AN INVESTMENT FOR THE STUDENT-ATHLETE

As explained in Chapter 8, the basic theory of human capital states that workers invest in skills in order to increase their future earnings. When workers invest in on-the-job training that will increase their earning power at competing employers, they "pay" for their training by receiving lower pay than they otherwise would. Therefore, looking solely at their wages or salaries understates the value of their total compensation.

---

[34]Connecticut, Pittsburgh, Rutgers, and West Virginia are the plaintiffs in the case. The judge dismissed a broader suit against the ACC. Virginia Tech was not named in the suit, perhaps because it was invited at the insistence of the governor of Virginia, who threatened to withhold funds from the University of Virginia if Virginia Tech did not receive an invitation to the ACC.

In this section, we examine the claim by Penn State's football coach, Joe Paterno, that, "An athlete who . . . graduates is overpaid,"[35] from a number of standpoints. Student-athletes who receive a degree see a significant increase in their lifetime earnings thanks to their participation in athletics regardless of whether they play professionally. Even if they do not graduate, student-athletes who go on to professional sports careers may be making such a significant investment in their skills as athletes that their scholarships overcompensate them. This section examines whether intercollegiate athletics is a good investment for athletes.

While in college, student-athletes may invest in their physical human capital and prepare for a career as a professional athlete, or they may invest in their intellectual human capital and work toward a college degree. If one judges success in either area by the likelihood of receiving a degree or making the professional ranks, then playing intercollegiate sports as a scholarship athlete does not appear to be a good investment.

The data in Table 11.3 suggest that professional athletics resembles the winner-take-all environment described in Chapter 8. The payoff to being a professional athlete is very high, but the odds of success are very low. Table 11.3 shows the number of freshman and transfer student-athletes (defined as those receiving an athletic scholarship) who entered Division I-A football and Division I basketball programs in 1992–93. Assuming that the number of openings at the professional level equals the number of students taken in the college drafts and that only students from Division I basketball and Division I-A football programs can have a professional career, fewer than 7 in 100 football players and about 4 in 100 basketball players end up having a professional career.[36]

A study by James Long and Steven Caudill contradicts the above reasoning and suggests that athletics may be a good investment even if it does not lead to

Table 11.3

College Athletes' Chance of Success in College Athletics

Sport	College Athletes[a]	Professional Openings[b]	Chance of Success
Football	2,290	155	0.067
Men's basketball	1,298	58	0.045
Women's basketball	1,211	56	0.046

[a]Number of freshmen, 1996, and one-fourth of the four-year total of transfers.
[b]Number of openings assumed to equal the product of the number of rounds in the professional draft times the number of teams in the league.
Source: Football: "Division I-A Graduation Rates" at http://ncaa.org. Basketball: "Division I-A Graduation Rates" at http://ncaa.org.

---

[35]Quoted in Sheehan, *Keeping Score* (1996), p. 286.

[36]If anything, these figures probably overstate the chances of a professional career, as teams draft more players than they have openings, and we are ignoring the use of foreign players.

a professional career. They find that men who participate in intercollegiate athletics earn more in later life than men who do not. (They find no statistically significant differential for women.) The study, however, is hampered by limitations imposed by the data. Data sets that identify whether a person participated in interscholastic or intercollegiate athletics and follow his or her earnings history are only recently available and are often imperfect. The data available to Long and Caudill did not permit them to control for either the sport the student played or the school attended. Their study thus treats squash players at Swarthmore and football players at Ohio State as one and the same.[37]

Because of the lack of appropriate data, both researchers and the popular media have generally not tried to measure future earnings and looked at the graduation rates of varsity athletes instead. Overall, the graduation rates of varsity athletes—and of football players and basketball players in particular—do not differ significantly from those of nonathletes and in some cases are marginally higher. However, this observation may be misleading. It does not, for example, account for the fact that, unlike other students, scholarship athletes rarely have to leave school because they cannot pay their tuition bills. Moreover, as noted in Chapter 8, athletes may leave college early for the (sometimes incorrectly) anticipated bonanza of a professional career. Equating the graduation rates of athletes and nonathletes also fails to account for the millions of dollars spent on academic support facilities for athletes, a service mandated by the NCAA. At the University of Michigan, for example, "the Student Athlete Support Program consists of a director, 6 full-time advisors, 3 assistant advisors, 70 tutors, 10 specialized writing instructors, and 15 proctors for supervised study sessions."[38] Finally, the aggregate statistic obscures the difference between major athletic powers and small, more recreational programs. Football players and basketball players at major programs are less likely to graduate than other athletes and are far less likely to graduate than the typical male undergraduate at their institution. Moreover, this gap is generally larger at the more successful programs.[39]

Table 11.4 shows the average graduation rates over the previous 4 years for the Division I-A colleges that ended the 2002–03 football season ranked in the top 25. Tables 11.5 and 11.6 show the average graduation rates for men's and

---

[37]James Long and Steven Caudill, "The Impact of Participation in Intercollegiate Athletics on Income and Graduation," *Review of Economics and Statistics*, v. 73, no. 3 (August 1991), pp. 525–531. See also Zimbalist, *Unpaid Professionals* (1999), p. 51.

[38]James J. Duderstadt, *Intercollegiate Athletics and the American University: A University President's Perspective* (Ann Arbor, University of Michigan Press, 2000), p. 199.

[39]See, for example, Dean Purdy, D. Stanley Eitzen, and Rick Hufnagel, "Are Athletes Also Students? The Educational Attainment of College Athletes," in *Sports and Higher Education*, ed. by Donald Chu, Jeffrey Segrave, and Beverly Becker (Champaign, I.L.: Human Kinetics Publishers, 1985), pp. 231–234; and Louis Amato, John Gandar, Irvin Tucker, and Richard Zuber, "Bowls Versus Playoffs: The Impact on Football Player Graduation Rates in the National Collegiate Athletic Association," *Economics of Education Review*, v. 15, no. 2 (April 1996), pp. 187–195. Amato et al. find that the graduation rate for players in Division I-A programs declines by 3 percent per bowl appearance. They find no statistically significant relationship for Division I-AA programs.

Table 11.4

Four-Year Average Graduation Rates of Freshmen for Schools with Football Teams Ranked in the Top 25 of Division I-A in 2002–03

Rank	School Name	Graduation Rate of Football Team %	Difference from Overall Rate %
1	Ohio State	41	−13
2	Miami	49	−11
3	Georgia	62	−2
4	USC	61	−10
5	Oklahoma	33	−14
6	Kansas State	57	+6
7	Texas	38	−26
8	Iowa	57	−4
9	Michigan	46	−25
10	Washington State	57	+1
11	N.C. State	47	−14
12	Boise State	48	+27
13	Maryland	50	−10
14	Virginia Tech	49	−20
15	Penn State	76	−2
16	Auburn	44	−19
17	Notre Dame	81	−13
18	Pittsburgh	35	−24
19	Marshall	51	+21
20	West Virginia	48	−3
21	Colorado	43	−20
22	TCU	56	−5
23	Florida State	49	−9
24	Florida	44	−24
25	Virginia	76	−14

Source: "Graduation Rates" online at http://www.ncaa.org.

women's basketball teams that made it to the "Sweet 16" (the regional semifinals) in the 2003 NCAA Division I basketball tournament.[40] The data show that most of the men's teams were more successful on the field or on the court than in the classroom.

Tables 11.4 and 11.5 show that 14 of the top 25 football programs and 10 of the top 16 basketball programs failed to graduate half of the players who had entered as freshmen within 6 years. Moreover, the athletes' graduation rates were almost uniformly lower than for the male student body as a whole.[41] In

---

[40]We say that a student graduated from college if he or she received a degree within six years of entering. For transfers, it means graduating within six years of the class that they would have entered with as freshmen.

[41]Only two basketball programs had higher graduation rates than for men as a whole, and only four football programs had higher graduation rates. For two of the football programs, the graduation rate for nonathletes was 30 percent or less.

Table 11.5

Four-Year Average Graduation Rates of Freshmen for Schools with Men's Basketball Teams in the "Sweet 16" in 2002–03

College	Men's Basketball Graduation Rate %	Difference from Overall Men's Graduation Rate %
University of Arizona	23	−27
Auburn University	43	−20
Butler University	92	+29
University of Connecticut	27	−38
Duke University	67	−25
Kansas University	73	+20
University of Kentucky	0	−52
Marquette University	64	−8
University of Maryland	27	−33
Michigan State University	56	−10
Notre Dame University	64	−30
University of Oklahoma	0	−47
University of Pittsburgh	0	−59
Syracuse University	40	−32
University of Texas	38	−26
University of Wisconsin	44	−29

Source: "Graduation Rates" online at http://www.ncaa.org

many cases, the differences were quite substantial. Six of the top 25 football programs had graduation rates that were at least 20 percentage points lower than for all men, and 12 of the top 16 basketball programs had graduation rates at least 20 points less than for all men.

Table 11.6 shows that female athletes generally graduated at rates comparable with, and sometimes superior, to those of female nonathletes. Seven of the "Sweet 16" women's programs had graduation rates of 75 percent or better for their players, while only 3 had graduation rates of 50 percent or less. Moreover, seven of the schools had graduation rates for their athletes that were at least as high as those for women as a whole. Of those with lower graduation rates, only three had graduation rates that were substantially below those of other women.

Studies cite a variety of reasons for the low graduation rates of football and men's basketball players, such as the fact that athletes are less prepared for college than their fellow students. A case study of students at Colorado State University from 1970 through 1980 showed that athletes there had lower SAT scores, lower grades, and lower high school class rank than the typical Colorado State student. The shortfall in preparation was particularly large for male athletes, black athletes, and members of the football and men's basketball teams. A more recent study of Division I-A football programs showed that similar gaps existed at many schools well into the 1990s: the average entering student had SAT scores 165 points higher than the average entering student with a football scholarship, and coaches who try to build a team that resembles the student body at large may damage their chances of winning by "unduly" restricting their recruiting, as teams with larger gaps in SAT scores generally had better records.[42]

Another more recent study claims that college athletes choose to not pursue their studies as the result of rationally maximizing their utility. It points out that it makes more sense for a student-athlete to focus on his prospects as a football player at Notre Dame, which sent 76 players to the professional ranks from 1979 through 1993, than at Bucknell, which sent only 1 player to the NFL during the same time period. In light of such differences in professional prospects, the authors of this study suggest that student-athletes make their decisions to attend a specific college—and to become part of a specific athletic program—as part of their broader career choices. It is therefore no more surprising for a football player from a traditional football power such as Tennessee to fail to make the NFL than it is for a premed student at a small liberal arts college such as Brandeis to fail to get into medical school. By this standard, it is remarkable that 85 percent of Notre Dame's football players received degrees within 5 years.[43]

Table 11.6

Four-Year Average Graduation Rates of Freshmen for Schools with Women's Basketball Teams in the "Sweet 16" in 2002–03

College	Women's Basketball Graduation Rate %	Difference from Overall Women's Graduation Rate %
Boston College	46	−39
University of Colorado	50	−28
University of Connecticut	67	−6
Duke University	87	−7
University of Georgia	6	90
Louisiana State University	82	+26
Louisiana Tech	47	−8
University of Minnesota	77	+23
University of New Mexico	73	+27
Notre Dame University	85	−10
Penn State University	71	−12
Purdue University	43	−22
University of Tennessee	69	+8
University of Texas	88	+14
Texas Tech University	86	+34
Villanova University	85	−1

Source: "Graduation Rates" online at http://www.ncaa.org

[42]See, for example, Purdy et al., "Are Athletes Also Students?" (1985), pp. 221–234; and Sigelman, "It's Academic—or Is It?" (1995), pp. 247–261.

[43]Lawrence DeBrock, Wallace Hendricks, and Roger Koenker, "The Economics of Persistence: Graduation Rates of Athletes as Labor Market Choice," *Journal of Human Resources*, v. 31, no. 3 (Summer 1996), pp. 513–539.

11.4 THE NCAA AND THE UNEASY COEXISTENCE OF ATHLETICS AND ACADEMIA

In this section, we do not view the NCAA as a profit-maximizing monopolist. Instead, we adopt a more benign interpretation of the NCAA and treat it as a regulatory agency, like the U.S. Food and Drug Administration or the Occupational Safety and Health Administration, with the goal of ensuring the safety of a product or the workplace. Problems, however, often accompany an agency's attempts to regulate an industry in which members seek to circumvent regulations. This section also discusses how the motives of colleges to build athletic programs—and to avoid or undermine regulation—stem from the same desire for prestige and recognition that motivated cities in Chapter 7.

As in baseball a generation or so earlier, the athletes themselves ran intercollegiate athletics during the late 19th century. Students operated sports clubs independent of—and sometimes in defiance of—faculty and administration. Indeed, most university administrations seemed disdainful at best toward the growing popularity of football among their students. In refusing to allow a group of students to travel to Ann Arbor to play a football game at the University of Michigan in 1873, Cornell President Andrew D. White proclaimed, "I will not permit thirty men to travel four hundred miles to agitate a bag of wind."[44] The very size of a football squad may have been determined by such hostility, as the Yale Football Association pushed for team size to be limited to 11 players because it feared that the faculty would oppose allowing a larger group of students to leave campus for away games.[45] While the informal organization of sport in America resembled its British antecedents, differences soon appeared between the British and American models of intercollegiate sport, which reflected the differing social milieux in which the sports took place. Students at the major British universities "were gentlemen first and students and athletes only incidentally."[46] While aristocratic Englishmen felt they were above engaging in intense competition on the playing fields, the more egalitarian Americans soon progressed from viewing intercollegiate athletics as an opportunity for friendly competition between schools to viewing them as sporting contests to be won.[47] The pressure to win increased when the control of college sports passed out of the hands of students and into those of faculty and administrators.

The shift of control began in the early 1880s, when many colleges established faculty oversight committees.[48] The rationale for such committees was concern over the growing violence in football.

Attitudes, however, soon changed. In the eyes of faculty, administrators, and alumni, teams came to represent the entire school. Just as a city could not be a

---

[44]Smith, *Sports and Freedom* (1988), p. 74

[45]Smith, *Sports and Freedom* (1988), pp. 73–77.

[46] Dealy, *Win at Any Cost* (1990), p. 60.

[47]Dealy, *Win at Any Cost* (1990), pp. 60–61; and Smith, *Sports and Freedom* (1988), p. 34.

[48]Princeton formed the first such committee in 1881. See Dealy, *Win at Any Cost* (1990), p. 68.

"world-class" city without a winning professional franchise, colleges came to believe that a winning team was part of a top-flight university. Schools, like cities, saw sports as a way to raise their profiles to the national level. Instead of attracting business, however, schools sought to attract students, prestige, and funds.[49]

Why Schools Promote Big-Time Athletic Programs

As early as the 1880s, colleges faced the same forces that cities did decades later when they began to bid against one another for sports franchises. At first, the two situations do not appear at all similar. Unlike professional franchises, intercollegiate athletic programs are inextricably linked to the universities that house them. While the NFL's Rams left southern California for a better deal in St. Louis, one could hardly imagine UCLA's football team making a similar move. Indeed, the NCAA discourages such moves even on an individual level, let alone a team level. As with cities, however, public goods and financial spillovers play a major role in motivating colleges to invest in big-time athletic programs. College teams give students a sense of identity and belonging that they do not seem to get in the classroom. Paul "Bear" Bryant, former football coach at the University of Alabama, justified the prominence of his program by claiming that "it was unlikely that 50,000 people would show up to watch an English professor give a final exam."[50]

The consumption of the public good may extend beyond the campus, as several studies have shown that colleges with "big-time" athletic departments attract more and better students.[51] Studies suggest, for example, that schools that belong to major athletic conferences attract freshmen with higher SAT scores, and that the more successful a school's football program is, the higher the scores rise. The reason for the higher SATs appears to be that success on the football field expands a school's overall applicant pool (at least for Division I-A programs), allowing the school to generate more revenue by admitting more students or to generate greater prestige by being more selective in its admissions process.[52]

The studies, however, rely on assumptions that may invalidate their conclusions. For example, when a study equates a big-time football program with one that belongs to a major athletic conference, it includes many of the nation's

---

[49]Dealy, *Win at Any Cost* (1990), pp. 51 and 68; Guttman, "The Anomaly of Intercollegiate Athletics" (1991), p. 21; and Lawrence, *Unsportsmanlike Conduct* (1987), pp. 6–7.

[50]Quoted in Zimbalist, *Unpaid Professionals* (1999), p. 223.

[51]For a particularly cynical view of "mission-driven athletics," see Murray Sperber, *Beer and Circus: How Big-Time College Sports Is Crippling Undergraduate Education* (New York: Henry Holt, 2000).

[52]See Melvin Borland, Brian Goff, and Robert Pulsinelli, "College Athletics: Financial Burden or Boon?" in *Advances in the Economics of Sport*, v. 1 (New York: JAI Press, 1992), p. 218; Robert McCormick and Maurice Tinsley, "Athletics Versus Academics? Evidence from SAT Scores," *Journal of Political Economy*, v. 95, no. 5 (October 1987), pp. 1103–1116; and Robert Murphy and Gregory Trandel, "The Relation Between a University's Football Record and the Size of Its Applicant Pool," *Economics of Education Review*, v. 13, no. 3 (September 1994), pp. 265–270.

premier state universities.[53] Finding that such programs attract more and better students may reflect the impact of the school's position in the state rather than the prominence of its football team.

A survey of 500 college-bound high school seniors in the spring of 2000 provides support to both proponents and opponents of college sports. The survey found that "73 percent of the respondents said their decision to attend a given college was not influenced by its position in the divisional hierarchy of the National Collegiate Athletic Association. And more than a third—37 percent—said they did not know whether their college of choice belonged to Division I, II, or III."[54] This result can be interpreted in several ways. On the one hand, the vast majority of students do not care about college sports. On the other hand, over one-fourth of college applicants admitted to taking the success of Duke's basketball team or Florida State's football team into account when deciding whether to attend those colleges. Implicitly, if 73 percent do not care, then 27 percent do care. Whether success on the field brings success in the admissions office remains an open question.

Even if it is possible to attribute successful recruiting to successful athletic departments, these same studies also have a dark side. They assert that the key to success lies in having a winning program in high-visibility sports such as football and men's basketball. Success in these sports is a **zero-sum game** in which one team's success is another team's failure. The expenditures the college must expend to establish and maintain a winning program may offset the benefits of a winning program to the student body as a whole.[55]

Identifying with a school's athletic program can extend beyond current or potential students to the institution's alumni and sometimes to the residents of a state or region or to members of a particular ethnic group. The devotion of alumni and other outsiders—in particular, those who can make sizable donations or allocate state funds—can cause schools to see athletics as a vital source of funds.

As explained in Chapter 7, state and local governments may choose to subsidize facilities that fail to make a profit if the spillovers into the overall economy lead the city as a whole to benefit. Like cities, schools may benefit from victorious athletic programs even if the programs do not show a profit themselves. The academic side of the university may realize spillovers from gifts proud alumni or state legislators make, prompted by a winning, if unprofitable, athletic program. The evidence regarding the impact of athletics on such giving, however, is decidedly mixed.

---

[53]This opens the door to the question of what constitutes a "major" conference. Robert McCormick and Maurice Tinsley, "Athletics and Academics: A Model of University Contributions," *Sportometics,* ed. by Brian Goff and Robert Tollison (College Station: Texas A&M University Press, 1990), pp. 193–204, used the Atlantic Coast, Southeastern, Southwest, Big 10, Big 8, and Pacific 10 conferences.

[54]Welch Suggs, "In Choosing Colleges, Students Give Little Weight to the Quality of Sports Teams, Poll Finds," *Chronicle of Higher Education,* March 14, 2001.

[55]See Borland et al., "College Athletics: Financial Burden or Boon?" (1992), pp. 218 and 227–230; and McCormick and Tinsley, "Athletics Versus Academics?" (1987), pp. 1103–1116.

Most studies of alumni refer to specific schools, which are difficult to generalize to different schools at different times. Moreover, the case studies provide contradictory evidence. Studies of Clemson and Mississippi State showed that successful athletic teams lead to greater alumni giving, but a case study of Washington State and a broader study by the Council for Financial Aid to Education showed that athletic performance has no significant impact. Moreover, a recent study commissioned by the NCAA found no statistically significant relationship between either a school's expenditure on its football program or the success its football program enjoyed and the amount of alumni giving.[56]

While studies fail to agree on the impact of athletic success on alumni donations in general, they have found an unambiguously positive impact on alumni donations to the athletic department itself. Numerous studies show that alumni donations to athletic departments and booster clubs rise with performance. Moreover, some studies find evidence that donations to the academic and athletic sides of the university are positively correlated. However, schools that depend on athletic success to bring alumni donations are under continual pressure to field winning teams, which brings the need to spend money to ensure athletic success. Schools must therefore spend money in order to make money, and these increasing costs may offset the benefits of the additional donations.[57]

Administrators Who Embraced Athletics—and One Who Did Not

Like big-city mayors who have tried to use professional franchises as engines for economic growth, many college administrators have embraced athletics as a way to elevate the status and financial standing of their universities. One such administrator, John Hannah, became president of Michigan State College (previously Michigan Agricultural College) in 1941, when it was a primarily agricultural and technical college with 6,000 students and a budget of $4 million. By the time Hannah retired in 1969, his school, now Michigan State University, had become a major research university with 40,000 students and a yearly budget of $100 million.

Hannah transformed Michigan State by first building it into a football power. In 1949, he maneuvered Michigan State into the Big 10 Athletic

---

[56]Robert E. Litan, Jonathan M. Orszag, and Peter R. Orszag, "The Empirical Effects of Collegiate Athletics: An Interim Report," Report Commissioned by the National Collegiate Athletic Association, August 2003.

[57]See, for example, Paul Grimes and George Chressanthis, "The Role of Intercollegiate Sports and NCAA Sanctions in Alumni Contributions," *American Journal of Economics and Sociology*, v. 53, no. 1 (January 1994), pp. 27–40; Guttman, "The Anomaly of Intercollegiate Athletics" (1991), p. 22; McCormick and Tinsley, "Athletics and Academics" (1990); Murray Sperber, *College Sports Inc.* (New York: Henry Holt and Co., 1990), pp. 70–81; Shulman and Bowen, *The Game of Life* (2001), pp. 220–226; Brownlee and Linnon, "The Myth of the Student-Athlete" (1990); Cletus C. Coughlin and O. Homer Erekson, "An Examination of Contributions to Support Intercollegiate Athletics," *Southern Economic Journal*, v. 50, no. 1 (July 1984), pp. 180–195; and Lee Sigelman and Samuel Bookheimer, "Is It Whether You Win or Lose? Monetary Contributions to Big-Time College Athletic Programs," *Social Science Quarterly*, v. 64, no. 2 (June 1983), pp. 347–359.

Conference (over the objections of the University of Michigan, which foresaw competition on the gridiron and in the statehouse), filling the place left by the University of Chicago which had departed the Big 10 a decade earlier. This transformation, however, came at a cost. The pressure to win pushed the university's coaching staff to cut corners in recruiting, leading to substantial penalties from the NCAA in 1953, 1964, and 1976.[58]

State universities were not the only schools to follow such a strategy. Before John Hannah began his work at Michigan State, Rufus von Kleinsmid sought to transform a small, Methodist school in Los Angeles called the University of Southern California (USC) into a major university while he was its president (1922–46). After earlier attempts at traditional fundraising had met with disappointing results, von Kleinsmid decided to build a successful athletic program and to link that success with the regional aspirations of newly affluent southern California. The new strategy succeeded where appeals to academic ideals failed, as USC's winning teams helped von Kleinsmid bring funding and renown to USC. Here, too, success came at a price: other schools accused it—frequently with reason—of sacrificing academic legitimacy for athletic primacy.[59]

Sometimes a school hitched its wagon to athletics for reasons beyond the ambitions of a single state or region. The University of Notre Dame used football to bring American Catholics—particularly in immigrant communities—into the American mainstream. *Life* magazine took the success of this strategy to an almost absurd extreme when it named Knute Rockne, the football coach most closely associated with Notre Dame's athletic success, as one of the three most important immigrants in U.S. history.[60]

Many schools found that athletic success did not translate into more generous funding. As the University of Oklahoma was enjoying an era of unprecedented success on the gridiron in the 1950s, including three consecutive unbeaten seasons from 1954 to 1956, its president unsuccessfully appealed to the state legislature to increase its allocation so that he could "build a university of which our football team can be proud."[61]

In 1906, James Angell discovered the danger of trying to deemphasize the role of athletics. As president of the University of Michigan, he managed to convince the presidents of the other schools in the Western Athletic Conference (later renamed the Big 10) to approve a set of measures that included limiting the football season to five games, limiting an athlete's eligibility to three years, and banning special facilities for athletes. Unfortunately for Angell, his proposals ran afoul of Fielding Yost, Michigan's athletic director. In 1908, Yost undercut Angell's efforts by convincing Michigan's board of regents to with-

---

[58]Beth J. Shapiro, "John Hannah and the Growth of Big-Time Intercollegiate Athletics at Michigan State University," *Journal of Sport History*, v. 10, no. 3 (Winter 1983), pp. 26–40; Byers, *Unsportsmanlike Conduct* (1995), pp. 41–45; and Sperber, *Onward to Victory* (1998), p. 364.

[59]John Thelin, *Games Colleges Play* (Baltimore: Johns Hopkins University Press, 1994), pp. 83–87.

[60]Thelin, *Games Colleges Play* (1994), p. 89; and Sperber, *Onward to Victory* (1998), p. 5.

[61]Quoted in Thelin, *Games Colleges Play* (1994), p. 115.

draw from the conference (and to play as an independent for the next 10 years) so that it could avoid the measures put in place by its own president.[62]

The Difficulty in Regulating College Sports

Shortly before he disbanded the football team at the University of Chicago in 1939, President Robert Hutchins suggested, "A college racing stable makes as much sense as college football. The jockey could carry the college colors; the students could cheer; the alumni could bet; and the horse wouldn't have to pass a history test."[63] Today, Dr. Hutchins's words seem almost innocent. In their desire to build or maintain winning programs, colleges have sometimes admitted marginal students and then gone to extraordinary lengths to keep them eligible.

The behavior of these schools resembles that of firms battling for market share. Firms have frequently turned to providing additional amenities when price competition has been suppressed by either regulation or cartel agreements. For example, prior to deregulation in the late 1970s, the airlines competed largely on the basis of punctuality, decor, and in-flight amenities. Unable to compete for athletes based on price, colleges have also used amenities as a lure. In the 1970s, the NCAA engaged in protracted negotiations with the University of Kentucky over "Wildcat Lodge," a mansion the university had converted into an athletic dormitory. The negotiations covered everything from the number of people to a bedroom (at least two) to the composition of bathroom faucets (no gold allowed). Eventually, "the NCAA forced the university to stop the cooked-to-order breakfasts and remove some of the $200,000 in furnishings, to bring the place more in line with the facilities in which the typical undergraduate lived."[64]

Schools have also tried to acquire winning teams by admitting talented athletes who do not meet their normal academic standards. In one extreme example from the early 1980s, more than 150 colleges pursued a star basketball player despite his having a combined (math plus verbal) SAT score of 470. His verbal score of 200 reflected his failure to answer a single question correctly.[65] In 2003, St. Bonaventure University was forced to withdraw from the Atlantic 10 postseason basketball tournament when it was revealed that the president of the university had approved the transfer of a basketball player who had not completed the requisite junior college courses.[66] In the wake of the ensuing scandal, the school's basketball coach, athletic director, and president were either dismissed or forced to resign, and the chairman of the board of trustees committed suicide.

Academic violations date to the very beginning of the intercollegiate competition. In the first intercollegiate football game, an 1869 match between Rutgers

---

[62]Byers, *Unsportsmanlike Conduct* (1995), pp. 37–38.

[63]Quoted in Sheehan, *Keeping Score* (1996), p. 261.

[64]Quoted in Alexander Wolff and Armen Keteyian, *Raw Recruits* (New York: Pocket Books, 1991), p. 107. See also Byers, *Unsportsmanlike Conduct* (1995), p. 101.

[65]Guttman, "The Anomaly of Intercollegiate Athletics" (1991), p. 22; and Zimbalist, *Unpaid Professionals* (1999).

[66]Instead of an Associate of Arts degree, the student had earned a certificate in welding.

and Princeton, the victorious Rutgers squad had the services of three students who were failing algebra and a fourth who was failing geometry.[67]

Admitting athletes who are academically unprepared brings with it the need to find ways to keep them eligible. Colleges have found a number of creative methods. A lawsuit brought in the early 1980s by Jan Kemp, an instructor in the Developmental Studies Program at the University of Georgia, revealed a veritable school within a school, in which students could "never pass a remedial course, never take a college-level course, and still maintain their playing eligibility for two years."[68] Georgia again found itself in hot water in 2003 when it was revealed that several basketball players had enrolled in a course that never met. The instructor in the phantom course was none other than the basketball coach's son.

Schools have also allowed students to maintain their eligibility—if not progress toward a degree—by "cherry-picking" dead-end courses such as golf, billiards, and slo-pitch softball. One all-American football player reportedly took summer courses in golf, music, and AIDS awareness, as well as a mass communications course in which every student in the class received a grade of either A or A − , to increase his grade point average.[69] Even legitimate courses have sometimes been compromised. During the 2003 season, another star football player passed a course in African American Studies without taking the midterm or final examination. Instead, he took two oral exams, an option not offered to the other students in the class.[70]

The many responses of schools to the attempt to suppress price competition has led the NCAA to issue a regulations manual that rivals the size of a major city's phone book. The 1997–98 manual for Division I schools alone is 482 pages long and consists of astonishingly detailed regulations. For example, it contains the following restriction on laundry labels (Rule Number 12.5.5.1):

> If an institution's uniform or any item of apparel worn by a student-athlete in competition contains washing instructions on the outside of the apparel on a patch that also includes the manufacturer's or distributor's logo or trademark, the entire patch must be contained within a four-sided geometrical figure (i.e., rectangle, square, parallelogram) that does not exceed $2^{1}/_{4}$ square inches.

To summarize, the NCAA, like any regulator, must deal with the fact that the institutions being regulated will go to great lengths to avoid regulations that limit their ability to maximize profits. As a result, the regulator may find itself bogged down in minutiae that seem to have nothing to do with its original reason for being.

---

[67]Zimbalist, *Unpaid Professionals* (1999), pp. 6–7 and 20; and Smith, *Sports and Freedom* (1988), pp. 30 and 71.

[68]Dealy, *Win at Any Cost* (1990), pp. 86–92.

[69]In "Black Eye for the Buckeyes," *Sports Illustrated*, June 16, 1999, the All-American football player denied receiving special treatment; and Zimbalist, *Unpaid Professionals* (1999), p. 35.

[70]Mike Freeman, "When Values Collide: Clarett Got Unusual Aid in Ohio State Class," *New York Times*, July 13, 2003, p. 8–1.

Academic Standards: Bulwarks of Integrity or Barriers to Entry?

The NCAA has attempted to prevent schools from jeopardizing their academic standards in pursuit of victory on the playing field by setting minimum academic standards for athletes. Again, however, these standards can be viewed in either of two ways: as an attempt by educators to maintain their academic integrity, or as an attempt by established athletic powers to erect an entry barrier that will prevent other schools from becoming competitive. Still others see the regulations as yet another barrier placed in the path of the black student-athlete. This section summarizes the NCAA's attempts to establish academic criteria for participating in intercollegiate athletics.

Attempts at Reform   As part of its attempt to reform college athletics in the early 1950s, the NCAA tried to require that athletes have the same academic credentials as the typical student at the schools they attended. The NCAA could not agree on a standard, however, until 1965, when it adopted the "1.600 Rule." This rule required that incoming freshmen who wished to participate in intercollegiate athletics have a predicted grade point average (GPA) of at least a C − (numerically a 1.6, hence the name of the rule). The NCAA predicted the GPA by comparing the athletes' class rank in high school and SAT scores with data from almost 41,000 students at 80 different colleges.

In 1971 the colleges in the Ivy League sought to have the NCAA tighten the provisions of the 1.600 Rule. They were upset that the rule was lower than the standard they had set for themselves, giving other schools an advantage in recruiting. Reopening the issue, however, did not bring the result the Ivy League desired. In 1973, athletic directors pushed through the "2.000 Rule." The name implied that students would be held to a higher grade standard. In fact, it was a significant dilution of the existing rules, as students simply had to earn a C+ average in any high school courses whatever. Many of the abuses cited earlier in this section, in which students were admitted to reputable schools despite glaring academic deficiencies, occurred in the 1970s and 1980s when the 2.000 Rule was in effect.

In an attempt to prevent academic scandals, such as those that arose in the early 1980s, the NCAA has formulated a series of reforms. The NCAA adopted the first of these, Proposition 48, in 1983 and began enforcing it in 1986. It set the pattern that has continued to this day.

Proposition 48 required that students earn a score of at least 700 out of a possible 1600 on their SATs (or 15 out of 36 on the ACT) and have a GPA of at least 2.0 in 11 core high school courses in order to receive an athletic grant-in-aid. The last provision was intended to prevent students from maintaining acceptable grades by taking courses with minimal academic merit. A subsequent revision allowed students who met one standard but not the other to be "partial qualifiers," receiving financial aid but unable to play or practice with the team for one year. The idea was to allow such students to establish themselves academically before engaging in athletics. Partial qualifiers also lost one year of eligibility.[71]

---

[71]Fleisher et al. *The NCAA* (1992), p. 61; Dealy, *Win at Any Cost* (1990), p. 115; and Zimbalist, *Unpaid Professionals* (1999), p. 30.

Some schools attempted to eliminate the partial-qualifier provision at the NCAA's 1989 convention. The result was Proposition 42, which, when amended at the 1990 convention, actually broadened the provision. Proposition 42 allowed a partial qualifier to be offered a scholarship from the school's general scholarship fund. The change allowed schools to circumvent the NCAA's limit on scholarships and to stockpile talented players.[72]

The NCAA again tried to toughen standards at its 1992 convention by approving Proposition 16. As later amended in 1995 and 1996, Proposition 16 created a sliding scale of SAT scores and grades, so a student could qualify with a 2.0 GPA and a 900 SAT or with a 2.5 GPA and a 600 SAT. The NCAA also raised the number of core courses from 11 to 13 and created a clearinghouse to evaluate the merit of the courses.

All of the propositions have generated controversy. In particular, opponents note the disproportionate impact of the rules on black athletes. They have charged that SAT tests are racially biased and that they reflect poor school systems rather than personal failings by the student. They conclude that any requirement that places weight on the SAT discriminates against black athletes.[73]

Proponents of the reforms regard them as a necessary counterweight to the emphasis on athletics. Sociologist and activist Harry Edwards has supported the proposals, claiming, "[B]lack parents, black educators, and the black community must insist that black children be taught and that they learn whatever subject matter is necessary to excel on diagnostic and all other skills tests."[74] Those in favor of reform note that, while Propositions 48, 42, and 16 disproportionately affected black athletes, graduation rates of black athletes have risen as a result of the new standards.[75]

In March 1999, the NCAA's ability to regulate academics was seriously threatened when U.S. District Judge Ronald Buckwalter ruled that Proposition 16 violated Title VI of the 1964 Civil Rights Act due to its disparate impact on black athletes. Although this ruling was later overturned by the Third Circuit Court of Appeals on a technicality, the NCAA recognized that a future challenge could upset its academic standards.[76]

In response to both the legal challenge to Proposition 16 and the concern over low graduation rates, the NCAA has passed the most sweeping changes

---

[72]Dealy, *Win at any Cost* (1990), pp. 120–121; and Zimbalist, *Unpaid Professionals* (1999), p. 29.

[73]See, for example, "What's Wrong with the NCAA's Test Core Requirements?" Fair Test: The National Center for Fair and Open Testing, at http://www.fairtest.org/facts/prop48.htm; College Board Online, "Students and Parents-SAT Information—Frequently Asked Questions. SAT Program—Is the SAT Fair? Aren't Minority Students at a Disadvantage?" at http://www.collegeboard.org/sat/html/students/mofaq013.html; James P. Smith and Finis Welch, "Black Economic Progress After Myrdal," *Journal of Economic Literature*, v. 27, no. 2 (June 1989), pp. 519–564.

[74]Simon, "Intercollegiate Athletics" (1991) p. 62.

[75]Anonymous, "March Madness" *The New Republic*, March 29, 1999, pp. 10–11; and David Goldfield, "Weaker NCAA Standards Won't Help Black Athletes," *Chronicle of Higher Education*, April 9, 1999, p. A64.

[76]"March Madness (1999) pp. 10–11; and Welch Suggs, "Fight Over NCAA Standards Reflects Long-Standing Dilemma, " *Chronicle of Higher Education*, April 9, 1999, pp. A48–A49.

to academic standards since Proposition 48. The latest standards, which went into effect August 1, 2003, place less emphasis on test scores and more emphasis on academic progress in college. The latest rules retain the sliding scale with two important changes. First, the number of required core courses increases from 13 to 14. More importantly, the role of the SAT has been reduced. Athletes can now be eligible to compete as freshmen with a cumulative SAT of 400 if they have a grade point average of at least 3.55. While it is easier to qualify as a freshman, it is now harder to maintain eligibility. Prior to this, students were able to maintain eligibility by finishing only 25 percent of the work needed to complete a degree after 2 years, 50 percent after 3 years, and 75 percent after 4 years. Now, students will have to have completed 40 percent of their work after 2 years, 60 percent after 3 years, and 80 percent after 4 years.

Academic Standards as a Barrier to Entry

As was the case for athletic scholarships, it is possible to view the restrictions put in place by the NCAA's reforms in one of two ways. Defenders of these standards, such as coach Joe Paterno of Penn State, fear that abolishing them would return colleges to the "win at all costs" atmosphere that characterized the 1970s and 1980s.[77] Former NCAA Commissioner Walter Byers went further and questioned the motives of the schools opposing standards. He believed that administrators of these schools did not feel that they could compete with the major athletic programs for athletes if their schools were held to the same academic standard as the established athletic powers.[78]

Some opponents of the eligibility requirements have accused the established football powers of erecting barriers to entry by other schools seeking to create powerful programs by denying schools the chance to admit superior athletes who cannot meet specific academic standards. Unable to pay students more and unable to admit weaker students, the less-established athletic programs find it difficult to break into the ring of successful programs, because sucessful programs would have an advantage recruiting athletes who meet the higher academic standards. In his study of competitive balance and eligibility requirements, E. Woodrow Eckard finds that, whatever their benefits, the restrictions on recruiting imposed by the NCAA have worsened competitive balance among the big-time football schools, with conference standings and national rankings becoming increasingly predictable.[79]

The use of entry barriers to reduce supply and maintain monopoly power occurs in many professional fields. Doctors, lawyers, accountants, and other professionals also benefit from rigorous accreditation standards. Accreditation requirements, for example, limit the number of law schools permitted to provide the necessary training, while the bar exams limit the number of law

---

[77]Joe Paterno, "Score on the SAT to Score on the Field," *Wall Street Journal*, March 16, 1999, p. A26.

[78]Byers, *Unsportsmanlike Conduct* (1995), pp. 73–74.

[79]E. Woodrow Eckard, "The NCAA Cartel and Competitive Balance in College Football," *Review of Industrial Organization*, v. 13, pp. 347–369.

school graduates who are permitted to practice the craft. Such standards may protect the public by winnowing out unqualified practitioners and ensuring that capable students receive adequate training. In so doing, however, they limit the degree of competition in the market and inflate the pay of workers already in the field.

11.5   THE FINANCES OF COLLEGE ATHLETICS

One of the raging controversies in intercollegiate athletics concerns whether athletic departments represent a profit center or a drain on college resources. On one level, the entire argument demonstrates the peculiar position of athletics. After all, universities seldom publicly debate the profitability of their departments of physics or economics, even though these departments play a central role in the school's academic mission. The debate over athletics, however, shows the discomfort that many feel with the role it plays in academe. At schools with unprofitable athletic departments, the faculty members often complain that athletics drain resources away from "more deserving" activities. At schools with highly profitable athletic departments, faculty members often complain that the profits show the misplaced values of the institution.

Do Colleges Make a Profit from Athletics?

Chapter 4 describes how the NCAA has acted like a cartel in maximizing the profits of its members, and earlier in this chapter we explained that a cartel allocates output and profits based on the efficiency of its members. In the case of the NCAA, this meant giving greatest TV access to the most popular football and men's basketball teams.

Tables 11.7a and 11.7b confirm the earlier findings, as they show that athletic departments with Division I-A programs are far more profitable than those with Division I-AA and Division II programs. On average, however, athletic departments are not self-sustaining. Division I-A, I-AA, and II schools all show losses without the infusion of institutional support. Even with the infusion of institutional funds, only Division I-A schools show a profit.

Table 11.8 shows that Division I-A athletic departments rely on football—and to a lesser extent—men's basketball to subsidize the remainder of their programs. Average profits at Division I-A football programs have doubled, from slightly over $2 million per school to almost $5 million since 1995. Over the same period, the profits of basketball programs at these schools have grown from slightly under $1.3 million to over $1.6 million. The average profit for all men's sports, however, is roughly equal to the profits of football alone, meaning that other men's sports have lost between $1.1 million and $1.6 million per year.

Women's sports have lost increasing sums. Despite the growing attention paid to women's basketball, it still accounts for roughly 25 percent of the total losses of women's sports, losing an average of almost three-quarters of a million dollars per school each year.

Table 11.7A

Profitability of Different Levels of Intercollegiate Athletics, 1995–2001*

	1995	1997	1999	2001
Division I-A	1,200	400	1,900	1,900
Division I-AA	−470	−740	−600	−1,190
Division II	−220	−470	−500	−440

*Measured in thousands of dollars. Includes institutional support.
Source: Daniel L. Fulks, *Revenues and Expenses of Divisions I and II Intercollegiate Athletics Programs: Financial Trends and Relationships—2001* (Indianapolis: NCAA, 2002). Online at http://www.ncaa.org.

Table 11.7B

Profitability of Different Levels of Intercollegiate Athletics, 1995–2001*

	1995	1997	1999	2001
Division I-A	−200	−800	0	−600
Division I-AA	−1,670	−1,960	−2,250	−3,390
Division II	−840	−950	−1,150	−1,300

*Measured in thousands of dollars. Excludes institutional support.
Source: Daniel L. Fulks, *Revenues and Expenses of Divisions I and II Intercollegiate Athletics Programs* (2002).

Table 11.8

The Profitability of Specific Athletic Programs at Division I-A Schools, 1995–2001*

Sport	1995	1997	1999	2001
Football	$2,313	$3,231	$3,736	$4,742
Men's Basketball	$1,291	$1,703	$1,570	$1,677
All Men's Sports	$2,511	$3,296	$3,896	$4,911
Women's Basketball	−$414	−$528	−$639	−$739
All Women's Sports	−$1,742	−$2,236	−$2,396	−$3,207

*Measured in thousands of dollars
Source: Daniel L. Fulks, *Revenues and Expenses of Divisions I and II Intercollegiate Athletics Programs* (2002).

When a school's football program runs into difficulty, its ability to fund other sports is jeopardized. The University of Colorado, for example, depends on the $23.7 million in net revenue from its football program to cover most of its $36.5 million athletic budget. Colorado is particularly dependent on football, as its men's basketball team loses over $1 million annually. When the University of Wisconsin's football program ran into financial trouble in the 1980s, the entire athletic program was thrown into chaos. Confronting multimillion-dollar deficits, it had to shut down several "minor" sports. More recently, the University of Minnesota faced a similar crisis. Facing the need to provide a $10 million subsidy to its athletic department, it radically reorganized its athletic department and dropped three sports.[80]

---

[80]Adam Thompson, "Colorado's Next Budget Closely Tied to Football," *Denver Post*, July 18, 2003, p. D-03; and Mary Jane Smetanka, "U Sports Make More Money, But Much More Is Needed," *Minneapolis Star-Tribune*, November 4, 2002, online at http://www.startribune.com.

Even highly successful programs seem to have trouble making ends meet. In 1999, the University of Michigan's athletic department, long regarded as a model program, with a tradition of athletic and financial success, reported a $2 million dollar loss. Nor did Kansas University's regular trips to the NCAA basketball tournament prevent it from facing deficits of $2.4 million over 4 years at the turn of the 21st century.[81]

Some observers are not impressed with such reports of losses. They claim that the deficits are artifacts of an accounting system that misclassifies costs and of an institutional structure that encourages unprofitable behavior. To a college administrator, costs reflect budget allocations, but to an economist, they reflect foregone opportunities. An athletic department may therefore run an official deficit without costing the institution any real resources. For example, colleges with excess capacity in their classrooms and dormitories face little opportunity cost of admitting another student on a full scholarship and may actually profit from admitting additional students on partial scholarships. However, colleges count scholarships as if they were paying for the student to attend college. Thus, a student-athlete on full scholarship at a school that charges $20,000 per year in tuition and room and board but with spare classroom and dormitory space counts that scholarship as a $20,000 cost. However, the otherwise-empty dormitory room costs the college relatively little. Having an extra student in a class may inconvenience the instructor somewhat, but it too imposes little cost on the school. The college experiences a cost only if the scholarship athlete displaces a student who would pay more.[82]

Do Athletic Departments Try to Maximize Profits?

Some economists posit that organizations such as collegiate athletic departments and colleges in general do not even try to maximize profits because they do not face the same motivations as firms in the private sector. In Chapters 2 and 3, we assumed that firms maximize profit:

$$\pi = TR - TC.$$

A firm maximizes π in the above equation by choosing the appropriate mix of inputs so that it can produce any level of output as efficiently as possible and by choosing the level of output that maximizes the difference between total revenue (TR) and total cost (TC).

Athletic departments have no reason to maximize profits, since neither they nor anyone else in the not-for-profit university has a residual claim on the difference between revenues and costs.[83] The behavior of athletic departments more

---

[81]Fred Girard, "Deficit Pinches U-M Sports," *Detroit News*, July 14, 1999, at http://detnews.com/1999/college/9907/14/07140181.htm; and Tim Griffin, "Big 12's Budget Balancing Act," *San Antonio Express-News*, June 6, 2001, online at http://news.mysanantonio.com.

[82]See Borland et al., "College Athletics: Financial Burden or Boon?" (1992), p. 218; and Fleisher et al., *The NCAA* (1992), pp. 83ff. This ignores the social cost of denying an academically gifted student a scholarship so that an athletically gifted student can receive one.

[83]See Borland et al., "College Athletics: Financial Burden or Boon?" (1992), p. 217; and Fleisher et al., *The NCAA* (1992), pp. 86–87. Fort and Quirk, "The College Football Industry" (1999), pp. 11–26, assume that athletic departments maximize profit, but this seems more appropriate for a specific sport than for an entire department.

closely resembles that of bureaucracies than that of profit-maximizing firms. William Niskanen described the behavior of bureaucracies and bureaucrats in public sector agencies; his theories apply equally well to the academic sector.[84]

Niskanen claims that, because bureaucrats do not maximize profits, they are insulated from the discipline of the marketplace. Bureaucrats do not sell their product directly to the public. Instead, they provide a product to a sponsoring agency in exchange for a lump sum budget allocation. Niskanen envisions a bilateral monopoly in which the bureau depends on the sponsor for its budget but the sponsor must get what it wants from the bureau. The bureaucrat often has the upper hand in the ensuing bargaining over resources for several reasons. First, as noted above, bureaucracies typically do not produce a product that can be easily subdivided by the sponsor or consumers. The bureaucracy thus faces an all-or-nothing demand curve such as that described in Chapter 6. Second, the sponsoring agency typically does not spend its own resources. Instead, it provides funds out of compulsory contributions from others. Finally, the sponsors are themselves often part of a self-perpetuating elite that is insulated from public opinion. Indeed, the bureaucracy may be the only group that knows its cost of production. Unfortunately, economists have found little evidence to support Niskanen's conclusions. As a result, much of the recent work on bureaucracies has sought to explain how legislators have managed to control them.[85]

Collegiate athletic departments, however, appear to fit more neatly into Niskanen's profile of a bureaucracy. An athletic department provides a set of sports programs—from Division I basketball or Division III volleyball—to a college in exchange for a budget. College administrators, who do not directly consume the product, provide this budget. They, in turn, raise funds by coercing payments from students (payments that, as will be shown below, often take the form of vaguely defined "general activities fees") or by obtaining a budget allocation from state legislators who are often rabid alumni. Athletic departments thus provide college administrators with sports in exchange for a set budget. Neither the administrators, who do not confront public opinion, nor the public they serve has the chance to choose bits and pieces of an athletic program. A college either has a Division I-A football program or it does not. Those who provide most of the funds, the students, are generally poorly informed about the cost of the athletic department's output and have minimal voice in the size of the budget. Expenditures thus rise to exhaust the available budget, as they did at the University of Wisconsin in the early 1990s. Despite a widely publicized fiscal crisis that led to the elimination of the baseball, fencing, and gymnastics programs, the expenditures by the athletic department actually rose.[86]

---

[84]See, for example, William Niskanen, *Bureaucracy and Representative Government* (Chicago: Aldine Atherton, 1971), pp. 15–18.

[85]Niskanen, *Bureaucracy and Representative Government* (1971), pp. 15–25; Ronald Wintrobe, "Modern Bureaucratic Theory," in *Perspectives on Public Choice: A Handbook,* ed. by Dennis Mueller (Cambridge, UK: Cambridge University Press, 1997), pp. 431–433; and Terry Moe, "The Positive Theory of Public Bureaucracy," in *Perspectives on Public Choice: A Handbook,* pp. 458–459.

[86]Telander, *From Red Ink to Roses* (1994), especially p. 185; and Thelin, *Games Colleges Play* (1994), p. 185.

Athletic directors, in their positions as bureaucrats, thus have an unusual degree of control over the resources at their command but no obvious way to use them. With no control over the residual between revenues and costs, they have no use for profit. To say that they maximize utility is at once an obvious yet meaningless statement, since it is not possible to know the arguments of an athletic director's utility function. Niskanen suggests several factors that may enter a bureaucrat's utility function, some selfish, others more altruistic. On the selfish side, bureaucrats want to maximize the prestige of their positions and the perquisites they enjoy while minimizing the effort they have to put into administering their programs. On the altruistic side, bureaucrats may be committed to serving the greater public good, which generally takes the form of dedication to their own contribution to social welfare through the program they run. Whether one believes in the bureacrat as a self-serving drone or a self-less public servant, the end result is the same: the bureaucrat has a fixation on the size of his or her budget. The bureaucrat is constrained only by the fact that in exchange for his or her budget, the sponsor must be supplied with the desired level of output.

In practical terms, athletic directors have no motivation to maximize the difference between revenues and costs, and so they seek new ways to spend whatever surpluses may arise. The payoffs to success noted in Table 11.8 may therefore overstate the benefits that accrue to a school, since much of this payment is used up in ancillary expenditures, such as transporting administrators, bands, and cheerleaders to the bowl game. Many of the surplus funds are also dissipated in the construction of lavish athletic facilities. For example, much of the University of Michigan's 1989 deficit came from its $12 million "Hall of Champions" and from the Donald B. Canham Natatorium. Anxious to complete the natatorium before he retired as athletic director, Canham did not wait for the university to conduct a fundraising campaign and took out a $9 million mortgage, sinking the athletic department deeply into debt.[87]

In addition, the trail of revenues and costs often crosses different budgetary units within the university, making it difficult to trace them to the appropriate source. Part of the University of Michigan's losses may be traced to the university's listed concession revenue of only $1.5 million, roughly $2.50 per fan at football games and $2 at basketball games, both unrealistically low figures. At Western Kentucky, the revenues from concessions are attributed to food services, even though no sales would have taken place without the football or basketball team.[88]

---

[87]See Borland et al., "College Athletics: Financial Burden or Boon?"(1992), pp. 216–217; Dealy, *Win at Any Cost* (1990), pp. 155–157; Fleisher et al., *The NCAA* (1992), p. 87; and Zimbalist, *Unpaid Professionals* (1999), p. 44. Such expenditures fit neatly into the common modification that bureaucrats maximize *discretionary spending* on projects or perks they desire rather than maximize their total budget. See Wintrobe, "Modern Bureaucratic Theory" (1997), p. 435; or Moe, "The Positive Theory of Public Bureaucracy" (1997), p. 459.

[88]Borland et al., "College Athletics: Financial Burden or Boon?" (1992), p. 217; and Fleisher et al., *The NCAA* (1992), p. 89.

The tangled web of collegiate finances has also allowed some schools to transfer resources to athletic departments without subjecting much of the funding to public scrutiny. The University of Georgia was among the first schools to separate sports from the rest of the university when the Georgia Athletic Association (GAA) was incorporated in 1929 to manage the athletic—meaning football—program at Georgia. The GAA was largely exempt from institutional control, a factor that would come back to haunt Georgia in the academic scandal of the early 1980s. The university did work with the GAA in one area. Despite drawing large crowds of fans, the GAA's expenditures outran its revenues. To close the deficit, the university—without asking for anything in return—dedicated half of each student's annual activity fee to the GAA.[89] Many schools have since followed Georgia's example, justifying their transfer of student funds to the athletic department as a contribution to overall student well-being. In the late 1980s, the University of Maryland raised about $2 million, almost a third of its athletic budget, in this way.[90]

The need to spend surpluses has even led to changes in the way college football has been played. Today we marvel at the few gifted players who can play both offense and defense. Not long ago, however, such "iron men" were commonplace. Having its roots in soccer and rugby, both of which have highly restrictive substitution rules, American football was a one-platoon game. The same player who had thrown a touchdown pass a moment before was now on the field tackling opposing runners. In 1965, after enduring years of intense lobbying from different colleges, the NCAA finally permitted free substitution in college football. This quickly led to the two-platoon system, with players who specialized in offense or defense, and then to situational players who are on the field for specific situations, such as defensive backs or linemen who play only in obvious passing situations.

The growth of specialized play has also led to specialized instruction and specialized coaching, with larger staffs, more equipment, and larger travel budgets. As a result, the athletic payrolls at most universities have exploded with the growing revenues. One thus sees *assistant* coaches at major football programs making more than many college presidents. The highest paid assistant football coach in the ACC earned over $200,000 in 2002, while the highest paid assistant in the Southeastern Conference made $225,000.[91] With assistants making this much, it is no surprise that some head coaches make salaries in the millions of dollars.[92]

---

[89]Thelin, *Games Colleges Play* (1994), pp. 78–82.

[90]Sperber, *College Sports, Inc.* (1990), p. 85.

[91]Mark Schlabach, "SEC, ACC Salaries a Surprise in Survey," *Atlanta Journal and Constitution*, June 20, 2003, Pg. 1D.

[92]Jim Tressel, the football coach at Ohio State, makes $1.75 million per year, and Tubby Smith, the basketball coach at the University of Kentucky recently signed a 10-year contract that could pay an average of over $2.5 million per year.

The rising payrolls have made labor costs the largest single expense for athletic departments. As Table 11.9 shows, at 30 percent of total expenditure, they are twice the size of the next highest expense, grants-in-aid. In contrast, professional baseball, football, basketball, and hockey all have labor costs that account for over 50 percent of included revenues. As we explained earlier in this chapter, the reason for the disparity stems from the monopsony power of the NCAA, which allows its members to depress the "pay" of their most valuable resource—the athletes themselves—well below their market value. As Niskanen points out, while bureaucrats—here the athletic directors and coaches—maximize budgets rather than profits, they still act like profit-maximizing managers of competitive firms when it comes to minimizing the costs of production.[93]

Minimizing costs creates surpluses that allow athletic directors to avoid difficult decisions and add to their own prestige by providing funds to subsidize nonrevenue men's sports, such as tennis or golf. It also helps them to satisfy the mandates of Title IX by making funds available for women's sports, which, as Table 11.8 showed, typically lose money. One problem with such subsidies lies in the fact that the participants in the nonrevenue sports are disproportionately white and middle income while participants in the revenue sports are disproportionately black and poor. Moreover, students in the nonrevenue sports have significantly higher graduation rates than do students in the revenue sports. Colleges are thus in the morally uncomfortable position of using poor blacks who play revenue-producing sports to subsidize the activities of relatively well-to-do whites in nonrevenue sports. A few black student athletes may earn a college degree that they may not have been able to receive otherwise. Fewer still enjoy lucrative careers as professional athletes. Many, however, end up with neither a degree nor a professional contract. [94]

---

[93]See Fleisher et al., *The NCAA* (1992), pp. 83–84; and Niskanen, *Bureaucracy and Representative Government* (1971), pp. 30 and 57.

[94]Zimbalist, *Unpaid Professionals* (1999), p. 51.

Table 11.9

Expenditures by Athletic Departments (%)

Salaries	30
Grants-in-aid	14
Team travel	7
Debt service and capital expenditure	10
Guarantees and options	4
Equipment and supplies	4
Contract services	4
Recruiting	2
Other	25

Source: Daniel L. Fulks, *Revenues and Expenses of Divisions I and II Intercollegiate Athletics Programs* (2002).

ANITA DEFRANTZ

BIOGRAPHICAL *Sketch*

Without Anita DeFrantz, the corruption and the image of corruption will run unabated. With her, I have a genuine hope for our Olympic athletes inspiring young people that they can all live within that one circle of humanity.

—RICHARD E. LAPCHICK[1]

One of the most powerful women in the sports industry had little intention of following a career in sports. Instead, she came to her position as the result of a couple of fortuitous accidents. Born and raised in Indiana, Anita DeFrantz attended Connecticut College, a small school better known for its academics than for its Division III athletics. While a sophomore, the first accident occurred. One day, she saw the school's crew coach carrying a boat and asked him what it was for. The coach noticed that DeFrantz, at 5'11", looked strong and athletic, and he soon had her on the water with the team. DeFrantz went on to be a six-time national champion and, three years after her chance encounter with the crew coach, she captained the eight-woman boat to a bronze medal in the 1976 Summer Olympic Games in Montreal, the first Olympics to feature women's rowing.

An accident of timing led her from athletic success to a professional career in sports administration. While preparing for the 1980 Games, DeFrantz got a law degree from the University of Pennsylvania and passed the bar exam. Her hopes for a gold medal were dashed; however, when President Jimmy Carter declared that the United States would boycott the 1980 Moscow Games to protest the Soviet Union's invasion of Afghanistan, DeFrantz then took a step that helped define the future course of her career. She put her legal training to use by suing the United States Olympic Committee (USOC). Her lawsuit claimed that the government could not declare a boycott of the Olympics and that America's Olympic athletes had the right to make their own decision about whether they attended the Games.

DeFrantz's lawsuit proved politically unpopular—some critics suggested that she join the Communist Party—and, ultimately, unsuccessful. Although DeFrantz lost her suit, she succeeded in catching the attention of the International Olympic Committee (IOC). It awarded her a medal for her effort to put Olympic competition above politics and helped her to begin a career in the Olympic movement. In 1984, while still in her early 30s, DeFrantz was named vice president of the Los Angeles Olympic Organizing Committee. After the Los Angeles Olympics were held, she joined the Amateur Athletic Foundation (AAF) and the USOC, rapidly rising in each to become the president of the AAF and a member of the executive committee of the USOC. Recognizing her talents, the IOC named her as a lifetime member.

DeFrantz's appointment again made her a pioneer. She became the first American woman and only the fifth woman ever invited to join the IOC. Since her appointment, DeFrantz has become an extremely influential member of the IOC, especially in matters related to women's sports and developing countries. She has been a leading advocate of funding for training facilities in countries that cannot afford to build them. In 1992, she became the chair of the IOC's committee on women's sports and played a critical role in having women's softball and soccer added to the 2000 Olympic Games in Atlanta.

DeFrantz's reputation for integrity and fairness helped her become the first woman to be elected vice president of the IOC's Executive Committee in 1997. After IOC President Juan Antonio Samaranch retired, DeFrantz ran unsuccessfully to succeed him. Despite this setback, she has continued to use her position to speak out as a voice for athletes.

[1]Richard E. Lapchick, "A New Vision for the IOC: Anita L. DeFrantz," *Sport in Society*, http://www.sportinsociety.org/rel-article19.html.

Sources: Sarah J. Murray, "Anita DeFrantz: Setting the Standard," online at http://www.womenssportsfoundation.org/cgi-bin/iowa/athletes/article.html?record=68; Richard E. Lapchick, "A New Vision for the IOC: Anita L. DeFrantz," *Sport in Society*, at http://www.sportinsociety.org/rel-article19.html; "Olympian Rise" *Houston Chronicle*, online at http://www.chron.com/content/chronicle/sports/special/barriers/defrantz.html.

SUMMARY

This chapter used the tools of economics to analyze the behavior of the NCAA, its member schools, and the athletes who participate in collegiate sports. At the outset, we noted that amateurism is a troublesome concept with a history that may be more mythologically than factually based. For a university, the tension between fielding the best possible team and maintaining academic standards can be difficult to manage effectively, especially given that there are economic, sociological, and ethical dimensions that may be impossible to balance simultaneously.

The NCAA also functions as a cartel in the college sports market. To gain access to the lucrative television contracts and big-name opponents, schools must join the NCAA. Unlike most cartels, however, individual athletic programs, such as football at member schools, are not permitted to earn profits, and they are limited in their ability to maintain control over residual revenues generated by their programs.

DISCUSSION QUESTIONS

1. Discuss the viability of amateurism in the United States today. Is it possible, given the attention that elite athletes receive, to have "pure" amateurs?

2. Other than to retain NCAA eligibility (which is an artificially created constraint), are there any compelling philosophical reasons that a person may choose to remain an amateur rather than receive pay?

3. Discuss the possible implications of allowing schools to pay student athletes whatever level of compensation necessary to attract them to their programs.

4. Discuss the positive and negative implications of removing all entrance standards for college athletes, assuming that they must also enroll as full-time students.

5. Discuss the positive and negative implications of permitting colleges to use paid players who are not students.

6. Discuss the factors that should be included in the decision process by an elite high school senior baseball player of attending a Division I baseball school versus reporting directly to the minor professional leagues.

PROBLEMS

11.1 Show, using supply and demand for labor diagrams for Divisions I and III, the effect of a new rule allowing Division III schools to pay athletes a one-time bonus for enrolling at their schools.

11.2 Use the prisoner's dilemma model to show why schools have an incentive to violate NCAA rules.

11.3 Use human capital theory to explain why colleges might not pay students their full marginal product.

11.4 Assume that you are the newly appointed head of the NCAA. Construct a framework for a new scholarship program that would entirely replace the existing system. Describe what should be its fundamental tenets if:

    a. The primary goal is to ensure that athletes were not exploited.

    b. The primary goal is to ensure that student-athletes receive degrees.

    c. The primary goal is to simplify the system and reduce violations.

    d. Your primary goal is to be reappointed.

11.5 What effect do the following have on a person's decision to invest in athletic training versus academic training? In each case, explain the direction and likely significance of the effect.

    a. Risk of career-ending injury

    b. The probability of success in athletics

    c. An increase in the cost of college tuition

    d. An increase in the demand for professional sports.

11.6 Use game theory to describe how an effort by two universities to recruit a top basketball player might result in both committing NCAA recruiting violations.

11.7 What unselfish and selfish motives might be behind the attempts by some schools to set academic standards for student-athletes?

11.8 In 2002 the Big East football conference announced that it was kicking out Temple University, one of the least successful football programs in the conference. Analyze this action in the framework of an efficient cartel.

11.9 How might failing to graduate from college be an optimal investment in one's human capital?

11.10 Why are the graduation rates for women's basketball players so much higher than those for men's basketball players?

Works Cited

"1999–2000 NHL Standings." *FoxSports.com* online at http://www.foxsports.com/nhl/history/standings/2000_standings_conference.sml.

"2002 MLB Franchise Values," *Forbes Magazine On-line* at http://www.forbes.com.

"2001–2002 NBA Franchise Values," *Forbes Magazine On-line* at http://www.forbcs.com.

"2001–2002 NFL Franchise Values," *Forbes Magazine On-line* at http://www.forbes.com.

"2001–2002 NHL Franchise Values," *Forbes Magazine On-line* at http://www.forbes.com.

"ABL Out of Money, Files for Chapter 11 Bankruptcy." Sports "ticker." July 5, 1999, online at http://www.bball.yahoo.com/nba/news/981222/ablbnkrpt.html.

Abrams, Roger. *Legal Bases: Baseball and the Law.* Philadelphia: Temple University Press, 1998.

Amato, Louis, John Gandar, Irvin Tucker, and Richard Zuber. "Bowls Versus Playoffs: The Impact on Football Player Graduation Rates in the National Collegiate Athletic Association," *Economics of Education Review,* v. 15, no. 2 (April 1996), pp. 187–195.

Anderson, Torben, and Sumner J. La Croix. "Customer Discrimination in Major League Baseball," *Economic Inquiry,* v. 29, no. 4 (October 1991), pp. 665–677.

Aronson, Eliot, Timothy D. Wilson, and Robin M. Akert. *Social Psychology: The Heart and Mind.* New York: HarperCollins College Publishers, 1994.

Ashenfelter, Orley, and George Johnson. "Bargaining Theory: Trade Unions and Industrial Strike Activity," *American Economic Review,* v. 59, no. 1 (March 1969), pp. 35–49.

"Asia: Downhill All the Way," *Economist,* February 7, 1998, p. 44.

Associated Press. "Court Backs N.C.A.A. on Proposition 16." *New York Times,* December 23, 1999, p. D5.

———. "New Ballparks Mean Higher Ticket Prices." *Sporting News,* April 4, 2000, online at http://www.tsn.sportingnews.com/baseball/articles/2000404/228259.html.

———. "Commissioner Spent $1.2 Million on Lobbying in 2001." *ESPN.com,* May 15, 2002, online at http://www.espn.com.

Austrian, Ziona, and Mark Rosentraub. "Cleveland's Gateway to the Future," in *Sports, Jobs, and Taxes,* ed. by Roger Noll and Andrew Zimbalist. Washington, D.C.: Brookings Institution Press, 1997, pp. 355–384.

Baade, Robert. "Professional Sports as Catalysts for Metropolitan Economic Development," *Journal of Urban Affairs,* v. 18, no. 1 (1996), pp. 1–17.

———. "Should Congress Stop the Bidding War for Sports Franchises?" Hearing Before the Subcommittee on Antitrust, Business Rights, and Compensation, Senate Committee on the Judiciary. "Academics," *Heartland Policy,* v. 4 (November 29, 1995), online at http://www.heartland.org/stadps4.html.

Baade, Robert, and Richard Dye. "The Impact of Stadiums and Professional Sports on Metropolitan Area Development," *Growth and Change,* v. 21, no. 2 (Spring 1990), pp. 1–14.

Baade, Robert A., and Victor A. Matheson. "The Quest for the Cup: Assessing the Economic Impact of the World Cup," forthcoming in *Regional Science.*

Baade, Robert A., and Allen Sanderson. "The Employment Effect of Teams and Sports Facilities." In *Sports, Jobs, and Taxes,* ed. by Roger Noll and Andrew Zimbalist. Washington, D.C.: Brookings Institution Press, 1997, pp. 55–91.

——. "Field of Fantasies," *Intellectual Ammunition,* March/April 1996, online at http://www.heartland.org/01maap96.htm.

Baker, William. *Sports in the Western World.* Totowa, N.J.: Rowman & Littlefield, 1982.

Bamberger, Michael, and Don Yaeger. "Over the Edge," *Sports Illustrated,* April 14, 1997, pp. 61–70.

Barra, Allen. "In Anti-trust We Trust," *Salon Magazine,* May 19, 2000, online at http://www.salon.com/news/feature/2000/05/19/antitrust/index.html.

Barry, Dave. *Dave Barry Turns Fifty.* New York: Random House, 1999.

"The Baseball Archive," 2000, online at http://www.baseball1.com.

"A Basic Title IX Presentation," online at http://www.bailiwick.lib.uiowa.edu/CHBGrant/Present.html

Bartlett, Donald, and James Steele. "Snow Job," *Sports Illustrated,* December 10, 2001, pp. 79–97.

"Baseball Agreement to Extend Through 2003," online at http://www.theolympian.com/home/specialsections/Mariners2002/20020831/41339.shtml.

Becker, Gary S. "College Athletes Should Get Paid What They're Worth," *Business Week,* September 30, 1985, p. 38.

——. *The Economics of Discrimination,* 2nd ed. Chicago: University of Chicago Press, 1971.

——. *Human Capital,* 3rd ed. Chicago: University of Chicago Press, 1993.

——. "A Theory of Competition Among Pressure Groups for Political Influence," *Quarterly Journal of Economics,* v. 97, no. 3 (August 1983), pp. 371–400.

Beckett's Baseball Card Monthly. Beckett Publications, April, 2003.

"Beijing Enters Play-offs to Be Olympics Host," *People's Daily Online,* March 24, 2000, online at http://www.english.peopledaily.com.cn/200003/24/eng20000324S101.html.

Benson, Marty. *1999 NCAA Division I Graduation Rates Report.* Indianapolis: NCAA, 1999.

Berk, Sheryl. "Golden Girl," *McCalls,* December 1998, pp. 110–112.

Bess, Phillip. "Urban Ballparks and the Future of Cities," *Real Estate Issues,* v. 21, no. 3 (December 1996), pp. 27–30.

Betzold, Michael, and Ethan Casey. *Queen of Diamonds: The Tiger Stadium Story.* West Bloomfield, M.I.: Northfield Publishing Co., 1992.

Bissinger, H. G. *Friday Night Lights.* Reading, M.A.: Addison Wesley, 1990.

Blass, Asher C. "Does the Baseball Labor Market Contradict the Human Capital Model of Investment?" *Review of Economics and Statistics,* v. 71, no. 2 (May 1992), pp. 261–268.

Borland, Melvin, Brian Goff, and Robert Pulsinelli. "College Athletics: Financial Burden or Boon?" In *Advances in the Economics of Sport,* vol. 1. New York: JAI Press, 1992, pp. 215–235.

Bovarsson, Orn B. "A Test of Employer Discrimination in the NBA," *Contemporary Economic Policy,* v. 17, no. 2 (April 1999), pp. 243–256.

Brown, Robert W. "An Estimate of the Rent Generated by a Premium College Football Player," *Economic Inquiry,* v. 21, no. 4 (October 1993), pp. 671–684.

——. "Measuring Cartel Rents in the College Basketball Player Recruitment Market," *Applied Economics,* v. 26, no. 1 (January 1994), pp. 27–34.

Brown, Robert W., and R. Todd Jewell. "Is There Customer Discrimination in College Basketball? The Premium Fans Pay for White Players," *Social Science Quarterly,* v. 75, no. 2 (June 1994), pp. 401–412.

Brownlee, Shannon, and Nancy Linnon. "The Myth of the Student-Athlete," *U.S. News and World Report,* January 8, 1990, p. 50.

Buchanan, James. "An Economic Theory of Clubs," *Economica,* v. 32, no. 125 (February 1965), pp. 1–14.

Burger, John D., and Stephen J. K. Walters. "Market Size, Pay, and Performance: A General Model and Application to Major League Baseball," *Journal of Sports Economics,* v. 4, no. 2 (May 2003), pp. 108–125.

Burk, Robert. *Never Just a Game: Players, Owners, and American Baseball to 1920.* Chapel Hill: University of North Carolina Press, 1994.

Burns, Ken. *Baseball* (film). PBS Video, 1994.

"Business of 1999 Bowl Games." *Fox Sports Biz.com* online at http://www.foxsports.com/business/resources/bowls.

Butler, Michael R. "Competitive Balance in Major League Baseball," *American Economist,* v. 39, no. 2 (Fall 1995), pp. 46–50.

Byers, Walter, with Charles Hammer. *Unsportsmanlike Conduct: Exploiting College Athletes.* Ann Arbor: University of Michigan Press, 1995.

Byrne, Jim. *The $1 League: The Rise and Fall of the USFL.* New York: Prentice Hall, 1986.

Cagan, Joanna, and Neil deMause. *Field of Schemes.* Monroe, M.E.: Common Courage Press, 1998.

Cassing, James, and Richard Douglas. "Implications of the Auction Mechanism in Baseball's Free Agent Draft," *Southern Economic Journal,* v. 47, no. 1 (July 1980), pp. 110–121.

Cayleff, Susan. *Babe: The Life and Times of Babe Didrickson Zaharias.* Urbana: University of Illinois Press, 1995.

"The Celebrity 100." *Forbes Magazine On-line,* June 19, 2003, at http://www.Forbes.com/static_html/celebs/index.shtml.

Channel Sports. "Beijing Welcomes Inclusion on Shortlist to Hold 2008 Olympics," *China Daily Information,* August 29, 2000, online at http://www.chinadaily.net/cover/ storydb/2000/08/29/sp-beiji.829.html.

Chema, Thomas. "When Professional Sports Justify the Subsidy," *Journal of Urban Affairs,* v. 18, no. 1 (1996), pp. 19–22.

Clotfelter, Charles, and Phillip Cook. "On the Economics of State Lotteries," *Journal of Economic Perspectives,* v. 4, no. 1 (Fall 1990), pp. 105–119.

Coase, Ronald. "The Problem of Social Cost," *Journal of Law and Economics,* v. 3 (October 1960), pp. 1–44.

Coates, Dennis, and Bradley R. Humphreys. "The Effect of Professional Sports on Earnings and Employment in U.S. Cities," *Regional Science and Urban Economics,* v. 33, no. 2 (March 2003), pp. 175–198.

——. "Professional Sports Facilities, Franchises and Urban Economic Development." *UMBC Working Paper 03-103,* 2003.

College Board Online. Students and Parents—"SAT Information—Frequently Asked Questions; SAT Program—Is the SAT Fair? Aren't Minority Students at a Disadvantage?" February 15, 2001, online at http://www.collegeboard.org/sat/html/students/mofaq013.html.

Coughlin, Cletus C., and O. Homer Erekson. "An Examination of Contributions to Support Intercollegiate Athletics," *Southern Economic Journal,* v. 50, no. 1 (July 1984), pp. 180–195.

Curtis, James E., John W. Loy, and John N. Sage. "Race/Ethnicity and Relative Centrality of Playing Positions in Team Sports," *Exercise and Sport Science Review,* v. 6 (1978), pp. 285–313.

Danforth, John. "Sports' Integral Role with a Community," *New York Times,* February 2, 1986, Section 5, p. 2.

Danielson, Michael. *Home Team: Professional Sport and the American Metropolis.* Princeton, N.J.: Princeton University Press, 1997.

Davis, Seth. "A Blight on the Mountaineers," *Sports Illustrated,* December 6, 1999, pp. 80–81.

Dealy, Francis. *Win at Any Cost: The Sell Out of College Athletics.* New York: Birch Lane Press, 1990.

DeBrock, Lawrence, Wallace Hendricks, and Roger Koenker. "The Economics of Persistence: Graduation Rates of Athletes as Labor Market Choice," *Journal of Human Resources,* v. 31, no. 3 (Summer 1996), pp. 513–539.

Depken, Craig A. "Fan Loyalty and Stadium Funding in Professional Baseball," *Journal of Sports Economics,* v. 1, no. 2 (May 2000), pp. 124–138.

Depken, Craig A., David R. Kamerschen, and Arthur Snow. "Generic Advertising of Intermediate Goods: Theory and Evidence." Unpublished manuscript, 1999.

Dey, Matthew S. "Racial Differences in National Basketball Association Salaries: A New Look," *American Economist,* v. 41, no. 2 (Fall 1997), pp. 84–90.

Dickey, Glenn. *Just Win, Baby: Al Davis and His Raiders.* New York: Harcourt, Brace, Jovanovich, 1991.

Dienhart, Tom. "New NCAA Rules Make It Tough on Small Schools," *SportingNews.com,* June 3, 2002, online at http://www.sportingnews.com/voices/tom_dienhart/20020603-p.html.

Dubois, Paul. "Title IX: A Critique from the Underclass," *Physical Educator,* v. 56, no. 3 (Fall 1999), pp. 159–167.

Dubow, Josh. "Non-BCS Schools Allege Antitrust Violations," *CollegeSports.com,* July 22, 2003, online at http://www.collegesports.com/sports/m-footbl/stories/072203aax.html.

Duderstadt, James J. *Intercollegiate Athletics and the American University: A University President's Perspective.* Ann Arbor: University of Michigan Press, 2000.

Du Pont, Pete. "Men's Athletic Programs Cut to Satisfy Quotas," *Human Events,* v. 55, no. 33 (September 3, 1999), p. 14.

Dworkin, James. *Owners Versus Players: Baseball and Collective Bargaining.* Boston: Auburn House, 1981.

Eckard, E. Woodrow. "The ANOVA-Based Competitive Balance Measure: A Defense," *Journal of Sports Economics,* v. 4, no. 1 (February 2003), pp. 74–80.

Ehrenberg, Ronald G., and Michael Bognanno. "Do Tournaments Have Incentive Effects?" *Journal of Political Economy,* v. 98, no. 6 (December 1990), pp. 1307–1324.

Ehrenberg, Ronald G., and Robert Smith. *Modern Labor Economics: Theory and Public Policy,* 7th ed. New York: Addison Wesley Longman, 2000.

El-Hodiri, Mohamed, and James Quirk. "An Economic Model of a Professional Sports League," *Journal of Political Economy,* v. 79, no. 6 (Nov.–Dec. 1971), pp. 1302–1319.

Euchner, Charles. *Playing the Field.* Baltimore: Johns Hopkins University Press, 1993.

Farber, Henry. "Bargaining Theory, Wage Outcomes, and the Occurrence of Strikes: An Econometric Analysis," *American Economic Review,* v. 68, no. 3 (June 1978), pp. 262–271.

Farber, Michael. "Giant Sucking Sound," *Sports Illustrated,* March 20, 1995, p. 104.

Ferguson, D. W., Kenneth G. Stewart, J. C. H. Jones, and Andre Le Dressay. "The Pricing of Sports Events: Do Teams Maximize Profits?" *Journal of Industrial Economics,* v. 39, no. 3 (March 1991), pp. 297–310.

Finley, Moses, and H. W. Pleket. *The Olympic Games: The First Thousand Years.* New York: Viking Press, 1976.

Fischler, Stanley. *Cracked Ice: An Insider's Look at the NHL.* Chicago: Master's Press, 1999.

Fisher, Eric. "Reds' Ballpark Honeymoon Cut Short," *Washington Times,* August 3, 2003, p. C3.

Fleisher, Arthur, Brian Goff, and Robert Tollison. *The National Collegiate Athletic Association: A Study in Cartel Behavior.* Chicago: University of Chicago Press, 1992.

"The Forbes 400 Richest People in America," *Forbes On-line* at http://www.Forbes.com

Fort, Rodney, and Andrew Gill. "Race and Ethnicity Assessment in Baseball Card Markets," *Journal of Sports Economics,* v. 1, no. 1 (February 2000), pp. 21–38.

Fort, Rodney, and James Quirk. "The College Football Industry." In *Sports Economics: Current Research,* ed. by John Fizel, Elizabeth Gustafson, and Lawrence Hadley. Westport, C.T.: Praeger, 1999, pp. 11–26.

Foy, Paul. "Romney Just Glad Olympics Worked," *2002 Winter Olympic Games,* online at http://www.olympics.hiasys.com/olympics_main/news/ap_olynewsscene02252002.htm.

Frank, Robert, and Philip Cook. *The Winner-Take-All Society.* New York: The Free Press, 1995.

Frederick, David M., William H. Kaempfer, and Richard L. Wobbekind. "Salary Arbitration as a Market Substitute." In *Diamonds Are Forever: The Business of Baseball,* ed. by Paul M. Sommers. Washington, D.C.: The Brookings Institution, 1992, pp. 29–49.

Freedman, Matthew (Ed). *2000 Inside the Ownership of Professional Sports Teams.* Chicago: Team Marketing Report, 2000.

Freeman, Mike. "When Values Collide: Clarett Got Unusual Aid in Ohio State Class," *New York Times,* July 13, 2003, p. 8–1.

——. "Pursuit of Victories Presses on Colleges," *New York Times,* July 18, 2003, p. 8–4.

Freeman, Richard, and James Medoff. *What Do Unions Do?* New York: Basic Books, 1984.

Friedman, Milton. *Essays on Positive Economics.* Chicago: University of Chicago Press, 1953.

Friedman, Milton, and Leonard J. Savage. "The Utility Analysis of Choices Involving Risk," *Journal of Political Economy,* v. 56, no. 4 (August 1948), pp. 279–304.

Frommer, Harvey. *Rickey and Robinson.* New York: Macmillan, 1982.

Fulks, Daniel L. *Revenues and Expenses of Divisions I and II Intercollegiate Athletics Programs: Financial Trends and Relationships—2002,* online at http:www.ncaa.org.

Gallico, Paul. *Farewell to Sports.* New York: Alfred A. Knopf, 1938.

Gavora, Jessica, *Tilting the Playing Field.* San Francisco: Encounter Books, 2002.

Gearey, Robyn. "The Numbers Game," *New Republic,* May 19, 1997, pp. 19–24.

Gilbert, Susan. "The Smallest Olympians Face the Biggest Risk," *New York Times,* July 28, 1996, p. E4.

Girard, Fred. "Deficit Pinches U-M Sports," *Detroit News,* July 14, 1999, online at http://www.detnews.com/1999/college/9907/14/07140181.htm.

Gius, Mark, and Donn Johnson. "An Empirical Investigation of Wage Discrimination in Professional Basketball," *Applied Economics Letters,* v. 5, no. 11 (November 1998), pp. 703–705.

Goldfield, David. "Weaker NCAA Standards Won't Help Black Athletes," *Chronicle of Higher Education,* April 9, 1999, p. A64.

Goldman, William. *The Princess Bride.* New York: Ballantine Books, 1974.

"Governor Mitt Romney," *Massachusetts Office of the Governor,* online at http://www.mass.gov/portal/index.jsp?pageID=agcc&agid=gov&agca=biographies&agcc=mittromneybiom.

Gramm, Cynthia, and John Schnell. "Difficult Choices: Crossing the Picket Line During the 1987 National Football League Strike," *Journal of Labor Economics,* v. 12, no. 1 (January 1994), pp. 41–71.

Green, Daniel. "Toss Up: Suddenly Women's Pro Sports Are Hot," *Working Woman,* April 1997, pp. 26–72.

Griffin, Tim. "Big 12's Budget Balancing Act," *San Antonio Express-News,* June 6, 2001, online at http://www.news.mysanantonio.com.

Grimaldi, James. "Olympics File Suit Over Web Domain," *Washington Post,* July 14, 2000, p. E4, online at http://www.washingtonpost.com/wp-dyn/articles/A404762000July13.html.

Grimes, Paul, and George Chressanthis. "The Role of Intercollegiate Sports and NCAA Sanctions in Alumni Contributions," *American Journal of Economics and Sociology,* v. 53, no. 1 (January 1994), pp. 27–40.

Guttman, Allen. "The Anomaly of Intercollegiate Athletics." In *Rethinking College Athletics,* ed. by Judith Andre and David James. Philadelphia: Temple University Press, 1991, pp. 17–30.

Gwartney, James A., and Charles Haworth. "Employer Costs and Discrimination: The Case of Baseball," *Journal of Political Economy,* v. 82, no. 4 (July/August 1974), pp. 873–881.

Hadley, Lawrence, James Ciecka, and Anthony Krautmann. "Competitive Balance in the Aftermath of the 1994 Players' Strike." Presented at the 2003 meetings of the Western Economic Association. Denver, C.O.

Hamilton, Barton H. "Racial Discrimination and Professional Basketball Salaries in the 1990s," *Applied Economics,* v. 29, no. 3 (March 1997), pp. 287–296.

Hamilton, Bruce, and Peter Kahn. "Baltimore's Camden Yards Ballparks." In *Sports, Jobs, and Taxes,* ed. by Roger Noll and Andrew Zimbalist. Washington, D.C.: Brookings Institution Press, 1997, pp. 245–281.

Hanssen, Andrew F., and Torben Anderson. "Has Discrimination Lessened over Time? A Test Using Baseball's All-Star Vote," *Economic Inquiry,* v. 37, no. 2 (April 1999), pp. 326–352.

Harasta, Cathy. "Romney Shows his Mettle," *Dallas Morning News,* February 17, 2002, online at http://www.olympics.belointeractive.com/otherstories/0217olyromney.218e4. html.

Harris, David. *The League: The Rise and Decline of the NFL.* New York: Bantam Books, 1986.

Hart-Davis, Duff. *Hitler's Games.* London: Century, 1986.

Hatab, Lawrence. "The Greeks and the Meaning of Athletics." In *Rethinking College Athletics,* ed. by Judith Andre and David James. Philadelphia: Temple University Press, 1991, pp. 31–42.

Hausman, Jerry A., and Gregory K. Leonard. "Superstars in the National Basketball League: Economic Value and Policy," *Journal of Labor Economics,* v. 15, no. 4 (October 1997), pp. 586–624.

Hayes, Beth. "Unions and Strikes with Asymmetric Information," *Journal of Labor Economics,* v. 2, no. 1 (January 1984), pp. 57–84.

Heilbroner, Richard. *The Worldly Philosophers.* New York, Clarion Books, 1967.

Heintel, Robert. "The Need for an Alternative to Antitrust Regulation of the National Football League," *Case Western Reserve Law Review,* v. 46, no. 4 (Summer 1996), pp. 1033–1069.

Helyar, John. *Lords of the Realm.* New York: Villard Books, 1994.

Hepp, Christopher. "Near Fabled Park, Ambience a Lure," *Philadelphia Inquirer,* September 29, 1999, pp. A1 and A6.

Hoffer, Richard. "The Loss Generation," *Sports Illustrated,* April 17, 2000, pp. 56–59.

"Hoop Dreams: New League Banks on Sisterhood," *Inc.,* June 1997, p. 23.

"How They Bring in the Gold," *U.S. News and World Report,* January 31, 1994, p. 16.

Hudson, Ian. "Bright Lights, Big City: Do Professional Sports Teams Increase Employment?" *Journal of Urban Affairs,* v. 21, no. 4 (1999), pp. 397–407.

Humphreys, Bradley R. "Alternative Measures of Competitive Balance," *Journal of Sports Economics,* v. 3, no. 2 (May 2002), pp. 133–148.

———. "The ANOVA-Based Competitive Balance Measure: A Reply," *Journal of Sports Economics,* v. 4, no. 1 (February, 2003), pp. 81–82.

Irani, Daraius. "Estimating Consumer Discrimination Using Panel Data: 1972–1991." In *Baseball Economics: Current Research,* ed. by John Fizel, Elizabeth Gustafson, and Lawrence Hadley (Westport, C.T.: Praeger, 1996), pp. 47–66.

Isidore, Chris. "Stadium Curse Still Haunts Firms," *CNNMoney,* January 3, 2003, online at http://www.money.cnn.com/2003/01/03/commentary/column_sportsbiz/ sponsor_stock_index/.

———. "Baseball's Shell Game," *CNNMoney,* December 7, 2001, online at http://www.cnnmoney.com.

Jenkins, Jeffrey A. "A Reexamination of Salary Determination in Professional Basketball," *Social Science Quarterly,* v. 77, no. 3 (September 1996), pp. 594–608.

Jenson, Mike. "Start of Women's Pro Soccer League Not Just Around the Corner," *Philadelphia Inquirer,* July 8, 1999, p. E1.

Johnson, Arthur. *Minor League Baseball and Local Economic Development.* Urbana: University of Illinois Press, 1995.

Johnson, John. "When a Professional Sport Is Not a Business: Baseball's Infamous Antitrust Exemption." In *Sports and the Law,* ed. by Charles Quirk (New York: Garland, 1996), pp. 149–165.

Johnson, Roy. "We Got Game (Finally)," *Fortune,* February 1, 1999, pp. 28–29.

Jones, J. C. H., D. G. Ferguson, and K. G. Stewart. "Blood Sports and Cherry Pie: Some Economics of Violence in the National Hockey League," *American Journal of Sports and Sociology*, v. 52, no. 1 (January 1993), pp. 63–78.

Jones, J. C. H., and W. D. Walsh. "Salary Determination in the National Hockey League: The Effects of Skills, Franchise Characteristics, and Discrimination," *Industrial and Labor Relations Review*, v. 41, no. 4 (July 1988), pp. 592–604.

———. "The World Hockey Association and Player Exploitation in the National Hockey League," *Quarterly Review of Economics and Business*, v. 27, no. 2 (Summer 1987), pp. 87–101.

Jones, Richard, and Don Walker. "Packer Boss Warns of Move if Stadium Doesn't Get Upgrade," *Milwaukee Sentinel Journal*, March 1, 2000, online at http://www.jsonline.com/packer/news/feb00/lambeau01022900.asp.

Kahn, Lawrence M. "Discrimination in Professional Sports: A Survey of the Literature," *Industrial and Labor Relations Review*, v. 44, no. 3 (April 1991), pp. 395–418.

———. "The Effects of Race on Professional Football Players' Compensation," *Industrial Labor Relations Review*, v. 45, no. 2 (January 1992), pp. 295–310.

———. "The Sports Business as a Labor Market Laboratory," *Journal of Economic Perspectives*, v. 14, no. 3 (Summer 2000), pp. 75–94.

Kahn, Lawrence M., and Peter Sherer. "Racial Differences in Professional Basketball Players' Compensation," *Journal of Labor Economics*, v. 6, no. 1 (January 1988), pp. 40–61.

Kahn, Roger. *The Era: 1947–1957*. New York: Ticknor and Fields, 1993.

Kanazawa, Mark T., and Jonas P. Funk. "Racial Discrimination in Professional Basketball: Evidence from Nielsen Ratings," *Economics Inquiry*, v. 39, no. 4 (October 2001), pp. 599–608.

Kantorczyk, Todd. "How to Stop the Fast Break: An Evaluation of the 'Three-Peat' Trademark and the FTC's Role in Trademark Law Enforcement," *UCLA Entertainment Law Review*, v. 2, no. 1 (Winter 1995), pp. 195–228.

Kaplan, Daniel. "$50M Makes Bank One Presenting Sponsor of Bears," *Street & Smith's SportsBusiness Journal*, June 23–29, 2003, p. 1.

———. "Stadiums Tilt NFL's Economic Playing Field," *Street & Smith's SportsBusiness Journal*, May 26–June 1, 2003, p. 1.

Keating, Raymond. "Sports Pork: The Costly Relationship Between Major League Sports and Government." *Policy Analysis*, no. 339. Washington, D.C.: Cato Institute, 1999.

Kidd, Bruce. "The Myth of the Ancient Games." In *Five Ring Circus: Money, Power and Politics at the Olympic Games*, ed. by Alan Tomlinson and Garry Whannel. London: Pluto Press, 1984, pp. 71–83.

King, Bill. "New Ballparks Sport Old Look: Empty Seats," *Street & Smith's SportsBusiness Journal*, May 26–June 1, 2003, p. 37. pp. 148

———. "Passion That Can't be Counted Puts Billions of Dollars in Play," *Street & Smith's SportsBusiness Journal: By the Numbers*, v. 9, no. 36 (2003), 148–149.

Klein, Eugene. *First Down and a Billion: The Funny Business of Pro Football*. New York: Morrow, 1987.

Kleindienst, Linda. "Broward Opposes Bill Levying Cruise Tax to Help Pay for Marlins Stadium," *Fort Lauderdale Sun Sentinel*, March 22, 2000, p. 1B.

Knapple, Jeffrey S. "Naming Rights Industry." In *Naming Rights Deals*. Chicago: Team Marketing Report, 2001.

Knight Foundation Commission on Intercollegiate Athletics. *A Call to Action: Reconnecting College Sports and Higher Education*. John S. and James L. Knight Foundation, June 2001.

Knowles, Glenn, Keith Sherony, and Mike Haupert. "The Demand for Major League Baseball: A Test of the Uncertainty of Outcome Hypothesis," *American Economist*, v. 36, no. 2 (Fall 1992), pp. 72–80.

Koch, James. "Intercollegiate Athletics: An Economic Explanation," *Social Science Quarterly*, v. 64, no. 2 (June 1983), pp. 360–374.

Korr, Charles. "Marvin Miller and the New Unionism in Baseball." In *The Business of Professional Sports*, ed. by Paul Staudohar and James Mangan. Urbana: University of Illinois Press, 1991, pp. 115–134.

Kowalewski, Sandra, and Michael Leeds. "The Impact of the Salary Cap and Free Agency on the Structure and Distribution of Salaries in the NFL." In *Sports Economics: Current Research*, ed. by John Fizel, Elizabeth Gustafson, and Lawrence Hadley. Westport, C.T.: Praeger, 1999, pp. 213–226.

———. "Winner-Take-All in the NFL." Unpublished manuscript, 2000.

Krashinsky, Michael, and Harry D. Krashinsky. "Do English Canadian Hockey Teams Discriminate Against French Canadian Players?" *Canadian Public Policy—Analyse de Politiques*, v. 23, no. 2 (June 1997), pp. 212–216.

Krautmann, Anthony. "What's Wrong with Scully Estimates of a Player's Marginal Revenue Product," *Economic Inquiry*, v. 37, no. 2 (April 1999), pp. 369–381.

Krautmann, Anthony, and Margaret Oppenheimer. "Training in Minor League Baseball: Are Players Exploited?" In *Baseball Economics*, ed. by John Fizel, Elizabeth Gustafson, and Lawrence Hadley. Westport, C.T.: Praeger, 1996, pp. 85–98.

Kuklick, Bruce. *To Everything a Season: Shibe Park and Urban Philadelphia, 1909–1976*. Princeton, N.J.: Princeton University Press, 1991.

Laband, David L. "How the Structure of Competition Influences Performance in Professional Sports: The Case of Tennis and Golf." In *Sportometrics*, ed. by Brian L. Goff and Robert D. Tollison. College Station: Texas A&M University Press, 1990, pp. 133–150.

Landes, William, and Richard Posner. "Adjudication as a Private Good," *Journal of Legal Studies*, v. 8, no. 235 (July 1979), pp. 77–94.

Landsburg, Steven E. *The Armchair Economist: Economics and Everyday Life*. New York: Free Press, 1993.

Lapchick, Richard E. "A New Vision for the IOC: Anita L. DeFrantz," online at http://www.sportinsociety.org/rel-article19.html.

———. *Racial and Gender Report Card* (2003 edition). Available at http://www.bus.ucf.edu/sport/public/downloads/media/ides/release_report.pdf.

Lavoie, Marc, Gilles Grenier, and Serge Columbe. "Discrimination and Performance Differentials in the National Hockey League," *Canadian Public Policy—Analyse de Politiques*, v. 13, no. 4 (December 1987), pp. 407–422.

Lawrence, Paul. *Unsportsmanlike Conduct: The National Collegiate Athletic Association and the Business of College Football*. New York: Praeger, 1987.

Lawson, M. J. "Going for Gold," *Accountancy,* v. 117, no. 1234 (June 1996), pp. 30–32.

Leeds, Michael A. "Bargaining as Search Behavior Under Mutual Uncertainty," *Southern Economic Journal,* v. 53, no. 3 (January 1987), pp. 677–684.

———. "Rank Order Tournaments and Worker Incentives," *Atlantic Economic Journal,* v. 16, no. 2 (June 1988), pp. 74–77.

Leifer, Eric. *Making the Majors: The Transformation of Team Sports in America.* Cambridge, M.A.: Harvard University Press, 1995.

Lo Franco, Robert. "Profits on Ice," *Forbes,* May 5, 1997, pp. 86–89.

Long, James, and Steven Caudill. "The Impact of Participation in Intercollegiate Athletics on Income and Graduation," *Review of Economics and Statistics,* v. 73, no. 3 (August 1991), pp. 525–531.

Longley, Neil. "Salary Discrimination in the National Hockey League: The Effects of Location," *Canadian Public Policy—Analyse de Politiques,* v. 21, no. 4 (December 1995), pp. 413–422.

———. "The Underrepresentation of French Canadians on English Canadian Teams," *Journal of Sports Economics,* v. 1, no. 3 (August 2000) pp. 236–256.

Lopez, Steve. "They Got Next," *Sports Illustrated,* June 30, 1997, pp. 44–47.

Lorge, Barry. "Kroc Wanted to Give Padres to City," *San Diego Union-Tribune,* July 29, 1990, p. H1.

Madden, Janice Fanning. "A Study of Racial Differences in the Records of NFL Coaches 1986–2001," online at http://www.findjustice.com/ms/nfl/frameindex.htm.

McCallum, Jack. "A Cut Above," *Sports Illustrated,* March 10, 1997, pp. 24–29.

McCormick, Robert, and Maurice Tinsley. "Athletics and Academics: A Model of University Contributions." In *Sportometrics,* ed. by Brian Goff and Robert Tollison. College Station: Texas A&M University Press, 1990, pp. 193–204.

———. "Athletics Versus Academics? Evidence from SAT Scores," *Journal of Political Economy,* v. 95, no. 5 (October 1987), pp. 1103–1116.

MacDonald, Don N., and Morgan O. Reynolds. "Are Baseball Players Paid Their Marginal Products?" *Managerial and Decision Economics,* v. 15 (September/October 1994), pp. 443–457.

McHugh, Catherine. "Ericsson Stadium," *TCI,* v. 31, no. 4 (May 1997), pp. 32–35.

Mandell, Richard. *The Nazi Olympics.* New York: Ballantine Books, 1972.

Mankiw, N. Gregory. *Macroeconomics.* New York: Worth, 2000.

"March Madness," *New Republic,* March 29, 1999, pp. 10–11 (from ProQuest).

Media, Peter S. Battin. *Television Sports Rights 2003,* June 18, 2003, online at http://www.gouldmedia.com/nv_rpt_tsr03.php.

Microsoft. "Testimony of Robert Muglia," February 1999, online at http://www.microsoft.com/presspass/trial/feb99/02-25muglia.htm.

Miller, James. *The Baseball Business: Pursuing Pennants and Profits in Baltimore.* Chapel Hill: University of North Carolina Press, 1990.

Miller, Marvin. *A Whole Different Ballgame.* New York: Carol Publishing Group, 1991.

Moe, Terry. "The Positive Theory of Public Bureaucracy." In *Perspectives on Public Choice: A Handbook,* ed. by Dennis Mueller. Cambridge, UK: Cambridge University Press, 1997, pp. 455–589.

Montville, Leigh. "Howlin' Wolf," *Sports Illustrated,* May 3, 1999, pp. 40–51.

"More Cinncinati Bengals Jokes, online at http://www.pasteeaters.com/funny_jokes/More_Cincinnati_Bengals_Jokes.asp.

Morgan, Jon. *Glory for Sale: Fans, Dollars, and the New NFL.* Baltimore: Bancroft Press, 1997.

MSC Sports. "New Park Financing: How the Deals Got Done," 1999, online at http://www.wcco.com/sports/stadiums.html.

Munsey, Paul, and Corey Suppes. "Ballparks," 2003, online at http://www.ballparks.com.

Murphy, Robert, and Gregory Trandel. "The Relation Between a University's Football Record and the Size of Its Applicant Pool," *Economics of Education Review,* v. 13, no. 3 (September 1994), pp. 265–270.

Nack, William. "This Old House," *Sports Illustrated,* June 7, 1999, pp. 100–116.

Nardinelli, Curtis, and Clark Simon. "Customer Discrimination in the Market for Memorabilia: The Case of Baseball," *Quarterly Journal of Economics,* v. 105, no. 3 (August 1990), p.575–595.

"NBA Average Salaries and Salary Caps." *Wall Street Journal Sports Almanac,* May 3, 2000, online at http://www.ea.grolier.com/ea-online/wsja/text/ch10/tables/sp013.htm.

NCAA. "NCAA Division I, II, and III Membership Criteria," 1999, online at http://www.ncaa.org/about/div_criteria.html.

———. *1997–1998 NCAA Division I Manual.* Indianapolis: NCAA, 1997.

Neale, Walter. "The Peculiar Economics of Professional Sports," *Quarterly Journal of Economics,* v. 78, no. 1 (February 1964), pp. 1–14.

"2002 WTA Tour Leading Money Winners," online at http://www.sportsillustrated.cnn.com/tennis/stats/2002/stats.womoney.html.

Niskanen, William. *Bureaucracy and Representative Government.* Chicago: Aldine Atherton, 1971.

Noden, Merrell. "Dying to Win," *Sports Illustrated,* August 8, 1994, pp. 52–59.

Noll, Roger. "The Economics of Intercollegiate Sports." In *Rethinking College Athletics,* ed. by Judith Andre and David James. Philadelphia: Temple University Press, 1992, pp. 197–209.

———. "The Economics of Sports Leagues." In *Law of Professional and Amateur Sports,* ed. by Gary A. Uberstine and Richard J. Grad, New York: Boardman, 1988, pp. 17-1–17-37.

Noll, Roger, and Andrew Zimbalist. "Build the Stadium—Create the Jobs!" In *Sports, Jobs, and Taxes,* ed. by Roger Noll and Andrew Zimbalist. Washington, D.C.: Brookings Institution Press, 1997, pp. 1–54.

———. "The Economic Impact of Sports Teams and Facilities." In *Sports, Jobs, and Taxes,* ed. by Roger Noll and Andrew Zimbalist. Washington, D.C.: Brookings Institution Press, 1997, pp. 55–91.

"Not About Money: HBO Declines to Renew Wimbledon Contract After 25 Years," June 28, 1999 CNN/SI, online at http://www.cnnsi.com/tennis/1999/wimbledon/news/1999/06/28/hbo_wimbledon/index.html.

O'Hara, Jane, et al. "In the Name of Greed," *Maclean's,* January 19, 1998, pp. 22–24.

"Olympian Rise," *Houston Chronicle,* online at http://www.chron.com/content/chronicle/sports/special/barriers/defrantz.html.

"Open to All: Title IX at Thirty." The Secretary of Education's Commision on Opportunity in Athletics, online at http://www.nacua.org/documents/Title IX_Report_022703.pdf.

"Osaka Vows to Battle on to Host 2008 Olympics," Reuters, Ltd., August 28, 2000, online at http://www.web4.sportsline.com/u/wire/stories/0,1169,2712403_15,00.html.

Panaccio, Tim. "Senators Owner Bryden Got Tired of Fighting Exchange-Rate Deficit," *Philadelphia Inquirer,* December 5, 1999, p. C5.

Pappas, Doug. "The Numbers (Part 2): Local Media Revenues." *The Baseball Prospectus,* online at http://www.baseballprospectus.com/news/20011212pappas.html, December 12, 2001.

Parrish, Paula. "Leap of Faith: Mitt Romney Embraces Challenges, and This Might Be His Biggest One," *Rocky Mountain News,* February 4, 2002, p. 8S.

Pastier, John. "Diamonds in the Rough: Two Cheers for the New Baseball Palaces," *Slate,* July 31, 1996, online at http://www.slate.msn.com/feature2/96-07-31/feature2.asp.

Paterno, Joe. "Score on the SAT to Score on the Field," *Wall Street Journal,* March 16, 1999, p. A26.

Pearce, David W., (Ed). *The MIT Dictionary of Modern Economics,* 3rd ed. Cambridge, M.A.: The MIT Press, 1986.

Pearlman, Jeff. "At Full Blast," *Sports Illustrated,* December 27, 1999–January 3, 2000, pp. 62–64.

Peterson, Robert. *Only the Ball Was White: A History of Legendary Black Players and All-Black Professional Teams.* New York: Gramercy Books, 1970.

"A Plucky Proposition," *Sports Illustrated,* February 16, 1998, p. 28.

Pluto, Terry. *Loose Balls: The Short, Wild Life of the American Basketball Association.* Upper Saddle River, N.J.: Simon and Schuster, 1990.

Poole, Lynn, and Gray Poole. *History of Ancient Greek Olympic Games.* New York: Ivan Obolensky, Inc., 1963.

Porter, Philip. "Mega-Sporting Events as Municipal Investments: A Critique of Impact Analysis." In *Sports Economics: Current Research,* ed. by John Fizel, Elizabeth Gustafson, and Larry Hadley. Westport, C.T.: Praeger Publishers, 1999.

Posner, Richard. "The Social Costs of Monopoly and Regulation," *Journal of Political Economy,* v. 83, no. 4 (August 1975), pp. 807–827.

Pressman, Stacey. "Slam Dunk." *The Weekly Standard,* April 8, 2003, online at http://www.weeklystandard.com/content/Public/Articles/000/000/002/515gdyfj.asp

Purdy, Dean D., Stanley Eitzen, and Rick Hufnagel. "Are Athletes Also Students? The Educational Attainment of College Athletes." In *Sport and Higher Education,* ed. by Donald Chu, Jeffrey Segrave, and Beverly Becker. Champaign, I.L.: Human Kinetics Publishers, 1985, pp. 221–234.

Quirk, James, and Rodney Fort. *Hardball.* Princeton, N.J.: Princeton University Press, 1999.

———. *Pay Dirt.* Princeton, N.J.: Princeton University Press, 1992.

Rader, Benjamin G. *In Its Own Image: How Television Has Transformed Sports.* New York: The Free Press, 1984.

Ralph, Dan. "Toronto Among Finalists to Host 2008 Olympics," *Canadian Press,* August 29, 2000, online at http://www.herald.ns.ca/stories/2000/08/29/f161.raw.html.

Rappoport, Jordan, and Chad Wilkerson. "What Are the Benefits of Hosting a Major League Sports Franchise?" *Federal Reserve Bank of Kansas City Economic Review,* First Quarter, 2001, pp. 55–85.

Rascher, Daniel. "A Test of Optimal Positive Production Network Externality in Major League Baseball." In *Sports Economics: Current Research*, ed. by John Fizel, Elizabeth Gustafson, and Larry Hadley. Westport, C.T.: Praeger Publishers, 1999, pp. 27–45.

Ray, Margaret A., and Paul W. Grimes. "Jockeying for Position: Winnings and Gender Discrimination on the Thoroughbred Track," *Social Science Quarterly*, v. 74, no. 1 (March 1993), pp. 46–61.

Reid, Ron. "New League for Outdoor Lacrosse Keeping Favorable Eye on Philly," *Philadelphia Inquirer*, June 1, 1999, p. E6.

Ribowsky, Mark. *Slick: The Silver and Black Life of Al Davis*. New York: Macmillan, 1991.

Rice, Lewis. "Games Saver." *Harvard Law Bulletin*, Spring 2002, online at http://www.law.harvard.edu/alumni/bulletin/2002/spring/feature_1-1.html .

Roberts, Gary. "Antitrust Issues in Professional Sports." In *Law of Professional and Amateur Sports*, ed. by Gary Uberstine. Deerfield, I.L.: Clark, Boardman, and Callaghan, 1992, pp. 19-1–19-45.

———. "*Brown v. Pro Football, Inc.*: The Supreme Court Gets It Right for the Wrong Reasons," *Antitrust Bulletin*, v. 42, no. 3 (Fall 1997), pp. 595–639.

———. "Should Congress Stop the Bidding War for Sports Franchises." Hearing Before the Subcommittee on Antitrust, Business Rights, and Compensation, Senate Committee on the Judiciary. "Academics," *Heartland Policy*, v. 4 (November 29, 1995), online at http://www.heartland.org/stadps4.html.

Robson, Douglas. "Sydney Finds Its Facilities Formula in Blend of Public-Private Financing." *Street & Smith's SportsBusiness Journal*, October 25–31 1999, p. 33.

Rosen, Harvey. *Public Finance*. Chicago: Irwin, 1995.

Rosen, Sherwin. "The Economics of Superstars," *American Economic Review*, v. 71, no. 5 (December 1981), pp. 845–858.

Rosentraub, Mark. *Major League Losers*. New York: Basic Books, 1997.

———. "Stadiums and Urban Space." In *Sports, Jobs, and Taxes*, ed. by Roger Noll and Andrew Zimbalist. Washington, D.C.: Brookings Institution Press, 1997, pp. 178–207.

Ross, Sonya. "Clinton Signs Bill Removing Baseball Antitrust Exemption for Labor Matters," *Associated Press*, October 28, 1998, online at http://www.fl.milive.com/tigers/stories/19981028antitrust.html.

Ross, Stephen. "Should Congress Stop the Bidding War for Sports Franchises." Hearing Before the Subcommittee on Antitrust, Business Rights, and Compensation, Senate Committee on the Judiciary. "Academics," *Heartland Policy*, v. 4 (November 29, 1995), online at http://www.heartland.org/stadps4.html, volume 2.

Rother, Caitlin. "Tab Climbs in Charger Ticket Deal with City," *San Diego Union-Tribune*, September 12, 2000, p. B1.

Rottenberg, Simon. "The Baseball Players Labor Market," *Journal of Political Economy*, v. 64, no. 3 (June 1956), pp. 242–258.

Rovell, Darren. "What's the Lease You Can Do?" *ESPN: Sports Business*, September 20, 2002, online at http://www.ESPN.com.

Rushin, Steve. "Inside the Moat," *Sports Illustrated*, March 3, 1997, pp. 69–83.

Ryan, Joan. *Little Girls in Pretty Boxes*. New York: Doubleday, 1995.

Sandomir, Richard. "NBC Confronts the Departure of Its Must-See N.B.A. Star," *New York Times*, January 13, 1999, p. D3.

Savage, Charles. "Panel OKs Cruise Tax; Broward Is Exempt," *Miami Herald,* March 29, 2000, online at http://www.herald.com/content/today/docs/013838.htm.

Scahill, Edward. "Did Babe Ruth Have a Comparative Advantage as a Pitcher?" *Journal of Economic Education,* v. 21, no. 4 (Fall 1990), pp. 402–410.

Schmuckler, Eric. "Is the NFL Still Worth It?" *Mediaweek,* September 28, 1998, pp. 26–32.

Schoenfeld, Bruce. "Hockey-Mad Canadians Hard-Pressed to Afford NHL Teams." *Street & Smith's SportsBusiness Journal,* April 24, 2000, p. 1.

"Scorecard." *Sports Illustrated,* April 26, 1999, p. 22.

Scully, Gerald W. *The Business of Major League Baseball.* Chicago: University of Chicago Press, 1989.

———. *The Market Structure of Sports.* Chicago: University of Chicago Press, 1995.

———. "Pay and Performance in Major League Baseball," *American Economic Review,* v. 64, no. 5 (December 1974), pp. 915–930.

Seiken, Eric. "The NCAA and the Courts: College Football on Television." In *Sports and the Law,* ed. by Charles Quirk (New York: Garland, 1996), pp. 56–62.

Seldon, Arthur. "Public Choice and the Choices of the Public." In *Democracy and Public Choice,* ed. by Charles Rowley (London: Basil Blackwell, 1987), pp. 122–134.

Seymour, Harold. *Baseball: The Early Years.* New York: Oxford University Press, 1960.

———. *Baseball: The Golden Years.* New York: Oxford University Press, 1971.

Shapiro, Beth J. "John Hannah and the Growth of Big-Time Intercollegiate Athletics at Michigan State University," *Journal of Sport History,* v. 10, no. 3 (Winter 1983), pp. 26–40.

Shaughnessy, Dan. *Evergreen: The Boston Celtics.* New York: St. Martins Press, 1990.

Sheehan, Richard. *Keeping Score: The Economics of Big-Time Sports.* South Bend, I.N.: Diamond Press, 1996.

Shepherd, William. *The Economics of Industrial Organization.* Upper Saddle River, N.J.: Simon and Schuster, 1997.

Sherman, Len. *Big League, Big Time.* New York: Pocket Books, 1998.

"Shirley Muldowney: 2000 Star Tracks Archive," online at http://www.nhra.com/drivers/driver.asp?driverid=976.

Shropshire, Kenneth. *The Sports Franchise Game.* Philadelphia: University of Pennsylvania Press, 1995.

Shulman, James L., and William G. Bowen. *The Game of Life.* Princeton, N.J.: Princeton University Press, 2001.

Siegfried, John, and Andrew Zimbalist. "The Economics of Sports Facilities and Their Construction," *Journal of Economic Perspectives,* v. 14, no. 3 (Summer 2000), pp. 95–114.

Sigelman, Lee. "It's Academic—or Is It? Admissions Standards and Big-Time College Football," *Social Science Quarterly,* v. 76, no. 2 (June 1995), pp. 247–261.

Sigelman, Lee, and Samuel Bookheimer. "Is It Whether You Win or Lose? Monetary Contributions to Big-Time College Athletic Programs," *Social Science Quarterly,* v. 64, no. 2 (June 1983), pp. 347–359.

Simon, Robert. "Intercollegiate Athletics: Do They Belong on Campus?" In *Rethinking College Athletics,* ed. by Judith Andre and David James. Philadelphia: Temple University Press, 1991, pp. 43–68.

Singell, Larry D., Jr. "Baseball-Specific Human Capital: Why Good but Not Great Players Are More Likely to Coach in the Major Leagues," *Southern Economic Journal,* v. 58, no. 1 (July 1991), pp. 77–86.

Slam! Baseball. "Average Salaries by Sport," April 6, 1999, online at http://www.canoe.ca/BaseballMoneyMatters/salaries_by_sport.html.

Slam! Tennis, February 12, 2001, online at http://www.canoe.ca/StatsTEN/BC-TEN-STAT-WOMONEY-R.html.

Smith, Gary. "A New Life," *Sports Illustrated,* March 28, 1983, pp. 60–67.

Smith, James P., and Finis Welch. "Black Economic Progress After Myrdal," *Journal of Economic Literature,* v. 27, no. 2 (June 1989), pp. 519–564.

Smith, Ronald. *Sports and Freedom: The Rise of Big-Time College Athletics.* New York: Oxford University Press, 1988.

Smith, Sarah, Joanna Cagan, and Miles Seligman. "The Miller's Tale," *Village Voice,* January 19, 1999, p. 189.

Smith, Stephen A. "Phenom Works to Capture His Lost Dream," *Philadelphia Inquirer,* January 14, 2000, pp. D1–D2.

Spence, A. Michael. "Job Market Signaling," *Quarterly Journal of Economics,* v. 87, no. 3 (August 1973), pp. 355–374.

Sperber, Murray. *Beer and Circus: How Big-Time College Sports Is Crippling Undergraduate Education.* New York: Henry Holt, 2000.

———. *College Sports Inc.* New York: Henry Holt, 1990.

———. *Onward to Victory: The Crises that Shaped College Sports.* New York: Henry Holt, 1998.

SportZone. "Nagano Olympics Has $32 Million Surplus," January 12, 1998, online at http://www.espn.go.com/olympics98/news/980709/00765455.html.

Staudohar, Paul. "The Football Strike of 1987: The Question of Free Agency," *Monthly Labor Review,* v. 111, no. 8 (August 1988), pp. 3–9.

———. "Labor Relations in Basketball: The Lockout of 1998–99," *Monthly Labor Review,* v. 122, no. 4 (April 1999), pp. 3–9.

———. *Playing for Dollars: Labor Relations and the Sports Business.* Ithaca, N.Y.: ILR Press, 1996.

———. "Professional Football and the Great Salary Dispute," *Personnel Journal,* v. 61, no. 9 (September 1982), pp. 673–679.

———. "Salary Caps in Professional Team Sports." Compensation and Working Conditions, U.S. Department of Labor, Spring 1998, pp. 3–11.

Steptoe, Sonja, and E. M. Swift. "A Done Deal," *Sports Illustrated,* March 28, 1994, pp. 32–36.

Stigler, George, and Gary Becker. "De Gustibus Non Est Disputandum," *American Economic Review,* v. 67, no. 1 (March 1977), pp. 76–90.

Stratmann, Thomas. "Logrolling." In *Perspectives on Public Choice: A Handbook,* ed. by Dennis Mueller. Cambridge, UK: Cambridge University Press, 1997, pp. 322–341.

Street & Smith's SportsBusiness Journal, By the Numbers, v. 5, no. 6, December 30, 2002.

Struck, Doug. "Hosts Left to Foot World Cup Bill," *Washington Post,* June 29, 2002, p. A1.

Suellentrop, Chris. "Mark Cuban: How to Meddle with Your Sports Team—The Right Way," *Slate Magazine On-line,* December 4, 2002, at *www.slate.com.*

Suggs, Welch. "Fight Over NCAA Standards Reflects Long-Standing Dilemma," *Chronicle of Higher Education,* April 9, 1999, pp. A48–A49.

———. "NCAA to Pay $55-Million to Settle Lawsuit by Assistant Coaches," *Chronicle of Higher Education,* March 19, 1999, p. A47.

Sullivan, Neil J. *The Dodgers Move West.* New York: Oxford University Press, 1987.

"Summary of New 2002–2006 CBA," online at http://www.roadsidephotos.com/ baseball/laborstatus.htm.

Swift, E. M. "The $40 Million Man," *Sports Illustrated,* June 10, 1996, pp. 44–45.

———. "Anatomy of a Plot: The Kerrigan Assault," *Sports Illustrated,* February 14, 1994, pp. 28–38.

Swindell, David, and Mark Rosentraub. "Who Benefits from the Presence of Professional Sports Teams? The Implications for Public Funding of Stadiums and Arenas," *Public Administration Review,* v. 58, no. 1 (January/February 1998), pp. 11–20.

Taylor, Beck A., and Justin G. Trogdon. "Losing to Win: Tournament Incentives in the National Basketball Association," *Journal of Labor Economics,* v. 20, no. 1 (January, 2002), pp. 23–41.

Taylor, Phil. "To the Victor Belongs the Spoils." *Sports Illustrated,* January 18, 1999, pp. 48–52.

Telander, Rick. *From Red Ink to Roses.* New York: Simon and Schuster, 1994.

———. *The Hundred-Yard Lie: The Corruption of College Football and What We Can Do to Stop It.* New York: Simon and Schuster, 1989.

Terry, Richard. "Tight End Mackey Blocks Commissioner Rozelle." In *Sports and the Law,* ed. by Charles Quirk. New York: Garland, 1996, pp. 187–189.

Thaler, Richard. "The Winner's Curse," *Journal of Economic Perspectives,* v. 2, no. 1 (Winter 1988), pp. 191–202.

Thelin, John. *Games Colleges Play.* Baltimore: Johns Hopkins University Press, 1994.

Thomas, G. Scott. "Surhoff Proves to Be '99s Best Investment," *Street & Smith's SportsBusiness Journal,* October 25–31, 1999, p. 1.

Thurow, Roger. "Thrown for a Curve," *Wall Street Journal,* August 28, 1998, pp. A1 and A6.

Tofler, Ian, Barri Katz Stryer, Lyle J. Micheli, and Lisa Herman. "Physical and Emotional Problems of Elite Female Gymnasts," *New England Journal of Medicine,* v. 335, no. 4 (July 25, 1996), pp. 281–283.

Tollison, Robert. "Rent Seeking." In *Perspectives on Public Choice: A Handbook,* ed. by Dennis Mueller. Cambridge, UK: Cambridge University Press, 1997, pp. 506–525.

Tomlinson, Alan. "De Coubertin and the Modern Olympics." In *Five Ring Circus: Money, Power and Politics at the Olympic Games,* ed. by Alan Tomlinson and Garry Whannel. London: Pluto Press, 1984, pp. 84–97.

"Two Leagues of Their Own?" *Business Week,* May 13, 1996, p. 52.

University of Pennsylvania Museum of Anthropology and Archeology. "The Real Story of the Ancient Olympic Games," 1996, online at http://www.upenn.edu/ museum/Olympics/olympicathletes.html.

"U. S. v. International Boxing Club of N. Y.," online at http://www.ripon.edu/faculty/ bowenj/antitrust/ibcofny1.htm.

Vamplew, Wray. *Pay Up and Play the Game: Professional Sport in Britain, 1875–1914.* Cambridge, UK: Cambridge University Press, 1988.

Veblen, Thorstein. *Theory of the Leisure Class.* New York: The Viking Press, 1967.

Veeck, Bill, with Ed Linn. *The Hustler's Handbook.* Durham, N.C.: Baseball America Classic Books, 1996.

Veeck, Bill, with Ed Linn. *Veeck as in Wreck.* Chicago: University of Chicago Press, 1962.

von Allmen, Peter. "Is the Reward System in NASCAR Efficient?" *Journal of Sports Economics,* v. 2, no. 1 (February 2000), pp. 62–79.

Vrooman, John. "Franchise Free Agency in Professional Sports Leagues," *Southern Journal of Economics,* v. 64, no. 1 (July 1997), pp. 191–219.

———. "NBA Average Salaries and Salary Caps," online at http://www.ea.grolier.com/ea-online/wsja/text/ch10/tables/sp012.htm.

Walsh, William D. "The Entry Problem of Francophones in the National Hockey League: A Systematic Interpretation." *Canadian Public Policy—Analyse de Politiques,"* v. 18, no. 4 (December 1992), pp. 443–460.

Ward, Geoffrey, and Kenneth Burns. *Baseball: An Illustrated History.* New York: Alfred A. Knopf, 1994.

Warner, Gene. "Hockey Team has $65 million Impact, Hevesi Says," *Buffalo News On-Line,* February 26, 2003, at http://www.Buffalo.com.

Weiler, Paul, and Gary Roberts. *Sports and the Law: Cases, Materials, and Problems.* St. Paul, M.N.: West Publishing, 1993.

Weiner, Jay. "Investigating the 'U': A Year Later," *Minneapolis Star-Tribune,* March 10, 2000.

Westcott, Rich. *Philadelphia's Old Ballparks.* Philadelphia: Temple University Press, 1996.

"What's Wrong with the NCAA's Test Score Requirements?" FairTest: The National Center for Fair and Open Testing, February 2001, online at http://www.fairtest.org/facts/prop48.htm.

Wicksell, Knute. "On the Theory of Interest." In *Selected Essays in Economics: Volume I,* ed. by Bo Sandelin. London: Routledge, 1997, pp. 41–53.

Will, George. *Bunts.* New York: Scribner, 1998.

Wintrobe, Ronald. "Modern Bureaucratic Theory." In *Perspectives on Public Choice: A Handbook,* ed. by Dennis Mueller. Cambridge, UK: Cambridge University Press, 1997, pp. 429–454.

Wolf, Jason. "Haskins Lied, Told Players to Lie in Minnesota Basketball Scandal," *Associated Press,* November 19, 1999.

Wolff, Alexander, and Armen Keteyian. *Raw Recruits.* New York: Pocket Books, 1991.

Yeager, Don. "Black Eye for the Buckeyes," *Sports Illustrated,* June 16, 1999, p. 96.

Young, David. *The Modern Olympics: A Struggle for Revival.* Baltimore: Johns Hopkins University Press, 1996.

Young, Scott. *100 Years of Dropping the Puck: A History of the OHA.* Toronto: McClelland and Stewart, 1989.

Zimbalist, Andrew. *Baseball and Billions.* New York: Basic Books, 1992.

———. "Competitive Balance in Sports Leagues: An Introduction," *Journal of Sports Economics,* v. 3, no. 2 (May, 2002), pp. 111–121.

———. "Salaries and Performance: Beyond the Scully Model." In *Diamonds Are Forever: The Business of Baseball,* ed. by Paul M. Sommers (Washington, D.C.: The Brookings Institution, 1992), pp. 109–133.

———. *Unpaid Professionals.* Princeton, N.J.: Princeton University Press, 1999.

Zimmerman, Dennis. "Subsidizing Stadiums: Who Benefits, Who Pays?" In *Sports, Jobs, and Taxes,* ed. by Roger Noll and Andrew Zimbalist (Washington, D.C.: Brookings Institution Press, 1997), pp. 119–145.

Zotti, Ed. "Hosting the Olympics—Not All Fund and Games," *Advertising Age,* February 7, 1983.

Index

Note: Page numbers followed by letters *f* and *t* refer to figures and tables, respectively.